To Velma,

With compliments,
Wilga M. Rivers

Watertown MA.
2004

THANK YOU

Down Under / Up Top

Creating a Life

By

Wilga M. Rivers

This book is a work of non-fiction. Names and places have been changed to protect the privacy of some individuals. The events and situations are true.

ISBN: 1-4140-2484-3 (e-book)
ISBN: 1-4140-2485-1 (Paperback)
ISBN: 1-4140-2486-X (Dust Jacket)

Library of Congress Control Number: 2003097827

This book is printed on acid free paper.

Printed in the United States of America
Bloomington, IN

1stBooks - rev. 03/01/04

Table of Contents

PREFACE: EXPERIENCES AND MEMORIES v

1 TANGLED ORIGINS 1

2 EXPLORING THE WORLD: THE ASCOT VALE DAYS 30

3 BANK STREET STATE SCHOOL (1923-30) 75

4 LEARNING TO LOVE LEARNING: EHS (1931-35) 114

5 SURVIVING THE DEPRESSION (1931-35) 159

6 ACADEMIC NOVITIATE (1936-39) 188

7 RURAL VICTORIA (1940-46) 228

8 EDUCATIONAL CONTRASTS: ST ANNES (1944-46) AND
  TAYLOR'S COACHING COLLEGE (1947-48) 270

9 VENTURING OUT OF THE NEST (1948) 302

10 NORTHERN HEMISPHERE: UP TOP (1949) 331

11 THE DREAM REALIZED: FRANCE AT LAST (1949-50) 397

12 LIFE IN PICARDY (1950) 435

13 SIX MONTHS ON THE SIDELINES (1950) 483

14 THE SUNNY SOUTH (1951) 515

15 MONTPELLIER: SECOND YEAR (1951-52) 559

16 WILGA: THE HITCHHIKING SPECIALIST (1952) 601

17 THE CIRCLE COMPLETED (1952) 629

APPENDIX I REMEMBER: GROWING UP IN AUSTRALIA.... 642

ENDNOTES 647

GLOSSARY 653

PREFACE
Experiences and Memories

Experiences, whether sensory, emotional, or intellectual, combine to form memories. Whatever we do (through physical action, thinking, dreaming, wishing, regretting, viewing, tasting, smelling, admiring) crystallizes in memories. But that is not the end of the story. The brain is dynamic, constantly interacting like the clouds in the sky. Clouds are combining in new ways every second — expanding, contracting, absorbing, scattering — so that, even if today's clouds seem similar to those of yesterday or last week, they are never identical; they are a new combination of similar elements

Nor are our memories static; they are continually growing, diminishing, fading, reviving, and combining with the information and knowledge we possess, as well as with other memories that are closely or tangentially associated. As Park has observed, "Traditional thinking, concepts and prejudices rise like a mist between us and the object of our observation; it is the way of human life."[1] New information seeps into our "recollections" too, causing us to reinterpret them subconsciously. Our memories are influenced by psychological states of wishing, expecting, or rejecting. They are also quite selective; things we do not wish to remember fade from our conscious memory. We may even deny them. Each time we review our memories and reflect on them, they are embellished and enriched or diminished to an acceptable or frequently recounted form that satisfies us more. In one way or another they are subtly changed over time. Shields asks: "What is the story of a life? A chronicle of fact or a skillfully wrought impression?"[2]

Yet these are our memories. They affect the way we act and plan; they decide what we will seek and avoid; and they influence our beliefs, often without our being fully aware of the extent of that influence. Our memories as they exist uniquely in our own minds determine who we are and who we think we are. What I am sharing in this book are *my* memories — those to which I have tenaciously clung, even though they may not always conform with the interpretations of other participants or observers. Because these are my experiences, my interpretations of those experiences and thus my memories (enhanced, enriched, pruned down, reinterpreted), they have shaped me and they continue to influence the way I think, live, and interact. These are the things I am now sharing with my readers.

Frame pictures this process quite graphically, when she says: "Writing an autobiography, usually thought of as a looking back, can just as well be a looking across or through, with the passing of time giving an X-ray quality to the eye. Also, time past is not time gone, it is time accumulated with the host resembling the character in the fairytale who was joined along the route by more characters none of whom could be separated from one another or from the host, with some stuck so fast that their presence caused physical pain. Add to the characters all the events, thoughts, feelings, and there is a mass of time, now a sticky mess, now a jewel bigger than the planets and the stars." Lily Maynard in Miller's novel, *The Distinguished Guest*, says that "anyone who writes a memoir has got to be a little bit of a liar"[4] or, to put it more kindly, at least intentionally selective in recall. Since I have never been a person who "tells all" or "lets it all hang out," I plead guilty to the latter. In this book I have consciously restricted myself to memories and experiences that may interest and amuse my reader; the rest, more deeply personal, are for me to ponder. This book is not intended to be an autobiography, but, rather, selections from a personal journal. Fortunately for this I have had access to large quantities of correspondence, diary notations and photographic material that have enabled me to recount my actual on-the-spot reactions in many situations.

Some may wonder at the title *Down Under / Up Top*. North Americans seem to have fallen into the habit of calling Australia Down Under, to which I usually reply Up Top, since the world being as it is this is a matter of relative viewpoint. My perspective has the support of that learned group, the Jesuits (or at least one section of them). When I lectured at Georgetown University in Washington, DC, I saw above the stage in the Hall of Nations a representation of the world with Australia up top! Aha! I thought, a hundred thousand Jesuits can't be wrong! Perhaps the Jesuits and I share some esoteric insight. Alternatively, one may consider me as having divided my life fairly evenly between the southern and the northern hemispheres.

In reading this book you will notice that I easily fall into using "we" to describe my childhood. Since my sister Linda was just sixteen months older than I, the two of us grew up very much as though we were twins, even wearing almost identical little dresses and receiving similar presents at Christmas. It is not surprising then that I now thank my dear sister Linda, even though she is no longer with us, for her patience in jogging my memory in taped conversations and in many informal talks that proved extremely useful for establishing elusive details. I am also grateful to the many friends who read early versions of the various chapters and encouraged me to continue writing.

In some places I have changed the names of persons I have alluded to, in order to preserve their privacy. If what I have had to say is purely laudatory I have kept their actual names.

I hope you enjoy reading about these experiences and I will be happy to hear from those of you who have shared to some extent in them.

Watertown, MA, 2003

1
TANGLED ORIGINS

One evening I was sitting as an observer at the back of a Spanish class, in the Harvard University Extension School, when the teacher began asking the class that familiar elementary-level question: "How many children are there in your family?" The usual ones, twos, and threes were cited, until one woman replied: "Eighteen." That should have capped it, except that the teacher decided to include me in her questioning. I replied: "Twenty-four." After the class, the woman with the seventeen siblings hastened over to me and exclaimed: "Do you really have twenty-four in your family? I've always had the most!"

This question of my peculiar family has always been a useful conversation starter at parties that were laboring along in stolid tedium. How could I have twenty-three brothers and sisters? The alternative response is that I have only one sibling, but more of that later. The air begins to clear a little when I explain that my father married two widows and my mother married two widowers, creating five families in all. The untangling of this unusual family history takes us back to the very early days of Australia's settlement by Europeans — to the stories told of the Rivers, Tanner, Lehmann, and Burston families in the mid nineteenth century

From Van Dieman's Land to Victoria

The first Rivers to find his way to Australia was John Henry, an English accountant. In the late 1840s he was in Launceston in Van Diemen's Land, as Tasmania was then called. In those early days, when New South Wales and Van Diemen's Land were still penal colonies, a number of early free settlers in Australia seem to have had rather loosely defined occupations. Of an adventurous and enterprising spirit, they were presumably trying out anything they could do in the rough and tumble life of the newly established settlements, where convicts, of course, performed the brute labor. After Melbourne was established in 1834, a number of free settlers crossed Bass Strait from Tasmania to try their luck in the virgin territory of Victoria, which was never a convict settlement. This exodus accelerated with the discovery of gold in Castlemaine and Bendigo in the 1850s. As a child I was well instructed to refer to my ancestor as "John Rivers Gentleman," and, even in the 1930s, letters for my father arrived addressed to Harry Rivers Esquire. Later I discovered, on reading Hughes's enlightening book on early Australia, *The Fatal Shore*,[5] just how important it was to the early settlers to distinguish themselves from the convicts, even though many of the latter had been transported from England for quite petty offenses or for political dissent. Many of the convicts were on ticket-of-leave, which required them to report regularly to the police; others in the early colonies were freed men whose penalty had been paid but who had decided to remain in the colony. Free settlers considered themselves the Sterling, as opposed to those born in the colony, that is, the Currency lads and lasses, referred to in early Australian ballads.

John Rivers married Eliza, the only daughter of Lieutenant Edward Rawling of the Fourth King's Own. Edward had reached Tasmania in the 1830's on the Second Fleet that brought convicts to that southern outpost and had decided to stay on and try his luck. John and Eliza lived for some time in Launceston, where my father, Harry, was born in 1853 in the Windmill Hill area. There were four other Rivers sons: my godfather Osmond, my uncles Percy, William, and Frank (who was born later in England), as well as two daughters. Families came fast in those days. In 1865, when my father was twelve, John decided that the family should return to England, to London where my great-grandparents were living.

To embark for the Old Country, or "home" as the early settlers thought of it, the Rivers family traveled from Launceston to Melbourne. It seems there was a horse broker in Tasmania who had very much wanted to adopt young Harry, but this was not to the liking of the family. This man followed the Rivers group to Victoria, trying to convince them of the wisdom of allowing him to adopt their son, but to no avail. As the ship was about to leave on the tide, he declared

2

from the wharf: "Mark my words! That boy will be back in Australia before the year is out." How true his prophecy was!

In those days the trip to England took up to six months on a sailing ship. It must have been a rough, uncomfortable trip, but long enough for my father to acquire a love of the sea. Perhaps because of this, young Harry, unable or unwilling to adapt to the damp and fog of London after the sunshine of his native land, tried to join the British Navy. In my childhood, he told me that he was not accepted for this service because he did not know the French alphabet. As an indication of the subtle and covert nature of motivation, was it my childhood disappointment at this early setback in my dear father's career that made me so determined, at the age of eleven, to study the French language? Or was it my youthful excitement on reading the popular French Revolution based novel, *The Scarlet Pimpernel,* [6] with its interpolated French expressions?

I have often pondered this alleged exclusionary oddity for entrance to the British Navy that my father encountered in 1865. It reminds me of the old Australian device, which lasted into the 1960's —the "dictation test" — for refusing admission to the country to any immigrant the Government did not like. The test could be administered in any European language of the examiner's choosing. If by some chance the would-be immigrant passed the first test, a second in a quite different language could be administered, and this process continued until the authorities obtained the result they were seeking. Perhaps, in those long-distant nineteenth-century days, this French alphabet hurdle was a way of separating out candidates who had not attended the "right" schools and who presumably did not have the "right" background? Be that as it may, Father promptly decided to return to Australia on his own, and this at the age of twelve. He persisted in his resolve despite violent opposition on the part of his family. Taking himself off to the wharves, he sought out the captain of the ship that had brought his family to England from Australia. This sympathetic man agreed to take young Harry to Australia as his cabin boy (in those days a kind of captain's protégé). This was surely an early indication of the Rivers' charm and persuasiveness.

It was certainly fortunate for Harry that the ship that had brought him from Australia happened to be still in the port of London. My reconstruction of this coincidence is that the time interval during

3

which my father's unhappiness with his new environment developed into a determination to return to the land of his birth was long enough for a sailing ship to unload and reload in the Port of London, sail to Liverpool or some other English port, unload, reload, and return to London to prepare for another long trip to Australia. However it came about, John Rivers supplied his son with a letter of introduction to a grazier in Victoria and off young Harry went to join the ship. Possibly this sheep-breeding family had some connection with the horse breeder who had wished to adopt Harry earlier. Whatever the connection, we certainly know that, like so many early established Victorian families, these graziers, the Clarkes, had started off in Tasmania and had already acquired considerable wealth in land there before moving to the fledgling state of Victoria. Father worked for them for a number of years, becoming eventually manager of one of their properties — but I am jumping ahead in my story.

As Harry left his family in London, his grandmother, who found it impossible to believe that he was really going to set out on his own at twelve years of age, declared: "We'll see! You'll be home again before nightfall, I'll be bound!" And he was. When he reached the sailing ship, it seems the weather was not right for immediate departure, so the captain gave him leave to spend one more night with his family. His grandmother was gleeful at his return, but not for long. Next day he set sail with the tide and, as had been predicted, he was back in Australia before the year was out.

Harry was never to see his family again, except for his brother Osmond. The latter emigrated to South Africa where he bred merino sheep in Potchestroom. From this distant spot he came on one visit to Australia where he became my godfather. As a child I loved to play with a gift he left us: a small South African gourd with nuts rattling inside, which was covered with blue and white beadwork in Zulu patterns. Despite the great distances, the Rivers family in the two hemispheres has kept in touch for 140 years. At first this was by correspondence only, but by the 1930s some of the younger generation in Australia were already visiting their cousins in London. Eventually one of my father's granddaughters married an English second cousin, Hugh Rivers, thus strengthening the link nearly a century after the separation. Hugh's father, my English cousin Osmond, also an Osmond godson, married a Danish widow in later life and I now have a widowed Rivers cousin-in-law whom I enjoy visiting in Copenhagen. So the family continues to rove and spread and keep in touch.

Young Harry had a great time on the ship to Australia. He and the other cabin boys got up to all sorts of tricks and games. An important event on a trip by sea from the Northern Hemisphere occurred when the ship crossed the Line, the Equator, and entered the Southern Hemisphere. King Neptune came on board and initiated all neophyte travelers by dunking them in water. This was already the tradition in the nineteenth century, although on a sailing ship the baptism may well have been in the sea, not in a convenient swimming pool like the one in which I was immersed on my first trip to England in 1948. The passengers and crew on Harry's ship refused to believe a little twelve-year-old cabin boy when he asserted that he had already crossed the Line. Determined to maintain his right to recross the Line unhassled, Harry sneaked down to the luggage room in the bowels of the ship, made himself a neat cubbyhole under the trunks and did not emerge until all danger of dunking was over. These were the kinds of stories that endeared my "dear old Daddy" to me in my childhood. Since my father was 65 years old when I was born, that is how my sister Linda and I viewed him.

The Bolinda Vale Years

On arrival in Victoria, Harry went to the Bolinda Vale estate, near Sunbury, and presented his letter of introduction to the Clarke family. William Clarke was already well launched in the sheep-breeding business when Harry came to Bolinda Vale in 1865. His father, Big John Clarke, had deputed him, in 1860, to manage this extensive sheep run in Victoria. Big John was already one of the richest men in Tasmania. He had made his fortune as a contractor for the British Government, handling supplies for officers and convicts.[7] At Bolinda Vale, Harry was welcomed as a jackeroo. Jackeroos were trainees in the grazing art, usually from "good" families, and this differentiated them from the "hands" on the property. At Bolinda Vale in father's time, there were five jackeroos who formed a close band. With one of these companions, by the name of McLarty, my father corresponded all his life. I remember being impressed in my childhood by the envelopes of Mr McLarty's letters, addressed to

5

"Harry Rivers Esquire" in big, black handwriting. Another of the jackeroos, William Maloney, went into politics and at his death was the longest sitting member in the Victorian State Parliament. The foundations for my father's future career as an expert on sheep and cattle were laid during those early years on the Clarke estate. Father began working at Bolinda Vale about thirty years after Batman stood on the banks of the Yarra Yarra river and declared: "This will be the place for a village," thus founding the city of Melbourne. The population in Australia was about a half a million in 1851, when the Victorian Gold Rush began, first in Castlemaine, then in Ballarat and Bendigo. By 1858, the Australian population had expanded to about one million, so we can imagine how sparsely populated Victoria was when Harry returned in 1865. As has been observed so frequently, many early Victorians who came in search of gold found instead the golden fleece.

The kind of formal education Father had as a child in Launceston and how much is not clear. We do know that private education began early in Tasmania. Among the free settlers and the administrative officials in early Van Diemen's Land, there was a great concern for education for their children in such a wild and unsettled environment. "Schools, private, denominational, parish and government, abounded,"[8] it seems. Already by 1838, there were thirty-four Anglican schools, supported by the government, as well as Wesleyan, Presbyterian, and Roman Catholic schools. "Private schools only required willingness, a brass plate, pupils and perhaps ambition. Sometimes these schools lasted a few months, and sometimes they were run by ex-convicts whose major concern was wealth."[9] John Franklin, who was Governor from 1837 to 1843, and who is generally regarded as the founder of state education in Tasmania,[10] considered that "education should be freely available, general and non-denominational."[11] Public education was already functioning in Victoria in the 1850's, and in all probability also in Launceston. As we shall see later, my maternal great-grandfather, David Burston, was teaching in a private school in Launceston at the time when young Harry was living there. Whatever the circumstances of his education, there is no indication that my father had any schooling beyond the age of twelve, when he sailed for England. This was the era of the self-educated individual and, with a good basis in

6

the "three R's" (reading, writing, and 'rithmetic}, intelligent individuals read and wrote and learned from life. Whatever early education Harry had, he was sufficiently self-educated in his mid-sixties to write regular reports and articles for four Victorian newspapers. These were the evening *Herald,* the morning *Sun-News-Pictorial,* the *Weekly Times,* and the *Stock and Land,* all published by Sir Keith Murdoch, the father of Rupert Murdoch. The last two of these papers were devoted specifically to the needs of the agricultural and pastoral communities. At that later stage of his life, in the 1920's, Harry had become a recognized authority on the care and breeding of cattle and sheep, especially merinos.

Early in Australia's history merino sheep (some, it seems, from King George 111's own flocks) had been introduced and crossbred with hardier Asian types to ensure their survival in the heat of the southern colony, where the grasses were also very different from those in the land of their origin. Enough purebreds were retained to reinforce the strain as needed.[12] Since merino sheep were already well established in Victoria by the middle of the nineteenth century, at Bolinda Vale Harry Rivers was immediately plunged into a growing industry of immense importance to Australia's future. We still have in the family the cane he used for droving flocks of sheep in those early days. On one occasion he was prevented from returning to the homestead for several weeks by flooded streams, thus missing the due date for paying the premiums on his life insurance. In those bad old days, this meant losing his entire investment. Needless to say, this misadventure, frequently recounted, destroyed the family's faith in insurance policies for many years to come

Early Victorian life was not without tragedy. In 1860, William Clarke of Bolinda Vale had married Mary Walker. In 1871, after ten years of happy marriage, the pregnant Mary was out for a drive in a landau one day, with her youngest baby and her companion and helper, Janet Snodgrass, when a rabbit ran across the road almost under the horses' hooves. As the horses bolted, Mary panicked and jumped out of the landau with her baby son. Badly injured, she died soon afterwards, to her husband's great grief. In the period of turmoil that followed, Janet stayed on to help William with his four very young children. Two years later, in 1873, William Clarke married Janet Snodgrass[13] who later, when William was knighted for his services to the state of Victoria, became the famous Janet Lady Clarke, after whom the women's residential college at Melbourne University, Janet Clarke Hall, was named. (In 1937-38, while a student at Melbourne University, I was associated with Janet Clarke Hall as an external student, thus renewing, if tangentially, the family link.) Janet Clarke was an outstanding woman, who became very active in public life, alongside her husband. Harry Rivers, who lived through these tragic events on Bolinda Vale, knew Janet well. Preserved in the family for a long time was a letter to my father from Janet Clarke, in which she complimented him on being able to cook the best lamb chops over an open fire of anyone she knew — an art that was, of course, indispensable for drovers, who spent long periods roughing it in the bush.

As a young man on the estate Harry became very friendly with Charlotte Gray,[14] the wife of the manager of one of the Clarke properties. Charlotte, who had married Gray at the age of sixteen, was nearer Harry's age than her husband's and he enjoyed dropping in for tea and a chat. Unfortunately, in 1873, when Charlotte was only twenty-three, her husband died suddenly. (Was he thrown from his horse, as so many others were?). Two years later, Father married Charlotte, taking on as his own three very young stepchildren, Edward, Alfred, and Minnie Gray. Later Harry and Charlotte, with their family, moved to another Clarke estate, Bald Hill, near Donnybrook, where he became manager. Charlotte and Harry were very happy together and had ten children from their union. (We have now explained thirteen of the twenty-four children, years before my mother comes into the picture.) As children of Father's second marriage, my sister Linda and I grew up with a painting by Father's eldest daughter, Florence, of a prize bull "on Bald Hill." In our youthful innocence, we always wondered at this title, since the huge bull stood out against a background that distinctly represented a hill with some trees — certainly not a "bald hill." Nobody bothered to explain to us literal-minded children that Bald Hill was the name of the property, not a descriptor of the scene in the painting. After Father's death this family heirloom, never Mother's favorite, mysteriously disappeared from view.

Father remained on the Clarke estates for a number of years and always spoke with great warmth of his experiences at Bolinda

Vale and Bald Hill. My sister Linda, born to his second marriage in his later years, was always playfully called Linda Belinda; it is possible that in Father's mind she was Linda Bolinda. Harry's recognized position as a valued member of the early Clarke entourage is verified by his appearance, wearing the obligatory top hat, in an old photograph of the guests at the wedding in 1886 of Amy Cumming and Rupert Clarke, the son of William and his first wife Mary Walker.[15] By that time Father, who would have been thirty-three, had left the estate and was making his way independently in the sheep industry.

Harry's Expertise in Sheep and Cattle

At Bolinda Vale Harry had worked with Robert Clarke (no relation to William Clarke), who was manager and general superintendent of the Clarke family's vast station properties and who was recognized in those early days as one of the most successful breeders of sheep and cattle. Through him, Harry received extraordinary training at an early age.[16] As his own career developed, he always kept his interest focused on sheep and cattle. He eventually became a broker and auctioneer of stock and country properties, traveling widely throughout Victoria. During this period the Rivers family lived in a number of locations in the state: Romsey, Ascot Vale, Seymour, Flemington, and Rutherglen (at that time a thriving mining town). Finally they moved back to the western suburbs of Melbourne, to Essendon and Moonee Ponds, where I was born much later. Harry and his family always lived close to the northeast railway line because of his activities selling stock in the north of Victoria or auctioning off sheep and cattle at the Melbourne sale yards which had been established at Newmarket in 1859. Moonee Ponds, which was then part of the City of Essendon (now renamed Moonee Valley), has been called "the stopover that stayed." In the 1850s, prospectors passed this way and "stopped over" at the ponds on the early leg of their long trek to the goldfields of Mt Alexander (now Castlemaine) and later those of Bendigo and Ballarat in central Victoria.[17] Before the construction of the railway line the Moonee Ponds had also provided a watering place for drovers and their stock on their way to the sales in Melbourne.

When I grew up in Ascot Vale in the 1920s Father was in his early seventies. He was a journalist by then. I remember him rushing off at night to catch the ten o'clock train to the city to deliver to the editor his latest reports for the morning papers on sales of sheep and cattle at the yards and any interesting news he had gleaned from the agricultural shows he had attended. He also wrote long articles for the *Weekly Times* on the care and maintenance of livestock and gave advice on problems raised by his country readers. As had Father's first family, we lived on the railway line to Sydney, at Ascot Vale, just one railway station from the Newmarket Saleyards. The yards, after some 130 years of continuous use, were finally replaced by a housing development in the 1990's. The sale yards were certainly an important feature of the local economy. As children we would watch, entranced, and count the segments of the trains that passed the end of our street, drawing up to a hundred trucks packed with bleating sheep on their way to or from the sales at Newmarket. By that time, in the nineteen-thirties, just over 100,000 sheep and lambs and some 6,800 cattle passed through the yards every week.[18]

At the yards, "little" Harry Rivers was considered "a very colourful...character...of a restless mercurial disposition," who never really settled down until after his second marriage to my mother, when he became a newspaper reporter. Full of energy, he was considered "an oracle on all stock matters" and a "good judge of both sheep and cattle."[19] Harry had a hobby of repairing shoes, probably a necessary skill in the early Bolinda Vale days, and he always put several thicknesses of soles on the special boots he wore to protect his feet from the cobblestones of the yards, something his sore-footed replacements lacked, to their great discomfort when he was on holidays.

At this stage Father was much sought after as a judge at agricultural shows. In Ascot Vale we lived about a mile from the Showgrounds. At Show time, we would see horse-drawn jinkers drawn up by the score at the Ascot Vale railway station, ready to take interested patrons down to the Showgrounds for the Royal Agricultural Show, a week-long affair that rated a public holiday in Victoria's calendar for so many years. One of my early memories is of Father taking me as a small child to preview cattle before the opening of the Show to the public. Small as I was, I was most

10

impressed with the enormous size of the prize bulls that Father daringly, from my youthful point of view, poked with his umbrella to make them turn round. (Dad's capacious umbrella was a ubiquitous companion for a person who worked outside in Melbourne's changeable weather.) At the Show, Father worked on his reports in a small roped-off enclosure. When we were a little older and my sister Linda and I had become Girl Guides, we always looked forward to the Show Day holiday, when our Guide Captain (our beloved Cappy) would take our company to mingle with the crowds and enjoy the fun of the fair. On these occasions, Linda and I were very proud to point out to the other children our important-looking Daddy. To demonstrate to unbelievers that he really was our father, we would crawl under the rope to wheedle from him an extra shilling or two. Because we had to be careful what we spent in those difficult early days of the Great Depression, Dad would give us perhaps an extra sixpence, with which at that time, fortunately, we could still buy something. We would spend this largesse on samples, which were distributed for pennies in colorful bags at the different product stalls at the Show.

What kind of a man was Harry Rivers? He was very open and sociable, a raconteur and, in the nineteenth century setting of home entertainment, a noted reciter of long narrative ballads, like "Clancy at the Bat," "Ypsilanti Wins," and "The Charge of the Light Brigade," which he declaimed with much verve on social occasions. With his large moustache and neatly trimmed beard, he had a strong resemblance to King George V, as people frequently remarked. His large family, by his first marriage, loved music and formed quite a family choir for singing around the piano. He raced horses in country races, and we still have a silver cup from the opening meeting of the Romsey Racing Club on May 24th, 1883, which declares Harry Rivers's horse, Judy Mo, to be the winner of the District Handicap Cup race. In fact the paddock in Romsey where he kept his horses long retained the name of Rivers Paddock. At one stage, he and his sons engaged in butchering in Rutherglen. An old letterhead from those days reads: "Our Boys' Butchering Co." Perhaps this was another skill he had picked up in his jackeroo days at Bolinda Vale. All his life, he had firm ideas on how animal carcasses should be cut up. Mother was instructed never to allow the butcher to "butcher" the meat, which father neatly cut up himself with great expertise. While living in country towns he took great interest in the organization of the local community and was at times a representative on the Shire Council. He was a Freemason (always leaders in the small communities in those days) and a committed Anglican. By the 1890s, he and his sons were stock and station agents, with an office on the corner of Bourke and Queen Streets in the busy center of Melbourne. With the training they received two of his sons and one Gray stepson continued as auctioneers and real estate agents, in a firm called Gray and Rivers that the family maintained into the 1990s.

With Linda and Wilga, the children of his old age, Harry was kind and affectionate and teased us into good humor in our childish sulks. Our half-sisters and brothers from his first marriage, who were nearly as old or older than my mother, were quite amazed at how mild and accepting of youthful vagaries their disciplinarian father had become in his later years. He loved to talk to us and tell us the stories of his life. Although I was only thirteen when he died, I remember well certain aphorisms about life that he communicated to me in my childhood. One of these was "You wouldn't worry nearly so much about what other people think of you if you realized how little they do." Another that greatly influenced me was: "You can do anything in this life if you put your mind to it." Both must have served him well in his self-constructed pioneering career.

The Spanish Connection

Although the original Rivers family was quintessentially English, there is a Spanish strand to the weave. It seems that during the Napoleonic Wars one of the Rivers sons fought in Spain with the First King's Foot (a name we found hilarious as children). While there he married a Spanish woman who had nursed him when he was wounded. That this is more than a legend is validated by the fact that, while most of the Rivers children since then have been blue-eyed, rosy-cheeked blondes, a child will appear from time to time, on both the English and Australian sides of the family, who is olive-skinned, dark-eyed and dark-haired. In Harry's first family, there was one dark-haired, dark-eyed daughter, May, who could have been a twin for the first cousin she had never met — Gladys, Harry's brother

Frank's daughter in London — who was as different from her sisters as May was from hers.

On the Lehmann Trail

It is now time to untangle another thread — that of the Lehmanns. The Lehmann family, my mother's maternal ancestors, lived in Leipzig, Germany, where my great-great-grandfather and his sons were piano builders. After my great-grandfather, John A. Lehmann, emigrated to Australia in the eighteen-forties, his brother offered to send him as many pianos as he liked, to sell or to use if any of his children proved to be musical. There is no record of my great-grandfather taking him up on the sales proposition, but I do know that my great-uncle, Alfred, who was a very modestly remunerated music teacher, had two beautiful pianos in a very small house. It is very probable that these came from the family in Leipzig. At the time when John Lehmann came to Australia, a number of Germans of traditional views were leaving their country. Many were dissatisfied with the imposition by King Friedrich Wilhelm 111 of Prussia of certain changes in the Lutheran liturgy, which were intended to bring Lutheran and Reformed (Calvinist) worship closer to one another. Those who sailed from Hamburg to Australia, as my ancestors did, would have taken up to nine months to reach their destination in the south seas. It was on this long voyage that my Lehmann great-grandfather, John, met and fell in love with my Köster great-grandmother, Marie Christine. They were married when they landed in Adelaide. Like so many other German immigrants at the time, they had set their sights on South Australia. Here settlements of their fellow countrymen had been established through the support and sponsorship of a sympathetic English patron, George Fyfe Angas, who hoped to be reimbursed when the settlers' farming enterprises prospered.[20] The typically German villages near Adelaide, like Hahndorf, preserve for us an insight into their immigrant way of life. In the South Australian Barossa Valley, now the center of the German-style wine industry, one of the leading vintners today is, by coincidence, a Lehmann.

John Lehmann settled in Adelaide, where he set up a butcher's shop — always a useful addition to a frontier town. Before long, like so many others, he was attracted by the Gold Rush to Castlemaine and

Bendigo, he and his family traveling the six hundred miles east to central Victoria by horse-drawn wagon. Along the rough roads they would, of course, have come across many other hopeful seekers. On the goldfields, while some sweated and toiled at digging and panning for gold others fed them and, in family photographs, we see our solid German forebears lined up in front of their Bendigo butcher's shop in traditional striped aprons. John Lehmann kept this shop in Bendigo for thirty years, long after most of the gold diggings had ceased to yield.

On the goldfields it was customary for the first gold won from new diggings to be made into jewelry for the women of the family. In this tradition, we treasure our great-grandmother Lehmann's earrings of pure Bendigo gold, shaped into delightfully delicate leaves with a tiny ruby in the center. The specks of gold in a small flask, which we admired with wide eyes as children, have, however, vanished with the passage of the years. Like so many other Australians we long possessed (from the Burston side of the family) and passed around wonderingly, worthless shares in gold claims at Coolgardie in Western Australia, which had never realized the dreams of their early investors. Through these relics we experienced some of the mysterious attraction of this almost mystical substance.

From Bendigo the Lehmann children made their way to Melbourne, where one son, Willy, became an architect, Charles and Alfred established themselves as music teachers, the elder daughter, Christine Marie, became a school teacher, and the younger sister, Mathilda or Tilly, kept house for two of her single brothers. There seems to have been an attraction to "single blessedness" in the family; three out of four of the children, Willy, Alfred, and Tilly, never married. Musical talent continued into the next generation, with Charles's son, also Willy, working as a percussionist in an orchestra all his life.

Our Mater, Christine Marie

The Lehmann who interests us in this story is my grandmother, Christine Marie, from whom I took my second name, Marie. In 1875, Christine married Harry Burston whose strand is yet to be taken up. Both Harry and Christine were teachers. In 1879 Harry was appointed Head Teacher at a small rural primary school at Upper

Diamond Creek, then an isolated place, ten miles by horse, buggy, or on foot from Heidelberg, which was itself a quite small town separated from Melbourne by miles of untamed Bush. Harry and Christine divided the teaching of all the grades between them, with Christine being in charge of the younger children. At the time, the state system of education was in its developmental stages. There was little education available beyond the eighth grade, when students who had not left earlier to help their parents on the farms and in the orchards would earn their much-prized Merit Certificate.

As I knew my grandmother in her retirement, she was a straight-backed, severe-looking person, with her head, surmounted by a neat cushion of hair, held high. She had survived a difficult life of struggle. She wore high-necked, black corsages, decorated with jet beads and a jet brooch, and was always respectfully called Mater in the German tradition. In photographs of the obligatory Christmas Teas at Mater's, we see her sitting bolt upright in her chair, surrounded, as a matriarch should be, by her obediently assembled children and grandchildren. She was very downright in the expression of her opinions, and she certainly impressed on me that "the King was only a man with a nose in the middle of his face the same as anyone else." An avid reader, in her retirement she went to the public library every week to pick up a number of novels, which she carried home in a little case. It was on one such trip, when she was in her eighties, that she was knocked down by a car and suffered injuries that in all probability shortened her life. We will hear more later of this strong woman, who battled on her own for her large family's survival in the bleak environment of sparsely populated rural Victoria at the end of the nineteenth century.

The Teaching Tradition

We now turn to the Burstons. My mother's grandfather, David Burston, was born in the Clifton area of Bristol, in Gloucestershire in England in 1823. His father, James, worked in the shipyards. Young David, who was first an accountant and then a teacher, was educated at Battersea College in London. In 1844 he married Sarah Spearman Diamond, the daughter of a shipwright. Attracted by news of the phenomenally rich finds on the Victorian goldfields, David and Sarah set sail for Australia in early 1852 on the *Medina*, with their three sons, Benjamin, John, and William. Because of the imminent birth of another child, they were forced to disembark in Adelaide, where three days later my grandfather Harry was born. He was christened in the Church of England at Hindmarsh, thus establishing another South Australian connection. A month later, the family continued their voyage to Melbourne on the *Verona* — a name familiar to me in my childhood as that of my grandmother's house in St Vincent Place, Albert Park..

David Burston first taught at St John's School in Launceston, Tasmania, from about 1854 to 1856 — in the very town in which my father, Harry Rivers, was born in 1853. Since Australia was very sparsely settled at that time it is not surprising that these early settler families found themselves in the same small pioneer towns. It is interesting to speculate that my grandfather Rivers and my great-grandfather Burston may well have known each other in Launceston in the mid eighteen-fifties. Whether this was so or not, my father had enormous respect for the famous Burston family of educators, to the point of giving his first daughter from the Burston connection the name of her maternal family — Linda Burston Rivers. In 1857 David entered the Victorian education service, teaching first at Tower Hill in Melbourne, then in various country towns.[21]

In August 1900, the *Australasian Schoolmaster* published an article on the Burstons in a series on "Noteworthy School Teachers." In this article the writer observed that David Burston was "the first master of the earliest established schools at Koroit and the picturesque Cudgee townships" (p.35). It is recorded in official reports that he was Metropolitan Singing Master in 1864-5. His arithmetic, however, does not seem to have been as strong as his music. At one point his departure from one school was "sanctioned without causing prejudice," on the understanding that when next employed (there was no tenure in those days, each appointment being a separate contract) he was to have one month's results "deducted for inaccuracies in the rolls." This being a period of payment by results there must have been some temptation for teachers who were parents of big Victorian families to blink at a little inaccuracy in the enrolment records. When I read this report I sympathized with poor David. I myself had trouble, during my service in the Victorian Education Department, in coming to a final total on attendance each month. On the last day of the month, the attendance figures had to be added up vertically and horizontally in order to arrive at a compatible figure for the bottom right-hand corner of the roll — a final figure that I must admit often eluded me. Amusingly enough, one of David's sons wrote an arithmetic textbook used for many years in Victorian schools. David Burston retired from teaching at the age of fifty in Warrnambool, where he remained to live out the last eight years of his life as a highly respected landowner in that prosperous area of the Western District.

The four Burston sons became notable leaders in the early days of the Victorian state education system, serving Victoria's youth in many capacities. Common schools were established in Victoria in 1862. Under the Victorian Education Act of 1872, public primary education became free, compulsory, and secular.[22] From 1863 on, the Burstons were well known as Head Teachers, textbook writers (specifically John, known as J. J.), and classifiers who decided promotions and appointments (William). All their wives were teachers. A number of their sons and daughters also became teachers, one, the son of J. J., making his application to be a pupil teacher in 1884 at the age of fourteen.

The eldest Burston son, Benjamin, began as a teacher of gymnastics and then singing, his pupils gaining many awards in musical competitions. As his wife and children were also very musical, he added to his residence a concert room where he and his family performed as a small orchestra. Unfortunately the leading violinist, his son Benjamin, achieved the dubious distinction of being one of the earliest school children in the state to be killed, along with several classmates, in a tragic collision of their vehicle with a train at a level crossing, while they were on their way to a school picnic. During his career Ben Burston occupied a number of positions as Head Teacher and was very well regarded. Just one blot appears on his Departmental record: in 1877 he was censured for making children cane each other and admonished for administering corporal punishment to girls. Before he retired, while he was headmaster at Bendigo East / Quarry Hill, he took the notable step for those days of establishing a library for scholars and teachers.

John Burston (J. J.) was Head Teacher in Ballarat and Bendigo and then came to the city, where for many years he was Head Teacher in St Kilda. Not at first attracted to a scholarly career, he spent five of his formative years working on a farm. He retained this love of outdoor life and became noted for his "robust and healthy constitution which enabled him to withstand the heavy strain of thirty-three years' continuous teaching practically without sick leave."[23] An excellent teacher himself, his notable contribution to Victorian education was the writing of widely used textbooks for the study of arithmetic, grammar, and science. He was the first teacher in the Education Department to become fully qualified as a science teacher. His arithmetic textbook, written in 1884 for "teachers of Victoria and neighbouring colonies," was an indispensable aid in schools for many years.[24] As a minor but unfortunate footnote in his inspector's reports, he was criticized on one occasion for somewhat neglecting his pupil teachers. The struggle between time for scholarly activity and the demands of supervision for a busy teacher, administrator, and parent were apparently as real then as now. J. J. loved writing and in his retirement he produced an advanced arithmetic text. My mother was very fond of her uncle, J.J., and stayed with him on occasions in his Melbourne home.

William Burston seems to have been a feisty character or at least a very determined one. He fought the Victorian Education Department for sixteen years over a resented inequity in his rank and position; he was, he considered, passed over for a merited appointment involving promotion. Eventually, by special Act of Parliament (the William Burston Act of 1906), he won promotion to teacher of the First Class and the salary to which he was entitled, with a considerable accumulation of back pay. Not surprisingly, he was the founder of an early teachers' union, the Victorian Male Assistants' Association, which was able to secure many improvements for men teachers in the Education Department. Women teachers had to wait nearly three-quarters of a century for equitable treatment.

Harry Burston and Christine Marie in Upper Diamond Creek

My grandfather, Harry (whom I will refer to as Harry B to distinguish him from my father, Harry Rivers) was "a skilful and lively teacher," according to his reports. He and Christine Marie (née Lehmann) taught together at Upper Diamond Creek for about nine years. A class picture from 1887 shows him with the fourteen pupils in his third, fourth, fifth, and sixth grades. The children are ranged in neat rows before the portable blackboard — the girls in their dark, long-sleeved dresses, covered by white pinafores, with long dark stockings, and the boys with jackets buttoned to the neck. They are holding their slates and slate pencils. Only my Auntie Del, a member of the teacher's family, is also holding a small, much used book. Harry B appears as a personable young man, with the customary moustache and square, well-trimmed beard of the period and a black bow tie at his neck. The photo was taken on a dirt road with a background of young, bark-shedding gum trees.

Harry B became the black sheep of the family in 1888 when he resigned his post and left the district for Tasmania with the female assistant from the neighboring school at Nillumbik (Diamond Creek), whose teaching he had been supervising. Christine, on a meager salary, was left to support a family of seven children, soon to become nine when twins were born after her husband's departure. To Harry B's credit, he did offer to take some of the children with him, but they elected to stay together with their mother. Subsequent to this unfortunate incident, Harry B's name was struck from the family records; his picture was cut out of the 1888 photograph of the Upper Diamond Creek classes with their teachers; and his existence is ignored in the 1900 article on the Burstons in the *Australasian Schoolmaster*.[25]

Christine Lehmann Burston, our Mater, ruled her family with an iron hand. With all due respect, she needed to, since after Harry B's defection she had to bring up her nine children alone, while working full time — and this at a period when there was no financial assistance of any kind for widows with dependent children. Her role was that of "work mistress," which in those days meant teaching the early elementary grades and teaching needlework to the girl pupils at all levels — a position later called "infant mistress." As a woman teacher she was not well paid. At the time, of course, women had few career options other than teaching. Even as fully trained teachers, they received only half as much pay as men teachers and could not rise to the eminence of Head Teacher. Women in the state educational service in Victoria had to wait until 1971 to reach parity in salary with men of equivalent rank and responsibilities. I myself, as a fully qualified high school teacher in Victoria in the 1940s, earned sixty per

19

cent of the salary of my male colleagues. We were told that this was because a male teacher had to support a family, but the same salary was paid to both single and married males. This disparity was based on the unfounded assumption that women did not have the ultimate responsibility of supporting a family. In fact many single women teachers had aged parents or other dependent family members to support — in Christine's case nine children. Until well into the 1950s, a woman teacher in the Victorian Education Department, who was foolish enough to marry but wished to continue teaching, lost all the benefits of her former permanent status. She became a "temporary" at a low salary with no benefits, even when continuing to teach in her former regular position. Certainly the records show that Mater, on retiring in 1906 after twenty-seven years of service, received a pension of thirteen pounds ten shillings per annum, whereas her brother-in-law Ben, after forty years of service, received in the same year a pension of two hundred and seventy-eight pounds. Even given the difference in professional status and responsibility, this makes a pro rata (year for year) differential of fourteen to one.

To return to Christine's story, her life after Harry B's desertion was devoted to the survival of her large family, teaching and taking in lodgers (usually single male teachers appointed to the area), while providing the best possible education for her own children — although not for all of them. Probably her precarious financial situation dictated this selectivity. She clearly had her favorites and this was much resented by the other children, as my mother frequently told me. Christine saw that her eldest and youngest daughters became teachers like herself and her third son an engineer. To achieve this end, those in the middle of the family had to be sacrificed. My mother, Nina, for instance, had to stay home every afternoon to look after the baby twins, thus missing out on arithmetic and reading, since these were taught at the same time every day on the regular Education Department schedule. Since, by the Victorian Education Act of 1890, children could receive a certificate of exemption from compulsory attendance at school as early as ten years of age to start work, after her basic literacy and numeracy education Nina had to stay home, so that her mother could continue to work. Any time she could be spared from her household and family chores, Mater would send her to help local ladies in need. This service was, of course, quite unpaid, as a generous gesture on Mater's part.

Nina and her siblings worked very hard in the demanding and punitive atmosphere that Mater established in the home. Perfection was expected; the rod was not spared; and boundaries, which had to be strictly observed, were set to curb their wanderings. Mother vividly recalled expending much effort washing, starching, and ironing heavy curtains or table linen, with irons heated on the stove, only to have them crushed in Mater's hands, if they were less than perfect, and sent back to be ironed all over again. The most the Burston children received in their Christmas stockings was perhaps an orange (a rare pleasure in that struggling household) and some nuts. The eggs from their hens were of necessity sold to the neighbors. Mother frequently recounted how she and her brother, Harry, once found two eggs in a nest that had been overlooked and were therefore not accounted for. They hid them until they could cook them surreptitiously and taste them as a luxury. Unfortunately, by the time they had the opportunity, during one of Mater's absences, to bring out their little treasures the eggs were addled.

My mother and her brothers and sisters led an isolated life in Diamond Creek, as the children of a school teacher who did not want them to marry into the uneducated and rough-living farming families in the area. This Magic Circle, as Mater called it, consisted of closely related nonconformists, considered quite unsuitable partners for the young Lutheran-Anglican Burstons. Any yearnings the Burston girls might have had for youthful dating with local swains was soon nipped in the bud by their mother. Two of the youngest daughters did manage to break through this ban later and married into the Magic Circle with rather unhappy consequences.

The Tanners

In 1902, at the age of twenty, Nina married Charles Joseph Tanner, a sixty-eight-year-old widower, retired teacher, and father of four adult children. Charles had been born in Shropshire in England, where his father, John, was a solicitor. When he was in his thirties, that is, in the 1860s, he had emigrated to Australia where he served as a teacher, and later Head Teacher, in country schools outside of Melbourne. He was considered "a good scholar and an excellent

21

teacher," whose students, in a period of payment by results, achieved an overall average of eighty percent in "a locality not favorable to good attendance or punctuality."[26] The children he taught were probably required to work very hard outside of school hours helping their parents on the surrounding farms and orchards

On his retirement, Charles Tanner settled in the Upper Diamond Creek-Hurstbridge area as an orchardist. Nina had been sent by her mother to nurse Charles's bedridden wife, which she did faithfully until Mrs Tanner died. Later, when she and Charles fell in love, Nina successfully battled her mother's opposition to marry this orchardist widower. As a husband Charles was very affectionate and kind to her, bringing her chocolate creams and roses with the dew on them and surrounding her with a loving care she had not experienced in her twenty years at home. From a very strict and constrained home life, where she had nothing of her own, she suddenly found herself mistress of a house and orchard, able to give her brothers and sisters apples and pears whenever she felt like it. She was encouraged in this bounty by her adoring, thoughtful, and indulgent husband. Later, there was the bonus of four children of whom three sons survived — my half-brothers Reginald, Leslie, and Harold. The first child, baby Nina, of whom Mother spoke frequently, died of rickets at the tender age of seventeen months. This unfortunate occurrence was all too common before the importance of vitamin C, now so frequently given in orange juice, was recognized. Of course, at the time there were no health centers where young mothers like Nina could get advice on the nutritional needs of their children. Nina had to depend on family lore handed down by older women neighbors. With Charles Tanner's four surviving children from his first marriage and a fifth who died young, this brings the total to 22 children so far in the family circle.

Nina loved Charles very much and she spoke of him frequently even fifty years after his death. When she died she was buried beside him in the Diamond Creek cemetery, where bellbirds chime in the tall gum trees.

1904 in the Valley

The Upper Diamond Creek-Hurstbridge area in Nina's and Charles's time (they had the picturesque, if vague, address of Second Watery Gully) was lush with beautiful fruit trees. J. J. Burston, in a poem written in the spring of 1904, gives a contemporary word picture of an area that has now been largely swallowed up by the suburban sprawl of Melbourne. Even in 1995, however, Second Watery Gully, when we sought it out along a rough, potholed road, still maintained its distinctively rural atmosphere as a backwater the municipality had forgotten.

THE ORCHARDS OF DIAMOND CREEK (Visited in Spring). J. J. Burston. 10/11/04

> Success to the famous orchard lands of Upper Diamond Creek,
> Restful resort of visitors who health and comfort seek;
> Thy pleasant hills and gullies fair the finest fruits produce
> While in the creek gold fossickers auriferous gravels sluice.
>
> From Greensborough to Queenstown's bridge in gorgeous array
> Continuous groups of orchard plots their foliage display;
> Where the road winds round the river banks for a dozen miles or more
> At every turn fresh beauties rise with fruit-gardens by the score.
>
> Thy orchard trees are white with blooms that promise luscious fruit;
> While golden wattle-blossoms deck the winding streamlet's route.
> The wooded bushlands still uncleared stand out in bold relief
> To the fruitful farms and furrowed fields where stands the oats in sheaf.
>
> The forest birds delight the ear with sweet melodious songs,
> And cheer the weary traveller who slowly plods along,

The cricket's chirp and locust's hum a drowsy
deafening din;
In the water-holes the croaking frogs their tales of
sorrow spin.

The magpie pipes his saucy strain, loud sings the
native thrush,
The twittering wren and flitting finch build nests in
every bush,
With hearty, merry, mocking laugh the jackass greets
the dawn,
And celebrates his doughty deeds at twilight, noon,
and morn.

But on this pleasant peaceful day a calmness rules the
air
While fleeting shadows softly sail o'er the neighb'ring
hill-tops fair,
Anon the glorious sun appears with brightest splendour
crowned
And quickens into vigorous life all the insect forms
around.
Here moth and butterfly are viewed with much
deserved disgust,
Their visits to the apple trees the orchardists distrust;
For their eggs upon the blossoms bright they cunningly
will lay,
And daily give the grower cause to use his pump and
spray.

The starling (insectivorous?) on insects now regales,
But, later on, the ripening fruit he feloniously assails:
Like the English sparrow, introduced for reasons
deemed the best,
The starling to the orchardist has proved a perfect
pest....

Another visit let us make, when the promised fruit is
ripe
And midsummer heat has made our throats dry as a
tobacco pipe.
The luscious juice of peach or pear will then our thirst
assuage,
While cherries, plums and apricots our digestive
powers will gauge;

Prime apples in great variety of every size and hue,
Like those which tempted Mother Eve will tempt both
me and you,
And lurking berries ripe and red the strawberry beds
will show,
On the raspberry canes and currant bush a heavy crop
will grow.

Success we wish to Diamond Creek. Success to the
growing fruit,
Sole industry which experience finds this hilly district
suit.
May every grower's wealth increase, and health attend
his toil;
Hard-earned whatever competence he wrestles from
the soil.

The Beautiful Widow on the Hill

Unfortunately, although perhaps not unexpectedly, Charles
died in 1909 when my mother was only twenty-seven. He left her
with an orchard and the responsibility of three young boys, one of
whom, Harold, she nearly lost to diphtheria. She often told us of the
harrowing night when she had to hold him tight in her arms, as he
struggled against choking, while she and a woman neighbor drove
him ten miles in a buggy to the Heidelberg Hospital. They arrived
with only minutes to spare to save his life.

For about six years Mother struggled on with the orchard, with
the help of a hired man. Making a living as a grower of apples and
pears was very chancy in that area, because of the great variability of

seasonal weather. As well as floods, frosts, and summer droughts, there were insect pests to contend with. Then there were the long hauls of the fruit to market over rough roads. As a young widow, Mother was of course ill prepared to conduct a fruit-growing business alone. Too many orchards had been established in the Diamond Creek area during the boom years at the end of the nineteenth century. Furthermore, unreliable buyers bought and sold the fruit to suit their own purses, with little thought for the continuing needs of the growers.[27] "Those land-owners who appeared to be well off and who advocated cultivation of the soil as an antidote to the dying out of the [gold] diggings," we are told, "did not realise the difficulties of the poorer type of settler who had not the capital to back him during times of stress, and in encouraging such settlers they were to some degree using them to maintain townships that would otherwise have died out. Yet the incentive to be independent was so strong that many new settlers did not seem to care if the problems were almost insurmountable."[28] Perhaps, like Charles Tanner and later Nina, they did not realize how precarious the situation of the orchard industry was. The coming into production of a large number of new orchards at the same time had caused a glut of fruit on the Melbourne market. Mother, along with many others, had the heartbreak of having to tip out beside the road loads of perfect fruit, meticulously picked and packed to avoid any bruising, because of the impossibility of selling them. Some growers, ironically enough, tipped them down the mineshafts.[29]

To add to the orchard growers' burden, in 1914 the fruit trees were struck by a most untoward frost that damaged every orchard in the area. The only one that survived happened to be protected during the night by a heavy discharge of smoke from a boiler at a nearby mine.[30] The natural calamity of the frost was the last straw for many. Inevitably, Nina was unable to meet payments on a loan she had taken out from a wealthy local citizen, who promptly decided to sell her property and orchard equipment over her head and put her and her young family out on the road. Despite her desperate personal pleas on his doorstep for time to work things out, this "devourer of widows' houses"[30] would not even come out of his house to discuss the matter with her. The orchard and equipment were put up for immediate sale. Paralleling her mother Christine's experience, Nina too was living

26

through a period when there was no help available for persons like her — widows with children in unexpected need. Now that she was practically penniless her dilemma was how to continue to feed and clothe her family and keep a roof over their heads. All through Nina's life her family came first and, in this predicament, as in later vicissitudes, her one thought was how to ensure their survival and progress.

The Chances of Matrimony

At this point the last threads of the tangle come together. Harry Rivers was by this time a stock and land appraiser and auctioneer with a noted company that sold country properties. After a long and happy marriage, during which he had brought up thirteen children, the three Grays from his wife's first family and his own ten children with Charlotte, he was now a widower of sixty. Always the life of the party, he happened to be in the Diamond Creek district on business when Nina's property came up for sale. At the local office of his company, his fellow workers teased him, as a single man, telling him about the beautiful widow up on the hill who would make him a very suitable partner. Ever one for a lark, Father entered into the jesting. After a certain amount of chiyacking his colleagues bet my father that he would never get to see Mrs Tanner and he cheerfully accepted the bet. Nina Tanner was, at this time, a very good-looking young woman but known to be extremely shy and retiring. Till the day of her death, she was wary of outsiders.

So Harry Rivers made his way up the hill, ostensibly to look over the property that was for sale. When he presented himself at the door, Nina refused to come out to see him. Instead, she sent the hired man to show him around. This apparently did not satisfy the strange man sitting determinedly on her veranda, so she next sent out her eldest son, who was nearly thirteen, to act as guide. Still the stranger, aware of the details of his bet, kept requesting to be shown the property by the lady of the house. Harry, ever patient, sat outside on the veranda for two hours while Nina sat inside, asking from time to time: "Is that man still there?" Finally, as the only way out of the impasse, she came out herself and agreed to show Harry the property. You will remember my reference to Father's hobby of mending shoes in his leisure time. One of his first observations on seeing Nina's three young boys running about was: "Those boys' shoes need mending!" After a pleasant stroll around the property and some agreeable conversation, Harry suggested he might come back again and check on a few more details and this he apparently did.

A series of letters from the next two months survives. The first, written on 26th October 1916, is marked "Strictly confidential" and is addressed to "Mrs N. B. Tanner, Balee, Upper Diamond Creek." The B refers to Nina's maiden name and shows that Father was already impressed to discover she was a Burston. The letter reads: "Dear Madam, Ever since that Sunday when I had an interesting conversation with you, admiration for your plucky determination to try and battle through is constantly cropping up in my mind and when I think of how you have struggled on in the interest of those three nice boys it excites my sympathy. If your first impressions of me are not unpleasant to you and you have not already bestowed your affection on any one other than your sons I would be pleased to further make your acquaintance if you will extend an invitation to me. If no reply comes to this, I shall understand that you have no desire to further acquaintance and will accept your decision in good part. In the meantime, I am yours very truly, Harry Rivers." Nina, somewhat surprised, naturally consulted her closest friend, her sister Adelaide, a single career woman who preferred to be called Del. Always the manager, Del urged her to look to the future and certainly to see Mr Rivers again.

Six days later, Harry wrote: "Mrs N. Tanner, Dear Madam, I was pleased to receive yours of the 30th ult. this morning and am glad to know that you are not unwilling to further acquaintance and sorry to hear that you are a sufferer from toothache. As you say I may call and see you tomorrow evening at 25 St Vincent Place, Albert Park [where Del lived with Mater in Melbourne], if you are well enough and free from the pains of bad toothache I will with pleasure call and see you." So Harry and Nina met again under the careful chaperonage of Del and Mater. Del took to him immediately and declared, "If you don't want to marry him, I'll marry him myself."

So the relationship blossomed. By November 9th, Harry is writing: "Dear Mrs Tanner, Unless something unforeseen occurs tomorrow (Saturday), I shall avail myself of your kind invitation and come up to see you on Sunday next unless the weather is too wet altogether. I hope you did not catch a cold in your face before you returned and that you are now in much better health through having your teeth extracted. If the boys are down by the Balee Ry Stn I will be pleased to have their company out to your place." On this occasion, Harry went for a ramble up the hill with Nina and, while sitting on a log, proposed marriage. By December 1st, Harry is writing "Dear Nina" and signing his letter "Yours ever affectionately," as he discusses renting a house in Moonee Ponds. His Dec. 4th letter to "My dear Nina" expresses hope that she has finished loading her belongings safely to move out of the Hurstbridge property.

Mother and her family moved in with Mater for a few weeks and, by December 21st, she and Harry Rivers were married. From this marriage were born two children, Linda Burston (Linda Belinda) and Wilga Marie (Billy Cockatoo or Chickabid), thus bringing our total to twenty-four children, of whom twenty-two survived into adulthood.

2

EXPLORING THE WORLD
THE ASCOT VALE DAYS

My earliest memory (is it mine? or have I heard it recounted?) is of being pushed around the streets of Moonee Ponds in a pram by my big Tanner half-brothers, Les, Reg, and Harold, who were from twelve to sixteen years older than I. One day, to their great consternation, I got out and wandered away. Frantically they searched for me up and down the streets and lanes. My "brilliant career" might have ended there, were it not that those were safer days. Otherwise, my earliest recollection is of a big, big dog that was tied up by the side of the house; he barked loudly and jumped up and down as I tried to walk past. I am sure now that he was trying to be friendly. At that time, however, I felt like Christian, in Bunyan's *Pilgrim's Progress*, who had to walk timorously between two roaring lions, only to find they were securely chained.[32] This early memory is confirmed by my sister Linda (sixteen months older than I), who remembers this dog, a kelpie, walking up and down behind the hen house with its tongue lolling out like a wolf. She also remembers huge hailstones. "The boys," as we always called my brothers, packed several of these together into a block of ice, pretending that this large ball had caused the rent in the canvas cover over the hen roosts. Naturally, we little sisters were wide-eyed at anything these giants might tell us. Down the street lived twin girls, Gus and Maude Morris who, not surprisingly, became of interest to Reg and Les. Soon the boys were taking the Morris sisters out on the pillions of their motorbikes, side-saddle, of course, and these were the girls they later married. I remember little else of my Moonee Ponds days. My memories really begin when we moved to 1 The Parade in Ascot Vale in 1923, the year I turned four.

The move to the Ascot Vale house was unforgettable. In exploring the new premises, my brothers found a small trapdoor, leading down into a cellar space under the pantry floor. This was altogether too tempting, with little Wilga wandering around getting under everyone's feet. Inevitably the boys yielded to the temptation to drop me down into the cellar, pretending they were going to close the trapdoor on me and leave me in the dark. I was terrified and naturally screamed blue murder. To this day, I startle easily at sudden noises and unexpected movements and, for many years, I had recurrent nightmares of doors or windows suddenly slamming open or shut. I would jump out of bed barely awake, only to realize, with my hand on the doorknob or the window catch, that once again this was merely a nasty dream.

The cellar incident was not the only near-disaster of my early childhood. One day my brother Les was chopping firewood in the yard. I was wandering around curiously, shadowing my clever older brother, when he suddenly swung back the axe, hitting me on the head. What consternation! With a cut above the eye and blood streaming down my face, I was brought inside, screaming with shock, while Linda cried bitterly in sympathy. Fortunately, as far as I can see, no permanent damage resulted.

The Context

In Ascot Vale, we lived on top of a hill, really the cliff of the wide Maribyrnong River valley, and from this elevation we looked down to the west toward the most magnificent sunsets you could ever imagine. 1923 was near enough to the tremendous volcanic explosion, which blew the island of Krakatoa out of the ocean and filled the atmosphere of the Southern Hemisphere with swirling masses of volcanic dust, for its effects still to be felt. The dust particles in the stratosphere distilled the most incredible colors from the sunlight. We would stand and watch until the brilliant oranges, reds, and greens had faded into purple mists.

My life in Ascot Vale revolved around school and family, in the house and in the garden. Father, by now a reporter for the four Murdoch papers, worked hard, but he was not a rich man. Once, at the Newmarket Yards, one of his fellow reporters remarked "Harry Rivers never made a fortune, but he surely spent one!" — referring to

31

the fact that he had brought up very successfully eighteen children, of whom six were not his own. Being big-hearted and fair, he found plenty of love for each of the children, treating them all with kindness and solicitude for their future.

The Ascot Vale house was a nine-roomed Victorian brick house with a slate roof. It had been built in 1882. Mother, although no amateur archaeologist, found years later, while digging in the garden, a silver sixpence dated 1881, which may well have been dropped by one of the builders. The house had a three-sectioned bay window in the front sitting room and a veranda with twisted columns, cast-iron lace decoration, and a beige, brown, and blue tiled surface. The house rested on deep basalt foundations, the great blue blocks of stone rising to three feet above the ground on the downhill side. Inside, the rooms had high ceilings, with plaster rosettes surrounding the light fittings, and six fireplaces, of which two were of marble (one black and one white) and two of polished cedar wood. There was a small entrance hallway leading into a long, nineteenth-century-style passage. Along both sides of the passage were bedrooms and the sitting room, always called the front room, which, as was the custom, was reserved for special visits and auspicious occasions. The passage led into a large vestibule with another small bedroom on one side and the living room on the other. A back door led directly from the vestibule to the garden. Off the living room was a long narrow kitchen, which had the nineteenth century relic of a gas-jet light on a rod that could be swung out from the wall. For many years, whenever there was a temporary cut in the electrical supply, we would light this jet with matches and enjoy watching the flickering semicircle of yellow flame with its core of blue. This made us feel very superior to our friends who had to depend on candles. The kitchen also doubled as a family dining room, except when we had visitors. These we entertained in the vestibule on a large dining table, which also provided us with an ideal surface for playing table tennis, doing homework, or ironing clothes. The latter chore soon became Linda's and mine, since it was the one household obligation that Mother disliked. Was this perhaps because of deep-seated resentment of Mater's harsh training in that task in her childhood? The bathroom off the kitchen was just what its name implies: a room with a bathtub, over which was a shower fired by a temperamental heater we fed with wood chips gathered from around the garden. There was no washbasin and the toilet, or lavatory, was outside at a back corner of the house. This was a cool, isolated, and tree-sheltered spot, which necessitated in the evenings a walk in the dark in leafy shade, which all kinds of scary ghosts and goblins might inhabit. Off the living room were two tiny rooms: a sewing room, well lit by a narrow floor-to-ceiling window, and a completely dark, cool pantry with lots of shelves for storage. There was plenty of room at Ascot Vale for the seven of us, with many corners where we could get away on our own to hide or read or dream.

My memories of this house, which we kept in the family for sixty years, range from listening to the rain drumming on the corrugated iron roof of the vestibule to setting out dishes, buckets, and saucepans in strategic spots in the house to catch the raindrops that seeped in from the shifting slates on the roof. Sometimes, in later years, I even had to climb onto the roof in the driving rain to slip errant slates back into place. Driven by curiosity, Linda and I would peep down through the trapdoor in the pantry to gape at the deep cavity between the basalt foundations or climb up ladders to gaze through the manholes into the cobwebby roof spaces. On boiling hot days we would relax in the cool, cave-like temperatures that the high ceilings and nine-inch, double-brick walls provided. In all seasons, of course, we could enjoy the spaciousness and beauty of the garden, our playground.

Our Garden

The garden in Ascot Vale was an integral part of all of our activities. As well-bred children we were not allowed to play in the street. The garden centered on a twenty-five foot high Illawarra flame tree, an Australian native not very well known in Victoria at the time, which must have been planted when the house was built in 1881. With its big fig-like leaves, it created deep shade. Its alternating branches, not far apart, mounted circling upwards around a strong central trunk, which made it ideal for little legs to climb. Once at the top, we would poke our heads out and call on all and sundry to admire our crinoline. After a few very hot weeks the flame tree would really flower. It would lose every leaf, every twig would glow red, and the tree would be covered with innumerable clusters of scarlet bells — a great red pyramid at which one could only gaze with delight. Then came the enormous task of clearing up the great piles of large five-lobed leaves. The brick incinerator would be burning until late in the night as we kept packing in the seemingly endless piles of leaves. Mother, ever tireless, would clean away every leaf until you could have eaten off the ground. When the leaves were cleared away and the red bells had fallen, there was the further magic of the red carpet they formed under the tree. Later, when the large black pods ripened and split open, they could be painted gold or silver and packed with satiny pincushions for presents.

As well as the flame tree, there were two huge orange trees, whose perfume, along with that of the nearby lemon tree, wafted into the house. An overarching almond tree at the back of the yard was a bridal veil of delight in the spring. There were seven spreading, climbable pittosporums with, hidden among them, a few kurrajongs, whose tiny, clustered bells were light green with tiny red markings. In front of the house, hanging over the street were two big Western Australian cedar wattles that bloomed in January instead of July, when most of Victoria's wattles bloomed. This summer flowering would greatly astonish passersby, who would unexpectedly find themselves walking over a carpet of fragrant, golden balls. Linda and I, sitting hidden in the branches above them, would drop pebbles into the creases of the men's hats as they paused or break off from the tree trunk globules of resin to chew.

Our front fence, with its high wooden pickets, extended each side from an imposing gate, with side posts crowned by carved wooden knobs that we found were remarkably shaped for small legs to wind around. Linda and I would sit on each side of the gate, smiling happily as we greeted passersby in the street. To our surprise, our elevated perch seemed to agitate some of the kind ladies, who would remonstrate with us. "Little girls! Get down! You're going to hurt yourselves!" they cried. "You'll fall!" How nervous older people get about silly things, we thought! Haven't they ever climbed trees? This was mild stuff to us. However, to placate them, or more probably to silence their nagging, we would obligingly climb down, only to remount to enjoy our elevated position as soon as they had turned the nearby corner.

Those who know me are well aware that I am an avid gardener and never happier than when pottering around among plants and trees,

34

caring for their many wants. Those of you who do not share this passion and do not know a pansy from a poppy or a hibiscus from a camellia may want to skip the next four paragraphs, where I will share the details of our Ascot Vale garden with fellow devotees.

In the middle of the front garden was a very large camellia bush. At some stage it had been grafted and it now produced double pink and white camellias, pink speckled or striped camellias, white camellias with one red petal and, from time to time, a pure pink or a pure white camellia, or even a pure red. These flowers were so delicate and beautiful that we loved taking them to school for the teacher or giving them to our friends. We always had floating bowls of camellias in the house and we would wear them as corsages when we went out. Unfortunately they were very fragile and breathing on them seemed enough to turn them brown. It was my responsibility to remove all the brown or browning heads from this very large bush to keep it looking beautiful. This was quite a task. One year I counted the number of heads as I gathered them and found I had taken two thousand off this one bush in one season.

Nearby was a laurestina, with deep green leaves, the whole bush covered in season with beautiful heads of white florets. Golden genistas bloomed prolifically and seeded themselves all over the garden. On one hot day each year their seedpods would start popping in the summer heat and all that day the garden would be full of a sound like miniature gunfire. On the back fence were cactuses that produced some of the largest cactus flowers I have ever seen, red and white, the latter like big waterlilies. At the side of the house, we also had a strange Western Australian centipede bush, with horizontal veins cutting across the long, narrow, tapering leaves. Little multicolored flowers would appear along the sides of the leaves at the ends of the horizontal veins and new leaves would branch off from the sides of existing leaves. Large, sprawling, and seemingly chaotic, it was quite a novelty to ponder.

Much as it would delight me, I will not go into all the treasures of that garden. I cannot, however, omit the arum lilies with their white, half-folded cones around long yellow pistils, which grew prolifically year after year down one side of the house along an ivy-covered fence. In the same area, the humble oxalis, a shamrock-like weed, spread in thick carpets. One summer my brother Harold tried to

35

eradicate it, bulb by bulb, over days and weeks without success, and now, to Harold's incredulous astonishment, I carefully cultivate it as an indoor plant, to brighten the dark Massachusetts winter with its delicate white flowers. Mother's perennial dahlias, tall, single, and multi-colored, flowered and flowered for months, always providing a rich supply of cut flowers for the house. Miniature sunflowers turned their faces to the sun down by the garden tap; and ivy geraniums, pink and mauve, grew on the wire netting beside the garden path. At one side of the house was a very fragrant woodbine tree — a novelty in those parts — keeping company with the free-flowering red and pink weigelas and a damson plum tree that practically dropped its luscious, ripe fruit into our mouths. Snowball bushes, with tiny, hard, white balls, proliferated, beside a gold-spot bush, whose leaves unfortunately burned black in the Melbourne sun. Along the lane beside the house, the fence was covered with an orange trumpet vine, which spread and spread. Nor must I forget the lavender-blue bells of the lofty jacaranda with its delicate fern-like leaves, in among which one could glimpse the pink of the flowering red currant climbing along its branches. These contrasted with the huge, purple, hibiscus-like flowers of the showy lasiandra. When the fragrant mock orange that sheltered the birdbath by the kitchen door had run its course, we acquired a tall loquat tree and we loved to gather from the ground its luscious, sweet fruit, sucking off the narrow band of yellow flesh from the center of hard kernels. At the back of the yard was a very large bay tree, whose aromatic leaves we could use for seasoning; this we called the "blowfly tree," because the blowflies, finding the perfume of its leaves irresistible, created a steady din with their incessant buzzing.

Later Harold built a diamond-shaped bed where the side lawn had been, with a pretty pink and white camellia in the center. Around the diamond there was a pathway for ease in planting and watering, with flowerbeds on all sides. In these beds we planted massed displays of multi-colored ranunculi, asters, pansies, poppies, snapdragons, or whatever took our fancy. We cherished a small daphne bush because of the exquisite fragrance that emanated from its unassuming pink and white florets; its only competitor for subtle perfume was a small boronia bush that bore tiny brown bells with lime-green interiors.

Our magnificent almond tree deserves special note. Its luminescent blossoms of the palest pink were, along with the modest snowdrops, the first sign of spring. We brought armfuls of blossom into the house to decorate the living room and the vestibule. We distributed beautiful sprigs to our friends; we took them to school. We dressed up and acted out our little dramas under the tree. We had nutting parties with our friends to pick almonds. We first ate green almonds that we gathered under the tree. Later in the season, we vigorously shook the dried almonds off the high branches, climbing onto the roof of the neighbor's garage with some trepidation (trespassing was considered a major delinquency) to gather those too high to reach with a long pole.

Auntie Tilly, our German-speaking great-aunt, would always come visiting when spring burst upon us, looking for her share of almond blossom to brighten up her little house. Tilly had a green thumb. Everything she touched grew in profusion. In her house she had innumerable pots on stands and flowering plants at the windows. Down the very narrow path at the side of her house were stacked more pots of plants, profusely growing from slips she had begged, or surreptitiously purloined, from friends and neighbors. All of these plants were lovingly tended and watered with great assiduity. For Tilly, everything grew vigorously, flowered, and seeded for the next season. This propensity to care meticulously for all growing things is something that I inherited from the same genes, I presume. As friends who have visited me in Massachusetts know, in the winter I dedicate one room of my house entirely to plants I am carrying over till the spring. Some years there are thirty or more plants, all wintering under my tender loving care — six-foot hibiscuses, baskets of hanging ferns and fuchsias, a rubber tree, a young kurrajong in a pot, dormant hydrangeas, and newly rooted slips of geraniums and impatiens. It is surprising how dejected they look when I return from a trip out of town, even though others have watered them. These pampered pets reward my efforts by blooming profusely on my veranda or in the garden during the summer.

We also delighted in our big pittosporum trees, with their multiplicity of spring florets in small, white clusters, their perfume pervading the garden. As time went on these florets produced orange berries, which split open to reveal a sticky red center; this stickiness eventually covered the ground under the trees and stuck to our shoes. Nevertheless, the pittosporum trees were our great playground; we climbed them and hid in them to spy on our pursuers when playing Cowboys and Indians. We swung on their branches or merely kept cool in shelters, or myah-myahs, we built of branches in their deep shade.

Mother, having grown up in the country, missed the ubiquitous gum tree. On one occasion she saw one in a little pot in the garden section of a store. Feeling nostalgic, she bought it for one shilling and sixpence. Into the garden it went, at the front corner of the house. We soon discovered why the Australian eucalyptus tree has rapidly covered the vast areas of the world into which it has been introduced — in Europe, Asia, Africa, and the Americas. It grows rapidly and will not quit, no matter what the adversity — drought, bush fire, or flood. Very soon our specimen towered over the house, dropping, as gum trees will, innumerable leaves into our irascible neighbor's gutters and down pipes, its bark, dry as tinder, hanging loosely in strands down its trunk. To reduce the nuisance to our neighbor and ourselves, we cut it down. The trunk was so thick at the base that we could not dig it out; all we could do was cut it through fairly close to the ground. So much for the gum tree! Finis! We were liberated! But not for long. Young shoots appeared all around the stump. Some of them, feeling a primitive urge to reach to the heavens, shot higher and higher and soon we had the equivalent of several gum trees reaching up into the sky. These were slashed down in their turn, without too much success, and the struggle continued. Years later, when I returned from three years in Europe, what was the first glimpse I had of my home as I was being driven up The Parade? Nothing less than the sight of our gum tree's third or fourth generation of branches asserting their right to clean, fresh air as they shot up into the sky.

As I grew older, Mother and I, the two garden-lovers, would often take a stroll in the cool of the evening to visit personally every plant and flower, discussing and marveling over their progress and enjoying the new beauties each day had brought.

Despite my botanical name, we did not have a wilga tree in the garden. Wilga is my namesake's aboriginal name; botanically it is Geigera Parviflora. It is a hardy, not overly tall tree with thick narrow leaves for survival in arid areas (the cattle eat its leaves in times of drought) and a drooping propensity, like a weeping willow. As a child, I was frequently reminded that, when the Prince of Wales visited Australia in the early 1920s, he was reported to have sat under "a graceful wilga tree." McCullough describes it in the following terms: it was "commonly held the most beautiful in this part of Australia [outback New South Wales]. Its leaves were dense and a pale lime green, its shape almost perfectly rounded. The foliage grew so close to the ground that sheep could reach it easily, the result being that every wilga bottom was mown as straight as a topiary hedge. If the rain began they would have more shelter under it than any other tree, for Australian trees were generally thinner of foliage than those of wetter lands."[33] It was not until 1988, in the Botanic Gardens in Canberra, that I actually saw my first wilga tree. It was a thrill for me, after so many years, to finally see the tree for which l was named.

So how did I come by my horticultural name in prescience of my love of all growing things? It seems that when Father was in his roaming country days he had known a squatter who had two lovely daughters, Wilga and Wita (a name ascribed since my childhood to a bird I have not been able to trace). When I was born, Father suggested that Mother choose one of these two indigenous names, in recognition presumably of Australia's growing sense of national identity. Fortunately, in my view, Mother chose the more melodious and evocative of the two, although I have spent my life combating school nicknames like Wigla and Wiggie, "Olga from the Volga" and Mulga (that small scrubby desert bush), as well as misnomers like Wilma, Wilda, Wilbur, Hilda, and Helga. As an Australian name, Wilga is recognized, but it is not common. Sometimes it is spelled Wilgah. My first "other Wilga" was Wilga Thomas, who was named after me. Her mother had shared a ward with my mother at delivery time and asked what my name would be. "Wilga Marie! What a pretty name!" she exclaimed. Not unexpectedly, then, I found myself in the early grades sitting across the aisle from Wilga Thomas, who left for Sydney when I was in the second grade, leaving the Wilga field clear for me, at least for a while. When, at twenty, I went to teach in the small country town of Kerang in northern Victoria, Wilga Thorne was in my first French class. Apart from a nineteenth-century Wilga, commemorated on a plaque at the entrance to Christ Church, South Yarra, a fair-haired Wilga who was the daughter of a professor of botany at Monash University, Alyssa Wilga Hart, my Texan goddaughter, and a Wilga in Kruiningen in the Netherlands, the daughter of Willy and Olga, who makes handmade dolls, this exhausts my homonymic acquaintanceship.

Under the almond tree was a chook yard with a fenced-in run. In the fence was a narrow, low-set door through which we had to crawl to search for eggs and give the chooks their daily ration of seeds, bran, and green stuff, with occasional grit to strengthen the eggshells. For Christmas dinner, we would kill an old hen. Mother was the one who had the courage to wring its neck, just as she was the one to chase mice around the kitchen with a broom and the one who would stand at the kitchen door during a thunderstorm admiring the lightning, of which I was terrified. These were all very courageous things in my eyes.

Our playhouse was under the flame tree. Made for us out of palings by our brothers, this was a small room with a door and a window, linoleum on the floor, curtains on the window, and an inactive little light bulb in the center of the ceiling to give the impression of light. In here we kept our doll's bed, a small pram, and little chairs. In pride of place was Linda's very precious doll's tea set of orange china (a gift from her godmother, Del). This we used for the little tea parties we offered to selected friends. The doll's bed, painted mauve, had been made for us by Mr Macintosh, the washboard maker whose big workshop was across the lane. Linda used it later to demonstrate bed making to Tenderfoot recruits in our Girl Guide company. In the playhouse this little bed did not lack occupants. We were very joyful when Santa Claus brought us dolls, with pink-cheeked china faces and eyes with real lashes that opened when you sat them up and shut when you laid them down. One Christmas I was given a fairy doll and Linda a little boy doll with short pants and a cap. I set my lovely creature up on the windowsill of the front bedroom and, to my great distress, she fell on the tiled veranda smashing her china face. These beauties were a big step up from the much loved rag doll, with its painted face — my first doll that Mother had made for me. I must admit that there are some distinct advantages to rag dolls. They are very cuddly and you can drag them around by a leg or an arm and chew them or drop them without worrying about breaking them. Another delightful object in the playhouse was a bag of scraps from mother's dressmaking and altering efforts, along with old, outgrown dresses, from which we could find materials for dressing our dolls. These fabrics also provided us with props for our constant acting efforts. Our button box, filled with buttons collected over many years by Mother from innumerable worn-out dresses and coats, filled many a wet afternoon with pleasure and delight as we sorted and grouped them and marveled at their intricate designs. As time went on our collection was augmented with the various commemorative buttons that Dad bought for various good causes as he came home from his work in the city. "Under the clocks" at the entrance to Melbourne's central Flinders Street station was always a happy hunting ground at rush hour for fund-raisers of all stripes.

Further diversion was provided by several short sections of chandelier glass, beveled to a triangular shape, that someone had given us. These were most magical. We would walk along the garden paths looking at the marvelous multicolored world, as the chandelier glass broke up the daylight into the colors of the spectrum. If we looked through one side of the glass, the normally level path before us would appear to mount precipitously and we would find it most difficult to walk along it; then we would giggle nervously and stumble when the path, seen from another side of the glass, descended steeply into the depths in a way that did not respond at all to the reality our feet were signaling. Like a pot and a spoon for a small child, a piece of chandelier glass is much more fun to play with than many expensive toys.

The playhouse was next to the shed, a workshop that was also under the flame tree. This was where Dad mended our shoes in his spare time and our brothers did all those useful mechanical things that boys seem to love to tinker with. Adjoining the shed was the washhouse, indispensable in this time of long, hard days of hand washing. Mother would soak the clothes in two deep wooden troughs, over which she would then scrub them on a corrugated, wooden washboard. Directly adjoining the troughs was a brick construction holding a large copper container, with a fire-hole and grate beneath it into which chopped wood was constantly fed to maintain a roaring fire. The intense heat kept the water at a rapid boil that whitened the sheets and drew the dirt from heavy work clothes. Meanwhile Mother constantly turned the clothes over with a solid, well-worn stick. Mother refused to use the traditional bluing powder to whiten the whites, maintaining that this eventually gave the linens and cottons a grayish tinge. A good swirling boil with the right kind of soap and some washing soda was all that was needed for the whitest of whites.

Each week Mother would spend one long washing day in this small, overheated, steaming place with unlined weatherboard walls and a corrugated iron roof. No wonder that, in the summer, she often preferred to do her washing by lamp or candle light at nine or ten o'clock at night, when the air was cooler. Our big yard was invaluable for hanging out the large family wash on long lines. On innumerable occasions we had to dash out to rescue the week's wash from Melbourne's inevitable refreshing showers. Mother, with her country upbringing, was always careful to bring the washing in before dark, so that there would be no danger of what was known as "snowdropping" (the stealing of clothes from the washing-line while the family slept). On many occasions when the weather had been damp, this meant hanging sheets, shirts, and underwear to dry on the backs of chairs before the fire.

In our Ascot Vale home, we hardly needed ice in the summer. In the garden was a very old tank on a raised platform, which collected water from the roof. From this tank we could draw really cold water, as we could also from the front garden tap, which was fed from pipes that went deep into the ground. After long use, the tank fell into disrepair and became a breeding ground for mosquitoes. As the number of larvae in the water increased, we knew it was time for this garden landmark to go. We also had a Coolgardie safe under a pittosporum tree. This goldfields type of appliance consisted of a metal cage with burlap sides and a shallow dish on top. This dish was filled with water and strips of cotton material hung from it on all sides, their wet surfaces keeping the burlap moist and the interior very cool, so that the milk, cream, and meat were kept fresh and sweet inside it. When we eventually did get an ice-chest, I would ride to the local ice works to buy a block of ice, which I would tie on the back carrier of my pushbike. Then I would ride home half sitting on the cold, cold ice.

The front veranda with its smooth brown, beige, and blue decorated tiles was another play spot. Its tiled surface was ideal for

42

tops that we whipped with cord on sticks, trying to see how long we could keep them going. We decorated the upper surfaces of our tops with colored chalks and watched them spin until the colored designs blended into pure white. The twisted columns supporting the veranda were frequently in use for tying up robbers hunted down by amateur cops. For these games, we would also hide high in the pittosporum trees and drop berries, overripe and sticky if possible, on our pursuers, if they did not find us soon enough. The little boys we played with would rapidly scale the back fence to escape — a feat a little beyond my sister and me — and the chase would continue around the lane that circled two properties to lead out again into the street.

The Neighbors

Soon we were playing up and down the lane with the children of neighbors. Fortunately the lane was little used by vehicles. Few people had cars at the time. The neighbors whose houses backed on to the lane were a very mixed group, from the Broses, socially up with their large, affluent-looking brick house and garden, to the Schwarzes, who were socially down. Their house was weatherboard, with a corrugated iron roof, and they had to use a small "dunny" at the back of the yard, from which voices would emanate, shouting: "Mum! Paper! Quick!" In one of the yards backing on to the lane was an elevated pigeon house and toward sunset we would see a flock of homing pigeons, wheeling in formation across the sky for their evening exercise. On Mondays, the Bottle-O, with his horse-drawn dray, would make his circuit around the lane to pick up the "dead marines" (empty bottles) from neighbors' weekend carousals, crying "Bottle-O! Bottle-O" all the way. Sometimes this was varied with a singsong "Rags, bones, and bottles."

The back lane, an open-ended "right-of-way" that circled our house and the neighbor's, was lined with paling fences, covered with reddish-purple bougainvilleas and pink, pea-flowered dolichos. This secluded area was the site for an occasional two-up game — that gambling diversion, illegal at the time, which is sometimes called Australia'a national game. The lane was also a resort for "runners" for starting-price bookmakers, also illegal, who took off-course bets on the horse races, basing the odds they offered on the wager rates announced on the radio at the beginning of the race. We would

43

sometimes see a "nit keeper" (or lookout) at the entrance to the lane on race days, watching to warn bookies and bettors of an approaching policeman. Despite the danger of prosecution, the proprietor of the nearby lolly shop and the greengrocer also accepted starting-price bets to supplement their income and bring customers into their shops.

Our brothers and their mates were frequently out in the back lane with their Harley Davidson and Indian motorcycles, which seemed to require constant revving up for adjustment. Noise seems to be one of the essential joys of motorbike riding. When the boys were not in the back lane fiddling and tinkering with their bikes, they were in the shed, refining some motorcycle part with a file. This devotion to motorbikes was transformed in later life into a passion for rebuilding and restoring old cars, a passion which they passed on to the next generation. Since Mother could never get the boys to come for meals when called, she resorted to a metal triangle, which was struck loudly with a metal rod to attract their attention. As children, Linda and I loved to strike the triangle. How we came by it is still a mystery to me.

Across the lane on the uphill side were a dentist and his wife, with two children, more or less our age. One of the cultural values inculcated into us early in life was not to ask personal questions. Unfortunately Mrs Rosen, the dentist's wife, being from a different culture, would stop us when we were on our way home from school and check on developments in our family affairs. As a consequence, we were forbidden to speak to the Rosens at all and this ban lasted a good twenty years. On the downhill side was a Scottish neighbor, Mrs Buchan, who hated trees, particularly messy ones that dropped leaves and twigs on her meticulously swept paths. After many years of bickering about this sore point, she poisoned the roots of a big pittosporum tree on our property boundary. First one half and then the other fell across our garden. To Mother killing a tree was akin to killing a living, breathing entity and not to be endured. Naturally after that, our relations with that neighbor were even more strained than before. Mr Buchan, who had spent a lifetime with the intimidating Mrs Buchan, was a very quiet man who spent his days on a ladder, painting and repainting their weatherboard house, working carefully around it and then starting all over again. If we slept in on Saturdays or Sundays, we had to be very careful about positioning the window

44

blinds, because Mr Buchan might very well be on a ladder just outside our bedroom window, painting his down pipes one more time. Under Mother's careful guidance, we adhered in our neighborhood relations to the old adage: "An Englishman's home is his castle," and the fortress walls were kept high. Fortunately, with all the treasures of our little domain, we never needed to stray very far from home for our childhood amusements.

Apart from the yard, we had a huge shed across the lane to play in. Its owner, Mr Macintosh, was a carpenter and blacksmith, who made washboards and wooden garden seats with metal supports. Before washing machines took over, dirty clothes were scrubbed over a trough of soapy water against the corrugated surface of a washboard, of either wood or metal. Mr Macintosh's trade called for frequently shaping wood, held in great vices, which resulted in deep piles of sawdust that were a great delight to climb over and sink into. Working with metal required him to keep a huge forge burning and later he would beat the hot metal into shape on an anvil. We loved watching all this from a safe distance. Sometimes Mr Macintosh would throw steel filings into the forge to delight us with their multicolored sparks. Not many children were allowed into this magical domain, but we had the run of the place. For little explorers there were mysterious, neglected, cobwebby back corners into which we could delve, while outside at the back was a tiny, overgrown area where untended weeds and grasses grew nearly as high as our heads. During Mr Macintosh's lunchtime, he would play guessing games with us. With a long stick, he would trace initial letters followed by dashes on the dusty floor for us to fill in with letters, to make the names of towns and cities. One day, when we were older, we brought Mr Macintosh into our living room to lie on the sofa with chest pains, and not long afterwards he retired from his work in the shed. It was a time of nostalgic sorrow for us when, some years later, we watched the huge shed being dismantled and modern houses, inhabited by strange new people, gradually taking its place.

My Tanner Brothers

My three Tanner half-brothers had a great deal of influence on me as I was growing up. Being so much older than I, they naturally seemed to be endowed with much wisdom. Because of their early

45

family circumstances, as fatherless country boys, and their own natural diffidence, they did not continue school after the eighth grade when they earned their Merit Certificates and were legally able to leave school. Father, being of the old school of self-educated men who had made their way through learning from life and practical experience, did not insist on further education for them beyond that stage. Work was the real purpose of life in his eyes. In any case, only a small percentage of Victorian youth went on to high school in the teens and twenties of the twentieth century. Mother always maintained that, had Father not died when Linda and I were in high school, we also would have left school early for the world of work. She was the one who was determined that we should continue with our education for as long as we could, partly because of her own deprivation in that area and also from a sense of competitiveness with her more educated brothers and sisters, who had been Mater's favorites.

My brothers were engaged, for the most part, in work of a practical nature, and I soon learned to appreciate the fact that there were many kinds of intelligence other than the verbal, academic kind. This conviction of mine predated by some fifty odd years Howard Gardner's theory of Multiple Intelligences. Gardner has identified eight kinds of intelligence: linguistic, logico-mathematical, spatial, bodily-kinesthetic, musical, interpersonal, intrapersonal, and more recently naturalist; there are surely others still to be categorized.[34] My second brother, Les, for instance, had an uncanny diagnostic ability with anything mechanical or electrical and Reg, as the years went by, became in his spare time a self-taught carpenter and cabinet-maker, demanding of himself great perfection in his work. Harold, similarly, could turn his hand to anything in the practical domain. This early experience in a family of mixed educational levels and occupations developed in me a great appreciation of diversity of talents and achievements, providing a strong antidote to any temptation to intellectual snobbery.

My eldest Tanner brother, Reg, was of an inventive turn of mind, a characteristic that showed up early, when he invented a little folding playpen to fence Linda in when she was a little girl. These types of contraptions are not a novelty now, but his construction was considered such an innovation in the early 1920s that it earned him a photograph and a report in the local newspaper. When he was in his late teens, he invented and built of wood a small sidecar, which he attached to his pushbike to take his little sisters out for rides. This again was his own invention, before such sidecars, attached usually to motorcycles, became fashionable conveyances for flappers. By the time Reg had moved on from pushbike to motorbike, he was, of course, taking out his girlfriend in his sidecar. In his teens Reg had begun studies as a draftsman and this initial training served him well in his endeavors, although he did not find his niche in that type of work. He continued to create useful and practical inventions to fill perceived gaps until just before his death at eighty, when, for his latest brainchild, the Inventors' Club in Melbourne named him Inventor of the Week. Since he had a garage that opened onto a very narrow country road, he worked out a system whereby the driver could drive a car onto a metal plate in the garage; this plate could then be turned around with one hand, even by a woman, so that the car could be driven out freely, without having to reverse and maneuver in a small space. This was the invention for which he received special recognition.

Reg's greatest weakness was his inability to assess reality. He was forever the Peter Pan of our immediate family, although he was the eldest. He was the epitome of Alexander Pope's epigram: "Hope springs eternal in the human breast." Till the day he died, Reg remained convinced that there was a pot of gold just around the next corner, even though he had never found it. He wanted more than anything to be an important international business executive, jetting from capital to capital and continent to continent, but he had never learned that you begin small to grow big. He firmly believed that if someone, anyone, would just lend him enough money (two thousand dollars, twenty thousand — whichever amount slipped through the conversation without being disputed) he would succeed this final time. He continued in this belief to the end of his life, even though everyone in his family and among his acquaintances had already lent him sums of money of various magnitudes, often sacrificially, to help him out of difficulties. All of this money seemed to disappear into a mysterious black hole. He never stopped working very hard indeed, as many hours as his body could stand, but always, like Sisyphus, pushing against gravity and gaining one step to lose two. He was,

47

however, a very pleasant-mannered, kindhearted man, who helped a number of people out of unfortunate straits, sometimes only to be cheated and robbed by the very people he thought he was assisting on their way. Somehow Lady Luck never found her way to his door.

Our second brother, Les, was quiet and thoughtful, with the dark hair and dark eyes of the Tanners and Lehmanns. He was an avid reader of mystery stories and Westerns. After leaving school with his Merit Certificate, he continued with technical studies to become an electrician. In his spare time, he was first a motorcycle fanatic, like his brothers and friends, graduating to a fascination with motorcars as soon as he could afford an old model. He never lost this devotion to old model cars, as newer and newer models appeared on the market, preferring in later years ones from early carmakers no longer in business. After the horrors of the Depression, when, like his brothers, he suffered long periods out of work, he became an electrical technician in a big garage, spending his days detecting and correcting faults in the electrical systems of motor vehicles. It was here, and with many of his friends' cars, that he demonstrated his extraordinary diagnostic skill. He loved music of the artistic popular kind, songs like "I heard a brown bird singing" or "Only God can make a tree." Whenever I hear the old song, "Moonlight and roses," so popular during my childhood, I think of my brother Les. In later years, when he was earning extra money shuttling between picture theaters in the evenings, transferring reels of films that were being shown concurrently in several places, he would mark on the radio program in the newspaper at what particular moment he could hear a particular song. He would then make a special effort to call in at our Ascot Vale home, just for the few minutes during which he could hear it, before rushing off again on his busy schedule. In those days there were, of course, no radios or cassette players in cars.

My third brother, Harold, began work delivering cables for the Pacific Cable Telegraph Company. A subterranean cable, completed in 1871, which carried Morse-coded messages via Batavia, Singapore, Malaysia, India, Egypt, and the Mediterranean to Europe, was at that time the fastest way to communicate with the rest of the world. However, like many of the young people of his generation, Harold was fascinated with the prospect of working on the land. He refused other opportunities, including an apprenticeship with a major printing

48

enterprise. So Father, who met many stockbreeders in his work at the Newmarket Yards, arranged for him to work for two pioneering brothers who owned property in the hills north of Melbourne, in the Lancefield-Emu Flat area. Life was very rough and ready for Harold during this period. He found himself working for a very hot-tempered, impatient man who swore and cursed at him, with very little concern for the feelings of an inexperienced city boy. He was sent out to work in an isolated area, slashing down wattles and gums on virgin land and living alone in a shack with burlap walls, with a weekly visit from a human being to replenish his food supply. Later he worked in the equally underdeveloped wheat-growing area in the northwest of Victoria, at Wycheproof, during a mouse plague. He would find mice running up his trouser legs and in among his possessions. He would open a drawer and there they were. Old kerosene tins full of water were set out to try to trap as many as possible. This mouse plague entered the world of perennial newspaper fillers and for years little items would appear in papers in various parts of the world about mice advancing on southern Australia, destroying all the wheat crops and devouring the vegetation. Years later, friends in France and in the United States would send me cuttings about this phenomenon, the last one coming from Iowa with a note attached saying: "Those mice again! Are they real?"

While in the country, Harold developed a love for music and discovered he had a good sense of rhythm and a gift for playing by ear. The boys had always played the mouth harp and they particularly loved mouth organs, which were so popular with young men at the time. Harold returned from his country experiences with an accordion, on which he would play for hours in the dark of his room. He loved tuneful Irish songs, like the "Rose of Tralee," and Stephen Foster's songs of the American South. I was in my Stephen Foster period myself and loved to sing "I dream of Jeannie with the light-brown hair" and "Beautiful dreamer."

Our brothers' great mate was Rupert Clampit, who was half Maori. He was an exceedingly good-natured young man, whom Harold had met while working on the land at Lancefield. We were all very fond of Rupert who was like another brother. He remained Les's mate until his death, by which time he had been for many years an orderly at a local hospital. The patients and staff must have loved him.

49

Nothing was too much trouble for Rupert if it would help someone. Rupert was our only youthful contact with a person of color and, because of this early friendship, we grew up color-blind in our relations with others.

With Rupert the boys went rabbiting. Rabbits were introduced into Australia in 1859 by a landowner from England, who liked to go shooting and wanted game in his paddocks. With the favorable climate, plenty of grass, and no natural predators, the rabbits soon proliferated and, already by 1868, they were reported as a calamity in the Western District of Victoria.[35] By 1951 they were estimated to be eating as much feed as 70 million sheep. The major effort to eradicate them with the myxomatosis virus soon reduced their number to about one-tenth of what they had been,[36] even if only temporarily. Certainly in our childhood, rabbits were everywhere and property owners were very happy to welcome onto their land anyone who would kill a few more of these destructive pests. Our brothers and their friends kept ferrets, which would go down into the rabbit burrows and drive the rabbits up into the paddock to be seized by dogs or else shot with rifles. We became accustomed to rabbit skins drying on frames in the shed (they brought in a few pennies) and we ate a lot of rabbit in rabbit pies and stews.

When I was nine or ten, we had a hutch with a couple of white angora rabbits with pink eyes; these seemed to us to be of a quite different species from those pesky wild ones. Rabbits like ours would certainly not have known how to survive in the wild. Hungrily, in trusting confidence, they chomped on the lettuce leaves we brought them and they loved to have us caress them affectionately. Because of the persistence of the problem despite quite drastic measures, such pets as these are now, of course, rare on the Australian scene.

Our Rivers relatives

Dad's daughters," as we called the six women from his first family, had nearly all "married well," to use the common expression of those days. They were mostly as old as or older than my mother, who, having been brought up in the country, felt intimidated by their urban sophistication, fashionable dress, and education. Some of them also resented their father having married again, considering it an insult to their beloved mother's memory, so our mother avoided them in her shy way. The exception was Lena, who had married a potato farmer, who scraped out a living in Kinglake, to the north of Melbourne. Once a year, at the time of the Royal Agricultural Show, Lena would come to stay with us for a week, with her son Jack, whom she always called Bub. Mother felt more able to cope with Lena, probably because of her country ways. Dad visited his sons and daughters regularly on Friday evenings and took his two little daughters to see them from time to time. The eldest daughter, Florence, had married a highly respected public servant, somewhat older than she was. He was a very dignified figure in my eyes. Because of the enormous discrepancy in our ages (probably more than fifty years), the family found it very amusing to urge me, as a mite of four or five, well trained in respectful behavior, to approach this venerable gentleman and call him Hal. "Go on!" they would say, "He's your brother!" They would push me in the door, with my courage screwed up. I would take one look at this "brother" of mine and the words of greeting would freeze in my mouth as I backed terrified out of the room. This, of course, entertained the adults. I also had a very handsome nephew, another Harry much older than I, who rose to the rank of Major in the Second World War. Harry thought it very funny to call this little tot "Auntie." It was not surprising, with my unusual family extending over several generations, that I had the unique distinction among my schoolmates of becoming a great-aunt at the age of fifteen, a claim my high school friends found hard to believe.

Despite Mother's nervousness and misgivings, Dad's daughters turned out to be very charming and sensitive women. We became very fond of them and of our half-nieces and nephews who were about the same age as Linda and I. Alys devoted her life to voluntary charitable service through the Woollies Appeal, of which she was the energetic moving force. Through her regular radio sessions, she appealed to the women of Victoria to knit layettes for the babies of women in need, with wool supplied by generous donors. After the Second World War, when the British were suffering considerable deprivation, Alys encouraged the women to knit furiously to meet the needs of bombed-out victims in London. These woollies she distributed herself in England, arriving on an ocean liner over a hold filled with beautiful hand-knitted garments of the finest

Australian merino wool. Her sister, Violet, was very active as the president of the women's association of the Church of Christ, of which her husband was a minister, working, as their ministers do, in a fulltime lay profession as the business head of the Rivers Locking System, invented by his wife's brother Hector. Eva's husband was a hotelkeeper in an ocean front resort and later at Beechworth, in Kelly country. He became famous throughout Victoria when he bet the garage owner in Beechworth that he could not wheel him in a wheelbarrow to the top of Mount Buffalo. This grueling winter odyssey was followed avidly by Melbourne newspaper photographers. People poured into Beechworth, staying at the wheelbarrow passenger's hotel and buying petrol from the wheelbarrow pusher's garage. Publicity is generally elicited in less arduous ways these days.

Dad's three sons were not undistinguished either in their own ways. His eldest son, Hector, being of an inventive turn of mind, invented a burglarproof lock, which was to be found on many of the big bank and insurance buildings in Melbourne. These locks, it seemed, were less favored by the Police and Fire Departments than by financial institutions, since they made it extremely difficult for police officers and firefighters to get into buildings so protected. The other two sons followed one of Dad's earlier occupations — real estate valuation and sale.

What was Ascot Vale like in the Twenties and Thirties?

Like much of the City of Essendon (now part of the City of Moonee Valley) Ascot Vale had a Victorian-Edwardian air, called these days Federation style, since many of the houses date back to the boom years of the last decades of the nineteenth century. The variety of houses in the area accommodated very mixed social classes. Iron lace abounded on balconies and verandas of the bay-windowed brick houses, like our house at 1 The Parade, with their gray-blue slate roofs and basalt foundations. These houses were set back behind iron-spike fences or wooden pickets, often gracefully undulating. Much of this iron lace trim is still a feature of Melbourne's western suburbs. It is cherished and sought after much more now than it was in my childhood, when the newer eastern suburbs were adopting more modern functional styles, with tiled roofs and picture windows to light up the space. The Federation-style brick was mostly cream-colored, with scattered patterns of a darker brown. Jumbled indiscriminately among the larger homes were single-fronted weatherboard houses with corrugated iron roofs, but always with the indispensable veranda to protect against the inclemency of winter and the burning heat of the summer sun. Most of the houses were single-storied, each on its own plot, as Melbourne houses tended to be. The interspersed two-story houses, with superb iron-lace balconies and veranda trim still catch the eye in a quite spectacular way. Occasional terraces of even smaller brick or stone cottages still stand cheek by jowl with the larger houses and are becoming chic acquisitions for young professionals. The colors of the Federation houses (mainly beige, russet, dark brown, green, and cream) are now called heritage colors and are the only ones authorized in the present enthusiastic restoration of this historic area. Each house, whether large or small, had its garden in front, with a yard at the rear for vegetables. All sorts of imported Northern European annuals and perennials brightened up the scene in massed display. Roses bloomed exuberantly. The enthusiasm for native Australian bushes and trees, like banksias and the pink-flowering ti-tree, dates only from the 1950s and 60s and has had a sporadic influence in the Moonee Valley area.

In my childhood, Ascot Vale residents came from all kinds of backgrounds. There were doctors, dentists, teachers, journalists, shopkeepers, carpenters, factory workers, railwaymen, and council workers, who dug up the streets and cleaned the areas along the railway line, planting pink pig-face to hold the earthen banks together. The educated and the uneducated lived cheek by jowl. The western suburbs in the 1920s were not a socially elite area of Melbourne, although they were not by any means like the inner city. Melbourne was already expanding to the east into the foothills of the Dandenongs and along the Yarra valley, and to the south along the shores of Port Phillip Bay. In Ascot Vale we heard around us varied levels of speech: there were those who spoke the King's English, according to Fowler, and the "I seen" and "I have went" types; some children swore and cursed fluently, although this was, of course, quite unacceptable in our home. We were a fairly monolingual society. The majority of our neighbors were of English, Scottish, Irish, or Welsh stock, with a Jewish dentist, some Italian greengrocers, mainly from

Naples, a few Greeks who ran the fish shops, and a Chinese laundry-man near the railway station. Men's collars had to be highly starched at the time and only the Chinese, it seemed, had this skill. As we entered the Chinese laundry to pick up our father's collars, we would come to a boarded-up counter, with a small sliding aperture. When we knocked, the little window would open and we would see a Chinese face backed by rows of pigeonholes containing white paper packets, each with a large Chinese character on it. It was all very mysterious and somewhat intimidating. The Chinese could also be seen in their conical straw hats, stooping over vegetable gardens on the Maribyrnong River flats. As children, we heard how hard they worked, so that they could save enough money to return to China to die or at least to pay for their bodies to be sent back for burial in the sacred soil of their ancestral homeland.

The Irish in the population were strangers to us, as Anglican (English), Presbyterian (Scottish), or Methodist (often Welsh) Protestants. "The troubles" in Ireland carried over into Australian society in bitter division. Children of southern Irish descent were shepherded off to Roman Catholic parochial schools, from whence they moved on to unisex Catholic high schools. We public school children just did not meet Catholic children, who even in some instances walked home on the other side of the road from us. We did hear dark rumors from time to time about their mysterious beliefs and practices. Despite this social separation, we loved to sing Irish songs, along with folksongs from England, Scotland, and Wales. There were a few other small groups who were Roman Catholic (small communities of Poles, Hungarians, and Italians), but these got lost in the population, whereas the Irish were very numerous, vocal, and active in politics.

The only Catholic I met in my first sixteen years was my friend in the sixth grade, Annie Jones. She was a redheaded Welsh girl, who told me: "I am a *Roman* Catholic." This expression was such a novelty to me that I went home and asked my mother: "What is a *Roman* Catholic?" Mother probably explained to me that this meant that she was "Irish," because to Mother all Roman Catholics, even little Welsh girls, were "Irish." On one occasion, during the big assisted immigration intake after World War 11, Mother even observed that the Italian immigrants in our neighborhood were all "Irish," and this made perfect sense to her.

The Americas did not enter much into our purview when I was a child. Our acquaintanceship with the United States was mainly through our passionate involvement with Buffalo Bill and his ilk at Saturday afternoon film matinees, with Bing Crosby and his crooning on the radio, and later Frank Sinatra, whose gliding from note to note was much criticized by musical purists. We had heard about the Sinatra fans or Bobbysoxers who swooned at his performances, but we considered swooning to be very Victorian (tight-waisted corsets and all that) and inexcusably emotional; we would have been ashamed to yield to such weakness. Of course we wore bobby socks ourselves; they were very comfortable in hot weather. Mass hysteria, however, did not fit in with our British "stiff upper lip" culture. We felt much more at home with the acerbic satire of Gracie Fields (despite her raucous Lancashire voice). We loved to hear her sing about Queen Anne Boleyn, who walked the Bloody Tower of the Tower of London, "with her head tooked oonderneath her arm, at the midnight hour," and King " 'arold with eyeful of arrow" at the Battle of Hastings. One of Gracie's most famous songs was "The Biggest Aspidistra in the World." Aspidistras, being a very tough, unkillable plant, had graced nearly every Victorian interior, including Mater's and our own, and were very familiar to us. Of course, we adored the cozy humor of Stanley Holloway, who amused us with his eminently imitable song about Albert who went to the Zoo with his mother, poked a lion with his little stick and ended up with his head in the lion's mouth. Sir Harry Lauder was still popular, although now well on in years, as he sang about Glasgow, "Good old Glasgow town," and, teetotallers though we might be, we daringly belted out: "When I get a couple of drinks of a Saturday, Glasgow belongs to me." Our first experience of the United States close up was when the American fleet visited Melbourne in the twenties and real American sailors walked our streets and flirted with the girls. We were able to visit the ships in school groups, after very long waits in line, and were awed by their size and complexity. We all bought little American flags that were on sale everywhere and waved them as the sailors paraded in the city.

Our street, The Parade, which unimaginatively led into The Crescent, was lined with alternating English oaks and elms, all well grown and wide spreading. Their heavy shade was much appreciated by the drivers of horse-drawn drays who stopped there to enjoy their midday sandwiches and a postprandial snooze. Horse-drawn vehicles abounded in my childhood. Bakers delivered daily loaves to their customers in horse-drawn carts. Ice cream carts, usually drawn by a small pony, were fragile-looking contraptions, with a swaying red and white canopy from which hung a little bell to call children out of their houses for their penny ice cream cones. The horses of the milk delivery cart could be heard clip-clopping along the street in the early hours of the morning, as its driver filled the metal billies we left out for our daily supply of milk. On main roads, we would see the brewery carts drawn by imposing Clydesdale draft horses, often with colored ribbons plaited into their manes and tails. Even the grocer delivered orders to our home in a horse-drawn vehicle. As children we welcomed him eagerly, because he would hide a paper cone of boiled lollies in among the groceries.

Nearer home, beautiful trotting ponies, drawing low-slung jinkers for their drivers, would go by on their way to the Ascot Vale Trotting Course, and horse-drawn floats would convey valuable racehorses to the nearby Flemington and Moonee Valley racecourses. At the Ascot Vale Railway Station black buggies, with patient horses flicking the flies off their rumps with swishing tails, would be waiting on race days to take patrons to Ascot or Flemington. I used to dream of being able to take a ride in one of these vehicles, observing the view over the horse's tail, but this was something, unfortunately, we could not afford. As the years went by, this line of buggies gradually grew shorter and shorter, as people took to other modes of transport, until there were only one or two old relics, with equally ancient drivers, waiting for patrons. Finally they were no more and the old memorial horse trough near the station gradually fell into disuse and disrepair. With so many horses about, we could go out in the streets and scoop up horse manure for the garden. With this, added to the droppings from the fowl yard, we had plenty of fertilizer to enrich the soil.

Fruit was sold in shops with open displays that spread out onto the footpath to attract customers, and in the city there were barrows that could be closed up at night and moved to another location if necessary. Fruit sellers were somewhat notorious for topping up the fruit; they would put the best and most flawless specimens on top and hide shriveled, bruised, or marked fruit beneath them. They had to be watched very carefully as they served you or you would end up with the poor fruit, extracted by sleight of hand from underneath. Mother, having been an orchardist, knew that damaged or bruised fruit were called "specks" and that a scrupulous greengrocer would sell them for less. The local fruit seller, a Mrs Pierce, was a rough-spoken, carelessly dressed woman, who swore like a trooper. It was she who took starting-price bets for the illegal bookmakers. When we asked her if she had any "specks" to sell, she would reply brusquely: "I'm the only speck here!"

The lolly shop was also a popular attraction. It had a bead curtain to keep out the flies and a little bell that jingled as we opened the door. We would run down there with a lidded billy to buy extra milk (pasteurized, but not homogenized as it is today) and, on the way home, we would suck out the cream from the top of the milk between the lid and the billy. We would, of course, be reprimanded for this if found out, since it reduced the quantity of cream available for the scalded cream Mother loved to prepare. Opposite the subway at the railway station there was a drapery store. This was a real country relic, which had the old system of overhead transmittal of money and receipts via a screwed-together container, which would be sent on its way from the sales counter to the office upstairs with a jangling pull on a wire. This was always fun to watch.

Linda was very protective of her "little sister" and being a little older was a little bolder. On one occasion a cheeky little boy from the neighborhood started throwing stones at me. Not only did Linda stop this nonsense, but, taking me firmly by the hand, she marched me down the street to the house of the offending young man. Knocking on the door with inward quaking (she must have been all of six years old), she addressed the surprised mother who answered the door with the firm demand: "Will you please stop your little boy from throwing stones at my little sister!" No wonder I admired her and thought she was the embodiment of all the virtues.

Our Playmates

As we were growing up, one strong stricture was that we were not to play in the street. There were certain children we could play with in our own yard or theirs and then there were the others (usually those who played in the street) who swore and were cheeky to adults. The exception to this exclusionary rule was the large family of very poor children who lived by the railway line on a short, dead-end street, closed in by a steep staircase (later a ramp) up to the main road. No vehicles came this way, although, when we were older, we used to love to show our prowess by riding our bicycles up this formidable ramp and then bravely freewheeling down at a hurtling pace. In this cul-de-sac we could chase each other for the three or four yards from the footpath to the railway fence in perfect safety, as we played "Charlie over the water! Charlie over the sea! Charlie broke the teapot and blamed it onto me!" never associating this chant in any way, of course, with Bonnie Prince Charlie, the King over the water.

The prohibition against playing in the street set no serious limitations on us, since we had our large backyard for our games. Here there was plenty of room for chasing games of all kinds: tiggy, hidey, and the like. We could climb the trees to our heart's content, even when we were quite small; the lower branches of most of them formed a skirt of green close to the ground, which made them accessible even for the very young. We could invite into our domain acceptable, that is, polite, well-brought-up children to play with us. They too enjoyed climbing our trees and playing hide-and-seek in the many hidden nooks the garden provided. Tipping over an old bench, we would pretend it was a rowboat. There was the lawn for Ring-a-ring-a-rosy, with a soft surface for us to all fall down (unaware that we were reenacting the horrors of the Black Death in Europe). In singing games like "Here we go gathering nuts in May," or its variant "Here we go round the mulberry bush," we were perpetuating in our southern land the childhood traditions of our Northern Hemisphere forebears, despite the vast differences in our seasons and native trees. As we chopped off the heads of our dancing friends in the popular "Oranges and Lemons, the bells of St Clement's," singing "Chip chop, chip chop, the last man's head, head, head off," we did not know we were singing about London's ring of Wren churches around St Paul's, so close to the execution site in the Tower of London. There was even enough space to play Musical Chairs. Some of our friends, like our half-niece Nancy, could turn catherine wheels on the lawn, whereas all that plump little Wilga could manage was "head over heels" and a few leapfrogs. With all that was around us, we had no need for elaborate mechanical toys.

On fine days we loved to organize backyard concerts and show how well we could dance, recite poems, or sing. Linda demonstrated her virtuosity quite early by singing all the verses of "Clementine." With its disrespectful verses (including some we made up ourselves) this was always one of our favorites. We would dress up in old clothes and discarded curtains to act out on the grass under the orange tree our favorite scenes from stories and films. On one memorable occasion, I acted out the death of Edith Cavell, the brave heroine of the First World War who, as a nurse in Belgium, helped escaping British soldiers who had become separated from their units by hiding them in her hospital. For this she was shot at dawn as a spy by a German firing squad. As she was our childhood heroine, we loved to reenact the very moving and dramatic scene of her death. I amazed my small friends, it seems, by gracefully collapsing, almost in slow motion, at the tragic end.

On wet days, of which there were many in Melbourne, we would move our Acts, as we called them, into the vestibule, where we also played fast and furious games of table tennis. For a more leisured and "intellectual" inside game, we would list under one letter of the alphabet our favorite colors, songs, books, flowers, girls' and boys' names, and film actors. The old Victorian parlor game of "Consequences" we found hilarious. For this we constructed a round-robin story phrase by phrase, folding the paper over after we had added our contribution and passing it on to the next person. The simple sequence "X — met —Y — where — when — how — why - and with what consequence?" kept us in stitches. Scrapbooks also kept us from being bored. We bought sheets of colorful "scraps" (garlands, flowers, faces) which we broke up to make very decorative pages, arranging and rearranging them until we were satisfied we had the prettiest possible layout. Or we immersed in water what looked like dried-up flowers from China and watched as they unfolded mysteriously to reveal an unsuspected beauty. For these dull days, there were also card games, like *Grab*, definitely our favorite as we

59

noisily seized the whole pile when we were able to throw in our matching cards. We certainly didn't need the not-yet-invented television or video games to keep us entertained.

Most of our childhood celebrations were inherited from our British forebears. We knew nothing of Halloween. November meant Guy Fawkes Day. "Always remember the fifth of November," we declared. Living in the distant Southern Hemisphere we still remembered the English rebel, who on November 5th in 1605 had tried, with "gunpowder, treason and plot," to blow up the House of Lords in London while King James 1 was in attendance. Naturally such a celebration involved lots of fireworks, which our brothers enthusiastically provided. Linda loved watching the catherine wheels whirring round, but I loved the sparklers you could hold in your hand and run around with, shooting sparks as you went. The rockets, however, terrified me. I would run inside and hide my head under a pillow because I thought they were breaking up the sky.

Our great playmates for a number of years were the Stebbinses: Joyce and Colin, who were more or less Linda's age, and Vivien, who was younger like me. Vivien and I were considered the littlies and, since five does not divide evenly by two, Viv and I counted as one person when sides were picked for cricket, which we played with a rather timeworn bat. Because of our insignificance, Viv and I spent a lot of time watching the others batting and bowling, as we waited in the distant grass for the ball to come our way. Fortunately for us, the inevitable Melbourne rain often cut the game short. Vivien, who was easily bored with waiting around, loved devising battle campaigns with his toy soldiers, which he deployed in the tall weeds. I seemed to spend much time crawling through the grass, following his obviously invincible maneuvers, which he explained to me in great detail. As we grew older, we found it a lot more exciting to play hockey with some strong sticks from the garden and a golf ball we had found somewhere. The numerous holes we dug out in our enthusiasm did nothing to improve the appearance of Mother's back lawn.

Since the talkies had just come on the scene in the late twenties, one of our favorite Saturday afternoon occupations was attending the matinee at the local picture theatre. Here a packed house of screaming youngsters would be watching that week's episode of the yearlong serial. Buffalo Bill would be fighting the Indians on his wheeling horse and, as the reel came to its end, the Good Girl (always blond) or the Bad Girl (always a brunette) would be expressing her utter terror as the wheel of her covered wagon slipped over a steep cliff. This happened, of course, at the very moment when the scalp-seeking Indians appeared over the mountaintop, racing nearer and nearer (to be continued)! We loved "the pics." as we called them. Colin was very artistic and at one stage he won a children's art competition, sponsored by the local picture theater. For painting a magnificent Indian face, with wrinkles, feathers and all, he was awarded a Shetland pony, with which we paraded up and down the street for a full week, vying for rides, before his mother decided that "Muggins always had to clean out the shed" where it was lodged. A bicycle, she decided, would be not only less trouble but would cost much less to maintain.

Mrs Stebbins was a milliner, so Joyce naturally thought that creating imaginative hats would be a fascinating career. Consequently she left school as soon as she legally could. At that time the law ordained for compulsory education: "Fourteen years old or Merit Certificate," the latter being awarded to successful examinees from the eighth grade. As soon as Joyce was fourteen her mother sent her to learn millinery from her aunts. Later she set Joyce up in a little shop, with a window full of very stylish hats of her own design. We were very proud of her. Since I was now in my first year of French, at high school, I was asked to supply a suitably impressive French name for such a fashionable shop. Soon "Chapeaux Salon" appeared in fancy lettering on the window to impress the passersby. This was my first practical use of French.

Our Home-Centered Life

We had our initial experience of radio with Dad's crystal set, which could be listened to only through a pair of earphones. Made for him by his son Hector, the inventor of the Rivers Locking System, it was lodged in a plain, varnished, home-carpentered wooden box, but it was a magical thing for us children. On Saturday nights it was Dad's exclusively as he listened to the wrestling matches. Fortunately there were two detachable earphones in the headset, so Linda and I could both listen to the Children's Hour, run by a Miss Kookaburra who laughed like a kookaburra at the beginning of the program. We vied with each other in showing how well we could imitate her. My demonstrations of a kookaburra laugh in later years have always been a conversation stopper. Those were the days when Australians listened religiously at 11 p.m., Australian time, to the BBC news broadcasts direct from London. Voices with distinctively Oxford accents would come to us distantly over what sounded like the waves of the sea intermixed with occasional voice-drowning static. In the same distorted way, we would hear the King's Message to the Empire from Buckingham Palace on Christmas night. It was about this time that Linda and I had our first experience with a magic lantern, that precursor of the slide projector. Our brothers set one up in their bedroom where there was a suitable blank wall for this new experience. We had been lent a set of missionary pictures and soon, to our amazement, we saw all these strange black people from distant Africa walking up the wall amid tropical trees or sitting outside thatched huts. Along with the hand-wound phonograph, these contraptions were our earliest introductions to communication technology. On the phonograph, two of our favorites were "When Father Papered the Parlor," a comedy record in which everyone gets papered instead of the wall, and an hilarious monologue on the effects of laughing gas, another recent invention, with increasingly crazy demonstrations of its effects. This recording soon had the listeners laughing uncontrollably.

The Ascot Vale house was warmed from open fireplaces. Sometimes, on a moonless night, I would have to go down to the end of the yard under the trees to get more wood. Since I couldn't tell anyone that I was terrified of the dark, I would practically close my eyes and dash down to the woodpile, grab the wood and dash back in one reflexive motion. Then I would stop with my hand on the doorknob to draw deep breaths to regularize my breathing before calmly walking inside in utter nonchalance. Since we were very poor in the Depression days, after Father died, we would burn every scrap of wood and garden rubbish we could find to keep us warm. Acrid smoke would billow out into the room, stinging our eyes and gradually coating the painted walls with soot. Sometimes the dead leaves we burned would ignite such a blaze in the chimney that a stream of sparks would fly out into the night sky along with the smoke, as though the chimney were on fire. As we huddled close to the living-room fire, we would scorch in front and freeze in the back. Eventually we would have to leave the one warm room to go to bed in cold, unheated bedrooms. A bottle of hot water wrapped in a towel would help warm the bed: stone ginger-ale jars seemed to keep their warmth the longest. Next day would come the disagreeable task of cleaning the ashes and dead coals out of the fireplace. (In later years, when I had achieved the luxury of a centrally heated house, I thought I had left all of these unpleasant features of open fires behind me, only to find that people wondered why I never lit fires in the very decorative tiled fireplaces in my house in Watertown, Massachusetts.) Since Mother hated cleaning out fireplaces and wood was expensive, fires gradually disappeared altogether from our lives. We soon became accustomed to studying in frigid rooms with warm, woollen rugs around our legs and gloves on to warm our fingers. Before we went to bed we would warm our insides a little with a cup of hot cocoa, Ovaltine, or coffee with chicory. The latter brew was made from an inexpensive liquid concentrate, which came in a bottle with a label showing some exotic turbaned person from some indeterminate country. This was the only experience I had with coffee in my childhood.

No one can think about Melbourne without commenting on its changeable climate. We often say we have the four seasons in one day, and there certainly are abrupt changes in quite short periods of time. On hot, north wind days, when a total fire ban may have been declared because of the tinder-dry grasses that can so easily ignite the volatile eucalypts, there may be a drop of twenty degrees Fahrenheit (or twelve degrees Celsius) in twenty minutes in the late afternoon, when the southerly breezes come in from the bay. This will be followed by a cool night, making for comfortable sleeping. I remember getting up early in the morning after such nights to close all the windows, through which the cool air had been gently flowing all night. The house would then keep cool all day. We didn't need air-conditioning in our Victorian house with its high ceilings and nine-inch brick walls. It was as cool as a cave in the hottest weather.

Sydneysiders often jibe that it is always raining in Melbourne. Although Melbourne does have rain at all seasons, it frequently comes as an early morning weep. As soon as you see "enough blue to make a

pair of Dutchman's trousers," you know it will be a fine, sunny day
after all. As children, we would often look out anxiously, in bitter
disappointment, at the continuing rain on the mornings of a Girl
Guide hike or a Sunday School picnic. Our experienced Guide
Captain or Sunday School leader would insist, however, that we start
out on our excursion despite this inauspicious beginning, knowing full
well that it would be sunny and fine by mid-morning.

Linda was always drawing something and naturally I followed
along, although I was not as gifted as she was in this area. Very soon
we were making our own Christmas cards, splashing them with gold
paint left over from Mother's efforts at painting picture frames. We
decorated our cards with snow on the churches and robins in the trees.
We had never seen or experienced snow, but this seemed the right and
proper way to extend the season's greetings at that time, when so
many people born in Australia still referred to a trip to the British
Isles as "going home." In similar vein we sang joyfully on hot
December evenings about "dashing through the snow" that "lay round
about, deep and crisp and even." We children never expected what we
read or sang to tally with anything in the real world. We had been
brought up on comics and books imported from the Northern
Hemisphere. Christmas and New Year cards with local motifs —
summer scenes in the Australian bush, Father Christmases surfing in
shorts, or koalas with red-tasseled caps — were not yet current, nor
were madonnas with aboriginal features.

*Nina Diamond Köster Burston Tanner Rivers (as Mother called
herself)*

Mother, it seemed, never stopped working. "My work is my
pleasure," she always said. Determined as she was that we would be
more successful at school than the children of her more educated
brothers and sisters, she waited on us hand and foot. She was no doubt
driven by the sibling envy, aroused by her mother's unconcealed
favoring of her older and younger children. Because of the harsh
discipline she had experienced in her own childhood, she was
determined never to strike us or administer any kind of corporal
punishment. The strongest form of discipline she allowed herself,
apart from verbal disapproval, was to threaten to send us to a
reformatory if we didn't behave. This was the big parental threat in

those days. In a quite extraordinary way she managed to get us to want to do what she wanted us to do without any of the conventional forms of punishment. With much love and the freedom she gave us to express ourselves individually and develop in our own way, she inculcated the values in which she believed. When, as a punishment, Dad would send us to bed without any tea, Mum would slip a tray to us later, without Dad knowing. On these occasions the vestibule was handy as a bypass from the kitchen to our bedroom. Once she even went around to the side of the house and slipped a meal in through our bedroom window. This subversive behavior came primarily from her deep conviction that small children should not be deprived of nourishment. Next morning our dear old Daddy would compensate us for our meal deprivation by cooking us a particularly nice breakfast, which we would enjoy, apparently chastened, with never a word about Mum's intervention. I remember vividly Mother's quiet devotion and thoughtfulness in bringing our raincoats and umbrellas to school for us if the weather had changed during the day. Later, when we were in high school, she would go to the railway station, waiting patiently for train after train in order to be there with coats and umbrellas when we arrived. Perhaps the best example she gave us for life was in her forgiving approach to misdemeanors and ill-tempered outbursts. When we came to apologize, she would say, "I don't remember anything about it." And she certainly didn't.

To an extraordinary degree Mother, with few outside interests, was devoted to the survival and wellbeing of her own small group, and she would do anything to ensure it. Life made this a tough assignment for her. She survived two periods of unsupported widowhood with young children by living doggedly from day to day. There were no government programs to help her out. Deep down she knew that if she could make it one day, she could make it the next and somehow, despite tremendously adverse odds, she did make it.

Mother was happy in her constant work, in her sense of achievement in her service for others. I remember her, in her ample black apron, singing in the kitchen as she washed the dishes. A particular favorite of hers was "Harrigan" and we soon learned the words:

"H - A— Double R — I,
G — A — N spells Harrigan,

It's a name that the shame has never been connected
with!
Harrigan, that's me!"
We were not Irish, but we sang it lustily and frequently. Then we
would belt out:
"Yes! We have no bananas,
We have no bananas today!"
or soulfully launch into Stephen Foster's "Old Kentucky Home":
"Weep no more, my lady,
Oh, weep no more today."
These popular songs would be interspersed with favorites from the
Edwardian period, like "After the ball is over" and "A bicycle built
for two."

Mother was not a fancy cook and she certainly knew nothing
about gourmet cuisine, but her home-style meals were very tasty.
Naturally we ate a lot of lamb like most Australians. The preferred
Sunday dinner in most households was roast leg of lamb, with roast
potatoes, green peas with mint sauce, and often some roasted
pumpkin for good measure. I have nostalgic memories of Sunday
evenings when Mother would have made a batch of her perfect scones
and we would eat them hot with cold lamb. Mother was a noted scone
maker, scones being considered at that time Australia's special dish.
"You'll never find a husband unless you can make a good scone and a
good cup of tea," girls were told. Good scones were light, made very
quickly with very little kneading. and cooked in a few minutes in a
hot oven. They required a deft and practiced hand. Mother's scones
were certainly delicious, because she didn't spare the butter and
popped in any scalded cream that happened to be on hand. With her
experienced orchardist's eye, Mother always selected the best fruit
and we ate vegetables aplenty. I can still see Mum sitting on the table
in the kitchen with her feet on a chair, cutting up perfect French-sliced
beans. We often helped by peeling potatoes and shelling innumerable
peas. From leftovers she made wonderful custardy and raisiny bread
puddings and her steamed puddings were light, the latter always
served, of course, with Golden Syrup. A steady supply of rock cakes,
full of currants and sultanas, was always on hand in an airtight tin to
satisfy the hunger pangs of small fry running in from school.

Until Father died, Christmas dinner in our house was a completely European affair. In the heat of midsummer we ate a long, hot meal, of which the *pièce de résistance* was, of course, a big suet pudding, heavy with currants, dates, raisins, and sultanas, which Mum had kept boiling in the wash-house copper since the early hours of the morning. When the brandy sauce with which it was served was ignited, it burned with a bluish light and a delicious odor that easily convinced one that taste and smell are interdependent. Hidden beneath its fruity surface were greatly coveted threepences, sixpences, and shillings, with the occasional two-shilling piece. If I was beginning to look a little unhappy because I had not found any coins in my portion, someone would distract my attention while Dad or Mum quietly slid a coin into the custard sauce on my plate. Auntie Tilly would always come to see us after Christmas, looking for the traditional piece of Christmas pudding in which she hoped to find a "thrippenny" or a silver sixpence to bring her luck during the year. In keeping with the spirit of the season, we always had to ensure there was something for her to find in her portion, even if we had to poke it in before we gave it to her. To digest the heavy meal most of the partakers would retire for a siesta, leaving great piles of dishes to be washed. After Dad died, Christmas dinners in our house reverted to meals much more suited to the summer temperatures, with cold salads, cold chicken or ham, or salmon mousse. We had not yet heard of Australia's now favorite dessert, the Pavlova, with its meringue shell filled with fruit salad (always with the tang of passion fruit) and topped with thick whipped cream. No wonder so many Victorians now celebrate a "Christmas in July" when they can enjoy traditional Christmas fare in comfort.

Mother was not really a dressmaker, but through necessity she became extremely competent at altering and refashioning, so that hand-me-downs fitted very well and were sufficiently refurbished to satisfy the young recipient. One thing Mother was very proud of, and this came from her strict upbringing with Mater, was her perfection as a bed-maker. In fact, so perfect were her made-up beds that she often could not bear the sight of our best efforts. While we were away she would surreptitiously strip the beds we had made and remake them in her incomparable way. Naturally this led us to leave our beds for her to make, since she evidently liked it so much. She also loved doing the washing up, for which she had her own meticulous method. She always rinsed the dishes first, then washed them, rinsing them again in very hot water in a large, shallow milk dish before drying them. It was in this old milk dish that on the orchard in the old days she had set the milk to wait for the cream to rise to the top. For fifty years it served so many useful purposes that, even today, I mourn its inevitable rusty demise. When slates slipped on the roof, we would rush with the milk dish to collect the persistent drips of water seeping in from Melbourne's drumming rain. Since Mother enjoyed having her hands in water, she also loved washing clothes. In fact, so great was her love of washing things that she sometimes gathered up unironed clothes and washed them all over again. In her last years she found clothes to wash every day of the week. She never lost her love of constant activity.

When I was a small child, Mother had to comb my long hair and plait it in the mornings. Since I had a very sensitive head, I would dive under the table to avoid the pulling effect, and Mother would continue trying to comb my hair from a distance. As soon as short hair came into fashion, I was, not unexpectedly, among the first to get my hair cut, although Linda kept her plaits much longer. For special occasions Mother would roll our hair in paper at night and in the morning we would have the most beautiful ringlets. My hair was very thick. On one occasion Mother gave me a two-shilling piece and sent me off to have my hair cut for a shilling by a men's barber, who charged less at that time than a salon for women. The barber was an immigrant with a heavy accent. As he cut my hair he kept complaining "Too Tick! Too Tick!" Finally, when I gave him the two-shilling piece, he refused to give me any change, saying: "You have hair twice as tick as anyone else, you pay twice as much!" Bewildered, I had to go home and explain to my poor mother, for whom every penny counted, why there was no change.

Being a countrywoman accustomed to very few facilities and services, Mother doctored us herself when we were ailing, with home remedies of the kind passed down from generation to generation by mothers, grandmothers, and neighbors. Much of this wisdom was gathered in a book, sold from door to door — a big black tome called *Vitalogy*, which contained some 900 pages of distilled wisdom. In our house *Vitalogy* was always referred to as *The Book*. Full of herbal and home remedies, it enabled us to attend to minor illnesses and physical problems with substances on hand. It was also a useful repository for Mother's little treasures, our Merit Cards from school, recipes cut from newspapers or a lock of baby hair. "Look up *The Book!*" was always the cry in an emergency. Doctors cost money and could be considered only if the problem seemed life-threatening. On one occasion my brother Reg, who was driving great distances hauling logs in the mountains, called in for his mother's advice when he was suffering great pain from sciatica. Naturally he could not afford to take time off from the physically demanding activities that were his sole source of income in order to sit in a doctor's very aptly named waiting room. So out came *The Book* and Reg swallowed, as it recommended, a teaspoonful of turpentine. This was such a shock to his system that he never complained of sciatica again. We learned many other things from *The Book*. One of the joys of *Vitalogy* for us as children was the layered anatomical pullouts, which showed us livers, kidneys, intestines, lungs, and other unmentionable organs. Through these sections we learned many things our mother had not got round to telling us about. As we browsed further, we discovered many deadly diseases of which we definitely seemed to have all the symptoms and absorbed some hoary old wives' tales from the nineteenth century. This valuable family possession is still extant.

With the responsibility of her three boys and the two little girls who came along when she was no longer young, it is not surprising that Mother suffered from stress, developing very severe headaches in mid-life. Since we could never afford doctors except in dire circumstances, Mother sought the advice of neighbors who suggested a nearby Chinese herbalist. He prescribed a special mixture of herbs that Mother had to pick up every month in a mysterious packet labeled with Chinese characters. This mixture had to be boiled for a full day. The unpleasant odor from this preparatory procedure pervaded the house and persisted for days. Several times a day, to relieve her headaches, Mother had to drink the resulting concoction, murky dark-brown in color and malodorous as it was. Despite its unpleasantness, she persisted with this regimen, which did seem to help her. A worse catastrophe was the extraction of all of her teeth when she was little more than forty. In those days, dentists were rabid teeth-pullers and Mother suffered dreadfully from this procedure, with very little if any anaesthetic or painkiller to help her. This was the only time when, as little children, we found ourselves without a meal on the table, as Mother lay in a dark room in utter misery and agony. All her life Mother hated her dentures and mostly refused to wear them, except when she was going out. When visitors came she had to be reminded to make herself presentable.

Auntie Del, Mother's older sister and "middle of the family" friend, was a frequent visitor to our home. Del was a smart, fashionably dressed, unmarried career woman — a rarity at the time. Also ahead of her time, she had a male "boarder," who accompanied her to all our family get-togethers. (Did she or didn't she? That we never knew.) Auntie Del was the first person I knew who wore powder on her face — this being the flapper age. She loved lapdogs, particularly small silky-haired terriers or toy Pomeranians with their long-haired tails curled up over their rumps. The dogs were always kept inside, which gave Del's living quarters a distinctly doggy smell. Successful at managing her own life, Del tended to try to manage the lives of those around her. She found it hard to keep from telling others what to do. "That's not the way to iron the collars" or "That iron's too hot for silk," she would say, if Mother happened to be ironing clothes when she came to visit. At this point, Mum would go on chatting, while unobtrusively putting the ironing away for another day. "You shouldn't clean those children's shoes," was another of her complaints. One day, overhearing this remark, Linda and I felt guilty and decided to clean our own, but Mum's emphatic reaction was: "You say you have so much school work to do, then go and get on with it. I can do this."

As a single aunt, Del took particular interest in her nieces, Linda and Wilga. Since she was Linda's godmother she brought her gifts for her birthdays. Although she tried to be even-handed and to include me on most occasions, I felt a little jealous and would say, "It's not my fault my godfather died when I was three," my godfather being Osmond Rivers of Potchestroom in South Africa. We still have the little silver handbags held by a silver chain, with our initials inscribed on them, that Auntie Del gave us one Christmas; we thought they were so beautiful and so elegant. She also gave us little colored hankies, mauve, blue, and orange, with a tiny trim around the edges, which we proudly tucked into our little silver handbags. In the days before telephones, family visits tended to be either as arranged by letter in advance or impromptu "dropping in." On one such occasion, when Auntie Del "dropped in," Linda was just going out to some activity with friends. When Del rebuked her for going out when relatives called, Linda replied, rather pertly, although honestly: "We choose our friends. We don't choose our relatives," to her godmother's considerable disapproval. Certainly, Linda always spoke her mind.

Our Introduction to Religious Life

As little children we were sent to Sunday school. Unfortunately, when I was about nine I was discouraged by a somewhat traumatic experience. Sunday School was at three in the afternoon and Mother often found it hard to get a hot Sunday dinner over by that time. As a consequence we were somewhat irregular in attendance. On this occasion, we did manage to leave on time and arrived at the church hall to discover that, during our several weeks' absence, classes had been promoted and moved from their familiar places. When I eventually found my teacher, who was sitting with a new group of unfamiliar children, she looked at me in surprise and exclaimed: "You're a stranger!" That was enough to discourage me from going back to Sunday School. I was extremely embarrassed and from then on preferred to stay home on Sundays to read the *Australian Journal.* Later, when I was in high school, a classmate asked me to come to her Sunday School, so I thought I'd try again. I waited outside the Sunday School hall, where she had arranged to meet me. All sorts of unknown children passed me in friendly groups, while I, feeling very conspicuously on my own, wished I could drop into a hole in the ground. My friend never arrived. After about twenty minutes I grew tired of waiting and made my way home. I was much too shy to go into a hall full of strange people by myself and announce who I was. That was the end of Sunday School for many years, until my late teens and early twenties when I was persuaded to teach Kindergarten and Intermediate classes.

We were not, however, bereft of all religious teaching. Mother taught us our prayers and Dad took us to church at St Thomas's, Essendon, which was actually in Moonee Ponds. Dad, being in his seventies and working hard all week, obviously needed as much rest as he could get. He would often sleep in on Sunday mornings, but about once a month he would rouse us to go to Church with him. He would walk up the aisle very proudly with his two little girls one on each hand. We would sit under the stained glass window of St Luke, the "Beloved Physician." Mother's experience of St Thomas's was not such a happy one. In the little Methodist Chapel at Upper Diamond Creek, which she had attended as a child, Mother had learned to sing in a loud country style that, unfortunately, seemed a little too attention-getting in our polite, suburban, Anglican setting, so we tended to try to tone her down. She soon became discouraged by our shushing and, from then on, she preferred to worship God while listening to the birds in our trees or preparing a hot Sunday dinner.

When Linda was ten and I was eight, Dad gave each of us a Bible as a present. Mine, I remember, had lovely colored pictures. Having heard what a wonderful book this was, Linda and I decided, as many children do, to read it right through — every single word. Linda began with the New Testament and was enjoying the stories of Jesus, while I, having been allocated the Old Testament, was laboriously making my way through the many "begats" and lists of tribes in the Book of Numbers. One answer to the problem of the boring or incomprehensible parts was to read them out to each other from bedroom to bedroom at the top of our voices. Despite these difficulties, we did not become discouraged but kept this Bible reading up for years until we had in fact read every word.

In the Victorian system of public education, we had one hour a week of Religious Instruction (Religy, as we called it), and from this I learned a lot. The classes were taught by local Sunday School teachers who were free during the day (only a few married women worked in those days) and by the occasional hapless, and sometimes inept, local minister. For me the most notable of these instructors was an Ascot Vale Sunday School teacher called Miss Fisher who taught us in the third grade. We loved Miss Fisher, who had a fascinating silver pencil with an appendage that jiggled as she made her points. She certainly must have had a way with children, since she was able to keep forty seven- and eight- year-olds attentive in their seats.

Learning Australian Values.

Mother remembered being told as a child about Ned Kelly, the notorious Victorian bushranger, and she often recounted to us the tale she had heard. Apparently the Kelly brothers came to a house in Hurstbridge to ask for food. When the owner of the house, who was naturally alarmed, went behind a door to prime up his gun the Kelly visitors heard the sound and shot him dead. This was only one of the many stories recounted of the mythic Kellys, Ned and Dan — the wild Irish boys. Ned and Dan were horse rustlers in the late nineteenth century, when Victoria was sparsely settled and the land was rapidly being taken over by wealthy landowners who had acquired it very cheaply. The Kellys were seen as "common thieves" only by some of the population. To others they had a Robin Hood quality. They stole horses, robbed banks, and defied the police, but they were very devoted to their mother and sister. Declared outlaws with a price on their heads, they were apprehended and imprisoned. The last straw for the Kellys was when the police arrested and imprisoned their mother, who had sheltered them when they were on the run. In their last standoff against the police at a hotel at Glenrowan, Ned and Dan wore the tin armor they had made for their protection, which is now in the Melbourne Museum. Having refused to surrender, they were killed by the police, as the hotel burned down. The indomitable Kellys have become folk heroes over the years and, when I was growing up, the expression "as game as Ned Kelly" was considered the highest compliment that could be paid for dogged determination against all odds. To us the Kellys represented daring, belief in individual rights, confidence in oneself and one's ability to carry things through, loyalty to mates, devotion to family. and risking danger while resisting petty authority. Our interest in this local hero was fueled by an early, somewhat tattered paperback, called *The Girl who Loved Ned Kelly,* which my brother Les had passed on to us. We devoured this book with delight as a somewhat illicit or at least dubious literary masterpiece.

The myth of the Kelly boys linked up with the sentiments expressed in Banjo Paterson's song, "Waltzing Matilda," which we sang enthusiastically on all possible occasions. Written in the rough and ready frontier days of the nineteenth century, "Waltzing Matilda" lauds the strong individualism and personal values of the "little"

Australian, personified by the swagman, who, free as air, refuses to give up his chosen way of life and submit to the petty dictation and arbitrary authority of the Establishment (the wealthy squatter) and the complicit police. Preferring death to curtailment of liberty and perceived individual rights, the swagman jumps into a billabong. (I often wondered if he swam under water to the other side.) This was the system of values we imbibed — standing on your own two feet, making your own way without allowing yourself to be deterred, derailed, or pushed around by self-promoting authority figures. Along with not asking personal questions or prying into other people's affairs, giving everyone a "go" (an opportunity to carry out his or her own projects and fulfill his or her own dreams), and accepting people as they are, respecting them only for their personal qualities, not for rank or status — these were our family and societal values. Mother never discouraged us from reaching for the stars. She admitted that she herself did not know how to get there and could not give us any advice, but she cleared all obstacles out of our way, insofar as she could, and let us fly.

3
BANK STREET STATE SCHOOL   1923-30

When I was four and a half years old I was taken to school. Bank Street State School, No. 2608, was founded in 1885, one of the earliest schools in the Essendon area. It was in a heavy brick building, with windows divided into small panes. In a small steeple was the school bell that rang for the beginning and end of school sessions, usually notifying Linda and me in the mornings that we were late again, as we raced up the street behind the school. At Bank Street, there was an asphalt playground around which marched, at the beginning of the day, a school band with bugles, kettledrums and a big bass drum. In front strode a Drum Major who was twirling and tossing a baton in the air as he led us in formation, grade by grade, until we broke off in groups to go to our separate classrooms. If we were lucky we could slip into the formation as it arrived at the end of the playground near the street and no one would notice our delinquency. After all, being late was a serious and punishable offense. In the center of the yard was a flagpole, where every Monday morning we assembled to declare our allegiance to the powers that be. We would put our right hand on our left breast (or, if very small, more likely on our tummies) and proclaim:

"I love God and my country;
I honour the flag;
I serve the King;
And cheerfully obey my parents, teachers, and
the laws!"

Not even our teachers believed that we interpreted this literally. When Linda reached the sixth grade she had no favorite teacher and was beginning to resent school discipline and authority, so she deliberately left out "teachers" and satisfied herself with parents and the laws. How many others, I wonder, made similar adaptations?

At "playtimes," in the middle of the morning and in the middle of the afternoon, we milled around in the small yard, playing the same age-old children's games that reappeared at the appropriate times of year in Anglo-Celtic cultures, without anyone apparently calling the tune. We chased each other around in games of Tiggy to keep warm in the winter and jumped on seats or other high points, shouting out: "I'm the King of the castle and you're the dirty rascal!" Or we played Skippy, jumping over the rope to traditional chants like: "Andy pandy, sugary candy, French, almond, raisin, rock," turning the rope faster and faster when someone cried, "Pepper!" When we were more adept, we showed off our prowess by jumping in the middle of two ropes, turning in opposite directions." Wash the dishes. Dry the dishes. Turn the dishes over!" we shouted, as the skipper drew herself together to jump into the ropes. For a change, we would skip to the left and right of a snaking rope in Railway Line. In warmer weather, we drew carefully with chalk on the asphalt of the playground the stylized designs for hopscotch that we had learned from older children; then we hopped carefully through the bases on one foot, kicking tors or small stones from one to the other. As we grew bigger, we loved to show how clever we were at leaping over bases, without losing our balance or our tors. We girls whipped our wooden tops with enthusiasm, while the boys avidly concentrated on their games of marbles. All around the walls of the building, about two and a half feet up, there was, more by accident probably than design, a row of bricks projecting an inch or two at a descending angle. This we found ideal for bouncing balls against and seeing how long we could keep up the returns.

Around the periphery of the yard were a few shelter-sheds, providing some protection from Melbourne's frequently inclement weather. The lucky few, who got to them first on rainy days, could sit down out of the cold and eat the lunchtime sandwiches they had brought in brown paper bags. The rest of us would have to sit at our desks and eat our lunches in dull classrooms. For liquid refreshment, we would make our own "lolly water" by shaking aniseed balls, which we could buy twenty for a penny, in a bottle of water. This we would pour into little aluminum pannikins that collapsed flat to fit in our pockets and could be pulled out, accordion-style, to make a container when needed. On fine days we preferred to run all the way home at noon to gobble down the lunch Mum had prepared and run all the way back, always with an apple in our hands — this was Mother's perennial health precaution from her orchard days. "An apple a day keeps the doctor away," went the old adage.

Always running late was a fault we inherited from our mother. Consequently, I have vivid memories of running to school and running for trains, even though all the clocks in the house were set twenty minutes ahead for just such a contingency. Of course there were exciting things to distract us on the way to school, such as long earthworms in the flowing gutters beside the road after Melbourne's "morning weep;" these we would examine carefully, having been told that if one end was chopped off another would grow in its place. Linda and I tried very hard not to be late, but inevitably, day after day, we would be running down The Crescent, under the subway near the railway station, the down slope giving impetus for the up slope, rushing up our school street and across the playground, puffing and red-faced, to arrive out of breath at the classroom door.

At the Ascot Vale State School, we were as mixed a socioeconomic group as in our neighborhood, although we didn't realize it at the time. We just knew that some children didn't have hankies and their noses ran and it was rumored that one little girl didn't have any underwear on under her dress. We vaguely knew that some children were given a little financial help but no one knew who they were. Every now and again we had to have our hair washed in kerosene and combed with a fine tooth comb, in case we had "caught something" from others at school. It was easy to see that some of the houses near the school were very much smaller than ours, but even in our own street there was considerable variation, from very small row houses to large ones like ours with plenty of garden. That was Ascot Vale. We were largely of similar ethnicity and culture. The Irish and Italian children attended separate religious schools. In this regard things have changed a great deal in Ascot Vale. It was something of a shock to our largely monocultural community when immigrant groups of many different ethnicities moved in after World War 11, in the

1940s and 50s. Now, of course, their presence is accepted as the norm.

When I was in the primary grades, our teachers had no doubts about the values and manners the community expected them to inculcate. These were honesty (no cheating, stealing, or lying); obedience to authority; hard work (no shirking); homework written out neatly or memorized, depending on the material (otherwise a period of being "kept in" after school); cleanliness (next to godliness); politeness (no cheekiness and no "bad language"); trustworthiness; punctuality; tidiness — these no one questioned. Truancy and dropping out of school were not a major problem. There was a Truant Inspector who took care of that and called at the homes of any children who did not have valid notes to explain their absence. We all had a healthy fear of the Truant Inspector, who was presented as a kind of bogeyman.

All the women teachers at Bank Street were single and their teaching was central to their lives. Since this was in the 1920s, many of them had lost the opportunity to find life companions because of the 1914-18 War, not only because of the great loss of life among young men of their age, but also because many of those who survived had found wives abroad. After all the war had been fought in faraway Europe and many relationships had not survived the years of separation. The same circumstance affected my generation twenty years later, although in this case some of the young women married American GI's and returned with them to the United States as war brides. In the 1920s the Education Department did not welcome married women. Only single women were put on the permanent departmental roll. Married women were paid lower salaries as temporaries and shunted from school to school as supply or substitute teachers whenever emergencies arose.

My earliest school memory is of walking home down Bank Street as a very small child, feeling that I was the only person really alive, actually sentient and conscious, on the street; all the others around me, I felt, were empty shadows. My mind, I knew, was active, thinking and observing, but it was difficult to conceive of these others as having identities or of being engaged in thought as I was. I was interested to read later that psychologists regard this as a natural stage of development of one's sense of personal distinctiveness. This feeling was not just a one afternoon experience, but remained with me, it seemed, for quite a while, as very young children experience time.

Another early learning experience stemmed from my disillusionment with promised wish fulfillment. As part of acculturation there are a number of occasions when custom requires you to make a wish: on eating the first cherry of the season, on breaking off the larger end of a wishbone, on seeing a black cat. Yet custom requires also that you tell no one of your wish if you want it fulfilled. I adhered religiously to this stricture on several occasions when I was quite small, until one day I blurted out that it was all a fraud. "Why?" Mother asked kindly. "Because I've wished I had a pineapple three times so far and I never get one," I complained. "Dear me!" said Mother, "If that's all you want, we'll certainly get you one right away." In this way I learned the truth of the Biblical injunction: "Ask and you shall receive."

Even walking home from school added to our learning experiences. Among local personalities who intrigued us was the real estate agent, near the railway station. This gentleman used to amuse passing children by showing us how to fold paper and make wonderful things like birds and flowers, sometimes with cutouts, sometimes not. Of course, like all school children, we already knew how to fold paper airplanes and send them sailing around the classroom; these, after all, were only the evolved descendants of the traditional paper dart. Then there was the old lady (how old I now wonder?) who used to look out over a gate between high hedges and who, from our too intense diet of fairy stories, we took to be a wicked witch about to seize us or turn us into stone with a glare. We would come up to her gate, with strong inner misgivings, then scurry past as if the devil were at our heels. In one large garden on the way home there were statues of two deer, one standing and the other sitting. We were never really sure whether they were alive or not, and we would watch for long minutes to see if one of them moved. Occasionally, while we held our breath, a daring little child would slip in and start up the long drive to pat one of them to find out the truth. Inevitably fear of the unknown and of trespassing on other people's property would take over, and the child would scuttle back to safety within the group. Weary of these diversions, we would dive into a patch of yellow-flowered sour grass, which we had discovered on a vacant, overgrown lot, and we would chew this with as much pleasure as any candy. Or we would play at battles royal with certain seeding grasses, trying to knock the long heads off each other's fragile wands.

No Ascot Vale story is complete, without mention of our most eccentric personality: Old Daddy Edwards. He was never known by any other name nor by any shortened form of it. He was a sandwich man, in the days when picture theaters would advertise their next film, particularly the matinees, on a hinged board with a hole in the middle so that it could pass over the head. Wearing this contraption a man or boy would parade up and down the main street, bearing news of the forthcoming feature. Our sandwich man, however, was unique. He was certainly one of a kind. With long hair and beard, in a period when this was rare, he dressed in a long robe, wore sandals and had his fingers covered with all kinds of exotic-looking rings. Considering himself the reincarnation of Noah, he had built a large ark on his small piece of land. In this boat he intended to save the local cats and dogs in a forthcoming catastrophic flood. In later years he collected old cars, which he set out on his block, each painted with the red, white, and blue of an enormous Union Jack. I don't know if these were supposed to float when the flood came. He was the delight of the young children of the neighborhood. When they had got over their initial impulse to mimic and tease him and had begun to talk to him, they found him a source of all kinds of incredible stories. We loved to hear him explain how he had come by those mysterious rings, which, it appeared, would give him privileged access to romantic places in faraway lands. Parents tolerated our speaking to this odd person, who was quite harmless and always clean and polite.

Educational Trauma One

A common subject of conversation among school children naturally is school and at regular stages I found myself in a little group of children who were boasting of their educational success up to that point. "I've never been left down!" they would boast. "Have you?" At this stage I would look away into the distance and appear uninterested. I had a secret shame that I knew must never be revealed. I had been left down in *Kindergarten*, of all grades. This had been a very tragic moment for me. I had been a very happy four-year-old, 4.8

to be precise, when a little ceremony had taken place in our class (the Bubs, as Kindergarten was called). It was decided to make the transition from the Bubs to First Grade a momentous occasion, so the first graders who were moving on were sent to escort the kindergarten children to their new home in the first-grade room. One by one my little companions, all forty-nine of them, were taken by the hand and led out of the room to greater things. I waited excitedly, and then anxiously, as the number of remaining children gradually dwindled to one — me, of course — and I cried and cried as they brought in the new little kindergarten children, so much smaller than I was, to take up the empty chairs. To my eternal shame, I had been "left down" after an enthusiastic three months of my school career. No one explained why. It was years later that I worked out what had happened. At that time children could begin school in Victoria at four and a half. School was open from February to December and I had been born in mid-April. Mother, determined as she was that we were to have every educational opportunity, had taken me by the hand on the day I was four and a half to enrol me in Kindergarten, where teachers had to adapt to new children arriving throughout the year. Unfortunately for me, four years eight months at the end of the school year was considered too young for first grade — hence the tragedy! I would have to stay another year in kindergarten. My dear sister Linda was sixteen months older than I and born in December, so from then on I was always two grades behind her — another wound to my juvenile pride. Why on earth, I wonder, don't teachers try to ease in some way these infant traumas, which leave emotional scars for years? Perhaps this experience explains why I have never stopped working hard, at no matter what job or task, in case I prove inadequate. From that point of view maybe it was a blessing.

While I was in Kindergarten, Linda developed scarlet fever, a dangerous illness in those days, which necessitated a period of treatment at the Fairfield Infectious Diseases Hospital. Because of a misunderstanding on mother's part, Linda had to spend a further six weeks in quarantine at home, in case she was still infectious. During this period, she was confined to her room, with the luxury of a fire in her bedroom and a little bell to call Mother whenever she was thirsty (one of the features of the illness). Linda was still in bed when my fifth birthday came around. For my birthday I had so much wanted pink lamingtons (small sponge cakes dipped in red jelly, instead of the usual chocolate, before being dipped finally in coconut). This was something we were not often given to eat. With Linda in quarantine, none of my little friends could be invited to our home, of course, so I spent my special day wandering around the yard on my own, eating my pink lamingtons and missing my sister very much.

Something else children liked to eat, but which we were rarely allowed, was a sweet cake called a bird's nest. It consisted of a meringue in the shape of a bird's nest, with toasted desiccated coconut representing the twigs; on top there would be several little birds' eggs with a bird sitting on them. All of this decoration was made of pure cane sugar and was not considered good for our growing teeth. It was also rather expensive, as small cakes go. Consequently, there were no birds' nests for us, which made them all the more desirable since they were unattainable. Frustrated, we would gaze into the shop window, pressing our noses against the glass, as we devoured them with our eyes.

By the time I was in the *first grade*, my father was seventy-two years old. This gave me, I thought, a superior position in schoolyard conversations. The children would sit around eating their lunches and comparing how old their fathers and mothers were. "My daddy's twenty-eight," one would say. Another would counter this proudly with: "Mine's thirty-three." "My Daddy's seventy-two," I would declare grandly, knowing I could cap them all. This would cause considerable bewilderment and the next day some would return to say flatly: "Mummy says he can't be your father! He must be your grandfather!" This disconcerting opinion would cause me consternation and tears, and I would run home to Mother protesting: "They say Daddy can't be my daddy, but he is, isn't he?" — at which, of course, she would give me explanations that soothed my ruffled feathers. It was the same scenario when I boasted that I had three brothers who had a different surname from mine. This once again put me in quite a different category from my little classmates. "Then they can't be your brothers!" my classmates would assert. This resulted in more consternation and bitter tears into Mother's capacious black apron as I wailed: "But they are my brothers! They are my brothers, aren't they?" Mother quickly reassured me with further explanations about the convolutions of our unusually tangled family, so that I could once again hold my head up proudly and boast of these anomalies.

Discipline was strict and traditional at Bank Street. "Spare the rod and spoil the child" was a firmly held belief. In the second grade, I remember being sent to be strapped with the boys (probably for talking too much — that most unacceptable behavior to which I have always been prone). Of course, I was the only girl waiting in the corridor. As we waited, the little boys were licking their hands and wiping them on their pants, as their big brothers had taught them to do, to lessen the pain of the strapping. I remember doing the same thing and wiping my damp hands nervously on my little dress as I waited. Linda also talked too much, but she went further than I did, questioning authority and asking why she had to do certain things. "Why?" was not a question teachers wanted to hear in those days. One such incident resulted in her having to write out the word "obedience" three hundred times, a disagreeable task she completed while running home for lunch, stopping at each telegraph pole to add to her list. Fortunately the "lines" (as they were called) didn't have to be written in copperplate.

Because of Linda's chattiness it was discovered that she was shortsighted. In those days good little girls and boys, who had done well on their tests and behaved in class, were moved to the back row, while the little scallywags occupied the front seats under the teacher's nose. The desks, each with an attached hard wooden bench, which accommodated two pupils, were set out in rows and often screwed down to the floor. Linda would do well on her tests and be moved to the back row. Since from that position she could not read clearly what was written on the board, she would have to keep asking her desk mate for the details of the task. At this point she would be moved to the front row for talking. Since from that position she could see well, she would get good marks on her next test and be returned to the back row. Cycle repeated. It took a medical examination (which, along with dental checks, was a yearly feature of school life) to decipher this mystery. From then on Linda wore glasses, talked less in class, and sat permanently at the back as befitted her intellectual ranking.

In the *second grade* I learned much. For one thing, we learned to sew. We began sewing from mark to mark on a piece of cardboard to make a picture of a cat or a cockatoo and then moved on to something much more splendiferous. We wound wool, often of different colors, over two hollow circles of cardboard from the inside to the outside. Then we cut the wool along the outer rim; we passed a strand of wool between the cardboard circles, tying our production together firmly with a knot, and hey presto! a lovely, fluffy ball appeared when the wool was brushed out. This beautiful creation gave us a great sense of achievement and we would happily make more and more balls to delight our parents and admiring aunts and uncles. Then we moved on to hemming, herringbone, and cross-stitch, but these were humdrum compared with our beautiful balls.

Learning by rote began early. By the second grade we were well into reciting multiplication tables in unison in a singsong. "Two *twos* are four; two *threes* are six," we chanted. We now know from psychological studies that a musical tune helps with rote memorization, so this chanting was an effective memory aid. On Friday afternoons, review time, the sound of this type of recitation could be heard throughout the school. Consequently, I can always summon up the correct product of two numbers up to twelve when required. Why didn't we learn the thirteens? Since thirteen is a prime, it could have been helpful. My birthday being on the thirteenth, I am very attached to that number and I count things out in thirteens whenever I can. Mental arithmetic was considered very important in primary school and each day began with ten minutes of rapid-fire calculation problems with books closed. Some children were so remarkably quick at this operation that many of us just couldn't keep up with them. With all of this early practice, I can still make mental calculations reasonably quickly, which is disconcerting to many younger people at checkout counters in supermarkets, who seem quite at a loss for a total when their computer breaks down.

Each day in second grade ended with the hymn: "Now the day is over / Night is drawing nigh / Shadows of the evening / *Steel* across the sky," or that was the way I understood it. I regularly looked out the window at this point, searching earnestly and with some puzzlement for the steel bars across the sky, which never materialized. Oh well, teacher knows best, I thought, even if outward reality does not seem to correspond with what we are learning.

The teachers at Bank Street were, of course, very diverse. Why do we remember some of our teachers so vividly and affectionately, while we still resent others or don't even remember their names? My kindergarten and first grade teachers are a blur in memory. In second grade, we had Miss Viant, who was short and stout and turned her toes out at a sharp angle. This greatly impressed us. It wasn't just that we were closer to her toes, but she also insisted that we turn ours out too, a habit I have spent years correcting, always with the guilty feeling that Miss Viant is watching me from somewhere, ready to pounce.

Teachers in those days seemed to do a lot of pouncing. Instead of aerobics, they must have gone to pouncing classes, learning how to do this very quietly and stealthily when pupils were least expecting it or most enjoying themselves. Enjoyment in school always seemed to some of them a sign of disorder. In the *third grade* we had a student teacher, Miss Carroll, who was "lovely." Unfortunately she had to teach the upper section of the third grade in a room that connected by an opening with the room of her supervisor, Miss Smith, who was very strict — "real mean" — and didn't let anything pass by her eagle eye. "Smithy" had her hair drawn back in a tight bun, wore pince-nez glasses and pursed her lips. Generation after generation of pupils came to recognize her obsession with spelling, writing, cleanliness, and manners. For those who met her standards she meted out merit cards of different colors, representing levels of achievement.[37]

When we were enjoying ourselves too much with "lovely" Miss Carroll, Miss Smith would pounce through the opening and bawl us out in the presence of our class teacher, requiring that we return to her version of order in quiet, respectful rows. Aware of this, children in the back rows of her classroom would hiss lightly to warn us when she was approaching the back of her room. If she happened to catch us red-handed doing something of which she did not approve (perhaps engaging in a little cooperative learning), we would be moved around the partition and made to sit at the back of her room, thus missing all the fun of our own class. "Smithy" was the epitome of what we called "crabby." Fortunately, because of the critical need for extra space, our section of the third grade was moved in the middle of the year to a classroom in a building in a nearby street, Regent Street. Here we could enjoy Miss Carroll's classes in peace.

I began my school experience at the end of the era of slates and slate pencils. These were actually more for fun and games after the first grade, but we each had one. We found them very useful when we wanted to draw things, because they were so easily erased with a damp cloth. By this time we were preoccupied with learning to write neatly with a rigid steel nib slipped into a wooden penholder, which we dipped into an inkwell anchored in a hole in the wooden desk. We tried hard not to get the teacher-made ink all over our fingers and our pages in the process. The nibs were made of two sections, divided vertically, which after a certain amount of use became crossed and dug into the paper. Often we had stuffed blotting paper — a necessity in those days — into the inkwell, so that we could watch it absorb ink and change color. This did not help with the dipping process. On Friday afternoons favored pupils were able to help the teacher make the following week's supply of ink, while the rest of the class washed out the dirty inkwells, all of this being a satisfyingly messy operation.

At the time we still used copybooks. At the top of each page was a line of copperplate script, perfectly executed, which we had to copy, equally perfectly, four or five times on the lines beneath. We began with pothooks and other basic elements, moving to separate letters repeated over and over, then we graduated to simple words (cat, cat, cat; mat, mat, mat), which led to profundities, like "the cat sat on the mat." Then, to expand our minds a little, we would copy out a number of times, in our version of copperplate, moral admonitions like "Wilful waste makes woeful want" or "Great oaks from little acorns grow." By the sixth grade we were copying out little moral poems, so that our mechanical writing exercise would continue to be edifying. Throughout her life my sister Linda retained her perfect copperplate handwriting. Even at eighty she loved beautiful handwriting and would "white out" or amend with a razor blade any blemish in her script. Her writing was frequently admired. My handwriting, on the other hand, always went a childish "every which way," until some time in midlife when I decided I was just writing at an angle that didn't suit me. I then practiced a circular movement and developed a rounder, anti-clockwise motion, rather than the angular left-lower to right-upper sloping movement required for copperplate. My writing now is always legible, if sometimes erratic as to direction of slope.

Educational Trauma Two .

It was working against my natural circular movement with a stiff steel nib that caused me to dig into the paper at school, so that in the second grade the teacher used to tell me that I wrote "with a telegraph pole." This criticism followed me up through the school, no matter how much I labored to produce the beautiful handwriting required by teachers. (Even in the 1950s there were still special handwriting classes in primary teacher training in Victoria to teach a uniform style.) Although analyzing people's handwriting to uncover character traits was not unknown, it did not seem to occur to teachers that this would also imply different natural styles of writing. Year after year they persisted, with class after class of pupils, in trying to force us all into the same copperplate mold.

All this is preliminary to my third grade experience of public humiliation. One thing we always tried to do was create a perfect first page in a new exercise book. We carefully covered the new book with brown paper to keep it clean, neatly inscribing our name on the front. Then we sweated and toiled to complete the first page in perfect handwriting (insofar as we were capable of it) without a single blot. With our usual worn old nibs and our pens dipped into inkwells low in ink, this was not the easiest task. On this particular occasion I had toiled laboriously over the first page of my book with my best "telegraph pole" writing, trying not to dig into the paper too much. Unfortunately, I was not able to prevent at least one blot, carefully dried immediately with blotting paper, from reaching my pristine page. Horror of horrors! What a to-do! Whatever got into my teacher's head, I will never know. She decided to "make an example" of me, to "show me up." How this could improve an eight-year-old's writing I still do not understand! She marched me up the passage with my exercise book to my sister Linda's classroom. There, with the cooperation of my sister's teacher, Linda and I were stood in front of the class, each holding our books open — Linda with her beautifully neat, copperplate writing on an unsullied page and little Wilga with her unfortunate first page, in her usual heavy writing, with the inevitable blot. Naturally Linda and I, being so close, were equally upset and we both wept — Wilga from the unjust humiliation after such a mighty effort and Linda because she knew how hard I had

87

tried. Presumably some arcane purpose was achieved by this harsh display. Whatever it was, I certainly never found out and continued, with more or less success, to try to improve my writing in my own way. On reflection, was it the long shadow of Miss Smith reaching to the annex on Regent Street and insisting on a pounce, just "to show them"? It was certainly more her style than Miss Carroll's.

It was about this time that Linda began playing the violin, beginning with a small instrument and learning by the colored dot system that helped her learn where to place her fingers to find the correct notes. Nothing quite equals the violin for the painful effect of early practice on other people's ears, and we certainly amused ourselves imitating the rather off-key, gliding sounds that came from her room. My brothers thought they sounded like an injured cow. However, Linda persevered, encouraged by her teacher, who played Saint-Saëns' "Dying Swan" for her — a piece of music Linda thought was the most beautiful thing she had ever heard. Her teacher also took her to her first orchestral concert in the Melbourne Town Hall. By these small acts she set a lifelong pattern of love of music for my sister. Linda's fourth grade teacher was also a violinist and, on the days when Linda brought her violin to school, her teacher would ask her to play for her during her lunch hour. Unfortunately, however, when Linda was being considered for her first violin examination, her teacher brought in an outsider to hear her play and this visitor remarked that Linda had talent, but not genius. This really dashed Linda's spirits. In the third grade she had read a story about two girls blessed at birth, one with talent who fast became rich and famous, but not celebrated, and the other with genius, who remained unrecognized initially, but in the end achieved the success she deserved. Poor Linda was very confused!

It was in the fifth grade that Linda made up her mind to be a teacher, an occupation so much in the family tradition. I was in the third grade at the time and I greatly admired my sister's decisiveness. I felt it was probably a good idea for me too, since Linda thought so, but I didn't have any convictions of my own at that point. Like most children, we loved to play school, and we always wanted to be the teacher, so that we could show how "crabby" we were and get to boss the others around. Career decisions, however, were hardly in my mind at that point.

While Linda practiced the violin, I took piano lessons with Miss Lily Baulch, an older lady who had on her piano a metronome, which rigidly kept us in time with its loud, authoritative beat. It was rather terrifying trying to keep up with it. Miss Baulch gave us certificates and prizes for assiduity rather than brilliant performance. We had to note down every minute we practiced. I was supposed to do a half-hour of practice every day, and I would sometimes catch up on delinquency by doing an hour and a half just before my next lesson. When I became a Girl Guide at eleven, I had to learn by heart the lives of St George, St Andrew, and St Patrick, whose crosses made up the Union Jack. I would set my Guide book on the music rest, and, while I concentrated on my memorization, I would play the scale of C Major over and over, since it did not require too much attention. In this way, without real musical talent, I gained certificates for my perfect practice record and, on one occasion, a prize. This was my first and last Elsie book, *Elsie's Children*.[38]

The series of books about Elsie Dinsmore were of Miss Baulch's generation, not mine, and they were insufferably moralistic in the Victorian style. Elsie was oh! so respectful and obedient to her parents! She ended up marrying her father's choice, his best friend, rather than the handsome young cad of her own age, with whom she had fallen in love without realizing he was an alcoholic. The book was obviously a product of the Temperance period. One night, as Elsie was riding home with her father in the late evening, the lights of his horse-drawn vehicle shone on her beloved, staggering drunk across the road. Then, of course, she realized that father knew best. We found all of this nauseatingly priggish.

Unfortunately, all of my assiduous practice led to very little real facility at the piano. I was fine at the intellectual exercise of music theory, but it was very apparent I had not been blessed even with talent, let alone genius. Years later, when I was teaching in the country, at Yarram, I decided I would really learn to play with ease. I practiced for up to four hours a day after school, but I finally had to accept the fact that I was no Paderewski.

Opportunities to develop other accomplishments were not neglected. Mother even sent us for ballet lessons and bought us toe shoes, so that we could stand on our toes — the great ambition of all little girls. For our lessons we went to the local Masonic hall, with all the lissome, waif-like, wanna-be Pavlovas. I was well built, to say the least, and standing on my toes did not seem to be my forte. However, we did enjoy the Scotch reels, Irish jigs, and sailors' hornpipes with which the sessions ended. After a very short time it seemed more immediately profitable and less expensive to seek culture elsewhere.

A popular Edwardian accomplishment had been Elocution, with a capital E. For this, quite an emotional, histrionic performance was expected. In the 1920s, no Sunday School concert (an annual event in those days) or other amateur show was complete without a hired elocutionist to move the audience. Special dramatic poems, not found in the school anthologies, were the favorites of these entertainers, whom as children we greatly admired. My childhood coincided with the tail end of the popularity of this art. Off we were sent for elocution lessons, where we learned to recite very melodramatically, with lively body language to increase the emotional impact. This probably gave us something extra in poise and confidence in public speaking, even if later we had to tone down the strongly declamatory style we were taught. Of the poems we learned to recite the one that sticks in my memory is the very moral tale of "Sugartooth Dick," who "for dainties was sick, So he slyly crept into the kitchen." This naughty little boy got his just deserts when he took down a jar in the pantry thinking it was full of custard, only to find, to his consternation and the audience's delight and presumed moral satisfaction, that it was mustard (which rhymed, of course). We were all supposed to learn a salutary lesson from his experience!

At school we also did much learning by heart of poems that we later recited in class as expressively as we could. This is an activity I have never regretted. Not only was it enjoyable, making us conscious of the verbal music and magic of poetry, but it also furnished us with a stock of delightful lines to recall and quote on many appropriate occasions. We wept for Little Boy Blue, whose room, after his premature death, was kept exactly as it had been during his short but vivid life, with his lonely teddy bear waiting in vain for the return of his Little Boy Blue. Later we thrilled to the dramatic shipwreck at the Inchcape Rock and the gallant, if futile, charge of the Light Brigade. These opportunities for emotional expression lightened the somewhat sober, moralistic diet of our traditional school readers, with their hares and tortoises and boys who

90

cried "Wolf!" More relevantly contemporary were the carefully selected stories and poems in the much-awaited *School Paper*, which came to us each month from the Education Department. These we kept carefully in a file to read and reread even in subsequent years, enthusiastically singing out of school the songs we so eagerly sought as a regular feature on the back page. It was the *School Paper* that introduced us to Christopher Robin saying his prayers and set us off in pursuit of more of A. A. Milne's delightful poems and his adorable children.

> "James James Morrison Morrison
> Weatherby George Dupree
> Took great care of his mother
> Though he was only three,"

we would declaim, and

> "I had a penny. A bright new penny!
> And I took my penny/ To the market square."

Or:

> "The King asked the Queen
> And the Queen asked the dairymaid,
> 'Could we have some butter for the royal slice of bread?' "

It was the *School Paper* that introduced us to some of our own Australian poets, like Henry Kendall, Adam Lindsay Gordon who died in the First World War and, of course, Banjo Paterson of "The Man from Snowy River" and "Waltzing Matilda" fame.

Spelling has never been a problem for me. We were well taught. For years we learned twenty spelling words every night. Their meanings had been explained to us and we were expected to be able to use them in context. We would often learn the day's list as we walked to school and we would meet other boys and girls, murmuring to themselves as they completed the same task. We were very disappointed if we didn't get all twenty right when we were tested at the beginning of class each morning. In this way, we developed a love for words and their meanings. Word contests and spelling bees gave us opportunities to demonstrate our prowess and we would have many occasions to try to use them in our frequent written compositions. Consequently, new words have always been a delightful discovery for me, and word problems in magazines are still a pleasurable challenge. All our lives Linda and I enjoyed discussing words and their vagaries at length when we were together. In fact, when quite young, I loved to read the dictionary and, because of this predilection, the other children were already calling me "the professor" when I was eleven,

Writing a composition each week — one that was carefully read and commented upon — stimulated our imagination. One of the most memorable at this early stage was a story I wrote about a coin that passed from hand to hand and pocket to pocket. Soon I was trying my hand at original narratives. The first story I wrote, in about fifth grade, was entitled "Topsy-turvy Town." This great masterpiece was about a town in which everyone walked upside down and everything was done in opposite fashion to what one would expect. One of Dad's sons from his first family was so impressed with this early production that he had it typed up in his office and circulated within the family. Unfortunately for posterity, this great literary work has been irretrievably lost. All I have been able to find is the second page, written painstakingly in careful, neat handwriting.

To celebrate great occasions the Education Department favored mass displays by school children at the Melbourne Cricket Ground. In 1927 we Bank Street children were involved in one such display — a living message, for the visit of the Duke and Duchess of York, later King George V1 and Queen Elizabeth (the long-lived Queen Mum). In those days of long sea voyages a royal visit to our distant outpost of Empire was something of an event. Massed on the huge oval of the Cricket Ground, all dressed in white, we created a gigantic "Welcome" for our Royal visitors. The Duke and Duchess were visiting Australia for the opening of the Federal Parliament House in the developing capital city of Canberra, which had recently been artificially created halfway between the rival cities of Melbourne and Sydney. In 1927 only small portions of Canberra existed for the Duke and Duchess to inspect, along with a temporary Parliament House, which, like many such buildings, remained "temporary" for more than sixty years. There was much excitement and controversy at the time about the new capital, which was planned by Chicago architect Burley Griffin, a student of Frank Lloyd Wright's, whose proposal had won a worldwide contest. The architect's name was finally immortalized in Lake Burley Griffin, created in 1964. In geography lessons we were learning to think of Australia as one nation and this visit was a unifying event. Avidly we followed in the newspapers the visits of the Duke and Duchess to the six widely separated state capitals of our vast country — the home at that time of only six and a half million people.

It was in the third grade that I learned at first hand about death. I had a blonde playmate called Edna Prosser, whom I loved very much. She came and played with me often in our yard, climbing trees and sharing secrets, as little girls do. One day when she was out with her mother, she started to run across the road and, despite her mother's anguished warnings, ran directly into the path of a rapidly advancing tram. She was killed instantly. This was a dreadful shock and grief to her classmates and particularly to me. Life seems eternal to the very young. The whole class was taken to line up as a guard of honor outside her modest, weatherboard home, with its tiny, pocket-handkerchief garden, as her coffin was carried out to the hearse. The finality of it all was hard to grasp. Sadly I returned home and wandered around the yard, putting flowers on all the places where I remembered her feet had trodden on the previous happy afternoon. More than seventy-five years later she still lives in my memory. Linda also lost a little playmate in the fourth grade, Flossie of the long flaxen hair, who died of meningitis, a disease about which little was known at the time, but whose swift effects were terrifying. In school on Friday, Flossie was dead by Monday. We were learning the grim realities of life.

Playing in the Sun

In primary school the game we played most was rounders, a similar game to baseball. In our class contests, in which everyone took part, I was never considered a great batter or bowler. Consequently, I spent a lot of time in the outfield waiting for the ball to come my way. I found this excruciatingly boring. To fill in time, I would make daisy chains or chew on bits of grass, so that when the ball did fly toward me, once every half-hour or so, I was naturally caught unawares. Seeing everyone looking my way, I would make a lunge at this object flying out of the blue at far too fast a pace and inevitably miss it. I was a typical butter-fingers, which I found extremely humiliating. Rounders, I am afraid, would never have stimulated me to a lifetime interest in sporting activity. Fortunately for my health and physical development, I was rescued by the game of field hockey in high school. This game, with its constantly evolving action for all members of the team, kept me alert and excited and became my passion for many years.

Much more interesting than rounders was learning to swim. Each week we were taken by tram to the Melbourne City Baths, where we disported ourselves in green chlorinated water, the girls segregated from the boys, of course. Mixed bathing did not come in until 1938. Learning to swim was very important in Melbourne, with its extensive sandy beaches around the bay, apart from the many opportunities to swim in nearby rivers. Of course, in those days, we all wore modest swimming costumes with short sleeves, round necks and little skirts, with light, waterproof swim caps to protect our hair from the salty water. We wore sandshoes on the beach and even had little rubber shoes to wear in the water to protect our feet from the numerous sharp rocks along the shores of the bay. Everyone in Melbourne was expected to learn to swim. Apart from compulsory swimming classes in schools there was a statewide Learn-to-Swim Campaign, with free lessons offered on the popular beaches. Newspapers promoted the campaign, and, along with swimming instruction, there were exciting sandcastle-building competitions. The elaborate structures the children built all over the sandy beach were a sight to behold against the background of the clean, blue waters of the bay, which sparkled in the sunshine. The prize-winning sandcastles were pictured in the evening newspapers.

The beach was also a favorite site for big picnics. My father's employer was Sir Keith Murdoch, who owned the Melbourne *Herald* and the *Sun-News-Pictorial*. There was a common saying that the *Herald* had its "tens of thousands of readers," while the *Sun*, with its many pictures, had its "hundreds of thousands of lookers." Once a year Sir Keith would organize a huge seaside picnic for the families of his employees. He would hire a big paddle steamer, the *Weeroona*, to take these hundreds of people down Port Phillip Bay to the ocean beach at Sorrento for a day in the sun. We found these excursions very exciting. They gave us our first experience of sailing on a ship, running all over the decks and up and down the companionways. Sunday School picnics at the beach were also a great event of the year. Our Sunday School at St Paul's used to go to Brighton Beach, which at the time was at the other end of the railway line from Essendon. Games, sandcastle-building competitions, and races were organized on the sand. Sometimes we would watch the strong, muscular, bronzed lifesavers practice their skills in reeling in swimmers in difficulty. We ate lots of sandy sandwiches, yeast buns, and ice cream from big churns and we drank great quantities of raspberry vinegar, all this fare prepared in the early morning by a dedicated team of Sunday School teachers. At one beach picnic a newspaper photographer took a picture of Linda in the sea. Although, to her disappointment it did not appear in the newspaper, I still have the photograph of a happy little girl in a high-necked, very proper swimsuit, clearly enjoying herself in the water.

Sunday School picnics were usually held on Melbourne Cup Day, a state holiday in Victoria. When portable radios became available, we would see the adults disappearing in the bushes at three o'clock to listen to the Cup race — a local obsession even for people not normally addicted to gambling. After all nearly everyone in Melbourne would have invested a few "bob" (shillings) in an office or workplace winner-take-all "sweep" on the race.

Like all Melbourne children, we loved the beach. We had forty miles of beautiful sandy beaches to choose from around the then pellucid, unpolluted Port Phillip Bay and lots of summer sunshine in which to enjoy them. Horrible sunburn also came with our long days of exposure to the direct rays of the southern sun. Some of these sunburns were very severe and memorable; we came home red as lobsters, unable to lie down or put on clothes with comfort. In a few days every bit of exposed skin would have peeled off. In those days we had not heard of the ozone hole over the Southern Hemisphere and the need for Australians to protect themselves from ultraviolet rays. We didn't stop to "slip on a tee shirt; slap on a hat; and slop on the sunscreen lotion." Mother was most unhappy when we came home sunburned, because she had always been very insistent that we take good care of our skin. She worried about the dried out, wrinkled skin, so prevalent among adults in Australia's withering summer climate. She persistently exhorted us to wear hats and we were constantly discouraged from frowning or wrinkling our foreheads. "Don't pull faces," was our childhood warning, "If the wind changes, you may stay that way!" As a result of this early conditioning, neither Linda nor I, in our older years, had many wrinkles, and people always remarked on our soft, smooth skin.

The Little "Twins"

When Linda was born, Mother was still grieving for her first daughter who had died so young, her little Nina. It was a delight to her to have a daughter. When Wilga came along, just sixteen months later, she treated her two little girls very much like twins. She tried to give us much the same things and for a while we were dressed alike. Because of this closeness we each tended to want what the other had, tolerating at most a difference in color. When we went to the lolly shop with a penny to spend on lollies, I would always wait to see what Linda chose and then generally buy the same sweets, knowing that otherwise I would be disappointed that I did not have what she had. Years later I discovered that Linda had apparently felt the same way. One Christmas, we went looking for a Christmas present for each other. Although we searched separately, keeping our choice a secret till Christmas, we ended up giving each other the same pretty blue and pink feather fan, because we had both found it the prettiest, most irresistible thing in the shop.

When we were about eight and nine, we went to our first fancy dress ball, a Bank Street school function in the local town hall. We were suitably decked out in hired costumes. I was attired as the Fairy Queen, in a white dress, with shiny silver trimmings and a scattering of silver stars, white tulle wings, and a tumbling white headdress with a silver band (hardly a crown). Linda was a butterfly, with golden butterflies embroidered on her yellow dress and a butterfly crown. We also wore the ballet shoes, now painted silver and gold by Mother, which we had retained from our earlier disastrous sortie into that area of the arts. With my usual "twin" complex, I thought I didn't look as pretty (perhaps as colorful?) as Linda, but I did have a wand which I could wave over my school friends in an attempt to turn them into birds or frogs. The following year Linda went to the fancy dress ball as "No More Strikes." She wore a dress made from sacking that was completely covered with dead matches we had saved over many

96

weeks or cadged from friends. I went as a postbox, wearing a stiff cardboard cylinder of the obligatory red of His Majesty's Mails (GR for Georgius Rex), with a real slot for other children to post their letters in. Unfortunately, this was not such a felicitous idea, since in order to attract the notice and appreciation of the judges by my authenticity, I had to remain motionless all night, or at least until the judging was over. This somewhat spoiled the fun, particularly as those mean judges did not reward my effort at its true worth.

When my brother Reg married Gus, one of the Morris twins from Browning Street in Moonee Ponds, Linda was selected to be a trainbearer (although in twenties style there was very little train to bear). She was decked out in a little pink dress with an edging of minute pink roses, with pink tulle around her hair. Naturally, although I was not part of the wedding party, I had to have an identical dress and I was very proud of my pretty appearance. Consequently I never understood why Linda got to sit for the official bridal photograph while I didn't. The fun of sliding over the highly polished floor at the reception with the other little children, in and out among the dancers, made up for some of this disappointment. The real excitement of the evening came when great numbers of paper streamers were thrown for the streamer dance and we could gather up and keep great armfuls of them. Later we laboriously untangled the streamers and rewound them to throw down our long Victorian passage at 1 The Parade — rewinding them again and again to enjoy the excitement of the ephemeral throw. Streamers were readily available at the time. Not only were they an integral part of weddings, along with confetti, but throwing them from quay to deck and deck to quay was also an indispensable expression of affection when friends were sailing away on ocean liners. The sight of a ship leaving, with the myriad intertwined, multi-colored streamers joining loved ones until the ultimate moment when, stretched beyond their strength, they broke and fell, was a moving and unforgettable moment.

Being so popular, paper streamers were not expensive and with patience could be reused. They became part of our decoration scheme for celebrations like Christmas. On wet afternoons we would sit for hours, folding different colored streamers over and over each other to make multicolored paper chains to loop across the vestibule, over window and door frames, and along the mantels of fireplaces. As the Depression drew ever closer and we had to watch every penny, Linda translated this love of streamers into a fancy dress for a junior high school "frolic," with a skirt and cloak made entirely of streamers and a pointed cardboard hat trailing even more streamers. She felt as pretty as a fairy princess.

After their marriage, Reg and Gus went to live in Glenbervie, a very new suburb about three miles further out from the city than Ascot Vale. Here the streets were not yet paved, although the railway line passed through on its way to northern Victoria. When we visited them, we had to make our way back to the railway station in the dark over a small creek at the bottom of a rough gully full of gum trees. From the branches above nocturnal mopokes called eerily: "More pork! More pork!" If it had been raining, the usually dry creek bed would be flowing with water and we would have to try to find stepping stones to cross it in the pitch darkness. It was quite scary for two young girls, but seeing our dear brother was important to us and we hated to take the long, equally dark route by the road.

In the *fourth grade*, we remained in the Annex in Regent Street. This made us feel very special. We were in our own little school of two classes and felt closer to each other and to our teacher. This was the year of the change of spelling. In the third grade we had learned to spell words like *honour* and *colour* with a "u" and words like *centre* and *theatre* with "re," in the British tradition. From one year to the next, we were suddenly informed that in future we would write *honor* and *center*. (We were not told that this was the American way.) Obediently we complied. The following year, to our surprise, we were switched back to *honour* and *centre*. I don't remember whether this switch included *travelled /traveled* and *defence /defense*. Was this due to a different political party taking over the Education Department? Be that as it may, this experience developed in me my first skepticism as a linguist. I realized from practical experience that such things as spelling were not based on immutable principles, written on tablets of gold when time began, but were arbitrary decisions on small, unimportant matters, made by mysterious others whose motivations I would never know.

In our primary school studies, we did not have exploratory science lessons, as children do today. We did, however, explore life around us in Nature Study. We observed how plants absorb water by standing snowdrops in our inkwells and watching them turn blue. We discovered that earthworms that have been cut in bits can reconstitute themselves; we came to recognize praying mantises, standing stiffly like twigs, and stick insects that constructed cocoons woven onto bits of stick, from which they emerged in time as moths that flew away. We also developed a passion for silkworms, the pupae of which were passed, as a special favor, from one child to another. Silkworms, we discovered, could be fed only on mulberry leaves that had to be sought out diligently as a rarity in our neighborhood. We watched them spinning their silk to make their cocoons and later we loved unwinding the silk from the cocoons onto spools — not that most of us ever did much with the yellow silk afterwards. Much easier to find and feed than silkworms were the colorful green caterpillars of the Emperor Gum Moth, with their red and yellow pimples; these fed happily and voraciously on the leaves of the ubiquitous peppercorn trees.

My first encounter with an IQ test was in the fourth grade. IQ tests were new to Australia in 1928. Naturally this revolutionary type of test aroused considerable interest among the teachers. As a matter of educational policy, we were never told our scores, but I did notice after the test that I was pointed out as an interesting phenomenon to various teachers who came to the door of our classroom. It was rumored that I had given correct responses to all the items on the test. I mention this here because of what happened to me at the end of sixth grade (which I have labeled *Educational Trauma Three*). I will keep you in suspense about that sad event for a few more pages.

Fifth grade, still at Regent Street, was Patto's domain. Miss Patterson was a warm and patient woman, who clearly loved children and sought to make school an interesting and enjoyable place for them. She introduced us to the Anne books,[39] which were for a number of years our joy and delight. Anne of Green Gables lived in Avonlea on Prince Edward Island. Although it was in Canada, PEI became for us a mythical place with no geographical location. Over a series of seven books and nearly as many years its inhabitants became our intimate companions as we moved into our teens. It was in Patto's class that I finally achieved the distinction of becoming top of the class. All through primary school I had had stiff competition from a perfect little girl, with neat flaxen plaits, who never blotted her copybook and always dotted her "i's." Not unexpectedly, it was she who usually came first in class. With my rapid completion of school work and my heavy, irregular writing, how could I surpass her?[40] Naturally, I was elated with my fifth grade success, but even more so when, on the way home, my dear sister came to meet me and gave me a Violet Crumble. I was so proud and happy that she was pleased with my achievement, for which at the end of the year I received a small silver medal inscribed with the magical word "Dux."

Hygiene was a preoccupation of our primary school teachers and Miss Patterson would tell her classes that she had a cold shower every morning and urge us to do the same. Linda took this seriously and was trying to suffer through a cold shower on a dreary winter morning in our unheated bathroom, when Mother came in and dragged her out. Mother was very scared of our "catching our death of cold," teacher's admonition or not. We were also learning in school life skills, such as thrift and care with money. We were each provided with our own little savings bank books from the State Savings Bank of Victoria, in which we were encouraged to deposit a penny a week, sometimes even a thrippenny bit, all carefully entered by our teacher in our bank books as a Monday morning ritual. I recently found my small savings bank book from my primary school days and discovered that, over six years, I had accumulated all of five pounds (or ten dollars), the equivalent of 1,200 pennies — a much larger sum then than now, of course. The thousands of Victorian schoolchildren who participated in this arrangement must have supplied the State Government with quite a tidy loan from their little frugalities.

Having been brought up on such adages as "Penny-wise and pound-foolish" and "See a penny, pick it up, and all the day you'll have good luck," we were amused, rather than surprised, by the old man of the neighborhood, rumored, probably quite correctly, to be very wealthy, who spent his days on quiet walks, poking among the leaves and papers in the gutters for small coins that might have been dropped. Values change. Sixty years, or three generations later, a professorial colleague of mine at Harvard was walking behind some students along a street in Cambridge when one of the students dropped a dime. Picking it up, my distinguished colleague hurried up to the student, saying: "Excuse me, you dropped a dime." "Oh!" replied the student, "You can keep it!"

For everyone the *sixth grade* meant Miss Falloon, very much of the old school. A long-time Bank Street teacher, Kate Falloon believed in much learning by heart and maintained stern discipline in her class of forty children. History was memorized sentence by sentence. When we arrived each morning, the history sentence for the day would already be written neatly and clearly for our copying at the top of the blackboard, as a teasing segment of a continuing serial. Whether we received any explanation of it I do not remember, but we would set about adding this new item immediately to our memorized sequence. Since sentence snippets about the past remained unchanged from year to year, it was easy to catch up. If you had missed some days of school, probably with the inevitable cold from which Melbournians so frequently suffered, all you had to do was consult your elder sister's or brother's or aunt's or uncle's sixth-grade exercise book and there you would have all the history sentences verbatim. On Friday afternoons, we recycled all our geographical and historical knowledge in a singsong chorus that echoed along the corridors. "*Mel*-bourne on the *Yar*-ra / *cap*-ital of Vic-*tor*-ia; *Lon*-don on the *Thames* / *cap*-ital of *Eng*-land," we cried, and "*Old*-ham, *Bol*-ton, *Pres*-ton, and *Hud*-dersfield," the cotton manufacturing towns of the Lancashire few of us would ever see, but whose names formed a melodious sequence. We then moved on to recite the series of history sentences up to that day's morsel (English history, not Australian, of course). Of all this memorized history, the only two gems I can remember are the rhythmic "Arthur Wellesley, Duke of Wellington" and "Elizabeth was vain and loved flattery," which, as sentence number one of that glorious epoch in English history, had been repeated over and over on many Fridays. Sixth grade also meant the "Qually" (Qualifying Certificate), for which Miss Falloon assiduously prepared us. She was noted for her almost total success with her very diverse band of pupils. It is recorded that in 1919 she got 44 out of 46 pupils through this examination.[41] I was in her class in 1929.

Minidrama: The Heinous Crime of Passing Notes

Under the old discipline, talking in class and passing notes were major misdemeanors. We all knew that. On this particular day, Miss Falloon found a scrap of paper with writing on it on the floor of her immaculate classroom.

"Who wrote this note?" she inquired sternly. Silence followed.

"Who wrote this note?" she repeated with some exasperation. There was only silence in the room.

"Very well," she continued, "Since no one is willing to admit to having written the note, I shall keep the whole class in every night after school until the writer of the note confesses."

At this point she looked penetratingly at me, a fact not lost on my classmates. So in we stayed for a good half-hour after school.

"Why don't you own up?" asked the girls with whom I was walking home from school. "After all, she knows your handwriting."

"But I didn't write it," I protested.

"Of course you did," said my companions. "Let's get this over with."

For several more days we stayed in after school, despite further appeals from Miss Falloon and a very pointed comparison of my exercise book with the writing on the scrap of paper.

"It isn't fair to keep us all in every day like this," said my home route companions. "It's your fault. Why don't you just confess and get us off the hook!"

But how could I? This was not the first or last time that a teacher posed a difficult moral dilemma for me. It would have been easier to tell a lie and say I had written the note. But I hadn't written it and I was not supposed to tell lies. Furthermore, I knew it was not a note, so how could I confess to writing a note that was not a note that I hadn't written. To complicate matters still further, I knew who had written the note that was not a note, but peer-group ethics precluded my telling tales on my classmates. On the other hand, by not confessing to writing the note that was not a note that I hadn't written, or alternatively telling tales on a classmate, I was keeping my friends in after school, unjustly and perhaps forever. This too was unacceptable. Finally, I decided the lesser of the various evils would be to explain the situation to the teacher, who would surely understand that a note that was not a note should not be treated as though it were a note and that would be the end of it.

So what was this strange piece of paper with writing on it that resembled mine, but was not mine? (After all, hadn't we all been taught to write in much the same style for six years already?) In our leisure moments we had been playing *Fortunes*. For this game, we wrote out "fortunes" on pieces of paper, which were then placed in a box, from which we drew out fortunes at random. On the day of the alleged misdemeanor, I had seen one of these fortunes flutter to the floor while the box was being passed surreptitiously from hand to hand under a desk. It was this scrap of paper that Miss Falloon had picked up on that ill-fated day.

I explained all this to Miss Falloon, who was forced in all justice to lift the after-school sanction, but who still felt some kind of example should be made of us all for our foolish conduct. "I understand you can tell fortunes," she observed icily. "Tell me my fortune then." Now we were in a real dilemma. Clearly she wanted to make us seem gullible for believing that we could foretell the future. How could we prove ourselves infallible? We put our heads together and came up with an ingenious solution. Many times, in developing our hygienic and moral sensitivities, Miss Falloon had told us things she did regularly. We could capitalize on these, knowing we could not be wrong. As safe "fortunes," then, we wrote a series of slips like "You will have a bath tomorrow morning" or "You will go to church on Sunday," and we knew that all was saved, at least temporarily. Of course, we never knew what the next aberration on the part of our teacher might be.

The Effects of the Great War (World War 1)

As we grew up in primary school, we were still close enough to the 1914-1918 Great War to be constantly reminded of it. Many of our friends' fathers had been involved in the military bungle at Gallipoli in 1915 that led to Australia's first blood bath. This episode resulted in the disastrous loss of the lives of so many idealistic and patriotic young men, who had left our shores singing and chiyacking, with hopes of high adventure. Anzac Day celebrations, on April 25th each year, were emotional occasions, as we listened to the Last Post played on the bugle and Rupert Brooks's moving words: "Age shall not weary them nor the years condemn. At the going down of the sun and in the morning, we will remember them." At school and around the Cenotaph in Queen's Park, the site of what remained of the Moonee Ponds, we heard accounts of their valor. The speeches were usually given by ex-servicemen, who told us in lurid detail how these young men, in their first military engagement, had tried to take the forbidding cliffs of Gallipoli under the full blast of Turkish fire. Family and neighbors treasured relics like shell cases and iron helmets and we heard of lost fathers and brothers and shell-shocked friends. We vaguely knew that something was going on at Versailles, but whatever it was did not seem to concern us very much.

We had a further reminder of the war each year on Armistice Day, when at the eleventh hour on the eleventh day of the eleventh month all work would cease, all transport would stop, and all heads would bow for two minutes of silence. Pins in the form of the red poppies of Flanders (the *coquelicots* I later admired so much in the fields in the north of France) would be sold by the Returned Soldiers, Sailors, and Airmen's League to aid disabled servicemen. At school local officials would give rousing patriotic speeches, the contents of which were fairly predictable. A spate of memorials was being built in cities and towns to honor those who had died in action. We became accustomed to seeing listings of battlefields where the Australians had fought in the muddy trenches along the Somme in Northern France and in Belgium. Names like Mons, Ypres, Amiens, Saint-Quentin, and Villers-Bretonneux became familiar to us. When I was in France as a student in 1950, I visited a friend in Saint-Quentin and saw the endless rows of white crosses in the Australian Cemetery nearby. I was also able to visit the school in Villers-Bretonneux, which had been rebuilt after the war with money raised by the school children of Melbourne, of whom I was one.

In this kind of post-war atmosphere, it is not surprising that I won a prize in the sixth grade for an essay on "Why I would like my brother to join the 58th Battalion" (the local battalion whose flags hung in St Thomas's Church in Moonee Ponds for many years). The title of this early piece of creative writing (the subject imposed, of course, by the prize-giver) still surprises me, since the sentiments it required me to express were hardly mine at that time or since.

Early Reading

As a family we did not own a great number of books. It was not that books were not valued, but they were not affordable. Books available at the time were for the most part hardbacks imported from England, there being only a few Australian publishers. For some obscure reason, this almost doubled the price. The paperback revolution was well in the future. In the pioneer conditions in which my parents had grown up, private libraries of any size were not an option. Mater had been a great bookworm and in her retirement she read bools constantly, but these were books from the local library. When she found out that Linda and I were avid readers, she delighted in discussing books with us. My mother, having had little education beyond the sixth grade, was not a reader of more than the daily newspaper and when she read aloud she read rather hesitantly. When she was bedridden in her mid-seventies, in the year before her death, I persuaded her to read the first and only book she had read in her life. It was Alan Marshall's memoir, *I can Jump Puddles,* [42] which described his growing up in Victoria at a similar period and in similar circumstances to her own. She really enjoyed this book, but, as her immediate memory was gradually deteriorating as a result of her illness, it was an experience she was not able to repeat. Father, although writing a great deal, was extremely busy for a man in his seventies. He attended sales at the Newmarket Yards, judged at country shows, and worked in between times in the *Herald* office from nine to five, with overtime reports to write at home in the evenings at least once a week. Naturally daily newspapers and the *Weekly Times* were all the reading he could cope with.

Linda learned to read before I did and from the start she adored reading; in fact, she was always known as a bookworm. She would become so absorbed in her reading that she would not hear anything addressed to her. Very early she started to practice her newfound skills by reading aloud to little Wilga and telling me in great detail the stories she had heard or read in school. I began reading as fast as I could. I remember the first book I was given by a cousin in 1924, when I was five. It was about *The Wise Gray Cat,* [43] who was so wise because she had lived seven of her nine lives. I don't remember much of what happened to the poor creature but, at that early period, just having her story around made me feel very proud. It was, after all, my first very own book.

Among the few books in the house there was, not surprisingly, a much-prized copy of Great-uncle John Burston's *Arithmetic*, along with copies of De Quincy's *Confessions of an English Opium Eater* (Routledge, 1886) and Daniel Defoe's *Moll Flanders* (1722). Where they came from I never quite made out. These rubbed shoulders with some old history books that had belonged to Charles Tanner in his teaching days and Prescott's 1848 *History of the Conquest of Mexico* (Routledge). At a later period, Great-uncle Alf Lehmann brought us several more nineteenth-century books with heavily embossed covers, gold edgings, and etchings of people in strange places. One of these books was called *The Young Llanero* and it gave me my first glimpse into the distant territory of South America. There was a blue and gold book, *On the Nile* by a Mrs Sarah Hunt (Nelson, 1880), with line sketches of life in Egypt at the time of its publication, and a London Missionary Society book by a Mrs Arnold Foster, which seems a strange attribution in this more feminist-conscious era. Mrs Foster's book was called *In the Valley of the Yangtse* (1899) and, although written in a rather boring style, it gave us some insights into the life and customs of traditional China. With these Uncle Alf included Lord Lytton's *The Coming Race* (Routledge, 1874), which had belonged to his brother Charles Lehmann, and which, I am afraid, was never read. This very eclectic set of family relics hardly provided a literary initiation for small children. A very old copy of Hans Christian Andersen's *Tales*, with a deep hole bored or burned into its leather cover, emerged at one stage from I know not where and was read much more than the others, albeit with some mystification at its gloomy tone. Perhaps it didn't transfer too well from a land of clouds and rain to a land of radiant sunshine. In the front sitting room, taking pride of place on the high-gloss, hexagonal table decorated with inlays of various woods, which we had inherited from the Tanner family, was a large book, called *Beautiful Britain*. In it were full-page, rather faded, black-and-white photographs of English castles and stately homes, showing both their exteriors and their very cluttered Victorian interiors. We loved to peruse this book on rainy Sundays. Along with my now much-read *Wise Gray Cat*, these constituted the family library.

Much more accessible than these nineteenth-century books were the children's comics and magazines we bought. These contained stories and serials as well as cartoon-strip adventures, all printed in black and white. They came by ship from England and, consequently, arrived at somewhat irregular intervals. We accepted as a natural fact of life that most printed materials described settings, seasons, and public holidays that had nothing to do with our

Australian scene. After all, hadn't we grown up on nursery rhymes about Banbury Cross, St Ives, and London Bridge falling down? In our winter months we read about summer and August Bank Holiday, whatever that was. We looked with interest and curiosity at the children cavorting in the snow, which we had never experienced in our warm southern land, although it was very familiar to us from the scenes on Christmas cards. We studied intently the pictures of the Man in the Moon in our comics; this face we could not detect on our southern hemisphere moon, since we were seeing it from a different angle from our European counterparts. We eventually found out that if you put your head on one side and tried to see the moon upside down the patterns did seem to resemble what was depicted in our reading material. This confirmed my developing conviction that printed materials were never intended to represent reality as I knew it; they were all fanciful and I loved fiction, anyway. Just as we did when reading about the Chinese or the Zulus, we flexibly adjusted our thinking and imaginings to the unfamiliar world of these interesting others.

As small children we read the *Tiger Tim* comic. Sometimes we were given for Christmas the *Tiger Tim Annual*, with its cartoon adventures of animal characters. No one knew as yet of Mickey Mouse or other Disney creations. Our Christmas annuals (and each comic produced one) kept us busy with word games and puzzles, where we found faces hidden in line drawings of forests, for instance, and made pictures by joining up numbered dots or worked our way through mazes. To fill spaces in the page layout, there were often small sketches that I loved to copy in black India ink, with a pen with a very fine nib, for the homemade Christmas and birthday cards we made for our friends. Another comic I loved was called *Film Fun*. It had much more exciting adventure stories than the more juvenile *Tiger Tim*. The serials kept me breathless from ship to ship, as I pestered the newsagent for news of the arrival from England of the next episode. One memorable serial that captivated me was called "The Human Mole." In this masterpiece the protagonist had built a steel capsule, in which he could bore under the floor of a neighboring building in the middle of the night and come up into the vault of a bank; then he could disappear just as easily with all the money. Hooray for the Human Mole! Here was someone who could flout

107

authority and get away with it. At that age I was not overly concerned with the morality of it all.

As we grew older we graduated to the *Schoolgirls' Own*, a weekly girls' magazine from England that contained lively stories of girls in an English boarding school, the games they played and the pranks they got up to. This magazine also arrived at unpredictable intervals depending on the schedules of various ships. Consequently, one issue might arrive before the preceding number and put us out of sequence in our serial story. The protagonists in these stories became very familiar to us by name and individual character. Betty Barton and Polly Linton, I remember, were the leaders of the bunch, Betty being the very good Senior Prefect type and Polly the madcap. Linda even drew a complete set of miniature portraits of them all, as she did later for the characters in the Anne books. Sometimes the magazine offered readers little gifts, which seemed to us an incredible windfall. One such gift, a set of tiny gold transfers of figures in eighteenth-century costumes, ended up as a decorative frame around Linda's bedroom mirror. For Christmas we would request the *Schoolgirls' Own Annual*. We did not hang up socks for Father Christmas to fill; they were far too small for our aspirations. We always hung up pillowcases, which could hold these big books that we awaited with such impatience. Not only did we get in these annuals more stories about our schoolgirl friends, but also quizzes, pictures to complete, or patterns for making gloves, scarves, or toys for presents.

From the Annuals, we moved on to some Australian children's books. We loved Mary Grant Bruce's *Billabong* books and Ethel Turner's ever-popular *Seven Little Australians.* Mrs Aeneas Gunn's *Little Black Princess* and *We of the Never Never* provided our first introduction to the intriguing and exotic Deep North of our own country and the distinctive way of life of its indigenous inhabitants. As we grew older, our brothers introduced us to Steele Rudd's *Sandy's Selection*, which gave us hilarious pictures of the life of our pioneer forebears, as they battled droughts, bushfires, sandstorms, and scrabble-hard soil. None of this was about our own reality either. After all, we were city dwellers who had never ridden a horse or seen a kangaroo outside of the zoo. We still read mostly about life overseas, however. We continued to beg, borrow, or steal any new books about our beloved Anne *(Anne of the Island, Rilla of Ingleside)* and her life on Prince Edward Island in Canada. We also read through the many Pollyanna books[44] about the American Glad Girl who saw everything through rose-colored glasses. If Pollyanna sprained her ankle, she would be glad that she hadn't broken her leg. This little ray of sunshine, who could find a reason to rejoice in anything and everything that happened, seemed rather cloying after the down-to-earth Anne, with her disappointed hopes and her very human mortification when things went wrong, but her adventures were entertaining.

We did not have libraries at school, although there was usually a classroom shelf with a few books from which to choose. Avidly we devoured everything on them. There were no municipal libraries either with their extensive collections of children's literature, as there are today. As we became teenagers, a local newspaper shop established in a back room the first local lending library of books for adults; this was very exciting and we patronized it assiduously. By insisting, however, on books as presents for Christmases and birthdays, we eventually built up a little store of our own to treasure. Mother's sister, our Auntie Del, gave us a display case, with shelves and glass doors, which she had rescued from a now defunct cake shop of which she had been manager. Rainy days were soon occupied with covering all our books with brown paper, very neatly folded and tucked in, with the titles carefully printed on the spines, so that we could line them up on the shelves of our very own library.

The brown paper procedure we had learned at school, where the teachers insisted that we cover every schoolbook to keep the exterior in pristine condition or to conceal the messiness of the second-hand books that were usually all we could afford. We all had to buy our own schoolbooks and, no matter what the financial sacrifice, Mother always stretched her meager budget to ensure that we had everything the school required. It was always a thrill when we went off to buy our new schoolbooks — those that could not be handed down from older brothers and sisters. The books passed on to us were usually the class-level readers published by the Education Department, which remained the same over a number of years. A very ancient hand-me-down I loved was an arithmetic textbook that had belonged to one of my brothers. It had a series of "moving pictures" carefully drawn into it. My brother had discovered that, if you had the

109

patience, you could make a series of little sketches on successive pages of a textbook, making minimal changes in subsequent drawings, and lo and behold! if you riffled the pages of the book the pictures actually moved. This was great! Without realizing it, we were junior Disneys and our little friends were fascinated. Naturally, with our love of books, we never sold any of our class texts at the end of the year and these added considerably to the collection on our library shelves. Because of the brown paper tradition, it wasn't till years later that Linda and I discovered how beautiful a row of books looked when their colorful dust covers or bindings were open to view.

On Christmas Eve, as midnight approached, we would wait anxiously for Father Christmas to come, pretending to be asleep, so that we could leap up and start reading our new books immediately. Mother, who was of course the gift distributor, would be in the washhouse doing her washing, to avoid the insupportable heat and rush of the Christmas Day ahead. Despite strenuous efforts to keep awake we would eventually succumb to slumber and Mother would always manage to sneak our presents in without waking us up. By three or four in the morning, however, we would be absorbed in our new books. We kept up the Father Christmas custom until we were well into our teens, as so many children do. It is hard to give up the excitement of waking to find presents hanging in a pillow slip from the bedpost. After my brother Les married Maude, his sister-in-law's twin, I inherited her bicycle, but it was not enough to receive this much coveted object in a mundane way, I had to receive it in a simulated surprise at the foot of my bed on Christmas Day. Years later I met Father Christmas at the Santa Claus Village in Lapland on a visit to Finland. Entering into the fantasy, I thanked him for having given me a bike one Christmas when I was a little girl, to which he replied without a blink: "Oh! You were *that* little girl!"

As soon as the bike came into my life, I became a very enthusiastic rider. My brothers started me off in the learning process, of course, by holding the back of the bike steady for me, until I could balance by myself. I perfected my early riding by making my way up and down our side lane, turning round in the small space at the end to ride back. This narrow lane was very useful for a beginner like me, because, if I wobbled off my path, I could always steady myself with my hand against the paling fence. After I had gained confidence and balance, there was no keeping me off the bike. This bike served me well later on, when we were living on very reduced means. It became my only means of transport for going to all sorts of places — daily to school and university or to visit friends, even on the other side of Melbourne.

On Sundays, we loved to stay in bed reading *The Australian Journal*. This inexpensive, paper-covered magazine was bought by my brother Les and then passed on to Linda and me. It provided an outlet for original writing for anyone who cared to send in a manuscript for consideration. Many Australian writers of the day were first published in the *Australian Journal*. Alan Marshall and Arthur Upfield, the popular writer of stories about the Koori detective, Napoleon Bonaparte, come readily to mind. At the end of each issue was a section we enjoyed, where the editors responded to those whose stories had been rejected with witty remarks like "*The freight train whistled twice* never made it to the station." These caustic comments we found very funny, since they didn't apply to us. When, after my Bachelor of Arts degree, I pursued my teacher training in 1939 at the Diploma of Education level in the Faculty of Education at the University of Melbourne, Professor George Browne recounted in class the details of a survey he and his colleagues had conducted to find out what people in Victoria were reading. To their astonishment they had discovered that the most widely read magazine was the *Australian Journal,* of which they had never heard. In fact they had been obliged to send out to buy a copy to see what it was! I certainly giggled when I heard of this incredible ignorance, since we had spent so many years reading our favorite magazine from cover to cover and stacking it up in piles as a family treasure. But then we were ordinary people, not the cognoscenti.

Moving On

At the end of the sixth grade came the famous, or infamous, high school entrance exam, which would pretty well determine the direction of our lives. If we were not admitted to high school after sixth grade, there were only two paths open to us. We could continue in primary school till the eighth grade, when we would be awarded our Merit Certificate and finish our schooling. Otherwise, the boys could go on to a Technical School to learn a trade and the girls to a

Domestic Arts School to be trained as dressmakers, milliners, cooks, or general housewives. After this cursory middle-school education, a girl with no particular career interests could go out into the world at fourteen, the school leaving age, and fill in a few years as a shop assistant or factory worker. It was generally accepted that she would eventually marry and be supported by her husband, so this period of work was regarded as more or less a waiting and looking-around period. Many parents still considered higher education, or even senior high school, a waste of time for girls, since "they would only get married."

If a girl wanted to be a teacher, nurse, or secretary (really a shorthand-typist), which were the only professional careers open to most young women at the time, she would have to pass the entrance examination to high school and continue studies there, if only for two or three years. The absorbing prospect of studying algebra and a foreign language set first year of high school off from the elementary school program or the technical school track. In high school too, students had different teachers for the various subjects and moved from room to room for different classes. To us this was an exciting prospect after six years of primary classes with one teacher in one room. Naturally, as the day approached for the entrance exam to Essendon High School, we were all agog and filled with trepidation.

Educational Trauma Three.

With eager anticipation I made my way to Essendon High School, along with the other nervous eleven- and twelve-year-olds from the primary schools in our area, and began the series of tests. I was enjoying the various tests, as I usually did, until I came to the IQ test. For this we were hustled into classrooms in batches of about thirty. This test being still fairly new in Victoria, there were no copies of the test for the students, just the one copy for the examiner. (The heaven of photocopying was not yet in sight.) Consequently the IQ test had to be read out to the group, while we inscribed our choices on the answer sheets. To this day, I believe I was in a dead spot in the room. Be that as it may, I could not hear the administrator of the test clearly, so I kept asking him to repeat the items. To this request, he would reply with growing impatience: "I am only allowed to say it once!" Naturally this state of affairs induced in me a growing panic and I heard less and less. As a result, when the scores were totted up, I turned out to be a moron, certainly not high school material. This was quite a contrast to my fourth grade experience. To my shame my name did not appear on the high school admissions list.

The administration of Essendon High School had reckoned, however, without the redoubtable Miss Falloon, no doubt already well known to them as a vigilant lioness protecting her cubs. After a couple of days, I heard to my relief that I had been admitted to high school on sufferance, because of her intervention. This shock to my self-esteem and confidence resulted in my working extremely hard all through my first year at high school and achieving the distinction of becoming top of all four first-year classes. Again the educational system had tried to put roadblocks in my way without success. The ever vivid memory of this experience had, I am sure, a major influence on my educational philosophy, which has always been based on a respect for all learners and what they personally bring to the learning process. As an educator I have continually searched for administrative frameworks, teaching approaches, and techniques that enable all students to realize their potential. I am more and more convinced that this cannot be done through large-scale, standardized, one-day-decides-all testing.

4
LEARNING TO LOVE LEARNING: EHS 1931-35

At the end of January, in 1931, I made my way with Linda to Essendon High School (EHS) for the beginning of the school year. I was very proud to be wearing my new school uniform. It was reassuring that Linda, who had been in high school for two years already, knew her way around. Now that I was a grownup eleven-year-old high school student, instead of walking to and from school, I took a train and bus on a term ticket that it was fun to flash at the railway porter at the exit. We entered high school at Form F (seventh grade) and would normally continue up through the school to Form A for Leaving Honours (twelfth grade). In each form there were several parallel classes of about thirty-five pupils. I was now in class with girls and boys from a number of schools in the western suburbs, not just local kids from our Ascot Vale streets.

Essendon High School (EHS), only eighteen years old at the time, consisted of a set of pleasant red-brick buildings, centered on an asphalt quadrangle, surrounded by airy classrooms with ample natural lighting. The quad, as we called it, would be awash with water on days when it rained and rained. Veranda roofs along the four sides kept us dry as we moved from classroom to classroom or milled around during morning and afternoon recesses. These breaks were no longer called "playtime" as in primary school. The change of name did not stop the more energetic of us from playing vigorous games of "tiggy," round and round the overloaded racks of damp coats in the entrance cloakroom, nearly skittling teachers who were unfortunate enough to choose that moment to try to pass through.

In contrast to the Bank Street School, which was built directly onto the street, EHS featured a lawn and garden, with trees and shrubs. A recently constructed two-story school hall was well lit by tall windows that opened outwards. I later found these window alcoves exciting to sit in, with my legs hanging out into space, as I studied for my exams, although this choice of nook seemed to agitate teachers passing below. The hall sported comfortable, cushioned seats that went up and down, like those in a picture theater. Known as the "new building," it also provided a corridor of extra classrooms, which were used by the senior classes. School assemblies were held in the new hall, where singing was also taught to us in large groups of four classes together. At school assemblies we now sang lustily, and with considerable pride, our school song:

> "Come, ye youths and maidens,
> And sing with joyous cadence,
> In honour of our school.
> No time have we for grieving
> While youthful garlands weaving
> With voices sweet and clear."

It hardly bothered us that the words were so floridly Victorian. The song concluded with "Strive to live worthily!" "Live worthily" was the school motto emblazoned on our school badges and to us its meaning was quite unambiguous.

As well as our class form room, we now went to different rooms for various subjects. There was a separate science room, with its funny smell of gas and chemicals, which was furnished with benches and high stools instead of desks. Bunsen burners, beakers, pipettes, and little sets of scales were the only equipment provided for demonstrations and experiments. During the more boring science lessons, we loved to pursue small globules of mercury that had accumulated in the cracks in the linoleum covering the benches; these rolled about and reformed into small balls when we tried to break them up. There was also a spacious art room where we could move the furniture around so as to get a better look at what we were drawing. (Movable furniture was a novelty in schools at the time.) Saucepans and funnels were among the beautiful objects we tried to convey in pencil on special art paper.

We now wore a school uniform, like the girls in the *Schoolgirls' Own*. We wore a well-starched, high-necked, white cotton blouse under a navy-blue tunic of mid-calf length, which had

115

to be kept despotted, and a blazer with the school badge. We sported a tie in the school colors — red and black just like the district football team, the famous Essendon Bombers — and this we had to learn to tie correctly and keep more or less straight. With these we wore long, black stockings and solid, black walking shoes. In winter we added a jumper, with around the vee of the neck the red and black, of which we were so proud. Our school hat was made of straw and shaped like a pudding basin (or, as some would have it, a "jeremiah" or chamber pot). It had a broad ribbon band in the school colors with the badge in front (that is, when you took the time to align the badge with the middle of your nose). The boys wore gray suits, with white shirts, ties in the school colors, and caps with the school badge. In countries like the United State where most school children do not wear uniform, people are often shocked at this presumed suppression of individuality. We did not feel that way at all. School uniform was, in many ways, a protection. We did not have to decide each morning what to wear and whether everything matched; we did not have to worry whether this was what we had worn yesterday, whether it was still in fashion, or what others would think of what we were wearing. We just put on our uniform, making sure it was clean and neat, and we were ready for school. Behind this uniform garb, we did not know which of our classmates were rich or poor, who could afford the most expensive clothes, and who were wearing hand-me-downs. This was a great alleviation of adolescent anxiety, for which, looking back, I am grateful. We were proud of our school uniform, which we wanted others to recognize, especially when we came across students from other schools. We were encouraged to behave outside the school in ways that would make people think well of our school (that is, we tried not to "disgrace our uniform"). Even with this apparent regimentation, there were still subtle ways in which we could individualize our appearance.

At high school there was a school orchestra, a school magazine that solicited our contributions, and a school play for which we could audition. Gathered in one classroom was an embryonic school library — just a few shelves of books — but these we seized on, until we had exhausted their possibilities. At eleven I set out to read as many Walter Scott novels as I could, since these were on the shelves. By the time I was fourteen I had read eleven of them —

116

Ivanhoe, Kenilworth, Rob Roy, The Bride of Lammermoor, all were grist to my mill. I also became acquainted with *The Secret Garden* and the Canadian *Girl of the Limberlost.*[46] The school even boasted a small book shop in a converted classroom, where we could buy our course textbooks. Each year the buying of textbooks, exercise books, atlases, art paper, graph books, rulers, compasses, and protractors by individual students was one of the considerable but obligatory expenses, along with a modest sports fee, of our otherwise free education.

For physical exercise whole forms, with their three or four parallel classes, regularly filed out into the quadrangle to do Swedish Drill with a lean, sprightly, white-haired visiting instructor called Colonel Bjelke-Petersen, who ran a physical education center for the citizenry of Melbourne. To the loud blare of Souza's Colonel Bogey March on a gramophone record and encouraged by the lithe example of the Colonel himself, we leapt and turned and spread our arms in unison, in ways that gave us plenty of aerobic exercise.

We now played in a much bigger schoolyard than at my cramped, overcrowded primary school or in sports fields in the back paddocks. EHS at that time was on the edges of settled suburbia, so there were wide, open spaces between us and the nearest small groups of houses. Wednesday afternoons were consecrated to sports, in which every student was involved. The girls played either field hockey or basketball in the winter, while the boys battled it out in eighteen-a-side Australian Rules football, with its spectacular long kicks and high jumps to seize the ball. Australian Rules was a product of our own state of Victoria. It was first played in the 1860's in Melbourne streets by small urchins, who kicked around little bundles of tightly wrapped newspaper tied with string. As a child I saw my brothers and other children still kicking around similar small bundles. During the spring term swimming or tennis, with cricket for the boys, absorbed our energies.

At high school we belonged to "houses" for intramural competition. The EHS houses were named after Victorian rivers. I was in Wimmera, the green house, while Linda was in Yarra and sported royal blue. Tambo (light blue), Kiewa (pink), Avoca (purple), and Campaspe (yellow) completed the series. When later the house names were changed to honor former headmasters, Hill, Searby, King, and so on, they seemed much less romantic and colorful. We applauded noisily at house debates and bickered happily with those less fortunate, in our eyes, in their house membership. In the spray of the indoor municipal baths we screamed our encouragement as our friends and housemates thrashed vigorously past. We shouted for our house team to win in organized track meets at local sports grounds, on tennis courts, or out in the paddocks, proudly flaunting our house colors. Apart from house matches, we played sports against other schools at different levels of competition. A Teams were respected for their skill, but we were far too busy practicing for our B, C, or D competitions to spend much time in hero worship.

I chose swimming as my sport in the warm weather and field hockey in the winter. Hockey soon became a passion and my best friends were all hockey enthusiasts. At that time there were very few specialized physical education teachers in the state system. All teachers were trained to carry their share of physical education classes and teach sports in which they had some expertise, as I myself was trained at a later date. Our hockey coach was a redheaded, bespectacled Irish teacher, Miss Kelly, who taught us English. On the field she urged us on with cries of "Roon, girls, roon!" She taught us not only the physical skills of the game, but also the strategies of this constantly moving, competitive sport. We learned the responsibilities and interdependence of teamwork, how to make decisions literally "on our feet," and how to execute them in the best interests of the team. We learned to appreciate the performance of better players, even if we did not win. It was a truly educational experience.

In the organization of the school, authority was delegated to some extent to senior students, who were selected by the Administration as outstanding leaders, both academically and morally, and designated Prefects. Their selection was in no way a democratic procedure. There were six girl Prefects, one of whom was appointed as Head Prefect, and six boy Prefects, again with a Head Prefect. The Prefects were expected to keep an eye on the behavior of other students and could impose penalties for misbehavior of minor importance, for instance, breaking school rules. They had the privilege of a small office, where they could relax or study during spare periods, and they were expected to take leading roles in school assemblies or special ceremonies. As a distinguishing mark they wore specially decorated pockets on their blazers. Head Prefects achieved the distinction of having their names emblazoned in gold on a permanent Honour Board. I was never a Prefect myself, nor was Linda, possibly because we were both very young for our classes and tended to behave in a less mature fashion than would be expected of Prefects. Along with our closest friends, we were too busy rushing around with our hockey sticks before and after school and during recesses to care about having to rein ourselves in and act as exemplars.

EHS was co-educational in principle, but careful lines of separation were drawn. Although classes were mixed, boys and girls sat on different sides of the room, occasionally hurling erasers at each other or passing notes when the teacher was writing on the board. There was, of course, a rule of silence in the classroom. Boys had special classes of Sloyd (woodworking), while the girls learned Cookery and Mothercraft. Girls and boys played in different yards, separated by a high fence, over which we could still hurl little stones, which would be returned in good measure by our unseen opponents, in what we called shrapnel fights. On the way home from school, the boys walked to the station on one side of the street and the girls on the other. There were penalties for walking home on the wrong side of the street with classmates or friends of the opposite sex. The prefects were expected to keep an eagle eye on us and report any infractions. If caught, we would be given the punishment of walking around the quadrangle ten or twenty times after school. Of course, some boys and girls slipped off together down small side streets, which the rest of us considered very daring. This was not a period of early adolescent "dating." For the most part our fraternizing with the opposite sex was in groups, at parties and picnics, on hikes in the bush, or at youth camps, organized usually by Sunday Schools or Christian Fellowships. Even Boy Scouts and Girl Guides did not mix socially in any official way, although we might occasionally meet when the Guides were invited to visit the Scouts' camp at a big Jamboree, for instance. In this segregated coeducational situation, we all knew who were the girls and boys we considered "boy-" or "girl-mad," but they were a small minority whose activities we wondered and whispered about.

On school excursions, boys and girls traveled in separate buses. EHS was trying at that time to ensure some future funding with a long-term project of cultivating a plantation of slow-growing pine trees in the mountains to the northeast of Melbourne. Here senior students, who went to assist and learn some rudimentary ecology, were segregated according to the "natural order" by suitable tasks. The boys cultivated the soil and planted trees, while the girls devoted themselves to the domestic tasks of feeding the toilers and keeping the campsite clean and neat, that is, when the girls were invited at all.

One way of approaching the boys was with our autograph books. We all had our battered little books and loved to collect little rhymes and aphorisms from our classmates and teachers. Those who could adorn their entries with little sketches were in great demand. Many of the rhymes we wrote in each other's books could be traced back at least a century to Great Britain, whence they came to Australia. "Roses are red; Violets are blue; Sugar is sweet; And so are you" is probably the best known of these. Looking through my old autograph book is a real nostalgia trip. The rhymes do not always fit in with present notions of political correctness, to be sure. I remember well the rhyme written in mine by the boy with whom I always vied for place in form — "Be good, sweet maid, And let who will be clever," he wrote. Intended merely as a little adolescent teasing, it certainly fitted in well with the attitudes of the time.

Learning Useful Womanly Arts

EHS boasted a Cookery Centre, where the girls studied to be good housewives. This small building, off on its own, was presided over by the elegantly dressed Miss Brown, who entertained some of the men teachers to lunch each day. This custom provoked whispered speculation among the girls. If we amateurs succeeded in cooking anything really tasty, it was whipped off from under our noses to feed Miss Brown's guests, while we would have to consume someone else's less than successful concoction. The first thing we learned to make was blancmange. This white, eggless custard, although simple in appearance, was quite tricky to prepare well. It had to come out smooth and not lumpy, and neither too runny nor too stiff, or it would be quite inedible. We then graduated to chocolate blancmange, popularly known as Yarra Mud. Next came macaroni cheese.

Unfortunately, early in life I had decided that I could not eat cheese, no matter how it was disguised, so there was no way I was going to eat this dish. Fortunately we had learned from older girls to take brown paper bags to our cookery classes, so that, if we had cooked something altogether too revolting to eat, we could slide it off the plate into the bag for safe disposal. Obviously my macaroni cheese was soon shoveled into a bag and on its way to the rubbish bin. Sausage rolls were always a favorite with Australian children and, when we learned how to make these, Linda and I enthusiastically decided to make a batch at home — just the kind of application teachers hope for. We did exactly what we had done at school, or so we thought, and into the oven went a splendid batch of sausage rolls. Out came some huge, indigestible specimens, because inadvertently we had used baking soda instead of baking powder. On his return home from work, our kindly Dad was obliged to eat this offering, so as not to offend his young daughters. Eventually we graduated to more sophisticated items like chocolate cake and steamed pudding, always served, of course, with Golden Syrup.

In further preparation for a woman's accepted role in life, the girls were given a course in Mothercraft. We learned to bathe the baby without letting the slippery little thing fall on the floor or drown in the tub, and we were instructed in the correct way to change its linen "nappies." For this we received a certificate from the Victorian Baby Health Centres Association, which presumably we could present to our future husbands to assure them of our competence. Naturally, in the 1930s, this course did not enlighten us as to how babies were conceived or how they came into the world. This information was still considered very hush-hush.

Learning Languages

One of the most formative things to happen to me at high school took place on the first day. All the incoming students were assembled in the quadrangle for allotment to language classes. We were invited to form French, German, and Latin groups, according to our personal preferences. Being determined to study French (perhaps because of my father's early experience of rejection because he did not know the French alphabet), I joined the French group. This was one thing I was determined to get from my high school experience.

Since far too many had chosen French, we were asked whether some of those in the French group would move over to German or Latin to balance out the classes. As a schoolgirl, I was usually amenable to any reasonable suggestion from authority figures, but on this occasion I hid behind the other students so that the teacher would not catch my eye and move me into one of the other groups. As a result of this early persistence, I ended up devoting my life to French studies, whereas I might quite easily have become a classicist or a Germanist.

I remember vividly my first French class at the age of eleven. The teacher was a young Australian, Kathleen Meldrum. I am sure she had never had the opportunity to visit France or a French-speaking country. The nearest French-speaking outpost, New Caledonia, was some seventeen hundred miles from Melbourne and most Australians at that time were barely aware of its existence.[47] Along with thirty-five or so eager pre-teens, I had the time of my life in Miss Meldrum's class. In vogue for language teaching was the Direct Method, with its emphasis on the continual use of the language in lively oral presentations of material related to the classroom setting. From the language they were hearing and trying to use students were expected to work out the grammar rules by a process of induction. In Victoria, we had little possibility of encountering French speakers out of class, of hearing radio programs in French, or of picking up French-language newspapers. There were no French films we could see in Melbourne in those early days of cinema. The Direct Method had, consequently, been modified to permit use of the native tongue for explanations, when this would speed up comprehension of more abstract meanings or the way the language was structured. Emphasis in the classroom, however, was on establishing direct links between word and meaning, without using translation, except as a last resort. The teacher would mime, draw, pass around objects, and give simple paraphrases in the language to help with comprehension. In keeping with the theory, we made picture dictionaries for our vocabulary, without English equivalents, of course.

We began by performing actions in response to commands in the language, explaining what we were doing in French as we went along. This was a form of the old game *Simon Says*, which we called *Jacques Dit*, and we loved it. For the first month or six weeks we saw no printed version of what we were saying or hearing. The only graphic accompaniment was in phonetic script, to encourage us in native-like sound production. We handled objects, describing them and using them to elicit oral comments, sometimes in some form of game. We drew large pictures, labeled them, and put them on the walls around the classroom. We sang songs. We danced (imagining we were ladies and gentlemen on the bridge at Avignon), and we learned poems. We read little stories, written in simple language with much redundancy, frequent reentry of a limited number of new words and plenty of dialogue, rather than trying to decipher long stretches of narration or description. These stories we acted out and improvised upon. Since films and videos were not available, our teacher would use large, colorful pictures to stimulate conversation and original writing. These pictures depicted such everyday situations in France as farmers' markets, schoolrooms, bakers' shops, farmyards or the family at dinner. Since there were no audio aids available either, we were entirely dependent on our teacher for the sounds and rhythm of the language. (This was pre-tape, pre-cassette, pre-video.) With Miss Meldrum we were lucky, because she did try to use oral French in her classes, encouraging us to do the same.

I was so excited after my first French lesson that I rushed home to share my experiences with my monolingual mother. It was a scorching summer day in late January and she was in the detached washhouse, with its heat-absorbing corrugated iron roof, stirring the household washing in the boiling water in the wood-fired copper. She could hardly have found my rendition fascinating, since she did not understand a word of it. As a loving mother, however, she listened interestedly and with pride as her excited daughter read her the first lesson from her French textbook.[48] My French was probably execrable, but I could not wait to share with my mother the exciting information that our flag was red, white, and blue, whereas the French flag was blue, white, and red. That night I diligently drew and colored the two flags, labeling them in my new language. Actually, in the book "our" flag was the Union Jack, of course. Like practically all our textbooks at the time, our French book, *Mes Premiers Pas*, was imported from London. In my school days we young Australians were accustomed to such anomalies in schoolbooks and it never entered our heads to question their validity. We just adjusted our thinking to the fact that printed material in textbooks did not relate to reality, but to some mysterious "educational" world, which we knew to be intrinsically important with a logic of its own. Fortunately the colors also applied to the Australian flag, although coincidentally as far as the textbook writer was concerned. In any case we had had plenty of experience in drawing the Union Jack whenever we drew the Australian flag.

Accompanying *Mes Premiers Pas* was a simple reader about Mrs Mouse and her family. A Direct Method reader, whimsically written, it did not have French-English word lists, but used abundant line drawings to illustrate new words and phrases, much like those we were accustomed to drawing in our own vocabulary lists. The simplified text was easy enough for us to read quite early in our course. For instance, we read:

> "*Le fils de Madame Souris est un bon pêcheur.*
> *Il pêche avec sa queue.*
> *Le voilà qui pêche avec sa queue.* (drawing)
> *Il a un ver.* (drawing)
> *Les poissons* (drawing) *aiment les vers.*
> *Ils mangent les vers.*
> *Voilà il a pris un petit poisson.*"

There were a few easy translation exercises at the back of the book but also lots of opportunities to illustrate the meaning ourselves. We found the book great fun at our childish level of French. It was certainly accessible and non-threatening.[49]

Miss Meldrum kept us involved and active in our French classes for a full three years and our motivation remained high. We all remember her with great affection. French was hardly the most obvious subject for young Australians to study. Now, in the twentieth-first century, Australian students are more likely to be learning Japanese, Chinese, and Indonesian, or heritage languages like Italian or Greek, than French. In 1931, however, with our England-centered program, the fact that England was across the Channel from France was sufficient reason to make it, in the eyes of our curriculum designers, the most important language for us to learn. Moreover, it was accepted without question as an important language for international communication.

How then did this young teacher arouse such enthusiasm for what to us was an esoteric subject? First of all, she loved young

124

people and she loved teaching. She used her imagination as she shared with us the knowledge of the language she possessed, even though in some ways it may have been imperfect. She had us doing things and living them in a vicarious way. She wove us into a group that worked together, talked together, and played together, and we became interdependent in our progress. Her approach to teaching the language was active, imaginative, and innovative and it clearly reflected her individual personality — all ingredients of effective language teaching, or of any teaching for that matter. She developed a rapport with us that made us want to communicate with her and with each other in situations that stimulated our interest and involvement. She aroused our motivation to continue with the language at higher levels. Certainly, when I began teaching French myself, I had in my memory a splendid model that I wanted to emulate.

Not being able to supply us with a native model, but desirous that we should feel that French was a living language through which real people expressed themselves, Miss Meldrum soon put us in touch with correspondents in the distant continent of Europe. This opportunity was a real excitement for us in our isolated situation. All correspondence had to be sent by sea mail, of course. Ships left erratically. Even if our letters actually caught a departing mail they would take about six weeks from mailing to delivery and this meant long waits of at least three months for replies. My first correspondent was called Marcelle (just like the wave!), but she lost interest in me and very soon passed my letters over to Christiane, with whom I corresponded for nearly twenty years, meeting her in La Rochelle in 1949. I enjoyed this relationship so much that I was very ready to take on Colette in Creil, when one of my classmates did not want to continue that relationship. This correspondence lasted equally as long, and I was able to stay with Colette and her husband on several occasions on my first visit to France.

I was thrilled, and felt very special, whenever I found in the letterbox these thick envelopes from France, smothered with exotic-looking stamps and filled with little sepia photographs with deckled edges, that seemed so much more artistic than our more prosaic-looking black-and-white, straight-edged ones. It was fun to be able to read these letters out in class and wave them gleefully and triumphantly at my family. (For a reason quite obscure to me at the time, I was carefully instructed to refer to them as "letters from France," not "French letters," which, it seemed, had a rather murky meaning.) We wrote our letters to our correspondents partly in French and partly in English, and young Christiane and Colette were very conscientious in pointing out to me my deficiencies in French. I took their comments to heart very seriously. From descriptions and photographs I soon got to know their families and I marveled at the *cortèges* in wedding pictures they sent me. I learned their different ways of celebrating festival days, including such new ones to me as St Nicolas's Day on December 6th and the First of May, with its traditional cards decorated with lily-of-the-valley. I even attempted correspondence with Erna Fabinger in the Sudeten area of Czechoslovakia. Erna sent me a brooch in the form of an umbrella at the time of British Prime Minister Chamberlain's visit to Munich to negotiate with Hitler about the future of the Sudetenland. This correspondence ended abruptly soon afterwards, when Hitler invaded Czechoslovakia and annexed the area. The correspondence with Erna, though short, was eye opening, because she informed me that in her secondary school commercial course she was learning four foreign languages: English, French, German, and Spanish — something quite unfamiliar to us in our Australian setting. These letter-writing experiences, not surprisingly, launched me on a lifelong interest in stamps and the different parts of the world they come from. I am still quite unable to throw away a new stamp that comes in my mail and I am saddened by the proliferation of metering.

The first teacher of French we encountered in high school who had had some experience of native French and whose accent was native-like was Miss Schmetzer, who taught us in our fourth year. A ladylike teacher, with white hair blue-rinsed, she dressed very tastefully. We called her the Mist in Purple or the Vision in Green, depending on her choice of dress for a particular day. When she had to pass through the cloakroom area, where we would be chasing each other around the coat racks, she would calmly hold her open hand at the vertical as she moved straight forward, saying quietly: "Girls, please, please!" She was the first person to introduce us to the intonation of the language — that song so strange to our ears. She began by having us repeat over and over again *"la mûre sauvage"* (the blackberry), with a rising-falling intonation, until we began to

126

giggle. Thinking it the funniest thing we had ever heard, we rushed out into the schoolyard, repeating our new chant at the top of our voices to amuse and impress the other students. Miss Schmetzer later introduced us to gramophone records of native French speech by a Monsieur Stéphane. This was a great classroom novelty in that era of sparse technology.

It was Miss Schmetzer who launched me into reading on my own. The Alliance Française had allotted a prize to EHS for the best French student. Since I was top of the most senior French class, I had been selected for the prize, but I had to earn it by writing a composition in French on a serious subject. Miss Schmetzer lent me a book on the life of Madame Curie to prepare me for this task. This was a real French book written for French people. It was while reading this book that I became aware for the first time that I was reading directly in French, without any form of mental translation. This was a very exciting moment that I have never forgotten. There seems to have been no one else in the competition, so in due course I was awarded my Alliance Française prize — a book in French, printed in France, called *Agnès et le Vaste Monde*.[49] I was very proud and felt very adult as I tried to read it with my newly acquired direct reading technique.

Linda was studying Latin, having been given no choice of language. Being such an enthusiastic student of French, I felt she had been deprived of one of the great joys of life, so during the summer holidays at the end of my first year of high school I took it upon myself to rectify this situation. I began to teach Linda French for an hour every afternoon and put her on a strict day-by-day study schedule. She was my first student of French! I began, of course, with the exciting information about the French flag being blue, white, and red and then led her on to an acquaintanceship with Madame Souris and her family. This regimen lasted a little more than two weeks, after which Linda rebelled and decided she preferred the pleasures of life in the summer sunshine to more close encounters with the Gallic mind.

I myself was not forever deprived of a classical education. In my second year of high school, when I was in a special scholarship preparation form, I was given the opportunity to take up Latin as a further language. I remember that the first line of our introductory Latin reader conveyed the important information that *Britannia insula*

est, Roma urbs est. The book was, of course, from a British press, and
no doubt better prepared us for reading Caesar than any reference to
Australia would have done. The writer of our main grammar text was
Professor Tucker, an Australian classicist at Melbourne University.
Although he adopted a strictly grammar-translation approach to the
language, he thought that Latin could be made more fun if the
sentences we had to translate from Latin into English or from English
into Latin were somewhat nonsensical, and thus, presumably,
amusing. While learning the first declension we would be translating
sentences about the cow jumping over the moon (*vacca* and *luna*
being by tradition some of the first words to be learned). I continued
studying Latin for two more years at EHS, moving on, as I advanced,
to more solid fare, like Cicero's letters, Livy, and Ovid.

Perhaps because I had started Latin a little late and was
competing with others who had studied Latin for one year more than I
had, I was never as strong in Latin as I was in French. A further
reason was undoubtedly that, in contrast to French, we were very
badly taught. The first Latin teacher I had was obviously not well, and
she would go into a corner from time to time and cough into her
handkerchief; we thought she had tuberculosis, which was a common
enough affliction at the time. The next to teach us was Mr Mack. He
was more interested in politics and the debating society than in his
Latin classes, which were merely providing him with a regular
income while he prepared himself for greater things. At a later date he
left the Labour Party to become head of the Democratic Labour Party
(DLP) — a breakaway anticommunist group that was determined to
force the Labour Party to reject its extreme left wing. Eventually Mr
Mack was elected a DLP senator, but he did not serve for very long.
Ultimately the DLP faded away, never having achieved more than
about twenty-five percent of the vote.

Those of us who had studied Latin with Mr Mack felt we
could never vote for him or his party, no matter what our political
views might be, because he had ruined our Latin. His classroom
routine was to go rapidly through the translation of the section of the
classical text we were supposed to have prepared for homework,
finding the subject of the sentence, racing over to the verb, finding the
objects, direct and indirect, then returning to other parts of the
sentence. He would then make some desultory comments on

grammatical relationships, sometimes asking one of the Latin stars to translate a sentence or two. This process of dismembering the text was mumbled in a monotonous voice for what seemed an interminable length of time, usually on a hot afternoon in a classroom on the western side of the building. During this procedure, we would be whispering to each other or sitting with our hands across our eyes while we snoozed in peace. My friend Rachel, who had the exceptional skill of being able to raise one eyebrow at a time, would be reducing me to giggles from across the room. At a certain moment, perhaps five minutes before the bell for the end of the lesson, Mr McManus would say: "Take down the translation." This was the signal for us all to come to life, pen in hand. He would then dictate the translation at full speed and we would take it home and learn it by heart. We could recite in English whole sections of the prescribed authors at will. All we needed to do during an examination was to identify the test passage by recognizing a few words here and there, work out where it began and where it ended, and then write down the memorized translation. Not surprisingly, we never acquired confidence in drawing meaning from Latin texts as consecutive discourse. We developed very little feeling for the distinctive points of view of the various Latin writers we encountered or for the way they used the language to express interesting meanings — and this I regret. We had little help in writing in Latin ourselves, although this became an important activity as we continued our study of the language in high school and later at the university. We were so far behind in this area that, when we had tried our very best, we ended up looking forlornly at returned exercises covered with red-ink corrections and we soon despaired of ever mastering the subtleties of the Latin subjunctive or the ablative absolute.

Because of my interest in languages I was advised to continue Latin as a subject for my Leaving Honours or final high school year. By this time I was at MacRobertson Girls' High School. However, Linda, who had preceded me at the school, talked me out of it because of her own unfortunate experiences and persuaded me to take European History with the popular Miss Searby instead. This meant that I was not prepared for first year Latin at Melbourne University, which was a requirement for my Honours French degree. Competing with students who had come directly into the class from Leaving

Honours, that is, with one more year of recent study, I was out of my depth at the beginning, although I struggled on to pass the course. Because of this checkered progress, I never derived from my Latin studies the pleasure I have experienced with other languages. Fortunately my university Latin instructor conducted lively classes, with a weekly conversation group where we played dice and pretended to be Romans. I would chime in with "Etiam" every now and again. This interactive approach to a supposedly "dead" language rearoused my interest. Later, when I had the opportunity to teach Latin, I had from my high school classes a model of what not to do and from Melbourne University some idea of what to do. I discovered the difference in interest and motivation that resulted from applying modern language teaching approaches to this intrinsically interesting and valuable subject. I have remained a firm believer in the value of studying Latin as a means of developing a feeling for the different ways languages work and for broadening the student's knowledge of the vocabulary and potentialities of the English language, as well as its insights into classical civilization.

Debating Issues

School debates, with teams of three per side, were held in the school hall as part of our house competitions. Here political and ethical issues were discussed in a very structured form of presentation and rebuttal. I had the privilege of representing my house in one such intramural contest. The debates were taken very seriously and required careful preparation and rehearsal. Our house won the debate and the experience gave me a great interest in thinking through controversial issues. As we grew older, Linda and I would frequently argue out positions on problematic matters with each other, sometimes for hours at a time. On one occasion in our teens we discussed, sometimes heatedly, throughout the afternoon and into the evening, the virtues and fallacies of a new economic system of Social Credit we had read about in a political pamphlet that came in the mail. In the vigorous give-and-take Linda would never admit when I had had convinced her by my reasoning. Sometimes I would be very surprised in the days that followed to hear her espousing just the view I had been presenting to her. Perhaps she still needed time to cogitate.

All our lives, when Linda and I were together, we enjoyed discussing issues in depth, pitting our brains against each other. Through the years we discovered that our thinking processes were very different. Linda needed to think things through step by step, whereas I had a tendency to leap certain steps to move the argument along; this could result in a few minutes of arguing at cross-purposes, before we worked out where we both were in the process. Similarly, in facing problems in other areas of our lives, Linda preferred to analyze the situation, proceeding logically and even writing out her analysis at times, whereas my thinking processes were more implicit. When seeking a solution, in the intellectual as well as the practical domain, I sometimes go out into the garden to do some weeding or even take a nap, and the solution comes to me without overt, detailed reflection.

Political Climate of the Thirties

The 1930s was a period of much political ferment and discussion. Mr Mack was not the only teacher at EHS to be interested in the political ideas swirling around us. Because we were still close to the period of the Bolshevik revolution and the establishment of the Soviet Union, with all the excitement and controversy these events generated, there was much polarized talk about socialism and communism. Like so many other countries, Australia had its small communist party, some members of which ran as candidates for the parliamentary elections, although with very little success. Usually with less than five per cent of the vote they lost the initial deposit required to participate. For years, as I grew up, I remember hearing after elections: "The Communist Party candidate lost his deposit." The left wing members of the Labour Party, although for the most part not communist, were usually referred to as "red raggers" (communist sympathizers or "fellow travelers") and there was much rumor and misinformation about people's political views. Our Geometry teacher at EHS, Mr Dee, had fought with the Australian Light Horse in the Great War and we used to love to get him talking about it on Friday afternoons, when the pace of school was slackening. He would tell us tales about his adventures in the deserts of North Africa. He was more popular with us than the subject he taught. It was rumored in the school that he was a "red ragger," not that any of us had any real information about his political views, which he did not voice in class. One day at the House debates he was bated by some senior boys for expressing dissenting views by being presented with a cauliflower bouquet tied with red ribbons.

Not long after this incident, Linda was having lunch with friends in the quadrangle near the Head Master's Office at the entrance to the school, when a strange man came marching in. Without paying the usual courtesy call at the Headmaster's office, he came straight up to Linda's group and asked: "Where is the Communist teacher in this school?" Linda, ever helpful, quickly responded: "Oh! Mr Dee. He's over there in the Men's Staff Room," pointing out the way. The stranger, who seemed to be in a great rage, strode over to the Men's Staff Room and demanded to see Mr Dee. Naturally, there was quite an altercation. Someone from the Headmaster's office took the matter up in short order and asked Linda's group who had pointed out Mr Dee as being a Communist. "I did," said Linda, honestly and innocently, at which she was promptly hauled off to the Headmaster's office and given a lecture on making statements about other people's views from mere hearsay, which was a lesson to us all.

Educational Trauma Four

Because Linda was born in December and I was born in April and the school year began at the end of January, she was always two years ahead of me at school, although she was only sixteen months older. This I could bear. However, when Linda went to high school and did well in her first year, it was decided to promote her to a special Remove Form that would prepare students who learned quickly to go directly into tenth grade the following year. This skipping of a form was in effect a double promotion that put her three years ahead of me and made her even younger for her class than she had been to this point. Naturally I felt it was most important for me to make up this difference. After my shock in the entrance examination, I had worked very hard in F Form and at the end of the year I was ranked first for all four parallel classes at that level. A special "scholarship class" had been set up for the next year at ninth grade level. To this new class were allocated the most promising students from the eighth grade level and a few outstanding seventh-graders.

Our form mistress was to be Miss Cuthbert, one of the strictest and most demanding teachers in the school. She was to prepare us for the statewide Junior Scholarship examination, success in which would give us some much-needed financial assistance in this Depression period.

Miss Cuthbert, who was noted for her unblinking eyes and stern demeanor, decided to interview personally all the girls and boys who had been listed to enter her special class. I was, of course, most anxious to be accepted, so that I could catch up on Linda. As a mere twelve-year-old, I was naturally intimidated by such an august figure. When my turn came, Miss Cuthbert looked me straight in the eye and asked me a very difficult question: "If I accept you into my class, will you promise to be a better girl than your sister Linda was?" (Because Linda was so young for her classes, she had acquired a reputation, of which I was not aware, for immature behavior and talking too much in class.) Miss Cuthbert's question posed a serious dilemma for me. Without being aware of it, she was challenging me either to tell a lie and be promoted (I knew it was impossible for me to be a better girl than my beloved older sister), or else to tell the truth and not be promoted. The latter alternative was unthinkable from my point of view, since it would continue the discrepancy of three years between us. The decision had to be made fast. Miss Cuthbert was waiting for an answer. I decided on expediency and made the promise Miss Cuthbert was expecting me to make. I immediately felt very guilty and treacherous. Crying forlornly, I raced down to the bottom of the schoolyard where Linda was talking with her friends. "I've just done a dreadful thing," I wailed. "I've promised Miss Cuthbert I'll be a better girl than you were and, of course, I can't possibly!" Knowing she was not the Miss Perfection I thought she was, Linda laughed and did her best to cheer me up, but this was another emotional wound that remained with me. Once again, a well-meaning teacher, insensitive to the circumstances, had deeply hurt a young student by what was probably intended only as a routine warning.

We were very fortunate to have Miss Cuthbert directing our studies at this formative stage of our adolescence. She was very serious about our education and imposed strict discipline. She herself taught us English, History, Geometry, and Algebra. She wore her hair drawn back tightly in a bun on the nape of her neck, and, as the day wore on, little wisps would escape and trail down her neck. She had gimlet eyes that saw through any attempts at subterfuge. But she taught us how to study. She would not accept anything but the most meticulous, thoroughly prepared work, submitted on time. I attribute to her the scholarly habits that have served me so well in my professional career and I remember her with great affection, although at that time I was very wary of her. She expected us to concentrate and provided us with interesting work on which to concentrate. Already as thirteen-year-olds we were studying such difficult texts in English Literature as Milton's *Lycidas*, *L'Allegro*, and *Il Penseroso*, and the undiluted text of *Paradise Lost*. Since both Linda and I were chatterboxes, Miss Cuthbert would often quote to us from Tennyson's *Brook* :

> "I chatter, chatter as I flow,
> To join the brimming river,
> For men may come and men may go,
> But I go on for ever!"

For history, Miss Cuthbert encouraged us to bring books from home, so that we could compare different historians' accounts of the same events (this was far from the rote learning of isolated snippets of history of Miss Falloon's class, just two years earlier). I remember taking to class some nineteenth-century history books that Charles Tanner had used in his teaching and reading from these to the class. They contained very colorful and exciting descriptions of such events as the Star Chamber, the Field of the Cloth of Gold, and the Spanish Armada, and I was very proud of my contributions. Miss Cuthbert made us think our way through Euclidean theorems and we began to understand the rationality of algebraic equations. Of course, we continued to write an English composition every week and we were expected to know our Greek and Latin roots and the extensive lists of long, often scientific, words that were derived from them. Along with French and Latin, Science, Geography, and Art, this gave us eight different subject matters to work on. Being a specially selected group we lapped it all up. Our academic studies were supplemented by Physical Education classes, Wednesday sports afternoons on the hockey field or in the swimming pool, and regular singing sessions with other classes in the school hall.

134

Educational Trauma Five.

At the end of that year we sat for the Junior Scholarship examination for which Miss Cuthbert had been coaching and drilling us so meticulously. Of the thirty of us, handpicked and thoroughly prepared, inexplicably not one was awarded a Junior Scholarship, of which there were quite a number each year. One of the boys in the class became the youngest lecturer in mathematics ever to be appointed at Cambridge University in England (always regarded by us in distant Australia as the apex of educational institutions) and I became a full professor at Harvard, yet neither of us, at age thirteen, achieved the distinction of winning a Junior Scholarship. Over the years I have wondered how such a highly trained, carefully selected group, prepared by such an experienced teacher, could possibly have failed so abysmally. We were all very successful in the next form and went on to perform well right through high school, many of us winning scholarships and awards later in our studies. I have been inclined to think that the administering body mislaid our set of papers or that there was some error in registering the results. Since public examination scores on written tests were recorded in those days by hand on paper lists, those registering the grades did sometimes enter totals on the wrong line and this could result in a series of grades from that point on being attributed to the wrong persons. There is always, too, the mental slip from eyes to hand that results in reversed or incorrectly copied figures, although one would expect this to affect only a small percentage of one class group. It was not customary in Victoria in 1932 to question official published results of examinations. At a later period a system for inquiries was instituted. This required payment of a search fee and errors were not infrequently discovered, resulting in official changes of grade. To this day, I am unable to understand what can possibly have happened in this case.

For me this failure was catastrophic, since I very much needed scholarship help at that time. My father had died during the year and it was becoming extremely difficult for Mother to keep both Linda and myself in school, despite the help being given us by our brother Harold who had come home from the country on my father's death. Although earning only the basic wage during that Depression time, he gave mother his wages and enabled us to keep going. Education was supposedly free. Yet there were sports fees, locker fees, a composite fee (whatever that was we were never sure), and excursion fees. We had essentials like books, uniforms, fares, and schoolbags to pay for, as well as occasional levies for participation in such activities as plays and musical events. All of this added up to quite a sum of money. These expenses were what the distinguished American educator, Harold Hand (who later became the adviser for my doctoral thesis at the University of Illinois at Urbana-Champaign) researched as "the hidden costs of public education." A small tuition fee was also initiated at about this time, probably because of financial problems during the Depression. Over and above all that, of course, we had to eat and be clothed.

Mother always maintained that Linda and I would not have continued our education after the age of fourteen had Father lived longer. Having lived during his formative years in the nineteenth century, he thought of girls as having only one future — getting married and establishing a family, as all the daughters of his first family had done. Like most men of his generation, he felt that too much education was "wasted" on girls. It was Mother, with her pride in the Burston educators in her family, who refused to contemplate our leaving school at the legal age of fourteen to help fill the family coffers. As long as we were interested in our work and doing well she was determined to manage somehow so that we could continue our studies. Hers was a "one day at a time" approach.

Breaking Rules

Similar to the rules that separated the sexes at high school were other rules that kept girls from different age groups apart. The younger girls were expected to eat their homemade sandwich lunches in the bare schoolyard, while the older girls, as befitted their increasing dignity, had the privilege of sitting on the lawn under the trees in front of the school. Since Linda and I were so close, it was not surprising that we made friends with two sisters of similar age, Mary and Marjorie Alexander. Mary was a little younger than I and Marj was a little older than Linda. With two other girls, Rachel Story, whom I met in the scholarship class, and Joyce Young from Mary's class, we formed a "gang" of six of diverse ages and classes. We were all crazy about field hockey and played together every time we could

136

get access to the hockey sticks, during breaks and at lunchtime, as well as playing together in teams, so it was inevitable that we would want to have lunch together. This simple and natural state of affairs meant that some of us at least would always be in the wrong place when teachers on yard duty came around, looking for victims to pick up papers and generally tidy the grounds. We loved to eat on the more comfortable lawn in the area designated for the older students; consequently, the four younger ones among us, the rule-breakers, were sitting ducks to be rooted out and put to work. Joyce had flaming red hair, which made us even more conspicuous, so we did what we could to hide her head under our skirts or blazers when the teachers on duty appeared on the scene. I'm sure the more indulgent teachers just ignored us, except when they had trouble finding other victims for the cleanup crew for the day. Despite these misguided, bureaucratic efforts by our teachers to control our relationships, Mary, Marj, Rachel, Linda, and I remained close friends for a lifetime.

In our scholarship form year, Miss Cuthbert devised a wise approach to accommodating youthful enthusiasms and affinities. Rachel and I were continually rushing into class late, puffed and red-faced from playing hockey vigorously until the very last minute. We would hit balls to each other all the way from the far paddocks, right up to the door of the hockey cupboard where the equipment was stored, always trying to get in two or three last passes. Miss Cuthbert grew tired of rebuking and punishing us, so she decided to put us in charge of stacking away the equipment. This gave us the key to the hockey cupboard and immediate access to the hockey sticks and balls whenever the fancy took us, even before school. This also meant that we had to wait, at the end of morning recess or lunchtime (hitting balls to each other, of course, while waiting), until the very last girl had brought back her hockey stick. This gave us a perfectly legitimate excuse for arriving in class a few minutes after the bell. There are other ways than sanctions for keeping both teachers and students happy.

Literature and the Arts

My early secondary education, like my elementary education, was very much England-centered, with some reference to Scotland, Wales, and Ireland, when these regions impinged on things English. We knew the geography of the British Isles in detail, as thoroughly if not better than that of Australia. In history and literature (poetry, novels, plays, essays), we studied England's role and contribution almost exclusively, learning about Australia very sketchily. My study of European and American history came later. Australian history seemed to end after the exciting stories of the early explorers, which were full of drama and colorful adventure. We learned little of our country's development into a federated nation. We read no Australian fiction or drama. Any attention to Australian poets had disappeared for the most part after primary school, when we had enjoyed the poems, redolent of the Australian bush and outback life, of Henry Kendall, Banjo Paterson, and Adam Lindsay Gordon. Fortunately this inappropriate emphasis in the schools has now changed. In our day we sang English folksongs and learned English legends. Later, when I went to England and visited Glastonbury in Somerset or the Lake District, I surprised my English friends by recounting to them things they did not know, like the legends of Joseph of Arimathea and the child Jesus or details of the lives of Wordsworth and Coleridge. They admitted that they knew much less about their background than I did.

I developed my love of poetry in my high school years. I have never regretted the time spent learning poems and long quotations from Shakespeare by heart. These beautiful lines frequently recur in memory and are a constant delight. Much has been lost by the almost complete elimination of memorization in schools. After all, memorizing is a normal activity for actors, musicians, and singers, among others. Consequently a generation has now grown up that has no reservoir of quotations to share, whether for illustrative purposes or for the sheer pleasure of verbal music or epigrammatic force.

Our incipient love of literature was not helped by our first experiences of real-life theater. In Melbourne at the time there was an obviously failed actor, who had carved out a niche for himself by producing each year for school children the Shakespeare plays that were on the tenth and eleventh grade English literature reading lists for the Intermediate and Leaving Certificate examinations. He himself played the leading roles. His histrionic performances were so bad, each year seeming worse than the last, that the theaterful of youngsters from the surrounding schools could only laugh and talk and chiyack, while the actors tried to impress them with the beauty of the language of the Bard. Attendance, unfortunately, was obligatory and students arrived by busloads. After the performance we were sometimes required to write an essay on our impressions, which we found quite difficult to do without being somewhat insulting to the hardworking cast, particularly the star himself. After one such disastrous afternoon of theater, Linda wrote a very honest critique and was severely rebuked by her teacher for not appreciating what the company had to offer us in the form of higher culture.

Fortunately for our love of the theater, during a later year at high school, Melbourne was honored with a visit from the great English actress, Dame Sybil Thorndike. We saw her perform as both Lady Macbeth and Medea. In the latter role, unfortunately, from our cheap seats in "the gods," we could see only her feet as she stood above the portico, apparently holding her dead children in her arms. We were very moved and impressed by her superb acting. We could not have been more thrilled when our teacher took us backstage to meet the great actress herself and receive the much-treasured gift of a personally autographed photograph. This experience stimulated our love of drama and I went on to win a Shakespeare Society prize for an essay on *Twelfth Night*. For this I was awarded a gilt-edged volume of Shakespeare bound in soft blue leather, which has been carefully cherished and much read over the years.

Our Art teacher was Miss Spring. She was not a pleasant person to deal with and could be very sharp, even nasty, to her students. No wonder we called her Spring Onions. Nevertheless, she took her work very seriously. Personally I feel I owe her a great deal. Over the years I have been most grateful to her for the thorough background she gave us, over a three-year period, in History of Art. We studied the basics of architectural design from the Parthenon to the Flamboyant Gothic of King's College Chapel, Cambridge University; we knew our Doric, Ionic, and Corinthian pillars, as well as our Romanesque arches and flying buttresses. Every detail of Salisbury and Exeter Cathedrals, as well as St Mark's in Venice, was familiar to us, along with the leading figures in European painting. I only regret that we learned very little about the growing body of Australian painting. When I visited museums in Europe, thanks to this early training, I knew what I was looking at, whether it was Fra Angelico, Rembrandt, Velasquez, Van Gogh, Constable, or Turner, and was able to appreciate the distinctiveness of the art of very different regions and cultures. It was not surprising then that, when I was studying in France years later, I chose History of Art as one of the subjects for my French degree. History of Art, however, was only part of our training. We learned to draw leaves and flowers, as well as teapots and the perspective of telegraph poles. We learned the principles of design, as we tried to fit patterns of eucalyptus leaves and gum nuts into triangles and circles and, eventually, into repetitive, reciprocal designs for textiles or wallpaper. We also drew posters for advertisements and learned to feel at home with watercolors. Although we did little "free drawing," we learned a great deal about the discipline that lies behind artistic expression and we learned to love art.

Educational Trauma Six

It was a pity that Miss Spring did not have the sensitiveness in understanding young people that she had in interpreting great art. Paralleling my humiliating experience in the fourth grade (the hullabaloo over my writing), I had a similar experience of humiliation under Miss Spring. I did not have the artistic talent of my sister Linda, who painted such beautiful scenes on her Christmas cards. On one very proud occasion she won a prize at the Royal Melbourne Agricultural Show for a pencil drawing of a merino sheep. Taking as a guide Dad's photographs of great merino champions, she worked in all the fine detail of curly wool and inward curving horns.

One assignment Miss Spring gave us was to design or copy an advertising poster. Ambitiously I chose the cover of a glossy magazine, *The Western Mail,* which showed a very colorfully nuanced picture of a black swan, reflected in sparkling water. I labored over this assignment for many hours and achieved a very creditable version in watercolor. When I had finished this mini-masterpiece, I signed my name in India ink at the foot of the page. Unfortunately at the last minute I dropped a blot of ink over my name.

Carefully I erased the blot with a razor blade and reentered my name. Instead of being impressed with the level of my achievement, Miss Spring found herself unable to believe I was capable of it. Zeroing in on the erased and rewritten name, she accused me of having submitted as my own a piece of Linda's work. This was a great grief to both of us, myself because my enormously painstaking effort was not recognized as such and Linda, once again, because she knew how much time and effort I had put into the work. I was, of course, shocked that my teacher believed me capable of such dishonest behavior. Explanations were made and authenticity sworn to by both Linda and myself and, somewhat reluctantly, Miss Spring was persuaded to give my work the grade it deserved. (The moral in this, as in the earlier traumas, is that teachers should avoid comparisons between siblings, who are after all quite different people bound together by strong emotional ties.) At the end of the year, when after much effort I had received a passing grade on my art examination, Miss Spring could not resist justifying herself by going out of her way to tell me that all of my work had had to be submitted to a second examiner. Fortunately, not all my teachers were so distrustful of young people, nor as careless in destroying their fragile self-confidence and undermining their self-esteem.

Our musical education was not neglected at EHS either. Once a week a well-known Melbourne singer and teacher, Madame Gregor Wood, soloist at the time at the central Scots Church, came to train us in the basics of using our voices effectively. She had to teach groups of a hundred or more in our big assembly hall, but by the force of her warm and encouraging personality she managed to keep the sessions from breaking up in chaos. With Madame Gregor Wood we learned to sing many charming songs in harmony. I remember particularly and often hum to myself: *"Waterlilies floating on the stream, Waterlilies, lift your heads and dream....,"* especially when I am walking beside the Charles River in Watertown, where the spreading masses of waterlilies in the shallows watch serenely as the scullers sweep by. We were especially charmed on those rare occasions when Madame Gregor Wood's husband, also an excellent singer, came with her and we could prevail on them to sing duets for us. This is another area of my high school education that has proved its usefulness in later life, enabling me to join local and church choirs in a number of places with confidence, even though I do not consider myself by any means a great singer.

At school Speech Nights, held at the end of the year in the Melbourne Town Hall, we sang for parents, teachers and friends, with the girls all dressed in white. On these impressive occasions, after student successes had been reported and rewarded, we were treated to a lecture, usually of an uplifting and exhortatory nature, on how the big, wide world was just waiting for our leadership. I was often told in my youth what a mess everyone had made of the world, and how it was up to my generation to get out there and straighten it up. This was a favorite theme also for school assemblies and Anzac Day celebrations. It came as something of a surprise to me, therefore, when, just as I thought I was of an age and preparation to do something about it, I began hearing that it was now up to the generation coming after me to be the great saviors of contemporary society. It certainly seemed that these moralizers left young people very little time to demonstrate their capabilities in such a complex area.

Becoming Scientific

As I proceeded into more senior classes, Geography and Geology attracted my interest. We had studied Geography each year through primary and secondary school, but now it became a much more scientifically-based, problem-solving activity, less focused on uninteresting, memorized details. We also learned much about drawing and interpreting graphs and surveyors' contour and hachure maps. For our examination requirements Geography had become a useful option, since it could be selected as a science subject by those interested in the humanities and as a humanities subject by those interested in the sciences. Consequently, those of us who were not particularly interested in Chemistry and Physics were permitted to choose Geography and Geology as the obligatory science components of our upper level certificates.

Because of my name, I have always been attracted by rivers and I find it a thrill each time I encounter one of the great rivers of the world: the Thames, the Euphrates, the Tiber, the Rhine, the Mississippi, the Nile, the Jordan, the Yangtse, the Ganges, or the Danube. (I have not yet reached the Amazon or the Congo.) From my

Geography studies I retained for life a deep appreciation of the life-cycle of a river. I loved to follow its development from the early stage, when it churns out a deep, narrow gorge through resistant rock and pushes all objects before it — boulders, tree trunks, and all the refuse of the forest — plunging impetuously in cascades down steep rocky slopes, until it finds more level ground where it can broaden out, receiving the collaborating waters of its many tributaries, then spreading its silt as it floods the low-lying fields near its banks. As a mature stream, it now winds and meanders gently and placidly through the lowland on its way to the sea, going around obstacles, rather than cutting through them, and taking short cuts that leave billabongs and lagoons in its wake. In this way it shares the riches of its long journey as it divides into the many fingers that deposit valuable soil on its intervening deltas. Finally it mingles its waters with those of the gulf or the bay, to begin again, through evaporation and rain on the mountain slopes, the eternal cycle of activity. What more inspiring metaphor can one find for the life of a human being in its many phases?

The geology we learned seemed much drier than our geographical studies, requiring, as it did at the time, a great deal of memorizing of characteristics of fossils, rocks, and minerals — their chemical composition and specific gravity (a term of whose meaning I am not very sure even today). I learned these by rote, along with the stratigraphy of Victoria (that is, outcrops of which rocks of what period are found where), while walking round and round a table on which I frequently studied, or round and round the orange tree in the garden. Examining the different kinds of crystals that distinguished the minerals was much more interesting. I still love mineral museums and have some interesting "pet rocks" and crystals on display in my home. In a more problem-solving mode, we made extraordinary discoveries about what had been going on under the surface of the earth for millions of years, as we drew sections from surface geological maps with the help of our protractors to get the angles of the displaced layers and faults just right.

One of the attractions of both Geography and Geology was the fact that both involved excursions outside of the classroom to see the reality of what we were studying. For city dwellers like us, these excursions were quite eye opening, as we went to out-of-the-way spots to see natural phenomena. One of the most exciting excursions was to the Lerderderg Gorge, on the Werribee River, which we reached by train and then on foot. This excursion was actually quite dangerous because we had to get around steep cliff faces on very narrow ledges, where the teachers had to reach out to grasp our hands to drag us safely to more stable terrain. This was no place for anyone afraid of heights. I doubt that teachers today would be allowed to take groups of students into such hazardous places for fear of liability in case of accidents. Our teachers, however, were adventurous and undeterred. On the way back from the gorge, we stopped to see the vertical, 120-foot high, volcanic formations at Sydenham, where new lava had cooled slowly, creating the spectacular Organ Pipes. On less strenuous excursions we would study river formations along the Maribyrnong — meanders, billabongs, and such like. We soon learned to distinguish granite from granidiorite, and mudstone from sandstone. Conglomerates were easy to spot. When we returned from our excursions, we wrote them up in our practical books, which we submitted as part of our final examination assessment. We spent hours making these as attractive as possible, with careful drawings and photographs. By now Linda and I were enthusiastic Girl Guides and we were delighted with the extra bonus of being able to get our Geologist badges for what we had learned in school.

It was in my Leaving Certificate Geography class one afternoon that I had my first experience of a minor disability that perturbed me considerably. Suddenly I found I could see only parts of my teacher's face and only fragmented sections of the print on the book in front of me. This was a most alarming experience. I thought with inner panic that I must be going blind. My eyes had "gone on the blink," as I call it — a minor migraine caused by glare to which I am now quite accustomed. Closing my eyes, I see zigzags of bright light and must rest, perhaps with an aspirin, until the zigzags disappear; this usually takes about twenty minutes. I have learned to be wary of this occurrence and, when giving public lectures, I often have to ask that bright lights not be trained on to me for the making of television or video records of my lectures. Another danger point is the flashing reflection of the sun shooting back from rear-vision mirrors of cars ahead of me and sudden blinding flashes from their chromium

144

fittings. This minor disability is, of course, nothing compared with what others have to contend with.

Room Thirteen

At EHS, Linda and I found it just as hard as at Bank Street to get to school on time. In the morning we would try to catch the half-past eight train, which would connect nicely with the bus at Essendon station and drop us off for school at nine o'clock. If we missed that train, there was another at a quarter to nine, which arrived at Essendon Station at about eight minutes to nine. If we ran hard from that train we might just jump puffing onto the bus, which would take us to within a block of the school. We would stand on the step of the bus, ready to race into school at about five past nine, which was LATE. Sometimes a kindly bus driver would take pity on us and take the bus a block out of its way to drop us at the door, just on time. Otherwise, the extra five minutes meant detention for an hour after school in Room 13. This room, with its sinister number, became very familiar to us.

On one such occasion, Linda signed the detention book on arriving late, but, since she had team hockey practice that afternoon, she chose what was, in her eyes, a much more important obligation and skipped detention until the next afternoon. When she walked into Room 13 on the following day she found the eagle-eyed Miss Cuthbert perusing the detention book. Looking at this apparent volunteer for detention, Cuthy remarked with some surprise that Linda's name was not in the book. Linda, being honest, replied in an explanatory tone: "No, because I should have gone yesterday." "Oh!" said Miss Cuthbert, "Then why didn't you go yesterday?" To which Linda gave what seemed to her a perfectly reasonable response: "Because it was hockey practice!" This not having the same force of logic for Miss Cuthbert as for Linda, she was assigned the punishment of walking around the quadrangle ten times. This made her a kind of exhibit of wickedness for her departing schoolmates. So round and round she went. This sight was too much for that other strict disciplinarian, Miss Spring, who was in charge of Linda's form that year. Up she came to find out what was going on. Linda explained, again quite reasonably as she thought, that it had been very important for her to be at hockey practice the previous day because she was in the first or A team with an important match coming up. "Really!" said Miss Spring, "We'll see about that! You can go into the second team or no team." To this, Linda, never the most tactful with teachers, asked rather pertly or pertinently: "But what about my sports fee?" As a consequence, Miss Spring saw that she was kept out of the first team for three weeks, which made the other members of the team most indignant. Without Linda's strong defense they were losing matches. This could not go on. One of Linda's team mates, who was in greater favor with Miss Cuthbert, begged Linda not to be late for at least three weeks. This accomplished, she was able to persuade Miss Cuthbert to let Linda back on the team before the next important match, which EHS won, to the delight naturally of the team members and of Linda herself.

This incident shows what a fuss teachers can make over little things that have, from the student's point of view, quite reasonable explanations, and how inflexible in their thinking they can sometimes be. Apparently our teachers had not found a solution for chronic latecomers like the Rivers girls. Room 13 was clearly not enough. Perhaps if they had allowed us access to the hockey sticks before school, as Miss Cuthbert had done, we would have been on time every day. Moreover, teachers varied a great deal in how strict they were about students' attendance at detention, sometimes even forgetting that it was their duty day; all of this made it difficult for students to gauge the seriousness of the offense in their eyes.

Swimming in the Maribyrnong

In my second year of high school I made friends with Rachel Story. I had begun riding my bicycle to school by this time and would frequently ride after school to her home on the Maribyrnong River for a swim. Sometimes when Rachel's bike was out of commission, she would lope along beside me as I rode. Rachel later became a Physical Education teacher and this early jogging was in keeping with her love of exercise. The Storys, with four boys and four girls in the family, had a little jetty with a diving board, just across the river from the munition works. Rachel's big, strong brothers, who swam a mile down the river every morning to begin the day right, used to teach young people from their church to swim and dive. They would attach a hook to the back of the learners' swimsuits and hold them in the

146

water with a kind of fishing rod and line until they gained enough confidence to launch out on their own. Those of us who could swim without surveillance would go right across to the munitions works, a couple of hundred yards across deep water. When we got to the other side, we would find ourselves knee-deep in gluggy mud — "clean" mud, as we called it. Having so much enjoyed my swimming in the Maribyrnong as an adolescent, I always like to swim even now with twenty feet of water under me and I love to duck dive, turn and turn in honey pots, play about in the water and swim around, mixing breaststroke, backstroke, sidestroke, and the Australian crawl. I love to float on my back and gaze up at the sky. I also love to stay in the water when it rains and I have even done so, perhaps foolishly, during lightning storms. After our swim in the river, we would walk back to the Storys' house through a grove of cherry plums that we picked and ate on the way.

Centenary Celebrations

In 1934 we celebrated Melbourne's centennial year. In 1835, John Batman had purchased from the Port Phillip Bay aborigines a certain amount of land in exchange for some clothing, flour, mirrors, tomahawks, and knives. For a future settlement he chose a spot near the bay on the Yarra Yarra River, declaring: "This will be the place for a village." (Yarra Yarra was the local aborigines' expression for "flowing water.") From this early settlement developed the city of Melbourne, capital of the State of Victoria, which separated from the mother colony of New South Wales in 1851.

For its centenary year, Melbourne was illuminated and decorated. The Duke of Gloucester, third son of King George V, represented the Crown at the ceremonies to dedicate the new Shrine of Remembrance, built in the form of a stepped pyramid as a memorial to Victoria's war dead. The Grenadier Guards, with their colorful uniforms, tall, black busbies, and stirring music, made the long journey from London, as did the popular English Poet Laureate, Sir John Masefield. On the local level, Sir McPherson Robertson, a wealthy confectioner, gave Melbourne various gifts, including a new bridge, a fountain, and a very modern, new central high school, called MacRobertson Girls' High School (MacRob), which I was to attend in 1935.

Linda was already enrolled as a student at Melbourne Girls' High School, the Education Department having centralized students in the final year of their secondary studies in two main locations, to which the best teachers at that level had also been relocated. This measure resulted from the drastic drop, in this Depression period, in the number of students staying on in each suburban high school to finish their education and qualify to matriculate at Melbourne University. Melbourne Girls' High School was at the time holding classes in a very old, rather dingy, nineteenth-century building in the city. There was great excitement when the girls were able to move into the new building, beautifully situated near the Albert Park Lake. In 1934, Linda was a member of the first cohort of students at MacRob. Having just been completed, the school was fresh and bright, with many colors of paint in the modern style. The school had been given the trade name of its benefactor. As a young man Mac Robertson had built up his business by personal effort from humble beginnings. We were frequently told how he had saved his pennies and bought his first pound of sugar, which he had turned into sweets. He had then bought two pounds of sugar with the proceeds. In this way he had slowly and painstakingly built up his hugely successful chocolate and candy enterprise. Sir McPherson Robertson's benevolent face beamed down at us in the entrance hall from a portrait that showed him carrying on a tray a model of the new high school in sugar.

There were all sorts of cultural and sporting events arranged for the Centenary celebrations. Particularly exciting for us as teenagers was the Centenary Air Race from England to Australia, with a prize of fifteen thousand pounds, again donated by Sir McPherson Robertson. This was the period of enthralling new adventures in flight. In 1928 Bert Hinkler had thrilled us with the first solo flight from England to Australia. In 1930 Amy Johnson had become the first woman to repeat this feat, while in the same year Australia's great aviator, Charles Kingsford Smith, after whom Sydney's Airport is named, had been the first to fly around the world. The winners of the Centenary Air Race were C. W. A. Scott and T. Campbell Black. Fortunately for us, we lived near the Flemington Racecourse where the winners of the air race were to be welcomed. Knowing from the radio when Scott and Black were expected to arrive, we climbed the flame tree in our garden to get a better view of their plane flying over. The flight from London to Melbourne had taken them less than three days, quite a miraculous time in those days. Since EHS was close to the Essendon Aerodrome, for the next few days we would rush excitedly to classroom windows or gaze up into the sky from the schoolyard as various competitors straggled in from London.

Guiding as a Formative Activity

By 1934 I was an enthusiastic Girl Guide in the Kookaburra Patrol of the Moonee Ponds Company. Linda was a Thrush. I was very pleased with my navy-blue uniform, of a respectable mid-calf length, with its numerous pockets and, later, the cloth specialist badges I earned, which were sewn on my left sleeve. I proudly wore the gold cloverleaf badge on my pale blue tie and clipped to my leather belt a pocket knife, with various kinds of blades to meet all emergencies. Our hats were pudding-basin style, with our Guide badge embroidered in gold on the navy-blue band. Our Guide Captain, always called Cappy, taught one of the elementary grades in a private school. She was also in charge of the Junior Sunday School at St Thomas's Church, where she directed a team of teachers for more than a hundred eight- to ten-year olds. A very kind, patient woman, she knew how to maintain discipline through her personal authority and obvious affection for us all. Being a good organizer, she designed exciting and productive activities, which kept us involved and united. We were all very fond of Cappy, who had a great gift for enthusing young adolescents.

On Guide nights we learned all kinds of useful things in our patrol corners. We tied knots (I still find the good old clove hitch very useful); we made beds (always using the square nurse's corner for tucking in the sheets); and we practiced first aid. We each had our own kits in readiness to treat sprains, burns, and snake bites. We learned how to build up a fire so that you could light it with one match. We were instructed in child care. We also had to learn by heart the life stories of the three saints whose crosses formed the Union Jack in the top left-hand corner of the Australian flag: St George of England, St Andrew of Scotland, and St Patrick of Ireland. St David of Wales had not been accorded this eminence. Of this memorization of the three life stories all I can remember is the first line: "St George was born in Cappadocia of Christian parents and those not of the meanest quality." We had to be word-perfect, despite the somewhat archaic tone of the script. Perhaps the rhythm helped. We also learned the Guide Promise and the ten Guide laws, which we summarized for recall in the jingle: "Trusty, loyal, helpful; Sisterly, courteous, kind; Obedient, smiling, thrifty; Pure as the rustling wind."

Once certain early tasks had been mastered, we were awarded our Tenderfoot badge, after which we worked for our Second Class badge and various specialist badges. In the latter category, I began with the Toymaker's Badge, for which I made a rag doll and a set of doll's furniture constructed of matchboxes, both of these masterpieces being now, unfortunately, lost to posterity. This, along with my Geologist's badge and my Interpreter's badge, for which I was tested by my French teacher, made up the sum total of my achievement in the area of badges, as I became more and more absorbed in my studies. Our Guide meetings always concluded with the full company gathering as Cappy read to us or encouraged us in discussion. Once a month we had a uniformed church parade at St Thomas's Anglican Church, where we proudly carried in the Australian flag.

Another important centennial event for young people was a World Jamboree of Boy Scouts and Girl Guides, which Lord and Lady Baden Powell, the founders of Scouting, attended. Naturally it was a once-in-a-lifetime experience for us, as young Australian Guides and Scouts, to be able to welcome Lord and Lady Baden Powell to an enormous international camp at Syndal in the Victorian countryside. In the 1930s Syndal was quite a rural area, although it has since been enveloped by the relentless sprawl of Melbourne's suburbs. Having grown up in a largely monocultural society, we found it very exciting to meet at the Jamboree so many young people from different countries, of different hues, speaking different languages, and wearing uniforms adapted to the traditional dress of their local communities. The tall Fijian and Tongan Scouts with their bushy hair, their traditional skirts, instead of trousers, and their bare feet particularly drew our attention. The Guides had a special day to meet Lady Baden Powell. For this the Moonee Ponds Company was out in full force. I had just earned my Tenderfoot badge, which unfortunately had not been immediately available. Cappy had managed to get one for me at the last minute, just in time for the great day, and it had to be hastily sewn on my sleeve in the swaying train to Syndal. It would have been such a disgrace for me, I thought, to come face to face with Lady Baden Powell without my first badge. What would she have thought of me!

My most vivid memories of my Guiding years are associated with our adventures on public holidays, when we would go out in the bush to establish a day camp at a favorite site near Vermont, then virgin bush although it is now quite suburban. Here our patrols (my Kookaburra group, Linda's Thrushes, the Magpies, Robins, and Emus) would choose their separate areas among the gum trees to set up camp. These campsites were later inspected and allotted points, so they had to be well organized and neat. As good citizens, we were always expected to leave our camp spot tidier than when we arrived. Our skill at lighting a fire with one match was immediately useful on these occasions, which were often used for testing new Tenderfoot aspirants. Building up our fire with twigs and bark from the eucalyptus trees, we would enjoy their aromatic perfume as we cooked snags (sausages) and lamb chops on sticks held over the coals. We boiled water for tea in a billy, just like the swagman in *Waltzing Matilda*. Of course, we were very careful to put out every ember and scatter the ashes so as not to leave any possibility of igniting a bushfire. We were well aware that in among the gum trees even a small piece of glass could focus the sun's rays on a dry leaf and cause terrible havoc. After our hot lunch, we would vie in tracking, following the blazes on trees and the more subtle signs left in the dust by other patrols. We were alert to watch out for snakes and, with our first-aid kits on hand, we were ready to apply a ligature and suck out the poison should the occasion arise. Since Cappy had encouraged us all to join the Field Naturalists' Society we also enjoyed bird watching, admiring the sudden flash of the gray and pink galahs or the multicolored rosellas. It was always a pleasure to listen to the caroling of the magpies, the ping-ping of the bellbirds, and the loud, rollicking laughter of a group of kookaburras. The song of the English thrush was quite easily distinguished. I always enjoyed watching the constant insect search of the lovable, ever-active Willy Wagtails, which had given me another of my early nicknames.

Sometimes we would go further into the Dandenong Ranges. As Melbournians, we have always been very fortunate to have such easy access to the beautiful fern gullies and tall gum trees of the Sherbrooke Forest, just thirty miles from the city's busy streets. To reach more remote areas, like Sassafrass, Olinda, Cockatoo, and Emerald, we traveled in the Puffing Billy, an old steam train on a narrow gauge line. Its sturdy engine tooted and whistled its way up the mountains, drawing behind it open carriages of city-dwellers, seeking pure air and the perfume of the gum trees, which are particularly fragrant after rain. Since the population of Australia was only six and a half million people at the time, it was easy to find areas of practically untouched native bush quite close to Melbourne. In the winter we were still able to pick small amounts of the plentiful pink, white, and red native heath, Victoria's state flower, now protected. Our national flower, the golden wattle, bloomed in profusion in July, lighting up the bush on gloomy winter days. This was a period when we could still go mushrooming freely, taking our baskets and climbing through post-and-rail fences into paddocks covered with mouth-watering wild mushrooms. When we cooked these mushrooms, we were always careful to slip a silver coin into the liquid in which they simmered. If it tarnished, we knew that we had included some toadstools or other poisonous fungi; if it did not, we could enjoy a delectable feast. It was sad as the years went by to see the close development of housing gradually invading our beautiful Dandenongs. Fortunately, action groups and the development of National Trust areas helped to save much of the native bush around the Sherbrooke Forest and further into the ranges, in what is still Melbourne's natural playground.

Great-grandfather Lehmann's butcher's shop on Bendigo
goldfields c. 1855

Harry Burston's class (3rd – 6th) Upper Diamond Creek
1887

Nina and the boys in a neighbor's Sunbeam car, c. 1913

Diamond Creek Township

Harry Rivers' office in Queen Sl, Melbourne. c. 1890

Harry & Nina with Linda & Wilga. 1920

The little "twins"   The Fairy Queen and the Butterfly

Dad at Newmarket Yards.   Linda in EHS uniform 1931
Will it rain? 1930

Linda seabathing in 1929

The Ascot Vale house in the 1920s. Camellia bush in the center.

Linda and Wilga with the   Harold in the Air Force 1943
indispensable bikes

St. Annes 1944
Dora, Wilga, and Muriel

5
SURVIVING
THE DEPRESSION
1931-35

When I reached the upper classes of the high school, Australia was well into the worldwide economic Depression and many students could no longer afford to stay in school. One of my best friends, who was top of her class, had to leave EHS after her eighth grade Merit Certificate and train to be a shorthand typist in order to earn money as soon as she possibly could, Only fifteen students from my year (there had been about 120 of us in our first year at high school) had been able to stay in school for their Leaving Certificate at eleventh grade level. They were quite an exceptional group. One became an Ambassador for Australia. Another became the spokesman for the Victorian Employers' Association, counterbalancing a boy from a class above us, our Headmaster's son, who was for many years the Secretary of the Australian Communist Party. One became headmaster of a school in Africa. Others went into industrial design or engineering. Some taught at university level, others at high school. This output was quite remarkable for a small high school in the lower middle-class western suburbs. At this time most professional people had studied at private, denomination-affiliated schools, situated for the most part in the eastern suburbs. These fee-paying, selective schools, many taking boarders, were well provided for, with beautiful buildings and grounds. They maintained very high academic standards and developed a permanent staff of very experienced teachers. Fortunately, because teachers in the state system earned promotion more rapidly by accepting to teach wherever the Education Department decided they were most needed, most teachers at State schools in the city and suburbs had already had considerable experience in country high schools. The few younger teachers who were appointed to the suburbs early in their careers had often been rated among the best of their group during their teacher training. For these reasons suburban high school students had, with some notable exceptions, very good teachers indeed.

Already, by 1933, as a restructuring economy measure, the final class (Leaving Honours at twelfth grade level) had been lopped off most of the Melbourne State high schools for the duration of the Great Depression. The few students able to continue were funneled into classes at the University High School (UHS), which was a teacher-training demonstration school, Melbourne Boys' High School, and the MacRobertson Girls' High School (MacRob). In these schools they were taught by some of the most experienced teachers in the Education Department. In 1935, when our time came to move on, my friend Rachel and I chose MacRob rather than the nearer UHS. We could not bear the idea that we might have to play in the UHS hockey team, always our great rival while we were at EHS. MacRob, against whom we had not competed, was quite a different kettle of fish to our adolescent minds. At MacRob we naturally found it very challenging to study with the most talented students from all over the city and suburbs. Accustomed as we were to demanding academic work at EHS, we had to work even harder to cope with the quantity and standard of work required of us at MacRob. After this intense experience, we found much of the early work at Melbourne University quite relaxing.

Victoria during the Depression

The Depression lasted years longer in Australia than in some of the other industrialized countries. As Park points out: "Many of the unemployed never had regular pay between leaving school and joining the A.I.F [Australian Imperial Forces] in 1939."[51] According to the 1933 Census, the City of Essendon had a male unemployment rate of 18.2 percent, most of which was concentrated in the Ascot Vale segment of the district.[52] Many of the unemployed were, of course, young aspirants to the job market.

This widespread lack of available jobs hit my brothers very hard. They were now well into their twenties, when they might have expected to be establishing their career paths. Because of the exigencies of this trying period, the three of them were out of work for up to five years each, apart from casual, short-term employment. Reg, who had been a storeman in charge of inventory, was called back for a month each year by his company for their annual check of stock. Reg very much resented this cavalier, self-serving attitude on the part of his employer. This apparent lack of concern for his wellbeing made him decide never to work for a boss again. This was a big mistake on his part, since he did not have a head for business. Despite strenuous efforts in all kinds of transport and a capacity to keep working for long hours, he never really made a success of his endeavors in later life.

Victoria had, at this time, certain "blue laws" that prohibited the conducting of any kind of business on Sunday. These laws, however, did not apply in New South Wales. Consequently, transport drivers who were close to the New South Wales border at midnight on Saturday night would make a dash to reach the state border undetected. This would enable them to complete their four hundred and fifty mile trip to Sydney by Sunday night, which was especially important if they were carrying perishable goods for the Monday market. Their trucks were usually not refrigerated. One Saturday night Reg, who was transporting fresh tomatoes from Melbourne to Sydney in an unrefrigerated truck, was caught in this bind on the Victorian side of the border. Naturally the Victorian police were on the lookout for just such situations and Reg, hurrying to reach the border after midnight, was arrested and thrown in the local lockup overnight. He had no choice but to leave his truck beside the road during this enforced delay. When he was released, he found to his consternation that his truck had been stolen. At a later time when he seemed to be prospering, he bought a second truck and employed a driver, who promptly tipped the uninsured truck and its contents over a steep incline into a ravine. Reg seemed to have constant bad luck, although he worked extremely hard. He pressed on despite these discouragements, always with a hopeful attitude and the best of intentions. He was very willing to lend a helping hand to anyone he met along the way. Sometimes it was these lame dogs who let him

161

down. One, who had just been released from prison and whom Reg had sheltered in his own home, left abruptly with booty from Reg's house. As time went on, Reg drove huge log-haulers in the mountains and big lorries transporting loads of new cars to sales destinations. In his later years, he delivered parcels by taxi-truck in the city and suburbs. Despite all his efforts, he never made even a modest fortune. He kept afloat but little more and then only with the help of constant loans solicited from everyone he knew. He was dogged all his life by unexpected misfortunes, which were often due to miscalculations on his part and false confidence in unreliable people. In his good-heartedness he was not quick to detect scams.

At the height of the Depression, Reg tried selling Rawleigh's pharmaceutical products and spices from door to door. The policy of the company at the time was to leave the products with customers, who would pay later. As the Depression deepened, many, unfortunately, were not able to pay. This resulted in bad debts for products that the representatives had had to pay for out of their own pockets. In the end Reg was left with a great number of products he had bought from the company that he could not sell at any price. Mother tried to help him out as best she could from her meager means, so we sniffed and inhaled Rawleigh products for our colds and rubbed them on sprains, bruises, and wheezy chests for years. We did everything we could to diminish the great pile of small packages of cinnamon Reg had given Mother in repayment of loans, putting cinnamon in apple sauce, pies, and cakes, but they seemed to last forever. When selling Rawleigh products did not work out, Reg was reduced to going from door to door, trying to elicit shoe repairs on commission for a shoe repairer, at a time when people were making every worn-out shoe do just another turn or two. The boys, like so many others of that period, would do anything they possibly could to avoid going on the dole, called euphemistically "sustenance." Taking the dole was considered the ultimate disgrace, especially when it required recipients to break stones along the roads like convicts. The word was avoided like the plague or uttered in whispers. To cheer themselves up during this seemingly hopeless period, people turned to dark humor. The most popular song at the time, which we sang loud and long, was:

"Ain't it grand to be bloomin' well dead!
Look at the tombstone. Jolly old tombstone!
Ain't it grand to be bloomin' well dead!"

By this time Les and Harold, still unemployed, had left for Myrtleford in northern Victoria, where they had found seasonal work on a tobacco plantation. Here they lived in tents with a large group of Italian immigrants, who spoke little English, ate strange foods, and sang in incomprehensible dialects around the campfire at night. Like so many immigrants at the time these new arrivals were used to living on very little. Mother's favorite plantation songs often came to mind as we thought of our brothers who were so far away. After Father died in 1932, the husband of Dad's daughter Alys obtained a position for Harold at the Spotswood Pumping Station of the Melbourne and Metropolitan Board of Works, keeping in good working order the machines that disposed of the water from Melbourne's streets and sewers. This was a lifesaver. When there were floods, there was instant overtime. Les, being a qualified electrician, found a job rather more quickly than Reg. With his expertise and his love of motorbikes and cars (he loved buying old model cars and getting them back into good working condition), he eventually found employment in a big garage, working on the electrical systems of cars and trucks.

Having suffered so much with unemployment, the boys never wasted a moment. When the opportunity arose, they took second jobs in the evenings as runners between picture theaters. Their work was to ensure, when films were being shown concurrently in several cinemas, that successive reels of film were available for use as soon as the previous reel came to an end. This meant constant dashes between cinemas. If the runners were late with a reel, there would be a blackout in the middle of an exciting episode and much booing from the audience. Because of the insecurity engendered by the Depression and the need to make extra money to catch up for the lost years, the boys kept up this cinema work and other supplementary jobs even after they had found steady employment.

As the Depression deepened people did all kinds of things to survive. One thing we very much appreciated in the winter term at EHS was the entrepreneurial effort of a housewife and mother whose house abutted the schoolyard. During the morning she would cook a large number of little meat pies, which she sold over the school fence

163

for a penny apiece, along with steaming penny bowls of homemade pea soup. Her husband, most probably out of work, must have blessed her. Those of us who lived through this period were marked for life in various ways. We find it hard to throw away things that "may come in handy," and this leads to a tendency to stuff drawers and cupboards with articles we never use and may even have forgotten we still have. We mend and patch things, instead of discarding them. We are innovative in making things do "one more turn." This period of constant penny-pinching did give us training in how to make money go around and taught us to save little by little for an uncertain future.

Despite being in his late seventies, Dad worked long hours at the Newmarket Sales Yards or in his office in the city. When he came home he would be very tired. It was his custom after his meal to settle down to read the newspaper or to listen to a radio program on his crystal set before going to bed. He always retired for the night reasonably early, because he had to leave early next morning for the *Herald* office or the Newmarket Yards. Before he left he would cook his oatmeal porridge in a little iron pot. Since getting up early in the morning and preparing a family breakfast were not Mum's forte (she liked to work late into the night), Dad would get us up and serve us breakfast from the porridge that remained in the iron saucepan. If we dallied he could not wait, so, unsupervised, we often dashed off to school with little or no breakfast, running to catch the last possible train to get the last possible bus to reach EHS on time. At school I was always rather amused at the enormous emphasis laid by some teachers on the need for a substantial cooked breakfast. When asked by well-meaning primary, and later secondary, teachers what I had had for breakfast, I would fib a little, since the truth seemed to upset them. Never having felt the need for anything but a light early morning meal, I was heartened, on discovering the French style of breakfast, to find I was not alone in my preference.

Death and Change

Father died in 1932, in the middle of the Depression. This was a great shock to us, because it happened so suddenly. Until the day he died, at seventy-eight years of age, he had continued to work full-time. That May day he came home from work and listened to the wireless as usual before going to bed. At five in the morning, Mother woke her two daughters to tell us that Dad was having a heart attack. We were sent off immediately to fetch the doctor. We did not, of course, have a telephone. In those days we had caring local doctors who knew us from birth till death — family physicians who came to the house as soon as they were called, at no matter what hour of the day or night. Dawn was just beginning to light the sky as Linda hurried home to tell mother the doctor was coming. Meanwhile I waited, anxiously and endlessly it seemed, under the street light for the doctor to pass by. Somehow I missed him and Linda had to come back to look for me. Father had died about twenty minutes after his attack. The doctor arrived too late. This sudden death was a dreadful shock for our mother. After the doctor had left, Mother leaned exhausted against the kitchen door and said: "Well, your daddy's gone to be with the angels, but I've just got to have a cup of tea!" Linda went outside and sat on a seat under the orange tree just as the sun was coming up and experienced a kind of peace. I, on the other hand, saw my father before he was laid out and that shocking image stayed in my mind for years. The next thing was to notify the family, so Linda and I were sent to Reg's place to tell him what had happened. Since we had to take our usual bus that went right past EHS, we were glad it was too early to run into any of our schoolfellows.

The body lay at rest in the coffin in the house, surrounded by wreaths, many of which contained lily-of-the-valley. For twenty years afterwards I could not stand that perfume — it aroused too many vivid emotions. Several times I slipped quietly into the room where my father was lying, so small and so white in what seemed to me to be an incredibly small coffin. As a consequence, for years I could not see my father in my mind's eye as I had known him in life. Often I would go into the front sitting room and gaze at the large photograph of him in order to refresh my memory of my living dad. I remember a few times when I thought I saw Dad coming home from the station when I walked down to the shops in the early dusk. After more than seventy years, he is still very present in my mind and his influence remains.

The coffin was kept open until Les and Harold could get back the next day by the slow steam train from their tobacco plantation at Myrtleford. Only then did the funeral service in the house begin. The house was crowded with visitors and relatives, and Dad's sons and daughters and their spouses were all in black. After the funeral endless cups of tea were served, in the Australian tradition. But Linda and I could not cry; that would come later when all the people had gone. The next day Mother and I went to the cemetery to see his grave covered over with stacks of wreaths. This was the only time we went to see Father's grave, because Mother did not believe in cemetery visiting, nor do I, knowing as I do that my loved one is not there, but only the worn-out body that let him or her down. At that time I was keeping a small daily diary, but this experience was too deep to be expressed in words, and in my little book I can see those two days with the empty spaces outlined in black.

When I went back to school several days after Father's death, one of the girls said to me, to my astonishment: "It's disgusting! You stayed home to swot for the test!" She was naturally shocked and embarrassed when I told her my father had died. It was very upsetting to me that the last term exam results I had reported to my father had contained a failure in Algebra (35/100). I had never had to show my father a failed grade before. The next term I made a strenuous effort to redeem myself, achieving 100 per cent in Algebra. To my eternal regret it was too late to run home to tell my dear old Dad the good news. Early algebra, as taught at that time, seems to have been one of those "all or nothing" subjects. I recently came across a carefully preserved piece of paper with the results of that set of tests for myself and five of my friends. Interestingly enough, four of us out of the six in this special scholarship class had grades in the thirties for algebra that term, so perhaps we were in need of a little clearer instruction.

Our little Dandie Dinmont terrier was very attached to my father. After his death Bobbie would go every day to the step leading from the vestibule to the bedrooms to wait for Dad to appear. He kept this up faithfully for six months, after which he gave up, hid under a bush, and died. An affectionate, little silvery-gray terrier, we had often teased him as children. We would rattle a biscuit tin at the end of the long passage between the bedrooms just to see him race from the vestibule to the front door, and then we would reverse the process. In a mischievous mode, I had sometimes amused myself by rattling the tin to excite him and then feeding him almond shells, which he gobbled up joyfully to please us. We missed him sorely when he followed our beloved father in death.

We were very fond of our father who loved us very much. His first family were amazed at how much more indulgent he was with us than he had been with them in his strict nineteenth century disciplinarian days. We were after all of the same age as his grandchildren. From Father we learned a great number of things, sometimes through proverbs. He would remark, for instance, in his down-to-earth, practical way, that "Pigs might fly, but they'd be most unlikely birds." People loved to pepper their speech with proverbs at that time and personally I still enjoy collecting new and unusual ones.

The Lehmanns Come to Stay

As the Depression deepened, work opportunities of any kind dried up completely. Not surprisingly there were no pupils for music teachers, who depended on mothers paying for lessons for their children after school. Great-uncle Alf Lehmann, a bachelor, and his unmarried sister, Great-aunt Tilly, who kept house for him, were both well on in years by this time. They had only meager savings and with no social safety net available they were soon in very difficult circumstances. Now that Father had died and the boys had either married or were working in the country, we had space in our nine-roomed house to help them out. So one day Alf and Tilly arrived with a few pieces of furniture and two beautiful, though ancient, pianos and settled in, until fortune should smile on them again or at least look less glum. Tilly was a very modest woman, whose wants were few. Having lived in a very small cottage, she felt more comfortable in small spaces, so she established herself in our bathroom. ("Bathroom" in those days was used in its literal sense, not euphemistically as at present.) The rooms in the Ascot Vale house were large Victorian ones. Consequently, the bathroom was a small room in itself, about eight feet by six, with two windows on opposite walls but no electric light. If we took a bath in the evening we used candles. The bath, with its wood-fired heater, was on one side under a window and, since there was no wash basin or toilet bowl, the rest of the space was clear. Auntie Tilly installed her bed on the side opposite the bath and brought in a small chest of drawers, after which she was as happy as a bird in the bush. With Tilly in the bathroom, we had, of course, to make arrangements with her whenever we wanted to have a bath or shower. Fortunately, with no wash basin in the bathroom, we had been accustomed, if we wanted to perform a briefer form of ablutions, to heating water on the stove and pouring it into mother's wash-up dish. The toilet was outside at the back of the house.

Tilly did not miss the switch-on light in her room. She was definitely a child of the nineteenth century. As a young woman, she had enjoyed the tambourines, drums, and lusty singing of the early days of General Booth's Salvation Army. Unable to adapt to a new age, she distrusted newfangled things like electricity and preferred to move around the house with a small oil lamp. This habit worried Mother, who had visions of the house going up in flames — surely the last thing we needed in our straitened circumstances. When later we installed our first telephone, Tilly would never go near it, being scared to death by this unnatural phenomenon of disembodied voices coming out of a strange, black contraption. Later still, in the fifties, when we drove her home in Harold's car with its built-in radio, she was astonished at the strength of the voice of the soprano we were listening to. As we drove up a parallel street she remarked in awe: "Goodness me! What a strong voice she has! You can still hear her from here!"

Uncle Alf's two beautiful upright pianos, with the ivories worn from much playing, were set up in our front sitting-room. Although he had won prizes in his youth for his playing, Uncle Alf had been too shy to take on the life of a concert pianist. Nevertheless, he always kept his skills at a high level for his own pleasure. His great treasures were two old, faded, sepia pictures of Beethoven and Liszt, warts and all. It was his great pleasure to go into the front room in the evenings and play Liszt in the dark. As long as I was very good and quite quiet, he would let me sit unobtrusively on the floor across the room, listening to this beautiful, personal concert. Uncle Alf and Auntie Tilly had been brought up bilingual in German and English and, while they were with us, I found it intriguing and amusing to hear Uncle Alf, when annoyed with Tilly, reprimanding her in German at the side of the house. Being of German parentage, he was very upset by the turn of events in Germany in the 1930s and he would often expostulate that it was all the fault of "those Nazzis."

How did we survive?

    After Dad died, mother was in very serious straits financially. The *Herald*, the main paper for which Dad had worked, paid his salary for six months after his death, but there was no pension fund, widow's pension, or other social program to help us out. Mother did everything she could think of. She even wrote to Dr Maloney, a State Member of Parliament, who had been a jackeroo with Dad at Bolinda Vale. He sent a sympathetic reply but offered no help. Father had been a Mason and we had always been told the Masons "looked after their own." So Mother wrote to the local lodge. It was, however, too long since Father had been an active Mason, and even then he had been a member in a small country town, so no one remembered him. The very small rent that Uncle Alf and Auntie Tilly could bring to Mother's coffers from their old age pensions was of very minor help. We would never have survived as we did had it not been for my brother Harold. Willingly he came home from the country to take the job at the Spotswood Pumping Station of the Board of Works, which my half-sister Alys's husband had been able to arrange for him at a time when it was almost impossible to find work. At first, it was a low-level job on the basic wage, stoking engines and greasing machines. As time went on he was able to work his way up in the Board of Works and was finally in charge of all the house and land specifications in the central office in Melbourne. Having to work three shifts at Spotswood, Harold had to bike to work early in the morning, in mid-afternoon, or late at night. If there were heavy rains and flooding he would be kept back to do double shifts or called back suddenly, even on holidays. I remember one year when Harold had to leave the dinner table in the middle of our Christmas celebrations to rush off to work, because a sudden tropical storm had flooded Melbourne's streets and particularly the low-lying suburbs near Ascot Vale. Harold was always a very kind person, ever seeking ways to help others. Often, when I was working hard in the early morning on my homework for MacRob, he would bring me my breakfast before leaving for work. On coming home from his late shift in the winter, he would bring me cocoa to warm me up, as I studied with a rug over my knees in the cold, unheated front room.

Although Harold was only on the basic wage when he was at Spotswood, he selflessly gave everything he earned to Mother to support the family, and this saved us from penury. Without him, we would never have been able to keep going through those difficult years and Linda and I would certainly not have completed high school. Fortunately, we had our own home, with its modest monthly mortgage. As Mother understood Father's will, the house was only hers in trust during her lifetime, after which it was to come to Linda and me as our inheritance. This was fortunate, since, had it been otherwise, she might have been tempted to sell the house at the height of the Depression to make ends meet. We finally retained the house for about sixty years.

It was very lucky for us at that difficult time that we had to find only a pound a month for the mortgage to keep a roof over our heads. Father had bought the house for 1,400 pounds in 1923, when one pound had been a substantial sum. By the 1930s, however, after inflation, one pound was no longer prohibitive. This mortgage payment, over and above basic living expenses, had to be found somehow every month. Fortunately, within two and a half years of Father's death, Linda was beginning to earn some money, a mere pittance actually, as a student teacher, but this enabled her to pay some board and buy her own clothes and necessities. Three and a half years after Father died, I had a fee waiver at Melbourne University and some private financial help to cover my living expenses and books. As soon as I began to earn money in my first teaching position in 1940, I sent Mother enough money every month to cover the mortgage payments. This pound a month mortgage remained the same through many years of further inflation until, in the 1950s, I persuaded Mother to pay off the small part of the principal still remaining after some thirty-five years. Mother paid this final installment with old pound notes she had squirreled away during the tough years — notes such as the astonished young clerk at the loan office had never seen. Even though Mother was by this time in the early stages of her final illness, she was so happy to be finally paying off the house that she insisted on going into the city herself to pay in the money personally, note by note.

If it hadn't been for Mother's primitive survival instinct and determination that her daughters would go as far as their abilities would take them, we would never have been able to become teachers, which, with nursing, was one of the very few career outlets available for educated women. Nothing was so important to Mother as seeing that we continued with our education as long as we could. Dealing with what life presented from day to day and pressing on somehow, Mother made it possible for us to concentrate on our studies, even when she could barely afford to feed and clothe us. After her experiences with her mother's family favoritism, she was also determined that her children would do better than those of her mother's "pets," that is, the older and younger members of her family. We were natural bookworms, especially Linda, and sometimes Mother thought we were studying when we were indulging in our favorite occupation — reading whatever we came across. In this, Mother was probably right since all reading is informative in one way or another. She would do anything for us that freed us up to study, finding her reward in our success. In a way she found her fulfillment in our fulfillment.

During this period of sheer survival we scrimped in every possible way. We went into the city early to join the crowds at "two-for-one" sales at a big shoe shop, rushing in with the mobs of waiting women, as the doors opened, to grab shoes that seemed to fit. We bought hats (still a necessity for properly brought-up young women in those days) for a shilling at sales. We bought cheap dresses at Coles and Woolworth's. Mother was not really a dressmaker, but she always rather enjoyed altering clothes. Her sturdy sewing machine was kept busy making us presentable. Dad's daughters, Alys and Violet, were very thoughtful in passing on to us good quality clothes they no longer needed (sometimes even a hat or two) and this helped. For everyday attire, of course, we were still wearing our school tunics and blazers. All this careful watching of the pennies gave us good training in budgeting. Its effects remain today. Like so many Depression-reared adults, we know how to defer gratification until they can pay for it in full.

We made every conceivable economy in food costs, while always being well nourished. Fortunately fruit and vegetables were not expensive in Melbourne, and Mother made sure that we ate a good share of these. From her orchard days she retained a strong attachment to apples and pears. Bananas from Queensland were cheap. We ate mandarins, apricots, peaches, cherries, and grapes in season. Of course, we ate plenty of potatoes. We particularly loved to pop these in the coals in the fireplace and extract them later as apparent lumps of charcoal, which we would split open to enjoy the delicious, slightly smoky taste of the white interior. Pumpkin, which was also inexpensive and readily available, was a very popular vegetable, either boiled or roasted with the meat. We loved "bubble-and-squeak," made from leftover pumpkin and potatoes fried in dripping in the pan. Dripping, from any roasted meat or fried chops, was always kept carefully in a basin, constantly replenished, and it was indispensable for preparing most dishes. Dripping with tomato sauce on slices of bread was a standby, being much cheaper than the piquant Vegemite that has become so indispensable to today's young Australians. Mulligatawny stew was a tasty repository for any and all leftover fragments of meat and vegetables. We also ate a lot of inexpensive sausages and mincemeat, tomato sauce again adding to the palatability of their rather bland flavors. Lamb was readily available in the form of delicious baby lamb chops or as the ubiquitous Sunday leg of lamb. Rabbits, shot or ferreted out in the paddocks by our brothers and their mates, were in these pre-myxomatosis days, a welcome change of diet. Pork was rare, except in the sausages. Mother had learned a great deal from Dad about which of the less popular, and therefore cheaper, cuts of beef were most tender, and we watched the fluctuating prices carefully before buying. Fish was not a regular part of our diet, except occasionally in fish and chips on Fridays, when the fish was freshest because of the Roman Catholic practice of the Friday fast. Stale loaves of bread were dipped in water and steamed in the oven to freshen them, the slices then being eaten with lots of apricot or plum jam, the latter usually made from plums grown in our own or our friends' gardens. Mother particularly loved fig jam with ginger. We bought broken biscuits (cookies) cheaply from the grocer and occasionally, to our delight, there would be some fragments of the popular pink-iced biscuits among the bits and pieces. Then we had the constant pleasure of Mother's excellent scones and rock cakes.

After Les married Maude Morris, the twin of Reg's wife, he came to tea every Friday night, which was Maude's "night out with the girls," and Mother cooked us pancakes. She cooked the best pancakes in the world from her own recipe, with ingredients tossed together by intuition rather than measure. We scoffed them down in quantity, with raspberry or apricot jam and lots of scalded cream. Mother always scalded the milk, boiling it in a saucepan over a pan of water and then letting it stand overnight, when all the scalded cream would rise to the top. This cream, which could be scooped off with ease, was a feature of our house. When I had to stay home with the flu, Mother would cheer me up by bringing me slices of cake, slathered over with her beautiful scalded cream, a procedure we called "gilding the lily." It is a memory that still makes my mouth water.

Like all Australians at the time, we drank enormous quantities of tea and we soon acquired a fine taste for good teas. Black tea from Ceylon was the most popular. I had my first experience with advertising "come-ons," through my love of hot cocoa on winter nights. The cocoa container told me that for twenty-five labels I would be given a free box of chocolates. This advertising ploy was new in those days and exciting news for me. It took years, I found, to drink my way through twenty-five tins of cocoa powder. The rest of the family, although not as addicted to the chocolate flavor as I was, helped me out. Even the boys, who were away from home, took pity on me, helping me to reach my total by buying a couple of extra tins of this particular brand of cocoa to give me the labels. After three years, satiated with cocoa, I made my way to the cocoa factory to redeem my labels and found, to my great disappointment, that I was only entitled to a small single-layered box of chocolates — almost nothing at all. It was an early lesson in not trusting advertisers.

With Mother's country background, her scant education, and her lack of experience outside of the home, all she could have done to earn money would have been to clean other people's houses. This was hardly an option. During this period of serious slump housewives could not afford such help, certainly not in our area of lower middle class and working class families. Furthermore, at this time wives stayed at home and looked after their own houses. When Mother could think of no other way to obtain the money she needed to keep us going, she took up seriously Australia's popular leisure-time preoccupation: "following the geegees": picking winning racehorses and backing your favorite, even if you did not watch the horses actually run. In the pre-television 1930s, many more people listened to the races on the wireless than went to the course itself. In our neighborhood, there was much discussion of the form and prospects of racehorses. After all, Ascot Vale was surrounded by three racecourses, if you included the trotting ponies, with dog-racing tracks in suburbs close at hand. There was also much reading of specialized publications, like the *Sporting Judge*, which provided detailed information to assist punters in choosing winners. Mother had formed a friendship with a rather odd person in the locality, whose name was Mrs Eel (or was it Heel, we never did know). Mrs Eel wore a strange old hat with a big hatpin stuck through it. Fashions in clothes were not her particular preoccupation, but she did know her horses.

Off-course betting was illegal in Victoria at the time, but it was widely indulged in by way of starting price bookmakers (SP bookies). These operators accepted bets at whatever odds were declared over the air at the time the race began. They accepted bets by phone or through agents among the proprietors of small shops. Sometimes they operated in back lanes or pubs. They always had to keep one step ahead of the police, who were not too vigilant since many of them liked "a flutter on the geegees" themselves. As happened in the back lane behind our house, the bookie would often have a lookout or "nit," keeping an eye open to warn bookie and patrons should any police be in the vicinity. I'm sure this element of sudden danger added to the attraction of the enterprise. Nowadays, in Melbourne, when anyone can go into a betting shop and lay an off-course bet tranquilly and legally, this romantic element of physical risk has vanished. Mother and Mrs Eel could place bets at the local fruit shop, with the rough-spoken Mrs Pierce, or with the lolly shop proprietor. These people had direct access to SP bookies.

Mother, who had a certain sixth sense, saw this "hobby" as an opportunity to support her family. As well as studying form, she also dreamed winners, often at high odds (twenty to one was her preference). She even dreamed with some success of outsiders that won the Melbourne Cup, the richest race of the year. Apart from dreaming winners, there were also the tealeaves, teacup reading being another popular fortune-telling pastime among women at the time. Mother's brother, our Uncle Alf, being an engineer with some knowledge of mathematics, would sometimes lecture her on her perverse hobby. "Nina," he would say, "You know perfectly well you can't win in the long run. The odds are absolutely against you!" Mother would listen politely, smiling inwardly, because she knew that it was her winnings that enabled her to pay the mortgage. She had to keep her family going somehow.

Mother had a strategy according to which she operated, sometimes on the racecourse and sometimes off-course. She would bet two shillings on a horse in the first race, usually "each way" (win or place), and preferably on a horse that offered profitable odds. If she won on that horse she would bet on a horse in the second race. If her luck held out, she would wager a little longer, but never beyond two losing races. After all, she could not afford to waste precious survival money. In this way she paid the mortgage and put extra food on the table. Once when Mother had won quite a lot of money (several pounds at least) on a winner at twenty to one, she was so happy that she threw her hat in the door with the money in it.

When Mother came home with winnings, we would have a special treat. The nearby cake shop sold pretty little butterfly cakes, their tops cut in two pieces set in a cushion of whipped cream. Obviously, fresh cream turns sour after the first day, especially in hot weather, so at nine o'clock on Saturday night, just before closing time, the cake shop proprietor, who did not open on Sundays, would sell any cream cakes at half price. Linda and I would wait outside the shop, with sixpence burning in our hands, to rush in just at closing time for our half-price treat, glaring at any late shoppers who might look as though they were going in to buy at the last minute. Sometimes we would rush in at five minutes to nine, but the proprietor, still hoping for a last customer, would shoo us out, if only for four minutes. Never have small cakes tasted as good as those Saturday night, slightly turned cream specials.

Mother's sixth sense showed up in other ways than dreaming winners. On one occasion, I had left my umbrella on the tram when I was going to a meeting. Losing anything was quite a tragedy in those days, short of money as we were. Mother had come to meet me at the tram stop, as she liked to do when we were coming home late in the evening, so I told. her the sad story. Seeing another tram coming, Mother said to me: "Ask the driver of that tram if he has it." I protested: "But that's so stupid. I lost it a couple of hours ago and this tram has nothing whatever to do with it." But Mother insisted: "Ask the driver of that tram." Reluctantly I asked the driver of the tram as it stopped whether someone had handed in an umbrella. Incredibly this turned out to be just the tram whose driver had my umbrella, which he was even then taking back to the depot to lodge in Lost Property. Mother was not at all surprised.

At one stage, a researcher in women's studies at Harvard asked me whether there had been strong women in my past who had influenced me in my career.[53] I realized immediately that both Mater and Mother had been very strong women, who, as single parents, had had the responsibility of bringing up children without outside support. They had both been able to do so very successfully by sheer force of will. Mother always said that she had been a widow much longer than she had ever been a wife. In both of her widowhoods she survived unexpectedly difficult circumstances beyond her control, because of the strong sense of responsibility she felt toward her children and her intense desire to ensure for them the best of all possible futures. In this way, but with a very different preparation for the world of work and a different approach to child-rearing, Nina's life paralleled that of her mother. We always found it amusing that whenever Mother hurt herself, by falling off a ladder or slipping on a wet pavement, she would just lie there and laugh and laugh for a few minutes, before attempting to pick herself up. This, I think, was a physical reaction that paralleled her emotional reactions. When things unexpectedly became difficult, she would take a breather and ignore the new circumstances until she had regained her equilibrium. This, it seemed to me, was a way of submitting to the inevitable without allowing things to overwhelm her, giving herself time to readjust to changed circumstances without bemoaning them. She would then pick herself up, refreshed and ready to move on purposefully with her tasks.

As time went on, we lost contact with Dad's daughters, since Dad was no longer available to take us to see them. We had no money for train and tram fares to go visiting in suburbs on the other side of Melbourne and Mother, being extremely shy and feeling intimidated by these self-assured city women, preferred to retire into her shell. One day in my later teens, when I was in the city with Mother, she pointed out two smartly dressed women, talking in the doorway of Buckley and Nunn's department store. "Go over and speak to them," she said, "They're your sisters." I felt very nervous and diffident, because these "sisters" were old enough to be my aunts and I hadn't seen them for years. To me, they looked so confident and well dressed, as though they were from another world. By this stage of the Depression, we were looking pretty shabby. At Mother's insistence, however, I went over to the two women and, tapping one of them timidly on the arm, I murmured: "Hello, Florence. Hello, Violet. How are you?" The two ladies looked very astonished at being addressed by their first names by a strange girl whom they didn't recognize. "I'm Wilga," I said. Of course, they were delighted. After that Linda and I tried to keep up the contact, which we did successfully in the case of the younger ones, some of whom had children about our age. When Linda was appointed as a student teacher at Ivanhoe Central School she was close enough to Violet's and Alys's homes to visit them. Soon we became friends with their children — our half-nieces and nephews or "funny cousins," as we preferred to think of them.

MacRob Days (1935)

The time came to say farewell to my classmates of four years at EHS and, with my friend Rachel, to wend my way across town to the sparkling new high school on the Albert Park Lake. For this we had to take the train into the city. There we boarded a tram filled with girls and boys in a multiplicity of uniforms from private and state schools along the tram line. Each of us was proud of the school we represented. I was particularly pleased with my distinctive new badge, representing the helmeted Pallas Athena, goddess of wisdom and the arts. Our motto was in Latin, *Potens Sui*, Power over Self (self-control, self-direction, self-realization). It was something to reflect on. This was the first school I had attended where the Principal was a woman — Miss Mary Hutton, whose portrait in oils still adorns the entrance to the school. She was pleasant, but distant. She spoke to us at assemblies, but in the day-to-day routine we saw much more of her second-in-command, the strict but fair Miss Gainsford, a mathematician who would later become Principal herself and who is also memorialized in oils. Life under Miss Hutton's low-keyed supervision went on smoothly, happily, and productively.

We were now at an all-girls school after a lifetime of coeducation. The first thing that struck me, and more so Rachel with her four brothers and their hoards of male friends, was the obsession girls who had been in single-sex education all their secondary school lives seemed to have with boys. To us they were part of the furniture, not objects of somewhat mythic dimensions. It was a little less distracting for us not to have boys in our classes to tease and chiyack with, but it made very little difference to our class work. At EHS, some girls had been obsessed with the other sex, but these had been few; we knew who they were and whispered about their probable activities. Here there seemed to be a slightly breathless interest in the unknown. As in other all-girls adolescent institutions there were some "pashes" (passions) of junior girls for senior girls, usually prefects or sports leaders who seemed goddess-like in their achievements, but these, being transitory and shallow, dissipated for the most part over the summer vacation.

This MacRob year was our pre-university Leaving Honours year when we would or would not gain university entrance, University Free Places (which waived fees only), or Senior Scholarships (the latter providing a small supplementary living allowance, over and above the fee waiver). Consequently, the girls in our class, all top students from the different high schools, were highly motivated. They were well trained in study skills and already accustomed to working hard. Some were very brilliant and all had passed through a fairly rigorous academic selection process as they progressed through high school. They expected and were expected to do well on the statewide examinations, written by committees of university faculty. At MacRob, we were given much out-of-class work to do that required serious reading and we had frequent research papers to write. There was now a library and we learned to use it in an autonomous way to seek out the information we needed. The amount of work we had to cover kept us extremely busy in the evenings and weekends. When we finally went on to the university, we were very well prepared to study on our own.

For Leaving Honours we studied four subjects (a few exceptional students studied five). I chose French, of course, along with English (both language and literature), European History, and Geology. It was not unusual for me that year to study four hours at night and another two hours in the morning before leaving for school. The morning hours I devoted to working my way through a very solid

178

tome on European History. It was our ambition to get First Class Honours in as many subjects as possible and win Senior Scholarships. For this we could afford to have perhaps one Second Class Honour on our record. There were Thirds and Passes, but these we were anxious to avoid, since they would do little to help us in the tough competition to gain much needed financial help for our future. Most of us were not from affluent families. We were encouraged to study hard by the extremely competent corps of women teachers, all single. These teachers were thoroughly versed in the subject matter they taught but, even more importantly, they knew how to present the material interestingly and how to engage their students in challenging and intellectually absorbing tasks. They were also very familiar with the requirements and predilections of the examiners.

Languages at MacRob

I now had a French teacher, Miss Frances Barkman, who had had more contact with authentic French than our beloved Miss Meldrum. It was during this challenging year that I discovered many of my linguistic deficiencies, but this did not lessen my enthusiasm. Miss Barkman was very exacting in her requirements. The Matriculation examination was fifty per cent translation of passages from French into English and English into French, the remaining fifty per cent going to original composition in French, dictation, and a quarter of an hour's oral interview with two members of a Melbourne University team. Miss Barkman gave us plenty of practice in these areas. To supplement our weekly assigned practice in written translation, Miss Barkman would frequently read to us at dictation speed a passage which we were to translate as it was being read. She would also give us much dictation, without repetition, at a normal speed of speech. Both of these procedures forced us to make decisions on written French very fast. At first I made many mistakes until I became familiar with this type of exercise, but it certainly prepared us for anything we might encounter in our final examinations. Each week, we were assigned a topic for an essay in French, which was corrected meticulously, with comments in red ink. For her own convenience, Miss Barkman had had made for our compositions some special, smaller-sized exercise books that just fitted into the small case she carried home from school every day. Every week we met in small conversation groups. In class we read in close detail prescribed short stories, poems, and a play. To develop our fluency in reading authentic French in texts of interest to us, Miss Barkman had a collection of magazines from France. We were encouraged to borrow these and take them home to read in our leisure time. I particularly enjoyed one magazine called *Lectures pour Tous*, which consisted entirely of short stories. It made me feel very important to be reading a real French magazine on the way home in the train. As I read it, I would hold it in such a way that the title of the magazine could be clearly read by the other (less "cultured"?) passengers in the compartment.

Thanks to Miss Barkman's hard work in helping me overcome my weaknesses, I was awarded First Class Honours in the examination, despite a strange experience at the oral interview at Melbourne University. Being only sixteen, I believed that university professors, especially examiners, were serious people who were looking for serious answers. I was somewhat perturbed, therefore, when the examiner began the conversation by asking me whether I preferred to die by being poisoned, shot, or hanged. Instead of launching into fluent French on some familiar topic, I was rendered speechless while I tried to decide by which violent means I preferred to die, when I knew I did not want to die at all. Now, in such a situation, I would respond: "I really don't want to die yet. First, I want to go to France and see the Louvre and the Eiffel Tower," (or the Côte d'Azur or the Châteaux of the Loire), thus leading into a topic about which I could talk more easily. The examiners were probably highly diverted by my nervousness as I tried to think of an honest answer to their foolish question. There should be no place for this sort of wry humor at the expense of candidates in oral interviews that may well determine a student's future opportunities. Another student was asked how to make bricks. She remembered from Sunday School that the Israelites, when captives in Egypt, had had to make bricks without straw and presumed that straw was a necessary component in brick-making. How else would she know? What the examiners made of this I cannot imagine.

Later when I myself was preparing students for such oral interviews, I would always give them several practice sessions in the art of diverting the examiner to a subject of their own choice, for which they would come well prepared. This is a conversational gambit that is quite easy to acquire. "What do you want to be?" the examiner asks, and my future occupational therapist or dental technician, whose future career choice requires specialized vocabulary and expressions, responds: "Oh! I love history. That's what I want to study!" The examiner, following the normal pattern of polite conversation, is now manipulated into asking: "What area of history interests you most?" To which my student replies: "French history, of course! I love to read about the French Revolution," thus leading the conversation into an area with which she feels at home. This preparation has worked very well for many of my students, one of whom even went to the lengths of taking into an oral examination a string bag full of fruits and vegetables in order to divert the conversation into a discussion on shopping. Another, who was not strong in aural comprehension but who came from a rather exotic-sounding small town in the Woop Woops, had prepared a very interesting spiel on her home area. Just the mention of its name, worked into the early exchanges, aroused the interviewer's curiosity and she was able to give quite an impressive performance. In this way students retain some control over what can otherwise be an emotionally devastating experience. It is up to the examiner then to lead the now confident and relaxed student out into more extemporaneous expressions of opinion.

In 1935, the Education Department decided to provide new opportunities for the study of languages beyond the traditional French, German, and Latin. Saturday morning classes in Italian and Japanese were offered in two centers for students from different schools. Naturally, I was one of the first to leap forward and seize the opportunity to study another language by enrolling in Italian. One of my friends studied Japanese and maintained her interest in that language over many years. Later, after a very successful career as a teacher of French and German, she once again took up the serious study of Japanese and was very influential in the 1960s in encouraging the teaching of that language in Victorian high schools. I found learning Italian very refreshing and a nice change of pace in my very busy study schedule. At the end of the year I was awarded a Dante Society prize to purchase books. With this money I bought an Italian-English dictionary, a copy of Dante's *Divina Commedia,* bound in blue mock leather, and a copy of Pirandello's *La Vita Nuda*. I was all set for a future incursion into the Romance Languages.

Hockey Again

My second great enthusiasm was abundantly satisfied at MacRob, where, along with my friend Rachel, I immediately became a member of the school hockey team. We now played against other girls' high schools. In vigorous house matches, as a Nereid I played against Naiads, Oreads, and Dryads, as was appropriate in a school with Pallas Athena as patroness. We now had extensive playing fields beside the Albert Park Lake. A short tram ride away were the St Kilda Baths, where we practiced swimming in the seawater of the Bay. Since sporting activity was considered such an important element in the education of every girl in the school, all kinds of sports, including lacrosse, were available. There was even a croquet court set up for the few students who for health reasons could not engage in vigorous physical activity.

Developing a Love of Literature

English expression and English literature were an important part of our Victorian curriculum. In 1935 they formed one compulsory, full-year subject for Leaving Honours, as for the preceding Leaving Certificate. I had always loved writing and I was an avid reader. With Miss Egan our love of literature increased. A big woman, who wore dresses with large patterns and tended in her enthusiasm to spit a little on the students in the front row, she made us fall in love with each text she introduced — whether it was Francis Bacon's *Essays*, Spenser's *Faerie Queene*, Chaucer's *Canterbury Tales*, Shakespeare's *King Lear*, Milton's *Samson Agonistes*, Hardy's *Mayor of Casterbridge*, Pope, Dryden, Shelley, Byron, or Keats. We could not get enough of our readings and her explications. We were sent to the library to read the critics in preparation for our essays on literary topics and in every way we were well prepared for our later studies in literature at Melbourne University. In fact, in second year Honours English classes at the University, I was still referring back to notes I had taken during Miss Egan's MacRob classes. Many of us were expected to get First Class Honours in English and we did. What could have stopped us? I attribute my lifelong love of wide reading in the literatures of many different cultures to the enormous excitement for literature that Miss Egan inspired.

We had clubs that met on Wednesday afternoons, where we could engage in special interests in a more recreational way. I belonged to the English Club, which produced scenes from *Romeo and Juliet* for the delectation of our parents and other students. It was my first opportunity to perform on stage and I was given the minor role of Juliet's father, who had to greet arriving guests with a call for "Lights! More lights!" I can remember my one-line part to this day. One of my friends had to play the silent role of a guest and pretend to respond to my silent greeting. Determined to speak in Shakespeare's words, she would look me straight in the eye as I greeted her and say softly: "You egg!" which she had found in another play. Naturally, in my nervous excitement, I burst into helpless giggles and nearly lost my important role.

The Earth and World Affairs

My next choice was, of course, Geology, which I had so much enjoyed at EHS and I looked forward to the excursions. These gave us ample opportunities to dig into the cliffs around Port Phillip Bay in search of fossilized sea urchins and to rummage eagerly among the rocks and pebbles along the shore for fossil sharks' teeth. Our teacher, Miss Richardson, was noted for the number of her students who were awarded First Class Honours each year, so we had every confidence in her ability to prepare us well. It was tough love with Miss Richardson; term exams were tough and grading was tough. It was well known that if you achieved a grade of 52 out of 100 on one of Miss Richardson's tests, you were on your way to First Class Honours. My first semester I made 48 out of 100 and burst into tears with disappointment. Miss Richardson came over to me, put her arm around my shoulders, and said: "But you did quite well!" as she went over some of the questions with me. I found it hard to believe that 48/100 was "doing well" in a course, but I renewed my efforts and wore more and more of a track around the beautiful hexagonal table in our front sitting-room, as I memorized the properties of rocks, minerals, and fossils and the stratigraphy of Victoria. That limestone is found in Lilydale is the only detail of the latter I can remember, probably because of the alliteration.

We enjoyed equally as much our European History classes with the striking, black-haired Miss Searby, whose father had been the first headmaster at EHS. A warm, approachable teacher she was very popular with her students, in whom she took a deep interest. This course took us all over Europe from the Fall of Constantinople in 1485 to the Treaty of Versailles in 1929, with Bismarck as the special study for the year. Miss Searby, in her delightful way, aroused our excitement about the exploits of Peter the Great, Gustavus Adolphus of Sweden, Garibaldi, and the Young Turks. As a result I acquired another life interest. I now had an excellent background on which to build for following world events and placing current problems in a regional and national historical context.

Christian Fellowship

At MacRob I met Miss Ruby Chapman, another person who had a strong influence on my life. Miss Chapman, who was a lecturer in biblical studies at a non-denominational institute in Melbourne, had been deputed to establish Christian Fellowships in the high schools, on a voluntary, after-school basis, to parallel the very successful Crusader groups in the private schools. One of the first high schools in which she established a Bible study and prayer group was MacRob. That year we already had a very fine instructor in the scheduled Religious Instruction period — Colonel Graham of the Salvation Army, who in his Wednesday morning classes kept the attention of thirty or forty senior girls. He made us think seriously at an adult level about religious questions and he had a considerable influence on my interest in spiritual matters. The family of my friend Rachel were dedicated Presbyterians and her brothers ran church youth groups, so Rachel naturally gravitated to Miss Chapman's group. I went along with her, as did my close friend, Peggy Jackson, who was a Baptist. I had also heard about the group from Linda. Not only were Miss Chapman's Bible studies interesting and thought-provoking, but she had tremendous faith in young people and her strategy for the development of the movement, despite very few resources, was to draw on us to expand those resources. She trusted young people and had great confidence in their ability to run things for themselves, even things they had never done before. She organized the first weekend fellowship camp I ever attended, at Montrose in the Dandenongs. In

184

the next few years she had us organizing and running camps ourselves for younger girls. We were given full responsibility for all the logistics of ordering food, arranging meals and living arrangements, designing recreational programs, and preparing Bible studies. This we were doing at seventeen and eighteen years of age.

The following year, when I was a first-year undergraduate at Melbourne University, Miss Chapman asked me to go to Coburg High School to address all the girls in a quadrangle assembly. I was to invite them to join me in establishing a Schools' Christian Fellowship (SCF) to meet after school hours. For a shy teenager this required screwing my courage to the sticking point. With Miss Chapman's prayers and my own to support me, I was able to make this first public speech and gather together a very enthusiastic group of girls to join the Fellowship. Looking back, I feel the influence of Miss Chapman in giving me confidence in my own abilities when attempting tasks that are beyond my experience, in speaking in public, and in trusting in God and His plan for my life. Through the SCF both Linda and I felt we had decisions to make. Consequently, we made our way to St Thomas's, Moonee Ponds, the church our father had taken us to in our early childhood, and asked for instruction for Confirmation.

Educational Trauma Seven: Fiasco of the exams

The excellent training I had received under Miss Cuthbert at EHS in organizing my work and making full use of the time available was reinforced at MacRob. Two hours of study before breakfast and four hours every evening was my regimen. Before our end-of-year exams we were given two weeks' leave from school to review our year's work. I spent this "swot vac" in our front room in complete isolation, working as usual on the hexagonal heirloom table. I followed a half-hour by half-hour study schedule I had drafted, from 7 a.m. till 10 p.m. each day, with an hour off for lunch and for dinner. This self-imposed schedule took me step by step through all my year's work in my four subjects. At the end of the two weeks I felt well prepared to face any examination paper.

I was well aware of how crucial the results of the exams would be for my future career. Because of our financial situation I needed a Senior Scholarship to enable me to go on to the University. For this, I would have to have a very good Honours record in all subjects. I have spoken earlier about my First Class Honours in both French and English. Then came the Geology exam. Incredibly I was caught in the confusion of a curricular change. A new Professor had taken charge of the Geology Department at Melbourne University and was now responsible for the examination questions. He and his favorite topics were as yet an unknown quantity to the teachers of the senior classes in the schools. There seems to have been a substantial lack of communication between the university faculty writing the Geology paper that year and the teachers responsible for preparing the students. The teachers were continuing to follow along the lines of the course of study of the preceding regime. Miss Richardson was well placed to know what was expected and her students' results had always been outstanding. This time, however, she seems to have been operating on insufficient information. For our Geology paper, there were no questions on rocks, minerals, or fossils, which had previously constituted an important part of the course and in the details of which we were well versed. Most of the questions were on glaciers and volcanoes, the detailed study of which had previously been considered the domain of Geography. Most of the knowledge we had so laboriously acquired was not tested at all. Not surprisingly we did not do well. This was through no fault of ours and certainly did not indicate lack of knowledge of the published course syllabus. The final grades, in my case Third Class Honours, did not reflect what we knew. We were drawing on what we remembered of material our teacher had treated rapidly, as a tangential part of the course, and recollections of the previous year's Geography course. It was too superficial.

The European History examination, for which I had worked so conscientiously and methodically morning after morning, was a similar catastrophe. The course requirements were obviously too extensive for a one-year high school course. We had had to study the history of the many countries of Europe, east, west, and central, over a period of nearly four hundred and fifty years (1485-1929), as well as the life of Bismarck as our special topic. Our experienced Miss Searby had concluded that this was altogether too much for us to digest. To lighten the load a little, she had decided, in the special topic, to concentrate on the first half of Bismarck's life — his rearrangement of Europe and unification of Germany. This seemed to her to be more interesting and of greater import than his political maneuvering later, when he was trying to maintain his power base in his home country. She had reckoned on a choice of questions, which would surely contain something about the influential first part of his life. Unfortunately for us, all the questions on our special topic were on the second half of Bismarck's career. As a group, then, we received no credit at all for our special study and this drastically reduced our grade. When we came out of the Exhibition Building at the end of the examination, Miss Searby was in tears. "None of you will get Honours," she wept, realizing that this could be an incredible blow to the career prospects of some of her students. "I just didn't teach you that part of the syllabus," she admitted. As a consequence of this debacle, I was awarded a Pass in European History, not Honours. It was not that my classmates and I did not have a very strong and extensive knowledge of European History, which it was the role of the examination to detect. Rather, we were victims of the system. The syllabus had been too all-encompassing and our teacher had engaged unsuccessfully in the normal professional game of guessing the contents of the examination paper, in order to keep the amount of work within reasonable limits for her students. What more could we have done?

With two First Class Honours, a Third, and a Pass, I could not win a Senior Scholarship. I was listed for a Free Place, which in our financial situation was quite inadequate, since it provided nothing for living expenses. At that time there were no student loan or work-study opportunities for undergraduate students. My hopes of continuing my studies at undergraduate level, then, were dashed. I had to find work immediately in order to keep myself and help the family. So I wended my way to the Education Department offices to seek a student teaching position in one of the primary schools, this being the first step to becoming a fully certified and salaried primary school teacher. In this way, I would follow in the footsteps of my grandmother, my aunts, and my sister. Linda had already been student teaching in a school for a year, while she studied at night the preliminary subjects required for her one-year course at the Primary Teachers' College. The only way either Linda or I would be able to study for a Bachelor of Arts degree would be through long years of night school.

6
ACADEMIC NOVITIATE
1936-39

The end of January 1936 found me making my way on my bicycle to the Maribyrnong State Primary School, where I had been appointed as a student teacher. I was to teach in the Infant School, which in those days drew together kindergarten and first and second grades as an autonomous unit within the Primary School.

I remember the mesmerizing effect of seeing well over a hundred small children at little desks on different levels in a great big room, where the Infant Mistress, an experienced educator of senior rank, conducted full-group sessions. Several student teachers kept watch from different parts of the room, observing the teaching and, from time to time, helping little people "who had to go." The student teachers later taught groups of thirty or more children in smaller classrooms. In after-school sessions we were carefully guided as to what we were to do the next day. We were then expected to plan our lessons in detail and write them up for approval. My task was to teach my little flock the Little Old Man Story. Reading was being taught through phonics and each letter of the alphabet was associated with an incident and sketch in the story of the Little Old Man. I remember that he went up a hill (sketched in colored chalk on the board within the outline of an aitch), puffing "Huh! Huh! Huh!" At one stage he came across a snake (S) that went "Ssss! Ssss! Ssss!" I really do not remember what else I did.

I had been at Maribyrnong for about two and a half weeks, when by chance I met my French teacher from MacRob, Miss Barkman,.

"Well, you'll be starting at the University in a few weeks," she said to me cheerfully. (Melbourne University's first term began about the middle of March.)

"Oh no!" I replied. "I can't possibly go to the university. We can't afford it!"

"Nonsense! Nonsense!' she replied, in her down-to-earth way. "Of course you must go to the university." She fished in her handbag, bringing out a piece of paper. "Here," she said, "is a phone number. Call this Mr Lightfoot at the Aspro Building and arrange to see him right away. I'll let him know you're coming."

Somewhat bemused, I took the slip of paper she held out to me and did as she directed. The friendly Mr Lightfoot asked me to bring my mother to see him. So into the city we went and crossed Princes Bridge to the Aspro Building, which was quite a landmark across the Yarra River. Mr Lightfoot made us feel at home immediately. He had spoken with Miss Barkman and already knew something about me — specifically, that I had a Free Place for Melbourne University, but no financial means for my living expenses and books. He asked my mother how much she thought she would need for my upkeep if I continued my studies. Mother, being very modest and used to making ends meet somehow, said quietly that she thought she could manage with four pounds a month. (It is hard to give any idea what this means in present-day terms, except that it was four times our low but indispensable mortgage.) So it was arranged that once a month I would go to the Aspro Building and ask for Mr Lightfoot. Either he or his secretary would appear with a form for me to sign and discreetly pass over to me my monthly allowance. Sometimes, if he could spare the time, Mr Lightfoot would invite me into his office for a chat on how I was progressing and how the family was managing.

The Aspro Company had been founded by the Nicholas family, who had been very successful in pharmaceuticals both in Australia and abroad. Later they drew some international attention when a daughter and a son of one branch of the family were married for a while to the musicians, Yehudi and Hephzibah Menuhin. A Methodist family, they believed strongly in quiet, personal charity, in "not letting their left hand know what their right hand did." They had a private fund through which they helped students recommended by their teachers as being worthy of their largesse to continue their

189

studies. Miss Barkman at MacRob happened to be one of their agents in the schools. Without their early help I would never have been able to progress professionally as I did. If I had had to do my Bachelor of Arts degree at night, I would not have been able to do an Honours degree, since this option was not available for night students. According to the system in place at Melbourne University in 1936, this limitation would have prevented me from continuing on to a Master's degree, for which the B.A.(Honours) degree was a prerequisite.The Pass degree would also have been a considerable impediment later to obtaining a teaching position in a university, although this never entered my mind as a possibility at the time. I was never told which other MacRob students received similar help. At one stage I did see a girl who had been in Linda's class and who was studying Law leaving the Aspro Building as I was coming in. This was a period when only a few women were enrolled in Melbourne University's Law School. I presume she also benefited from the same generosity. When I finished my studies, Mr Lightfoot told me the Nicholas family did not expect any form of repayment, but they hoped I would later do for someone else what they had done for me. I searched for quite some time for a way to carry out this wish, until I found a fund in America that provides a financial subsidy to black students with outstanding high school records who cannot afford to continue their studies at community college or college level. This was exactly what the Nicholas family had done for me. It has been a delight for me to be able to support this fund for more than thirty years.[54]

Melbourne University at Last

The tide having turned, I was able to resign after six weeks of primary teaching, proudly taking home my first salary. I was now ready to move on to Melbourne University. Fortunately the Uni, or the Shop as we called it, was only about three miles from Ascot Vale and could be reached conveniently on my sturdy old bike; this was a considerable economy. I enjoyed riding along the wide boulevard-like Flemington Road, looking out over the broad expanses of Royal Park, with its gum trees and open sports fields. As I rode I would sing at the top of my voice, knowing that my singing was amply covered by the noise from the six lanes of cars and the bells of the green and yellow trams on their fixed tracks. On the last Friday afternoon of each month, I would turn my bike eastward instead of westward and make my way down Flinders Street, through Melbourne's city center, in rush-hour traffic. I would dive in and out among the impatient, revving cars in the narrow space between parked vehicles and the lines of trams, all crowded to capacity with home-bound workers. Crossing over the Yarra I would pick up my allowance at the Aspro Building. I would then bike back to my home in the western suburbs, patting my pocket from time to time to make sure that the precious pound notes had not worked their way out as I pedaled along.

Arriving at the University to enrol, I had to work out what I would do next? There was no form of student advising in 1936 and Mother certainly had no idea of what went on at a university. For the first time I did not have Linda's lead to follow. I obtained a copy of the official Courses of Instruction booklet and immediately turned to French. To my delight I found something called Pure French Honours. It would allow me to spend five-eighths of my time on French studies. What more could I wish for? I immediately made my way to the Registrar's office and enrolled myself without hesitation in this wondrous program, which seemed to have been designed just for me.

I found out the differences between the Pass degree and the Honours degree for the Bachelor of Arts. Honours degree candidates took only eight year-long courses, as opposed to ten for the Pass degree, but much more work was required of them. They studied a number of extra course segments in their major area. For my Honours degree I would have five courses in French, two in English (my minor), and one in a related subject, for which I selected Latin, which was a prerequisite for French Honours. In French, we covered the major developments in literature and language from the medieval period to the 20th century, as well as having three years of thorough study in areas of language use. We Honours students also wrote a thesis in our third year, without guidance or assistance of any kind. Mine was on André Gide, who was still writing in the 1930s. The Honours degree prepared us for immediate entry into the Master of Arts program, where we would write a longer thesis, again without any guidance, advice, or contact with the department after the approval of the subject. (There was no further course work.) On the

191

other hand if Pass students wanted to write a Master of Arts thesis, they would have to complete an extra year of courses to make up for what they had missed of the Honours program. Pass students thus had much more time for socializing and enjoying life than Honours students. They often wondered aloud why we Honours students bothered to take on so much extra work when we didn't have to; we, however, were enjoying the challenge and the intellectual stimulation.

Because of our financial situation and the absolute necessity of being able to support myself at the end of my studies, I still felt somewhat insecure about my future. At the suggestion of the Headmaster of the Maribyrnong school, I had gone nervously to see the Chief Inspector in the Education Department to ask him whether I should sign up there and then for teaching in the state high school system after my studies. With my Free Place and the Nicholas supplement I did not need any financial assistance from them, but I needed the assurance of a position on graduation. After all, Australia was still suffering from the Depression and I had my own family's experiences as a warning. The Chief Inspector told me distantly that he could not guarantee that the Education Department would want any high school teachers when I finished my degree (looking back this was, of course, nonsense), and that I should act immediately. Not knowing any better, I signed on the dotted line, thus committing myself to teaching in the Department for three years after completion of my studies. This limited my options. Later, when I thought I might be interested in studying law or politics, I was unable to do so because the Education Department had to approve of my choice of subjects as being useful for teaching. I was, however, sure of a post after completing my B.A.(Honours) and Diploma of Education. This naturally had a calming effect on a somewhat bewildered sixteen-year-old, making her way unpiloted in a strange world.

In any case, I was to find out before too long that Melbourne University was not very hospitable to women students who wanted to enter previously all-male domains. It was still the general opinion that, for females, teaching and nursing were the most appropriate fields. A few women did make it into the legal and medical professions and one friend of mine became a lecturer in the Engineering school. It was not an easy journey for them, however. One fellow student from MacRob had been so academically successful that she had had to do Leaving Honours for two years in succession, while she waited to reach the university entrance age of sixteen. She had studied five different subjects each year, attaining First Class Honours in every field. At the University she had wanted to enter the Pure Chemistry Honours program. Although she had been a top student in Chemistry in her first year, the head of the Chemistry department declared that no woman had ever done Pure Honours in Chemistry in the past and, while he was there, none ever would. Consequently this brilliant scientist was forced to do Combined Honours in Chemistry and Physics (Combined Honours being considered at the time as somewhat lower on the totem pole than the Pure Honours degree). In subtler ways older professors, through remarks in big lectures, often made women feel they were there on indulgent sufferance. Of course, "everyone knew" that they would only go off and get married, devoting themselves thereafter to cleaning the house, cooking, and child rearing. Women who managed to have both a career and a marriage with children were very rare indeed. A few strong single women, who had fought their way up, were the only role models for ambitious female students.

In 1936 Melbourne University campus centered around a shallow lake, surrounded by huge, sprawling Moreton Bay fig trees. It was pleasant to walk around the lake and sit and dream in their shade. Commencement came in April, soon after classes had begun, and it was conducted with the usual pageantry. To celebrate their new status, the graduating engineers traditionally jumped into the lake to fight the medical students, with mud flying and water splashing all over the onlookers. The opportunity to return to childhood was irresistible and cause for great hilarity among the bystanders. It was a great loss when the picturesque lake was filled in to pack the crowded campus with still more buildings.

Around the perimeter of the main campus were the residential colleges, each with a denominational affiliation, which offered tutorials to supplement the lectures at the university. These were the Anglican Trinity College for men (and, associated with it, Janet Clarke Hall for women), the Roman Catholic Newman College (with St Mary's for women), the Presbyterian Ormond College, and the Methodist Queens College. These institutions also taught the theology of their denomination. The buildings of the Colleges competed in grandeur from Gothic to modern and they still form a spectacular semicircle that adds to the beauty of the university area. The non-denominational Women's College was built while I was still at the University, but the inspiration for International House came later.

Arts students spent most of their time in the lecture theaters and classrooms of the yellow sandstone Arts Building, with its tall clock tower, or walked around the Gothic cloisters leading to the library. The library was small by today's standards, but it was a treasure trove for us at the time. In my second year the Student Union was built. This gathering place for students was a new concept in those days and soon we were spending much of our time there, in facilities such as we had never dreamed of before. It was here that a great deal of our real education took place. Like young students everywhere and in every age we argued our way through many thorny issues and wrestled with many philosophies, very often during meals and spare hours in the Union. I did not see as much of the Union as some of my friends, however. On my stringent budget I just could not afford cups of coffee. When my friends would leave the library for an afternoon break, I would profess not to like coffee and stay at my books, dreaming only of the steaming brew until they returned.

Since Melbourne University was situated to the northwest of Melbourne near the Carlton and United Breweries, there was always a strong smell of malt and hops in the neighborhood. Carlton at that time was a rundown, older part of Melbourne. This was before its gentrification and the establishment of the variety of ethnic restaurants that make it such a favorite area for dining out nowadays. Within easy walking distance of the university, there were many old Victorian houses with iron lace on their upstairs balconies and, with the passing of the years, these have become much sought after as dwellings for professional people who work in and near the central city. As we walked the short mile from the University to the Public Library, where we could supplement the rather small collection of books in our university library, we would often see big, lumbering wagons, laden with kegs of beer, drawn by huge, strong-muscled Clydesdale draft horses. We would pass the old Haymarket, with the arch of its entrance gateway adorned with a horse's head in high relief, and, turning away from the busy fruit and vegetable stalls of the Victoria Market, we would reach the Melbourne library. There we

194

would work at long tables, with green shaded lamps, in the circular reading room under its high dome. Deep in thought, we would stare at the several floors of book stacks that circled the great chamber, where a dropped book echoed accusingly in the deep silence.

To my surprise riding a bike, as I had done for so long, was just not acceptable for a young lady at Melbourne University in the 1930s. Attitudes changed during the war when fuel for cars was rationed and car drivers had to resort to attaching smelly, smoky charcoal-burners to their vehicles to keep them going. Among the day students only two of us rode bikes — a missionary's daughter and I. A bobby-soxed youth worker from the YWCA rode in to night classes, as my sister Linda did later, after her Primary Teachers' College training. Naturally we soon got to know each other. The general attitude toward our unconventional behavior was expressed by a fellow student, a private school girl, who openly remarked that I must be very "common," since I rode a bike. At one student Stunt Night I was satirized on stage because of my bike riding and my unfashionable appearance. At the time (1937), I was still making do with the clothes I had worn to my father's funeral in 1932, especially my old school blazer and a navy-blue beret. The wealthier students, with little experience of Depression struggle, apparently found this remarkable and incomprehensible. Some of my friends, having found the skit hilarious, insisted on my seeing it. I laughed with everyone else, until one girl asked: "Didn't you recognize yourself?" Insecure and uncertain socially as I was, I was so mortified that I could have hidden in a hole in the ground. From then on, I insisted to my friends that I was not interested in clothes, nor in what others thought of me; my mind was on higher things. I was an intellectual, no less. These protestations were, of course, to cover up my feelings of embarrassment and inadequacy. As soon as I began to earn money and no longer had to scrimp and stretch all my resources, I became very attentive to my general appearance, to color coordination, to mixing and matching, and to choosing appropriate accessories.

To understand this strange attitude to a simple form of transport like riding a bicycle one needs to remember that in 1936-39 only a small percentage of students at Melbourne University were former state high school students. Most of these would have been on some form of scholarship or student aid. Depression conditions had weeded out many promising students and there were no loans or opportunities for students to earn money. The majority of the students had attended fee-paying private schools, being the children of more affluent families. Of these, only the Methodist Ladies College prided itself on being open to students from various socioeconomic levels. Most of the students were not from "our side of the river," that is, from the working-class western suburbs. Since their families had been much less affected by the Depression, they were inevitably much better dressed than we were and they could afford to indulge in the more costly social activities, like balls and weekends with the Ski Club. We must have seemed terra incognita to many of them. Since there were no facilities for parking and locking up our bikes, we three riders had a private agreement with the janitor of the Arts Building to discreetly sneak our bikes, unobserved, up some back steps into a disused, unlighted doorway area, where they would not be an eyesore. At least our bikes were safe in this out-of-the-way spot, which most students and professors did not know existed. We were even given keys to the building, which gave us greater flexibility in our study hours.

At the end of my first year, having done well in my studies, I was very pleased to be awarded a non-resident bursary to attend tutorials at Janet Clarke Hall, with its resonances of my father's early acquaintance at Bolinda Vale with the lady herself. Non-resident students were called "outpatients," by the resident women. This was the first time in my life that I had ever had access to any kind of supplementary help with my studies and I was determined to get the most out of it. Of course it was expensive to live in Janet Clarke Hall or pay for tutorials as an external student, so not surprisingly most of my fellow students were affluent, private school girls, more accustomed to some tutoring and less appreciative of what to me was a great opportunity. An old French lady gave us extra work in translation. Serious translation of all kinds of texts into another language is a very demanding and never-ending apprenticeship, so I never missed a session. After the tutorial the non-resident students would walk back along a narrow path to the main campus in a chatty, laughing group, and I would trail along some distance behind, knowing that I was not welcome to join their "in-group." However, I was determined that no amount of snobbish exclusion would hinder me in my search for as much knowledge as I could ingest and my Honours degree — my passport to the future.

Not surprisingly, in a very short time I had begun to form my friendships within the group of convent school girls. The Catholic schools, apart from a few very wealthy ones that reflected the social stratification of Catholic society, had always accepted a wide swathe of students from different socioeconomic levels. Since all Catholics at that time were expected to send their children to be educated by the Church, there were many Catholic schools in the suburbs on both sides of the river. I found this group much more open and willing to accept all comers. My dearest friend for years was Marie Pietszch, of Polish origin, whose two brothers and a sister had entered religious orders, as a second sister was to do later. Having grown up in such a religiously divided society, this close contact with devout Catholics was a new experience for me. Marie, who was doing Combined Honours in Classics and French, was just my age — sixteen. I remember that, young as she was, she was also a competition-level golf player. With her strong background in Classics and French, she went on to become an accountant and auditor, which demonstrates that a solid liberal arts education is a good preparation for work in other fields. Through Marie, I found myself spending most of my lunch hours and spare moments with a happy, vivacious group of Catholic girls, most of whom were studying French as well. Their interests lay with the Newman Society activities, whereas, with my ISCF experience I had joined the Evangelical Union (EU). Through the EU and the Student Christian Movement (SCM), I became friends with a very varied group of students, men and women, from different faculties — Science, Medicine, Music, Architecture, Law, and Theology, as well as Arts. Soon I had found my feet and was very much at home in my various friendship circles.

Through my friend Phyllis Lawson, who was blind, I made friends among a group of blind students. Phyllis was the most determined and indomitable person I had ever known (after my mother, of course). Never, throughout life, would she allow her visual impairment to hinder her in carrying out what she had planned for herself. Phyllis, who was taking French courses too, took notes in lectures with a small portable brailling apparatus. In this era, before white canes or guide dogs, she needed help in moving around the campus, so we spent a lot of time together, doing the same things at the same time — library, lecture theater, Union. In later life she established in Melbourne the well-known Lady Nell Seeing-Eye Dog School, on the Council of which I served for a number of years. When she married, I was one of her bridesmaids and later the godmother of one of her sons.

My most vivid and characteristic image of Phyllis comes from a weekend at a student camp, where we were experimenting with horse riding. Phyllis, determined as ever to do everything that everyone else did, wanted to try to ride too, so we mounted her on a horse. We were walking beside her, chatting, when the horse suddenly broke into a trot and made off. The unexpected movement took Phyllis by surprise and she fell off her unaccustomed perch onto the ground some distance ahead of us. We were naturally very distressed and began running toward her. Before we could reach her, Phyllis had seized the saddle and was trying to get back on the horse without assistance. This was typical of Phyllis's spirit — nothing ever kept her down. Despite many life experiences and personal setbacks that would have daunted others, she doggedly persisted and overcame all obstacles with intelligence, courage and grit.[55] From Phyllis I learned a great deal about how to be a friend to persons with physical disabilities. I learned to accept them as perfectly capable companions, including them as full partners in all activities and only assisting unobtrusively when there was a real need.

In between hours of study in lectures and in the library, I was, of course, pursuing my leisure interest of field hockey. Since I was never of top competition quality, I mostly played in the C Team, with invitations to play in the B team when they needed a defensive back to fill in for an absent member. Since there were no other universities in Melbourne at that time, the C team often played against teams from factories, where the players had plenty of spunk, but not too much technique. Hockey sticks flailed as the two teams clashed and the language was often colorful. As always, it was exhilarating and refreshing to be out in the fresh air, even in wintry weather, driving up our adrenaline with vigorous physical activity.

It was at Melbourne University, too, that I developed my interest in classical music, unexpectedly enough through a gift from the Americans. I had rarely had opportunities to listen to classical music, apart from Uncle Alf Lehmann's occasional solitary performances in the darkness of the front room. There had been my lessons in piano with Miss Baulch, who concentrated on technical production and music theory, rather than musical appreciation. At home we listened to light popular music on the radio, with a preference for tuneful songs. The Carnegie Foundation had made a gift to Melbourne University of a collection of excellent records of classical music by famous orchestras, under the baton of equally famous conductors. These came in monthly boxes. The University decided that the best way of making this music available to the greatest number of students was to arrange two-hour sessions in a small lecture theater for students to listen to the records. Since some of my friends were anxious to attend, I went along too. The music was played without any form of introduction or explanation. I remember that I found the first session excruciatingly boring, this being the first time I had listened to classical music for such a long period of time. However, I continued to go with my friends and, as time went on, I began to enjoy it. From this experience developed my lifelong love of classical music, particularly chamber music, with the cello being my favorite instrument. In my first year of teaching in the country, I followed up on this newfound interest by enrolling in an adult education correspondence course in musical appreciation. I hope the Carnegie Foundation boxes were as successful with students in other countries as they were with me. From my point of view it was certainly money well spent on their part.

French Studies

The French Department at Melbourne University in 1936 was not enormous but it had achieved prestige because of the intellectual strengths of the small number of scholars who were there, as well as the outstanding researchers it graduated. In charge was Professor A. R. Chisholm. Chizzy, as we called him, was a small, gnome-like man with a skin like tanned hide. A literary critic of considerable perception and subtlety, highly regarded for his work on Mallarmé and Valéry, he had an enduring influence on his students, a number of whom became leading Mallarmé and Valéry scholars themselves. These included such well-known figures as Lloyd Austin of Cambridge University, Gardner Davies, Australian Cultural Attaché

199

in Paris and ambassador to UNESCO for many years, and James Lawler of the University of Chicago. Professor Chisholm's influence spread beyond the university through a regular literary column he wrote for the Melbourne *Age*. He had a strong interest in Australian as well as French literature, particularly the work of Christopher Brennan, the Australian poet who discovered Mallarmé while he was a temporary expatriate in Germany in the 1890's.

Chizzy was also a phonetician. We all used his small, red-covered book on French phonetics, the study of which was considered at the time the best way to improve pronunciation. Professor Chisholm belonged to the earlier generation of French professors, who spoke (and wrote) excellent French but with a noticeable accent that was strongly influenced by their native English. On one occasion, in later years, I attended a function where Chizzy was welcoming to Melbourne in flawless French a new Cultural Attaché from France. After a few minutes, the Cultural Attaché, beside whom I happened to be seated, turned and whispered to me in French: "Would you mind translating what Professor Chisholm is saying, please. I don't understand English very well." When Chizzy gave lectures on literature to the Pass students, he spoke in measured tones with his anglicized accent, so that even the weakest Pass students had no trouble taking full and careful notes. When he lectured on Baudelaire, Mallarmé, or Valéry, of whose *Cimitière Marin* he gave us a word-by-word exegesis, the Honours students were spellbound. Some of the other lecturers had much less elevated ideas on how to teach literature. Their courses for Pass students (attended also by the Honours students) consisted of little more than word-for-word translation by the lecturer himself of sections of the text that had previously been assigned as preparatory reading. Long poems of the Romantics and even whole novels underwent this treatment. Translation in all its manifestations was certainly in vogue.

The next most impressive person in the department, and one who had a lasting impact on us all, was a mercurial Frenchman of Armenian origin, Nazar Karagheusian (Kara, as we called him). A small, dark-haired, dark-eyed, vivacious man, with hair limited to a little behind each ear, he spoke fast, gesticulated often, and smiled a lot. He had an enormous sense of fun, which livened up French Club activities. Climbing a mountain during the night to see the sunrise was one activity he enjoyed. He was a single man, who lived with his mother who ran a prosperous *haute couture* salon in Melbourne called La Rue de la Paix. His lectures on seventeenth century French literature (Corneille, Racine, and Molière) were invaluable at this stage of our studies, mainly because they provided us with our first opportunity to listen to fluent native French for a full hour, even if we were not always sure of the details. Full of quirky humor his lectures were very entertaining.

One of Kara's major contributions to the program was his stimulating conversation tutorials. We were too far away to go to French-speaking areas for visits or study abroad; the voyage to France by ship in the late 1930s (there being no commercial air flights) required thirty days each way. Such luxuries had to be left for our later years. Kara, then, was France for us, and what a lively, unpredictable France that was. His way of stimulating conversations was to express outrageous, controversial opinions, thus arousing strong motivation in us to express contrary opinions in the most voluble French we could produce. One example remains with me. "I love impressionist art," he announced. "In a book in the Public Library I come across a reproduction of a lesser known Pissarro. This is a great painting, really one of Pissarro's best! I just love it. Yet here it is, shut away in a book that is, quite obviously, rarely borrowed out. No one looks at it! Should I leave it there, neglected and unappreciated, closed away for years, or should I take a knife and cut it out, so that I can frame it and enjoy it every day. It was painted to be appreciated. Surely I, who really care for it, have a right, even a duty, to liberate this painting and place it where it can be constantly enjoyed in the light of day. Now what do you think I should do?" Naturally we young Australians, brought up with undisputed ideas of right and wrong, were scandalized at such unorthodox sentiments coming from an apparently responsible adult and we immediately leapt into the fray. Words and fur were soon flying. Goal of the conversation tutorial achieved.

Another Karagheusian mystery was a big box in his office. Painted black, it had the exotic words "Consulate for Salvador" in bold white letters on one side. In Australia in 1936 few people had had any contact with Central America and we had to think hard to even remember where El Salvador was. Was he or was he not consul for this mysterious little country and why? Or was this another of Kara's little jokes? He later explained, on being questioned, that there was certainly very little call for his consular services. However, his consular status ensured that he would be invited, along with other members of the Consular Corps, to any garden parties or receptions to celebrate national days or to meet visiting dignitaries. This seemed typical of Kara's general modus operandi.

Kara loved his students. I was able to observe this side of him in action in his kindness to my visually impaired friend Phyllis, to whom he frequently gave special tutoring in his office to help her overcome obstacles that might arise because of her lack of sight. She had a regular visiting reader, but one to whom texts in French were something of a challenge. When Kara retired, he returned to Paris, where he kept open house for any passing Australian students of the two thousand whom he had taught and never forgotten. "Chisholm-bred" he called us and we were proud of the appellation. Young Australians like to travel, as I call it, at "ground level" (that is, in the most inexpensive way conceivable) and Kara regularly had former students in their sleeping bags on the floor of his Paris apartment, recuperating from their travels and eating whatever they could find in his larder. One day, about twenty years after I had taken his classes, I was in Paris on my way to the Orangerie Museum to see the Impressionists, when I met Kara in the street. "Miss Rivers!" he cried joyfully. "No!" he insisted. "No Orangerie this time. I must show you *my* Paris!" With his usual generosity, he took me under his wing for two days, showing me less known areas of Paris and wining and dining me in Armenian restaurants. When I later sent him a postcard of thanks, I put under my signature "1/2000," knowing he would be thrilled by the allusion. What a preparation knowing Kara was for living in later years in Watertown, Massachusetts, one of the most Armenian towns in the United States.

Chizzy had an equally long memory and warm affection for his students. At one time when I was in London, I walked onto the platform of a station of the Underground and saw, just in front of me, the unmistakable figure of Professor Chisholm. Thinking to reintroduce myself as a former student, I tapped him on the arm and said: "Professor Chisholm." At this, he turned round with a happy smile and, without hesitation, cried: "Ah! Miss Rivers!" At that stage

I had not seen him, except for the most casual contact, for nearly twenty years. Along with many others, I was delighted later to be able to contribute to the cost of an oil painting to memorialize him in the Foreign Languages Building, constructed after my time at Melbourne University.

Medieval French literature (*Aucussin et Nicolette*, not surprisingly) brought us under the spell of Professor J. G. Cornell, whom we loved, not only because he was an excellent and caring teacher, but also because he was very handsome and courteous and spoke such beautiful French. Unfortunately, he left us at the end of our second year to take charge of the French Department at the University of Adelaide. His successor was much more boring, despite the exciting literature of the sixteenth century he had to deal with, notably Rabelais and Montaigne. It was the latter course that precipitated my next setback.

On Saturday mornings Mr Seel taught us phonetics in three-hour sessions. He was a part-time lecturer who was rumored to be a lawyer the rest of the week. A dissipated-looking man, he had bags under his eyes and a weary look as though he were recovering from a night out on the town. His clothes were always baggy and rumpled. Saturday morning was not his best time for teaching, because he had his mind already on the racehorses on which he would be betting in the afternoon. His large field glasses would be sitting prominently in front of him on the table as he lectured. At the stroke of twelve, he would grab them and his overcoat and dash out the door on his way to the real business of his Saturdays. On one occasion, just before he left, I presented him with a dilemma. As a very innocent seventeen-year-old, I had come across, in the novel I was preparing for a literature class, an expression that I could not find in the dictionary, except in its constituent parts. (I later learned to be wary of French expressions not in the dictionary.) It was, I remember, *fille de ruelle* . "Girl" and "lane" were recognizable, but what on earth could it mean? So I took it to Mr Seel, who after all was a native speaker of French, and asked him what it meant. I think he thought I was playing games with him. Looking at me suspiciously, he asked incredulously: "You really don't know what that means?" "No," I replied quite honestly, at which he turned quickly away with the words: "If you don't know what it means, I'm not the one to tell you!" Hardly informative, but a comprehensible reaction at the time.

Jay Wold and I were the only students committed to the Pure French Honours track. Jay's background was very different from mine, in that he came from an immigrant family from central Europe, whose members spoke five languages fluently and used languages other than English at home. I always felt that this gave him an advantage over me. I came from a background where no one in my immediate family circle had ever learned another language or used one in daily life. Even Auntie Tilly and Uncle Alf Lehmann used their second-generation bilingual German very little and then mostly in exasperation. However, I plugged along, seeking every opportunity to learn more. Like me, Jay was from a state high school, University High School (UHS). He also found, I suppose, that he was not easily accepted into the social circles of the private school students, despite the prestige of UHS.

Jay and I soon made friends with two other students of French, who were determined to develop their knowledge of French language and culture to the highest level: Bill Gardner Davies and a Chinese Australian, Violet Young. The four of us formed a group anxious to seize every opportunity to improve our spoken French through constant practice. What better way than to attend the meetings of the Alliance Française? Bill was so deeply devoted to the French language that he refused to use any other medium of expression, even with his family who didn't speak French, or so he told me. Whenever I met him around the university, he would speak only French. Sharing his enthusiasm, I reciprocated. We soon discovered that the Alliance Française, as well as producing French plays from time to time and arranging musical evenings and lectures in French, organized *causeries* (or conversational circles) every Thursday afternoon, where local French speakers would give up their time to talk with learners like ourselves. These we never missed. The President of the Alliance Française at the time was Madame Albertine Gay, the wife of a Swiss who imported watches. She was very warm, welcoming, and friendly. Very much the life and inspiration of the gatherings, she soon made us feel very much at ease in this conversational setting. Our little foursome so much enjoyed talking in French that, after a *causerie* or a monthly meeting of the Alliance Française, we would often stand on a street corner, sometimes for a full hour, continuing a furious discussion and reluctant to break up and go home.

Another regular French-speaking participant in the *causeries* was Monsieur Fraillon, a retired railway man who had been awarded the Croix de Guerre in the First World War. A man of deep culture, over a long period he took a particular interest in my progress with the language, even inviting me to visit him in his home so that he could give me further help. A French Protestant, he first invited me with Violet and Jay to read the Bible in French on Sunday afternoons. Here we met in a room with walls covered from floor to ceiling with shelves of books. This was an eye-opening experience for me with my modest background. On one visit he even gave me two precious books from his shelves, one recounting De Beauvoir's voyages around Australia in the nineteenth century and the other a copy of Chateaubriand's *Histoire du Christianisme* in its heavy original binding. A strong believer in the way handwriting reveals character, he once analyzed my handwriting. He also analyzed the handwriting of Flaubert, when I was exploring the possibility of writing a thesis on that writer. From his analysis he decided Flaubert was not the type of author I should be studying (for my moral health, I presume).

A significant part of my final year was spent on my Honours thesis on André Gide, whose radical ideas on personal morality threw me into a whole new world of thinking. This was my first chance to develop on my own initiative a larger piece of research than the usual course paper. Because Gide was still writing at the time, the Melbourne University Library did not have all of his latest works. It made me feel very important when the Library had to send to France for books just so that I could complete my undergraduate thesis. Altogether, then, I was not at all disappointed with my choice of major studies and derived much more than knowledge of French language and literature from my three years of study.

Being very young for my class (only sixteen when I began), I had the distinct impression of having to work much harder in order to show my real abilities than those who were more mature. I certainly found quite soon that I had had few life experiences and little cultural preparation to help me understand the subtext of French literary works and their place in the European intellectual tradition. To meet this challenge, I filled in on my own, as best I could, the gaps in my knowledge of philosophy and cultural history, all of which made my education richer and established firmer foundations for my future autonomous study and scholarly work.

English Literature, my Second Love

I chose English literature as my two-year minor study. Here I experienced some of the worst teaching of my university career, specifically in the large first-year literature lecture for all Pass and Honours students, where a very pleasant female lecturer, who was a completely incompetent teacher, utterly bored all comers. Of course, the French Department could hardly boast of its own program when one remembers those incredible, year-long, literature translation sessions. Fortunately, in the second year, we attended lectures given by the professor who headed the English Department. A lively lecturer, his one weakness was inflicting on his young captive audience what would now be considered "politically incorrect" expressions of his personal anti-religious and male chauvinist opinions. The second-year Honours seminar, for which we read all of Shakespeare's plays and sonnets, was much more valuable. The lecturer was Mr Mack, a specialist in drama, who was noted for his scathing reviews of theatrical performances. We also experienced his sharp tongue. Nevertheless, I consider one such session to have had a most important influence on my writing. I wrote a paper for Mr Mack, the subject of which I do not remember. I do remember, however, the session when he returned the papers. Conscious that I had to write an "introduction," I had tried in my inexperienced way to impress the reader in what must have been very florid prose. Mr Mack took up my paper and tore the introduction to shreds (metaphorically) before the whole class as pretentious verbiage, which, while sounding impressive, really did not say anything that warranted its writing. I could have fallen through the floor, but I learned a very good lesson. I am now very careful to study my writing to see that I am really saying something and not just blowing hot air. Even as I write this page, I can feel Mr Mack peering over my shoulder in a very salutary way.

My last experience in the English Department was attending a seminar on Chaucer by an Australian poet of some reputation. As Honours students in French, Jay and I were permitted to audit this special literature course for the Pure English Honours students and, as avid learners, we seized the opportunity. Unfortunately, the highly respected poet never arrived on time and it was soon apparent that she put very little effort into preparing her lectures. Moreover, she was far too bound by the text and lost in labored detail to be able to elaborate extempore and still keep her students awake. The lecture was scheduled for Saturday mornings and one by one the Pure English Honours students assessed its worth and ceased to appear in the classroom. Finally the only two students in the room were Jay and I, both auditors from Pure French. We both felt sorry for her and hated the idea that one morning she would come into the room to find no students awaiting her. We continued to provide her only audience till the end of the year. Looking back, I wonder if she would not have preferred to find the room empty, so that she could recuperate time to devote to her own interests. From my point of view anything I could learn was grist to my mill, even if I had to suffer extreme boredom to extract the few grains of wisdom from hours of attendance. Interestingly enough, my notes on English literature texts from Miss Egan's class at MacRob were still useful to me in my second year at the university, particularly the notes on Chaucer and Shakespeare. This reinforced my conviction that I had indeed received a very solid educational preparation at high school. Apart from the excellent teaching we had experienced, we had also learned how to use libraries for reference in establishing a knowledge base and were well prepared for autonomous research for writing papers or preparing for examinations.

Educational Trauma Eight.

For my final examinations for my Honours degree, I had worked very hard reviewing all my courses and was well prepared to answer any questions that might be asked. Unfortunately, I knew too much. In essay-type exams, it was customary to set six questions to be answered in a rigidly observed three hours. With timed exams, it is essential to organize one's time very carefully; this I knew full well and I have frequently preached it to my own students. Personally I see no virtue, however, in rigidly timing an examination, if one is hoping to find out what a diverse group of students, who think and write at different speeds, really knows. In the exam on 16th Century French

Language and Literature, I found the questions on French language so interesting that I wrote on them exhaustively and this took up two and a quarter hours of my three-hour allotment. I obviously could not do justice to the literature section in three-quarters of an hour. As a consequence I received second-class honours for this paper. Had it not been timed, I would probably have received a first. Since this final examination was the only assessment in the subject for the year, there was nothing with which to compare my grade. This ruined my chances for a First Class Honours degree and I had to settle for a Two A, or higher Second.

From this unfortunate experience I learned an important lesson for my own career as an instructor. As a consequence, I never give timed exams. Some students can complete a traditional three-hour essay-type examination in less than three hours; others may require four. What point is there in assuming that all students can put down on paper their accumulated knowledge in exactly the same number of minutes? The aim of the examination should be to assess students according to what they know, not just on their writing speed. A timed system favors the fastest writers and sometimes those who have the ability to write attractively, while burying in extensive verbiage their disregard for details and alternatives or their shallow grasp of the topic. If the option of working at one's own pace in an untimed exam is open to all, this is a perfectly equitable system. In my experience the slower, and often more meticulous, writers rarely need more than twenty minutes or half-an-hour of extra time, sometimes only a few minutes, to make their points clear. Without pressure to finish exactly as the hour strikes, all can demonstrate the extent of their knowledge. With this system students feel more relaxed about examinations, which, because of their uncertainties, are always somewhat nerve-wracking. The same rationale applies equally to multiple-choice tests, in which, with rigid time limits, one is testing reading speed and a temperamental willingness to gamble on quick guesses, rather than taking the time to make decisions based on actual knowledge. After all, with four choices, even random guessing would produce about twenty-five per cent of correct answers, so why not just guess?

Apart from taking a relaxed approach to timing, many examiners now prefer to distribute for advance preparation a list of questions, only some of which will be asked at the examination. As students prepare the questions they find they provide a framework for guided study. This was the system adopted, as early as 1949 at the University of Lille, by Monsieur Antoine Adam, the well-known seventeenth-century specialist. Other instructors prefer to distribute take-home exams, which require more thoughtful judgments and organization, to be completed at the student's own pace. Questions asked can then be much more demanding. These various possibilities counteract the effect on students' results of hastily prepared questions of which examiners may not have realized all the ramifications nor the amount of time required to do them justice.

When we came to our final exams, Jay carried off the First Class Honours and the prizes that would enable him to study in France and these he had, of course, earned through diligence and concentration. At that point I seemed to see my own possibilities of studying in France fly out the window. Determinedly, however, I tucked such long-term dreams away in the dark recesses of my memory for future realization. By this time Jay had worked out the easiest way to complete requirements with the least possible effort. In the end he wrote his undergraduate Honours thesis, his Master of Arts thesis, and eventually his thesis for his Doctorat d'Université in Paris (a degree mostly completed by foreigners at that time), all on one fifteenth-century poet. He explained to me that he had deliberately chosen this poet as his long-term research project, not for the scholarly attraction of his work, but because his entire production consisted of thirty pages of poems. He tried to persuade me of the advantages of this kind of strategy, but I was always more anxious to extend the bounds of my knowledge, and I selected authors, not for their brevity, but for their intrinsic interest and their potential for leading me along unknown paths.

At the end of my studies for the Bachelor of Arts with Honours, my sponsor, through Mr Lightfoot, gave me the fee for graduation — ten pounds at the time — for which I was most grateful. My family, particularly Mother, was very proud to see me in my black gown with the blue-lined hood of the Faculty of Arts. I was the only university graduate in Mother's family apart from my engineer uncle, her brother Alf, who had been one of Mater's favorites. For Mother this validated her own line as equal to those of her more favored brothers and sisters. It was at this graduation, where the

209

Bachelor's degree candidates were capless and the Master's candidates were distinguished by their mortarboards, that I decided that, come hell or high water, I too would eventually graduate with a mortarboard. This seemingly minor distinction reinforced my determination to continue my studies to the Master's degree somehow or other and eventually study in France, although I did not know how. I was now nineteen.

Learning to Teach

The most pressing issue on graduating was to prepare myself to earn my living. Although an Arts degree develops one's intellectual powers and helps one mature, its benefits are not obviously vocational. Since my contractual agreement with the Education Department to enter high school teaching still held, even though the expenses of my studies continued to be covered by my Free Place, I now undertook under their auspices my graduate teacher-training year, the Diploma of Education (Dip Ed).

My interest in educational questions had been stimulated and confirmed as early as 1937 by a big event in Melbourne: an international New Education Fellowship (NEF) conference. To our delight this conference brought to our campus such well-known American progressive educators as I. L. Kandel and Harold Rugg of Teachers College, Columbia University, and British leaders like Sir Cyril Norwood of St John's College, Oxford, Beatrice Ensor (the Founder and President of the NEF), and Susan Isaacs, the child psychologist at the Institute of Education at London University. Other scholars came from Japan, Denmark, Finland, Switzerland, and South Africa, among others. For us, in our isolated island-continent, this conference brought riches beyond our imagining, and the stimulating presentations of these committed leaders confirmed the enthusiasm of local educationalists for student-centered education. As Beatrice Ensor summed it up, "We must encourage the primary function of education as opportunity for the growth of the individual and the development in him [or her] of qualities of character."[56] The Conference attracted nearly 9,000 new members to the NEF and many thousands of others attended single lectures. As the biggest educational gathering Australia had ever seen, it gave a tremendous boost to our own educational ideals of a "fair go" for all students.

Having attended the Conference and listened intently to the message of its lectures, I was well prepared for the kinds of approaches that were presented to us in our Dip Ed classes.

Prior to the beginning of lectures in the Faculty of Education in 1939, I was assigned by the Education Department to observe and do some supervised teaching for three weeks in the eighth grade of an elementary school in Errol Street, North Melbourne, not far from the University. The teacher in charge of the class was extremely conscientious in his supervision, perhaps I should say excessively so. When I taught my first class for him, he sat at the back of the room with the lesson plan I had written in my criticism book open before him. Throughout the lesson he wrote extensively in my book, which I found rather disconcerting. Although I was inexperienced, it seemed to me that the lesson was going reasonably well. At the end of the class came the moment for the supervising teacher to discuss his evaluation of my performance with me. I was horrified to see that he had written a full three pages of criticism, which he went through detail by excruciating detail. So far, so good. Having come to the end of these three pages, he smiled encouragingly and said; "Now, I didn't want your professor to get the impression that the lesson was a really bad one, so I didn't write everything in the book. Here, however, are the other things I noticed which you will need to work on." Whereupon he produced several more legal-sized sheets of paper, covered with close, neat writing; these he also discussed with me item by item. Naturally, I was most discouraged to think I could have made so many errors in teaching in just one forty-minute period. How would I ever learn to teach? I wondered.

I have kept this incident in mind as I have observed and supervised trainee teachers over the years. Conscious of the fragile egos of young teachers facing their first classes, I have always tried to be as encouraging as possible, pointing out no more than two or three important aspects of their teaching that should concern them immediately. It is much more likely that new teachers will be able to improve in two or three ways, while they are concentrating on teaching their next lesson, rather than having to sort out from a deluge of criticism what they should attack first. I usually begin my discussion of the classes I have observed by asking the young teachers how they themselves feel about their performance. I have found that teacher trainees can usually identify the important weaknesses in their teaching in such self-comment. This approach encourages them to ask about areas where they feel they need the most help. I then commend them on the successful aspects of the class, adding a few comments of my own on areas for improvement. We finish them with a discussion of any questions they might like to pursue. Students will remember self-generated evaluation much more than a mass of bewildering suggestions from someone whose teaching style may be quite different from their own

The Professor in charge of the Faculty of Education was a jovial man who was very interesting to listen to. We soon found out that he had been to the United States, where by some strange quirk of destiny he had been made a blood brother of the Blackfoot Indians. This story was incorporated into his lectures year after year. Although he was a very amusing lecturer and raconteur, I discovered, on reading my notes, that there was not a great deal of substance in what he had told us. His lectures, however, stimulated our motivation to read about various educational theories and the institutions in which these ideas had been worked out in practice. The assignment system of the Dalton School in New York, where students worked individually or in groups on discovering knowledge through resource centers, with teacher guidance only as they felt the need, was very much under discussion at the time, as was A. S. Neill's "free discipline" approach at the Summerhill School in England. We enjoyed reading about Neill's learner-centered ideas in his entertaining Dominie books, where he recounted experiences with students in his early years as a rural schoolteacher in Scotland. Through our course readings we imbibed many of the progressive education ideas of John Dewey and, to my delight, we used as one of our textbooks the report of the 1937 NEF Conference.

In my Dip Ed year I studied the history of education, comparative education, educational psychology, general classroom practice and management, and the specific methodologies of the three subjects I would be called upon to teach — French, English, and Latin. Those of us contracted to the Education Department had also to learn how to teach physical education and various sports (in my case, hockey and swimming), since we would be expected to carry our share of teaching in these areas. On Saturday mornings we also had a special session on Blackboard Writing, which we found rather hilarious and reminiscent of primary school. An attempt was made to "correct" our Australian accents by a lecturer in Voice Production.

Interspersed with lectures were periods for observation of demonstration classes in our teaching subjects. These were frequently at UHS, but we also visited outstanding educational programs in the Melbourne area, including the progresssive education system at the Melbourne Church of England Girls' Grammar School (MCEGGS) where Miss Dorothy Ross, a local leader in the NEF, was working out the practical applications of many of its principles. Supervised student teaching took us off campus for several two-week periods in selected schools. Later we spent a six-week period in one school, where we not only observed specific classes but were given full responsibility for some extended segments under the supervision of the class teacher.

The formative influence on my career as a language teacher was Mr Wilfred Frederick (Freddy, of course), a handsome, fair-haired man, with a charming manner, a great sense of humor, tremendous enthusiasm for lively modern-language teaching, and a sincere interest in all his students. He inducted us into a modified form of direct method teaching, which involved maximum use of the new language in class with resort to the native language when a brief grammatical explanation or translation of an abstract concept would save class time. Freddy believed strongly in sensitizing students early to the new sound system through an oral beginning, during which the International Phonetic Alphabet (IPA) provided the only graphic representation. He emphasized active use of the language by students and teacher in communicative exchanges on classroom topics.

On looking back at my methods course notes, I find that in 1939 Mr Frederick placed the reading objective first, as being most appropriate for our isolated Australian situation. His approach to reading, however, was active and oral, so that students learned to think in the language, rather than translating. Reading of the text began with echo and chorus reading, with running commentary by the teacher in the language and vigorous discussion of the content. This prepared students for silent reading, skimming texts to find details and much individual out-of-class reading. Second in order of objectives he placed "understanding" (now usually called listening comprehension),

213

then speaking, and last writing (which was writing down what one could say). He advocated a carefully integrated syllabus on the foreign culture, which would begin in the first year and develop over the six-year high school language experience. He introduced us to the use of gramophone records of native speech — the newest aid at the time. Our term assignment, apart from short papers, was to start immediately collecting in a book, for later class use, as many ideas, bits and pieces of realia, and short texts as we could find, thus establishing a habit of keeping authentic materials in an accessible place. I found my own book very helpful during my early years of teaching.

With enthusiasm and admiration, we watched Freddy's own teaching at UHS, where I also spent one of my shorter student-teaching periods. Freddy certainly practiced what he preached. When he came to see our inexperienced, amateurish classes, he wrote very helpful evaluation notes, with many suggestions for activities and techniques for making them more interesting and effective. It is a pleasure to reread these lengthy commentaries, which are as fresh and full of useful ideas today as they were in 1939. It is not surprising that one of our prescribed reading texts was Harold Palmer's *The Principles of Language-Study*.[57] It was from Mr Frederick that Miss Meldrum at EHS and many other Melbourne language teachers at the time had learned their active classroom methods.

Freddy made us believe that we could do anything in a language classroom — stand on our heads, sit on top of the piano, mime meanings of words, or sing more or less in tune. If we did not feel foolish, he told us, our students would not find it odd either. He also taught us that a good teacher never sits down, a dictum to which I adhere to this day (except for small seminars), often to the amazement of my overseas students. It certainly results in a quite different classroom perspective and control than does the sedentary position.

Of course, we soon fell under Freddy's spell. As he had taught us, we drew pictures and performed actions as dramatically as possible to convey meaning, we encouraged our pupils to make picture dictionaries without native-language glosses and we sang French songs to brighten the language learning. We used the language as much as possible in class. We began with a purely oral period of at least a month, using phonetic symbols as a memory aid. Since developing an ear for the sounds and rhythms of the language from the beginning was considered of paramount importance, we encouraged students in the production of pure vowel sounds (monothongs) by singing them up and down the scale. During this oral period, we taught without a textbook, concentrating on the performance of actions in the classroom, which, in the Gouin tradition,[58] students described in the language as they performed them. The vocabulary they learned sprang out of their discussions of their immediate environment or scenes in large wall pictures that depicted everyday life in France. We encouraged our language learners to do much individual, out-of-class reading of specially written texts, with frequency-controlled vocabulary for various levels of difficulty, so that students progressed at their own pace to more difficult reading. On one occasion the red-headed instructor in methods of teaching English, having seen me teach a French class in Freddy's style, told me he was waiting to see me teach English with as much verve as I did French. Even the Latin teacher who supervised my teaching practice in that language believed that "speaking Latin should become as natural as breathing," as it certainly was in Europe for many centuries.

When I published my third book, *Speaking in Many Tongues: Essays in Foreign-Language Teaching* (Newbury House, 1972), I dedicated it enigmatically to L. B. R., W. H. F., and D. J. R. L. B. R. was, of course, my sister Linda; and D. J. R. was D. J. Ross, the well-known Headmistress of the MCEGGS, of whom more will be written later. Who else could W. H. F. be but Freddy himself, who had inspired me to make language teaching in the active mode the central focus of my career. When I delivered a copy of the book to him personally, he exclaimed, with self-deprecatory jocularity: "Wilga, you are my only fan!"

One of Mr Frederick's most enthusiastic disciples was Mr Manuel Gelman, who later became a formative leader in the Modern Language Teachers' Association of Victoria (MLTAV). Mr Gelman took over the foreign language methods teaching and the supervision of teacher training pactice at Melbourne University after Mr Frederick moved on, to apply his educational ideas as Headmaster of one of Melbourne's leading boys' public schools,[59] Wesley College. From this position Freddy returned to Melbourne University, at a later date, to take charge of the School of Education. When I was doing my Dip.Ed., Mr Gelman, then at Coburg High School, was one of the teachers whose classes we observed. I later did my six-week student teaching segment with him at that school. With both Freddy and Manny as my exemplars, I could not but absorb the most active of teaching techniques and the enthusiasm I developed carried me over into my first cold bath of full-time teaching at Kerang in 1940.

Jay was doing his Diploma of Education too, with a view to teaching, but he seemed to lack a certain something that makes a good teacher. He told me that, when he was out in schools during his teaching practice sessions, the boys in his classes would throw paper darts at him and that he could see their point of view. When final results came out, he had failed in Practical Teaching, which precluded him from obtaining a teaching position with the Education Department at the end of the year. Miss Alice Hoy, the student adviser, always called Shippa, because of the A.Hoy on her door, asked him to come to see her to discuss his results. To console him, she told him that a certain university lecturer in the English Department, Miss Janus, had also failed in Practical Teaching. Jay came to me to ask what I thought of Miss Janus's teaching. Not knowing the context of his question, I responded quickly: "Janus? She was the worst lecturer I ever had!" "I thought there was a catch to it somewhere," Jay replied glumly.

Since the war had begun by this time, Jay, to avoid as he told me the physicality of army life and the violence of fighting, took the route of student deferment. First he wrote his Master's thesis in French, but the war continued. Next he began a Bachelor of Laws degree, which took him another three years, and then he continued on with a Master of Laws. After all these years, the war being over, he was able to prepare to leave for France on his earlier scholarship. Because the war had begun the very year we graduated and the normalization of regular sea transport to Europe at the end of the war was very slow, Jay was not able to take up his studies in France much earlier than I did (that is, in 1949), despite the fact that I had had to save every penny of my fare myself and find out for myself how to get work to support me during my studies abroad. Ironically Jay, with all the financial help he received from prizes and grants to continue with his studies, never made any academic or scholarly contributions

216

in later life. He never held a teaching position nor did he publish the results of any research. Instead, he settled for a routine bureaucratic post in a state government department, rising in rank through seniority so that eventually he had the right to the desk by the window, where he could enjoy the afternoon sunshine. In 1938 it must have seemed obvious to our professors that, of the two of us, the man would be the one to profit most from study abroad, and he would certainly seem the most likely to enter upon an academic career.

By this time Linda had been able to attend daytime university classes for a year. Throughout her student teaching and her year at Primary Teachers' College, she had taken undergraduate courses at night. At Teachers College she was given a second year to study full-time in the Faculty of Arts, with the assistance of one of the newly instituted student loans. Repaying this loan took her many years on a young female teacher's salary. The four subjects she completed during this full year of study shortened by several years the period for completion of her degree at night. Altogether her Bachelor of Arts studies took her seven years of tenacious perseverance. Once she had completed the degree, however, she was able to move from primary to secondary teaching.

Extra-Curricular Interests

Apart from studies, a great deal of my time at Melbourne University was spent with my friends in the Evangelical Union (EU). We arranged public lectures each week by Christian leaders, which launched me on another of my life's activities — writing. I was deputed to write reports on these lectures for the student newspaper, *Farrago*, and I tried to make them interesting to students not generally attracted by such topics. We had informative and thought-provoking Bible Studies, led by the principal of an institute for biblical studies. We also attended regular prayer meetings. I also continued my weekly bike trips to Coburg High School for the meetings of the Christian Fellowship I had established, which had attracted some very enthusiastic members. In the egalitarian atmosphere of the EU we formed a close-knit fellowship of students from different backgrounds. We sometimes spent a few days together in fellowship camps and I would bike across the city at night to go to parties in their homes in the eastern suburbs. This group gave me a center where I could be myself and feel appreciated.

In my awkward adolescent years this accepting fellowship was a boon to me. Like my mother I had always had a shy streak, hidden under social affability. I suffered acutely from insecurities as to what people thought of me. I would indulge in periods of what I called "glooming." If I felt I had made a faux pas or said something a little out of place at a social gathering I would suffer from intense mortification, forgetting all the enjoyable aspects of the evening. Growing up in our uncomplicated and inward-looking home circle, I had had little training or experience in how to behave on social occasions with a group of strangers. I had to learn by watching others and seeing how they behaved; this learning was frequently post hoc, hence the mortification. I have always hated pushing myself forward, as I have frequently had to do, introducing myself and explaining my legitimate presence. Later, as a one of the few females at university gatherings, I often had to make it clear that I was a professor, and not a faculty wife or an administrative assistant, in order to enter into professional discussion with male colleagues. This was even more difficult in the gender-divided Australian society of my early professional life, where men tended to talk to each other on one side of the room and women on the other.

Some of my EU and SCM friends became interested in the Oxford Group (later Moral Rearmament — MRA) and accepted its tenets of the four absolutes by which they should conduct their lives: — absolute purity, absolute unselfishness, absolute honesty, and absolute love. It is a question worth discussing as to whether absolute love is compatible with absolute honesty. I suffered further mortification through friends in this group, who felt they should tell me the truth about how they felt about me. I well remember one such experience. I was just getting into a train, when a well-meaning older student, whom I greatly admired, felt that in absolute honesty she should tell me that she had never really liked me. I have often wondered what good this true confession accomplished, except to make me feel even more insecure.

It was through the EU that I attended my first inter-university, interstate conference. I had rarely traveled before, even within Victoria (except for day trips into the mountains close to Melbourne) and never to another state. Nor would it have been possible for me to do so on this occasion had it not been for the generosity of a Christian doctor, who was a generous sponsor of our activities. It was he who paid my expenses to attend a conference at Katoomba, in the Blue Mountains, where we hiked and climbed, in awe of the magnificent scenery. Here I met fellow students from every state in Australia and enjoyed many in-depth discussions. It was a most exciting time, while being spiritually and intellectually enriching.

There was trauma too. In my last year at the University, Victoria had some of the worst bushfires in its history. In January 1939, fires were raging throughout the Dandenongs and the air in the city was hot and full of the smell of acrid smoke. Seventy-one people died in the flames. The worst day of the fires has ever since been referred to in Victoria as Black Friday (January 13th). Some of my EU friends were involved in a Crusader camp for private school boys and, when the campsite was threatened, the boys and their leaders had to take refuge in a creek while the bushfires raged around and over them. Fortunately none of them was injured, but the same year one of our most popular members was burned to death at his family's vacation home in the hills, although not in a bushfire. Apparently he had knocked over a lamp when he fell asleep over his books in a makeshift room which had been added to the house for his convenience. This came shockingly close to home.

Initiation to the World of Work

Of necessity, I had to find work whenever possible in order to contribute anything I could to the family coffers. In Victoria, at the time, it was difficult for a student to find work during the year. Labor laws to protect working men and women from competition with young, untrained people, who would be paid lower wages, were strictly enforced. At Christmastime, however, when the university examinations were over, there were several opportunities for casual labor — one was in the Post Office sorting the Christmas overload of cards and letters; another was as a salesperson in a shop for three weeks, to help cope with the Christmas rush. Some students also found work for a few weeks in January picking fruit. I had experience with the first two of these occupations and, when the war began, with factory work in the munitions buildings, to which we used to swim across the Maribyrnong from Rachel's place. One summer, I obtained a further few weeks of work tutoring the daughters of one of the professors.

My experiences in the post office were eye-opening. I was assigned to the registered parcel section. Since more people than needed had been taken on that year, there was only enough mail for about four hours of work during an eight-hour shift. If we exceeded the four hours, there would be nothing left for the next shift to do, so we had to work slowly to leave them enough work to justify their jobs. Yet it was strictly forbidden to read books or newspapers during our idle periods. We were supposed to spend any spare time studying the routing book, which explained the shortest routes by which to send parcels to small towns we hadn't known existed. This reading soon exhausted its potential as a time-filler, so I would read a book, with the routing manual so placed that I could draw it over my book should a supervisor appear. It was quite a surprise to see parcels labeled "Fragile" being tossed across the room from dispatcher to dispatcher, occasionally falling on the floor. I also discovered why letters are frequently "lost in the mail," at least for a few weeks. Sometimes this is due to the "stuck in the bag" phenomenon. The dispatcher would hastily shake the letters out of the bags for sorting and throw the bag aside. At times a more careful dispatcher might notice a letter that didn't slide out easily and fish it out, exclaiming: "Good Lord! I wonder how long that letter's been stuck in the bag!"

In an inner suburban Woolworth's store I learned other lessons. At that time there was in operation a "Buy Australian" campaign to discourage people from buying less expensive Japanese goods. (This was the period when the Japanese imitated European goods in cheaper versions.) A high proportion of the goods we sold at Woolworth's were Japanese made, so one of my tasks was to take the "Made in Japan" labels carefully off the goods in my section. As we were never allowed to sit down behind the counter, even when there were no customers, we had to learn to ignore fatigue. My fellow worker on the counter, a young teenager, was rather rough-hewn and every second word she uttered was an obscenity; she was, however, very good-hearted and we had many laughs together. She had never met a person like me and I had never met a person like her. She often wondered why I did not swear vigorously, as she did. In a very few days we began to recognize the local housewives, who enjoyed the companionableness of shopping in the local area. During the morning they would arrive with their hair in curlers and in the late afternoon they would pop in for something they had forgotten with nicely curled coiffures. The job was not very well paid, and I remember working from eight o'clock in the morning till ten o'clock at night on Christmas Eve — on my feet all the time as I served the rush of last-minute shoppers — all for the lordly sum of five shillings. This was equivalent to fifty cents, or about 3.5 cents an hour — a very basic wage, even in 1938 terms.

My January assignment of tutoring the daughters of a Professor in a house on Professors Row, near the University entrance (an area that has since become a hockey field), was equally disillusioning. It seems the girls had not done as well in school as their father would have liked, so he had insisted they be coached for the coming year during their vacation. This they very much resented. It soon became apparent why the girls had not done well during their school year. They showed little interest in their studies and sat silently through my teaching each morning, with their minds on the pleasures of leisure in the afternoon. After all, It was Dad's idea, not theirs. However I labored on, since the pay was somewhat better than at Woolworth's.

Continuing Community Contacts

Having sought confirmation in the Anglican Church, Linda and I became very active in the activities of St Thomas's Church in Moonee Ponds. Our minister, Rev. Hedley Raymond, was a very welcoming person and, since I had no father, I found him a very helpful surrogate. This was the period when a minister brought with him to a parish a free worker, in the person of his wife, who was expected to take a lead in the various organizations. Mrs Raymond was one of the earliest vicar's wives I knew to restrict her activities in the parish to only a small number of tasks of her own selection, instead of being at the beck and call of all. She performed these tasks very well, while conserving time to devote to her family. She did not feel obliged to wear herself out running everything and attending everything. This new, liberated approach surprised some of the congregation; consequently, there were underground murmurs of criticism from those who knew her less well. I was one of those who had the opportunity to get to know Mrs Raymond well from working closely with her and I came to admire her for her personality, her dedication, and her spirituality.

One of the tasks Mrs Raymond undertook with great love and commitment was the organization of the Sunday School Kindergarten, which in those days consisted of over a hundred young children from about five to seven years of age. For this onerous task, Mrs Raymond had the assistance of ten helpers, of whom I was one. We soon came to appreciate her gifts as a teacher of young children, her ability to train teachers, and her solid knowledge of the latest approaches to child learning. Every Monday evening she conducted a preparation session for her helpers. Here she taught us child psychology, according to the theories of Susan Isaacs, who was recognized as the leading child psychologist at the time. She would then explain the spiritual message of the lesson for the following Sunday, as set out in the Diocesan Sunday School guide, *The Trowel,* and outline the activities in which we would engage the children after the spiritual devotions and the telling of the week's story. Mrs Raymond often did the story telling herself, keeping her little listeners enthralled, but we also had the opportunity to practice this art, which has been useful to me on many occasions. At the end of our Monday training sessions we would make posters of songs or pictures for children to color in, or we would put together craft materials for sand tray constructions or the making of models related to the week's lesson. Through these working sessions we learned a great deal about the interests of young children and how to involve them in learning through doing. Naturally, when Sunday arrived, everything would be thoroughly prepared and the session, with the hundred odd effervescent and enthusiastic youngsters, would go smoothly and enjoyably. This was also a lesson in thoughtful organization and attention to detail. For three years I profited from this training. When Mrs Raymond took a weekend each Easter season to visit her family in Tasmania, I would have the privilege and the valuable experience of taking over the Monday preparation and the Sunday session in her place. Here again, I was being given opportunities to develop useful life skills at the relatively early age of seventeen.

Through my St Thomas's contacts, I also learned to appreciate people of very different intellectual and physical capacities. One of my close friends had a cleft palate, which was much more common in those days when treatment of such problems was less advanced. Another, with whom I frequently walked home from church, was at borderline level in intellectual functioning, but she had a warm heart and a great capacity for friendship. Yet another suffered from severe cerebral palsy, with great limitations on the use of his limbs and vocal chords. He became a skilful gardener and remained a devoted member of St Thomas's Church all his life. These friends helped me to appreciate the very varied contributions human beings bring to community life and to our mutual experience of social wellbeing.

We learned at St Thomas's that prayer is like breathing. One can pray anywhere, not just in sacred places. Consequently Linda and I were often to be found, after Friday night late-closing time, on our knees praying among broken or partially repaired umbrellas in the Puckle Street shop of Miss Noel, a single businesswoman whose lifelong interest was supporting missionaries, both spiritually and financially. Outside, young people would be promenading in the busy street and the Salvation Army, with their drums, trumpets, and tambourines, would be singing hymns and proclaiming through megaphones their message of personal salvation. Inside we were learning to take time out from the busy rush and commerce of crowds to find time for reflection and developing serenity of soul.

During my University years I was also developing new networks of friends through the Church Missionary Society League of Youth. This group of dedicated Christian young people met frequently. There were meetings in various suburban areas, with Bible studies and lectures by missionaries on leave, who kept us up-to-date on the needs of people in developing countries. From time to time we united in citywide rallies. In January we enjoyed attending the League of Youth camp at the Upwey Convention in the Dandenongs, where we slept on hard camp stretchers in fairly primitive housing, eating under a big tent where we kept the innumerable small bush flies at bay with switches of eucalyptus leaves. Once we had become accustomed to stoically enduring the many mosquito bites and the mass-produced meals of scrambled eggs, fried tomatoes, and boiled sausages, we had lots of fun. As well as attending the lectures and

Bible studies in the open-sided convention hall, we enjoyed walks in the bush and many long talks with like-minded young people. The chairman of the convention, Dr Kay, was an elderly man who had very strict ideas on the way young people should behave and dress. Much of this we took with a grain of salt, especially his nineteenth-century idea that young women should wear long-sleeved dresses in the middle of summer. He was a medical doctor, and I had personal contact with him one night when I jumped up in alarm from my stretcher with a beetle in my ear. I was rushed to Dr Kay who extracted it for me and all was well. At these summer camps I made many valuable, long-lasting friendships. When the war came in 1939, we farewelled a number of the young men in our group who had joined the Australian Armed Forces. Some of them never returned

War Shatters our Tranquillity

In my last year at the university, Mr Lightfoot decided that my mother was becoming overburdened and needed a holiday, so he gave me ten pounds to take her away for a few days. This was a great surprise to my mother who had never been on a holiday in her life. Accustomed as she was to constant work, she could not imagine what she would do if she went away. The only holidays we had experienced had been one or two weekends at my mother's brother's (Uncle Alf's) seaside house, which was next to a gasometer, the strong odor of which permeated the property constantly. Uncle Alf's house was near a sandy beach on a rocky shore. It was fun climbing around the rocks at the base of the cliffs, stopping to look intently at the marine life in the still rock pools, but when we dashed shoeless into the sea we found the rocks hiding in the shallow water sharp and cutting. It was better to get out of our depth in the water as soon as possible, so that we could swim without constantly grazing our legs against them. Fortunately our frequent experiences of swimming in the Maribyrnong, with twenty feet of water beneath us, gave us confidence for swimming well out into the waters of the bay.

With Mr Lightfoot's largesse in my pocket, I decided to take Mother to Warburton. In this beautiful mountain resort, she would be surrounded by the bush land of her youth in which she could walk and relax. After much hesitation, Mother agreed. This was at the beginning of September 1939. In late August Germany and Russia

224

had signed a non-aggression pact and the world was apprehensive. Talk of war had been in the air for some time. The final precipitating incident was when Germany invaded Poland on September 1st. On September 3rd, Great Britain and France declared war on Germany. Soon afterwards we huddled around Father's old crystal set to hear Robert Menzies, the Prime Minister of Australia, declare that, since Britain had declared war, we Australians, as members of the British Commonwealth, would likewise declare war on faraway Nazi Germany. We were well aware that land-hungry Japan, so much nearer to our shores, was also beginning to build alliances and flex its muscles, but at that time we strongly believed that British forces would come to our aid should there be any serious emergency in our region.

In a family discussion we debated what we should do in this new and threatening circumstance. Should Mother and I go off for this once-in-a-lifetime holiday at such a critical moment or should we stay home? Fortunately commonsense prevailed and I took Mother off on the train to Warburton, where, not surprisingly, a great deal of our holiday was spent listening to news reports of the rapidly evolving war situation in Europe. Warburton was, and is, a beautiful spot and our guest house was surrounded by thickly forested mountains. Mother ventured out a little into the bush, but she felt much more at home helping the guest house proprietor in the kitchen. It was, nevertheless, a change of scene, with reduction in intensity of activity. For a short while, we were able to keep at bay the pressures of our daily lives.

As my last year at the University drew to a close, I waited for my teaching appointment for 1940 to be announced by the Education Department. This was a great mystery. Although we had been able to submit some preferences as to locale in advance, we knew that beginning teachers were usually sent to fill the gaps after those with longer service had received their promotions or selected transfers. Our first appointment could be anywhere in Victoria and would be announced baldly in a list in the newspaper. Meanwhile I had one more long summer vacation to enjoy among my family and friends before launching out on my teaching career.

As Linda and I had become more gregarious during our university days, Mother's shyness seemed to increase. She could

225

handle her small group and battle on, but newcomers into the circle meant further adjustments with which she could not cope. If we wanted to invite friends home, she would always try to put the visit off till "next week" "Not now. Later," she would say. We would gently insist and the fateful day would arrive. Our friends would walk in. Mother, who had spent days making sure that every speck of dust had been picked up and the house was as perfect as she could make it, would be nowhere to be seen. She would be fussing in the interior of the house on some detail of the dessert or some spot where she felt the cleaning had been less than perfect. She would not have changed out of her work clothes. Perhaps two hours after the guests had arrived, she would appear, pleasant, and smiling, serving a well-cooked meal and plying our guests with second desserts. Our friends never realized how much effort had been required on her part to "screw her courage to the sticking-point" to come out to meet them.

Mother was not perfect by any means. She tended to nag, or perhaps I should say she stuck rigidly to her viewpoint and refused to be budged by argument. At times this obstinacy made me feel I wanted to throttle her. Yet often she was intuitively right. She could be quite tempestuous (after all we were growing up during her menopausal years). At such times Father would just walk away. He hated to get involved in family rows. He would pick up his wallet, and later his walking stick, and go to visit one of his daughters. By the time he returned the tempest would be over. I soon learned my father's strategy and I also tend to withdraw and come back later to avoid violent argument, which I find emotionally wrenching.

For so long during her years alone, Mother had had to be strong against all circumstances, with no supporting figures, that it had become a mental and emotional habit. This inflexibility became more affirmed as she grew older. She could never allow doubt or uncertainty to weaken her resolve or she might go under. Even when things became easier for her, with her children now earning their way, she had to hang on to certitude in case some chasm might open beneath her feet, and this at times had disastrous effects. Her virtue of tenacity, rooted in insecurity, became unfortunately a vice as she aged, causing unhappiness for some of those closest to her

Remarkably, Mother's deep-rooted attitude that all life was sacred and every effort must be exerted to sustain it continued throughout the period of the war. She knew in her bones that life was about living, not killing and maiming. Despite all the increasingly intrusive propaganda and the buildup of "enthusiasm," she stubbornly maintained her pacifist stance to the end of the war — killing was wrong and there were no two ways about it.

7
RURAL VICTORIA
1940-46

During January 1940 I waited with some apprehension for the publication in the newspaper of the school to which I had been appointed for the coming year. This could be anywhere in Victoria, as the Department saw fit. More experienced teachers, higher on the Department roll, were usually appointed to the city schools, so I expected to do a stint in some country town. When the list was published, I scanned the fine print anxiously and found I was to go to Kerang High School. Now, where on earth was Kerang? I had heard of Terang in southwestern Victoria. Perhaps Kerang was close by? I searched in my school atlas and at last I found Kerang in the northwest of the state near the Murray River, about 180 miles from Melbourne. What kind of a place could it be? Like so many Melbournians who had been affected by the Great Depression, we did not yet own a car; for that we had to wait until the 1950s. Consequently, I had never ventured far from the city. A brief visit as a child to Lancefield, to go rabbiting with friends of Harold's and the one visit to Warburton with Mother the previous year were the sum total of my experiences at any distance from Melbourne, so this was a great adventure. Moreover, I had never lived away from my family before.

With some money Mother lent me, I was able to equip myself at Woolworth's with a few light dresses and a raincoat — the latter an essential, along with an umbrella, for a Melbourne girl. Being from the showery coast, I found it hard to believe that it rarely rained in the arid northwest plains. My constant compulsion to carry an umbrella whenever a small cloud appeared in the sky later became a source of some amusement to my Kerang acquaintances. At the end of January

228

I set off with my few belongings, not forgetting my books for study. I was still determined to write a Master of Arts thesis somehow. Flaubert had been approved as my topic and I could expect no more help or guidance while I researched and wrote it.

The journey by train to Kerang was long — six and a half hours, which usually extended to eight, since the Victorian country trains were notorious for running late. Being summertime, it was hot and dry. The steam train chugged along, belching out much cindery smoke that traveled down the train, catching in our eyes if we looked out of the open windows in search of a breath of fresh air. As it was wartime, coal was in short supply, so wood was being used and we stopped several times on the way, not just to take on water to cool the engine but also to allow the driver to chop more wood to keep it going. To confuse any enemies who might try to invade our country, the government had decreed that the names of all country towns be taken down from the railway stations and along the roadways. Despite this stricture I soon found that you could work out where you were easily enough by studying the signs on the businesses in the towns we passed through. There was always a "Kyneton Funeral Parlour" or a "Castlemaine Bakery" to clarify things. Since these trains had no restaurant cars or snack bars, the passengers soon became hungry. At certain larger country towns, notably Castlemaine and Bendigo of goldfields fame, there would be a stop of perhaps ten minutes. As the train drew in, everyone would race to the restaurant for the popular take-away food of the day: a hot meat pie in a bag with a cup of steaming tea with milk. The tea was served in cups of incredibly thick railways china and we would blow on it, or even pour it into the saucer, to cool it quickly to a drinkable temperature, before dashing back to our carriage. There we would enjoy the luscious pie, with its delicious, thick gravy seeping slowly into the brown paper bag, from which we could lick it up afterwards to prolong our pleasure.

Soon we were traveling through incredibly flat land, where the eye could see right to the horizon, which was outlined by a few very distant trees. The railway line made its way in a perfectly straight line, exactly as it had been drawn on the original map, and there were very few physical features to distinguish one part of the countryside from the next. About thirty miles from Kerang appeared what looked like a rather high pile of road metal; it was called Pyramid Hill. Later I discovered this was the nearest approximation to a hill or a mountain most of my Kerang students had ever seen. As we moved into an area of very low rainfall (fourteen inches per year on average), the air grew steadily drier and stiflingly hot. It was well over 100 degrees Fahrenheit (38 degrees Celsius). This dry heat of the arid interior was very different from the late summer humidity in Melbourne by the sea. I soon found out that temperatures in the Kerang area, with its continental climate, reached very high levels in January and February (the highest I experienced was 114 degrees Fahrenheit or 43 degrees Celsius), while winter brought biting black frosts.

What was the town of Kerang like when I finally saw it? It was an isolated town of some three thousand inhabitants. At that time the population of Australia was about six and a half million people, half of whom lived in Melbourne and Sydney. Once you left the coast and passed through the nearer arable areas, crossing the Dividing Range into the more arid plains, the small towns were widely separated. They were, however, important market centers, even though they might have only a thousand or fifteen hundred inhabitants. Kerang with its three thousand was a "big" place and a marketing and shopping center for farm folk from an extensive area around. The students at the high school came from considerable distances, often traveling for an hour or more each morning and evening in school buses. Since milking machines were not yet readily available, some would already have milked cows by hand for several hours before leaving home and could anticipate the same chore on their return. It was not surprising that some students would drop off to sleep in class as the day wore on. The students were, of course, high-spirited and riding the buses was much the same as it is today. One girl, in those early 1940s, even sued a bus driver for physical assault because he had put his hands on her shoulders to try to make her sit down in the bus, instead of running around while it was in motion. Other students rode to school on horses that could be spared from the farm. One small mite of a boy (later a nuclear scientist), came in on a big draft horse, to the amusement of the other students. Another always wore a very shapeless, countrified hat as though he were harvesting; you expected to see him sucking on a piece of straw as well.

Kerang's main competitor was Swan Hill, about forty miles to the north on the Murray River. Since there were only one or two trains a day and few private cars, going to Swan Hill and back for a day visit was quite an enterprise. We looked on it as a special trip. Our main contact with Swan Hill was for regular sports events between the two high schools, when the visitors from the bigger town usually carried off the trophies. Soon after my arrival I was, with my usual sports enthusiasm, training the girls' field hockey team, and I would insist on their running around the sports field several times each morning before school to keep in form and prepare to take on their rivals from Swan Hill.

The town of Kerang consisted of several business streets, centered in a gridiron pattern around a freestanding clock tower. This central structure was a monument to Karlie MacDonald, a young language teacher at the high school who had drowned in the Lodden River, while trying to save one of her pupils who was in difficulties during a swimming lesson. At the school, I came across a number of French textbooks with her name inscribed on them. It was very moving. The shops in the business area were built in the typical early Australian style, with corrugated iron roofs extending over the footpaths to protect shoppers from the harsh sun and the occasional shower of rain. Beyond the modest shopping area, with its one department store run by the local Hawthorne family, were residential streets with their competing churches. In very short order, one was abruptly faced with the great expanse of farmland and pasture.

The farming areas alternated between the deep green of the irrigated paddocks and the brown of the dry, unwatered land. I found a similar situation in Israel in 1981, with rich, irrigated land on one side of the road and brown, thirsty fields on the other. It was a pleasure to walk in the sunshine along the levees on either side of the irrigation channels, stopping to look at the slow turning of the wheels that measured the amount of water flowing through. Here I could also watch birds, particularly ibises, dipping their bills in the cool water. On the rare occasions when the fields beyond the levees were flooded by freak storms, rabbits were driven out of their burrows onto whatever higher ground they could find. Here they gathered so close together on small mounds that they formed a solid mass. At night if we were driving into Kerang, we would frequently see, in the beams of the headlights, the flash of white tails as innumerable rabbits scattered back to their burrows in the paddocks at the side of the road. Another danger of driving in that open country was "Kangaroos Crossing." Drivers unlucky enough to hit a frightened kangaroo or have one land on top of their car could suffer serious personal and vehicular damage.

After the 1914-18 War, the Victorian Government had distributed many blocks of land to "soldier settlers." Some of these settlers had known or learned enough about farming to be able to grow waving fields of wheat, but others had failed dismally, deserting their cleared blocks. The latter soon reverted to their original aridity, but with loosened soil. In the Kerang area, with the availability of the waters of the Lodden River, a tributary of the Murray, more were successful at this time than in the Mallee areas further to the west. There farmers clearing their blocks had found a great sale for the roots of the straggly Mallee scrub. When I was growing up, knotty, irregular Mallee roots were greatly prized for Melbourne's fireplaces. Little did we realize, as we enjoyed their warm blaze, that we were participating in the rape of the land. As the Mallee topsoil was left unprotected by this natural growth, the dry winds blew much of it away till the hard, rocky subsoil was laid bare. In Melbourne, in those years, we frequently suffered from "red rain," due to the admixture of this red soil blown south from the Mallee. Dust storms blew over Kerang too at times, darkening the sun with their clouds, silencing the birds, and leaving layers of grit on everything in the closed houses. In a letter home, on Feb. 17, 1941, I wrote: "Yesterday a dust storm came up, not just a quick one — up and over, but an all-day affair — muggy, dirty and hot as an oven." On March 29th that same year I wrote: "There was a beautiful dust storm. One of the reddest I've seen yet. The sky was absolutely lurid. We could see through the windows the dark red glow."

About five miles from Kerang there was a necklace of lakes, with gaunt skeletons of red gums standing knee-deep in the water: First Reedy Lake, Second Reedy Lake, and Third Reedy Lake they were called. These lakes were surrounded by thick lignum, a tall, straggly, almost leafless shrub, through which it was difficult to force one's way. A little further afield were Lake Charm and Duck Lake. The lakes were cool for swimming and were favorite destinations for picnics. My old bicycle, which had served me so well at Melbourne University, was soon put to use as I explored the environs of Kerang.

The great event of the year in Kerang was the opening of the duck-shooting season on the last day of February. For this, the town was crowded with duck shooters from Kerang and neighboring areas, and even from Melbourne. At midnight on the long-awaited day, all the shooters would be out on the lakes and swamps waiting for the opening shot to be fired. By four o'clock in the morning there was a continuous roar of shots, as though one were in the midst of a great battle, and this continued throughout the day. Of course, on this great day, half of the boys were away from school, out with their fathers in the swamps. Those who were in class were already tired out, having spent the early hours of the morning watching for ducks and shooting their share. This rite of slaughter has now disappeared from the calendar, but at this time Kerangites all over town looked forward to dining on roast duck. Even in our boarding house we were served duck, since some of the male boarders had gone out to the swamps in the night. In the following days bad colds and bronchitis, from wading in the lakes and sitting in class in wet clothes, spread rapidly through the school. This was a bad area in any case for upper respiratory tract infections. I once had a heavy cough and cold that lasted for three months, after which the local doctor, who was about to leave for service in the Armed Forces, gave me an experimental injection of manganese that kept me clear of colds for a good fifteen years. I was lucky he was still in Kerang when I needed him.

A Country High School

Kerang High School was a single-storied brick building that accommodated about 215 students in grades 7 through 12. At the back were playing fields and in the front were gardens cared for by the different student houses. At Kerang the houses were named for rivers: Avoca, Murray, Campaspe, and Lodden. I soon became House Mistress of Lodden and worked after school in the garden with some of the older boys who were nearly my age. I was 20 at the time and the oldest of my students was 18. We found gardening together lots of fun.

The Headmaster of Kerang High School was, of course, a man. No woman was able to become Head of a departmental coeducational high school in Victoria till the late 1960s. Kerang's Headmaster, Lieutenant-Colonel Brooke, was soon called up for wartime service with a Light Horse division. The only thing I can remember about Colonel Brooke, apart from the semantic link of our names, was that he apparently had no sense of rhythm and was noted for the fact that he had once marched a whole company around on the wrong foot. Our main administrative contact was with the Senior Mistress, Bea Gerrand, who took her mentoring role very seriously. Many were the times in my first year when I huddled over the staff room fire with her, during a shared spare period, and received unobtrusive guidance on how to take full responsibility for a class. I know I owe her a great deal.

I had brought my enthusiasm for all things French to this country area, where the students soon informed me that "The cows don't speak French, Miss!" To counteract this attitude, I wanted to make them feel from the first lesson that they could communicate in French about something of importance to them. I decided to teach them to say in French something they could try out on their mothers when they raced into the farmhouse on their return from school. Since it was still summer and the first day of school was exceedingly hot in this dry area, I taught them to say in impeccable French: *"Bonjour, maman. J'ai soif"* (Hi, Mum. I'm thirsty).

To make their contact with French culture more real and personal, I immediately tried to set up correspondence for them with actual French boys and girls of their own age. (I was still enjoying my own correspondence with Christiane and Colette.) Having no access to outside sources to arrange these exchanges, I took a map, closed my eyes, and jabbed with a pin at the map of France. My pin penetrated the name Clermont-Ferrand, a town I did not remember hearing about before. However, one town seemed as promising as another as a source of authentic contact, so I encouraged my students to write letters, which I sent off addressed vaguely to the "English teacher" at the lycée in this unknown place. Most teachers are keen for their students to establish contact with native speakers of the language they are learning, and Australia must have seemed to the recipient of my letter a rather exotic place at that time. Thanks to a prompt response, my students were soon engrossed in establishing these distant epistolary contacts. From Australia, the problem for country-to-country correspondence was, of course, the difference between the Northern and Southern Hemisphere school years. Even when I would set the operation in motion at the very beginning of the Victorian academic year, that is, in February, the students would just be beginning to set up a relationship when the European schools closed for the summer. The most enthusiastic of the French students would continue to write during the northern summer, but not all, to the disappointment of my Australian students, fully engaged at that time in the activities of their school year. Furthermore, since costs for the recently established airmail to Europe were prohibitive for fat letters packed with photographs, we had to depend on irregular ship schedules, published in the newspapers. One-way delivery could take from six to eight weeks and a response might require several months. But what excitement it was for the students when the replies arrived! They now knew there actually were people who spoke and wrote French.

I had hardly had time to build up some enthusiasm for the study of French in Kerang when France fell before the German forces. "There isn't a France anymore, Miss," my students jubilantly informed me, "so why should we learn French?" This was hardly auspicious for my future endeavors. I rapidly linked up with the Free French movement in Australia (later *La France Combattante*) and soon, for supplementary reading, my students were finding out about General de Gaulle and the growing *maquis (*underground) in France from *Le Courrier Australien,* the Free French newspaper. Enthusiastically they drew Crosses of Lorraine on all their books. Personally I was devastated to have my very happy relationship with Christiane in La Rochelle and Colette in Creil interrupted. Both of them managed to send me accounts of the increasingly disturbed situation around them, before the dark curtain came down between us. Colette's last letter, before the Occupation cut off mail connections, was a long account of the terrible mass exodus from Paris before the advancing German army, in which she had found herself engulfed. These letters I shared, of course, with my students. They were thus able to experience vicariously this incredible turmoil, through poignant contact with real people, whose current experiences contrasted so vividly with their own peaceful existence in our quiet, rural setting. I heard through the *Courrier* of a way of sending correspondence into Occupied France, via neutral Portugal, and I immediately tried to reach my dear friends through this channel. My letters probably didn't make it: I never received replies.

In my classes I continued the Freddy tradition of motivating students through active involvement in language use from the earliest stages. As well as the usual diet of readings, grammar, and exercises, we had much acting out, singing of rollicking songs, and making of big vocabulary-labeled scenes to hang on the walls. We made our own cards for our family and friends for different festive occasions. Like students from time immemorial we danced on the bridge of Avignon and raised the rafters as we tried to rouse Brother Jacques to ring the bells for Matins or called to our neighbor, Pierrot, to lend us a quill pen as we waited in the moonlight. I enlivened the class with my ideas of French culture with a great deal of provincial folklore. I was very proud of a book of colored drawings of the various regional costumes and coifs, which illustrated my presentations. In those days I always began the first-year class (seventh grade) with a completely oral-aural month, when the only written French the students saw was in phonetic symbols, as we concentrated on aural comprehension and pronunciation. I found many of my young students acquired a very acceptable French accent in this first year. It was noteworthy, however, that as they grew older they became much more self-conscious about what their peers thought of them and, not wanting to stand out as different from the others, they tended to slip back into the anglicized accent they heard around them. Later, when they were older, they began again to try to sound more like authentic French speakers.

Since reading was considered a top priority for French in our isolated situation, I provided my students at a very early stage with a shelf of graded readers that they could read freely on their own. My favorite for the beginning students was one of a series by Marc Ceppi, Inspector of French in the Channel Islands, which, within a very limited vocabulary, with new words introduced at a slow digestible rate, told a delightful and whimsical tale about a little earthworm. The mere repetition of the words "*le petit ver de terre*" was fun and good pronunciation practice. (I had always loved earthworms, anyway.) As the oral reading method advocated, I taught them to read directly from the French text without mental translation, by keeping the reading practice within the class setting at first. I read aloud to them while they followed in their books, until they had acquired some skill in drawing meaning from linking ongoing units of discourse, and I had them read after me to keep them thinking in meaningful segments, not single words. They learned to tolerate ambiguity, as they worked out the meaning of new words in context. We also had sessions of reading aloud in pairs, the room being filled with a general buzz of gentle murmuring. At this time, "silence in the classroom" was the rule in a well-ordered school. There is a great difference between constructive and destructive classroom noise, for sure, yet whenever my class settled down to quiet, enjoyable pair work in reading it seemed the wandering Headmaster would appear around the corner to see what was going on. The readers I provided for the students' selection contained short, exciting narratives at a level they could read easily. They loved to borrow these to test their growing skill in independent reading. They would come back enthusiastically to tell me how well they had got on and the interesting things they had discovered. Of course, they would recommend the most enjoyable and accessible of these readers to their classmates.

We wrote skits and acted them out. The first-year students even produced a short play of their own concoction — *La Grande Querelle* — for the edification of other classes. For listening to authentic French we would turn on the radio for an hour on Fridays, when we would hear the excellent and varied broadcasts prepared for schools by our dedicated colleague, Manny Gelman. Manny provided this service of authentic materials, with accompanying booklets, for many years. Without this support many isolated teachers like myself would have been very much on their own in providing anything resembling authentic aural material. The broadcasts also helped us as teachers to keep up our own skills in listening to native French. Since even gramophone records of native speech were not readily available to us for developing listening comprehension, I would read aloud in class conversation-filled narratives that the students would try to follow without a written text.

I also taught English at all levels, both expository writing and literary texts, with a strong admixture in the early grades of vocabulary building from Greek and Latin roots. It was in an eighth-grade English class that I had one of those pivotal educational experiences that one never forgets. It was early in my first year. I came across a word in the text we were reading that neither I nor my students had ever encountered before. It was, I remember, the word "kale," which I now know to be a kind of cabbage that we didn't find in our Australian greengrocers' shops at the time. Naturally the students asked me what the word meant. As a young, inexperienced teacher, I had to decide there and then whether to bluff my way out of the predicament with some invention or to tell the class that I didn't know, thus blasting away forever any impression of my omniscience. The latter seemed to me a daunting admission for a very new teacher to make. I decided to be frank and tell them I didn't know, but we would all try to find out the meaning of the word for the next day. To my surprise I didn't lose their respect at all. This was one of the liberating moments in my teaching career. It freed me from considering my teaching role to be one of expounding on all wisdom for the uninitiated from my obviously encyclopedic and infallible knowledge. Instead, I was learning alongside my pupils. As Seneca observed, the person "who is too old to learn is too old to teach."[60] This change of attitude enabled me, early in my teaching, to launch out and explore unfamiliar areas, without fear of being "caught out" by my students, and to take on in later years the teaching of areas new to me in the rapidly evolving fields of linguistics and psycholinguistics.

I had such fun teaching English literature to students nearly as old as myself that in my first term I began to lose control of one of my upper-level classes. Like many beginning teachers, I had the urge to be loved by my students and to be considered the most popular teacher in the school. Experienced teachers realize that popularity comes from other factors than being an amusing buddy to one's students and never displeasing them. In this class we were reading a very amusing poem when I found myself having a fit of the giggles, along with the students, and, egged on by them, I was unable to regain my usual composure. I began to realize that something was wrong with my approach, as apparently did the watchful administration, who were anxious that this senior class should do well in external examinations. Quietly and gently, Miss Gerrand suggested that I might be happier switching to one of the more junior classes in the second term, so that I could start over again, which I did with much more success. I find recounting this experience to young teachers to be very encouraging to them. In their sometimes unpleasant initial experiences they often do not realize that all teachers have had to learn their craft over a long period of successes and failures and that, even in their later careers, experienced teachers do not always find everything plain sailing.

I well remember one particular student, Charlie, who came from a dairy farm. He spoke in that slow country drawl, which one often heard in Australia from isolated farm folk — the type of speech featured in the popular radio serial at the time about the adventures of Dad and Dave. A very serious, hard worker, Charlie had great difficulty with spelling. On one occasion, when writing from dictation Browning's "Home Thoughts from Abroad," he spelled Trafalgar "Figal." In those days we had never heard of dyslexia, but I knew instinctively that this boy was very intelligent, although he had some unusual problems. As a country boy he was determined to get his Merit Certificate, which signified success at eighth-grade level and was still, in the 1940s, held in great esteem on the farms. As the Education Department established the content of the Merit examination, it was essential for Charlie to pass a dictation test — his Waterloo! I remember standing over him and practically bellowing every syllable into his ear, so that he would attain this much coveted height of academic achievement. He loved me for my attention to his needs and my faith in him, and he was successful in the final exam. The following year I met him at the Agricultural Show and he came up and exchanged a few words with me in his reticent way. After a while he asked me: "What are you doing tonight?" and I thought my great romantic moment had come. "Nothing in particular," I replied. "Probably some reading." He paused for a moment, then out came the slow drawl: "*I've* got to go home and milk the *cows*."

When I finally made it back to Kerang after more than fifty years, I was anxious to see Charlie among others, but unfortunately he died of cancer during the night of my arrival. When I visited his family, his bright, attractive granddaughters asked me what kind of a scholar their grandfather had been. "He was a very hard worker," I said. At this they promptly produced the report books, in which I had entered his grades and some remarks on his progress, and most proudly of all his Merit Certificate, on which I recognized my own signature. It was a very moving moment. His wife said to me: "You know, when Charlie had to find out anything he always went to books, and he would work over the text, making diagrams to picture the farm machinery or the crop rotations he was seeking. It might take him time, but he always figured out the information he needed." A true dyslexic, Charlie would never let anything get past him and I admired him for it.

Among my colleagues at Kerang I found Mr Chalmers, who had been one of my geography teachers at EHS. It was a strange experience to be now his colleague. One of Mr Chalmers' professional hobbies was taking the Departmental roll, on which all the teachers in the service were listed in order of seniority, in four classes with subsections. Since batches of young teachers were added to the roll in alphabetical order as they entered the service, being an Aaronson rather than a Zultas could affect one's opportunities for promotion for many years to come. Mr Chalmers kept a personal copy of the roll on which he crossed out with red pencil all the "dead'uns" and the chronically ill teachers on leave. He carefully studied the home situations of those above him on the list who might be seeking promotion by applying for the advertised vacancies. He found out, mostly by information on the grapevine, whether they would be discouraged from applying because it meant displacing school-aged children or moving a long way from aged and ailing parents. Mr Chalmers knew well that promotion on the roll came more rapidly to those who were willing to take positions in the country or in tougher, less desirable, inner-city schools. In this way he prepared himself meticulously to apply only for positions for which his applications might be successful and which would advance him most rapidly.

Under this rigid roll system inspectors, who came to rate our teaching, played an important part in our promotions. We usually began our career by being evaluated as C in quality of teaching, even if we had been rated A in our training year. This convenient bureaucratic artifice made us unpromotable for a year or two. Over a period of several years we would gradually work up to a B, or even an A, and this made us eligible for a position in a higher section of the roll. After promotion, we would inevitably be rated C again to slow our promotion chances to a decent interval of years. This led to steady and orderly promotion, irrespective of quality. In this way all but the most hopeless teachers gradually made their way into more senior positions. Not surprisingly, this somewhat quality-blind process led at times to the application of the Peter Principle of promotion to the level of one's incompetence. The recognizably and undeniably incompetent were shunted off to the correspondence school, where they would have no discipline problems, as they corrected the written assignments sent in by those who had to study out of school because of distance or disability.

My first close encounter with the inspectorial system came toward the end of my first teaching year. Naturally Freddy, in our teacher-training course, had discussed with us aspects of good and bad textbooks for teaching French. The one I found myself using at Kerang seemed to epitomize the worst features of language textbooks. For teaching French to Victorian children, it used artificially created and simplified reading texts on such subjects as the Melbourne Botanic Gardens, the Shrine of Remembrance, and Flinders Street railway station. This choice of subject matter was predicated on the notion that one should proceed from the familiar to the unfamiliar, so that students would not be disconcerted by the strangeness of a new language and culture. This premise is debatable as a way of beginning a new language in which are embedded distinctive cultural meanings. Apart from that, in a country town like Kerang, texts on Melbourne resulted in a three-way situation. For the majority of my students Melbourne was absolutely terra incognita. Most of them had never traveled further south than Pyramid Hill or Bendigo. They were learning French by reading and talking about sites unfamiliar to them They could well have studied Melbourne's landmarks in English if that was considered important. Reading about such places in French contributed nothing to their knowledge of things French, except for a few culturally context-free items of vocabulary, like *street*, *tree*, or *train*. Content of this type could only reinforce the students' naïve assumption that French was just a rather esoteric and roundabout way of talking about things and that there was a word-for-word correspondence between French and English. The worst example of this approach of moving from the presumably familiar to the new in language textbooks was a book used in some Melbourne schools called *Kangourou*. In this book students read legends of the Australian Aborigines in French, legends that were as foreign to them

241

as would be stories of the French *Loup Garou* (bogeyman). All this was a long way from the present emphasis on teaching about another culture as an important element in learning to use another language.

To return to the French textbook being used at Kerang, apart from its Melbourne-based content, it began each lesson with a short reading passage with a great list of unfamiliar vocabulary. In successive chapters there would be reading passages with more long lists of new vocabulary but with no reentry of the words from the previous passages. All the exercises were mechanical: fill-in-the-blanks and prompted transformations of discrete items abounded, with no encouragement to use the new language creatively. Naturally I thought we could do better in selecting a textbook for the following year, so I promptly changed the book to be ordered. The Inspector for French appeared in Kerang on his annual visit and, after studying the book list for the following year, he summoned me to the headmaster's office. "Why did you change the French textbook for next year?" he inquired. I immediately launched into what I considered to be a perceptive analysis of all the weaknesses of the text I was using, asserting that it was clearly a very bad book from the methodological point of view. "I think you had better reinstate the order for next year," he said with an air of finality. It was only after his departure that I learned that the textbook had been written by his wife, who had recently died. Climbing up the departmental ladder had its hazardous moments.

For teaching we were expected to have training in three subject areas; for me these had been French, English, and Latin. Since Latin was not taught at Kerang, I was asked to teach a Geography class, which I did under the mentorship of my former Geography teacher, Mr Chalmers. Since I have always had a strong interest in things geographical, I derived great pleasure from teaching it and learning more and more as I went on. This launched me on a trajectory, which resulted in my developing skills in teaching Geography from seventh grade to twelfth grade in the various schools in which I taught. Later I even taught the geography of India to students in Hyderabad in South India, who were preparing for external examinations conducted by Cambridge University in England. Looking back, it is surprising how the segments of my career came together.

Living in Community

Naturally I had to find lodgings of some sort in Kerang and, never having lived on my own before, I chose a boarding house near the school — Miss Raven's. Miss Raven took in up to twelve boarders, in a rambling old Victorian house with a large dining room that also served as a living room. Miss Raven, who belonged to the Salvation Army, had previously worked in a home for delinquent girls under their aegis. We had the impression that she treated her women lodgers very much as though they were young delinquents. She treated men with much more respect and a little apprehension. Her old mother, who helped her, acted rather like a spy. Moving noiselessly, like a shadow, she kept an eye on any illicit doings (that is, any infringements of Miss Raven's unwritten, but strictly enforced, rules). Miss Raven's previous experience had taught her to be extremely frugal and she tried to run the establishment on a shoestring, although we paid good board, even paying the full amount during school vacations. Miss Raven believed strongly in the therapeutic value of cold showers for her guests throughout the winter, this in an unheated house, even when there had been a black frost during the night. Clearly this was a money-saving rather than a health measure. While we showered, Miss Raven's old mother would wander around listening to the length of time we were running the water.

Miss Raven was particularly sensitive to our use of electricity. The vestibule where we would iron our clothes on a large table was lit with a ten-watt bulb. Since there were no drip-dry or non-creasable fabrics in those days, everything we wore had to be ironed. At the time, I had my first "little black dress," with tiny red roses embroidered around the neckline. I remember trying to iron black fabric in the dim light, in which it was impossible to see the creases. One of my mother's great concerns had always been our care of our eyes. She would become quite alarmed if we continued reading into the twilight without turning on the lights, so having "good light" for reading was always considered a priority as I grew up. I was then, as now, a voracious reader. In my bedroom at Miss Raven's, I was most surprised to find that the light by which I would prepare my classes, correct students' exercises and tests, work on my MA studies, and read books for pleasure at night had only a forty-watt bulb. In my innocence I thought this could only be a slip on Miss Raven's part.

When I went shopping, I thought I would save her trouble and expense by buying a sixty-watt bulb to replace it. Furthermore, Miss Raven believed that, even as responsible adults, we should have lights out by eleven o'clock in the evening, which seemed to us a rather unreasonable rule in a boarding-house. I have always read late into the night. As much as I tried to be accommodating, I found it very hard to conform to this restricting rule. At the time I was reading a long novel that had to be returned to the library the next day. With my newly acquired "bright" light of sixty watts, I prepared for a few happy hours beyond the regimented eleven o'clock "lights out" by laying a towel along the crack below the door and stuffing the keyhole. I didn't think it important that my room had a small door with a glass window, which looked out across a vacant lot toward a rather distant neighbor's house. Next day, there was a great to-do! Old Mrs Raven had discovered my newly installed sixty-watt bulb, and the neighbor had reported seeing my light burning until two o'clock in the morning! Clearly a major crime had been committed. Miss Raven accused me of robbing her by using twenty watts more electricity for longer hours than she permitted. I offered her some extra money to placate her, but what worried her, she said, was my deliberate dishonesty, which changed her opinion of me forever. This was no doubt an echo of the way she had spoken to the delinquent girls in the past. Had I been a more experienced boarder, I would have walked out and sought a flat of my own where I could do as I liked. This being so soon after my quitting the cozy family nest, however, I was uncertain of my ability to live by myself, and there was also the question of the expense so early in my first year of wage earning. In my indignation, I bought myself twelve large candles. These I melted at the base and set out on a sheet of cardboard. That night I enjoyed a good read until two or three in the morning, leaving the stumps of the candles for the Ravens to see as evidence that I had become autonomous in my search for "good light." I am sure they must have been alarmed that I would burn the house down.

This and other experiences soon taught me that I had made a mistake in being too friendly with the Ravens at the beginning of our acquaintance. I had, for instance, tried to help them by picking up groceries when I was in town on my bike, and soon after my arrival I had said: "Just call me Wilga." My colleague, Carmel Moloney, much the same age as myself, had kept her distance. She was always addressed as Miss Moloney and had apparently inspired a different kind of respect and a slight degree of awe by refusing to be considered "just family." I had much to learn about dealing with strangers. This was the period of clear-cut fasting rules for Catholics — no meat on Fridays was the edict. Since such a practice was not part of Miss Raven's Salvation Army culture, she would sometimes forget and serve meat on the wrong day. Carmel, being a devout Catholic, kept a close eye on this behavior. One Friday some young Catholic boys from a farm out of town, who lunched with us during the week, were tucking into their hot meal of lamb chops when Carmel came in from school. She took one look, swooped down on them, snatching their hot lunch from under their noses, and marched into the kitchen, demanding an immediate substitution of fried eggs. The poor boys, who had obviously not been brought up as observant Catholics, looked most disappointed as they saw their nice hot lunch disappear before their eyes. Miss Raven would never have dared to argue with Miss Moloney.

Every meal at the Ravens was an exercise in arithmetic. Each piece of bread and each scone or piece of fruit had been carefully counted out — twelve people = twelve lettuce leaves, twelve scones, twelve pieces of bread (or maybe eighteen, if there were no scones), twelve pieces of fruit, and so on. Each meal began with our counting everything, so that there would be no confusion as to exactly how much was our share. At one stage, one of the boarders, a high school girl whose parents had a property some miles out of town, asked her father to bring in a load of apples from his orchard to supplement our frugal diet. How disappointed she was when this made no difference whatsoever to our daily ration! This being Australia in the early 1940s, meat was expected three times a day. Since Miss Raven bought only the cheapest cuts of meat we nearly wore out our teeth and jaws trying to chew the tough steaks and mutton chops she provided

The only heating in the boarding house in the winter was a fire in the living room, which had become a place for vigorous conversations in the evenings. After our evening meal at six, either Miss Raven or her mother would build up and light the fire, leaving just two small pieces of cut wood as a supplement. This was presumably in the hope that we would take the hint and go to bed early, thus saving electricity. As soon as the Ravens left the room we would seize half of the wood on the fire and set it aside to supplement the two small pieces they had left us. The fire would burn up brightly, the extra pieces rapidly disappearing, despite our doling them out as slowly as we could to prolong the warmth. Soon we were left to watch the dying embers. At this stage, we would amuse ourselves by challenging each other to burn a loose section of one of the chairs to keep us warm. Later that first winter, we had as boarders four tall, strong workmen who were building a road out of town. These family men rapidly concluded that Miss Raven had either forgotten to bring in extra wood or expected them to carry it in themselves from the substantial woodpile in the yard. We regulars said nothing to disillusion them, but we smiled broadly to ourselves as they brought in great pieces of wood with which they built up a roaring fire. They kept feeding the fire all evening, leaving several unused slabs piled up beside the fireplace. Miss Raven must have nearly had a heart attack when she came in next morning to clean the grate. At least while the road was being built we were able to keep warm. Probably Miss Raven felt intimidated by these confident men, who were so much bigger than she was. She dared not deprive them, as she so obviously was prepared to do with insecure young women like the rest of us.

At this stage of my life I was convinced that I could not eat cheese in any form. I had decided I did not like it, although I don't think I had ever tasted it. At school we had regular lunch duty, staying in the staff room to answer student questions, apply the occasional Band Aid, respond to parents on the phone, and check on the cleanliness of the school yard after lunch. On my first duty day Miss Raven, who was accustomed to the routine of her teacher boarders, supplied me with some sandwiches and the inevitable apple for lunch. To my horror, on opening my lunch packet I discovered thick slabs of bread enclosing equally thick slabs of "mousetrap" cheese, as we called it — the common, unlabeled cheese, sold in large chunks, that was the cheapest variety. At this point I decided that since so many people ate and liked cheese, I would just chew on it and endure it, trying to find out what there was about it that appealed to other people. Each week, then, I would chew reflectively on my mousetrap cheese sandwiches and try to decipher this mystery. This hesitation to confront the formidable Miss Raven and ask for something other than cheese to eat ultimately resulted in a real love for cheeses of all kinds, smells, and flavors — except, of course, the mousetrap variety. That is one thing for which I can thank the redoubtable Miss Raven.

Then there were the Kerang mosquitoes that bred in the lakes and swamps. In the evenings particularly they came zooming in and they loved my blood. Soon I was a mass of scratched red lumps. At the time I was sharing a room with Irene Parker, the Art teacher. She told me that whenever she heard them zinging around the room after we had turned off the lights she would just turn over, because "they would always find Wilga." How right she was! Here I learned another very useful lesson — not to scratch mosquito bites! If I could endure the stinging stoically for half an hour, I found it would go away and I would have no further problems with that particular bite. This worked much of the time, although I must admit that sometimes such self-control was quite beyond me.

One thing I had yet to learn was that casual conversations, no matter how animated and intense, are not necessarily world-shaking or of lifelong import. It was tempting to remain in the evenings and join in the social exchanges among the boarders, but deep in my heart I knew that I had my MA thesis to write, that this was of deep concern to me, and that I would not be satisfied until I had finished it. I was also determined that I would somehow find my way to France after the war ended. So I had to screw my determination to the sticking point, pick myself up, and leave all this fascinating socializing behind me, along with the glowing fire. I would install myself in my bedroom, wrapping a rug around my legs as I had learned to do in the cold depression-era Ascot Vale house, and settle down to my task of reading Flaubert's correspondence. At first, I had only the ledge on an old-fashioned dressing-table to write on, so I bought a folding card table in town to accommodate my papers and books. Of course, there were piles of essays and tests to correct for my classes. As a teacher of English, I had an essay a week to read from each of my students. Every morning before breakfast I would work for two hours, trying to read in that time forty pages of Flaubert's correspondence or sections of *Salammbô* or *La Tentation de saint Antoine*.

Extra-Curricular Life and Activities

Life was not all work fortunately. At first I missed the busy social life among young people my age that I had enjoyed with the various youth groups to which I had belonged in Melbourne. A reminiscence of this exciting life came in regular letters, written in purple ink, from one of the boys I had been friendly with in the Melbourne group. Later, as the war in the Pacific spread, I tried to cheer up this friend and other young men from our group, who were serving in New Guinea, with lively correspondence. I seemed to spend a lot of time, as I still do, writing letters. Among others, I wrote to Mother, Harold, and Linda every week — a habit I continued for sixty years. Of course, there was no telephone in the Ascot Vale house when I first went to Kerang. Our home phone service wasn't installed until 1941, when my letter-writing habits were firmly established. We had never been able to afford a phone before, so we were spared the old wind-up type of instrument. Even when we did have a phone, long-distance calls were considered too expensive for use except in urgent circumstances.

It was by letter that I heard of Mother's adventure with the would-be burglar, a naive bungler who hadn't realized what he was up against in breaking into Mother's home. This was before the installation of the telephone. Mother, who was home alone, had put together the money to pay some bills and was coming down the long passage to the vestibule, when she saw, to her amazement, a man with his foot over the windowsill of my brother's bedroom. Outraged at this violation of her home space, she immediately dressed him down in plain language. "How dare you break into my house!" she cried. At this outburst the intruder stuttered and stammered that he was not breaking in; he was just coming to see if his dog had wandered in. "No, you're not," Mother yelled. "You're just a common burglar! I'm going to ring the police." With that, she marched back up the passage, before realizing that, with no phone nearer than the railway station, she would be leaving the coast clear for the intruder. Back she marched determinedly, but by then the burglar had got the message and had disappeared. It was hard to stand up to Mother's expressions of righteous rage.

248

In 1940 in Kerang, there were no young men of my age in sight. In the various wars in which Australia has been involved country boys have always been among the most patriotic. Before long, many of the boys in our senior classes were leaving to enlist in the various branches of the fighting forces, several of them having discovered that they could join the Navy at as young an age as fifteen. By 1942, twenty-year-olds were being called up, but many anticipated the call and chose to enlist earlier, in order to be able to select the branch of the services they preferred. There were only twelve students in the senior form by 1942, most of them girls. Some of our male teachers also joined up, as did some of the male boarders at Miss Raven's. As available teaching staff became scarce, classes grew in size, some having as many as sixty pupils. The largest class in French I had was a first-year group of fifty-five. Included in the number were twelve students who were not studying French. These students, whom I was "baby-sitting," sat at the back of the room while I taught the others. Keeping an orderly classroom in these conditions was quite a test of skill for a young teacher.

I was not allowed to feel lonely in Kerang. With typical Australian country hospitality, the parents of some of my students and some of my friends at church, who lived on farms perhaps fifteen or twenty miles out of town, were very welcoming. I would ride out to their farms for the weekend on my trusty bike, and I soon learned a lot about milking machines and the pleasure of drinking warm, foaming milk just extracted from the cow's udder. Some of my hosts were wheat farmers with that ruddy complexion of people who spent most of their days out in the hot sun. With them I rode out on farm wagons to gather stooks of hay and I went rabbiting with their children. Sometimes I would watch the workings of the irrigation system, bringing water from the Lodden. As I was essentially a city girl, this was all very new to me. I became a close personal friend for a lifetime with some of these farm friends, whose warmth and open acceptance were boundless.

It was through one of these families that I came to recognize the difference between "shy" and "quiet" students. One thirteen-year-old boy, Jim Welsh, was very quiet and I would tease him in class to get him involved. I could see that he glowed and enjoyed the attention. One of my colleagues, who considered herself something of

249

a psychologist, told me that my teasing would cause him all kinds of psychological problems. Shortly into the first term, I received a call from his mother. "Miss Rivers," she said, "Would you like to come out to the farm for a weekend visit? You know, Jim never talks much about his teachers, but he has been pestering me to invite you for several weeks." In this way I learned to trust teacherly intuition in dealing with individuals, rather than being unduly influenced by the ever-changing generalities in educational psychology books. This "quiet" boy, who was not shy, later became quite a leader in his country area.

Soon I was fully involved in town activities and sometimes I was out every night of the week. I joined the local Choral Society. Enthusiastically we visited outlying townships to sing art songs and sections of Handel's *Messiah* to receptive farm folk, who were unaccustomed to concerts in their local halls. After the performance, our hosts would ply us with four-inch high sponge cakes, oozing with thick whipped cream taken straight from the separator. I also joined the Music Lovers Club and, to prepare myself better for participation, I registered for a correspondence course in Musical Appreciation offered by an adult education group in Melbourne, from whom I received regular boxes of records and discussion materials. Taking my courage in my hands, I prepared a lecture for the Music Lovers Club on French music from Couperin to Debussy and Saint-Saëns, passing by Berlioz and Gounod, illustrating my talk with recorded music. I also acted in play-readings with a local acting group. In a country town we had to create our own amusements. To fill my time profitably I took up German and learned to touch-type, practicing on the school typewriter every evening after school. I also learned to crochet, knit fancy patterns and do more complicated embroidery. I took a first-aid course as part of the National Fitness Campaign and learned to play tennis. Later, when I was in France, my friends at Douai would argue among themselves as to whether I was a true "intellectual," since I could do and apparently enjoyed doing so many practical things.

Before long, I was organizing at the Anglican Church the Senior Girls' Friendly Society for young women in their late teens and early twenties, as well as directing the Sunday Kindergarten, along the lines Mrs Raymond had taught me. Like my mentor, I was

250

soon teaching several young helpers how to instruct and keep the interest of five to seven-year-olds. Whether our spiritual messages got through, we were never to know. On one occasion when we were celebrating the Harvest Festival with little hymns and stories, I asked the children to stand up and thank our Father God for giving us our daily bread. One little fair-haired boy refused to stand up, despite several urgings. When I asked him why he didn't want to stand up and thank God for our bread, he stubbornly insisted: "No! No! We have the baker!" (who, in those days, brought the bread daily in a horse-drawn cart).

The War from a Distance

School children were soon involved in the war effort and our pupils raised money for the War Relief Fund in every imaginable and unimaginable way. One year my form of seventh graders raised the most money, half of the school total, that is, a sum of twenty-five pounds (equal to a month and a half of my salary at the time). This they did by buying and selling everything they could think of. Some made lollies and cakes to sell; others cooked hot saveloys and sold them on bread during the morning break. One boy cut off his horse's tail and sold the horsehair; others sacrificed their pet lambs; one little boy from an itinerant family, not to be outdone, brought along a number of plants to sell — we didn't inquire too closely into where he had acquired them. Some students contributed money they had earned working on the farms during the summer holidays. Students picked up waste materials throughout the town and sorted aluminum, copper, glass, or old newspapers to raise money to send to the Red Cross. Others collected eggs for the hospitals. The boys also made walking sticks for the wounded in their woodwork classes, while the girls knitted innumerable rugs, pullovers, mittens, mufflers, and balaclavas to keep Australian soldiers in the European zone warm in the northern winter. As Australian involvement in the war switched to the Pacific, many of our troops were transferred to Papua New Guinea. At this stage our servicemen much preferred gifts of cold-water dyes, which were very popular among the Papuans for dyeing their grass skirts. The Australians were able to barter these for souvenir grass skirts for their sisters and girlfriends

My brother Harold joined the Air Force in 1942 and, while he was serving on the island of Kiriwina, off the coast of Papua, we sent him dyes on several occasions. In return we received a voluminous grass skirt, which was a great novelty to show our friends until it became tattered and disintegrated. We also admired the large abalone shells with beautiful, iridescent mother of pearl interiors he brought home. On leave, he would show us the banknotes that had mildewed in his pockets from the intense humidity in Papua. While there he also sang in the choir of the "Coral Cathedral" that Australian airmen had built with the help of the Papuans. Our Australian troops greatly admired the Papuans, whom they called "fuzzy-wuzzy angels," because of the gentle way they carried the wounded for long distances over the steep mountains of their tropical land.

After Japan's attack on Pearl Harbor in December of 1941 and the rapid advance of Japanese troops through Southeast Asia, Australians began to feel very vulnerable to attack. Plane-spotting assignments were set up for volunteers from the town. We were trained to recognize the silhouettes of our own planes (Wacketts, Wirraways, Douglases, Lockheeds and Catalinas) and those of the enemy. Should we spot an alien outline in the sky, we were to call the information in to the authorities immediately. We spent many fruitless hours at this task. I found it much more interesting to watch the many constellations in the brilliant southern hemisphere sky and the wide sweep of the Milky Way, all so clearly visible over the flat plains. These long nights under starlit skies aroused my interest in identifying the various constellations, an interest I continued to develop later during my years at Yarram and Sale in Gippsland. As a Girl Guide I had learned to find the South Magnetic Pole from the distinctive positions of the Southern Cross and its pointers, Alpha and Beta Centauri, and Orion was familiar to me. But now I came to know many more. One evening, as I was whiling away my airplane-spotting session in pleasant conversation with Perce, the local pharmacist, he thought he heard a foreign plane and rushed to the phone. What an achievement — something finally to report! In his excitement Perce forgot about the radiator beside the phone, which was keeping us warm on that frosty night. In his haste he burned his trousers. All this for what turned out to be a false alarm!

Linda was not idle either during the war. Since all the male youth leaders at our church were away, she began a group for adolescent boys, called Volunteers for Christ, for whom she organized regular meetings and activities, including long bike hikes, in which I participated when I was in Melbourne for holiday periods. The boys continued enthusiastically in this group for several years, some until they enlisted in one of the services. Being typically high-spirited and mischievous teenagers, they sometimes embarrassed us with "innocently" destructive behavior, like throwing stones at the ceramic insulators on the poles carrying the electricity wires or picking bunches of protected native flora to present to us as gifts.

As the war progressed, the Australian Government became anxious about the general health of the nation and instituted a National Fitness Campaign. During my teacher training year I had been instructed in how to run physical education classes and I knew what was required for a thorough workout. Soon I was involved as a leader in the campaign, and once a week I would have a group of local housewives and young working women skipping and jumping to music and performing all kinds of exercises on the floor of the Parish Hall. This would be interspersed with some simple folk dancing. I also taught my Fitness class swimming in the warm months — teaching Learn-to-Swim classes for beginners as well as advanced life-saving techniques. I thoroughly enjoyed this community activity and continued teaching this class during the three years I was in Kerang.

At the high school, besides my field hockey responsibilities, I also taught swimming as part of my teaching load. Although I myself was not a diver, I was very proud of the fact that I had trained the school diving champion from her first dive to her championship display. Of course, the young champion was a natural diver and it is often easier to tell people what to do than to do it oneself. Until the age of eleven I had been able to dive; then, for some reason, I did not dive for a season. When I next tried to dive I could only do belly-whackers. Later when I was teaching diving, quite successfully, I felt I should be able to follow my own instructions. I stayed back after my students had gone and tried several dives. Result: only belly-whackers, so I gave up and satisfied myself by jumping into deep water and enjoying long swims.

Very soon after my arrival in Kerang, I started an after-school interdenominational Christian Fellowship for the girls from the high school. We met for an hour at Miss Raven's and she played the organ to accompany our singing of lively choruses. After a while she felt, quite rightly, that this might not be very appropriate for a boarding house, where other boarders had different interests. At that stage we moved to the home of a Methodist lady in town. To brighten up our activities, we rode out to the lakes on our bikes for picnics. On one memorable occasion several groups lost touch with each other and we got lost in among the thick, tangled lignum around the lakes, which made for a frustrating afternoon. However, a few dips in Reedy Lake soon cooled us down. This fellowship group continued for the three years I was in the area and some of the girls have remained in touch with ever since.

One of the girls in this group was called Wilga. Despite its native Australian origin, the name has never been very common in Australia, and after my little classmate, Wilga Thomas, who had been named after me, moved to Sydney, I remained sole possessor to my knowledge of the Wilga field. When I met my first French class at Kerang, I began by asking their names. I was quite taken aback when one of the girls said her name was Wilga. So surprised was I that I asked her to repeat her name and even spell it for me. The girls in the class, having noticed that I had written W. Rivers on my books, wondered among themselves whether that could be my name too. "After all, she made such a fuss about Wilga's name," they said. Wilga turned out to be one of my best French students. At one stage, I arranged for Wilga to come to Melbourne to participate in a fellowship camp. It was her first visit to the city and I remember her amazement on seeing from the train, in some of the outer suburbs, streets that went straight uphill from the railway line. After all the only hill she had ever seen until then was the "heap of scrap metal," Pyramid Hill, just south of Kerang. Wilga Thorne, later Wilga King, taught mathematics at Swan Hill High School for many years and we remained friends until her death in 1999.

Another group I linked up with at Kerang was the Kerang Fellowship, an interdenominational group that organized a Convention in Kerang each year to which enthusiasts came from areas on both sides of the Murray River, including several tall, rangy young

254

men from Deniliquin in New South Wales. These young men had agricultural deferments, since continued food production was in the national interest. With the paucity of male company, we looked forward to their participation in the convention from year to year. Not all the churches in town agreed with the aims and approach of the Kerang Fellowship, because of its evangelical beliefs, and this applied to the Anglican priest. However, some of his flock managed to keep a foot in both camps without losing his confidence. We enjoyed some outstanding preachers and Bible teachers through the Convention and had meetings together during the year. On one notable occasion, I set out with one of the leaders of this Fellowship to try to sell Bibles in the different farmhouses out of town. This was quite a daunting experience, because of the great diversity in our reception. Some of the farm folk responded to us pleasantly, but others peered suspiciously through narrowly opened doors or rejected our visits outright with a certain amount of vituperation. I began to feel some sympathy for the Jehovah's Witnesses I myself had rebuffed in the past.

Independence and Maturity

It seems I was growing up. When I went home for the first ten days' holiday period at the end of the first term, my sister Linda, who was accustomed to her "little sister" following her lead and deferring to her advice even in the choice of a new dress, was very shocked at how independent I had become. It took her a long time to adjust to the change. Even later in life, she sometimes still referred to me as her "little sister" and recalled the shock she had sustained at that time. Soon I acquired the confidence to stand on my own two feet.

Deep-rooted in my psyche was my determination to go to France to study and improve my knowledge of the language and culture. Since I had no possibility of obtaining any scholarship help, I would have to do it on my own. No one in my immediate family had ever traveled abroad; they had rarely traveled interstate. I had no personal contacts abroad, apart from my long-time correspondents, Christiane and Colette. There were the English second cousins with whom some members of the Rivers family had kept in touch; these I intended to look up in London. I had no idea how I would get to France, nor how I would support myself while I was studying. I knew however that the first thing I had to do was to save enough money for the return fare (by ship, of course). I also knew that young Australians who set off on the Grand Tour to Europe were advised to make sure that their fare for the return trip was tucked away in the bank. Without this precaution, it might take years to be able to save enough while abroad for the return voyage and they could be stranded. All the time I was at Kerang, and later in Gippsland at Yarram and Sale, I saved for the realization of my life's dream. With my Depression-era upbringing and mentality, thrift was already ingrained. Whenever I was tempted to buy a cup of coffee or an ice cream I would tell myself that I could have it in London. So gradually the pennies accumulated. Since women teachers earned only sixty percent of a male teacher's wage, my men friends who had a similar ambition could save from that extra forty percent. Later, when I was abroad, these male friends could afford to travel around Europe in buses or trains while I hitchhiked. By my second year of teaching I was earning 400 pounds a year, or eight pounds a week, after insurance and superannuation. There were taxes to pay and the one pound a week due to Miss Raven for board and lodging. I also sent Mother four pounds a month to pay off a loan, cover the house mortgage, and help her continue with less stress and anxiety. In addition I tried to tithe for my church and charitable causes. General living expenses could not be ignored, as well as clothes and fares to Melbourne for the holidays. Despite all this, I managed to save to realize my dream of studying in France.

During my three years at Kerang, my enthusiasm for and dedication to student-centered teaching grew. Older teachers tried to discourage me, telling me that I would soon lose the "stars in my eyes" that I had acquired during my Diploma of Education training. With experience, they predicted, I would soon recognize the realities of the perversity of youth. Fortunately I never did.

The Great Return

One of the most exciting days of my life came in early January of 1995, when I returned to Kerang for the first time in fifty-five years. I had indicated to some of my former students, with whom I had kept in touch, that I would like to see Kerang again, and in no time they had passed the word around: "Miss Rivers is coming back!"

The word spread throughout the area, to Swan Hill, Bendigo, and even to Melbourne, and there was great excitement on both sides. By now, my little seventh and eighth graders were gray-haired grandfathers and grandmothers and many of them had retired.

I traveled by a now faster train to Kerang in just over three hours. As I got further north, I could see green irrigated paddocks with black and white Frisian cattle and scattered Border Leicester sheep. The broad land I remembered was still flat to the horizon, with trees planted along watercourses and irrigation channels. All was not well, however, in this formerly lush, green area. Over the years over-enthusiastic and uninformed irrigation, along with careless clearing of catchment areas. had ruined much of the land. Excess water, equivalent to doubling the rainfall, had caused the water table to rise, leaching salts out of the soil. As the salts rose to the surface, they poisoned the paddocks, which as a result had become overgrown with blackish-brown salt bush. Some farmers had abandoned their land, leaving it to rot, but others were working hard to redeem their farms, by establishing drainage channels to drain the saline water from their paddocks and run it into Lake Tutchewop. The drained water in the lake was more saline than the sea, and there was talk of using it for setting up a farmed barramundi and tuna fish industry. As the water table was lowered from beneath, fresh water from the Grampians range was being brought in via the Lodden River and other watercourses to refresh the surface soil, which was becoming green again wherever this system had been applied. It would be a long process, however, to restore what inexperienced farmers had damaged.

It was a pleasure to visit the farm of my former student, Netta Schulz at Murrabit West, who with water from the Murray had created around her house a veritable little Eden of park-like land with weeping willows, a rose garden, a water-lily pond and a small Japanese garden. Everywhere along the roadsides were the mauve and white flowers of agapanthus plants that had been encouraged to grow wild. The grand old red gums along the Murray River separating Victoria from New South Wales were sturdy and seemingly eternal. Nearby, Second Reedy Lake had now become the largest reserve in the world for white ibis. At sunset we watched from a hide as small squadrons of these big birds flew in from all directions, along with a few pelicans, to settle in the gathering dusk on the dead trees rising out of the water.

The reunion itself was held in the Uniting Church Hall, where cups of tea and sandwiches were available all day, from ten in the morning till five in the afternoon, for one continuous party. This was catered for by the ladies of the church, including the ninety-three year old mother of my former student and longtime friend, Wilga Thorne King. Spirits were high and the conversation never stopped. Despite the gray hair and wrinkles there was still a twinkle in the eye or an expression on the face that recalled the little tykes and teenagers of 1940 to 1942. Some of the girls (now women, of course) were, to their great disappointment, committed to Pennant matches of lawn bowls on that day, but an early thunderstorm caused a cancellation and they excitedly rushed over to the reunion. Some who had specialties honored me with beautiful flower arrangements or bark pictures. Others recalled their classes. They had brought their treasured report books with them and were proud to point to my signature. "Remember the jellyfish column," some of them cried. "Yes! the jellyfish column!" others chimed in. This I had forgotten, but it appears that I had established a system, whereby those who had come to class without doing their homework had to sign their names at the side of the board as a confession that they were "spineless invertebrates." This seems to have been remembered more than the rules of the agreement of the French past participle. They also remembered the little old man who had a dog called Parmi (French for "a-mong") and one even drew a picture in our remembrance book of this critter. I remembered that this was one of Freddie's little jokes that I had exported to the country. One former student, unable to be present that day, phoned to tell me that I had affected his life three times. The first time, he said, was when I taught him French at Kerang; the second time was when, by chance, I taught him in a course for returned servicemen in Melbourne after the Second World War, enabling him to qualify for university admission; and the third time was after his retirement, when he was motivated to take up French again for personal reasons. He went to Paris and studied conversational French at the Alliance Française, so that he would be able to talk to the villagers when he visited the place where his father fought in the 1914-18 World War.

A visit to the high school showed how life in this small country town had changed. The trees our young boys had planted during the war years were now well grown and there was quite a garden environment around the school. The present headmaster was part Indian and part Black, from Guyana, and had studied in England; his Kenyan wife was part Indian and part Portuguese. Education Department policies had changed and the headmaster now appointed his own teaching staff according to the needs of the school, which had become a Technical High School. The curriculum was much updated to suit the interests of late twentieth-century youth. Courses were divided into semester segments. Musical Appreciation was now entitled "All that Jazz," and Geography courses had such titles as "From Moscow to Beijing." Indonesian and Asian languages figured prominently among the students' choices. Kerang had changed as Victoria had changed, becoming much more multicultural and attuned to world trends and movements.

What had not changed in Kerang was the sense of community and the warm-hearted friendliness and openness of the local families, which I have since found notable in their annual reunions in Melbourne, for which many of them now make a one-day return trip by train. Despite their many vicissitudes (Kerang now has the highest rate of cancer deaths in Victoria, for instance), they pull together and enjoy life and each other's company, without stinting on time or energy for joint undertakings.

Wilga as Depth Charge

The war was still raging in the Pacific in January 1943 and drawing nearer and nearer to Australia's shores. Australians had become very aware of their vulnerability in the previous year when Darwin was bombed and midget Japanese submarines were discovered in Sydney Harbour. There was a stepped-up effort to build up stocks of munitions of all kinds. With so many men and women serving in the armed forces, there was naturally a shortage of workers, so a call went out for people to help in this endeavor. Teachers were asked to do some form of national service during their long summer vacation. I opted to work in the Maribyrnong munitions plant, which was close to my home in Ascot Vale and easy to reach by bike. This job took me into the completely new environment of blue-collar work.

259

In my three weeks' stint at the munitions plant, I worked the three shifts — early morning to early afternoon, early afternoon to late evening, and late evening to early morning. This was a new experience for me and my fellow workers soon initiated me into the "fair play for other workers" frame of mind. My first job was to put dints in hinge pins for depth charges, destined to blow up submarines. This meant receiving a huge number of brass pins, which I had to dint throughout the day with a small press. After reflection I found that if I lined them up and then pushed them under the press in quick succession I could dint a much larger number in the time allotted. Very soon, however, the union representative told me to "cut it out," since I would only push up the number of pins other workers would be expected to dint (that is, the tally, which was checked every hour). She explained that others, especially on the night shift, would not necessarily be able to complete the tally at the level I was setting. Later when I worked the night shift, I myself experienced the period of slump in the early hours of the morning when one's pace certainly slackened. This fellow worker, who worked very fast herself, was the sister of a well-known professor at Melbourne University. In order to keep the tally at a reasonable level for others, she regularly took herself off to the restroom with a newspaper to fill in some time. I soon discovered a different way to use up some of my time. I found that I could roam around the plant at will and observe other people's occupations if I merely carried an empty box in my hand. With the empty receptacle, I was always presumed either to be going to get more material to work with or just coming back from delivering finished parts to the store. In this way I was able to slow down my output acceptably, while getting a little exercise and familiarizing myself with the operations of the works.

Near my work station were huge lathes, which seemed to be continually breaking down. The woman who worked on the nearby lathe spent a considerable amount of her time leaning against her machine, waiting for the maintenance crew to come and fix her problem. The lathe certainly looked impressive, and when the lathe operator left I was asked to take her place. I now had this huge machine to operate according to an ABCD schedule (A: turn this lever up; B: put the material in position, C: turn on this switch, and so on). It was hardly a difficult routine, except for the machine's predilection

260

for breaking down. I was now making brass rings for some other obscure purpose of depth charges. But all good things come to an end, including the camaraderie I was enjoying in the factory. After a few more days of summer leisure it would be time for me to return to teaching for the new school year.

Wonthaggi Interlude

After three years of teaching at Kerang, I had decided on a change. My dear friend from MacRob days, Peggy Jackson, had married a Baptist minister, Les Rawlings, and with their young son they had gone to serve in a parish in the coal-mining town of Wonthaggi, about 86 miles from Melbourne. Seeing a vacancy advertised by the Education Department at Wonthaggi Technical School, I thought it would be fun to be in the same town as Peggy and Les for a while. It was in an area of the state I had not visited before, and it also meant a complete change of climate. Naturally I did not find it difficult to get an appointment in a coal-mining town. In late January I moved on to South Gippsland. Since this was a technical school, I was soon teaching English to big, adolescent boys who were very expert with their hands or with machines but had much more difficulty with pens and books. Very practically minded, some of them were already making more money than I was, by running "a book" (illegal off-course betting) on the horse races.

I immediately decided not to set arbitrary standards. I would meet the boys where they were and select material they could relate to. I was really enjoying teaching my Wonthaggi students when I was suddenly informed that the Education Department had changed its mind. The central office in Melbourne had decided that Wonthaggi Tech was overstaffed for its enrolment and that my presence was required elsewhere. Since the Wonthaggi headmaster had not, of course, been consulted, he was somewhat annoyed and disappointed by this sudden staffing change, especially when his counterpart at the Higher Elementary School (HES) in Yarram began phoning to ask where in heaven's name Miss Rivers had got to. To this the irritated Wonthaggi headmaster replied, "She's not a flying angel." The boys I was teaching were very disappointed that I was leaving, so they decided to give me a "big" farewell gift. Gathering together their small contributions, they went down the street to Woolworth's and bought the biggest things they could find for their money — three heavy, machine-cut, glass salad bowls of different sizes (these incidentally I used for years). They then asked one of the teachers to write a thank you speech for them, which he did on a very long sheet of paper in red ink. During my last lesson, one of the boys practically sat on a very large lump covered with a coat, until the end of the lesson, when he read the speech, rather haltingly, to the great applause of his classmates. It was very moving indeed.

In my three weeks at Wonthaggi, I had just had the time to join the choir at the Anglican Church and try my hand at pancake tossing for Shrove Tuesday, when I had to get out my atlas again to see where exactly Yarram was. All I remember otherwise of this short interlude, apart from some pleasant visits with Peggy and Les, is the jocularity of the minister's wife. On one occasion she made us giggle during choir rehearsal by whispering that the words "Ponder anew" in the hymn would make a very good name for a baby elephant. Another choir member, also teaching at the school, introduced me to William Walton's *Façade Suite*. All too soon, I had packed up again and was off to meet the classes waiting for me in my new, unchosen town.

I was glad to have spent some time with my friend Peggy who faded into eternity in her early thirties with Hodgkin's disease, about which little was known at the time. I remember she had about thirty tests to try to find out why she was just getting weaker and weaker, but all to no avail. She was a beautiful person in every way.

Yarram Yarram on the Tarra Tarra in the County of Buln Buln

Yarram, it turned out, was a town of some 1,500 inhabitants, at the foot of the Victorian coastal range, about sixty miles further east than Wonthaggi along the Gippsland coast. To get there, I had to take an evening bus through the Foster Hills — a rather hallucinatory drive through gaunt, treeless slopes that loomed ominously in the early darkness. The bus driver drove me to my new boardinghouse in Yarram and, as we drew up to it, his headlights shone on a sign saying "H. Henley. Undertaker."

Despite this somewhat disconcerting arrival, I found myself much better accommodated than at Miss Raven's. Mrs Henley was from Herefordshire in England, and she soon explained that hers was a dialect that omitted and added aitches. She was Mrs 'Enley and her 'usband was 'Arry. I soon became accustomed to her calling loudly to her eighty-year-old deaf 'usband: "'Arry, get the haxe," and I frequently had to make my way through the coffins in his workshop to tell the 'ard-of-'earing 'Arry that dinner was ready. When there was a burial, Mrs 'Enley would type up a notice to say that "the internment" was at such and such an hour. Since it was wartime, the spelling slip seemed all the more hilarious.

Mrs Henley was affability and generosity itself. She had room for three boarders and she always took in teachers, more for the company than for the extra money. While I was there, one of my co-boarders was a primary school teacher and the other was the domestic science teacher at the HES to which I was now attached. We three would work together on our preparation and corrections until about ten o'clock each evening. Mrs Henley would then serve us a luscious supper and settle down for a little chat. She told us she had never realized that teachers worked so hard until she had teachers as boarders. Every weekend she baked a great supply of iced cupcakes, shortbreads and sponges that she filled with rich whipped cream. These she served as an English tea on our return from school at four o'clock in the afternoon and again for our supper snack in the evening. Of course we had a hot dinner in between. Before long we were putting on weight in a way that had never been a problem at Miss Raven's.

We were awakened in the mornings by the radio news turned up to a volume that 'Arry could 'ear and this penetrated the thin walls of the house, serving as a wakeup call. Mrs Henley always left the radio at the same high volume to accommodate 'Arry and turned it off when the news was over, because half-heard music irritated her husband. Every Tuesday she would go out to play cards with her friends and this provided us with an opportunity to turn on the radio to enjoy a surreptitious evening of music. 'Arry was, of course, 'ammering coffins and didn't 'ear a thing. We always set the radio back to the right station at the right volume and turned it off between the time when we heard Mrs Henley close the garden gate and the moment she opened the front door. Thus it would be ready for the morning reveille. One evening, however, we did not hear the click of the garden gate and, as the key turned in the front door lock, we switched off the radio, turning the dial quickly to the morning news station and guessing at the volume. Next morning, we giggled in our beds as Mrs Henley wondered loudly to 'Arry what could possibly 'ave 'appened to the radio that it had lost so much volume.

The Henleys' only son had enlisted in the armed forces and been sent to fight in Burma. Unfortunately he had been reported missing in action in that disastrous campaign. This was naturally a great sorrow to his parents. Mrs Henley believed strongly that he was still alive; she just knew it intuitively, until one night when she had a very vivid dream, almost a vision. In her dream, her son came to her to say goodbye and she knew then that he had not survived.

The Henleys were kindly folk who must have made the lives of innumerable lonely, homesick teachers a little happier in their home away from home.

Back to Teaching

At the Yarram HES, which catered only for four levels, from seventh to tenth grades, we were a small but congenial group of teachers. We each taught our own subjects across the four levels. The school had about 120 students, coming by buses, as at Kerang, from the dairy farms and rural townships of this rich pastoral area. Since I had become by now a Geography as well as a French and English teacher, I was immediately recruited to assist with this core subject. At Yarram we were fortunate to have a trained Geography teacher, well versed in the latest methods of teaching the subject. It was he who taught me to teach Geography from a basis of scientific principles, rather than as a grab bag of disparate facts. This problem-solving approach, relating facts to the whole context in order to deduce other facts, involved reasoning rather than memorization, making application much more interesting. We would study a whole locality, with its hinterland. Then we would work out where the most likely place for a port might be or, to reverse the process, we would begin with a port, with its latitude and longitude, and consider the factors that made it an important port. We would draw information from climatology, ocean currents, prevailing winds and their relationship to mountain ranges, with their tendency to collect rain or dry the air, inferring what could or would not grow in such an area. I became expert at drawing circles on the board (Giotto's Os we called them) to demonstrate how climate evolved from the earth's relationship to the sun. All of this involved a lot of interesting preparation for me, broadening considerably the bounds of my knowledge, synthesizing what I knew and filling in the gaps my previous studies had left. Of course, I continued to enjoy teaching French and English.

At Yarram I experienced once more the shocks and errors that external examinations can generate. My tenth graders were preparing for their Intermediate Certificate, which was very important to them since for many it would be their school-final examination. My top student in French was a girl named Sue, a very composed young woman, with blond hair tied back in neat plaits. An earnest student, she was very meticulous in everything she did, always dotting her i's and crossing her t's. In French she never forgot to put in the right accent or add the right gender or number agreement. Yet little Miss Perfection failed her external examination, something which was beyond the realm of possibility. To this day it remains a great mystery to me. There is no way that she could not have produced a nearly perfect examination. By the time I saw the results published in the newspaper I had left Yarram. At that time, published exam results were considered immutable. It was not until several years later that I found out that it was possible to request (and pay for) a reexamination of an individual student's paper. Had I known this at the time, I would certainly have challenged Sue's failure, which must have resulted from a total entered on the wrong line, an inaccurate copying of her examination number, or even a misplaced paper. (The completed examinations were sent to Melbourne for correction from proctored country centers). Fortunately for Sue, she was continuing on to a senior high school where she would still have time, in her Leaving and Matriculation studies, to make up for any deficiencies in her record.

The washback effect of the form of the examination on the curriculum meant that we had to spend a great deal of time translating from English into French. For the Intermediate exam there would be five complicated sentences to translate, with the kinds of exceptions to rules and aberrant spellings students were likely to forget. Preparing for this kind of test was presumed to teach them the French language. I preferred to teach French for communication and enjoyment, but I knew that students needed to be well prepared for this tricky type of question. I had to work out a way to have the best of both worlds. Previous examination papers revealed that there were always five linguistic traps per sentence, for a total of twenty-five points for the question. Part of the preparation I gave my students was to examine each sentence closely and find all five traps first before trying to translate it. Once these "problems" had been identified and dealt with, the student needed only to pay careful attention to the routine parts of the sentence to be successful. I was not convinced that this little "treasure hunt" had much to do with using French, but at least it would help my students to gain necessary points toward a passing grade. In this way I managed to prepare them for this absurd type of test, while leaving time for them to have fun actually using the language. This was probably why a colleague once remarked that the girls liked French because I made it like crossword puzzles. Fortunately there are many ways of gaining students' attention. To each time its appropriate means.

Since the Yarram HES was in an old school building that had once been a primary school, it had a Headmaster's residence attached, as was so common in rural schools. Our Headmaster, Mr Doherty, was a genial Irishman, who liked to do his administrative work in the comfort of his own home across the schoolyard. Consequently that was where the one school typewriter was usually to be found. If we wanted to type something up during a spare period, we would wend our way across the yard to the Headmaster's house, where Mr Doherty's old mother would greet us with little homemade biscuits and some of her traditional Irish raisin pop. This drink was cool and so delicious that I asked her for the recipe. When I went home for the Easter vacation, I hastened to try out my new summer drink. As she had suggested, I soaked grapes in water in a bucket with sugar and lemon juice. After several days of soaking (and the fermentation I had not counted on), I bottled the liquor that emerged. All the family declared the first bottle to be deliciously refreshing, as I had promised it would be. The contents of the second bottle went right up our noses and my brothers declared the third bottleful to be particularly exhilarating. A few days later the fourth bottle burst with irrepressible force. By then it was clear that my first venture into liquor-making had been all too successful. To avoid any further catastrophes, I took the bottles gingerly to the bottom of the yard where I carefully worked out the corks, with the bottles pointed away from me, and the liquor swept out with a hiss. Thus ended my experiment with Irish moonshine

Having so much time to myself at Yarram, I decided to take up the piano again, at the point where my lessons with Miss Baulch had left me years before. I was able to practice on a piano in a local hall, so I took lessons and practiced up to four hours a day. Alas! It seemed I really had no inborn talent. By the end of the year it was obvious that, much as I love to listen to music, I was not going to become the much-sought-after social performer I had hoped to be. I decided to stick to my last and return to languages, playing around again with German.

I first saw snow at close quarters, while at Yarram. On cold winter mornings we could see snow on the tops of some of the mountains that formed a backdrop to the town, but in Yarram, as in most of temperate Victoria and certainly in Melbourne by the sea, it did not snow. We had, of course, read about snow in our school textbooks where French-speaking children played in the snow and constructed snowmen or English poets raved about its purity and beauty. One day the father of one of the pupils at the Yarram school, who had passed through a light snowfall while crossing the mountains on business, had thoughtfully filled a basket with the novel white stuff and dropped it off at the school to be passed around the different classes. We took handfuls of it; we felt its texture; we sniffed and tasted it in great excitement. I did not see snow again, except in the distance on mountain ranges, until I encountered light falls in England and France, which were certainly nothing compared with the great snowfalls that drape the New England scenery after a February blizzard.

Leisure Hours in Gippsland

In sharp contrast to the flat, dry country around Kerang, Yarram gave me access to some of the most beautiful scenery in Australia. By this time I had found my own company to be sufficient and I did not wait to find companions for my roamings. I would bike out of town for about seven miles to the foot of the road up the mountains. From there I would ride and then walk my bike for about three hours up the steep, winding track to the Grand Ridge Road.

267

Here I would picnic and then freewheel for three quarters of a mile downhill to the Yarram Road. The beautiful eucalyptus forest, with its spectacularly tall, slender trees, and the magnificent views over Central Gippsland made it an outstanding experience. On other days I would go to Bulga Park, via the Minnehaha Falls. Here a suspension bridge over a narrow gorge provided a wonderful viewpoint for looking right down into the hearts of the huge tree ferns. Or I would visit the breathtaking Tarra Valley National Park, a virtually untouched area of waterfalls and fern gullies, which few people visited at that time. Here I could see the original Gippsland forest as it must have been for centuries before the arrival of the first colonists. For a complete change of scenery, I would go south to the Ninety Mile Beach, where the ocean rollers swept up on the dazzling white sand, at the foot of the grass-covered dunes. There would not be a soul in sight in either direction. It was my private little heaven. After a hot ride I could lie on the wide, sandy beach enjoying the cool sea breezes and watching the boiling surf turn over and under, as it rushed back to reform in tremendous waves that crashed up on the beach. Or I could amuse myself jumping the waves as they dashed at me with overwhelming force. On these trips I would sometimes see beside the road echidnas and wombats, burrowing rapidly out of sight to avoid disturbance; and once I saw a baby frogmouth owl, for all the world like a large ball of fluff as it sat motionless on a bough. Every weekend became a fascinating holiday.

By a strange happenstance, my former student from Kerang, Wilga Thorne, had been appointed for her first student-teaching position to a small school near Alberton, some three hundred miles from her home, but just fourteen miles from Yarram. Thus the two Wilgas, alone in strange places, could meet and socialize. She would ride in halfway to Yarram on her bicycle and I would ride out on mine. Then we would have a picnic in some spot in the forest or explore the little fishing cove at Port Albert. These opportunities to share our leisure strengthened our bonds of friendship and alleviated our feelings of isolation.

At the Anglican Church in Yarram, I met the McDonalds. The Rector himself was a kindly man, but the worst preacher I have ever encountered in my church-going career. I remember the relief with which we heard him say, on one very hot summer morning, "For obvious reasons I will dispense with the sermon," as he mopped his brow with an ample white handkerchief. His best sermons were verbatim readings from the newsletters of missionaries in far-distant lands. It was his energetic, unselfish wife who held the church together. Welcoming and hospitable, she soon made newcomers feel at home. Before long I had found a friend in her daughter, Mary, who suffered from mild cerebral palsy which had rendered her left arm useless and left her with a limp in her left leg. Her speech, however, was not affected. In addition she had a form of epilepsy that caused her to "go away" for a minute or two every now and then. She would stand, quite vacant for a brief interval, then return as her usual determined self. I became quite accustomed to just waiting until she "came back." Mary never let her disability hinder her in her indefatigable service for others, which she has continued wherever she has been for the sixty years we have been friends. During my year in Yarram, her energies were going into sorting out from the town's refuse old newspapers and cardboard, bottles, tin cans, old batteries, and aluminum, copper, and other metals. These we could sell to raise money for the war effort, while providing the nation with needed raw materials. Mary and I would spend every Wednesday evening together in this enterprise. Unfortunately, sometimes thoughtless people would neglect to separate their garbage from recyclable items, so this became a rather dirty, smelly job. I can still see Mary in her apron, cheerful and tireless in the midst of it all, working long hours at sorting, sorting, sorting. Mary was never able to work independently for her living, but many are the people in trouble, the aged and the sick, who have blessed her as their ever-available guardian angel.

Fortunately I am a collector of people and I still treasure these fortuitous friendships with very diverse individuals, who represent the different facets of my experiences in creating a life.

8

EDUCATIONAL CONTRASTS:

St Annes 1944-46 and Taylor's Coaching College 1947-48

A Decisive Turning Point

At Yarram I was in the Anglican Diocese of Gippsland, whose Bishop at that time was the Right Reverend Donald Blackwood. A gentle, compassionate man, he had a deep spiritual influence on the churches in the diocese. On one occasion he visited the Yarram church, where he spoke of the need for more teachers for the small, developing, diocesan boarding school for girls, St Annes[61], in the cathedral town of Sale, which was further east along the Gippsland coast. I had always attended state-run high schools and I associated private schools with snobbishness and exclusivity. This rift between the students in state-organized, tuition-free educational institutions and private, fee-paying schools was endemic in the Victorian populace at the time. It had never occurred to me to teach in any other schools than those of the State Education Department. Not only was it a family tradition, but it also provided me, a child of the Depression who had grown up in a family of reduced financial circumstances, with a permanent lifetime position that promised steady promotion and a guaranteed pension at the end of my career. These were all very important considerations in the eyes of lower middle class families. Yet, as I listened to Bishop Blackwood, I felt a distinct sense of calling, as though God were asking me to give up all

I had worked for and the growing prosperity it set before me to launch into unknown waters where there was no promise of permanency or security. Leaving the Education Department service and offering to teach at St Annes at this stage of my career went against logic and all my previous mindset, yet it came to me as a very persistent call that I felt I could not refuse. After much prayer I decided to follow this inner conviction and resign from the Department to go to Sale the following year.

Naturally the Bishop and the retiring Headmistress of St Annes, Miss Constance Tisdall, were very pleased with my decision, but not so the Education Department, which saw me as a very promising young teacher with a bright future in the service. As it happened one of my former Latin teachers from EHS, Miss Walker, was a senior Departmental Inspector at the time. She decided to come and see me personally to talk over with me a decision that she saw as a great mistake on my part, the biggest miscalculation of my life, and one which would vitiate my whole future. However, despite her arguments, my inner conviction that this was the path for me won out.

Time has shown that it was Miss Walker who was making a big mistake, not I. Looking back, I see this as a decisive turning point in my life. Having made the decision early in my career to liberate myself from psychological commitment to a secure future along a well-defined path, I was free to make a variety of choices at later stages. This liberation enabled me to shape a very eventful life, which led to experiences and professional opportunities I could not have envisioned at the age of twenty-four in that small country town in southern Victoria. In the Education Department at the time no extra advancement came from doing further study or seeking broader teaching experience abroad. Taking leave without pay for such purposes was a possibility, although it was not encouraged. Those who had the temerity to do so returned to find themselves at the same point on the roll as when they had left, while those who had stayed at home had forged ahead — in other words, they had lost rather than gained ground. Many, returning from study and experience abroad to this patently unfair situation, switched over to the private school system. Because of this bureaucratically simpler but blinkered approach, the Education Department lost many gifted teachers over time. I still had my eyes set on studying in France. These were not the

271

thoughts that occupied my mind as I made this important decision at this point in my life, but they were factors that made me very glad later that I had made this choice, before becoming irrevocably committed to an inflexible system. St Annes at Sale now became my next destination.

Round-the-Clock Education at St Annes (1944-46)

A town of about five thousand, Sale was the hub of South Gippsland, on Victoria's southeast coast. St Annes Church of England Girls' Grammar School was a very young school in 1944. It had opened its doors in 1924 with four pupils, of whom three were the daughters of the then Bishop of Gippsland, who was the leading force behind its establishment. This small group, rising to eleven during the year, was taught by a Deaconess in the church hall. St Annes initiated secondary classes only in 1931 and by 1944, when I arrived, there were 154 students in the primary and secondary classes, of whom sixty were boarders. The retiring Headmistress, Miss Constance Tisdall, who had interviewed me for appointment in 1943, had been born in Walhalla in Gippsland. With her sisters, she had already established a respected girls' private school in Melbourne, called Rosbercon. Miss Tisdall had "vowed never to take charge of a church school nor to bury herself in the country."[62] Fortunately for St Anne's, she had yielded to persuasion when approached in 1934 to lead this struggling young school. It was Miss Tisdall who established the commitment of St Annes, from its early days, to student-centered education. Her educational aim at Rosbercon had always been: "by wise guidance and watchful care on the part of the teachers to foster in each girl a love of learning and to give her the opportunity of developing her special gifts, so that she may be able to take her place in life and fulfil her duties to the community."

At St Annes, Miss Tisdall added to these aims, "the necessity of considering the country background of the girls, and the importance of ensuring that their education would enhance the role they would play in rural communities."[63] This addition was important since most of the girls at St Annes came from quite small country towns and remote farms. To ensure that the school provided education for some girls from poorer rural families, Miss Tisdall introduced two "domestic scholarships." These bursaries enabled girls from very isolated places to earn money by helping in the kitchen and performing supervised household duties, while boarding at the school and enjoying the benefits of the rich education it provided. They were fully integrated with the life of the school and by 1949 one of these girls had become Head Prefect. It was this school that Miss Lorna Sparrow inherited when she came to Sale as the new Headmistress in 1944. The continuing war in the Pacific was still at its height, along with the problems and deprivations it engendered. By this time the St Annes girls, in their bottle-green tunics with fawn blouses, were a familiar sight in the town of Sale. The work of the school was becoming well known and appreciated throughout the diocese of Gippsland. This recognition was due in large part to the unremitting efforts of Bishop Blackwood, who worked hard to keep even the outlying areas of his diocese aware of what was going on in the center at Sale. Inevitably, because of the war situation, the developing school was suffering more than its normal share of the growing pains of lack of space, lack of personnel and lack of funds.

At the age of thirty-one, Lorna Sparrow was the youngest Headmistress of an independent girls' school in Victoria. Since nearly all of Miss Tisdall's staff had retired with her, Miss Sparrow found herself with an almost entirely new teaching staff, of which I was a member. Fortunately, before leaving her home state of South Australia, she had recruited several young teachers to come to St Annes with her. Although there were only nine teachers to cover all subjects and levels, we were all very well qualified and dedicated to our work. In the very enclosed situation of a boarding school in a strange place, we came to know each other very well and we enjoyed spending time together. Looking back, it is clear that the girls in this small school were receiving an excellent education that took into consideration their different temperaments and capacities and respected their needs and interests, while allowing them much leeway for idiosyncratic development. This approach was made possible because of the size of the school and the high degree of individual attention. Miss Sparrow felt very much at home with Miss Tisdall's established educational philosophy, as I certainly did. She continued to develop an education that enriched each individual. As one example of this approach, the most important prize of the year went, not to the student with the best academic record nor to the leading sports luminary but, on the vote of the girls themselves, to the one who had contributed most to the community as a leader in daily life and service to others. One year, I remember, this prize went to a girl whose dream was to be a hairdresser. Successful hairdressers are all therapists, in my experience, and are specially gifted with social skills.

The nine teachers in residence in 1944 included a kindergarten teacher, a music teacher, a physical education teacher, an elocutionist, a boarding house supervisor (who taught some shorthand and typing) and two student teachers. All the subjects in the senior school were taught by Miss Sparrow, Kath Woodroofe (later a Lecturer in History at Adelaide University), the student teachers and myself. Since it was wartime, supplementary staff was practically unavailable. Despite her administrative work as Headmistress, Miss Sparrow taught thirty-nine forty-minute periods a week in mathematics, sciences, economics and religious studies, as well as conducting the religious devotions that began each day. In my second year, I taught forty-two periods per week of French, English, and Geography. These ran from ninth grade to twelfth grade level (or Matriculation as Leaving Honours was now called). Several of my classes were doubled up, with two levels in the one room. If we were to cover all subjects of the curriculum for all girls at all levels, there was nothing else we could do. We were well aware that all over the country, in our wartime situation, people were trying to cope in no matter what domain, with very few hands to take up the many tasks. Naturally, we were kept very busy out of class; over and above our boarding school duties, we had so many lessons to prepare and so much in the way of homework and tests to correct for so many classes. In those days much written work was assigned and there were regular tests every three weeks. These were not multiple-choice or fill-in-the-blank tests, but essay-type and problem-solving tests. Fortunately, in such a small school, classes were not excessively large as they had been in the state system. Being constantly present in the boarding house, the teachers were able to give personal help to girls who were slower learners or guide those with exceptional talents in individual projects.

As part of the students' development, Miss Sparrow set up an Advisory Council of faculty and student leaders (prefects, captains and vice-captains of forms and houses and representatives of school committees), of which I was the first chairperson. It was the task of this Council to decide on the administrative details of running the school and the boarding house. From its second year on, this Advisory Council was student-managed. This system of governance gave the girls valuable experience in formulating regulations for harmonious community living and supervising their observance. The girls also took responsibility for the organization of leisure activities, such as fancy-dress balls and fund-raising fetes. All the students were encouraged to engage in social service, either for the Red Cross, the local hospital, or in support of church missions and they regularly contributed to an Appeals Fund. Some taught Sunday School in the various churches.

We were very close to the girls, as we were to each other, living our lives parallel with theirs for twenty-four hours a day in a restricted space. We had meals with them in the refectory and supervised them in their dormitories. On Sundays we escorted them to church services, walking two by two in crocodile, and we accompanied them on outings and picnics. In the refectory the junior and senior parts of the school ate together, so we came to know all the girls very well. I remember one very homesick five-year-old who wept bitterly for weeks after her arrival at boarding school, so much so that the girls called her Waterworks. The parents of another girl, who was a weekly boarder, phoned her every morning at the end of breakfast and we became accustomed to hearing: "Penny X, to the phone please." Penny went home every weekend and, although a perfect angel in school, apparently played old Harry while she was at home, so that her parents were at their wits' end. Then, early on Sunday afternoon, she would pack her case and demand to be taken back to school, where she became again her angelic school self.

Through a Saturday Club, the girls organized their own leisure in the weekends. In these pre-television days, producing skits and vaudeville-type mock melodramas was popular as homegrown entertainment, especially if the amateur actors could take off their teachers in the process. In every way possible, Miss Sparrow encouraged student initiative, a trait that would serve them well later in their lives in their small communities.

As Resident Mistresses, the teachers also collaborated with the girls in organizing after-school clubs that catered for a variety of intellectual and aesthetic interests. I was in charge of the International Club, where we studied the background of countries in the news or those from which our families had come. A list in my files shows we were interested in South Africa, Canada, India, the United States, England, Scotland, Ireland, Poland, Norway and Japan, the last three being much in the news as the war dragged on. The students, researching in pairs, prepared presentations on their chosen area, after which there was always lively discussion. Ironically enough, I remember stating very firmly at one of these meetings that I had no interest whatsoever in visiting the United States, because I thought that, as a new country, it was altogether too much like Australia. Little did I realize that I would be spending a large part of my life in that country. I also coordinated the program for the Literary and Debating Club, where we discussed books we had read, had poetry readings and wrote and read our own poems and limericks — a form of verse that was very popular at the time. The girls also gave prepared and impromptu speeches. After a visit to the local law court, they argued their way through their own court case, about a charge of physical assault, intentionally but factitiously perpetrated on the school premises in front of unsuspecting witnesses, who were then called upon to testify. A bewigged judge and barristers, who cross-examined the witnesses, added solemnity to the occasion. They practiced their journalistic skills in preparing a news sheet, *The Green Grubs' Gossip*, for distribution among the other students, green being the color of their school uniforms. They graduated to full-scale debates among themselves and occasionally against the local high school. On one memorable occasion, the girls debated with the boys in a Home in the neighborhood. The subject discussed was "That protection is in the best Interests of Australia" — a perennial subject of controversy for Australians.

Lots of fun and games enlivened life in the boarding house, and this reminded me of my earlier reading of the *Schoolgirls' Own*, with its accounts of pillow fights and secret feasts in English boarding schools. Since space was scarce, as the school population grew, there was a continual search for further buildings in town that could be used by the school. In my first year I lived several blocks from the school with a group of girls whose dormitory was in the Church Registry building. Here Miss Adria Weir, an Archdeacon's daughter who had been associated with the school since its inception, was House Mistress and took responsibility for the girls' living arrangements, while I continued my resident duties at the main school. In the Registry there was a small kitchen and occasionally the girls would organize midnight feasts there, to which we would be invited in hush-hush secrecy.

When we were on duty during the weekends, we sometimes took the girls on extended hikes in the country. Here they would have the pleasure of picking wild blackberries and the mushrooms that popped up plentifully in the paddocks along the road, or they would push on further to the ocean coast at Seaspray, where they could cool off in the waves. Sometimes we took the girls on longer trips by bus, particularly in my case for the Geography excursions required for their external examinations. On one occasion, we visited the nearby open-cut brown coal mine and briquette processing plant at Morwell, as well as the associated electrical generating plant at Yallourn. While we were walking along high walkways, looking down on the huge generators, one of the girls suffered from a bout of acrophobia. Petrified into complete immobility, she had to be coaxed away step by step, with her eyes averted from the abyss. We also organized one very memorable, full weekend bus trip for the Geography and Geology classes during which we were able to complete the work for several of the required field excursions. We studied the terraces, torrent gravels and silt jetties of the Mitchell River on the way to the beautiful holiday resort of Lakes Entrance. Here in one direction we could see a string of lakes stretching as far as the eye could see, with green banks separating them, and in the other the offshore bar, with the walls of the artificial entrance, beyond which the blue waters of Bass Strait stretched to the horizon. We hunted for fossils in the sea cliffs. I have always found that nothing makes the long evolution of different species really come to life so much as the experience of finding actual fossils in layers of rock. To keep expenses down we slept on stretchers with straw mattresses at a camping ground and we picnicked by the roadside or on the beach as often as possible. On these trips, the girls were always extremely well behaved, not only because they were having such fun together, but also because the relationships developed through our close contact in the boarding school were very familial and cordial. After several of these exciting, curriculum-related junkets, Miss Sparrow quietly inquired as to the availability of material for field excursions in natural features much nearer to home — like, for instance, the meanders and billabongs of the local Thompson River and its confluence with the Latrobe. How unexciting, if useful, we found this excursion to be, after having traveled so much further afield!

One important realization that came to me while teaching at St Annes was the fact that we often teach students more brilliant than ourselves and that this need not be a scary experience that shakes our confidence. These highly intelligent students will learn with or without our help and sometimes despite us. By recognizing this fact, we are liberated from our sense of insecurity. We can then devote our attention to helping them to develop their special talents and explore their interests. We can release them from some of the guided learning their fellow students need and enjoy, while using them in unobtrusive ways to help in peer teaching. Above all we take care to see that they do not become bored with the educational process but develop autonomy in self-education. Although many of the St Annes girls came from isolated and often culturally limited situations, there were, as in any group, some who were more intellectually gifted than others, being endowed with particularly inquiring minds and independence of thought. The open educational climate that Miss Sparrow encouraged was an excellent milieu within which these girls could develop and flourish. The boarding school provided many opportunities, through constant association of students with teachers, for individual encouragement and stimulation. I remember sharing with one thirteen-year-old girl, who later became a university-level reading specialist, the latest novels I was reading and I very much enjoyed discussing them with her afterwards.

Since most of our teaching group were in their early twenties they felt and acted much more like friends or older sisters to the girls than distant mentors or disciplinarians. The girls shared with us their personal traumas and their growing pains in learning to live in a community. The physical setting of the school was conducive to this feeling of being an extended family. On the outskirts of Sale, it was on the shore of a lake, with reeds and birds and shady trees. Walking the two miles around the lake was a favorite way to relieve stress and draw in new strength with the cool fresh air. Adolescent girls living in such a hothouse of relationships developed passionate and changing attachments, "pashes" we called them, which sometimes took on intense emotional importance in their lives. In the middle of one such experience, one fourteen-year-old girl, unable to control (or understand) her emotions, decided to commit suicide. I remember following her out to the lake late one evening and gradually talking her down, until she returned exhausted to her dormitory bed. In my last year a new sports mistress, with unexpressed and unresolved personal problems, joined me to accompany the girls on their walk to church. Her face was so flushed that she had turned up the collar of her coat and turned down the brim of her hat to hide it from comment or inquiry. It appeared that she was taking barbiturates and had taken a handful of pills that morning (this in a period when taking drugs was a rare phenomenon). I was very much afraid that she might do herself serious harm. On the way home I insisted that I would not leave her side until she gave me the bottle with the remaining barbiturates. Naturally she protested that this was no concern of mine and that I had no authority to boss her around. Nevertheless, I continued with the technique of seeing whose will was the stronger and followed her to her room, refusing to move until she gave me the offending bottle. Finally my will won out, or her own fright at her condition caused her to give in, and she handed over the bottle, which I promptly emptied down the toilet. As far as I know, that was the end of her flirtation with dangerous substances.

As a group, we resident teachers had fun together in our leisure and went on bike rides and picnics when not on duty. On one such picnic, Morphett, the Physical Education teacher, and Woodroofe, the History teacher (we called each other by our family names, as teachers and nurses often did at the time), decided to accompany those of us on bikes in a hired horse-drawn jinker. Neither of them had had any experience with horses before. An odd couple, Morphett was very small and thin while Woodroofe was a very big woman, so the weight was rather poorly distributed in the jinker. When we arrived at the picnic spot, they calmly tied the horse to a nearby tree and proceeded to ignore it. When we suggested that horses rather like a chaff bag and a drink of water after a working period, they looked very surprised that animals needed more care than bicycles or cars. When we got back late after such excursions, we

279

would usually come into the school through the kitchen door, so as not to disturb the sleeping girls. Here we would nearly trip over large pails of fresh milk for the next morning's breakfast, with the rich cream accumulating on the surface of the unhomogenized liquid. This was too much for tired and hungry young women, so we would get ourselves plates of cereal and pour the thick, rich cream over it. Next morning, not surprisingly, the cook would be complaining about the dairyman delivering such thin milk.

With the continuation of the war, commodities became scarce and were rationed. We had coupons for butter and sugar, as well as for clothes. Because sugar was in such short supply, we ate rhubarb sweetened with honey, which I found to be a most unpleasant combination. Apples were readily available from orchards in the local area, so for one full year we ate apples continually in every possible shape or form, often sweetened with honey too. We ate stewed apples, apples baked in their skins, apple Brown Betty, apple pie, apple snow with beaten egg white, apple dumplings, apple flapjacks, steamed apple pudding. For twenty years afterwards I couldn't bear to eat an apple.

Miss Sparrow was remarkably adaptable and could turn her hand to anything. The school was indeed fortunate in having her services at this time, when there was not only a shortage of teachers but also of domestic and maintenance staff. Since no cook was available in the weekends, as often as not Miss Sparrow herself, with the help of the young music teacher or some of the older girls, cooked the meals. As staffing problems increased, she arranged for the girls to share the housework. On many occasions she herself wielded a paintbrush or a garden fork as she prepared the school for the opening of a new school year or a new term. She rarely took off weekends or holidays. Even during the summer vacations she continued to work on problems of new living or classroom space. Her energy seemed boundless.

As at Kerang and Yarram, there were no young men of our age in sight. As Japan swept closer to our shores, advancing through Southeast Asia, Indonesia, and Papua New Guinea, more and more young Australians were called up or joined the forces of their own volition. As a group of young women who enjoyed male company, we made what efforts we could to meet some of the servicemen who came to the nearby Air Force Training Base. This seemed to provide some prospects. On one occasion we invited a group of airmen to a party at the school, after the girls had gone to bed. (The girls were, of course, peering out of the windows to see who our guests were.) We put a lot of effort into making this a very successful party, but unfortunately the young men left town the following week. We discovered the base was being used for three-week training sessions for airmen about to be sent into action. One week for the new arrivals to settle into the base, a second for us to get to know them, and a third to say goodbye hardly gave us much time to develop lasting relationships. Finding it too difficult to keep up with this rapid turnover, we had to look elsewhere. The churches were doing their bit with socials for visiting servicemen in church halls. One of our teachers did meet and marry a young man from a nearby farm, a Methodist as she was, who came home on leave from time to time. We were not bereft of friendships in Sale, however. We were frequently invited by hospitable townspeople who tried to make us feel at home. One couple in particular, the Valentines, who had a strong interest in St Annes, which their two young daughters attended, proved to be great fun and remained among my very good friends for many years.

During the 1914-18 World War, there had been, in my home area of Essendon, a certain number of hostile chauvinistic actions taken against shopkeepers with German names, like Plarre's, our local pastry cook, who suffered broken windows and noisy invective. Some of these loyal German-Australian citizens had taken the expedient of putting Australian flags in their windows and even anglicizing their names. German sausage had changed its name at that time to Belgian sausage. During the Second World War there was less of this kind of petty harassment. With the rapid onrush of events, Australia's attention was soon focused on the war in the Pacific. This was much nearer to our shores and more personally threatening than the war in Europe. The atrocities committed by the Japanese against Anzac prisoners of war in camps like Changi, in death marches and in the dreadful ordeal of the building of the Burma Road aroused strong emotions in Australia. This led to at least ten years of anti-Japanese feeling after the war, an attitude long since buried as trade and tourist relationships with Japan have become of such importance to

Australia's economy. Many Australians have visited Japan and Japanese students have lived with Australian families. The beautiful Queensland coast is now a favorite resort for Japanese holidaymakers. This familiarity has greatly modified attitudes.

Quite early in the war, we became accustomed to the Italian prisoners of war who were sent to Australia, most of whom settled in quite happily to work on outlying farms to which they had been assigned. They had not necessarily been very enthusiastic about fighting in Europe to begin with and most enjoyed their quiet life in peaceful surroundings. One of our boarders at St Annes, who came from an isolated farm at Ensay, recounted how her father, a Presbyterian, had asked his Italian workers if they would like to go to church on Sunday. "Yes," said the Italians readily and jumped in the car for the outing. On arrival in the small town, my friend's father stopped at the Catholic Church and said: "Your church — Catholic Church. We're Presbyterians." The Italians however refused to budge, shaking their heads. When their driver repeated the information, fearing they might not have understood, the Italians settled back comfortably and replied firmly: "In Italy, Catholic; in Australia Presbyterian." A number of these Italians preferred to remain in Australia after the war, when large numbers of their fellow countrymen were immigrating to our shores.

Although there were great numbers of Americans in Australia at the time, I personally met none of them, living, as I was, in my little country backwater. On my vacations in Melbourne, I would hear about the effect of their presence. After the fall of Singapore, Australians had been forced to realize that they could not depend on faraway England for their defense and that the alliance across the Pacific with the United States was of primary importance. Australia was, and is, conscious of the fact that it was the forces of the United States that saved them from invasion at the Battle of the Coral Sea and finally brought the war in the Pacific to an end. Many of our friends and brothers, including my own, had fought beside the GI's in the war zone. After General Douglas MacArthur set up his headquarters for the direction of the Pacific war in Brisbane, there were swarms of American GI's on recreational leave in the big cities, many of whom married young Australian women.

Finally the war in the Pacific came to an end. VJ Day we called it (August 15th, 1945). There was great excitement at St Annes. Students and teachers together, we ran around the lake loudly ringing the school bell and singing popular wartime songs such as *The White Cliffs of Dover, The Last Time I saw Paris, Roll out the Barrel, A Nightingale Sang in Berkeley Square* and the very singable *Marines' Hymn.* That these songs referred in the main to the war in the Northern Hemisphere mattered little to us; our boys had fought there too and we were accustomed in our studies to seeing everything from the perspective of the "Mother Country." They had become our songs as well. We shouted and cried and tooted car horns, as we expressed our great joy and exhilaration at this liberation from worry and strain. Eagerly we anticipated the return to normalcy in our lives and our communities

In Sale I made my own connections with the Anglican Church, apart from the formal links of St Annes as the diocesan school. Our heavy program and our boarding school duties left us little time for extra church activities, but I was soon singing in the choir. This time we had a first-class choirmaster, as befitted a cathedral, if only a small one. I think there are few groups who become as closely knit in bonds of friendship as choirs, where sopranos feel a special bond with the tenors and the altos with their supporting basses. There is always a great feeling of camaraderie at choir practices.

I particularly enjoyed my walks home from evening practice. Because of the heavy frosts in this part of Gippsland, the winter skies would be very clear and cloudless. It was on these walks that I taught myself how to distinguish more and more constellations, until I could recognize much of the map of the heavens. Orion's Belt was always easily located. The next, most easily identifiable, for those who knew how to find it, was the Southern Cross, with its pointers, Alpha and Beta Centauri, circling around the South Magnetic Pole. Most children learned to recognize early the Seven Sisters (the Pleiades), with the seventh tiny star which you really had to look for, as it blinked faintly in modest reticence. These were good starting points for identification of new groups of stars. Venus was prominent near the Moon, as the Morning or the Evening Star and the reddish gleam of Mars made it easy to detect. I would try to find the Gemini, usually low on the horizon, and the splendor of the Crown, but I particularly

283

loved the great question mark of Scorpio, sprawling across the sky. "Shooting stars" and meteorite showers were quite common and very occasionally to the South I would see traces of the Aurora Australis.

Dargo Weekend

At Sale, as at Kerang, I had opportunities to experience country life, on invitation from some of the girls' parents. I enjoyed watching harvesting or sheep shearing or orphaned lambs being fed from a bottle. Some of the St Annes girls lived in very remote, sparsely inhabited places, one of which was Dargo, way up in the mountains. I had learned about the Dargo High Plains in geography lessons at school, as an area where cattle roamed free during the summer months but had to be taken down to lower levels in winter, because of the snows. It was the kind of country one associated with daring stockmen like the Man from Snowy River. Two of the girls on domestic scholarships at St Annes came from this exotic place, which had previously been their whole world and about which they talked incessantly. I was delighted when they invited me to visit their home town during a school break.

The little township of Dargo boasted two hundred closely interrelated inhabitants, who were scattered on surrounding farms. To reach it from Sale was quite a trip by train and bus. Dargo itself was situated on an elevated river flat, with the river running through the middle of the township. When the bus stopped in Dargo, I found on one side of the road a General Store with Post Office, which offered mail service twice a week, and on the other a small hotel. Hens and chickens and an occasional pig were wandering in their own preoccupied way down the middle of the road. There were no houses in the town itself, as far as I could see. A tennis court and a cricket ground, for the convenience of the surrounding farm folk, and a Mechanics Institute Hall on the outskirts completed the ensemble. The surrounding paddocks were dotted with little groups of sheep and cattle and there were patches of maize, potatoes, beans, and pumpkins.

I carried my weekend case into the hotel to find no one in sight. I soon discovered that this old, well-worn hotel catered for very casual living; it was a do-as-you-please, come-and-go-as-you-like kind of place. If I wanted to go out before the proprietor had decided

284

to get up, I had just to get myself some breakfast — helping myself to whatever I wanted. Because of measles in the family the girl who had invited me, Francie Traill, had unfortunately been quarantined at her grandparents' place just at the time of my visit. She had urged me to come all the same, assuring me that her cousins would look after me. The only time I was able to see her during my visit was when I was driven a few miles out of town to a bridge over the river, to which she had ridden some distance on her horse from her grandparents' farm.

As Francie had promised, I was soon welcomed by a group of cheerful young people from the surrounding farms. Most of the people in town, I soon discovered, were Traill cousins. Very soon my new friends were driving me up the mountains to see a magnificent view of dark mountain ranges behind dark mountain ranges, stretching far into the interior. The view was breathtakingly spectacular, yet when I commented on its grandeur, one of my local hosts responded carelessly: "Oh! We see it every day. We don't even notice it." For this trip about eight of us stood packed on the truck bed of a pickup without working brakes. "That's alright," they cried out cheerfully, as we began the steep descent, "We'll drive in second gear." And we did, the driver shwooshing happily around the steep curves of the mountains, as we laughed and sang and swayed together. Curves there were aplenty. On the road down from Dargo toward the coast there is one hill with a hundred turns and curves in a four-mile stretch. With this carefree group, accustomed to wild driving, we survived the hair-raising ride in one piece.

My new friends were determined I should have a good time, so they asked me whether I would like to go to a dance or see a film. I expressed a preference for the former, which, they said, would be no problem. To arrange a dance all they had to do was put the lights on in the Mechanics' Institute Hall and all the young people from the area, seeing the signal, would come. It took about an hour for everyone to primp up and get to the hall, where a local girl played dance music on the piano. At one point her friends decided it was hardly fun for her not to be able to dance at all with her fiancé, who was visiting Dargo for the weekend. Another local girl, who knew how to play only one danceable piece of music, then took over and played her piece over and over again to give her pianist friend time to enjoy herself.

The next day being Sunday, I was told there would be a church service in the evening at the Church of England. "No need to leave for the service at any specific time," I was told. "We just wait until we see the minister drive past." It seemed this would give us plenty of time to get to the service, since it would take a little while for the itinerant preacher to pump up the lamps to light the church. Unfortunately, the only working lamps for the service were at the front of the church, so to see the words of the hymns or to follow the prayer book we had to turn our backs to the altar and to the minister. I am sure the Lord was accommodating.

Hospitality at Dargo was warm, openhearted, and generous. Now, with the extension of modern amenities, technology, and ease of travel, it would be hard to find such a close-knit, self-sufficient, fun-filled community. For me, as a Melbournian, this visit was a very happy, if somewhat unusual, adventure.

MA Continues

All the time I was at St Annes, despite my time-consuming obligations, I was continuing my discipline of working two hours every morning before breakfast on my MA thesis. With Chizzy's approval, I was now working on Racine, since the actual body of text was more definitive and more easily accessible than for Flaubert. This was important because I was in a situation where I did not have ready access to library facilities. My correspondent, Colette, sent me several books of recent Racine criticism, which I found invaluable. Otherwise, I had to rely on whatever I could borrow on library loan, or what I could study in haste during infrequent vacation visits to the Melbourne University Library and the Melbourne Public Library. My topic was Racine's conception of fate, as exemplified in the corpus of his plays. For this I needed to study the conceptions of fate in the original Greek and Roman writers from whom Racine had taken his themes, Aeschylus, Euripides, Sophocles, and Seneca. I studied these works in a fairly literal translation, which I had been able to buy in a secondhand shop in Melbourne. It seemed to me that this translation might bring me nearer to the original formulation than someone else's poeticized interpretation. Steeping myself in these seminal works was, I found, providing me with the opportunity for a fourth level of education and an autonomous one where I followed my intellectual

286

interests wherever they led. Marie Pietzsch's brother, who was a Jesuit, wrote me a very thoughtful and erudite sixteen-page letter on the differences between the Jesuit and Jansenist beliefs on predestination and destiny as God's plan for our lives, which I found very illuminating. Sale became quite cold in the winter, particularly at night, with heavy white frosts that remained on the lawns until early afternoon. Every morning I would get up at six and make myself a cup of hot beef tea in the Registry kitchen. Then, wrapping a rug around my legs as I had been accustomed to do at Ascot Vale during the depression years, I would settle down to close study of Racine's plays in my unheated Registry bedroom.

After three years of heavy teaching loads, piles of weekly English essays to read, French exercises and compositions to correct, regular essay-type examinations and tests, time-consuming preparation for the upper level geography and English literature classes, preparation for the International Relations Club meetings, and boarding-house duties, I began to realize that, even with my two hours of study most mornings, I was nowhere near completing a Master of Arts thesis. A thesis requires, over and above careful reading, time for reflection and concentrated writing in order to develop a new approach to the subject. It became clear to me that, now that the war was over, I must begin planning not only how to complete my M.A., but also how to get to France somehow for further study. I was becoming more and more conscious of my need to immerse myself in French language and life. (We were not yet using the term French "culture" as it is used today.) I decided, with my meager savings, to take a year off to complete my thesis, during which time I would live at home with Mother and Harold, who was now back from New Guinea. In Melbourne I would try to find some supplementary funds through incidental teaching or tutoring. Had I remained in the Education Department, I would not have had this freedom to decide what I would do next with my life. With my experiences of the Depression and the war, I had learned how to live very economically. I was sure I would be able to survive for a year or two, working freelance, without cutting too deeply into the small nest egg I was putting aside toward my fare to Europe.

Under Miss Sparrow's careful planning and management, St Annes was recovering from the exigencies of the war period and teachers were once again becoming available. Furthermore, most of the girls I had taught for three years, often for three subjects while being also their Form Mistress, would be moving on, some to further study, others to return to their small towns and farms. It seemed my departure at this point would not be too disruptive for our small community. By this time, Linda had felt a very strong call to work as a missionary with the Anglican Church Missionary Society (CMS). Despite very strong, violently expressed opposition from Mother, and some discouragement for medical reasons by CMS, she had finally left home and was well launched on her missionary training. I knew that Mother would appreciate having me home again to fill the gap. With a certain thankfulness for the diverse experiences the school had given me, some real regret, and not a little trepidation about my dimly perceived future, I once again stepped out into the unknown. Soon I was back in the city, with its movement and bustle of crowds of people and its intellectual stimulation.

Teaching for Success: Taylors Coaching College (1947-48)

As soon as I found myself back in Melbourne, I applied for a teaching position at George Taylor and Staff University Coaches, usually referred to as Taylor's Coaching College, located centrally in the city. Taylor's prepared paying students to pass all kinds of public examinations, including those for the all-important Matriculation and Leaving Certificates. I knew that during the month of January Taylor's would be busy coaching large numbers of students, who had failed to pass their exams in the previous December, for the February Supplementary Examinations (Supps). This second chance in "Supps," now abolished, was an established feature of the Victorian State exam system at the time. Taylor's always needed experienced teachers for this extremely busy period. After Supps I was hoping to be able to work part-time in their regular yearly program. This kind of work would bring in some money while I was writing my Master's thesis, without requiring a full-day commitment. George Taylor employed me as soon as I presented myself and I began teaching almost the next day in a kind of educational institution that could not have contrasted more with the system at St Annes.

At Taylor's, education could certainly be described as student-centered, although in a very different sense from St Annes. George

Taylor, an excellent teacher himself, was a charming, affable man, who was as tough as nails in business dealings. With his equally skillful and determined partner, Inez Sexton, he had made a most profitable educational enterprise out of giving students exactly what they wanted and were paying for — success in their exams. Taylor's provided classes for the Matriculation examination (now the Victorian College of Education Higher Certificate), which was required for university entrance, and in the eleventh-grade level Leaving Certificate, which admitted students to a certain number of non-university tertiary institutions and was required of applicants for many positions. They also provided coaching for other job-related examinations, such as those for police officers, and arranged for private tutoring in any subject requested. In January, the business premises in the center of the city (it is hard to describe them as a school in the traditional mold) were buzzing with worried and discouraged students, anxious to get back on the scholastic track.

The first thing Mr Taylor required was that all Supps students pay for a review of their results in the December examinations. This very practical move was derived from his long experience with the system. To my surprise, but not George Taylor's, twenty-five percent of the students would drop out of their courses at this stage, having found that there had been mistakes in the grading, calculation, or registering of their results, and that they had in fact passed. Since the exam papers were corrected and results entered manually by a huge team of graders, the possibilities for error were multiple. This staggering percentage of error was an eye-opener to me and explained some of the mysteries I had encountered in the results of some well-prepared students in the past, including myself.

Intensive teaching for Supps, every day for a month, with earnest students anxious to recoup their academic losses, brought spectacular results. After this January experience I was invited to stay on as one of the regular staff. We were paid by the hour and, apart from a regular schedule for classes taught, we could work on a time-sheet system for as long as we liked at whatever hours we preferred. We prepared study materials, corrected assignments, or wrote examination questions for practice exams. This flexible schedule suited me very well, allowing me to spend most of the day concentrating on my thesis, while I earned money at Taylor's in the late afternoon and evening when most of the classes met.

The system that had made Taylor's the word for assured success in examinations is worth describing. Taylor's coaching college was a business and was run on business lines by its extremely practical and no-nonsense founders. It consisted of a day and an evening school. The day school mostly attracted high-school-aged students who were not learning successfully, either because they had not adapted well behavior-wise to regular school routine or because they needed more guidance in their studies than the schools provided. Since there were no out-of-class facilities at all, these students came to the college on the upper floors of a city building for their classes and then went their way. It was not considered the responsibility of the college to do more than teach them good study habits and challenge them academically with the material required for their examinations. This day school was not the most important part of the college from the business point of view. The evening school, by far the larger section, attracted a great number of motivated students from all over the city and suburbs. It also enrolled country students who studied by correspondence.

My period at Taylor's, 1947 and 1948, was at the height of the education boom for servicemen and women returning to civilian life. The Australian government was providing funds for returning enlisted personnel to study and qualify themselves for professions of all kinds. For entrance to these areas of study, they needed their Leaving and Matriculation Certificates. Many, like my own students at Kerang and my friends in the CMS League of Youth, had not completed high school before enlisting; others had never expected to do so, having had to leave school early during the Depression to earn money to help their families. Mostly in their twenties, they were now eager to get on with their chosen careers as soon as possible. These students were not interested in playing around. They realized they needed what Taylor's had to offer as essential educational background for their career-related studies. They wanted to complete the work successfully as soon as possible and get on with their delayed civilian lives. Having left school in their formative years and having become accustomed to an organized life in the services, they flourished under the discipline of Taylor's system. Consequently I found myself teaching what can only be described as extraordinarily motivated students, avidly exploring the new areas of knowledge and opportunity their teachers were opening up to them. I remember distinctly one evening in an English Literature class when one of my students asked me: "What is poetry really?" I explained as best I could, but explanations cannot give the essence of poetry and its appeal to the individual. I then went on to teach *Hamlet* for an hour, after which the student, a very bright, intelligent young man, came back to tell me: "I think I know now what poetry is." These kinds of experiences make teaching worthwhile. These young men and women were most grateful for all the help and attention they received from the college and their teachers. Later I met a number of them, now successful in various walks of life. Several, curiously enough, were my own students who had enlisted from Kerang High School.

George Taylor was one of those teachers who could teach anything, even if he had to keep one page ahead of the students. In earlier years when the college was establishing itself he and Inez had frequently had to teach subjects new to them. George had always reserved for himself the teaching of the essential subjects required of all students, like Leaving Certificate English and Matriculation English Expression. And he saw that his students passed. In my first year he asked me to assist him in this core teaching. Classes were not small. There might be a hundred students in a Leaving Certificate English class, yet all the assigned work was carefully corrected and evaluated. Part-time teachers were employed to help with this mammoth task. In my second year, I was very flattered when I became the first teacher to whom George had ever delegated the responsibility for these essential classes, so vital for his students' success. Inez Sexton, similarly, had always had the responsibility for Leaving and Matriculation English Literature, and in my second year she also passed these over to me. I had won the confidence of both of them in my ability to teach effectively.

What was the secret of George and Inez's phenomenal success in preparing other teachers' failures to be their successes? I have before me a small leaflet for students from the Taylor's of that day. In it their system and the students' responsibilities are outlined in such clear language that students could not have the least doubt as to what they were to do and how to go about it. George and Inez were certainly ahead of their time in their careful attention to helping students develop good study habits, realizing long before most other educators what a crucial role poor study habits had played in the earlier "failure" of their students. It is essential to refer to George and Inez together in the one phrase. It soon became obvious to all of us that Inez had no intention of standing by while the man in the equal partnership received all the recognition and made all the decisions, as was so frequently the case in Australia in the 1940s. She made sure that, as George's collaborator, she was always by his side in the office when matters of importance were to be discussed and vital decisions made. She kept a careful eye on everything that was going on and never relaxed her vigilance.

Taylor's system was based on what were called "The Big Five,"[65] and the rationale behind each of the five was explained to students at the beginning. First, the *General Instructions* explained the Taylor system, how to read one's individual timetable for work, how to return assigned work, and how to get help with difficulties. *Particular Requirements* pertained to specific subjects: the scope of the work required for the course, how and in what order it would be presented and should be studied, references needed (if any were advised beyond what was in the Assignment), and how this subject matter might be studied most efficiently. Then came the *Assignment*, one of the key elements in the system. The Assignment was a detailed step by step Study-Guide, which led the students through their study of the topic, directing them where to go for facts, how to extract them, and in what form to represent them, so as to make the student's notebook "a summary and a mnemonic aid."[64] Next, and equally as important as the Assignment-Study Guide, was the *General Summary*, which consisted of many pages of clear notes "to supplement, elucidate, or dispense with the text-book as the case may be, and show the essentials of the subject in the simplest and yet the most thorough manner." The *Time Table* gave the student a carefully planned schedule to which to adhere to ensure completion of assigned work by specific dates, so that all work might be covered and reviewed by the time of the external examination. Any students following this carefully devised five-part system of Taylor's could not fail to learn how to organize their work for successful completion of their studies.

I soon found that Taylor's would pay any money for the writing of the Assignments and Summaries; in other words, there was no limit set to the number of paid hours the writer of an assignment or summary might take. I myself wrote a number of these for English literature and stylistics. The writer was required to research the subject and then write up the essential information in the long Summary (often a small booklet). The Assignment would then be carefully drafted to lead the student through the material, not for rote memorization, but in a way that demanded careful reflection and planned application. No one ever hurried or hassled the Summary or Assignment writer. The work had to be the best and most comprehensive possible, no matter how many hours it took, because it would then become a part of the study kit of many students for many years and be reprinted whenever the topic reappeared in the course requirements. All of this work was carefully reviewed by Miss Sexton or Mr McDougall, the Head Master, and sent back to the writer for further work, until it seemed perfect. Reference books were made available to us when required or we could clock hours of research in the Public Library. We wrote in a small faculty workroom, where Mr McDougall kept a careful eye on us through the glass wall of his office. Under Mr McDougall's dour gaze, no one would dare chatter or waste time. Under these conditions, I wrote very long Summaries, with Assignments, on Shakespeare's *King Lear*, Milton's *Samson Agonistes* and his minor poems, Thackeray's *Vanity Fair*, and an anthology of modern poetry, as well as analyzing the styles of writing of a number of essayists in a prescribed anthology of twentieth-century prose. No doubt these productions continued to be used for a number of years. It was a more challenging and enjoyable occupation than spending hour after hour correcting and commenting on assignments from correspondence students, which was the chore of some of my colleagues.

The final keystone in Taylor's system was the October practice examination. For this test all the questions were written by very experienced teachers on the staff, who knew the types of questions that the official examiners were likely to ask in the December examinations. The questions on the topics that had been on exam papers in recent years were, of course, freely available to teachers in the schools. One of the ways of ensuring as many passes as possible in public examinations had always been to give the students much practice on questions that had been asked in the past, with particular emphasis on predicted questions for a specific year. Independent schools could also obtain from their association an October pre-test. Taylor's went one step further, however, than the usual classroom teacher. As well as correcting the complete in-house October Test for each student, with hints on how to improve their answers, Taylor's sent with the returned tests sample answers written by the staff. The year I set the questions for the Matriculation examination in English Literature for the October pre-test, my predictions for questions on the final exam paper were so accurate that the students could not believe that I had not been on the Board of Examiners. Consequently, each of my students had had a dry run for most of the questions, with advice for improvement and a sample answer. It was no wonder that they did extremely well on the examination. An external examination which has such enormous consequences for each candidate's future career lays itself open to attempts of this kind to beat, or at least keep up with, the system. From my experience it was clear that the students got their money's worth from George Taylor and Staff.

George Taylor was very flattered one day to receive a request from Government House for private coaching in French for the son of the Aide-de-Camp to the Governor of Victoria. He and Inez, determined to put their best foot forward in this undertaking, asked me, as their most experienced French teacher, to take on this tutoring, which would involve private lessons with the young man for an hour every weekday. Naturally I was pleased at the prospect of earning more money, especially as my thesis was now in its final stages. So the young sixteen-year-old student and I met. I was enthusiastic about having a student whose motivation was to be able to use the language in a future career in the diplomatic service. I soon discovered, however, that this might well be the motivation of my student's parents, but his own motivation was to live it up as much as possible. He seemed to go to parties till late every night (or, rather, early every morning), arriving bleary-eyed and half-asleep, with tennis racket in hand, for his daily lesson. I applied my best skills in attempting to instill something of the French language into this young man, who would drop off to sleep before my eyes. I tried raising my voice. I tried opening the windows to see if fresh air would effect any change. Nothing seemed to help. He remembered nothing from the previous day, and he had not, of course, made any effort to learn anything overnight. I could hardly shake him physically or use a hammer to beat some knowledge into his head. Finally, I gave up what had become a very painful way of earning much-needed money. I told George and Inez regretfully that I could not, under any conditions, continue with this assignment. I don't know how the Aide-de-Camp received the news. Perhaps, knowing his son better than I did, he was not surprised.

Study Again

Now that I had most of my daytime free, I had plenty of time to concentrate on organizing my thoughts and my notes and drafting an argument for my thesis. I went at it with a will. Although I was now back in Melbourne, there was still no kind of guidance from the French Department nor opportunities for discussion of the direction I was taking. I was writing my thesis in French, never having been to France for that final superb polish of language I coveted. Nor did I have any personal contact with a native speaker with whom I could check a point or two of expression or a subtle choice of words. For these things I had to rely on thesauruses and dictionaries (the bigger the better).

Melbourne University had changed considerably since my undergraduate days. In place of the lake with its Moreton Bay figs there was now a rather banal-looking Commerce Building. Into the front of this building had been inserted, rather incongruously, the gracious nineteenth century facade of a Melbourne bank, which was certainly more beautiful than its host building. At least this awkward incorporation had preserved the lovely Victorian facade from the wrecker's jackhammers. The old Gothic Wilson Hall in which we had graduated had burned down and been replaced by a beautiful modern building, its interior dominated by an enormous modernistic mural. To accommodate the influx of adult ex-service men and women, Quonset huts, no longer needed by the Army but useful as temporary classrooms, had been moved into the space behind the library. Languages had finally won their own space in a new building, with a round tower-like section, soon called Babel. All of this development centered around an expanded and refurbished Student Union building. To the original series of denominational residential colleges and the younger Women's College had now been added International House. Its construction reflected the growing postwar trend, already increasing exponentially, for students from many countries, particularly in Southeast Asia, to choose Australia for their advanced training.

Much as I loved my old university campus, the Melbourne Public Library proved to be a much more convenient and attractive working space for writing my thesis. For one thing it was closer to Taylor's than the Melbourne University Library. This was important since I walked everywhere. I loved the quiet isolation of its polished wood tables, with their personal, green-shaded lights under the great rotunda, and the intense silence, which would be positively shattered by the sound of a dropped book or the scraping of a chair. I soon became accustomed to the proximity of other regulars, studying goodness knows what — the ancient Assyrian alphabet or the aquatic habits of the muskrat. For a break, I would wander out into the garden to eat my home-made sandwiches and watch the birds and the passing crowds. As my thesis reached its final stages, I spent many hours trying to improve it stylistically before submitting it, being very conscious of the fact that I lacked that internalized feeling for authentic expression that comes from a sustained period of immersion in the language among native speakers.

I tried attending the Alliance Française as a way to get some opportunities to use French, as I had during my student days. Now, however, the habitués had changed. The meetings seemed to be the domain of little cliques of French women of a certain age, as the French say, who chatted among themselves, with hardly a sideways glance at any strangers in their midst, and to whom I certainly could be of little interest. Feeling very isolated in the midst of a crowd, I would listen to the occasional lecture and applaud the actors in a home-grown play, then leave as silently as I had come. Like my mother, I have always been shy about trying to break into established social circles, except, of course, in professional contexts. When lecturing or at language-teaching meetings, I have learned, over the years, to put on my professional persona and make the rounds, greeting all and sundry and asking them questions that lead them into further conversation. I am also quite experienced at acting the hostess myself at a mixed assemblage of people, who do and do not know each other. From my own experiences, I am sensitive to the situation of newcomers who need to be rescued unobtrusively from that feeling of isolation on the periphery of a group. At this stage, then, I felt chilled out of my earlier favorite haunt, the Alliance Française.

Pressing on without any advice or assistance, I spent the last two months checking every word and expression in my MA thesis, trying to detect whether it sounded like an Anglicism or not, something that is very difficult for a person who has mostly learned and used the language among fellow anglophones. In some trepidation, I turned in my carefully handwritten thesis and waited several months for a bald, bureaucratic statement that it had been accepted at the Honours level. The only comment I ever heard about it was a remark from some person that Chizzy had been heard to say that it would be very useful to students. The thesis was, of course, lodged in the Melbourne University Library, where after a period of years it was found to be missing. It seems that at least one student must have found it useful over the years.

As soon as I had submitted my thesis I went about satisfying another persistent desire of mine — to learn German. Since I was also interested in how languages are taught, I decided it would be a good idea to combine both my interest in the language and my interest in language teaching by enrolling for individual instruction at the Berlitz School. In this way I hoped to experience personally the famous Berlitz way of teaching languages and get to see their materials, which at that time were only available to their students. How disappointed I was at my first meeting with my native German instructor! Closing the door, he told me: "I don't believe in the Berlitz method, so I will teach you my way from the book I have selected. Please don't mention this to the administration or I will lose my job." As a result, instead of learning something about the Berlitz method, I was submitted to the good old German method of Plötz and his successors — the grammar-translation approach. My instructor being a very thorough teacher, I learned a great deal from him about the German language, even if I did not become very fluent in its use.

France, but how?

My thesis finished, I was able to wear, at my graduation, the mortarboard to which I had so aspired. My next most urgent problem was to work out how I was going to get to France to study. I did not feel I could approach any of the very few people I still knew in the French Department at Melbourne University to seek advice. I was far too shy and intimidated for that. I had always felt somewhat on the outer as a single female without connections. Quietly I set about finding out how to get to France in my own way. No one in my immediate family had traveled abroad, so I hardly knew how or where to begin. I knew that just saving my return fare was not sufficient; I would also need to find some way to earn my living while abroad. I began with the logistics of getting there. As soon as I heard that in 1948 ships would begin to sail again from Australia to Europe, I made my first move. At least I could find out how much my fare to Europe by ship would cost, so that I could see where I stood. To my surprise I found that cargo ships, which took some passengers and spent several months drifting around the Pacific, were more expensive than regular ocean liners. I lingered in front of the windows of shipping companies, which showed models of their passenger ships, with cut-out sections showing the interior of some of the cabins. Plucking up my courage, I went in to the Orient Line office and checked out the cheapest available fare, which happened to be in a six-berth cabin over the engine. It would cost me fifty-eight pounds for a one-way trip. There and then I decided to book myself a cabin, eighteen months ahead, on the Orion (named for my favorite constellation). Leaving in December 1948, it would be one of the first ships to sail for London since the beginning of the war.

Next came the question: What could I do to support myself while I was abroad? I knew that, even with very tight control of my earnings and with the small amount I had managed to save while teaching in the country, I would have very little above my return fare. One day, on the radio, I heard an interview with a French woman; Madame Jeanne Chaton is my long-term memory of her name. It was announced that she was an officer of the French Association of University Women, so it seemed to me that she might have some information that would help me make a start on my puzzling project. I wrote to Madame Chaton, care of the radio station, and asked her what steps I could take to find some teaching in France, so that I would be able to continue my studies there. She kindly wrote back, telling me about the system of *assistant(e)s de langue anglaise* in French schools, which supported exchange students from English-speaking countries with residence and teaching in schools during a period of study in France. She also gave me the name and address of the Office des Universités et Ecoles Françaises in Paris that organized these exchanges. On further inquiry from the French Consulate, I found out that these exchanges were arranged with institutions, not individuals, and that, at that time, about five hundred of these assistantships went to British students and about six to Australia. Clearly this meant that the top student of the year in the French Department of each of the six Australian Universities (there was only one university per state at the time) would obviously be the nominee for this opportunity. I was way out of the loop for anything for Melbourne University, so what should I do next?.

Taking my lead from Madame Chaton, I wrote directly to the Director of the Office des Universités et Ecoles Françaises in Paris, Monsieur Renard. In my letter I made the case that it was very important for the future of the teaching of French language and culture in the South Pacific that a person like myself have the opportunity to deepen her knowledge of these areas through drinking at the source in France itself. I thought this approach might appeal to the French and it seemed to do so. I do not know how many personal letters of this kind Monsieur Renard received each year from such unexpected places as the Antipodes, but he replied very courteously. He sent me an application form with the suggestion that I submit my candidature directly to his office, with the possibility of a position in September.

This was most exciting, except that, as we Antipodeans so frequently do, I had not taken into account the fact that the Northern Hemisphere scholastic year began in September or October, while the Southern Hemisphere year ended in mid-December. In a teaching institution like Taylor's, with my responsibilities for required courses for the December exams, it would be quite unethical to resign at the busiest time of the year. Moreover, there was the problem of the voyage. Not only did passenger ships take thirty days for the voyage to Europe, but my ship booking, for December 1948, was on one of the first ships leaving for Europe since the end of the war, so there would certainly be no chance of a booking in August. I also needed the extra four or five months' work at Taylor's to save my return fare. I decided to try to find through an agency some teaching in England for a few months after my arrival on the Orion, intending to negotiate with Monsieur Renard's office from there for some teaching in September 1949. In 1947 this all seemed very far off anyway.

A teacher employment agency gave me some leads on teaching vacancies in England, and I decided to apply to Abbotsford School in Kenilworth in Warwickshire. (Shades of my Walter Scott days!) The Head Mistress of the school seemed to be interested in my qualifications and experience, but she was not willing to appoint anyone without a personal interview — a point of view I quite understood. I kept the address and the correspondence on hand for future reference.

The big adventure loomed much closer and became much more real to me when, twelve months before the departure of the ship, I was required to put down twenty-five percent of the fare, non-refundable, as a deposit. "Are you really going?" my family and friends asked me, not believing that I could go ahead with such a leap in the dark. I was convinced, however, that this was the next step in God's plan for my life and that I could trust Him to lead me in the right direction. So out of the bank came the precious deposit. From then on, I knew I was really committed and the countdown began. Excitement grew as the date of departure approached. The Reverend Hedley Raymond, my vicar at St Thomas's Church, who had been a father figure for me during my adolescence, wrote me a letter in which he referred to the fact that I was "going Home," a common expression among older Australians at the time. "I am *not* going home," I commented to Linda, "I'm going to England, and later I intend to come home to Australia."

Through all this time of decision-making Mother, who was always so undemanding for herself, never held me back. "Go! Go! I can manage," she would say. I think she was rather intrigued by what she perceived as my adventurousness. Harold had returned from the war and was now living at home, which helped considerably with finances. Linda was engaged in a long period of theological and practical training for her service in the mission field with CMS.

Mother, who strongly opposed Linda's plans, had tried strenuously to dissuade her. However, she never tried to discourage me in my plans to leave for Europe, knowing how important to me was my dream of studying in France, which she saw as advancement as opposed to "throwing one's life away" in some distant land, as Linda proposed to do. Mother lived through her children but, at least in my case, unselfishly. Always interested in what I was doing, she loved to hear of my adventures and proudly recounted them to her relatives and acquaintances.

As my departure date approached, talk of war in Korea became widespread. Because of Australia's alliance with the United States, this would involve Australia also. I could foresee another long period of war when Australia would be cut off again from the rest of the world. In that case I might have to stay in Europe for years, which was far from my intention. Should I or shouldn't I go? Time passed relentlessly and finally my departure date approached. By this time the General Secretary of the Inter-Varsity Christian Fellowship (IVCF) in England had offered to send someone with a placard to the boat train in London to meet me and see that I was safely lodged on arrival. There were always the Rivers cousins in Ealing I could look up once I was there, as some of Dad's grandchildren from his first family had already done. Some possibilities were emerging from the mists of the future. Resolutely, I packed my big cabin trunk and boarded the Orion on December 3rd, 1948, after an emotional farewell from family and friends on the wharf. There was much throwing of streamers and clutching on to them as they slowly stretched and stretched and finally broke. The venture into the unknown had begun.

9

VENTURING OUT OF THE NEST   1948

While I was abroad from 1948-52, I kept a regular diary. This chapter summarizes my impressions on first encountering different cultures. It is mainly in the form of quotations from the original to preserve the flavor of my reactions. Explanatory interpolations are in square brackets

3rd December, 1948.

It was strange, after all the bustle and excitement of preparations and farewells, to be actually on the *Orion* — ship of dreams— and setting out on the great adventure. As I stood on the deck and my family and friends waved and threw paper streamers from the pier, I didn't feel lonely and friendless, as I had thought I might. It was fun that we had one streamer that held till the very end without breaking. I kept thinking of the song "With a full crew aboard and our trust in the Lord." As long as I could see the wharf, I kept waving and then went to the other side of the ship and kept on waving until we were far away.

It was dreadfully cold and windy out at sea, so I retired to my cabin to settle in. I found I was sharing it with "a lot of Pommies,"[65] as one of the English women remarked. Two of my cabin mates were older women from Yorkshire, who were returning to England after visiting immigrant children. One, about seventy-three, was subject to heart attacks, so her family had broken out a bottle of brandy to fortify her for the trip (or so she told us). Both of these women spoke in broad Yorkshire dialect, so I could see myself assimilating some of their expressions by the end of the trip: "How is weather the day?"

"Ee, Laass, but ah aam!" As I had been allotted a top bunk, one of the Yorkshire ladies sagely remarked that: "You haaf to go oop to laa down" and "you haaf to coom daan to get oop!" It wasn't long before my Yorkshire companions were asking the table steward when we were going to have "good old Yorkshire pudding" with our roast beef, and sure enough it soon appeared. The older lady paid me what she considered a compliment when she commented, in her broad Yorkshire accent, that I talked "very clear." "You don't talk like an Australian," she said, "You talk just like me!" I soon found the English to be very accent conscious, although more tolerant of dialectal variations from their own shores than the speech of "colonials." One man, visiting from first class, congratulated me on "not having one of those dreadful Australian accents." I am becoming accustomed to this kind of backhanded compliment, at which the English seem to excel.

I am very intrigued by the lilt of the English intonation I hear all around me; it seems to use so much more of the musical scale than our more level-toned Australian [which, I was later informed, seemed "flat and monotonous" to English ears]. As I go up and down the companionways, I imitate to myself the intonation of some sentence I have just heard. What intrigues me, however, is the great variety of accents among the passengers, from the Cockney accent of the stewards from Southend to the Yorkshire accents of my constant cabin companions, the broad Scots from Glasgow, and the soft, cajoling brogue of the Irish.

A number of my fellow passengers are disgruntled immigrants returning to England. Some came out on the Orion and are making the return voyage home on the same ship, having decided during the time it took for the ship to turn around and reload that Australia was not for them. Their fares have been paid by the Australian Government [under the immigration plan Australia initiated after the war]. One woman who has stuck it out for five months explained that she had not expected Australia to be so different from England and so "behind the times." She thought everything would be modern and up-to-date. I explained that she couldn't expect a young country with a future and everything to build to be like an old country with a past. Fortunately these vocal malcontents are counterbalanced by the number of contented long-term residents who are returning to their country of origin just for a visit; the latter speak well of their experiences in their new country. It is instructive for Australians like me, born and bred in a more or less homogeneous environment, with no experience elsewhere, to hear the viewpoints on Australia of such a variety of people.

By occupation and purpose the passengers are a very varied group. There are business people expecting to make useful contacts in Great Britain or in other countries of Europe (some from the Australian paper-making industry, for instance, are on their way to Sweden). There are students, university faculty on research leave, exchange teachers, artists, missionaries, entertainers going to London to try their luck, Greeks returning to Greece, Albanians to Albania, even a group of young Australians traveling to Czechoslovakia to join the Communist state — a real pot-pourri of different types and interests. We refer to some of the entertainers as the Exquisites. They are glamour boys, with dark hair, dark eyes, beautifully tanned bodies amply displayed, gold and silver chains and bracelets, large, showy dress rings, and floral or canary-colored shorts [this, at a time when men mostly wore gray, navy, or black, or at a pinch summer white]. There are also the sporting types, straight from Sydney's Manly Beach — bronzed almost to a mahogany hue and proud to display their bodies. Many are family people with small children being taken "home" to meet their grandparents. With so many young people on board, there are plenty of shipboard romances. [On a thirty-day trip young lovers had time to get engaged before reaching Ceylon, married by the captain as the ship approached Aden and divorced on arrival in London.]

My cabin, having six berths, seemed very crowded at first, especially with six sets of cabin luggage to be stowed. In the end this has turned out to be an advantage. Because of the crush three people decided to seek more ample accommodation elsewhere; one of the old ladies spends all of her time on deck with her friends, and my remaining cabin mate has turned out to be such a bad sailor that she spends almost all the time in her bunk. Her frequent request is for "a coop o' tea and some draa toast," this being all she can keep down. Fortunately I seem to be a good sailor. I had just an initial bout of seasickness on the first day when I rushed to the rail to feed the fish. With three people less in the cabin, my friends have started to compliment me on the roominess of my quarters, and I have been able to move to the top bunk by the porthole, where I can get the breeze and watch the sea not far below.

Since our cabin is over the screws there is an increase in vibration when the ship makes full steam ahead. The engines immediately beneath our feet cause a steady shaking, with a distracting rattle at times. The nightwatchman told me he had never heard such a racket and that the screws ought to be oiled. Not having the faintest idea what the screws were, I hied myself off to the office of the Purser (the ship's troubleshooter) to recommend that they oil the screws. With that and a screwdriver borrowed from a deckhand to fix a few rattles in the cabin, things have improved tremendously. I waited all day for an invitation to join the engineers!

Of course, there are many activities and competitions on board, from deck quoits, deck tennis, and table tennis to swimming, chess, drafts, and the favorite English pastime of darts. We can enjoy mock horseracing, films, dances, and community singing on deck, the latter sometimes impromptu. Add to this lively conversation with my many new friends, reading, knitting, and writing my diary, and I have little time left to be bored. At a fancy dress party, a group of us appeared as Snow White and the Seven Dwarfs. With crepe paper jerkins and stocking caps, and myself as Dopey wandering around agape at all that was going on, we won first prize for our sustained performance. We have put together a choir to prepare a choral performance to celebrate Christmas, and we enjoy Sunday services under the direction of a friend of mine from Sydney. Often I do nothing. The pleasure of wasting time ts just too attractive. With so much time to relax we have far too much to eat. We have rapidly become accustomed to the English plan of early morning tea in our bunks and four meals a day, two of them of four courses, with all of this supplemented by continually available snacks. Regular walking around the restricted second-class deck space (about a third of the ship), up and down the companionways and around the decks at several levels, has become more of a necessity than just a pleasurable activity if we are to retain our figures. Alys [my Rivers half-sister] asked me to take a fur coat to London for her daughter, Jeanette, on the understanding that I could wear it while on ship. With this beautiful, lustrous, brown coat I can weather the briskest of sea breezes, even stormy winds.

To build further on my German lessons at Berlitz, I have brought with me a copy of *German without Toil*, from the Assimil self-teaching language series. The Assimil method is based on the memorization of dialogues in common situations, and I amuse myself in my long leisure hours memorizing this material, answering the practice questions that follow, and making up my own little dialogues.

Watching the sea never becomes boring. Occasionally we see albatrosses, gliding down toward the ship with perfectly straight, apparently rigid wings. At times the sea is a deep, dark blue, like ink, relieved on calm, restful days by a tracery of foam from the little waves. Sometimes we see islands on the horizon — isolated, barren, rocky fragments appearing hazily in the distance, almost like cloud formations. At night we can watch the stars as they seem to rise and fall in the sky, with the gentle swaying of the ship. At other times we watch the moon rise over the sea — a large orange globule creating a path of silvery light.

The really exciting moments of the trip soon are the landfalls in a series of interesting ports. Outer Harbour, on our arrival in Adelaide, was not impressive — a long low skyline, too flat to be interesting, and a dingy little wharf, but here I was able to visit two of my former colleagues from St Annes in an excited and exciting reunion. The day began with the trauma of losing my purse, with all my money, possibly in a cafe, soon after my arrival and finding myself penniless in a strange city. Here I discovered, early on my trip, how kind strangers can be to the lost and lorn. Before the day was out I had been given so much money to see me through that it almost made up for what I had lost.

The coast of Western Australia was undulating, rocky and uninhabited as we drifted by, with little low hills and beaches at intervals. I kept thinking this was how the early explorers, like Dampier in the seventeenth century, had seen it. It was an utterly peaceful feeling, just gliding along, watching the rise and fall of the sea line over the rails of the deck. At Perth I was met by May Rivers Stillman [my half-sister] and her husband, Geoff, who took me to see Auntie Del [Mother's sister] who is now permanently bedridden. [Having sold her house to go three thousand miles from the rest of her family to housekeep for a brother in Western Australia, Del unfortunately had a stroke that caused paralysis of the right side of her body. Her brother had by this time remarried and disappeared from the scene, so she was now on her own and installed in a nursing home.] Although confined to her bed, Del, in her usual forceful way, still rules the roost from the sidelines, instructing all new nursing personnel and patients in the regular routines of the ward, with no tolerance for deviation. She has also taught herself to write with her left hand to keep in touch with us all. This reunion was an emotional occasion that meant a great deal to her. She considers us, her nieces, to be her family.

On the way back to the ship, we saw the beautiful Romanesque buildings of the University of Western Australia. [This was a university at which I was to lecture many years later, although I did not dream of such a possibility then.] Built uniformly in light golden stone, and set in lovely gardens, it was very different from the now crowded, higgledy-piggledy campus of Melbourne University. The classic view of Perth across the Swan River from King's Park was spectacular, with wide stretches of water where the Swan broke into a series of lagoons. King's Park was just by the narrows between one lagoon and the next, so that we could see the city and suburbs right round the edges of the water of both lagoons. King's Park is well worth the visit, enabling us to see so much of the native scrub land and distinctive flora of Western Australia preserved in its natural state.

On my return to the wharf at Fremantle I nearly missed my ship to England. As May, Geoff, and I were attempting to take family photographs in the crush of the streamer-throwing and streamer-holding crowds, an old lady stepped between us, becoming entangled in a streamer. While we cast apprehensive glances at the Orion, she made slow and deliberate efforts to disentangle herself from the restricting streamer without breaking it. By the time she had extricated herself and the photos were taken, the regular gangway had been taken up. I had to race to the other end of the ship to get in by an emergency gangway at wharf level, just making it before this also was withdrawn. My shipboard friends watched all this with apprehension from the safety of the deck. Soon we were steaming peacefully out of the narrow entrance in the mole of Fremantle's artificial harbor. [How

307

many times in my life have I arrived at the very last minute for trains or airplanes since then! I even have recurrent nightmares about such situations, waking in alarm just as my dropped suitcase has burst open, with contents tumbling down the stairs a minute or two before departure time. Deep-seated habits to profit to the full from every minute are hard to change.]

At teatime we found a very battered table steward waiting on us. His face was bruised and scratched and he was no longer the fresh-looking young fellow to whom we were accustomed. Fremantle had been too much for him. It appeared that he and his cabin-mate had had a few drinks and, on their return, began to squabble. The other fellow threw a boot in our steward's face, but he returned the compliment with something harder. As a consequence the original aggressor was left behind to recover in a Fremantle hospital. So the vicissitudes of life intrude on our seemingly serene and timeless voyage.

12th December [In the Indian Ocean]

The sea is fascinating. Yesterday I hung over the rails watching the deep inky blue, with patches of turquoise where the foam had broken. Little flying fish flew over the surface for distances of ten to fifteen yards, for all the world like little birds.

But this morning provided the thrill of the voyage. I came up on deck after breakfast to survey a dream-like scene. Smooth, oily water, moving in the gentlest of undulations, shone like molten silver to the horizon. In other directions it looked brown like sand dunes. Closer in to the ship the water was deep blue, the waves showing ripple marks as though they had been combed. There were few breaks in the waves, but where a little foam broke through it slid down the wave in a circular form like a lace doily. The haze over the sea was very brilliant and the cloud formations on the horizon were luminous and breathtakingly beautiful against a light blue sky. This was the Indian Ocean in the tropics, in the same latitude as Sumatra. I wonder if I shall ever see it like that again. Since then we have passed right through a low-hung rain cloud. The luminous quality has gone and the sea is gray and dull. Tonight we cross the Equator into the Northern Hemisphere.

13th December

When we crossed the Equator, King Neptune came on board with all his minions, and those of us who had never crossed the Line before were duly dunked in the swimming pool, in accordance with sea tradition. This was a source of much hilarity and we were awarded elaborate certificates to attest forever to our temerity in invading the territory of the God of the Seas.

14th December.

This morning, at about 6 o'clock, I went on deck, just too late for the sunrise, but I saw the sea in another light. As I looked toward the sun it shone like lustrous ivory silk. Later, when a storm came up, the silk turned to gray. It is interesting watching the rain falling from distant clouds, and seeing storms approaching from the horizon, until we are in the midst of one and there is a gray haze from the ship to the cloud. There is so much of interest in sailing across an extensive ocean. We do not feel the heat particularly, because the lower decks are cool and there is a continual sea breeze from the movement of the ship.

Today the idea of eventually doing a Ph.D. was suggested to me by a young Australian who was off to the London School of Economics for advanced study. This kind fellow traveler even offered to find me work in London, and invited me to live with his family while I undertook further study. The proposal is tempting but I still have my sights set on France — France and France only. Meanwhile there is much of the world to see.

15th December (Linda's birthday)

[We arrived at Colombo, a boatful of excited travelers, among whom were many young Australians with very little previous experience of the ways of other peoples. In our country, for instance, we knew nothing of tipping and haggling was unheard of. How the merchants and rickshaw men in Colombo must have looked forward to the arrival of each new boatload of naive young Australians, as a source of income of which they had been deprived during the long years of war.]

I woke at about five to see lights on the shores of Ceylon, so I hurriedly dressed and went up on deck, hoping to see the sunrise and watch our arrival in the port of Colombo. At about half-past five I saw Australia's red ensign hoisted at the rear of the boat and it gave me a feeling of pride to see it flutter in the breeze. About six the pilot came out in his boat and we knew we would soon be in the harbor. The sky was heavily clouded so I saw no sunrise. The lighthouse light was flashing from the shore and the buildings gradually became more distinct. Colombo's harbor is protected by breakwaters, each with a small light at the end. Before long we were safely in through the entrance and could see the masses of shipping at the docks and in the harbor. With the assistance of tugs, we ourselves were soon moored in mid-stream to another vessel. As our passports had to be stamped before we could land, we waited in the ship's cafe until the arrival of the Ceylon police, who looked very natty and efficient in their khaki uniforms.

Soon after breakfast I was ready and caught a launch to the shore. Colombo looked like any other port from the sea, drab and uninspiring, but the scene was very different after we had left the wharf. As we made our way to the coach for our trip to Kandy, we passed rickshaws waiting for passengers and were besieged by Cingalese offering us hats, fans, stamps, magazines, or bananas. It was our first introduction to an Eastern city and we were amazed at their persistence. Our coach was an object of great curiosity and a mixed group assembled to watch — young, old, handsome, repulsive, some chewing betel nut, some selling newspapers.

Our trip to Kandy was an experience not to be missed. First of all, we went through the poorer parts of Colombo, past bullock carts, Cingalese riding to work on bicycles, Tamil Indians with bright red or blue caste marks on their foreheads, or locals carrying baskets with all kinds of food on their heads. We continued over the Victoria Bridge into the countryside.

The road was almost completely lined with little villages, where people went about their tasks in leisurely fashion. All through the day, there seemed to be plenty of people with time to stand around. Most houses and shops had open fronts, so that we looked directly into the shop or into the living quarters. Some were very neat and decorated with flowers, others dirty and dark with narrow entrances. Some houses painted a bright blue were, we were told, the houses of Muslims. The women in the streets were dressed in bright-

310

hued skirts or saris. The most popular dress for the women was a long colorful skirt, after the style of a sarong, with a short white blouse with a wide, round neck. The men were also dressed colorfully, many with long, loose trousers gathered in at the ankles. The shops sold everything, fruit (bright orange pawpaws and bananas predominating), cakes, sweets, bottles of cordial, ironmongery, basketware, and meat hanging in the open air. In some shops men were busy on sewing machines. We passed village scribes, with lines of waiting clients, and even some women carefully examining their daughters' hair. Occasionally we would see a Buddhist priest in brilliant saffron robes, sometimes using an umbrella as protection from the sun. Fortunately we were blessed with a wonderfully cool, clouded day, so our view from the bus was not blocked by a lot of umbrellas. Everywhere there were crowds of people and especially children, some of the dearest, quaintest little mites with bright dark eyes, engaged in the usual childish occupations.

In between villages we got a fair impression of typical Ceylon scenery. It was so different at times from the Australian scene, with coconut palms, bright crotons with gold and reddish leaves, banana palms with their long, broad, flat leaves, tall, thin-trunked rubber trees, and the bright-colored flowers of the hibiscus. At other times the natural forest could easily have been Australian, with a tree that gave a similar impression to the mountain beech and the distant palms recalling our tree ferns. Once we passed an elephant dragging logs of wood. As we crossed streams we saw women washing their clothes on stones, beating them and scrubbing them, then laying them out on the rocks to dry. We even saw a woman having a bath, pouring water over herself and her clothes, then putting on a clean dress and removing the wet one from underneath. We passed many flat, low-lying paddy or rice fields, rich green with water lying on them. They were irrigated in an unusual sunray design from a corner of the field and sometimes terraced up the lower slopes of a hillside. The rubber trees had blazes low down on the trunk and a small cup to catch the latex. Higher up we came to tea plantations. We were surprised to find low, scrubby bushes with taller trees planted in between to shelter them from the sun.

We stopped at a tea factory and a rubber factory and saw the processing of the raw products. The tea factory had a strong odor like tea that has been brewed too strong and too long. The tea is first soaked in a stewy mess, then fermented for two hours, after which it is dried in twenty minutes. It is then poured on the floor. Barefooted women sit on the floor beside the heaps, taking baskets full of the dried tea on their laps and picking out all the waste sticks and the coarser pieces. Then the tea is packed in chests ready for transport. The rubber comes in two forms, the purer latex or sap of the rubber tree and the coarser rubber, which is scraped from the tree to which it has adhered. The latter is purified by a chemical process and made into sheets of yellow crepe rubber. Men sitting on the floor cut all the flaws out of the sheets before they are packed.

Back we went to our coach and on up the mountain, loving the beautiful mountain scenery and looking at more villages as we passed. In one we saw a little girl on stilts, dressed in a richly colored, beaded suit, obviously on show. We arrived at Kandy at about 12.45 p.m. and were taken to the Queen's hotel for lunch.

First we went upstairs to a washroom where a Cingalese woman brought us fresh water. We found we were expected to give her a tip. Then we went to the dining room for lunch. The waiter asked us if we would like a fruit drink first. We said no, but he was very pressing so we agreed, just to please him. We were to hear more of this later. We had a good four-course meal — soup, fish, roast pork with applesauce, and finally a most delicious fruit salad served from a watermelon shell. The mixture of tropical fruit flavors was delightful. Then we thought we had better tip the waiter, so the four at our table decided to give him 1 rupee 50 centimes (about two shillings and threepence) between us. We were making our way to the door when he came running after us to tell us that the fruit drinks at the beginning were 2 rupees 40 cents extra (about three shillings and ninepence)! We felt we'd been had somehow. Some of the other girls fared worse. Four of the girls decided to give their waiter a combined tip of two rupees. One of them gave the rupees to him for the group. To their surprise he proceeded round the table with a large silver plate. Feeling intimidated, they gave him an extra rupee each, a total of six rupees or nine shillings! These Cingalese certainly know how to handle the uninitiated!

Outside the restaurant we started to look for postcards. The merchant wanted the equivalent of fivepence each for them. I realize now that we should have offered him half and haggled over it, but this comes hard when you are not used to it.

We then set out for the famous Temple of the Tooth, the important Buddhist shrine that contains a tooth of the Buddha. We found the temple to be a very dingy, gray stone building. The front steps passed between pools of water in which there were sacred turtles. The ancient facade is preserved in the outer passageway. The stonework was cracking and the appearance was rather dilapidated. We were taken down a corridor where the wall was decorated with paintings of the Buddhist Hell, showing the torments to be suffered in the flames for major crimes, like lying, stealing, and murder. This Eastern art seemed strange to us and the sequence rather disjointed. Further on, we came to the main entrance to the temple, where we were required to take off our shoes. This was not a very attractive prospect as the place seemed so dirty; however, since we wanted to see further, we complied. We then went down some steps into the interior courtyard and approached an ornately painted shrine said to contain the tooth. It seems that this tooth came from Burma and has only been in Kandy since the beginning of the twentieth century. It was at one time crushed to pieces and thrown in a river. One day a Buddhist priest, wandering in meditation beside a stream, saw the tooth on a leaf floating down the stream. Knowing intuitively that it was a tooth of the Buddha, he rescued it and it was later placed in the shrine at Kandy. The decorations of the shrine are very colorful, and there is a massive barred and locked door to protect the relic. We did not see the tooth, which is taken out only once a year for an important procession. Every year since the tooth has been in Kandy it has begun to rain as soon as the tooth has been placed on the elephant's back for the procession, and then it has continued to rain for twenty minutes. As we walked around the portico surrounding the shrine we saw devotees with rosaries and prayer books. People went forward to the door of the shrine and knelt on hands and knees in adoration. We then went on to see a big golden casket, taller than a man, before which was a shelf with offerings of flowers, chiefly frangipani and lotus. This casket is said to contain the smaller bones of the Buddha. One of the priests gave each of us a frangipani flower. As we were about to leave we found we were expected to tip the priest! So we brought out our few remaining sterling coins — threepences and sixpences. In another part of the building we saw a Burmese Buddha in the conventional lotus position. Many women were standing about in groups. I saw a most beautiful woman with a baby and immediately wanted to take her photograph, but she turned and walked away. We were struck with the number of beautiful women we saw in Ceylon. As we went out we had to tip our guide, sixpence each, and the man who minded our shoes was waiting for his share, but we were getting tired of this, so only one of us gave him a sixpence. Outside were blind beggars and others with distorted limbs, all looking for alms. We were beginning to realize that you need to carry a lot of small coins with you in the East.

Next we went to the beautiful Peridenya Botanical Gardens — one of the showplaces of the island. As we went in, the gardener made for us, wanting to show us around, but being by this time tip-shy we hurried off in the opposite direction. This led us to a spectacular garden, planned in a regular design with neatly trimmed colored borders — a beautiful sight well worth seeing. We next visited the orchid house, where there were not many orchids blooming, but we did see a pitcher plant which eats flies. There were colonnades of Javanese almond trees of most peculiar shapes and striking avenues of coconut palms. The gardens were bright with bougainvillea, hibiscus, jasmine, and crotons. Some little boys passed us in the back of a bullock cart. When we waved and shouted "Hello!" one of them put out his hand! We found a certain useful place locked, but, since it was necessary to get the key from the gardener and apparently tip him before you could get in, we managed quite well without it. At the gates there was a man trying to sell us jewels and a blind beggar wandered up and down the side of the coach calling "Alms! Alms!"

Further down the road, we stopped to watch some mahouts washing their elephants in the stream. They performed a few tricks for us, the mahout being swung onto the elephant's back by its trunk, whereupon he rode up the bank to be paid!

Along the road back to Colombo we found the fences decorated, mainly with shredded palm leaves but in some cases with white streamers and even silver tinsel. There was to be a special Buddhist procession that evening for the full moon. The most striking feature of the return drive was the tooting. The animals and people seemed to have no idea of saving their own lives, so the driver, if he was to reach his destination in a reasonable time, had to toot nearly all the way. We were amused to see that some of the bikes had bells on each handlebar. The locals seemed to delight in the noise. One of our group had driven by car to Kandy and found the roads so crowded with vehicles and people that it was difficult to get through. A woman stepped out in front of the car and was struck but not seriously. She had been carrying a bag of flour, which split open and went everywhere. The car was immediately surrounded by angry Cingalese, who demanded he pay seven rupees before he could continue, although it wasn't his fault.

We had been warned that, in these Eastern cities, it is not safe to eat just anywhere and we knew that we had to be careful with salads and uncooked foods, so for our evening meal we made our way to the Nanking Cafe, which a local contact had recommended. The walk along the street to the cafe was an experience in itself. The shops were still open and, in a short walk, we were offered dresses, jewelry, carved elephants, a tune on a pipe, rickshaws, money changing, and sandals. After a tasty, but very filling meal, we left the cafe to find three rickshaws waiting for us. They must have watched us through the window. We eluded them and were determined not to ask any Cingalese the way back to the ship, being sure that we would have to tip them.

Soon we heard several loud explosions and were told that the Buddhist full moon procession was passing nearby, so we hurried over to see it. The women were all in white, the little girls wearing white bows on their black plaits, and all were carrying flowers. Next came an elephant, decorated and carrying an elaborate little shrine on its back; then more marchers and a decorated shrine brightly lit. After more of the procession came women with ropes of flowers by which they were drawing a shrine with a full-size standing figure of the young Buddha. This shrine was decorated brightly with electric light globes and was the climax of the procession. Immediately afterwards came the anticlimax — a wagon bearing an advertisement for the electrical firm which had provided the lighting for the procession.

By this time we had very little money left, so we went back to the wharf by public bus. The walk from the bus stop to the wharf through dark, shadowy streets was a little eerie. We passed mutilated beggars again, and we were highly amused when one man called after

315

us: "Goodbye! Tomorrow you go. Australia dinky-di!" We decided that he must have guessed we were Australians, as an American would have taken a rickshaw, an Englishman a taxi and only a fool of an Australian would be walking! We were determined, however, to have a short rickshaw ride before we left, so we walked back a block from the ship. There we asked a rickshaw man if he had any friends who would help him take the whole group. Although he said no, his friends began racing toward us from all sides. We asked firmly if they would take us to the wharf for one rupee fifty and they agreed, so off we jogged in style. They didn't hurry themselves, and it was peculiar to be sitting up in a chair pulled along by a running man.

19th December

It was a thrill this afternoon to see Africa. The outline of a cape appeared mistily on the horizon through the bright rays of the westerly sun, looking at first like a low cloud formation. Then a section of the Somalilands, Cape Guardafui, loomed up out of the mist. Gradually the nearer, lower coastline came in sight, apparently a rocky island, sand-capped, in a bay with wide, sandy beaches. There we saw a wonderful sight: as the setting sun was sinking behind a long bank of cloud lying low over the coastal hills, it created a golden rim around the cloud bank, while through a break lower down the golden rays spread out over this new continent. Gradually it grew darker and mistier and we felt the relief of the coolness. That is all we shall see of Africa until we come into port tomorrow after crossing the Gulf of Aden.

20th December.

Today we passed several groups of islands in the morning and in the afternoon we saw a great rock loom up on the horizon. This was Aden [now Yemen]. A huge barren mountain of rock, it was surmounted by the masts of the cable station. As we rounded it we could see modern administrative buildings coming into view and the great cross on Chapel Hill. Across the gulf we saw a remarkable view of the mountains, deep blue against darker blue, so that each group of mountains appeared like a section of stage scenery. We have seen this flat impression on several occasions. A few local craft were to be seen in the bay with their distinctive curved-D sails. On landing at 5.30

p.m., we went straight to the shopping center. The shops remained open as long as the ship was in port. They were bigger than in Colombo, and the traders were a mixed group of Indians, Somalis, Cingalese, Jews, and Arabs. In the streets we saw some people dressed similarly to the Cingalese, but there were more fezzes and turbans. Outside each shop was a verandah with steps from which traders called out to us and offered their wares. Some shops, we found, had fixed prices, but in most cases it was necessary to haggle for the goods.

You soon see how these people enjoy bargaining; they put their whole selves into it. It proceeds like this: you are offered a silver filigree bracelet at, say, fifteen shillings, which is more than it is worth. Its various qualities are praised to you — there's never been anything like it, it appears. You automatically say: "Too much! Too dear!" Then it may be offered to you for fourteen and sixpence. You continue to look interested, but poor, and then, saying with some finality: "Too much," you turn away. The trader appears to shrug as though that is the end of it. Then as you walk away, a beseeching voice is heard: "Missie! Missie! I not want make money out of you. I want please you. What you offer? What you think it worth?" This puts you in an awkward position, since you haven't the faintest idea of its value. "Eight shillings," you venture. The trader recoils as though mortally offended. "But, Missy, you not see its value. That below my cost price. You give me twelve and six." He practically wraps it up for you, but you repeat firmly: "Eight shillings is all I'll give you." He looks disappointed in you and almost offended. Then he tries again: "You give me sixpence above my cost price, You give me eleven and six." Then, as though in a fit of philanthropic magnanimity, he says confidentially: "I want you to have this. I give it to you for ten shillings." (At this stage one trader actually offered to throw in his sandwich lunch along with the article.) "Right," you say, and the transaction is completed. As you are going away, he comes up and says very softly, as though to a fellow conspirator: "I want you to have this, but you no tell anyone that I give you this for ten shillings." If you say, "Look, old chap, you sold one of these to a friend of mine for nine shillings," his eyes light up and he laughs joyously as though it's a great joke. If you took away their haggling, life wouldn't be half the fun, quite obviously. I got quite good at it in Aden, that is, for a beginner. They will only come halfway, so it's important to begin lower than you are willing to pay.

After we had been wandering around the shops for a while, we took a taxi to Aden. In Colombo you are pestered with rickshaws, but in Aden it's taxis — beautiful new cars, long and sleek and very cheap to ride in. We fixed the price before we got in to make sure — a rupee a mile for twelve miles for five of us. We traveled a little way around the coast from Steamer Point. Unfortunately, because of our half-hour's shopping, we found it was already getting dark. However, we enjoyed the view over the bay with its multiplicity of ships and smaller craft. Then we went uphill over the barren, sandy mountain slope to the edge of the volcanic crater in which Aden is built. We came down into the Arab quarters in the dark, the rocky walls of the crater closing in on us. All along the road we could see doors open in the wall, and we looked into what appeared more like stables than anything else. There were few women about, but those we did see were heavily clothed and veiled in black. We saw quite a few open-air cafes and local shops, and little groups of men sitting on the ground around a lamp, sometimes playing cards.

Leaving the town, we went out to the Tanks. These have been excavated and are believed to have been built for the Queen of Sheba. They are deep, wide tanks constructed in the ground, with steps leading down into them. Lots of little boys and girls ran up to us calling out: "Baksheesh! English money!" and offering to guide us. After our experiences in Colombo, we avoided them, but one very polite, clean little boy just came along with us. His name was Abdullah and he was nine years old. It was very engaging to hear the purest Scottish burr coming out of this little black face. It seems he has been learning English at a school run by Scottish missionaries. We asked him quite a few questions and he gave us interesting information. After seeing the Tanks we walked back in the dark through groves of lilac. One of our group gave Abdullah threepence and I gave him a penny, but immediately we were surrounded by crowds of other children seeking coins. They even poked their hands through the car windows at us. We journeyed back to Aden in the dark, shopping at a Jewish shop on the way. As we still had about an hour before departure time, we wandered in and out of the shops near

318

the ship, amusing ourselves haggling for things we didn't really want or need, until it was time to return to the boat.

21st December

Today we went down into the bowels of the ship on steep steps into the hot boiler room, where oil is fed to the boilers and steam created to drive the turbines. A tremendous propeller shaft of about 190 feet, in 30-foot sections, is rotated to turn the twin screws or propellers at the aft of the ship. (Ha! So these were the famous screws that needed oiling!). It was terrifically hot in the boiler room, 110 degrees Fahrenheit [about 42 degrees Celsius], but the temperature would be much higher during the hottest part of the voyage. We also saw the generating plant where all the electricity for the ship is generated. At one stage we were right on the bottom of the ship. I tried to locate the rattle that has been disturbing us at night in our cabin, but it was drowned, I'm afraid, by the terrific racket! It was all so loud that we couldn't even hear what our guide was saying, so I grabbed odd firemen and engineers and asked them questions.

23rd December

This morning we came up on deck to see the barren mountains of the Sinai Peninsula, mauve and misty in the morning light, and we thought of Moses and the giving of the Ten Commandments. There seemed to be a division of opinion as to which of the peaks was actually Mt Sinai, however. The peninsula is bare and rugged with wide, sandy, coastal plains. We watched the closing in of the mountains on either side as the Red Sea narrowed toward Suez, and we wondered just where the Israelites might have crossed over. We could see little apart from the contours, since the coast was too far away. But we did have the joy of seeing a wonderful sunset over the hills near Suez — a brilliant orange sunset leaving streaks of glowing color over the dark outline of the hills, just as you see it in those hand-colored picture postcards that you never believe to be real.

We had drawn into the harbor of Suez, but we had to wait about five miles from the shore. We could dimly see the opening to the Canal. Very soon it was dark (about 5.15 p.m.) and we watched the lights around the harbor, the searchlights, the incoming planes, the movements of little boats nearby, and the winking of red and green lights on the buoys. The ship was soon well anchored and will remain here until six o'clock tomorrow morning, when we are scheduled to enter the Canal.

24th December

Soon after 5.30 a.m. on Christmas Eve I was up on deck with some friends to see the entrance into the Canal. It was very chilly, so I wrapped up well in Jeanette's fur coat. The lights around the harbor looked very attractive in the darkness. The sky was too heavily clouded for us to see the sunrise. At last we moved toward the entrance, past the miscellaneous shipping of Suez — trading vessels, RAF launches, and native craft. The town of Suez was near the entrance to the canal and on the left was a monument to men who died in the 1914-18 war — a simple obelisk flanked by two tigers ready to spring. We entered a narrow passage with the sides reinforced with cemented stone. Unfortunately breaks that had not been mended were clearly visible. Buoys on either side marked the limit for safe sailing. The shores were so close to the ship that it was like traveling in a train. The right-hand bank was dry desert with occasional tussocky clumps of grass, so we concentrated on the left bank and were rewarded with a breath-taking sight of Suez. On the bank was a neat, well-built section of buildings, a church and the minaret of a mosque behind other structures. Behind that again came the blue waters of Suez Bay, and on the far side was the main section of the city, flanked by rocky hills. The strata of the rocks could be clearly seen and the unusual quality of the light gave it all a fairy-like, mysterious air. Off to the right ran a long line of date palms marking an oasis in the surrounding desert. We drank it in for a long time, although the foreground changed as we moved. We passed little mud-brick homes. Some of these were very broken down, with well-wrapped Arab people, looking like bundles of rags, watching us, and rugged camels for all the world like caterpillars on stilts. Other houses were better kept with neat gardens of vegetables and young date palms. Local craft passed with hallooing Arabs and many greetings. All the way through the canal the ship traveled at a maximum of five miles per hour, so we had plenty of opportunity for observation. Another ship was ahead of us and others behind, all keeping a specified distance apart, as we moved in a stately procession.

Soon the canal broadened out as we entered the Little Bitter Lake, where the path for the ship was still clearly defined with buoys. The waters here were smoothly undulating and sometimes oily, looking light blue and silver in the morning light, with occasional rainbow patches. Egyptian trading vessels hurried past, in appearance like converted landing barges and loaded with miscellaneous junk, old iron, tires, etc. The waters broadened out further as we entered the Great Bitter Lake, whose shores were almost invisible on the skyline. Then they narrowed again into the Canal. The rest of the day was fascinating; we couldn't bear to leave the deck. Here would be a pile of old rusting iron — the remains of a wrecked oil tanker of the war period that the Egyptians had not yet cleared away. Then we would pass an Air Force Camp, the men running to the gates to wave and call out: "Merry Christmas." Every now and then would come a landing stage with a French or Arabic name — a well built little station with a wireless pole and meteorological devices and a surrounding village, where people were waving to us from their windows or from the jetty. On the low-lying land beside the canal were innumerable vegetable and palm gardens, before the land merged into sandy desert. Across the desert would come a steam train and occasionally, where the road ran beside the canal, we would see sleek, smooth-running cars. At one stage we passed a most impressive War Memorial at the top of a sandy hill. It consisted of twin columns surrounded by a platform flanked by sphinxes, with the words "Défense de Suez 1914-18" across the front.

The most beautiful place along the way was Ismailia. We approached it across the waters of Lake Timsah and it formed a most attractive skyline. It was much larger than the other places we had seen, with many casuarina-like trees and palms, lovely buildings with wide, cool verandas, a most attractive church with a statue of Joseph holding out the Babe, and a picnic ground down by the canal. Here were little shelters, each like a half sphere, where people could picnic in comfort, looking out over the water. Further on we came to the place where the Palestinian railway crosses the canal. The line runs over a swing bridge, which was swung back into mid-stream for us to pass. Later on, we saw the Palestine train racing across the desert. More local craft passed us, with big, billowing sails, and in a wider section we were passed by a ship going in the opposite direction.

Once again it was dark early and we saw the sunset over the canal. This was particularly attractive as the canal ran beside a lake with a high embankment in between, the waters of the lake stretching out to the west. In the darkness we could see the headlights of the ships following us through the canal.

That night, Christmas Eve, we were to dock at Port Said. As martial law had been proclaimed in Egypt and we would be there at night, we were advised, for reasons of security, to form groups of men and women for going ashore. As we drew into Port Said at about 8 p.m., we were struck by the tremendous amount of shipping in the harbor. Because of the tense situation, we were held up for a while, waiting for the Egyptian police to stamp our passports, which we had to hand in before disembarking. The Egyptian police looked very smart and very severe in their red fezzes and we soon found they were not easy to deal with. We waited a long time in the passport queue for them to come, then a long time for them to stop arguing about what they intended to do. When my time came, the policeman looked through my passport several times, then fixing me with a steely gaze he asked: "What is your religion?" I stammered out "Anglican" and passed through. I believe they were particularly on the lookout for Jews, so probably the unusual name "Wilga" had caught his eye as a possibility. Later I found out that quite a few of the passengers were asked the same question. An even longer wait followed as we queued up for the gangway, while the police argued with the purser about what the proceeding should be before we were allowed off. During this halt, a passenger who had been celebrating "not wisely but too well" entertained us with song and alarmed us by making insulting references to the Egyptians in a loud voice. At last the Egyptians decided to take up our passports, giving us numbered slips in return, and we were finally able to leave the ship.

We crossed to the shore over a winding pontoon bridge, between boats of persistent traders, and made our way to the huge store of Simon Arzt, whose neon sign had attracted us from the boat. The goods were attractive but very expensive for poor tourist-class passengers, so we satisfied ourselves with sugared almonds and chocolate. In Colombo we had been pestered by rickshaws, in Aden by taxis, and here in Port Said by horse-drawn cabs with tinkling bells. The streets once again were full of traders, who tried to sell us fezzes, silver filigree work (bracelets, necklaces, rings), dates, and Turkish Delight. It was the same old story — goods offered at twice their value and haggling to reach a suitable price. As we wandered down the streets, we had hardly looked in a window before the proprietor or his assistant would rush out to ask us in for a look — "No harm in a look! You come in." Outside a perfume shop it was "No charge for a sniff!" At one shop they were beginning to close up, but as soon as they saw us coming the shutters came off again. Some of our group were looking for oranges. Eventually we found a street barrow man who immediately gave us sections of orange each and began selling us half a pound of peanuts as a pound's worth. To us, they seemed very crafty in their selling and you certainly needed to keep a sharp eye on them.

In the streets we met groups of English soldiers. Some, who had celebrated Christmas Eve with much liquid refreshment, were wandering around in large groups singing "Good King Wenceslas." Others were thrilled to see English-speaking people and got into conversation with the passengers, giving us their views of the local situation.

In Port Said there are very good shops where you can find anything you could possibly want. There are also a great number of open-air cafes with tables on the footpath. We were interested to notice the traffic lights were in the center of the intersection. We didn't notice this the first time but walked blatantly across the street against the red light, right under the nose of the Egyptian policeman in charge. The streets are narrow, with small shops all along the way, but they seem rather dimly lit after the beautiful modern lights we saw along the roads in Aden. Eventually the time came to return to the boat, which was supposed to leave at 11 p.m., so we returned over the pontoon bridge, gave in our slips and got back our passports.

On deck we found an Egyptian magician in action. He was squatting on the floor doing the most amazing things, each preceded by the catch-words: "Gilly, gilly, gilly!" He produced chickens out of eggs, changed chickens into eggs, duplicated things, made them vanish, everything in a most effortless way. It was truly amazing. In the street two of our friends met a man who changed coins they were holding in their hands, produced chickens out of a passenger's inner pocket, changed their florins into pennies and, asking if he could keep them, did a disappearing trick himself.

When the visitors had to leave the ship, we made our way to the rail to watch the fun. The traders in their little boats were doing a brisk trade with the passengers, mainly in poufs, handbags, suitcases, Turkish Delight, dates and fezzes. They would call out the price; the haggling would proceed; then, when a satisfactory price had been agreed to, they would send the article up to the deck in a basket on a rope they had thrown onto the roof. If the article was satisfactory, the money would be sent back in the basket, or else the article would be returned. It was amusing to watch the vendors. If you offered a ridiculously low price, they crumpled up and pretended to be flabbergasted. At last the ship began to move and the traders were left behind.

25th December

We had a festive Christmas on board. It began for me with Early Communion in the First Class Library. The ship had been decorated with all the traditional iconic elements: sleighs with reindeers, Father Christmases, bells, holly, and kangaroos as a gesture to the background of the majority of us. There were Christmas trees with gifts for the children and the King's Christmas message from Buckingham Palace was broadcast over the radio. It was strange to hear this annual message at a reasonable hour, without having to get up in the early hours of the morning as we had always had to do in Australia. Of course, there was far too much to eat — turkey and ham, Christmas pudding brought in flaming with ignited brandy, mince pies, nuts, fruit, and Christmas cakes with pink and white almond icing. Christmas crackers rounded out the fun and even some of the inevitably inebriated thoroughly enjoyed our choir's concert of Christmas carols.

Such a huge celebration had to be walked off, so I set off on a brisk walk with a friend around the decks. Since the tourist section occupied only about a third of the ship's length, the tour of the decks followed a pattern of going right round one deck, then going downstairs to the next, then up again and around the deck, and so on. We often envied the first-class passengers their extensive length of deck, which on most days they hardly seemed to use. Going up and down so many steps no doubt improved our workout.

26th December

Last night the ship began rolling very badly. We had struck a storm in the Mediterranean. There were crashes as things fell off shelves and dressing tables and crockery broke in the pantry. Water poured in through portholes, even through some that were closed. In the early hours of the morning a steward came into our cabin and clambered up on my bunk to tighten my porthole, saying it was just as well he had come since it was none too tight. My Yorkshire cabin mate was sick in the night, but the turmoil didn't affect me. It was fun looking out of the porthole and watching the high waves.

The storm continued this morning, Boxing Day. As we were getting up we found it hard to keep our feet and were often thrown across the cabin as the ship rolled. The morning was chilly and gray, the sea reflecting the dreary color of the sky. At Early Communion the celebrant found it hard to keep his feet. Since many people were seasick again, the dining saloon was half empty for breakfast. It had been swamped in the night, because the stewards, who had been celebrating Christmas, hadn't closed all the portholes. The tablecloths had been soaked to stop things from slipping and they were even wetter by the time some of our breakfast had swung off the plates

By this time I was making friends with some of the new passengers who had come on board at Port Said. First I began talking French with a Greek, with a French mother, who spoke French and Arabic but was not too sure in his use of English. Charles gave me quite a few insights into Egyptian life: the extremes of wealth and poverty, the unbelievably low wages for working people, and the unpopularity of King Farouk's divorce from his beautiful, much-loved queen. He explained the Egyptian viewpoint on the Palestinian Arab-Jewish problem, which was so different from what I had read in the Australian newspapers. Charles soon introduced me to George, a Greek from Alexandria, again a French speaker, who knew even less English than his friend. Through them, I was getting quite a lot of practice in speaking French again. Charles and George introduced me to an Egyptian gynecologist and obstetrician, Dr Diaa Seif El Din, who was traveling to London to prepare for his FRCS [Fellow of the

Royal College of Surgeons] exam and hoping to teach at the University of Cairo on his return. Talking with Diaa, I learned a great deal about public health in Egypt, significant medical problems, Egyptian history and culture, politics, and the Palestine war. Diaa spoke excellent English, with a precise, clipped accent, having done all his medical studies in English. This close association with new friends from a very different background was certainly broadening my perception of things. That slight distrust of foreigners, which the isolated Australian of 1948 inevitably felt, was gradually fading away as I met and conversed with such friendly, alert, educated people from a very different culture.

After our adventures with the storm, we had begun to think that "wintering beside the Mediterranean" was a myth. However, our first beautiful, warm, Mediterranean day soon changed our minds as we basked in glorious sunshine on the top deck. Sailing tranquilly along the Algerian coast we experienced that complete peace and relaxation one feels only on a ship.

29th December

I went up on deck this morning to see us draw in to the enormous rock of Gibraltar. At first we saw the great rearguard of rock like two towers with smooth slabs of rock in between. At the foot were the lights of a big encampment. As we came around the rock we saw the town at the base of the rock masses, with its many administrative buildings and barracks. On the crest of the rocks great guns pointed out to sea. In the foreground were many ships and tankers. Around a huge bay stretched the coast of Spain, then through a small gap we glimpsed the misty hills of Morocco on the other side of the Mediterranean. On the far coast of Spain a little light through the gray clouds fell directly on a small town and a rainbow circled the hills. It was one of the most attractive harbor views of the trip. Unfortunately we were not allowed ashore as the ship was only staying for an hour and a half. Nothing deterred, the Spanish traders rowed out from the shore with their wares — scarves and shawls, many with long silken fringes, mats, silver bracelets, nylon stockings, Spanish wine. There was not the haggling of the Eastern ports nor the same persistence and slick salesmanship. They called out their prices; at first these were high but, as sailing time drew near, they were gradually reduced. When it was time to sail, the sailors turned the hoses on the men in the small boats to drive them away. I slipped off down to the front of the boat, to the First Class end, to take a good snap of Gibraltar.

As the ship drew away, we were surrounded by hundreds of seagulls — a tremendous cloud, sometimes swooping down to pick up some refuse that had been thrown into the water. The sea seems to be quite a rubbish bin and it is surprising what is thrown in to it at times. Later I watched the passage through the narrow straits out of the Mediterranean. We were very close to the Spanish coast, which at this point was rather bare and uninhabited, with very evenly folded hills running down to the water. At last we saw Cape Trafalgar. After dinner we hurried on deck to see the flashing light of Cape St Vincent, and we were very disappointed to realize that Browning's "Home Thoughts from the Sea" was all poetic license. We passed Trafalgar at 10.45 a.m. and reached Cape St Vincent at 7.15 p.m., so it would have been quite impossible to see them both at once, while Gibraltar is right around the corner and quite out of sight! Then I remembered that Keats similarly got Cortez and Balboa mixed up. However, the poetry is still inspiring.

Diaa, who has been a chess champion for four years in Cairo, offered to teach me to play chess so that I would never be beaten — rather a heavy assignment, I thought. I accepted the offer eagerly, since I had always wanted to play chess. Diaa was a most patient and clear teacher. He began from the beginning, explaining everything in a most encouraging way and I began to get the hang of it. [After that I played chess with Diaa as often as I could till we reached London. This shipboard acquaintanceship was the beginning of a most enjoyable friendship.]

30th December

We are now approaching the Bay of Biscay (or the Bay of Biscuit, as one of my Yorkshire cabin mates calls it), which we are told will be very rough. The ship is taking it slowly now, and the fire doors are closed in the passageways as we have run into a little fog. The sea is higher now that we are in the Atlantic and the ship is rolling rather badly.

327

31st December

The Bay of Biscay certainly lived up to its name as a bay of storms and gave us all we could have expected. The sea was very high and the ship rolled in a most disturbing fashion. As you walked along, the floor came up to meet you, especially going down stairs. It was impossible to walk straight down the passages or across the room. In the corridors the walls just came to meet you and, at some stages, you pushed your way laboriously along, jammed against the wall; then as it swayed back you walked straight across to the opposite wall. You found yourself crossing the room in a rush, most unexpectedly at times, and running into people or a wall. In the lounge and in the cafe, ropes were run around central pillars making a kind of boxing ring in the middle, so that people had something to hang on to. It was hilarious in the diningroom. Half the passengers, being seasick, were absent, but the rest were curiously exhilarated and excited. There was much more noise and laughter than usual and many crashes, as dishes rushed off autotrays and sideboards. The edges were up around the tables to stop dishes from slipping off and the tablecloths were wet again to stop things shifting. When the ship lurched you had to be careful that your soup didn't swing off the plate. As you looked across to the portholes, you could see all sea, and then all sky. It was most amusing.

I spent the afternoon on a glassed-in deck watching the sea rise and fall, occasionally seeing a small ship breasting the waves. That night I played chess with Diaa. All around us were other groups at tables, playing cards, drinking, or just gossiping. The tremendous movement of the ship continued, yet not once did our chessboard become disarranged. Diaa was marvelous. He held the sides of the board, raising it as the ship rolled and then lowering it as the ship subsided. People's cards and drinks flew. Once or twice I was even lurched off my balance nearly on to the floor, but when I sat up again Diaa was sitting in the same place, quietly smiling, with the chessboard straight, and all the pieces in place!

We hardly slept that night. It was like sleeping on a whale's back, or perhaps an elephant's. The bunk just wouldn't keep still! I had become accustomed to the cradle-like rocking, but not this tremendous swaying. Fortunately I couldn't fall out of the bunk, since my steward had tucked my bedclothes in so tightly on both sides.

The fun continued on Friday morning. At times it sounded as though a cabin might be coming to pieces next door, so loud were the crashes. At one exciting moment two glass-topped tables from the lounge raced down the stairs to the landing, smashing the tops entirely. After that, all the tables were lashed together beside the wall, as the deckchairs had been lashed on deck. By the afternoon, however, as we reached the English Channel, things calmed down and many people reappeared from their cabins. It is surprising how immediately a seasick stomach responds to calm sailing.

By now we were approaching the English coastline and we could see the lights quite close at hand. I saw the pilot boat come out from Southampton. It seemed possible that we would be in the harbor at about 2 a.m. Having greeted the New Year, I retired to rest, to the terrific racket of the clashing of propellers under our cabin.

1st January, 1949

This morning we found we had nearly run aground on a sandbank during the night, hence the commotion beneath my cabin! We had expected to be in Southampton this morning, but we were out at sea again. It appeared it had been too rough for us to take the pilot on board, so we had had to take to the Channel again. As things calmed down we began to make our way into the strait beside the Isle of Wight.

With a freezing wind blowing, it was exceedingly cold on deck, but we all put on our warmest coats and headscarves and endured the blast to see all we could. We found the English coastline interestingly different with the dark patches of leafless trees, the little towns of close-packed houses, all two-storied and verandaless (so different from our Australian houses), the bright soft green of open patches of turf, little church spires, and one lovely view of Carisbrooke Castle, a gray ruin standing out clearly in an open green field.

At last we were in the enormous harbor of Southampton, with its skyline dotted with cranes and the many big ships in the docks. We were all excited to see the Queen Mary, a huge white liner with three orange and black funnels, drawing out of the harbor, followed not too much later by her two-funneled sister ship, the Queen Elizabeth. We were welcomed by a little bright sunshine, followed immediately by a shower of hailstones to remind us not to be too optimistic Then there was a terrific squall of bitter cold wind, rain, and sleet. What a welcome! I had arrived in the land of my ancestors, and France could not be far behind.

10

NORTHERN HEMISPHERE

UP TOP   1949

"**Y**ou're an Aussie, aren't you?" the luggage porter commented. "I want to thank you personally for what you Australians have been doing to help us out," he continued, referring to the quantities of food and clothing Australia had been sending to England since the war. This attitude, I found, was widespread. The help he referred to included, of course, the shipload of hand-knitted woollen garments from the women of Victoria that my sister Alys's Woollies Appeal had generated. I had arrived in a drab postwar Britain, with widespread evidence of wartime destruction, food-ration coupons still in force, and on all sides teeth-gritting determination to bring things back to normal. The reddish-purple fireweed, the colorful loosestrife, growing profusely among the stones and rubble of bomb-damaged buildings, attested to nature's cooperation in that effort and raised people's spirits. As I soon found out, however, no amount of devastation could mar the beauty of the English landscape — that countryside with which I had become so familiar through the works of Wordsworth, Hardy, and Housman.

The English people I met were very friendly and helpful to arriving visitors and relatives from abroad. A letter of welcome from my English cousin, Winnie Rivers, awaited me as the ship docked. My Australian half-niece, Jeanette, the owner of the warm fur coat, came to collect it and offer me a London guide, with the promise of showing me some of the sights of that great city. She herself had taken the long route from Australia, traveling on a French cargo ship that had taken three or four months, in and out of various ports of Southeast Asia, to find its way to Europe. When the boat train reached

331

London, the Inter-Varsity Christian Fellowship (IVCF) representative was there, with a card held high, to escort me through the corridors of the London Underground to the right train for Cheam. I was to stay with the family of Dr Douglas Johnson, the General Secretary of the Fellowship, who would soon give me useful information on how to find a teaching position in the middle of the English school year. Since I had arrived in London with my return fare in the bank and about forty dollars in my purse, finding work was of immediate concern.

Cheam was a delightful place with roomy houses, surrounded by extensive gardens and orchards, situated along restful English lanes with protective hedges. Along these lanes well-groomed residents walked their well-bred and well-fed dogs — Pekinese, Scotch terriers, spaniels, French poodles, and a few larger breeds that needed their exercise twice a day. In rambles deeper into Surrey with the Johnson children, I began to appreciate the English countryside even in winter, when it was so different from the evergreen Australian bush. We wandered in the leafless woods, strolling among the tall, slender trunks of the silver birches and larches, through which we glimpsed occasional flashes of scarlet holly berries on dark green bushes. We walked along trout streams, watching the rippling eddies over the stones, and we explored pretty little villages, like Friday Street, with wild ducks swimming on a large pond that reflected the trees of the nearby wood. These were peaceful moments. I began to look forward with eager anticipation to what spring and summer might bring.

I was soon in contact with my Rivers relatives in Ealing in West London. These were the families of my father's brothers and sisters who had returned to England with my grandparents in the 1860s. They became a great support to me during my time in England. Aunt Lucie, my father's sister-in-law, was about eighty, a small birdlike woman with a will of iron, who still ruled the household and directed the activities of her three single daughters. Gladys, the primary school teacher, was dark-haired and olive-skinned; she had inherited the Spanish gene as had my half-sister May. Winnie, fair-haired and kind, was very like my half-sister, Violet; and Margaret was an energetic organizer and career woman. These three women had grown up in a period when English people

332

did not travel very far from their home base, so there was still talk in the family about the time "when Margaret went to Norway." The son, Osmond, or Os, who also lived in Ealing, was always called Wiz for obvious reasons. A leading coachwork designer for custom-built Rolls Royce and Daimler cars, he had won his first award for car design before he was twenty. Wiz was an entertaining raconteur with a dry sense of humor. His wife, Betty, friendly, chatty and very welcoming, was Welsh, related to the famous, fiery Welsh evangelist, Hugh Price-Hughes. She confided to me that she was rather relieved that I was not wealthy, as so many of the Rivers relatives who had visited them previously had seemed to be. The family was for most part strongly Anglican. They were musical too, both Jean and Hugh, Betty and Wiz's children, being organists and choir directors. In more recent years, Jean's daughter, Anne, who was a small baby on my first visit, became one of the first women to be ordained in the Anglican Church of Scotland, where she lives with her husband, a doctor in Edinburgh. There was also, I found, a Roman Catholic branch, descended from an Irish ancestor, which included ecclesiastics as well as a daughter who had converted to Protestantism and written a book about her spiritual journey, entitled "From Rome to the Light." As time went on, I saw a great deal of Betty, Wiz, Jean and Hugh, who later married an Australian second cousin, Violet's daughter Margaret, who also visited London. When Hugh emigrated to Australia, his sons revived the inheritance of the Rivers name in Melbourne, since, of my father Harry's numerous family, all the sons had had daughters and only the daughters sons.

Impressions of a New Arrival

Coming from a young, sparsely populated country of great distances, I was very struck by the convenience and efficiency of the London transport system. My first train from Southampton to Waterloo station, besides being extremely comfortable and attractively furnished, served a copious English tea even to the third-class passengers. That there were only first and third classes on the trains, with no second, came as a surprise. Somewhere on the journey from the nineteenth century, one class had apparently got lost. Everyone, it seemed, except the very wealthy, traveled third class, without feeling that this cast any aspersion on their status. The underground system was very dependable with frequent service, most conveniently placed stations and interchanges, and directions so clear that no one, not even a new arrival from the Antipodes, could possibly get lost. In the streets polite and youthful-looking bobbies, in their distinctive tall helmets, were always nearby to help. Double-decker buses ran in all directions, while faster coaches, making less frequent stops, carried people over longer distances. For further convenience in transport, there were the upright, black taxis, with capacious interiors and loading platforms in front beside the driver for luggage; these were easily flagged down and charged very little for the trip. The traffic in the streets behaved in a most civilized way, as did the pedestrians, despite their legal privilege of priority when crossing the road. As an Australian, I soon found I had to become more disciplined too. I was unaccustomed to queuing politely and accepting refusal from bus drivers when the seats in the vehicle were full. Early in the piece I made a dive for a departing bus. I seized the pole on the back platform and steadied myself with a sense of achievement, only to be told by the driver that I had jumped the queue most impolitely (I hadn't noticed it was there) and that I must get off at the next stop. Despite my profuse apologies and protestations that I had just arrived in London and had much to learn, I was promptly deposited at the next stop, which happened to be a request stop. Since it was rush hour, I had to wait patiently and watch many buses pass before a driver with enough room for me took pity on my plight.

Houses in England were also strange to my eye. They did not have wide verandas to keep off the heavy rain and the burning sun as at home and, unlike most Melbourne bungalow-style houses, they were two-storied or even three-storied with attic rooms at the third level. That English people preferred to sleep upstairs I presumed was a tradition coming down from the bad old days of footpads and petty thieves abroad at night. Most noticeable to an Australian, though, was the fact that so many houses were alike. Streets and streets of houses were identical, often in long terraces or semi-detached pairs. Even in more affluent areas where the houses were detached, they were still quite often exactly alike. This contrasted vividly with the Australian predilection for individual designs for their one-family homes, each standing out as different from its neighbors. A builder soon informed me that this sameness kept the prices down, since all the pieces —

doors, window frames, and window glass, for instance — were interchangeable and could be bought in wholesale quantities.

Meal times posed another problem for me. In my Australian milieu, we had "tea" at six in the evening, and this was the hot meal of the day. "Supper" for me was a social affair, at ten thirty or eleven in the evening, after a party or meeting. For this savories, sausage rolls, cream cakes, and luscious, light sponge cakes would be served, with the inevitable "cuppa" (cup of tea). The English system of a rather substantial "tea" of sandwiches and cake or biscuits (and a pot of tea, of course) strictly at four, with a hot supper at eight in the evening was new to me. When I was invited out to tea by my London acquaintances, I presumed I should arrive at six p.m. Very soon I discovered I had accepted two "tea" invitations for the same day. For one, having been invited with precise details, I arrived at four, whereas for the other, to my hostess's considerable annoyance, I arrived at six. Gradually I adapted to the English system of four meals a day, often with a cup of tea in bed before rising as well.

Then there was the Australian custom of making first contact by phone with persons I had been asked to look up or who had asked me to do so on my arrival. In the England of 1949 this was apparently very poor manners. I should have written a note first and then phoned, it seemed. I was also often late in arriving. I soon found, as I did later in New York, that, because of the enormous size and spread of the city and the vagaries of public transport, I would have to calculate the time it would take to reach a certain destination and then double it, if I were to have any hope of being there at the specified hour. These things were carefully explained to me by the exasperated English, who seemed to consider Australian ignorance of such matters to be further evidence in support of their already deep-seated conviction that "colonials" were unmannerly or "mal élevé" in the French sense.

For we were considered to be "colonials," as I was soon made aware, even though Australia had never been an English colony and had established its nationhood, with its own constitution, in 1901. One older lady told me very kindly, "You know, when I meet you colonials, I am so proud of what our ancestors did!" Whose ancestors? I thought to myself. Hers appeared to have stayed in Kent; it was my ancestors of whom we should have been proud. Then there was the perennial subject of Australia having been a convict

335

settlement in its early days. Even as recently as 1993, an educated Englishwoman, a colleague in the language-teaching profession, greeted me at our first meeting at an international conference with the cheerful assertion: "Whenever I meet you Australians, I can hear the ball and chain clanking behind you." If I replied that my ancestors had actually been teachers, not convicts, I was cajoled with: "Don't get defensive. We don't mind." In this way the English endeared themselves to the "colonials" visiting their shores.

The wife of a retired headmaster of a private school in Cambridge, on hearing that I was seeking a teaching post, took me aside with the best of intentions to warn me that I could not expect English schools to take my Australian academic degrees seriously. When I asked her how big she thought Melbourne University was, she replied: "Well, Melbourne has only about twenty thousand people, doesn't it?" I assured her, to her considerable surprise, that my Australian degrees were accepted by British universities, under an agreement of reciprocity, and that Melbourne University had about twelve thousand students at that time. I had expected more knowledge of Australia from educated people than from schoolchildren, who later asked me: "Do you have grass and all that in Australia? Isn't it just one big desert?" I often wondered what they thought the sheep and the kangaroos ate. This surprising ignorance was usually followed by: "Do you live in houses like us?" One of my Australian friends developed a quick response to this question by showing, with a swing of her arm, how she was accustomed to swinging back the tent flap to face the world in the morning; another Australian friend simply agreed that she lived up a gum tree. This was in the British Empire period. I would hope that present-day English youngsters, with such a heavy consumption of films and television programs, have more knowledge of other parts of the world than their predecessors of 1949.

Naturally I was very excited to see all the sights of London of which I had heard or read for so many years. Having listened for so long, amid the static, to the chime of Big Ben as the prelude to the BBC radio news, it was a joy to see this icon rising over the Houses of Parliament in the Palace of Westminster. Here I visited the House of Lords, the House of Commons being still a shambles from the bombing. From my intensive studies of British history in Australia, I recognized in paintings and statuary, in corridors, galleries and around the walls of chambers and antechambers, so many famous figures — kings, queens, prime ministers, generals — and so many scenes of battles and celebrations that were familiar to me. In God's providence, St Paul's, that Christopher Wren masterpiece, was still standing amid the ruins caused by so many nights of bombing. Since this was a building I had studied in my History of Art classes in high school, I found every detail absorbing. Fortunately, some of the Wren daughter churches surrounding it were also relatively unscathed — the ones I had sung about in my childhood in "Oranges and lemons! the bells of St Clement's." Jeanette took me to see the Tower of London with all its very familiar historical associations. I could almost see Anne Boleyn, with her head "tooked" underneath her arm, as in the Gracie Fields song, walking the Bloody Tower, which faced the Traitors' Gate, that last passage for so many who were to lose their heads on the Tower Green. We gaped in amazement at the Crown Jewels, admiring the Black Prince's egg-sized ruby and the Star of Africa diamond, amid the other three thousand diamonds and precious stones in crowns, orbs, scepters, gold bracelets, spurs, swords and maces. Then we had, of course, to take our own photographs of the Beefeaters, guarding the Tower in their black and red Tudor uniforms.

Other Australian friends from Melbourne University days undertook to show me the sights as well. So many of my Melbourne friends seemed to be in London at the time that I could hardly be lonely. We would meet, like so many other tourists, at the foot of the Nelson Monument in Trafalgar Square among the pigeons, or we would drink tea as we watched the Tower Bridge over the Thames open to let the ships sail through. We found our way to Piccadilly Circus, with its statue of Eros, and watched the Changing of the Guard at Buckingham Palace, just like Christopher Robin. Westminster Abbey, whose Gothic architecture I had also studied in detail in high school, apart from its beauty as a Christian sanctuary, also provided me, through its monuments and plaques, with a refresher course on the great personalities of British history, literature, music, and art. Unfortunately the Abbey was just too cluttered with statuary, so that the full effect of single pieces was lost, with one statue obscuring others. Sometimes it seemed that the largest memorials had been erected for the least famous. The window commemorating Bunyan's *Pilgrim's Progress,* for instance, with scenes from that well-known book, was partly hidden and could easily be missed altogether.

Through Dr Johnson and my Australian friends I also met a number of people engaged in Christian work among youth, which had always been one of my great interests. An Australian friend, working with youths in the East End, took me to Woking, for my first visit to the poorer sections of London, where low-income workers lived in narrow streets in huge blocks of buildings called Courts and bathed in public washhouses. This area provided a considerable contrast to the beauty of Cheam.

Earning a Living

Since my arrival in London I had been active in applying for teaching positions, responding to notices sent to me by the Truman and Knightley agency. I had written particularly to boarding schools in different parts of the country, but January was, of course, the wrong time of year for most of them. After several disappointing rejections, "Position already filled" for the most part, I received an invitation to come for an interview for a position in mid-February and a week of immediate supply teaching at the Mundella County Secondary School for Girls in Folkestone. Two weeks after my arrival in London, then, I was on the train to Kent.

In the English system of the time, children had to pass an entrance examination at eleven for acceptance into Grammar School, which was the preparatory school for the School Certificate examinations required for university entrance. Students who did not pass this eleven-plus exam were assigned to Secondary Modern Schools, comprehensive high schools not yet being widely available. If they could afford it, parents whose children were not accepted for Grammar School could exercise the option of sending them to a private school. The Secondary Modern School coped with the rest and had to cater for a wide range of scholastic abilities and life interests. Many of the children were not particularly attracted to formal study. Some felt rejected by the system and were more or less waiting out their school years until they could leave at the permissible age of sixteen. There was much thought and discussion at the time about appropriate schooling for these children.

The journey to Folkestone by train gave me my first prolonged view of the English countryside. Here it was at its gentlest in this "garden of England," with its rich, green fields, often bounded by little hedges, its occasional woods, old-fashioned cottages, and hop gardens, with their long rows of tall training sticks and their quaint conical oast-houses for storing the hops.

Having settled in at a boardinghouse in a pleasant street, I set off to explore my environs and see the sea. After all, Folkestone was a popular winter resort, so there should be a beach to walk on. What was my disappointment to find, instead of lovely sand, nasty little round stones. I had never seen a shingle beach before. The stones were difficult to walk on and, if your feet went too deep, little ones came over the edges into your shoes. However, it was pleasant, as always, to watch the waves. The sea itself does not change and I had become addicted to its rise and fall on my long sea voyage. Here I could listen to its roar as the waves rushed up on the shingles. As I returned to my boarding house that first evening, the moon was full, and I remembered that my last full moon had shone on the Buddhist procession in Colombo.

Folkestone was a well-planned, orderly place that was part of the estate of Lord Radnor, who decided everything down to the smallest details. The streets were wide and tree-lined and there were beautiful public gardens. On the cliff tops were lawns, promenades, seats and platforms with balustrades looking out over the Channel toward France, for which there was a ferry service from Folkestone. It was still too misty, however, to see France itself. That would have to wait for another day. Along the cliffs at intervals, extending into the distance, were Martello Towers, whose thick walls and moats had guarded the English coast against invasion in Norman times. Along the channel beaches to the north you could still see the barbed wire that had been laid out, a few years earlier, as protection against an invasion by Hitler's forces.

The school at Folkestone was by contrast disappointing. It was in a rather dilapidated Victorian building of an old model with no corridor, so that you had to pass through a series of classrooms to get from one end to the other. For my immediate supply teaching, I found, I would be taking the place of the Physical Training teacher who was away for a week. I would be teaching Folk Dancing,

Gymnastic Exercises, Netball (a game akin to basketball but with a larger court), and some English and Scripture. As of mid-February there would be a position available for me when the Domestic Science teacher went back to college. I would be given two-hour sessions to fill in with "something useful"; what that would be was left entirely to me. It certainly sounded like a job for a Jill-of-all-trades, but at least I would be earning some money. I was accustomed to the well-structured system of education in Victoria, but here, it seemed, I would have to adapt to a situation of complete freedom with regard to what I taught. Since I was an experienced teacher, I felt quite capable of rising to this challenge. I soon found, however, that this complete lack of structure or guidance left weak teachers, some very poorly trained, to muddle along, filling in time and often never bothering to draw up or think out a syllabus at all. Teachers in their first year were left to work out their own salvation through trial and error, from which their students suffered in the meantime; and there was little articulation between levels, so that the same topic or text might well be taught and retaught in successive grades. With more experience of this type of system over the years, I have found that it cedes responsibility for the syllabus to the textbook writer. The textbook becomes the kingpin in teaching and selecting suitable textbooks the most important decision of the year. This has led to the preoccupation of many classroom teachers with counting pages and "covering the book," rather than concentrating on cumulative learning of subject matter. There is a lot to be said for an incremental syllabus, which has been well worked out through discussion among experienced and thoughtful teachers, as a guide to those who are new and less well-trained, so long as it leaves plenty of room for individual application and extension. At least, for the sake of the students, there should be mentoring of inexperienced teachers and those less competent.

I soon discovered I had more to worry about at Folkestone than deciding what I would teach. The war now over, the recently elected Labour Government had passed an experimental New Education Act, which advocated "free discipline" as the best way to give students space and time to develop their own personalities, interests, and social skills. I was all for providing students with an educational environment in which they could become what their inborn capacities and traits would have them be, but a school that

340

promoted "free discipline" needed a Head and teachers who had enough personal authority to gain the respect and attention of the students. Unfortunately, this was a quality the Mundella Headmistress and some of her teachers lacked. As a result free discipline at this school, instead of contributing to the students' individual development of inner control and the flowering of their capacities and talents, resulted in a kind of chaos and bedlam. Children rushed about the playground shouting and running into people. During class they walked around the room as they felt inclined, all talking at once to the teacher or to each other. Even when they remained in their places, they read books or comics if they couldn't be bothered listening to what the teacher had to say or didn't feel like working on the tasks she proposed. Naturally this did not suit me at all. I loved to teach and to see students opening their minds to new information and the fascination of new ideas, as they tried to do new things. Here, I could see, I would have to take a very firm hand in the classroom to get anything done at all and the girls were certainly not accustomed to that. On the other hand they were very friendly, and they loved to tell me about their wartime experiences when they had been evacuated, not so many years earlier, from the dangerous channel coast to the relative safety of South Wales.

As the replacement for the Physical Training teacher I had no difficulty with the students, since this gave their energies plenty of room for expression. I had never played netball, or even basketball, but they had, so I blew the whistle for them to start and then blew it again very quickly when they paused and looked at me for some fault. We managed very well like this until the gym teacher returned. I then had the opportunity to teach my old love, field hockey. However, for my daily classes of English and Scripture I needed to establish some kind of classroom order. (Scripture as a subject had been introduced by the Labour Government, in its postwar education bill, to bring to government school children some of the education in values the children of the more affluent were receiving in private schools.) It was difficult to buck the atmosphere created in other classes in the school, but I managed to get some attention in my own domain. Unfortunately, I taught next door to the class of a particularly incompetent, emergency-trained teacher, whose children created a constant din, ate their lunches in class, and even jumped out of the windows as the mood took them. All of this was, of course, of great interest to my own class. The Headmistress was trying to get rid of this teacher and had tried unsuccessfully to palm her off on a primary school in the district. When I took her quite small class while she was out job seeking, I found that, for me, they were little angels and a very easy group to manage. Her problems with them were obviously a matter of her own teaching skill and her inability to arouse their interest in anything beyond themselves.

This constant struggle at Mundella did not seem to me to be the educational experience for which I had saved up over so many years in Australia. I had hoped to learn something while abroad, not to be spending my days in an exhausting battle of wills. I realized that it would take a while for order to be established in some schools after the revolution of the New Education Act, but I felt that personally I did not have the time to wait. So I went to see the Headmistress. After a long discussion (and a rather emotional one on my part — I was still at the stage of bursting into tears after about half an hour of stressful negotiation), I succeeded in making my personal problem clear to Miss Lennon. She agreed to let me off my commitment and arranged for me to go to a school in nearby Sandwich. Here the headmaster of the coeducational Secondary Modern School had more personal authority and an educational approach that, although very definitely student-centered and progressive, was somewhat less radical.

I learned a great deal about humankind in my boardinghouse in Folkestone. In boardinghouses in England one encountered a number of aged, somewhat eccentric people living out their lives with some company. One old lady, Miss Buss, who was over eighty, was very curious by nature. She was always bursting to know what was going on but somewhat befuddled by what she was told. She had a face rather like a Dismal Desmond dog, square-jowled and long, and spoke in a gruff, monosyllabic way. During the evenings when I might be reading or knitting, she would apparently be reading too, except that she never seemed to finish the page. When I looked up, she would be observing me over the edge of her book. She had two main conversation openers: "It's cold, isn't it?" and "What time is it?" although she had a watch. She could not make me out at all, looking upon me as some variety of foreigner, used to totally different ways. When I came home one day from a visit to Canterbury, she asked:

"Did you have any lunch?" "Yes," I replied. "But how did you know where to go?" she grunted. I tried to look perfectly serious as I explained, "I saw the word Restaurant over a window, so I went in!" Another night she asked me: "Do you go to the same school as Mrs H?" (Mrs H was also at Mundella.) I replied in the affirmative. "In the same room?" she asked. "No, I teach, you know," I informed her. "How do you know what rooms to go to?" she ruminated. Miss Buss could not bear to have her routine disrupted. At nine o'clock every night, the landlady would put her head in the door and say, "Your bottle, Miss Buss." Miss Buss would take her hot-water bottle, which she duly filled, and get her regular glass of milk. One night when the landlady wanted to go out, she put her head in the door at a quarter to nine, saying: "Your bottle, Miss Buss." When she had popped out again, Miss Buss looked at the clock, looked at her watch, looked at me, and said: "Hum! Clock's slow!" After she had returned from the little ceremony of getting her glass of milk, she kept grunting and grumbling for the next half hour: "It wasn't nine o'clock, was it? No, it wasn't nine o'clock!"

Another fellow boarder was Mrs Tyrrell, equally advanced in age. She was partially deaf and recovering from a cataract operation. One day she decided, without warning, to go away. She packed her possessions and her jewelry in a case, which she left at her daughter's workplace. With it was a note saying that she was glad her daughter had been good to her, but she felt she was only a burden on everyone, so she was going away and they were not to look for her. The daughter was naturally most upset and immediately got in touch with the police. By two o'clock in the afternoon the police had traced Mrs Tyrrell as far as the train to London. They were trying to establish more details when lo and behold! the old lady got off a London train on her way home. It appeared she had intended committing suicide in the London traffic, but, finding it was too well organized to run her over, she had had to put her project off till another day.

When Miss Buss worked out that I was departing suddenly for Sandwich, she was determined to get to the bottom of all this. She stopped me on the stairs with the question: "What *is* this that you do?" "Supply teaching," I replied brightly, with a brief explanation. "Oh! supply teaching, is that it? Supply teaching, supply teaching," she murmured, memorizing it as she went up the stairs. It was just as well

I was leaving, because it seemed I was forcing Miss Buss to perform more mental gymnastics than she had for years.

As in my earlier teaching appointments I found wonderfully kind and hospitable friends during my sojourn in England. "Valentines" they were to me, like Sybil and Neville Valentine in Sale, who had "adopted" me and brightened my life while I was at St Annes. In London there was Mrs Winifred Upton of Twickenham, who wore a big, flowing, black cape. She had asked me to consider her house a home away from home and to feel welcome to come at any time for a day's visit or a weekend as one of the family. I was happy to accept her at her word. Even during my brief stay in Folkestone, I found another Valentine, a Mrs Rootes at the local Anglican church who was similarly hospitable, offering warm English friendship. Hospitality, especially to the displaced and wandering, is surely a God-given grace.

Now that plans were in place for transferring to Sandwich, there was still Folkestone to enjoy. By this time I had bought a second-hand, "pre-loved" bicycle, a real bargain, which I decided to call after the local saint, Eanswythe, who had founded the first religious community for women in Folkestone in 630 AD. I found there was a Miracle Pond in the town, through which St Eanswythe had caused pure water to flow, as she commanded it to follow her from the river up the hill to the monastery to provide for the wants of the sisters. I hoped she would help me as much, and I soon found my black and silver Eanswythe most useful for exploring the environs and going back and forth to school.

A sundial on the esplanade along the cliffs showed directions and distances to nearby places. We were 6.5 miles from Dover, 63 miles from London, 30 miles from Calais, 52 miles from Dunkirk from which a number of soldiers had been evacuated to Folkestone during the sudden retreat in 1941, 140 miles from Brussels, 165 miles from Paris, and a mere 15 miles from Canterbury (that magical name)! Of course, Canterbury had to be the first place to visit. These other exciting places would come in time.

Mater Angliae

The bus to Canterbury took me along a delightful country route, up hill and down dale, sometimes through wooded country, sometimes through orchards, with broad panoramas of fertile farmland. From the front seat in the upper level of the bus I had a magnificent view of the neat little villages with winding streets through which we passed to pick up passengers at the local hostelries. The very names of the latter were so English: the New Inn at Etchinghill (more than likely quite old), the Prince of Wales at Rhodes Minnis, the Rose and Crown at Stelling Minnis and even the Abbot's Fireside. Each inn had a smartly painted inn-sign with the subtly advertised name of a brewer at the bottom. At last we came riding into Canterbury, like the Wife of Bath, past the open cattle market where the Kentish auctioneer was calling out bids in a rapid patter.

Canterbury had been badly damaged by bombs and other missiles. There were many gaping holes, with signs telling who had conducted business formerly at a particular spot and their new address. Fortunately the Cathedral had escaped harm, although not all the churches had been so lucky. Opposite the cattle market was the shell of St George's, where Christopher Marlowe had been christened.

Canterbury was a quaint old town with narrow, winding streets, frequently overhung by the first floor of half-timbered Tudor houses. I began my visit with the Church of St Dunstan-without-the-Westgate, an old church built of flint stones set in cement — a combination not unusual in Kent. The list of vicars dated back to 1284. Here was the family vault of St Thomas More. Passing the House of Agnes, reminiscent of Dickens's *David Copperfield*, and the Falstaff Inn, I came to the massive Westgate, which has guarded the passage of traffic from London to the Kentish ports and from the Kentish ports inland since 1380. Nearby was the Holy Cross Church where mystery plays had been performed in the Middle Ages. In St Peter's Street, right in the middle of a busy shopping center, was St Thomas's Hospital, established in the 13th century as a hospice for pilgrims to the shrine of St Thomas A'Becket. Was this where Chaucer's pilgrims gratefully lay down on straw mattresses after their long journey? Along the Stour were the gabled houses of the Flemish Huguenot weavers who had come to Reformation England to avoid persecution in Europe. Further along the river were the overgrown ruins of the Franciscan Friary. In the Dane John Gardens was a great Roman burial mound near the city wall and moat. Every spot along the way was for me like turning another exciting page of a history book.

At last I reached the splendid Cathedral itself, the center of my Anglican faith. I approached it down Mercery Lane. This delightful, narrow, old-fashioned street led to the elaborately carved Christchurch Gate — a fitting preliminary to the striking sight of the beautiful eleventh-century cathedral, built on the site of the palace King Ethelbert gave to St Augustine and his monks in the sixth century to establish a church. Here Christians have worshipped since Roman times. The cathedral's towers and turrets and the pinnacles of the buttresses point like impressive fingers to the heavens.

For me the interior of the cathedral was breathtaking — so clean and light and spacious. It gave an impression of immensity, yet it was not over-cluttered with monuments and plaques like Westminster Abbey; the great pillars and soaring arches remained the central focus of attention. Adding to the impressiveness of the interior was the brilliant concept of a series of steps mounting toward the high altar from the nave to the choir, then up to the sanctuary, so that the altar is finally twenty-five feet higher than the nave. It was on this higher platform that the jeweled shrine of St Thomas A'Becket stood when this was one of the premier places of pilgrimage in Europe. To the side is the old staircase, with its steps worn away by the thousands of pilgrims, who for four centuries made their way up it on their knees. To the left of the choir is the spot where Thomas A'Becket was killed by the King's men, after he came down from the sanctuary to see what they wanted of him. Nearby a chained Bible, a relic of the days when Bibles were rare, is a reminder of the fact that Canterbury was one of the first churches in which the Bible was read in English.

The windows in Canterbury Cathedral are more than magnificent; of medieval glass their colors gleam like jewels, although the secret of the composition of the glass has long since been lost. Many of these windows contain glass of a deep blue, called Canterbury blue, which was specially made for the cathedral by French craftsmen from Chartres. In these beautiful surroundings lie such famous people as the Black Prince, Henry the Fourth and, of more recent memory, the much-loved Archbishop Temple, whose worldwide vision is commemorated in chapels with copies of the Bible and the Anglican liturgy in many languages.

Since I have great affection for the Romanesque style, called Norman in England, I was particularly moved by the small chapel of St Mary Undercroft, where the Black Prince loved to worship. Until the time of the Reformation, when Henry V111 raided the coffers of the church to enrich his own, this lovely chapel, entered only by the most important people in the realm, was bedecked with jewels and rich decorations. I shall never forget the sight, as I looked through the low Norman arches of the dark crypt into this perfectly shaped, illuminated chapel, so replete with historic memories. Nearby huddled a small chapel for the Huguenot refugees, in which services were still being said in French. To conclude my visit I walked in the quiet of the cloisters, a truly meditative spot. Archbishop Temple once wrote: "It is the bounden duty of every English-speaking man and woman to visit Canterbury twice in their lives." I am glad I have had that privilege, and that, on the second visit ten years later, I was able to hear the clear tones of the choristers rising to the Gothic arches as they sang Evensong — an experience that illuminates the meaning of the word "ethereal." *Ave, Mater Angliae*, as Canterbury's ancient motto reads.

Introduction to the Cinque Ports

Before leaving Folkestone, I paid a quick visit to Rye, one of the Cinque Ports, a medieval trade alliance around the Kentish coast. To reach this ancient paradise for smugglers of silks and perfumes, I traveled across the Romney Marshes, now, thanks to the numerous drainage channels, providing excellent pasture for the Romney Marsh sheep. The isolated little houses reminded me of stories of the marshlands that had fascinated me in Australia, like Constance Holmes' *Lonely Plough*. As a result of the draining of the marshes, the sea had retreated about two miles, so that Rye was now "a city set on a hill." Local teams were playing football where the sea used to lap against the cliffs. Remnants of the old defensive walls provided a reminder of the constant raids from across the Channel in earlier times. Soon I was in steep, narrow Mermaid Street, with its ancient cobblestones. Up this thoroughfare, the smugglers used to sneak with their haul to the Mermaid Tavern, an old half-timbered inn still in existence. This cobble-stoned street retains so much of its old character that, almost expecting to see a smuggler come surreptitiously around the corner with his sack on his back, I found a car parked by the curb to be a shocking anachronism. I was very amused by the clock in the old church, the pendulum of which hangs right down into the interior and swings steadily as it has been doing for hundreds of years. This must have a more hypnotic effect on the congregation than many a sermon. Restful to the eyes and mind was a lovely window of rich blues, greens and reds on the theme of the Benedicite, with medallions showing all the things that are called on to bless the Lord — birds, animals, fire and heat, rain and snow, lightning, seas, angels, saints, and all people. This was an intriguing and very detailed illustration of a subject rarely seen in church windows.

It was a lovely sight to look back at Rye in the dusk across the marshes. There it was, perched like a fairy castle on its hill, while mists rose from the valley below, making it appear to be floating in the clouds.

Sandwich, my next destination, was further north along the coast. It was another of the Cinque Ports. As I traveled there by train to take up my position at the Secondary Modern School, I thought of our very Anglophile Australian Prime Minister, Robert Menzies, who after his retirement was made Warden of the Cinque Ports, an honor that had been bestowed on Winston Churchill before him. The rather uneventful journey, through rough coastal land, was enlivened for me by the rushing past of one of the fast boat trains to Folkestone Harbour for the ferry to France. Soon after, I caught a glimpse of the white cliffs of Dover and Dover Castle itself, looking out across the Channel. These were intimations to me that I was not too far from the fulfillment of my dream to work and study in France.

Teaching in Sandwich

Monday morning (January 31st) found me making my way once again, in some trepidation, to a new school. How would I like it this time? Would there be "free discipline"? Would they be expecting me? The answer to the last question was no. The headmaster at the Sandwich County Secondary School was completely taken aback, since the County Council had failed to inform him that I was coming. However, as his male Physical Training teacher was to be away for a week, he was quite happy to have someone to keep the PT classes quiet.

I began, on the absent teacher's schedule, with two spare periods. Since I could not teach the classes of from twenty to forty boys soccer, rugby, or gymnastics on the rings or the horse, it was arranged that, during the scheduled PT periods, I would give talks on Australia. The boys were thrilled and listened most attentively to quick surveys of Australia's geography, history, climate, agriculture, and industrial production; descriptions of its unique animals, birds, and vegetation; the ways of life of its original inhabitants and the preoccupations of its majority population, particularly the sports that absorbed them. They probably found my Australian accent intriguing too. They asked innumerable questions, the first of which was usually: "Have you seen Don Bradman?" (Bradman was Australia's most famous cricketer.) This was followed almost immediately by "*I* have! At Canterbury!" This match between the cricket teams of England and Australia had been a red-letter day in the boys' lives. They wanted to know if I spoke Australian as well as English, whether Australians lived in houses as they did (the old, old question), and whether we had roads and railways. To them Australia must have seemed as exotic a place as China. They soon began to see it more clearly however. The talks on animals and birds, illustrated with imitative sounds from me, were among the highlights, and I was expected to be an authority on the average length of snakes, which are rare in England. When I told them of the low prices for fruit in Australia, that we grew oranges, grapes, peaches and apricots in our gardens and that there was no rationing of sweets, some were ready to pack up right away. (Looking back, I wonder if any of them did.) I found that even my fellow teachers thought Australians did not play football, so I had to explain something about Melbourne's strenuous Australian Rules game in this home of rugby and soccer. Altogether, during my first week at Sandwich, I talked to fifteen different classes on Australia, most of them twice, and some three times. The repercussions were felt everywhere, as the students rushed to tell the other teachers what they had heard.

As this was a Secondary Modern School, the students were not strong in academic studies (those who were had been admitted to the Grammar School and a second selection had gone to the Technical

School). They were, however, enthusiastic and interested. Their behavior was exemplary, and I felt that here was a school with a reasonable, friendly discipline where I could feel much happier and achieve much more than I could have at Mundella. Part of the noticeable difference was due to the fact that a majority of the children in the school were country and village bred, coming from all directions each day on nine buses. At Sandwich the students had ample school grounds in which to stretch their legs and let off steam and the classrooms looked out over fresh, verdant fields and haystacks, whereas the poor "townies" of Mundella had been surrounded by high, brick walls and a limited area of gray asphalt. The head of this mixed school of six hundred, Mr Cook, was a very genial, understanding man, with a strong interest in providing an education that would meet the needs and interests of different types of students of varying skills and abilities. I could feel that he had a genuine respect and affection for his students.

As a result of a phone call from my landlady at Folkestone, I had found excellent lodgings at a guest house that catered particularly for the golfing enthusiasts who frequented the world-famous Royal St George's Golf Course. This course was a favorite of the Prince of Wales (later the Duke of Windsor), who also had a lady friend living nearby. The guesthouse was very comfortable with excellent food. My life seemed to be settling down at last to some semblance of normality. At least I knew what I would be doing for the next three weeks, and this would give me a respite in which to continue my search for something more permanent.

Mr Cook had no specific work for me to do after the first two weeks. Since he had discerned my genuine interest in educational practice, he gave me free time to wander around the school observing how different teachers were handling the diverse problems of educating students from such a wide swathe of educational backgrounds and interests. I moved around discreetly, observing a Secondary Modern School in action. I sat in on classes, asked students questions, and had long discussions on aims and techniques with teachers who were developing experimental programs to provide for the non-academic type of student. Some of the students in one class were practically illiterate at fourteen, but by law they had to remain in school until they were sixteen. Of these some were gypsy children who had moved in and out of different schools all their lives, with no continuity of education. The problem for their teacher was to find very simple, introductory reading material that would, nevertheless, keep the interest of adolescents. In another class, the teacher was building integrated reading, writing and speaking development on individual students' interests. I remember vividly watching a fourteen-year-old boy give a presentation on pigeons. His passion in life, it seemed, was breeding carrier pigeons. Although he had never been particularly interested in or successful at academic reading or study, he had devoted hours to seeking out information about pigeons, filling an exercise book with diagrams, pictures, and written text. Now, probably for the first time in his life, he was teaching an interested class about the one subject he knew and cared about. The success and satisfaction I was observing may well have been the first that this boy had experienced in his school career. It was very impressive. Mr Cook also found time for long discussions with me about my impressions of what I had seen around the school. For me it was a most valuable week and consolidated my own commitment to student-centered education.

As soon as I had obtained some kind of short-term teaching to see me through, I began to correspond again with the headmistress of Abbotsford School in Kenilworth, Warwickshire, who had expressed interest in employing me while I was in Australia. I was anxious to know whether she still needed teachers. With my childhood background of avid reading of the novels of Sir Walter Scott, the very name Kenilworth, and particularly the image of Kenilworth Castle, evoked for me very romantic associations. I remembered sharing in the ecstasies and tragedies of Robert Dudley, Earl of Leicester, one of Queen Elizabeth 1's favorites, and his unfortunate wife, Amy Robsart. Where would I find anything more typical of "Olde England"? It was an exciting prospect. The headmistress, Mrs Hall, replied immediately to my letter. It so happened that her primary-level teacher, Miss Cay, was to be away for a while in the spring to nurse her aged mother, so I would be able to integrate into the school in a useful capacity as of the month of March. This would be a new experience for me, since I had last taught primary-age children during my three weeks of student teaching preceding my university studies in 1936.

With my next move settled, I was determined to see as much as possible of the south coast. Sandwich gave me easy access to the kinds of historic places that we Australians dream of but do not have in our own country. There were first century defensive castles, seventh century abbeys, fourteenth century guildhalls, and the harbor and castle at nearby Dover, about whose white cliffs we had sung during the war. There were also the popular holiday resorts along the coast, like Ramsgate, Margate, and Dickens's Broadstairs. I was just beginning to become acclimated to the region and was thoroughly enjoying my explorations when the time came to take myself off to the Midlands.

Experiences in the Center of England

On arrival in Warwickshire, I was not disappointed with my choice. Kenilworth, a picturesque town of about ten thousand, had in 1949 a quiet, backwater atmosphere, which has surely changed since the establishment of the University of Warwick, with its numerous students and faculty. The central feature of the town at the time was the enormous, overgrown area of common land, known as the Abbey Fields. A few low, crumbling, moss-covered walls remained as a reminder of the great Abbey, plundered and destroyed by Henry V111 on one of his reformist, coffer-filling forays against the property of the monastic orders. Across the Fields ran a great gully, full of trees and grassland, now a spring picture drenched in golden buttercups and white daisies. Here there were public recreation facilities, tennis courts, playing-fields and swimming baths and, on occasion, a traveling Fair with all the trappings — big dipper, dodgem cars, merry-go-rounds and all kinds of sideshow stalls. Around the Fields were houses, each with a superb view of parkland. Some of the houses on the far side of the Fields were thatched and half-timbered, which added to the old-world effect. On one side of the Fields was an open ford, where a stream flowed out; this was great fun to splash through for drivers who hadn't recently washed their cars.

Further along the road were the woods at the back of Kenilworth Castle and then the Castle itself. Penetrating the woods brought you out on a great open field, commonly called the Echo Field, which faced the hillside on which the Castle had been built. If you shouted across the Echo Field, the ruined walls of the Castle would send back a splendid extended echo, as your shout rebounded from wall to wall. Kenilworth Castle had been built in an excellent strategic position almost in the center of England, where roads diverged in all directions. Kenilworth was, in fact, halfway between Meriden, where the remains of a cross marked the center of England, and Leamington Spa with its Midland Oak, also claiming to mark the true center of the realm. In this famous castle the Earl of Leicester had entertained Queen Elizabeth 1 on several occasions at great expense. Henry 1, King John, Simon de Montfort (the pioneer of representative government in England) and John of Gaunt were other great names associated with it. Over the centuries it had been the site of both nation-shaping activities and political machinations.

I was now settled in one of the most beautiful areas of Britain — "leafy Warwickshire," as it was aptly called. The surrounding area was grazing country, with an undulating landscape of low, rolling hills and attractive panoramas as the road crested the hilltops. The fields were bounded with low brushwood, blackberry bushes, or hawthorn hedges and studded with spreading trees. Frequently there were avenues of trees arching across the roads. With occasional little streams in the valleys, the grazing cattle and sheep, the many trees and the hedgerow-bounded fields, so much smaller than the extensive paddocks of Australia, the effect was of a pocket-handkerchief countryside, with many little picture postcard vistas.

Abbotsford School, a small boarding school for girls with a large number of day pupils, was established in a rambling, old building straight onto the street. It was situated just at the traffic lights on an extremely busy corner where four roads converged. A continual stream of commercial and private vehicles panted and revved as they waited for the lights to change. Great lorries hurtled past on their way to the industrial cities of Coventry and Birmingham. As they turned the corner, their powerful engines would drown out our voices and teaching would have to cease until they had passed. When the Fair was in session in the Abbey Fields we received the full blast of loud hurdy-gurdy music through our classroom windows. In the evenings, we could hear clearly the ribald songs of drunks staggering past, after they were forced to leave the pubs at ten o'clock.

The girls at Abbotsford had not been accepted into Grammar Schools after their eleven-plus examinations. Their parents had chosen to pay for private education for them, even in a school that was not fully accredited, in the hopes that eventually they would be able to catch up with the academic stream. Since Coventry was only five miles away, many of the girls had spent long periods in and out of bomb shelters during the Blitz. They were to some extent what was called "Coventry-shocked" and found it difficult to concentrate for very long. I am sure the racket from the street outside did not help. They were, however, friendly and anxious to please. They spoke with distinctively Midland accents. I soon found I had to adapt my Australian accent in some ways (replacing the Australian front "a," as in "bat," with an English back "a," as in "father," in words like *castle* and *France*, for instance) so as to make myself more clearly understood.

The Headmistress, Mrs Hall, had lived for many years in India where her husband had been in business. Now, in her widowhood, she was making her living by running a private school. She had no very clear ideas about education (certainly no aspirations to innovate) and was not well organized. Often timetables for classes and examinations did not work, because they had been slapped together in a hurry, and sudden changes were likely to be imposed on us without warning. She was test-obsessed and grade-conscious, so that in English classes, for instance, not only was there an excessive number of tests, but regular numerical grades had to be provided for every segment of the subject: grammar, composition, spelling, dictation, reading, or whatever. All these marks and reports had to be entered in several different places and then added upwards and downwards and crosswards and backwards. She had a very disconcerting way of announcing "the end" of a correction period, without due warning, so that the teachers had to spend many long, late nights meeting these abrupt deadlines. Her answer to behavior problems was the traditional one of order marks and detentions, which were handed out liberally. She also had a very short fuse. At times she would flare up in a most disconcerting way about something quite unanticipated, while at other times she was very affable.

I had been allotted classes in English, Geography and Scripture at various primary and middle school levels, but most of my time was spent with a small class of eight- and nine-year-olds, as a replacement for Miss Cay during her enforced leave. These little ones had been completely traumatized by their teacher, who was a stereotypical "old maid," tall and thin with a very pale face and gray hair drawn back in a severe bun. When she returned to school after her mother's death, she told me bluntly: "I do not like children." She looked like a wasted ghost, and walked rather like one in a gliding fashion, with her head averted and eyes cast down, so that she would not have to greet anyone. As a result of her attitude to her pupils, I found some of them were writing their letters back to front and hardly dared put pen to paper. With a little tender loving care, they were recovering from their fright and beginning to enjoy learning when Miss Cay reappeared, at which point they promptly slid back downhill. "I knew you were pampering these children with your B's," she told me. "See! they're worth no more than D's."

Any description of Miss Cay can only seem exaggerated and fanciful to anyone who did not know her. She had a very narrow mind and lived a very narrow life. She had fixed notions and found it impossible to absorb new ideas or develop new habits. She never read a book, but listened to children's serials on radio and a few mild plays — never anything provocative, controversial or philosophical. She had deep-rooted likes and dislikes, even for foods she had never tasted. She always sat very straight at table, never asking for anything, but waiting in pained silence for it to be offered to her. "Would you like some milk?" we would say, or "Toast?" or "Marmalade?" This became a daily game of "Guess what?" She always had her bath at the same time on the same evening of the week and cut her toenails after school on Friday afternoons. Woe betide anyone who dared to take a bath at the particular time on the particular day that she considered her "hour." She followed immutable routines and had unchanging habits, always sitting in the chair in the staff room in which she had always sat and at the place at table to which she was accustomed. On arrival at Abbotsford, I had found a chair always empty in the staff room, so I took to sitting in it during our breaks and I put my books on a vacant section of shelf conveniently nearby. When Miss Cay returned she didn't say anything to me, but she took to leaving her classroom just on the bell and rushing down to the staff room as fast as she could to plonk her books on *her* little bit of shelf, before I could get there, and to sit in *her* chair, which I had so unknowingly appropriated. I soon got the unspoken message.

Miss Cay had an inordinate love of sweets, which were still rationed, so every Saturday without fail she set off for Leamington Spa to do her shopping and assiduously queue up for her ration of sweets, even when she did not want or need them. As far as I could see, she had no social life. She knew no one in the area; she rarely went out, not even to see a film at the local cinema. She disliked the theater, even Shakespeare, whose plays we all enjoyed seeing at nearby Stratford-on-Avon. Officially a Roman Catholic, she had long ceased to believe in the doctrines of her church or attend masses. She taught a few Scripture classes but said, quite openly, that she did not believe what she was teaching. When roused to protest in general conversation, she would make her point, then proceed to repeat it over and over firmly for ten minutes. She could be completely exasperating, sticking to the same complaint with unbroken persistence. Disliking children as she did, she naturally preferred the goody-goody ones; any child with a little life or energy was in her eyes "very naughty." She also disliked men and considered marriage "idiotic," although we couldn't help feeling that she had probably never known any men well, apart from her father and brother, and had probably spent her entire life in girls' schools. Now that her mother had died, she had dropped all family contacts and did not intend to let any relatives know where she was. She was, of course, most methodical and meticulous with her work, but every time I saw her a phrase from the Book of Proverbs kept springing to my mind: "Dead while she liveth! Dead while she liveth!" One Sunday morning, the cook's holiday, I went into the kitchen to boil my breakfast egg and, seeing Miss Cay standing at the stove watching a little pot, I asked her to slip in an extra egg for me. "Of course not!" she responded, "I'm cooking mine." Rather annoyed by this lack of cooperation, I seized an egg and without thinking dropped it in the water. The consternation on Miss Cay's face had to be seen to be believed. What was she to do? How could she possibly tell which of these white eggs bobbing around in the water had been there for exactly three minutes?

The Dickensian atmosphere at Abbotsford School was augmented by the presence of Mrs Otis, whose task was to teach the senior Geography, History, and Scripture classes. Of an indeterminate age, probably in her sixties but seeming much older, Mrs Otis was obviously teaching purely as a source of income, not from any particular interest in or dedication to education. It appeared she had a daughter, a Cambridge graduate, whom she never saw or heard from. She seemed to know nobody locally and rarely went out, except occasionally to the cinema, although I did go bike riding with her on one or two occasions. Personally I have always found that a person with rich and varied interests outside of the classroom is a much more interesting teacher. Mrs Otis was the type of person you would hate to tangle with. She could be very rude to people, as she often was to our French visiting assistant, Jacqueline Persillet. She would take Jacqueline to task very severely over quite unimportant things she was perceived to have forgotten or performed incorrectly. Mrs Otis was undoubtedly taking out her insecurities and personal unhappiness on the most vulnerable in her entourage, and this included her students. She spoke very slowly and, when she got started, worked very slowly, so that she always seemed to be working. She smoked like a chimney and was always in need of more cigarettes. While the rest of us were completing our corrections and preparations between tea and supper, she would be out searching the town for cigarettes, which were still in short supply. She would then begin her work well after supper and continue with it, while listening avidly to radio serials and smoking tenaciously, till the early hours of the morning. As a result she was always late for breakfast. She could often be seen carrying her breakfast on a tray to the staff room just as the girls were filing into their morning assembly at 9.30 a.m. She would make quite a fuss about other people being lax or behind with their work, yet her marks and reports were never ready on time.

Like Miss Cay, Mrs Otis obviously did not like children. She could be a real ogress and bite their heads off at the least provocation. When in a good mood she could be very affable with her colleagues, but many of the children were quite terrified of her. She told us that she had once been governess to Somerset Maugham's children; if so, they were certainly to be pitied. One feature of Abbotsford School was an old-fashioned system of order marks for misbehavior or for work not learned or completed, and once a month there was an after-school detention session to punish those who had accumulated five order marks. We took turns to supervise these sessions. I can still see Mrs Otis when it was her turn. As soon as the poor little detainees came up to her to be tested on what they had been learning, they would take one look at her hard, unblinking eyes and immediately forget everything. Back they would be sent to learn their work all over again. At these sessions seven-year-olds would sometimes be kept in for an hour and a half and still not "know their work." This kind of performance seemed to give Mrs Otis great satisfaction.

Another feature of Abbotsford "education" was a weekly Monday morning assembly, when the pupils who had received less than C's for their past week's work would be brought out in front of the whole school to be humiliated for their laxness and incompetence. The same unfortunate girls, who found academic work difficult, would have to suffer through this agonizing ceremony week after week, no matter how hard they had tried. I remember vividly one of the girls in my English class, who worked very hard but lacked scholastic ability. Every Monday morning she would be positively panting with anxiety and tension as she was dragged up for public disgrace; you could see her practically holding her breath until she could get back and hide herself among the other girls.

Not all the teachers at Abbotsford School were sadistic, fortunately. Some members of the resident staff were very reasonable and pleasant. Miss Steele, a Scottish teacher, was very congenial and even-tempered and we often played tennis together. There were several local non-resident teachers, married with families in town, who brought in a natural, happy breath of air from the outside world. I soon became friendly with the Games Mistress, Mrs Lawrence, and often visited her at home and shared outside activities with her. Our association began soon after my arrival, when the hockey team lost a match 22 goals to nil. As an experienced player and teacher of field hockey, I expressed my astonishment that any hockey game could end with such a score. In well-played field hockey one to zero, or at most two to zero, would be a normal score. When Mrs Lawrence was away with the flu, the hockey team approached me to help them with a little coaching. One sight of their normal play horrified me, as I watched them rushing around the field purposelessly, waving hockey sticks in the air in a most haphazard fashion. I promptly marched them into a classroom for a chalk-and-talk lecture on the basics of the game. I explained to them the roles team members in different positions fill and their interrelationships (who keeps an eye on whom, who passes the ball to whom), the general strategy of a match, and the tactics for applying this strategy. Then we practiced playing hockey, not racing round a field hitting balls. In their next match the Abbotsford team lost eleven to zero, which showed considerable, if still inadequate improvement. At this point Mrs Lawrence came back and confessed to me that she had never played hockey in her life. She had been coaching the team from the rules book, which, of course, says nothing about strategy and tactics. After that we became good friends and I continued to help her with various sports.

After the return of Miss Cay, my regular classes being no longer available, I spent most of my time in the spring sunshine, as an assistant physical education instructor, teaching swimming, diving, and tennis. I knew enough about the latter to be able to demonstrate good serving and to correct faults in general play. I had never, however, had the opportunity to learn to play tennis seriously, apart from a few lessons on serving and a certain amount of practice with friends who did not mind playing with a less than expert player. However, because of the reputation of Australia at the time as a world champion tennis country, it was obvious to the girls that I too must be a whiz at tennis. To my consternation the school champion insisted on playing a match against me, which I knew I would lose disastrously. What about my reputation among the girls? Fortunately, Miss Steele agreed to play doubles with me against the two best girls in the tennis team. As luck would have it we managed to hold our own reasonably well, so that my reputation was not utterly destroyed in the area of sports.

My closest friend at Abbotsford School was Jacqueline and we have remained friends for over fifty years. When I came to Kenilworth she had only recently arrived and knew few people. A graduate of a tertiary-level Commerce School in Paris, she was in England to perfect her English for career purposes. She became later Personal Secretary to a leading French Government official, a *hsut fonctionnaire*. It so happened that I was given a bedroom that connected with Jacqueline's, so that I had to pass through her room whenever I went in or out of my own, and we shared a penny-in-the-slot electric fire. We frequently chatted with each other and soon found we had much in common. We went for long walks together in the mild evening twilight and enjoyed exploring the countryside. Kenilworth, with its leafy lanes, lent itself particularly well to this pleasant rambling, and there was always the satisfying conclusion of a walk across the Abbey Fields on the way back. I talked English with Jacqueline while she was in England, since that was why she was there, on the understanding that later, when I went to France, she would talk to me in French. By this time I was listening regularly to broadcasts from France on a rented radio, in order to improve my listening comprehension, and I was pleased to find that I understood Jacqueline perfectly well when she spoke to me in French and she understood me equally well. This was encouraging.

Jacqueline was a somewhat shy, reserved young woman, a little bit of a dreamer, or perhaps she seemed so because she still had to think carefully about what she heard and said in English. She was given tasks like taking Mrs Hall's morning cup of tea to her in bed and looking after the youngest boarder, a little girl of about six, who cried a great deal from homesickness. Jacqueline got her up in the mornings, put her to bed at night, and kept an eye on her during the day. She would have been a very unhappy little girl without Jacqueline's kindness and concern. Jacqueline was also expected to prepare tea for the resident teachers after afternoon classes. Most English people at the time were convinced that no French person really knew how to make a good cup of tea, and our teachers were no exception. The staff room drama on the occasion when Mrs Otis decided, quite unjustly, that Jacqueline had made the tea without waiting for the water to boil had to be experienced to be believed. Mrs Otis came down on her like a ton of bricks as she had been accustomed to do with her students and the incident was never forgotten, as an example of Jacqueline's (and, by extension, generic French people's) general incompetence.

Because the school had no grounds to speak of, the only way to give the girls some exercise at lunch break was to take them walking in crocodile (that is, two by two). Most of the teachers treated this as a routine chore. They would develop a set pattern. On Mondays Miss A would take the girls down Streets L, M, and N and back by O and P. On Tuesdays Teacher B would take them down Street Q, turn into Street R, walk along Street S, and return by Street T. For the girls this was mindless, mechanical, and utterly boring. I decided on my duty days to take them on "mystery hikes." All this meant was that they never knew till they reached the corner whether they would turn right or left. "Are we turning right or left, Miss?" they would ask eagerly, "Right or left?" I would keep them in suspense until we reached the corner, saying only at the last minute:"Tuuurn left!" Then excitement would build till we came to the next corner: "Are we going left or right, Miss? Left or right?" It was a simple enough illusion, but it really worked to break the monotony.

On my duty days the girls loved to talk me into going to the Echo Field behind Kenilworth Castle; this was about twenty minutes' walk away. Once there, they would disperse and call across persistently at the castle walls, delighting in the bouncing echoes. Naturally they had no intention of coming back to me after a few minutes in order to cover the twenty-minute return to school on time. Finally, I would succeed in reassembling the crocodile, and they would have to walk very fast, arriving at the school breathless. Here they would line up in two lines, while I walked down the middle to a chorus of: "Thank you, Miss! Thank you, Miss! Thank you, Miss!" Then there would be a rush of hot and bothered girls into their classrooms. They also adored the Abbey Fields — very close to the school actually, but equally tempting, with low moldering walls and little wildflowers. Wandering about and making daisy chains, they would become quite deaf to importunate cries of "Come back, girls, quickly! Come back!" Again there would be an excited and breathless rush into class on our return.

In her unpredictable way, Mrs Hall called me one night to her office and, most unexpectedly, blew me up for not teaching the girls anything. I was, of course, astonished and wondered what had provoked this sudden outburst. Indignant and determined to vindicate myself, I immediately went down to my classroom to get a sample of exercise books from my pupils' desks, to show her what we had been doing. Somewhat surprised at what she saw, and a little mollified, she mumbled: "The girls like you, so I had to presume that you weren't teaching them anything."

Discovering England and the English

Life wasn't all Abbotsford School, fortunately. I was determined to see as much of England as I possibly could and I used every opportunity. I also enjoyed a rich social life, thanks to colleagues, friends of friends, and my Rivers relatives, as well as the networks of contacts made for me by the student organizations with which I still kept in touch.

Kenilworth was ideally situated for my explorations. Three towns — the big industrial city of Coventry, world capital of the bicycle industry at the time; Leamington Spa with its eighteenth century elegance; and Warwick with its many artistic treasures and its continuing aura of powerful families who had affected history — were each about five miles from Kenilworth. Close at hand to the west was the Forest of Arden and Shakespeare's Stratford-on-Avon and to the east the well-known Rugby School, whose famous Headmaster, Thomas Arnold, had so much influenced the development of English education in the early nineteenth century. Here the game of rugby had evolved in 1823, when one student ran with the ball in a game of football, thus setting off a worldwide obsession. Like so many young people of my generation, I had grown up avidly reading *Tom Brown's Schooldays*, which was based on life at Rugby. For me the very name of the school exerted an irresistible attraction. These and so many other interesting places were within the one county of Warwickshire, which was also noted for some of the loveliest villages in England.

I began my explorations with a bike ride to the Forest of Arden in search of Shakespeare's Rosamund, Celia, Bottom, and company and relaxed on a log in the deep shade as my imagination took over. I could easily see Titania lying asleep between the roots of the big, gnarled, moss-grown oaks. In nearby Henley-on-Arden, I cooled off with the "best ice-cream in England." (They had a diploma to prove it.) Of course, I loved Shakespeare's Stratford, with its modern Memorial Theatre beside the Avon River, which, with its small craft and swans, flowed gently and smoothly between banks of green sward. Here, during that spring term, I was privileged to see *A Midsummer Night's Dream, Othello,* and *Cymbeline*, with Diana Wynyard and Godfrey Terle in the leading roles.

During the Second World War, Coventry had become a household word because of the incessant bombing and the dreadful devastation it endured. Yet, already by 1949, the people of Coventry had lined whole streets, where great shopping centers had previously stood, with temporary buildings and cleared away rubble to create new public gardens. The blasted center of Coventry was ablaze with tulips and daffodils, sent by the Dutch to brighten the desolation. In the violent bombing attacks on heavy industry, it was inevitable that the beautiful should suffer with the useful. As I saw it in 1949, all that was left of Coventry Cathedral was a mere shell with the lovely Gothic spire still rising above the roofless ruins. The area within its walls had been cleared and lawns planted in the nave and aisles. Most impressive of all was the ruined sanctuary, truly eloquent in its simplicity. On the altar, constructed of remnants of the previous structure, stood two charred beams forming a cross. Before them was a shining cross of handmade fourteenth-century nails, with behind it the words: FATHER FORGIVE. One lonely figure remained standing near the sanctuary — a sorrowful figure of the Welcoming Christ. On the walls around, where the Chapels of the Guilds had previously been situated, the Coventry Hallowing Prayers had been affixed, each dealing with a different aspect of life: industry, the arts, commerce, healing, government, education, and recreation. As you turned from the ruins to the fine spire that was still standing, you read the words of the prophet Haggai: "The latter glory of this house shall be greater than the former, saith the Lord of Hosts, and in this place will I give peace." The vaulted crypt, where the people who were sheltering on the night the cathedral burned to the ground saw only a little trickle of molten lead coming under the door to warn them of their plight, had been converted into a Chapel of Unity for all denominations. In 1949 services of Holy Communion were being held in a very simple Chapel of the Resurrection at the rear of the Cathedral ruins, with three bright crosses of nails shining out against the wall over a Holy Table of fresh new stone. As a stranger who had not shared in those dreadful nights, I knew I could not really enter into their sorrow, yet, looking out over this courageous cathedral, I loved it and felt I belonged. When the new, very modern Coventry Cathedral was built, the ruins of the old one were retained as a continuing memorial, and this I was privileged to see at a later date.

Royal Leamington Spa, just four and a half miles by bus from Kenilworth, soon became very familiar to me as a shopping center. This was where Miss Cay spent so much of her time queuing up to redeem her sweets coupons. In the eighteenth and nineteenth centuries Leamington had grown from a village of some three hundred people to a grand and fashionable resort. Thanks to its saline spring, with a mineral content considered very efficacious for the treatment of such problems as rheumatism and arthritis, it was much patronized by George IV, Queen Victoria, and the "beautiful people" of their day. Leamington was well planned with wide sweeps of road, graceful curving crescents and beautiful mansions set back in gardens; the streets were tree-lined and there were lovely public gardens, so that the leisured classes had plenty of space in which to promenade. Even when I saw it, in the mid-twentieth century, many people still went to Leamington to "take the waters." In the Royal Pump Room special treatments and massages were given, under medical advice, as an accompaniment to the swallowing of pints and pints of spa water. The latter, I found, like so many things that are good for you, to be rather nasty — very salty and peculiar. As with other spa resorts, there were also regular entertainments. In its time Royal Leamington Spa had been as famous and as popular as the Bath of Jane Austen's day.

Forming a triangle with Kenilworth and Leamington was Warwick on the Avon. A gracious old town, Warwick was consciously proud of its past and tenaciously determined to keep its character. The narrow, winding streets, with their centuries-old houses took me into a world far removed from the bustle and tear of modern life. Here it did not seem strange when the road led to an unchanged heritage from the fourteenth century — Lord Leycester's Hospital. This hospice, or almshouse, was a magnificent half-timbered building, the black and white timbering arranged most decoratively, with bright-colored coats of arms and texts adorning the outer walls and with the typical bulging balconies of the period. My visit there was a prelude to an afternoon spent at Warwick Castle, redolent of history lessons on Warwick the Kingmaker. The magnificent, fourteenth-century stone fortress still stood intact, because the Earl of Warwick, during the revolutionary period of the overthrow of the monarchy, had had the foresight to support Cromwell. The high, tree-crested stone walls, the courtyards and defensive towers, the grand interior of the baronial mansion, the art galleries and museums were all breathtaking, as were the huge, lofty rooms with their rich carpets, French tapestries, crystal chandeliers, beautiful painted and sculpted ceilings, handsome period furniture, and oak paneling. Corridors were lined with ancient weaponry and armor, and everywhere there were magnificent portraits in oils. It was here that I was able to see for the first time original portraits by Rubens, Van Dyck, Holbein, Gainsborough, and Reynolds and came to realize how infinitely superior they were to the reproductions on which I had been bred. Outside I wandered around the formal Italian garden with its interesting topiary and wandering peacocks. It was a place to which to return again and again.

Soon I was experiencing the miracle of spring. As an Australian I was accustomed, of course, to the evergreen sameness of the eucalyptus forests. I had heard and read about this sudden outburst of new life, but I had experienced it only partially in the leafing out of the few European trees planted as showpieces in Melbourne's parks and gardens. "Spring" bulbs flowered in Melbourne, along with the camellias, during the winter months. The total experience of dead-appearing trees bursting into green leaf, just as the bare earth was blossoming, was new and wonderful to me. I described it to my family in the following terms (May 22nd, 1949):

"I do wish you could be here now that Spring is in the air. The trees are leafing out again, in a variety of fresh, new greens, and the birds are singing everywhere. In the gardens great use is made of wallflowers for mass coloring — great beds of golds and browns — with tulips and forget-me-nots. I would love to take you for a drive along the Kenilworth-Coventry road at the moment. I can imagine our cream Ford going along the road with me at the wheel, and your exclamations of delight as you looked out the windows. First, you would see green fields, mostly divided into small sections by hawthorn hedges. Along the roadside are splashes of white may. In the gardens are drooping the pendulous, golden, wisteria-like blooms of the laburnum, and mauve and white lilacs are in bloom. The rhododendrons are beginning to peep through and there are rich red peonies. The road itself is covered in by trees; broad-spreading English trees extend for a couple of chains on either side of the road — oaks, elms, limes, poplars, silver birches and the white and pink of the flowering horse-chestnuts, which make such a wonderful display. Interspersed is the vivid reddish brown of the copper beeches. Suddenly under the trees a misty carpet of blue appears — the bluebells of the English woods, single blue hyacinths growing wild in profusion, with a delicious mauvy-blue haze seeming to hover over

365

them. As you look ahead you see, continuing for several miles, an archway of trees forming a cool passageway of verdure.

"I heard my first nightingale the other evening! It was a thrill. Just at dusk he began singing on a tree outside Jacqueline's window and continued for about an hour until it was quite dark. Imagine a thrush and blackbird combined but with a richer, fuller tone and a dash of canary thrown in. A rather small bird he is too. You can imagine how pleased I was when he came again last night and conducted a long conversation with a friend in a nearby tree. I hope he comes every night. There's something very serene and soothing in his song. Then we have our cuckoos. One begins early in the morning a fair way away, but his "cuc-koo" can be heard so clearly, made a little mysterious by the distance. He may "cuc-koo" sixty times in succession. In England, there are little traditional sayings for everything. For the cuckoo they say: 'In May sings all day; in June changes tune; in July must fly'." One day in July, as I was taking shelter from torrential rain under a rather thin tree, a lady sheltering near me remarked: "It's St Swithun's Day, isn't it?" This allusion meant nothing to me until my English friends explained the traditional belief that if it rains on St Swithun's Day it will rain a little every day for forty days afterwards. This didn't happen the year I was in England, but I'm sure this hasn't prevented English people from making similar remarks on St Swithun's day every year since, just as Americans look to the ground hog to predict the end of winter.

As the spring season progressed, I became enraptured by the multiplicity of English wildflowers, the names of many of which were familiar to me through my reading of English poetry and novels. From the early snowdrops and bluebells, the bright yellow buttercups, wild forget-me-nots and violets, the little pink briar roses, the red poppies among the white daisies, the pink and red campions, the rich reddish-purple willow herb, the marsh marigolds, the small white flowers of shepherd's purse, and the little celandine, so beloved of Wordsworth, I collected them all. I pressed them with care, searching out the names of those I did not know, until I had a book with over one hundred and thirty carefully preserved and labeled specimens. I came across my first molehill, which illuminated for me the English expression I so commonly used. Then there were the squirrels — not the pretty red ones I had seen in children's books, but the gray ones which had driven them away. The first one I saw was flat on the tree trunk, looking rather like a platypus with its thick tail. It disappeared swiftly as it heard me approach, just as the same gray squirrels do, when I am walking along the Charles River in Watertown. Gray squirrels collecting hickory nuts in the garden are now a regular feature of my life in Massachusetts.

My English friends soon introduced me to English rituals. Mrs Upton invited me to join her Oxford-Cambridge Boat Race house party at the end of March. Since our hostess was working full-time, we all joined forces on arrival in a frantic cleaning bee, polishing all the family heirlooms. Soon the house filled up, even to the attic, with high-spirited guests, all of whom set off next morning for Mortlake to see the end of the famous race. As Mrs Upton's son, John, who was in Australia at the time, was an Oxonian, we all wore red ribbons, proclaiming us to be the JUP (John Upton Fraternity) and waved the dark blue colors of Oxford.

The boat race, I found, was not just a university affair, but London's day out. Factory girls arrived with their hair tied up with huge bows of light or dark blue crepe paper, according to their Cambridge or Oxford preference. Sailors sat along the walls of houses and little boys crowded the banks of the river. Peddlers hawked colored ribbons of all types and sizes and ice cream vendors did a roaring trade. On the bridge was one of many BBC television cameras, since this was the first race ever to be televised. It was a delightful spring day and the race was a perfect excuse for basking in the sunshine. We saw the crews set out for Putney for the start of the race, accompanied by river patrol boats, dinghies, dredges, huge ferry boats — anything that would float— all packed with people who would follow the race along its course, as we did, by portable radio.

At last the sounds of the barracking of the supporters traveled along the river toward us and the two boats came into sight around a bend for the final dash to the post. The long, slender boats were painted white and the oars too were white, with the appropriate university color on the blade. With the crews in white, rowing strongly and rhythmically, it was a pretty sight. They shot past us, absolutely level, in an exciting finish (the closest since 1871, we later heard); then, in the last few yards, Cambridge shot forward in an easy dash to win by a quarter of a length. My first Oxford-Cambridge Boat

Race was over and my newly adopted university had let me down. Notable after the race was the sober English crowd that plodded back to the station, so unlike our Victorian Henley-on-the-Yarra boat race crowds. There was no demonstrating, no signs of exaltation, but a perfectly matter-of-fact preparing for the next stage of the day. This was particularly noticeable as we crossed the overhead bridge and looked down on the crowds, six or seven deep, who silently lined the railway platform.

Thirty guests then descended on Mrs Upton for a "General Post" lunch (for which we moved to different rooms of her rather small house for the various courses). To facilitate movement and ensure mixing, Mrs Upton had temporarily taken the interior doors off their hinges. No wonder her friends kept insisting that she was not typically English. This exhilarating lunch was a happy prelude to rowing on the Thames near Richmond in the afternoon, enjoying the weeping willows in their early spring green, the white swans gliding by and the cheeky ducks cavorting and converging in an idyllic English setting.

In April, I participated in my first international conference of some four hundred people, from seventeen different countries, at the IVCF Conference Centre at Swanwich in Derbyshire. Nowadays, with rapid transport so freely available, one can easily meet delegates from 80 or 90 countries at big international conferences of several thousand people, but for me in 1949 this was a most exhilarating experience. In the relatively homogeneous Australia of the time I was not in the habit of meeting Africans, Indians, and Middle Easterners. In general conversation I learned a great deal about problems and achievements in areas of the world that had been blurry entities to me in the past, and I heard many details of the discrimination many of these future leaders of their people were enduring in the England of that day.

Apart from the excellent speakers and the Bible Study leaders, what impressed me most was the smooth organization by the English executive. Everything went like clockwork, organized from beneath the surface, so that the participants hardly realized that anything was being organized at all. Committee meetings and conferences among overseas delegates were going on at all times in a most unostentatious way. The genius behind this impeccable organization was the General Secretary, Dr Johnson, with whom I had stayed in Cheam. Although he was working solidly all through the conference, probably fifty per cent of the participants did not know of his existence or even notice his presence. While a group photograph was being taken, I said to Nora Nixon, the Graduates' Secretary, who later became a dear friend, "People like you and Dr Johnson should be in the front row." "You'd never get Dr Johnson there," she said laughing. "Who's Dr Johnson?" asked a couple of girls standing near us. I learned a great deal at this early stage from people like Dr Johnson about tying up all administrative details and keeping a close eye on turns of events, so that the organizational structure is unobservable to those profiting from it. In my later experience I soon found that good organizers go unappreciated, because, due to their foresight, nothing appears to go wrong and problems that do arise are deftly and unobtrusively handled behind the scenes. It is poor organizers people are sorry for; they seem so harried and overloaded.

Beyond all our conferencing, we were able to see something of the Peak district of Derbyshire, with its famous stone outcrops or Tors. We drove up hillsides that provided wide vistas out across the beautiful dales with their close patchwork of cultivation. Here there was no dearth of stone. In the villages stone walls separated the houses, and the fields that looked tiny to an Australian were also separated by little walls of stone, so different from the hedges of Warwickshire.

For my Easter vacation I decided to attend a short conference for teachers of Scripture at St Hilda's College in Oxford, since I found that, wherever I went, I was being asked to teach this subject, which was new to the curriculum. The visit gave me an opportunity to see at close quarters this great old university and experience something of its life, even if in a very abbreviated form. When I arrived at St Hilda's, spring was still very much in the air and the trees were blossoming in the college gardens. The first thing to do, obviously, was to join a punting party on the Cherwell. Passing under attractive stone and trellis bridges, we admired beautiful views of the towers of Magdalen and Merton Colleges. (I had no idea then that Merton Hall in Melbourne would later play such a pivotal role in the evolution of my career.) With amateurs wielding the punt, we sometimes turned in circles, while other punts passed us derisively, and on one occasion the pole got stuck in a tree. Later we lost it in the water. Eventually we got the hang of the art and drifted lazily and evenly down the stream. In the intervals between study sessions I was able to visit some of the colleges and the New Bodleian Library. I was very excited that after the Conference I would be setting out, with a friend from Sandwich, on a carefully planned cycle tour of Devon and Cornwall, for which I had already made all the overnight bookings in youth hostels. It was to be a once-in-a-lifetime opportunity to visit these picturesque areas. Unfortunately, the end of the conference was marred for me by a splitting headache. Despite this painful problem I packed and prepared for an early departure the next morning.

Minor disaster.

I did not sleep well that night because of a drawing sensation behind my ears. You silly ass, I thought, you've overdone it again. I sometimes felt like this when I was thoroughly overtired. I wondered how I would get through the next few days, with the hectic dash I had planned from Exeter along the south coast and up through Dartmouth. I got up early to be on time for a morning train to London, but I felt dreadfully ill. I was very worried and my glands were enlarged. Could it be swollen glands, I wondered, or mumps? It was a most inconvenient time to need help, since the conference participants and organizers were all packing up and moving out, with hardly time to say goodbye, let alone listen to my complaints. Yet it was obviously inadvisable for me to set out for Devon until I had found out what was wrong and also in case the room had to be fumigated. The most distressing part for me was that by this time my biking friend from Sandwich would be on her way from Dover to London, a trip of nearly a hundred miles, to meet me at Waterloo Station. How could I let her know what had happened? Fortunately a friend from the conference offered to go to London earlier and meet her at the gate to explain.

I felt alternately awful and quite all right as I waited for the doctor, who took one look at me, felt the lumps and said "MUMPS! Three weeks!" What on earth was I to do next? The only thought that came to mind was to get somehow to Ealing to Betty Rivers, Osmond's wife, who had said I was to look on their home as my own. I would take it from there. The Conference organizers (among them my dear friend, Nora Nixon) decided to pay my taxi fare all the way to London. Soon I was on my way miserably and painfully to Ealing, wondering what on earth Betty and Os would think of me, landing in on them like this. Slowly I munched the sandwiches with which I had been provided and pitied myself deeply.

I stumbled into Os's place, astonishing him by saying: "I shouldn't have come," and bursting into tears. The family were all sympathy and packed me off to bed immediately. By this time I looked dreadful and felt worse. Afterwards I found out that my Rivers cousins were actually in some consternation, since Osmond had never had mumps and he was older than I. One consolation was the news that my Sandwich friend had been successfully contacted at Waterloo station and had decided not to continue on her own. Some of my time on my first day in bed was spent on the mundane task of writing cancellations to all the youth hostels at which I had made advance bookings.

This period of enforced rest gave me a great opportunity to get to know my Rivers family better. Betty was most kind, not only looking after me but also keeping me company, so that I learned a great deal more about their story. Betty read me a narrative she had written about her Welsh family, as well as some of her daughter Jean's delightful poems. I heard much about Osmond's (Wiz's) work as chief coachwork designer at Hooper and Co, a company that concentrated on custom-built, personalized cars (Daimlers and Rolls Royces) for the wealthy in England and abroad, particularly aristocrats, ambassadors, and members of royal families. At that time Wiz was concentrating on rebuilding the vehicle the king would use that year for the Trooping of the Color, since he could no longer ride a horse. Wiz had designed cars for all the members of the British Royal family (from Queen Mary, through George VI, Princess Elizabeth, and the Duke of Windsor), for Princess Margrethe of Denmark, as well as for the King of Arabia, as a gift from Winston Churchill. He was a well-known figure at European Motor Shows, where he knew all the other designers. With gossip about the family, letter and diary writing, reading a book or two, and visits from other Rivers relatives, the time passed quickly. At the end of the three weeks, I was able to return to Abbotsford School on the normal date for the new term.

Thanks again to my Rivers relatives, I had another interesting experience of the "olde England" I had read about and pictured in my imagination. A Mrs Gumbley, a friend of the Rivers family, invited me to Haseley Manor, where her husband was the gamekeeper. She herself had been seamstress to the daughter of the manor, who had disgraced herself by marrying a ne'erdowell and had not inherited the property. The new owner had bought it as a wedding present for his daughter, who had married a wealthy man with several residences of his own, so it was now quite deserted, with its thirty-five bedrooms and many other rooms. All this had quite a romantic sound. The Gumbleys lived in a very pleasant cottage on the manor grounds, where Mr Gumbley's responsibility was to keep an eye on the game on the property. Beyond that he had plenty of time to enjoy his really magnificent surroundings, with its acres and acres of meadows, great avenues of lovely trees, extensive lawns, tennis courts, and great groves of rhododendrons and beech trees. From the side lawn, there was a clear view across to Kenilworth Castle. In front of the house was a great round lawn where, in the days of its magnificence, all the game would be placed at the return from the hunt. The whole setting recalled irresistibly a Wodehouse or Galsworthy novel.

Mr Gumbley was an out-of-doors type of man, sturdy and tanned, with a faraway look in his deep brown eyes, a gentle manner, and a really rich Warwickshire accent, which initially I found difficult to understand. I first saw him surrounded by his dogs. From his lifetime in the woods he had come to understand the calls of the birds, even the faintest ones, and could tell from the cries they were making whether they were in danger and what was threatening them. He had some interesting stories to tell about "new-rich" employers who were ignorant of things "gentlemen" were bred to know, as he put it. He told me about one American who came as a guest to Warwick Castle. For the shooting party he had bought the best of everything. Then he made the faux pas of suggesting that it would be much easier for the hunters if the gamekeepers drove the game across the front lawn for the hunters to shoot, rather than expecting them to go out into the woods and fields to find them. Mr Gumbley later worked for one "new-rich" employer who wanted to set himself up as a real gentleman but found it hard to overcome his ingrained "business instincts." On one occasion, Mr Gumbley had to remind him that, on employing him, he had promised him a suit of clothes as well as his salary. To which the businessman had replied astutely: "Do you have that in writing?" Mr Gumbley had responded in his quiet way: "I have your word as a gentleman, sir." Not surprisingly he got his suit of clothes without further demur. I felt a book could have been written about Mr Gumbley's life, which would surely have been more interesting than mine.

Wales — Another Country

For the Whitsuntide break in May — a much anticipated public holiday period in England, I decided to expand my horizons by visiting an old friend from my St Thomas's days in Moonee Ponds, Jean Bloomfield, who was visiting relatives near Caernavon in North Wales. I had a soft spot for the Welsh, having sung rousing Welsh songs since childhood. "Men of Harlech" was always one of our favorites, as well as the many beautiful and harmonizable Welsh hymn tunes like "Lead me, O Thou great Jehovah." I was looking forward to seeing them on their home ground. The journey to North Wales on a packed train, in which I had to stand for two hours, took me through an extensive and dreary area of factories and railway freight centers, through Birmingham and Stafford, with its potteries, to the major junction of Crewe. This area of intense industrial activity was an important part of the England of that period. After passing through the park-like county of Cheshire, I found myself crossing the Sands of Dee. How many times had I or my pupils recited the famous lines of Charles Kingsley, "O Mary, go and call the cattle home, And call the cattle home…across the sands of Dee." These grasslands beside the Dee estuary, with cattle and sheep grazing, had, I found, a great deal of surface water and many tidal pools, so it was easy to picture Mary going too far for the cattle and becoming disoriented and delayed by the fog :

> "The western tide crept up along the sand,
> And o'er and o'er the sand,
> And round and round the sand,
> As far as eye could see,
> The rolling mist came down and hid the land:
> And never home came she."

I soon knew I was in Wales when an airman on the train began to sing in Welsh to the "Guide me, O Thou great Jehovah" tune, Cum Rhondda. Later, I found myself in a bus where everyone spoke another language. The Welsh, being happily bilingual, would speak to each other in Welsh, then turn and in the same breath speak to us in English, with that very musical lilt they carry over from their own tongue. The hillsides were a picture with tall white daisies, foxgloves, and yellow lady's slipper. Soon we were skirting the walls of the famous Conway Castle, one of Edward 1st's line of border fortresses built to keep the Welsh under control. With mountains on one side and rocky cliffs down to the sea on the other, we looked toward the Isle of Anglesey. Soon we were at Caernavon, whose castle, since the thirteenth century, has been the site for the proclamation of the monarch's heir as Prince of Wales.

The village of Waenfawr, where Jean was staying, was typically Welsh with its low stone cottages enclosed by stone walls. Everywhere there was stone, from the rocky outcrops on the hillsides, with the occasional white goat clambering over them, to the high stone walls, ivy- and moss-covered, that surrounded the fields. In some areas where there were slate quarries the boundary walls would be built of slate upon slate. The fields were colorful, with a patterning of different shades, depending on whether they were under grass, planted with crops, or lying fallow. Wildflowers luxuriated in the fields, where purple heather, golden gorse, and scotch thistles were beginning to take over. In the gardens, rhododendrons were flourishing, along with spectacular lupins, of which I had never seen the equal. The inhabitants of Waenfawr possessed a great community spirit, possibly because of their isolation, with everyone seeming to know everyone else, so that a drive in a bus became a friendly race between the bus driver and the local car drivers. The village hospitality was as warm as their spirit, and we appreciated their ready invitations to visit them in their homes.

As we climbed higher on the mountain slopes on our walks, with the sea on one side and Mount Snowden, the highest mountain in Britain, looming above us, I began to understand the passionate devotion of the Welsh to homeland and freedom. Among the Welsh I met in 1949 there was a very nationalistic spirit. They did not like to see English people, "foreigners" as they called them, settling in their towns and villages. They greatly cherished their independence and were whole-hearted advocates of the continued use of the Welsh language and the maintenance of their distinctive culture. Very lively people, they loved singing and their Methodist chapels rang with tuneful harmonizations and rousing sermons in Welsh from eloquent itinerant preachers. No wonder Jean preferred the Methodist church, even with the service in Welsh, to the Anglican one. At one Anglican service we attended, there were ten or twelve people in the congregation waiting for the service to begin. The minister arrived late and clumped into the sanctuary in his overcoat to arrange it for the service. After about ten minutes of this fussing around, he began the liturgy. This was hardly conducive to a worshipful spirit and provided a real contrast to the fervency of the traditional Methodist services of the Welsh. One realized the sterility of a system where a parish appointee could stay for life, no matter how he performed.

Of course we visited Caernavon Castle. With its hexagonal towers it had rather the appearance of a cardboard castle in a child's play set, of which it might well have been the inspiration. Primarily a defensive fortress, it had strong battlements, with slit openings for archers and guardrooms within the walls themselves. Along the walls were quite wide paths so that troops could move quickly from one spot to another to combat an assault from any direction. From the castle walls there was a magnificent view over the Irish Sea and the Menai Straits to the Isle of Anglesey, as well as an unobstructed view over all the surrounding hillsides. It was a wonderful strategic position for spotting the advance of hostile bands. Like Conway and Warwick Castles, Caernavon was one of the structures familiar to me from the *Beautiful Britain* book over which Linda and I, as children, had pored for hours on wet Sundays in Ascot Vale.

Decisions, decisions, decisions

The weekend over, I had to hasten to London for an interview with the headmistress of a multi-national Swiss finishing school on the shores of Lake Geneva, with whom I had been corresponding about a position for the coming year. Earlier she had written asking whether I had a strong Australian accent, since this would be considered unacceptable to the parents of her students. Consequently I had been busy practicing "How now, brown cow?" and "The rain in Spain falls mainly on the plain," although the possibility of either subject arising in the conversation was most unlikely. I was at the time awaiting a reply from the French Government on the question of an appointment as an assistant for English teaching in a French school, so the timing put me in something of a dilemma. This was not the only time when turns in my career have depended on a choice between simultaneous opportunities. To be sure of my options I had had to contact Abbotsford School by phone to check on the day's mail before going to London. Sure enough a letter had arrived just that morning, saying that I would be proposed as an "assistante de langue anglaise" at the Lycée de Jeunes Filles (Girls' High School) at Douai, where I would be able to pursue my studies at the nearby University of Lille. Now came the real problems. What kind of place was Douai? What would the school be like? Should I or should I not turn down the Douai school for the Swiss school if I were offered the job? All this had to be decided in a hurry, so I consulted the ever-helpful and knowledgeable Dr Johnson.

Douai, it seemed, was in a mining area well to the north of France. It promised to be very wet and foggy for a large part of the year (a considerable contrast to Geneva in attractiveness), but, as I kept assuring myself, they spoke French there and that was what I was looking for. Moreover my schedule would be so arranged that I would be able to continue my studies. The major question that was unanswered in the letter from Douai was whether this would be a paid position or "au pair" (fed and lodged in exchange for services), which I certainly could not afford. There seemed to be so many things to find out before the three o'clock interview, that I began to feel a little bit churned up inside.

This had not been one of my better days. To begin with, I had left my camera at the Rivers's home in Ealing and I had had to go through endless corridors in the Underground to return for it; in my confusion, I had overridden my stop on the bus and been obliged to walk back quite a distance. Furthermore, I had left my umbrella in the train and had had to make do with a dilapidated old one that Betty had lent me, which didn't go at all well with my smart, white interview outfit. Inevitably, this being London, it began to rain.

Back I went to consult the ever-patient Dr Johnson about the money situation. He suggested I ask a friend of his at the Institut de France what the usual arrangement would be. Great idea! I immediately rushed to the Institut where I found, to my dismay, that they were still on holidays. (Why shouldn't they be, since I was still free myself?). Nobody else I knew seemed able to supply this vital piece of information, so I made my way, only half-informed, to the interview with the representatives of the Swiss school. The interview went very well; they were clearly interested in me and the position seemed most tempting. Despite the opportunities I would have in Switzerland to learn to ski, I felt that full-time work in a French-speaking school, even in the fog and damp of Douai, would be better for my language development. At the Geneva School the pupils were mostly speakers of English, and they alternated weeks of teaching in English and French. In all fairness, I told the ladies interviewing me about the offer I had received from the lyceé at Douai and promised to let them know as soon as I could what I proposed to do.

I had still not found out about the financial arrangements for the French appointment, so I next tried the French Embassy. Yes, it seemed I would be paid a salary, but no one had any idea how much! They suggested I ask the British Ministry of Education, which regularly sent about five hundred assistants a year to France, so I raced off to Curzon Street. Here I had difficulty convincing the appropriate official that he could have any idea how much English-language assistants in French schools were paid. Finally, after checking his files, he told me the salary English appointees received — twelve pounds a month at the time. This was at least enough to keep body and soul together, even if not in princely style. With this indispensable piece of information in place, I decided on Douai. I could now calm down and concentrate on plans for spending at least one year in France. My long-time ambition, it seemed, was about to be realized.

When it became clear that I would be going to teach at Douai during the following school year, Jacqueline's father wrote from Paris to say that I could stay in their apartment whenever I liked and treat it as a home away from home. This kindly welcome on his part greatly relieved my anxieties about launching out on my own into unknown territory.

The summer months now loomed before me, and for these I needed somewhere to live and some means to support myself. Fortunately I had been invited to help with a couple of summer camps for girls, run by my Christian Fellowship contacts, both in highly desirable locations for a visitor to Britain, namely the Lake District and Somerset. That left me with a three-week period for which I needed to obtain some paid occupation. I advertised in a newspaper for a position for a capable woman, willing to undertake any kind of suitable work. My English friends were horrified. "You are not a capable woman," they told me to my surprise. "You are an educated lady!" It seemed that my ad would be very misleading. The only reply I received, from a restaurant in Penzance in Cornwall, was scrawled on a torn piece of paper. It offered me a position washing dishes. I knew I could do that, so I wrote back inquiring further. Apparently my return letter had revealed that I was not a "capable woman" after all, but an educated lady, so I heard nothing further. I kept up my search, advertising this time in a church newspaper. Several answers came in offering me various kinds of household responsibilities for which, having been so spoiled by a mother who did everything for me, I did not feel I had sufficient experience. One, from a farmhouse in Devonshire, was for someone to help the lady of the house for a short period, while she adjusted to caring for a new baby. That seemed about my level. I could happily do as I was told. The position was in an area outside of Plymouth in beautiful Devon countryside, so I accepted with alacrity.

My summer now in place, I could enjoy the rest of my stay in Warwickshire. Jacqueline and I had always wanted to see the Cotswolds, so off we went. On the way we passed through the fruit-growing area of the Vale of Evesham, where we watched strawberry pickers at work. Here I saw my first gypsy encampment with its assembled caravans and caught a glimpse of my first wild pheasant. The solid, gray stone cottages of the Cotswolds with their slate roofs and their neatly constructed stone fences, which alternated flat, horizontal stones level by level and then crowned them with an edging of vertical stones, gave the region a distinctive coloring and individuality of appearance.

By now I had made the acquaintance of a young Australian engineer, who was working on jet airplane engines in Coventry and I was flying around the area on the pillion of his new, shiny, black and silver Triumph motorcycle — a new way of viewing the countryside. Alan lovingly kept his machine clear of any speck of dust, just as my brother Reg had cared for his motorcycle in my childhood.

Chester for the weekend

Some Victorian friends, fellow passengers from the *Orion,* invited me to visit Chester with them for a weekend. Although it was only three hours away by train, my English acquaintances were astonished. "You can't go all the way to Chester just for a weekend," they exclaimed. As an Australian, I couldn't see why not. Soon I was on my way to that beautiful old city, still surrounded by intact defensive walls. Here there were lots of black and white half-timbered houses, profusely decorated with elaborate woodcarvings, and the unusual Rows, with their small shops on two levels. I admired the medieval cathedral with its very individualistic carvings in stone, through which the masons had expressed their artistic creativity. Most noteworthy of these was the "Imp of Chester" peering down on the congregation from the clerestory, with its chin on its hands. In the Bishop's Garden grew a Glastonbury Thorn bush — an offshoot of the one that grew from Joseph of Arimathea's staff when, according to legend, he brought the boy Jesus to ancient Britain.

To crown the weekend, we took a side trip to Wales at Rhyl. What would my English friends think of that, I wondered. At this popular seaside resort, the tide was so far out that we could scarcely see the water. As I looked around I realized that what many English people looked for at a seaside resort was not the opportunity to swim in the sea but roller coasters, donkey rides for the children, and "Choc Ices." I began to understand those English paintings, always an enigma to me in Australia, of English trippers taking the sea air fully clothed, as they strolled along the wide sands or reclined on deck chairs in front of brightly colored bathing boxes. I had soon discovered that around the English shores the water was usually far too cold for enjoyable dipping and the sea breezes were brisk. At nearby Abergele, we visited a stereotypical, picture-postcard castle, which looked very romantic against the hillside with its turrets and crenelated battlements, but which, strangely enough, was not at all strategically placed. From the hill slopes above the castle's strong, seemingly impregnable walls, enemy forces could easily have fired their arrows or lobbed cannonballs directly onto the defenders! On entering the structure I soon found the answer to the enigma. It was a fake castle, built by a nineteenth-century industrialist enamored of

379

medieval glory. The towers of the castle's defenses were completely empty — within them there were no worn spiral staircases that had felt the tread of knights in armor and defensive archers. Instead, the castle was one big amusement park, a kind of forerunner of Disneyland and the numerous theme parks of the late twentieth century.

Being so near to Liverpool, we seized the opportunity to visit the thirteen miles of extremely busy docks of that great port — loading docks, graving docks, dry docks, and warehouses, with great heaps of timber and coal waiting to be loaded. I had seen so many ships in Melbourne with the provenance of Liverpool painted on their hulls that it was a thrill to be here and watch the great cranes and the stevedores loading and unloading goods for and from all parts of the world. This was before the container era that opened the way for the completely automated loading and unloading I was later to see in Singapore. The Mersey Tunnel, to take traffic under the river, had been one of the first of its kind and was considered a great achievement of engineering at the time. With its dim interior, intersecting roads and system of traffic lights to divert the vehicles in different directions, it was quite a novelty to me. We were able to visit the very modern Liverpool Cathedral. This was the first Anglican cathedral to be built in Britain since the Reformation and the only one to have been followed through its long years of construction by one architect, Sir Giles Gilbert Scott, who had been associated with the project since 1904. Miraculously the Cathedral was still standing unscathed amid the widespread destruction of the surrounding area. Lit by very modern stained-glass windows, its airy, spacious interior, rising to an awe-inspiring height, was crowned by a beautifully vaulted ceiling. The nave was constructed in such a way that the view of the sanctuary was unimpeded by columns or other supports, thus allowing three thousand people at the one time a clear view of the services. The red sandstone of its interior construction, lightened by horizontal lines of white mortar, gave it a most distinctive appearance. I was pleased to see that, at least in 1949, it was refreshingly uncluttered by over-elaborate memorial statuary and verbose plaques. There was about it a modern simplicity, with great structural and sculptural beauty.

Winding down

Back at Kenilworth to finish off the school year, I was soon engulfed by paper — examination papers, reports, all kinds of letters and clutter to be sorted prior to my departure. This seems, on looking back, to have prefigured a lifelong pattern. Sadly, I said goodbye to my sturdy Eanswythe; it seemed impractical to take her with me to France. My colleagues gave me an appropriate farewell gift of half-a-dozen high quality tennis balls and a strong eye shade. After all, I was a tennis champion! Then I was on my way to Ambleside in the Lake District, where I was to help with an IVF summer camp for about eighty girls, in a hostel on the shores of Lake Windermere in the midst of the mountains. I could hardly have been invited to a more exciting spot.

The summer of 1949: Lakes, lakes, and lakes

I soon found that our days at the camp at Ambleside were mainly taken up with trying to see how many lakes we could reach. (Our studies were in the evenings.) Apart from some organized trips, the craze was for hitchhiking in small groups, and some of the girls had already made it to Scotland — a hundred miles to Gretna Green and back. We traveled in lorries, furniture vans, paper trucks, and in kind people's cars — whatever came our way.

My first foray was to climb the Langdale Pikes, which overlook Ambleside. A group of twelve of us caught a bus to Dungeon Ghyll at the foot of the mountains, where it promptly began to rain heavily. It continued to rain on and off during the morning, but such things did not discourage intrepid climbers like us. We began climbing immediately and were soon clutching at bracken on a steep slope. As we went higher, we climbed over a stone fence and were soon picking our way up over boulders. The climb was strenuous but worthwhile, as the view opened out before us. We could see right down the valley, with its patchwork of fields, marked out with hedgerows, to Lake Windermere and, shining in the further distance, a thin silver strip that was Coniston Water. Ahead and on either side were bare, rocky hillsides and layer after layer of mountains, from the greeny brown of the nearer slopes through darker browns and grays to the faint bluish outlines on the horizon. One lovely view was of Blea Tarn, a charming little circle of water dropped right in the midst of the

381

hills, with a few picturesque firs at the water's edge. On the slopes were dirty-looking, thin-legged mountain sheep, many black, with rust-red identification marks across their rumps and their long tails swinging behind them as they ran ahead of us. At last we reached the very top of the Langdale Pikes. The climb had been quite an achievement, but a very blowy, cold success it was indeed, as we looked down the slopes to the glint of water from a little pond called Stickle Tarn. As a low cloud swept in from a nearby height, we were forced to leave the magnificent view of rocky ranges and begin our trek downwards. Going down required as much care as coming up, as we picked our way between boulders and slithered on moss. One girl, who had previously cut her knee on a sharp rock, now left her shoes in a bog. Fortunately we were able to rescue them for her. After a quick picnic lunch on a windy slope, we continued down to Borrowdale. In this awe-inspiring setting I naturally thought of Wordsworth and Coleridge. On these heights, you could understand Wordsworth's consciousness of the omnipresence of God and Coleridge's obsession with the supernatural. The heights could be very eerie and mysterious in the misty air. Unfortunately for my own meditations, I lost a heel on the last part of the descent. I staggered on, however, and was soon initiated into the art of "hitching." We were fortunate enough to be picked up by a lorry with an empty tray. We all piled on and whizzed up Borrowdale and on to Keswick, alongside Derwent Water, where misty mountain slopes swept down to beautiful pine-clad shores.

We were a disreputable-looking group when we finally reached Keswick, about sixteen miles from our hostel. By this time, having tasted the delights of hitch-hiking and found we had some talent for it, we had no intention of walking or paying our fare on the bus, so we started along the road to Ambleside, breaking up gradually into twos and threes. It seemed a shame to leave the beauty of Derwent Water behind us, and I kept taking backward peeps as we went up over the hill. Soon the last couple in our group whizzed past us in a car, waving cheekily! Before another ten minutes were out, however, my companion and I had managed to stop a lorry and were invited into the large cabin. The view was not what it might have been from a tourist coach, but the driver considerately took us right to our door in Ambleside.

On a borrowed bicycle, I went with a friend down the road to Grasmere, on the way passing by Rydal Water, an attractive small lake with lots of reeds and rushes. At this slower pace, more close to nature, I found the countryside had a "storybook" quality, with its low, age-old stone fences, picturesque stone bridges, and gray stone cottages. Grasmere turned out to be a larger lake than those we had already visited, its beauty enhanced by the setting of hills reflected in its dark depths. Wandering down a back lane in Grasmere, home for so many years to Wordsworth, Coleridge, and De Quincey, we came upon Dove Cottage, where Wordsworth had lived with his sister, Dorothy, and to which he had brought Mary as his bride. It was an attractive little, whitewashed cottage with a small stonewalled garden and an impressive view over the peaceful lake.

As we continued to pedal up steep hills, I kept my eyes open for new wildflowers for my collection. Since my companion cyclist was a botanist, this was a great opportunity to get their names straight. By now, the rain was pelting down, so we explored a local village church for a few moments of respite. Since the showers showed no signs of abating, we put on our macks and pedaled off into the driving rain. I must say that my flowers seemed to be enjoying this customary local weather more than I was. Soon we were soaked through, and from then on we found the ride quite exhilarating and refreshing. We passed Esthwaite Water, which I saw through one eye and the driving rain as a very misty stretch of water. Passing the hilltop where Beatrice Potter, the creator of Mopsy, Flopsy, Cottontail, and Peter Rabbit, had lived, we made a dash down a very steep slope to the shores of Lake Windermere. Here we cycled blithely along under the shelter (or drip!) of the trees to the Windermere ferry, a flat raft drawn by chains. This brought us back to our hostel, absolutely soaked and dripping, after a most memorable day.

Not all days were wet or momentous. Sometimes, on a wander from the hostel, we would come across little tarns that were pure beauty in themselves. One tiny tarn, no bigger than a dam in a paddock, was covered with white waterlilies in bloom and surrounded by flowering rushes, and in the boggy patches in the hills there were many kinds of mosses, with sundews and butterwort, both of which have sticky, insectivorous flowers. This was a contrast to Ullswater, the second largest lake, seven miles long, where Wordsworth saw his "host of golden daffodils…fluttering and dancing in the breeze." At times, we came across quite deserted lakes, with rugged, unclothed hillsides sweeping down to the water, or with windswept firs, braving the elements on narrow promontories jutting out into the water. Occasionally steep, narrow waterfalls and magnificent views across deep valleys and mountain ranges would raise our spirits to a new high.

As the days went by, we learned much about the art, or science, of hitchhiking, and we were even picked up at times without our signaling, so well accepted was the practice. On one occasion as we were making our way to Kendal, on the Scottish border, we saw an emptyish-looking car approaching, so we signaled. Sure enough it pulled up and a sturdy Westmoreland farmer, with humorous, twinkly-brown eyes, called out: "I can't really give you a lift, can I? There's no seat in the back." Wedged between him and the door we saw a huge milk can. Glancing at the sacking in the back, we chorused happily: "Oh! that's all right! We can sit on the floor." After all, we couldn't let a really good hitch escape. Since the driver was a Kendal farmer, he took us all the way to our destination. He became so interested in talking to us about Australia and Devonshire, the home area of one of our group, that he sat and talked to us for a good ten minutes after our arrival. He even offered to take us back that afternoon, if we could be on a particular stretch of road between four and four-thirty. I soon discovered that the people who picked us up enjoyed what we had to offer in the way of companionable conversation and new information. We were giving something in return for their kindness. The driver of one car that took us all the way back to Ambleside asked us: "What *is* on here, anyway? I brought seven girls home from Keswick the other day in the back of my van!" "Oh!" I said cheerily, "We were wondering when we'd be getting to the second round." One curious vehicle in which we rode was a snub-nosed contraption, with a semi-detached trailer tray, for moving heavy loads around a factory floor. It was being driven across country to its new home and could only move at a maximum of twenty miles an hour. In this vehicle we were forced to go up and down the Westmoreland and Cumberland hills at very reduced speeds, sometimes no more than five miles an hour. We felt superior to our comrades, whom we saw trudging wearily along the highway, until we saw some of them sailing serenely past us in a very comfortable limousine. At other times we traveled on loads of road metal and in delivery vans, jammed with sacks and loaves of bread. Such was the luck of the hitchhiking game!

One experience that particularly etched itself in my memory was a lonely, late afternoon climb through the Honister Pass. As we continued uphill, we were closely hemmed in by the steep mountain slopes. To increase the mysterious feeling, we saw a great white cross, erected high on the mountain slope, perhaps to mark some disaster that had befallen climbers at that spot. The slopes were greener here, almost a yellowy-green in the dull light, but a vivid one. The small track wound on through the bottom of the valley beside a small, very rocky stream, and the hillsides rose sheer on either side. There was something most peculiar about it — lonely and unprotected. To increase the sense of unreality, the high slopes against the sky created a flat effect, as though they were merely some massive painted scenery erected in a lifelike drama. You felt the urge to push them over to see the actors dressing on the other side. In this lonely spot we felt quite alone and out of the stream of daily life — an effect that did not seem to be completely dispelled by the occasional passing car or fellow hiker. The road gradually became steeper and the slopes more and more rugged, with great avalanches of scree poised perilously on their sides. At last we came to the toughest pinch of all — a hillside that must have been at a gradient of one in three. Cars came down very slowly and cyclists walked. By now, it was beginning to rain heavily, and soon we were so wet through that it didn't seem to matter any more. My last view of the Pass was dark and forbidding in the growing dusk and the driving rain, with the little road winding bravely down.

So many lakes, tarns, and waters that I visited deserve full description, but soon our camp was disbanding, and I had to pack my things to move on to the next camp to which I was committed. This was at the other end of England in Somerset.

We be Zomerzet we be

After a very lengthy bus trip which took me on a tour of the Border Counties, I arrived in Bristol just as the sun was setting over the Severn. I did not know at that time that Bristol was my *heimat,*

385

from which my Burston ancestors had traveled to Australia a century before. However, in Bristol I learned one lesson that has served me well in my later travels. The coach had run late and arrived in Bristol at 9.25 p.m. I had to disembark, get my luggage and make it to Temple Meads Station (wherever that might be) for a 9.38 train, the last one that night that went anywhere near my destination, Burnham-on-Sea. I had been foolish enough to load myself with three large pieces of luggage and I had only two hands. Here I was, with no time to spare, no idea where to go, and too much luggage, while the taxi rank was around the corner in the next street. In this quandary, I asked a passing stranger how I could get a cab. Seeing my plight, he said he would send a taxi around to me. There and then I resolved never to travel with more luggage than I could carry myself in an emergency — a rule to which I have adhered ever since.

I was in the taxi by about 9.32, and the taxi driver gaped somewhat when I told him I had to be at Temple Meads station for a 9.38 train. Fortunately the station was close at hand. With the help of the driver who carried some of the luggage, I was able to buy my train ticket, run through interminable passages, fling myself on the train and pay the taxi driver out of the window, just as the train jolted into action. I could now rest a moment and gather myself together, especially as I was in a very slow train, stopping at all stations.

After a few minutes, I became conscious of an old couple sharing the compartment with me, who were apparently talking a language of which I could not comprehend a word. "Dear, dear!" I thought, "How will I be in France, when I can't even understand the English." Then I remembered that in one day I had passed from the north to the south of the country. My ear, in just a short period, had become attuned to the rich, full tones of the north. After a few minutes of listening, however, I began to follow. Later, when I got into conversation with my travel companions, the old man told me: "We be Zomerzet, we be!" This was certainly new territory.

Burnham-on-Sea, where the camp was being held, was a rather ordinary seaside resort. In England, where there are so many shingle beaches, people rave about "the sands," and here there were certainly very extensive sands. Otherwise there were two drawbacks. First, swimming was dangerous (shall I say impossible) except for one hour before and one hour after high tide and secondly, the sand was so dirty that we came out of the sea looking very murky. (Was this early pollution?) As high tide might be in the middle of the night or at four o'clock in the morning, there were often days when we could not swim at all. One week this was the case for three days in succession. Consequently the camp program had to be fitted around the high tides, which might be at ten or eleven in the morning one day or at one in the afternoon the next. There being nothing of great interest to walk to near Burnham, outside activities were reduced to team games, treasure hunts, sandcastle competitions, and occasionally longer excursions out of town.

One extraordinary day has always remained with me. We went for a coach excursion across Somerset into Devon. The day was beautifully sunny, yet quite cool. Somerset, I found, was very compact and neat, with rich pasture lands, subdivided into tiny fields by darker hedgerows, with grazing cattle and sheep, and occasional golden hayfields, dotted with drying stooks. The countryside was gently undulating and very attractive. I could quite understand the devotion of the natives to their "Zomerzet." It was interesting to realize that this area was part of the Wessex of Thomas Hardy's novels. There were occasional small villages, which were most striking, with delightful thatched cottages that gave them a distinctively rural air. At times we caught glimpses of the sea, with views over magnificent coves, surrounded by red-hued cliffs. The sea was pearly-blue to the horizon, with just that faint mistiness that creates a fairylike impression. All of this, with the green countryside and spreading English trees, was most colorful and dreamlike. We stopped at a suitable beach with wide sands strewn with brightly-colored deck chairs and some sleepy-looking donkeys waiting for riders. Here we ate the inevitable ices before taking a dip in the Bristol Channel, where we could look across to the low outline of Wales. This was the first time I had swum at an English beach since my arrival. Back in the coach, we were soon on Exmoor, with its great bare hillsides. Here the sight was more than magnificent. The hills were radiant with purple heather, interspersed with clumps of low-growing yellow gorse. The coloring was so rich that one could have feasted on it. It was here that we passed the Doone Valley of Blackmoor's book, with great rugged hillsides enclosing valley farmlands. As we looked down the valley, we could see the little church where Lorna Doone is supposed to have married John Ridd. Some of the gradients on the road were very steep and on the hillsides we saw some of the horses that are bred on these moors.

Soon we passed from Somerset into Devon, as the milestone informed us. At last I was in "Devon, glorious Devon," and I don't think any other adjective adequately describes it — magnificent coloring, lovely, calm blue seas, beautiful rich farmlands with happy, prosperous-looking sheep and cattle grazing peacefully. My mind ran to Devonshire teas, Devonshire cream, and Devonshire cider, which I had time to taste only in imagination.

As we came down a steep hill in low gear, we caught glimpses of leafy gullies with faint indications of rapids in their depths and found ourselves in Lynmouth, a sweet little town on a cove, overlooked by a rugged cliff. On the shore was a quaint lighthouse, inhabited mainly by pigeons, but which surely had had an indispensable function in its time. In village fashion the streets of Lynmouth were very narrow, with quite a few thatched cottages to give it an air of being rooted in time. Unfortunately, since the tide was out, all we could see of the cove itself was yards and yards of rocks extending out from the shore.

Turning inland, we followed the course of the Lyn for some way, driving alongside a very deep wooded gully with water flowing over rocky rapids at the bottom and flashes of ferns that made it look quite like the fern gullies of my native Victoria. Soon we were back on the moors, having tea among the heather. On closer inspection, I found there were two kinds of heather — a finer, lighter type that was pinky-mauve (this was the commoner one), and a prettier reddish-purple bell heather, a little like Victoria's state flower, the native heath. Both had a sweetish perfume and a papery feel. For a while we roamed the hillsides, while I, as an inveterate photographer, took snaps. It was certainly a day to savor in memory.

Having seen the enormous modern cathedral at Liverpool, I was determined to see the smallest cathedral in England at Wells. Fortunately it was nearby, so I set out with an English friend for a day's exploration. First we visited the limestone caves at Wookey Hole, a name which seemed to me almost like baby talk. Here were huge underground caverns through which flowed the River Axe, with even more caves, it seemed, under water. These great chambers, which had been inhabited by people from 250 BC till 450 AD, ranged in height from fourteen to seventy-five feet, some with enormous unsupported roof-spans of more than 130 feet. Some had to be entered by boat, often through entrances very little above water level. In places the river shone a clear green with the light reflected off the mossy rocks. I was, of course, thrilled to see my first stalactites and stalagmites, whose origins I had studied in my geology classes. In one large cavern many of these age-old formations were broken. Apparently, an 18th century poet who was building himself a grotto had had many of them shot off with muskets. One large sphinx-like stone was said to be the petrified image of a witch, who had lived there with her goats and terrorized the villagers. To escape exorcism she had fled further in to the largest cave, where the river flows through, and she was never seen again. Excavations have turned up the bones of a woman and some goats, with various household articles and a crystal bowl, so perhaps there is some basis for the story. Even without such stories, it was very eerie, yet magnificent, there under the hills by the subterranean river.

Now it was time to see Wells Cathedral, which we approached by way of the moat around the Bishop's palace. This stretch of water is a relic of the original springs that fed the sacred well of ancient Wessex for which Wells was named. On the moat float the famous white swans, who over generations have learned from their mothers that, when hungry, they have only to pull a rope which rings a bell for food to be thrown out to them from a window — a very successful precursor of Pavlovian conditioning. Soon after the establishment of this system, apparently, the cheeky little ducks learned the trick too, so the rope had to be shortened. As a reminder of the constant wars of earlier periods, there is a drawbridge to protect the Bishop's palace. After all, this is the country of King Arthur and his knights and of King Alfred who, after his defeat by the Danes in 878, sought refuge on nearby Athelney Island. It was there that he burned the famous cakes, while deep in thought planning his comeback victory. The ancient cathedral of Wells, begun in the twelfth century and continued in the thirteenth, incorporates an interesting evolution from Norman to Early English Gothic architecture. The interior is supported by solid Norman pillars (or piers), the strength of each of which is disguised by twenty-four narrow columns surrounding it. The lovely

389

light-cream color of the stone makes the interior look as fresh as if it had just been built a year or two ago. The combination of light color and light-pillared columns creates an airy effect, which is beautiful in its simplicity. The quiet, secluded cloisters, where the monks used to walk as they read their missals, lead to another little architectural gem — the Chapter House, where the fan tracery of the ceiling springs out all round from a central column as if from a tree. Along the walls are low stone ledges where the original members of the Chapter used to sit. If beauty elicits adoration, then these medieval monks certainly had everything to help them in their meditations. The famous cathedral clock, dating from the fourteenth century when the monasteries were the source of all knowledge, is quite an attraction in itself, with little men on horseback who ride round in opposite directions as the hour strikes. A twenty-four hour clock, it shows, not only the time, but also the minutes, days of the month, and phases of the moon. Another little man, Jack Blandifer, strikes the quarter hours on some bells with his heels, striking another bell with a hammer for the hours. Outside the Cathedral, two knights strike the bells of a connected clock with battleaxes. With one thing and another, we had to keep very alert to see all that was happening and were as excited as any of the children in the watching crowd

We still had a little time to visit nearby Glastonbury, on the Isle of Avalon, the heartland of King Arthur and his knights, where the mysterious sword, Excalibur, was brandished by a hand from a lake. This is the land of the elusive and beckoning Holy Grail, the cup from which Christ drank at the Last Supper. Legend has it that the Grail was brought by St Joseph of Arimathaea to this area, to which he fled with Mary, the Mother of Jesus, and some other followers of Jesus after the Crucifixion. The holy vessel, although now lost, will, it is believed, be eventually returned to Glastonbury. According to ancient legends, St Joseph was a tin merchant, related to the Virgin Mary, who came frequently to these parts to buy the local metals and, on one occasion at least, brought the boy Jesus with him. Hence William Blake's famous lines: "O did those feet in ancient time, Walk upon England's mountains green, And did the countenance divine Shine forth upon our clouded hills." St Joseph is also supposed to have brought with him two cruets, one containing some of the sweat and the other some of the blood that fell from Christ on the cross.

At the church at Glastonbury, we were fortunate to come upon a very old clergyman, who, delighted with our interest in the place, called in an even older vicar. Together they gave us a very informative personal tour of the church, which they obviously loved. They explained the stories commemorated in the stained glass windows and showed us the empty stone sarcophagus, which is believed to have held the silver funeral casket of St Joseph of Arimathaea, since stolen. Various symbols carved into the stone sides of the sarcophagus identify it as St Joseph's. A window dedicated to the Abbots of Glastonbury incorporates a red rose that is supposed to have grown from the spot where some of the blood of Christ was spilled on the ground from the cruet. In the coat of arms of the Abbots there is also represented a piece of the Holy Thorn tree that grew from the staff St Joseph brought with him from the Holy Land. As Joseph, Mary, the mother of Jesus, and the rest of the party reached the top of nearby Wyrral Hill, overlooking Glastonbury, we are told, Joseph drove his thorn tree staff into the ground and said: "We are weary all." It does not seem to surprise the local population that St Joseph in his weariness expressed himself in English. From the planted staff grew a thorn tree of a kind not known in England, which blooms each year on Christmas Day, in honor of Jesus' birth. Pieces of the Holy Thorn were given away over the centuries to other churches and abbeys. Since the original tree was deliberately slashed down at the time of the dissolution of the monasteries, the present thorn tree at Glastonbury has been grown from a slip brought from descendant stock provided by another religious institution in England. Much of this legendary history was familiar to me from Anglican Sunday School in Australia, so I was surprised to find that it was quite new to my English companion. She was equally surprised at my knowledge of the history, geography and literature of England, not realizing that here I was at "home," these having been the standard diet of my Australian education in the 1920s and early 1930s.

The ruins of Glastonbury Abbey are supposed to be over the spot where the first Christian church in England was built in the first century by St Joseph of Arimathaea himself, hence our Sunday School interest in the place. This story is probably as likely as the other fact hinted at by our guides — that the Virgin Mary is also buried at Glastonbury. This glory Glastonbury must share with a number of other places in the world, including, I understand, Saudi Arabia. Here we also saw the alleged tombs of King Arthur and Queen Guinevere, and I remembered that in legend a boat with black sails had carried the great king off to the Isle of Avalon. Certainly Glastonbury was one of the richest spots for legends and stories that I had visited.

Cleaning the Manor House at Higher Fuge

It was now time to move on to my last summer job, where I was to help a young mother with cleaning, washing, and other household tasks in an eighteenth-century manor house (really a large-sized farmhouse) at Higher Fuge, near Plymouth in Devon. The young couple for whom I worked were Plymouth Brethren – a very strict Protestant group. Although I began work early each day and was kept busy till evening, they gave me a full day off per week. In addition, however, since they believed in Sabbath observance, not only for themselves but also for their manservant or their maidservant, according to the scriptural injunction, I was also free on Sundays. My employers, the Knights, were cheerful, friendly people and, as is usual on farms, food was fresh and plentiful. I worked alongside Mrs Knight in her daily tasks. As I had planned, I induced her into explaining exactly what she wanted me to do and how, so I was soon quite proficient as a household help. In fact, after the first week the Knights were so pleased with my work that they increased my salary by thirty percent. Mrs Knight very much enjoyed my company, since she was on her own most of the time with her six-months-old infant. We laughed and talked and walked together, especially in the late summer evenings.

The Knights' house had very large rooms, as I soon discovered when I set about cleaning them. Most of the downstairs rooms were stone-flagged fortunately, which made the task much easier. Since no water was laid on, this had to be brought in from a pump, bucketful by bucketful. Off the kitchen was the stone-floored, fly-wired dairy cum pantry, with stone benches on which the dishes of milk were left standing. In the old pre-mechanical fashion, the thick cream was allowed to rise to the surface, to be skimmed off and scalded to produce the thick Devonshire cream, which is always served with Devonshire Teas. All this reminded me of mother's shallow milk dish, which had served so many purposes in our house for some fifty or sixty years, and her scalded cream that was the joy of our home life. Here at Higher Fuge we had thick clotted cream all the time with our bread and jam, even for the seven o'clock morning snack I took with Mr Knight and his two helpers before they began the milking. We were not worried about cholesterol in those far-off days. For the milking Mr Knight used a small single-unit machine, keeping the milk cans cool in a nearby well. Since, in country style, the stove was kept hot all day, there was always plenty of boiling water for our many cups of tea.

The Knights' kitchen, unfortunately, was not fly-wired. Consequently, whenever there was anything sweet left out, we were visited by innumerable, very persistent wasps, which despite our efforts refused to leave anything they had selected, even at mealtimes. Wasps were a new type of pest for me, so I was inevitably stung before long. It seemed I had a spot of jam on my apron, on which a wasp had immediately settled. When I happened to pass my hand over my apron — and the wasp — the horrid little thing promptly retaliated, and so I learned painfully about wasps. With a little ingenuity I worked out a drowning trap for them. I would leave on the windowsill an empty jam bottle, not properly washed out, which I half filled with water. The wasps, drawn inexorably to the jam, then fell in the water and, to my delight, were "drown-ded." Since there was no electric lighting at the farm, we had to pump up old-style mantel lamps, or use candles. To go out to the shippon we carried hurricane lamps. At first, I thought the word "Shippon" was a corruption of "sheep pen," but I soon found out that it was the Devonshire expression for "cowshed' or the Scottish "byre." This shippon was very old and picturesquely inconvenient.

I had become accustomed to the English system of four meals a day, but now there were five. There was the pre-milking meal at seven, with breakfast at nine, at which we had a Bible reading and discussion, followed by prayers This brief devotion was always led by Mr Knight, since women in Plymouth Brethren circles did not participate vocally in services. (The very name "Brethren" seems curiously dated to a twenty-first-century feminist ear.) The midday meal was a hot dinner, which provided me with a little spare time, as we waited patiently for the men to answer our call to come in and eat.

Tea was served promptly at half-past four — usually bread and jam with lots of thick cream and cakes cooked with plenty of farm butter. At 8 or 8.30 p.m., we ate again, and this was followed by evening prayers. The work was not hard, but continuous. I found that I quite liked housework, now that I had actually done some. I seemed to have inherited my mother's love of having her hands in water, whether for washing up or the frequent washing of clothes, there being, of course, no washing machine.

The Knights treated me like a friend, not a servant, and also as a fellow Christian, which was an exceptional acceptance in view of the very strict views of the Brethren as to who was in and who was out. On Mr Knight's recommendation I was even allowed to break bread with his fellow Brethren at their Sunday meeting (although, as a female, I could not speak up, of course). The meeting was conducted along Quaker lines, in silence, with no structured service. We would sit in silent meditation; then a male member would rise and suggest a hymn, which we would sing, or another would lead us in prayer. One person might read a Scripture passage and expound on it, while another responded with a further passage or some exposition that continued the theme. They would then break bread from a simple loaf that was passed around and drink unfermented wine from a common cup, which they would carefully avoid offering to any younger people of whose commitment they were not sure.

My opportunities to enjoy my surroundings were mostly limited to the late evenings, but with the long, English summer twilights I still had time for walks after the evening meal, when Mrs Knight sometimes came with me. For these walks we wandered out past the orchard and a coppice beside a pond. We continued down a lane between really high hedges, nine or ten feet high that surrounded the fields in which Mr Knight had been thatching his hay ricks (that is, putting trim, straw hats on his haystacks).

I also had some experience helping with baby John, another first for me, changing nappies and giving bottles. How he loved food! When he saw his bottle he protested loudly until it was put in his mouth and grumbled and squawked in annoyance if you took the bottle out to force him to take a breath. When he had finished he expressed his disappointment lustily. This did not last long, however, and on the whole he was a perfect cherub and remarkably quiet. He was obviously going to grow up as a strong, silent farmer like his father.

In her considerate way, Mrs Knight found out the days when there were the best bus tours in the area and gave me my weekly days off accordingly. On the first of these trips, I set off, with a most substantial lunch packed in a basket, to visit Cornwall, which I had missed out on earlier because of my unhappy experience with the mumps. The coach traveled along the rugged, rocky coast of the English Channel, past many little pocket beaches. We then came to Dartmouth on the estuary of the River Dart. Dartmouth is spectacular, with its huge Royal Naval College on the cliff side and the two guardian castles of Kingswear and Dartmouth on either side of the harbor entrance. In the Middle Ages, these two fortresses had been linked by a great chain to prevent enemy vessels, particularly French ones, from entering the harbor. We then crossed the Devon countryside to take a ferry at Plymouth into the mysteriously different Celtic county of Cornwall. The Cornish proclaim themselves to be separated from the rest of England by the River Tamar and feel more affinity with the inhabitants of Little Britain (Brittany) than with their English neighbors. In fact Breton and Cornish fishermen had always understood each other quite well when they spoke their ancient Celtic tongue. Old Cornish lore held that "the Devil never ventured to cross the River Tamar from England into Cornwall for fear of being put into a Cornish pasty."[66] We were in a land of tiny coves and quaint fishing villages, which, though very picturesque in summer, looked to me as though they would be very cold and unprotected in winter. In Loue, with its pocket beach and rugged cliffs, the garden-less houses huddled together in such an unplanned way that the streets seemed to be unevenly shaped spaces between the dwellings, with washing strung on lines from house to house. Even the ancient Guild Hall was difficult to find in the mass of houses. Undoubtedly this was a place where smugglers could easily disappear if pursued by Revenue officers. I climbed the steep, stepped streets of picturesque Polperro, whose tiny harbor is entered by a mere cleft in the cliffs. Here I was so fascinated by the little streets among the houses that I nearly missed my coach. On the return trip we saw the dreadful wartime destruction of Plymouth that rivaled that of Coventry. Whole areas of the town had been literally laid flat, with the central shopping and business district completely wiped out. On the Hoe overlooking the Channel, we saw the famous bowling green where Sir Francis Drake was playing when he was told of the sighting of the Spanish Armada. Sure enough, under the shadow of the statue of Sir Francis, men were playing bowls in the sunshine.

On other trips I visited the great high plains of Dartmoor, where wild Dartmoor ponies were grazing among the blooming heather and gorse, and the numerous beehives were profiting from the summer pollen; I explored picturesque little villages like Widdecombe, famous for the song about the seven men who rode the one horse to its Fair, and here I tried out the village stocks to see how I would enjoy such public punishment; I picnicked at Dartmeet in a sylvan glade at the confluence of two rivers. At Paignton, I visited Mrs Knight's family, near the completely thatched village of Cockington and wandered around the harbor in the moonlight, looking across the water to the fashionable resort of Torquay. One highlight of my Devon summer was an afternoon blackberrying with Mrs Knight. Lovely big, luscious blackberries were everywhere in the high hedges. On the way home, we strolled through a delightful Devon wood with the leaves of several seasons thick underfoot. On our return, we had the fun of bottling the blackberries in the huge kitchen. It was a fitting conclusion to an idyllic summer.

Now the time had come for me to organize my departure for a new country — one seemingly unknown to me, yet so well known from nearly twenty years of reading and study.

11
THE DREAM REALIZED FRANCE AT LAST 1949-50

As the boat train drew into the St Lazare station in Paris, I nervously clutched a small photograph of Mr Persillet that Jacqueline had given me, hoping that I would recognize him on the crowded platform. Sure enough, there he was, at the early hour of six in the morning, smiling a welcome. Overnight in the boat train, I had shared a carriage with French students who were returning from a stay with families in England to improve their English. I had been very amused to hear them complaining how hard it had been to understand the English because they spoke so fast, and this had left me wondering how I would find the French in their own land. I was considerably relieved to find that I could understand Mr Persillet perfectly well and that he had no trouble understanding me. With Mr Persillet I had my first French breakfast of fresh croissants and *café au lait* at a sidewalk table outside a small cafe. Mr Persillet was soon entertaining me with stories of his wartime experiences as a draftsman in the Chausson Autocar company, which after the fall of France had quickly been taken over by the Germans to serve their military purposes. It had not been difficult, he found, to hoodwink the German supervisors. He would pin the work imposed on him for the German war effort over the work for his French company; then when the Germans were out of sight he would take out two drawing pins, allowing the German blueprint to roll back, so that he could continue with his regular work. Memories of the wartime occupation were still very vivid in the minds of the French.

Christine and La Rochelle

My next destination was the picturesque, historic city of La Rochelle, where I was to meet my beloved correspondent of fifteen years, Christiane. For this I had to cross Paris to continue my journey from the Austerlitz Station, to which Mr Persillet escorted me by bus. This being my first experience with people driving on the right side of the road, we seemed to be waiting for the bus on the wrong side. (This disorientation affected me for some time — I would look carefully to the right before stepping out in front of irate, tooting drivers on my left.) From the bus, I gazed wide-eyed at the spacious, tree-lined boulevards that contrasted so sharply with the narrow, crowded streets of the City of London, and I marveled at such imposing sights as the ornate Opera House and the huge Place de la Bastille, with its high column supporting the statue of the Republic.

The train journey to La Rochelle gave me an opportunity to absorb the distinctive features of the French countryside, at least in the west. Every skerrick of ground appeared to be cultivated, crops bordering directly on to pasturelands or the next crops without an inch wasted, so that there seemed to be little room for the fences or hedgerows so typical of rural England. The dividers I did see were barely a foot high, mere indicators of boundaries, and there were miles and miles of low-growing grape vines and hectares and hectares of sunflowers. Everything looked very trim, neat, and well cared for. Houses huddled together in small hamlets in the midst of surrounding fields, or in villages centered around the spire of the parish church (*"le clocher de mon pays"* of the folk songs). The roads were distinctively bordered with the ubiquitous tall, thin poplar, as much part of the French psyche as their bread and wine. *"Je suis triste comme un peuplier,"* one of my French friends would sometimes say ("I'm as melancholy as a poplar tree"). In the railway carriage a vigorous political discussion soon broke out between strangers. This sounded quite fierce, as both sides maintained their position, all talking at once in a rapid flow of words. How different this was from the polite or non-existent interchanges of the more phlegmatic and introduction-conscious English travelers! It was clear that the Anglo-Saxon taboo on talking about politics (and, I was later to discover, religion) did not apply.

Christiane met me with her two-year-old son, Hervé, a little pet whose baby hair had not yet been cut. To Hervé I rapidly became "Iga." We made our way up a narrow staircase to the one bedroom, third-floor apartment of a hardworking, two-job couple. Since there was no room in this small space even for Hervé, who stayed with his grandmother about two kilometers away, I was lodged in a nearby boarding house. I soon discovered that in postwar France everything was to be had for the buying for those who could pay the price, whereas with the high cost of living, low wages, and hours of work, which were much longer than workers in Australia were accustomed to, life was a constant struggle for young couples like Christiane and André. Women having to work to keep the family afloat is commonplace nowadays, but in 1949, with my Australian background, this was a relatively novel experience for me.

Since Christiane worked at the Prefecture from eight o'clock in the morning till six at night and André was on early and late shifts, Christiane left me on my first day to explore La Rochelle on my own. This was a pleasure since La Rochelle was a very beautiful and historic city — a picturesque, medieval fishing port, with its ancient ramparts nearly intact and its landscape dominated by a great, ornate clock tower. The narrow harbor entrance was protected by two thirteenth-century towers, one tall and turreted and the other a perfect round tower, these two having been linked in olden days by a chain that blocked entrance to the harbor by unwelcome ships. In the little enclosed port were many small fishing vessels with multicolored sails. I thoroughly enjoyed exploring the town with its narrow, cobbled streets, some with washing hanging from one side to the other. The whitewashed houses, airy and cool, were built straight onto the street, so that you could look in on the inhabitants through the open windows, just as they could watch the passing scene in the street outside. I strolled through the little shops, hidden deep behind great stone arches, and from the promenade around the shore I looked out to sea. La Rochelle, I found, rejoiced in a most extensive series of well-kept parks extending in a semicircle behind the town. Some had attractive beds of low-growing plants of varicolored foliage, planted so that the colors formed a pattern (this was my first experience of the French garden). Others were like miniature woods, through which might flow a slow-moving stream, covered with a green carpet of water plants and leaves from overhanging trees, with weeping willows, rustic bridges, and occasionally a small thatched cabin adding a pastoral note to the scene. Children paddled in wading pools, peacocks wandered at will, and hundreds of people relaxed in the warm sunshine.

In the late afternoon I was able to watch the return of the fishing boats — the fishermen in their blue dungarees and jerseys and their navy-blue berets presiding over their racks of shining silver sardines. On the quay a crowd of fish vendors, many of them women, clamored for their share of the catch, which they wheeled away to sell from barrows in the streets, and you could hear their cries of "*Sans sel*" (unsalted) ringing out around the town. One old lady had enlisted the aid of a big dog with a rope attached to his collar to pull her barrow. Around the little port sat groups of sailors' wives, knitting, sewing, and chatting. Many of them were Bretons with long, black skirts, full sleeves of black velvet and a very high coif of stiff lace rising about eight or nine inches in the air. These were the Bigoudènes, who during the summer months sold all over France the lace they had made in the winter. I also noticed the number of women in full mourning, a custom that had already disappeared in Australia. Here bereaved women were dressed, not only in black clothes and stockings, with black bag and gloves, but also with a long, light, black veil floating from the back of a black hat. With the accepted social rules of two years of mourning for a husband, a year for a close relative, and six months for a grandmother or grandfather, the women, once they had reached a certain age, were more or less obliged to stay permanently in black.

In earlier centuries, and especially during the reign of Louis XIV, La Rochelle had played a very important role in maintaining a balance between the kings of France and England, siding with one and then the other, and thus being in a position to exact privileges not enjoyed by other French cities. During the Reformation La Rochelle became a great center of Protestantism, until, defeated by the forces of Richelieu, it lost its independence. Many of the Protestants then left to found New Rochelle in Canada. In 1949, there was still much war damage in evidence, since La Rochelle, being an important submarine base for the Germans, had been one of the last cities to be liberated. Stirring stories were still being told about the resistance of the

400

Rochelais to the Germans. They were especially proud of their wartime Mayor, Léonce Vieljeux, who at the age of seventy-nine had resisted the Germans to the death. When the German Army took La Rochelle, he was ordered by a German soldier to take down the French flag flying over the Town Hall and put up the German flag. To this the Mayor replied: "I am a colonel and I am not accustomed to taking orders from a sergeant. Send your colonel to me." When the German colonel came with the same order, the Mayor replied with dignity: "I shall take down the French flag, but it is for you to run up the German flag." He continued in his quiet way to resist the Germans so effectively that he was eventually arrested and sent right across France to Alsace, where he was shot.

It was on this first day of solitary wandering in La Rochelle that I experienced that psychological block about speaking a foreign language to native speakers that afflicts so many non-native speakers. I had spoken French for years in Melbourne in the sheltered environment of the Alliance Française and I had had no problems with Jacqueline or Mr Persillet, nor with Christiane on the previous evening. Now, however, alone with strangers, I found the words stuck in my throat. I could not bring myself even to enter a cafe and order a cup of coffee. I had a delightful day by myself in a beautiful setting, but I ate only grapes that I could point to on a market barrow and I drank water from a tap in one of the parks (despite the many warnings I had received not to drink from the public water system in France). By the time I got back to Christiane's place in the evening, when she returned from her long day at work, I was so tired, exhausted, hungry, and frustrated that I burst into tears on seeing a friendly face. "But you speak French perfectly well," said Christiane, more than a little mystified by my emotional trauma. I have always kept this experience alive in my memory as I have continued to teach language. I try to keep in mind that what students need, when confronted with native speakers, is not just communicative ability but confidence in themselves, a certain daring and an awareness that the psychological shock they may experience is not uncommon, but part of the acculturation process. If they have had plenty of experience using the language in real communication from the early stages of learning, they will soon recover from any initial tongue-tying embarrassment.

By the second day, thanks to an introduction by a colleague of Christiane's at the Prefecture, I was eating my meals at a *"pension bourgeoise,"* in the open dining room of a boarding house. Regular customers came each day, during the customary two-hour lunch period, for a home-style, single-menu (*table d'hôte*) lunch, reasonably priced. Bread and wine seemed to be the personal responsibility of the guests and it was amusing to see the regulars arriving with their preferred amount of long, thin French bread and their own half-full bottle of unlabeled wine (*vin ordinaire*). At that time, the empty bottles of ordinary, home-table wine were exchanged at the store like milk bottles. At the pension, I had a great opportunity to listen to much informal discussion in French at the long communal table. I soon found that adjusting to flying conversations among a number of people was quite an art and that French spoken while laughing or with the mouth full presented quite a challenge for comprehension. Gradually, in this friendly atmosphere, I acquired the confidence to enter into the free-for-all and make my contribution. It was hard not to feel subconsciously at this early stage that we were all playing a game and that, if I could not think of a French word, I had only to insert some English word and all would be well. Blank stares soon taught me that this was not the case and reminded me that I was the only one thinking in English.

Having much time to myself, I began going to the cinema and I soon discovered that French films were a great help for attuning my ear to natural French speech. At first I was a little disappointed that I could not understand every word. Later, on my return to Australia, I realized that I did not get every word in an English-language film either. Sometimes one expects more from oneself and one's students in another language than in one's own. I also began to read books avidly — a lifelong addiction for me. Soon attentive reading was helping me build up my passive as well as my active vocabulary. I was determined to listen, talk, and read in French as much as possible during my precious time in France.

From Hervé I received my first lessons in comprehending baby French. His little utterances drew my attention to some interesting aspects of the French language. I found his way of dividing syllables very distinctly a little disconcerting at first: *"Voi-là le cy-cli-ste,"* he would say. He was learning very early that the

French syllable typically begins with a consonant and ends with a vowel (which contrasts with English syllabification) and that the ends of words when pronounced are clearly articulated, not mumbled or swallowed, as they so often are in English. I wished that these things had been brought to my attention when I was learning French and I have tried to emphasize them with my students ever since. Hervé became very attached to a handkerchief I had brought him from England with some boys in a boat; this he affectionately called "*le mouchoir de le bateau*," thus demonstrating that he had yet to acquire the contracted form "*du*."

Soon I was understanding practically everything I heard, unless I was taken unawares by someone rushing up to me in the street and asking the way when my mind was on other things. In that case they might have to repeat what they had said, but the same thing sometimes happened, as I was well aware, in my normal English-speaking environment. I continued for a while to be a little shy when talking to shop assistants, but I have always found shop assistants somewhat intimidating. Even from them, however, I learned things of interest. I had never learned in my studies that *Merci* in French had meanings other than a plain "thank you." One day I went into a shop to buy a new film for my camera. I asked politely for a *pellicule*. The shop assistant produced the right film, but when I said "*Merci*," quite politely as I thought, I was most surprised to see her quietly put it back on the shelf. I left the shop a little dazed, wondering where I had gone wrong. In this way I learned, in the context of experience, that my polite "*Merci*" had meant "No, thanks" to her.

Already at La Rochelle I began to discover the warmth and support that came from being accepted into a French family and the way in which this acceptance extended to all the ramifications of the extended family group. On many occasions, I have had reason to be thankful for this solidarity and sense of mutual responsibility. Jacqueline had notified her cousin, Suzanne, of my visit and, just as Jacqueline's father had shepherded me around Paris so readily, Suzanne had contacted me soon after my arrival in La Rochelle. She immediately made me feel very much at home, inviting me to her apartment and showing me around her city. Through her I was able to understand in French terms so much more of what I was observing. This kind solicitude, on the part of Suzanne, as well as of Christiane's

403

family, contributed considerably to my rapid adjustment to the new language and the culturally distinctive ways of its speakers.

Colette and Creil

My next destination was Creil, north of Paris, to see my other correspondent of equally long duration, Colette. Despite some trepidation on my part at having to search for someone I had never met on the crowded Paris-Austerlitz platform at rush hour, we recognized each other instantly from the many photographs we had exchanged over the years. Colette was just as I had imagined she would be, very natural and sincere. There was much excitement on both sides as I met her husband, Georges, and her 21-month-old son, Jacques. More baby French to master! I thought. This time I was "Dida" and had to divine meaning when only the last syllables of words were pronounced, sometimes repeated as in "*-toto* "for Daddy's *auto*(mobile). To add to the confusion "*-ture* "for *voiture* (his baby carriage) was also used for a *couverture* (blanket). As with Hervé, I noticed how this small child, having picked up the perceptually salient last syllable, which takes the stress in French, began these final syllables correctly with a consonant (something anglophone students find so difficult to do).

Since Colette and Georges had quite a spacious apartment, there was plenty of room for me to stay with them. Like so many French women at that time, Colette had a *femme de ménage* (cleaning woman) who came in every morning to clean up after us. I found French women seemed to have an aversion to doing the washing up and would leave it piled up in the sink, even over a weekend, for the cleaning woman to attend to on Monday morning. Coming from Australia, where even the Prime Minister helped his wife with the washing up, as visiting dignitaries had often observed, I found this rather amusing. Both Colette and Georges were excellent conversationalists, so there was hardly a dull moment during my stay. The conviviality was assisted by Georges's excellent selection of wines. As a salesman for Alsatian wines, this was his area of expertise.

Having been in France for such a short period, I would still occasionally switch into English without realizing it, until a certain puzzlement on Colette's or Georges's face would bring me up sharp.

Sometimes they would try out on me little bits of English, pronounced with strong French accents. I began to understand why Colette had once remarked that she understood the English of a French speaker more easily than that of a native English speaker. Later, at Douai, I had a French student who pronounced "potatoes" like "buttered toast," which, after all, is mostly a problem of the consistently syllable-timed rhythm of French, with equal stress on each syllable until the strong stress on the final syllable. This immediately struck my ear as the "typewriter effect," contrasting with the stress-timed rhythm of English (as variable yet smoothly regular as the waves of the sea); the latter is as hard for French speakers to acquire as their syllable-timed rhythm is for English speakers.

I had one unfortunate linguistic experience soon after my arrival, when Colette asked me to top and tail the beans for dinner. Not quite catching what she said, I murmured a vague assent and went to my room. Poor Colette, being convinced that my comprehension was perfect, was very disconcerted, even annoyed, when she found the beans were not ready. I soon learned to be more explicit about what I did and did not comprehend. Gradually, however, with constant practice, I began to think in French and express myself freely, even dreaming in French, which some consider the ultimate test. With Colette, I shopped in my first open market, where we sought out our fish and vegetables amid bootlaces, fur coats, flowers, cakes, tinware, and electrical goods. I enjoyed a typical, leisurely, three-hour Sunday dinner with Colette's parents, the Gaillards, who, having heard of my doings over the years, felt they knew me equally well. I had by now discovered that eating was a national pastime in France and, with the conversation that goes with it, was taken very seriously — a pleasant discovery for a chattering Rivers.

Creil being very close to Chantilly, I was soon taken to see that most elegant of *châteaux*, where the hearts of the members of the powerful Condé family are interred. It is spectacularly built on an island in the midst of a moat filled with water. We admired its white and gold decorations, beautiful painted ceilings, and magnificent pictures and furnishings, its great flights of stone steps, sweeping lawns, marble pools, promenades, and statuary — all very regular and classical. And most exciting of all, for a person from a very new country, was the magnificent, illuminated Book of Hours of the Duc de Berry, with its fascinating fourteenth-century scenes of life around the château during the various months of the year, under the influence of different signs of the zodiac. We made our way home through a typical French forest of close-growing trees, many with ivy-covered trunks, and the leaves of many seasons carpeting the ground. Crisscrossing the forest were innumerable training tracks for racehorses preparing for their contests on the famous Chantilly Racecourse nearby.

Paris, Eternal Paris

Soon I had become enamored of Paris. Colette had wanted me to get an impression of the whole of the city and we really did see everything. London had been very interesting to me, but Paris was, without hyperbole, beautiful. It was majestically planned, with wide, tree-lined boulevards, clean buildings, and great squares that gave an uncluttered view of the architecture of the city. The wide river, with its numerous and varied bridges, set off the beauty of the architecture, and walks along its banks refreshed and relaxed those who came to sit and fish or dream in the midst of the rush of city life. Even I eventually bought a little artist's notebook and a set of paints and settled down to create my own impression of the Pont Neuf. Other painters came to look over my shoulder and appraise my efforts. "Very primitive!" they murmured, which I took to be a stylistic compliment. I was soon becoming quite familiar with the great monuments and spacious gardens for which Paris is so famous. This extraordinary city made me realize that over the centuries the French had learned to live, not just to exist and work. I knew I would have to come back to it again and again in future years.

Georges, being anxious that my experience of the city should be complete, had booked a table in a smart little restaurant in Montparnasse, where we dined to the strains of a fine orchestra and laughed at the comedy routines. Here I had my first opportunity to listen to the topical and politically charged patter of the *chansonniers* — a test of a foreigner's listening comprehension of rapid French if ever there was one. At the end of a delightful meal, where I enjoyed my first snails, Georges thought it would be helpful, since I was to live in France, to explain to me that, from the French point of view, I had been very impolite throughout the meal. In my experiences with

French I had never been told that I should keep my hands on the table during a meal; consequently, I had been on my best boarding-school behavior all evening and kept them politely folded in my lap. This was valuable information. He also commented that I sang when I spoke French. It was then that I realized that I was singing the wrong song. Not having learned a great deal about intonation in my French studies, I had been singing an Australian song, instead of a French one, and so I became much more attentive to the rise and fall of the voices around me. Thus informed, I was ready to enjoy the rest of the evening at several nightclubs in Montmartre, where Georges continued to acculturate me to life in this new country.

Curiously enough Jay, my fellow student in Honours French at Melbourne University, was established in Paris at this time, after having sat out the war as a law student. In 1948, he had finally been able to take up his Traveling Scholarship for study in France. He was now enrolled as a doctoral student at the Sorbonne, writing his thesis on the same thirty pages of poetry on which he had written his two previous theses. Still without ambition, he told me that he was doing the doctorate only because he had won the scholarship in 1938. His mother had come with him and they had an apartment outside of Paris. His mother did not speak French, so he spoke Polish with her. When not with her, he spent his days in solitude in the library, doing research for his thesis. Consequently he had very little opportunity to talk French or to get to know French people. He had made no French friends and had never been invited into a French home. His contacts were mostly with fellow Australians or Polish relatives. As we sat on a seat in the Luxembourg Gardens, watching people sauntering by and children sailing little boats on the water around the fountains, we heard snippets of French from the passing crowd. "That's all the French I ever hear," said Jay. This seemed to me a model of what not to do if one wished to perfect one's knowledge of another language and culture. I realized I had spoken more French in four weeks than Jay would in a year and a half in Paris and I still had my period of residence at the school in Douai ahead of me. Naturally Jay also wanted to show me something of Paris. Together we visited the Sacré Coeur Church and saw Montmartre by daylight. Continuing on to visit the Latin Quarter, I had my first exciting glimpse of the Sorbonne, with its great courtyard and its amphitheatres for public lectures. In the chapel I paid homage to its famous patron, Cardinal Richelieu. With Jay I walked the length of the Boulevard Saint-Michel, along with so many other students, lingering in its bookshops and peeking at the old books and pictures in the open bookcases of the *bouquinistes* along the parapets of the Seine. Several months later Jay and I had the opportunity to renew our old student connection with Bill Gardner Davies, by then Australian Press Attaché in Paris and Australian representative at UNESCO. He invited us to a reception he and his wife were giving for Australian students at Christmastime. Already, in early autumn, Jay was breathlessly finishing his thesis and could hardly wait to get back to Australia.

My London cousin, Wiz, had now arrived in Paris for the French Motor Show, in which English, French, German, Italian, and American designers took part. (Japanese carmakers were not yet on the scene in 1949). With Wiz, I was invited to some grand dinners with leading car designers. At the actual show in the Grand Palais I was able to escape the milling crowds by accompanying Wiz on to the Daimler stand, amid the glamorous models displaying the very latest Paris fashions, some of which were most attractive and others just peculiar. The models had been brought in to set off the equally glamorous cars for a publicity newsreel. I hoped my homegrown image would not appear in the background. I remember one striking car, a French body on a Cadillac chassis; it was painted mauve, with mock bamboo weave decorations in white, and had a most luxurious interior of very soft off-white horsehair, with light-colored fittings. Like Wiz's designs, all these models were custom-built.

Douai and the Lycée de Jeunes Filles

The last week in October, when school was to reopen, was soon upon me and it was time to take the cold bath of total immersion in French language and culture at the lycée at Douai. This would be my first French experience without the supportive understanding of affectionate friends. I felt a little apprehensive, although my four weeks of talking French continually had built up my confidence and fluency. As I waited for the train to Douai at the Gare du Nord, it was exciting for an Australian to see long, fast express trains rushing by en route to exotic destinations like Copenhagen, Budapest, Moscow, or

Frankfurt, all of which I hoped to visit some day. Douai, it seemed, was on one of the main lines running north, which would make travel in and out of the town quite convenient.

Douai was in Flanders, as its tall Flemish *beffroi* (belfry) indicated. A town of about forty thousand at that time, it was situated in the midst of rich coalfields, with the resulting high slag heaps in the environs. The miners were mainly Polish immigrants. The extensive fields of this area, flat to the horizon as at Kerang, were largely planted with sugar beet. Since it was a strongly Catholic area the great church of St Pierre was a central feature of Douai itself. As with so many other towns in the North, there was still much evidence of bomb damage. The trees along the streets in town, which were severely pruned back each autumn, looked very distorted, like espaliers looking for a wall. Along the Scarp River, a little out of town, was a green area of grass and trees, with walled gardens where townspeople who had no space for such luxuries in the town itself grew their own vegetables.

The environment in Douai was pleasant enough, except for the climate; it was so frequently cold and foggy or rainy. The *brume* (general mistiness) of the North had its attractiveness but it became a little depressing over the long haul. My folding umbrella became indispensable as we rushed off twice a week for the train to Lille to attend our university courses. When it wasn't raining or foggy in Douai there would be torrential showers in Lille, and vice versa. We were continually getting wet and sitting in damp clothes. After classes in Lille, we would patronize the sellers of hot roasted chestnuts and *frites* (fried potato chips), who would be doing a brisk trade in the early winter darkness, and we would warm our fingers on the paper cornets in which our treats were served. The enticing smell of these delicious snacks pervaded the streets, masking to some extent the perfume from the public urinals. On our return to Douai, we would rush home in deep fog for a hurried, truncated, gobbled-down, half-cold dinner. We had to wait till spring for any break in the weather. Then, although it was still cool, the sky would be covered with very light gray clouds, with here and there patches of the palest blue. When the sun really came out, it was suddenly summer, with temperatures of seventy degrees (20 degrees C) and the locals would feel the "heat" and be waiting anxiously for a cool change.

The Lycée de Jeunes Filles, being in a disaffected Benedictine monastery, was surrounded by high brick walls, with iron bars on the lower floor windows where the building was directly onto the street, and heavy locked gates with a bell pull to alert the concierge. The monastery had been a place of refuge for English Catholic priests during times of persecution in the seventeenth century and the Douay translation of the Scriptures, used for so long by English Catholics, had been written at the nearby Lycée for boys (also a former monastic building). When the local hydroelectricity supply failed, as it did from time to time, and we had to eat by dim candlelight in the old refectory, the atmosphere was quite medieval. The four-storied school had two courtyards: a *Cour d'Honneur* with lawns and lovely lime trees for more special occasions and, for regular recreation periods, a rather plainer school yard that also had lots of trees. My window looked out over the latter and across to the turret and cross of the disaffected chapel, where later in the year the *Petits Chanteurs à la Croix de Bois* (the Little Singers with the Wooden Crosses), sang so appropriately. The red autumnal leaves of the creeper on the walls mellowed the scene.

There were about six hundred girls in the lycée, just over a hundred of them full-time boarders. The long dormitories were curtained off into quite large cubicles, with hot and cold water and all necessary facilities. My cozy little room was equally well furnished and quite warm, with central heating through hot water pipes for the winter ahead. Under Madame Arripe, the Principal, the lycée was run on very conservative lines. It was not a convent school but it might as well have been. The regimen was silence: silence in the classrooms, silence in the library, silence in the passageways, silence in the refectory, silence in the dormitories. The girls went to bed like mice. I rarely heard them as they filed past my room at night. They would bring their shoes to the entrance of their dormitory cubicles, clean them in silence and then retire to bed immediately. It was very different from the fun and games in the dormitory at St Annes. They rose at 6.45 a.m., when they all had to run around the quadrangle in their gym suits before they did anything else. I would hear them on the coldest winter mornings as I snuggled down under my blankets.

Classes began at 8 a.m. and continued till 4 p.m., with a recreation break at 10 a.m. and a two-hour lunch period. After a short

410

break for an afternoon *goûter* (snack), the boarders would do their preparation for the next day from 4.30 p.m. until dinnertime at 6.30 p.m. Day students could stay at school to do their preparation if they wished, and presumably those who went home had to study for a similar amount of time. After the evening meal the girls were given half an hour to socialize in the *salle de récréation*. Seizing this opportunity they certainly let their hair down and talked at the top of their voices, because another silent prep period would follow, with bed, in silence, at 9 p.m. On some festival days, Madame la Directrice would dine with the girls in the refectory and lift the rule of silence until, as the girls chatted excitably, the decibels increased so much that she could no longer stand it. She would then signal to the *surveillante générale* (the senior supervisor in charge), who would bellow across the room: *"Voulez-vous vous taire! Voulez-vous vous taire!"* ("Silence! Silence!") and stalk around the room glaring at any girls still bold enough to want to whisper to their neighbors. There was an absurd sense of hierarchy at the lycée that resulted in an unusual degree of respect for the Principal; this was exacerbated by the rarity of her appearances among her flock. The girls called her God and her secretary, who rigidly preserved her privacy, the Archangel. One girl told me, "When the Principal speaks to me in the *Cour d'Honneur*, I positively quake!"

My schedule, I found, was a light one, just twelve hours of English conversation classes and a Saturday afternoon English Club, hence no prolonged lesson preparation or corrections. There were no classes on Thursdays. My timetable had been designed to give me plenty of time to continue my studies at the University of Lille, which was twenty miles away, about half an hour by train. The classes I had to teach were in the mornings, which made it easy for me to eat a quick lunch and be at the station for the 12.30 train to Lille. This train always left promptly to the minute, arriving at Lille at three minutes to one precisely. French train drivers were proud of their punctuality. It seemed they earned a special bonus if they had never been a minute early or a minute late during the year. My conversation classes ranged across the middle and senior schools, from eleven-year-olds to eighteen-year olds, and I was asked if I would like to earn a little more money by teaching a group of eight- and nine-year-olds for two half-hours a week in lunch hours. This involved some elementary

English, mostly acquired through games and songs. With my recent experience with this age group in England, I felt quite ready for the assignment. I also gave private lessons in English for two hours a week to one of the girls, whose mother was a Countess. Through this contact I came to know a Royalist family who kept on the mantelpiece an autographed photograph of the Pretender to the French throne, the Comte de Paris, with his eleven children. Through them, I discovered there was a Royalist Society and a Royalist news sheet to which they subscribed. My French resident colleagues were rather amused by this information, since they had presumed such an anachronism to be non-existent.

My colleagues who were *maîtresses d'internat* were university students. They received their board and lodging and a small salary to look after the various aspects of the boarding side of the school, supervise student preparation and recreation periods, or help in the financial office. There were also non-resident supervisors for the day school, to supervise changes of rooms and spare periods, but we rarely encountered them. We saw very little of the lycée teachers either, except at lunch tables. Since they had few responsibilities apart from teaching their classes for twelve or fourteen hours per week, they came and went at their own convenience. The *maîtresses d'internat* were pursuing advanced studies and this system gave them plenty of time for their work. There were six of them at the lycée: Jacqueline, Micheline, Gisèle, Paule, Yvonne, and Monique. Mostly in their early twenties, they were of very varied personalities and temperaments. They were all very friendly and anxious to enjoy their leisure moments in good company. Along with a German-language assistant from the Saarland, Christel, and an English-language assistant from Britain, Ena, we formed a very merry bunch, and we laughed and talked and partied together most amicably. Whenever any of us had a birthday or name day or any other anniversaries (even the anniversary of my departure from Australia), we would break out a bottle of wine and celebrate with much laughter and light-hearted banter. There were always some of us who were not on duty to keep the ball rolling. From them I learned to follow rapid-fire informal French and I soon acquired the requisite student slang.

Jacqueline, the youngest among us, had a strong northern accent and she often used regional expressions. We became

412

accustomed to hearing her rejoicing on her return from a visit home about how well she had eaten and what fine wine she had drunk: "*Qu'est-ce qu'on s'est mis!*" she would exclaim, with a satisfied gleam in her eye. "*Qu'on s'a bien amusé!*" she would add. Since she was actually *au pair,* that is, she received board and lodging for her services but no salary, she always ate well, seeing this as a way of increasing the recompense for her work. Micheline was always laughing and joking; she was the *bout-en-train* (life of the party). Gisèle, who was older, was a little sadder. She was trying to pass a *concours* (a competitive examination) in the Classics, the results of which were determined by the number of Classics teachers required in the lycées across France in a particular year. This might be as low as ten or fifteen, so that what we would regard as the pass mark was a moving target. Since she had not been included in the cut for a couple of years, she felt her knowledge of and interest in the Classics were slowly declining, which made her less competitive against the students who had just completed their studies. Very frustrated, she would often cry herself to sleep at night. Eventually she gave up the struggle and became an elementary school teacher. Gisèle was a Protestant and came with me to services at the Temple when she could. Through her I became acquainted with the Huguenot cross, which has a small dove suspended from the base of the cross and is frequently worn by French Protestants.

Paule was training to work in school management and was an intern with the housekeeping and financial office (*l'intendance*). I soon became very friendly with Paule and we have remained close friends ever since. A Picardian from Saint-Quentin, she was always very interested in the songs and folklore of her region. After lights out, we would hear the students in Paule's dormitory singing regional songs in four voices. Like all Northerners the girls loved to sing. The region was famous for its Chorales. As Christmas approached I became acquainted with the Picardian Christmas carol of *Le P'tit Quinquin.* It was Paule I called on to enlighten me when I had filled my little notebook with newly acquired French words and expressions whose meanings I could not find in the dictionary. The result was a hilarious session, as I produced slangy or vaguely obscene words in quick succession.

Monique was engaged to a resident supervisor at the boys' school. For some reason I never quite fathomed she was disliked by the others, who deemed her *trop bourgeoise* — the ultimate expression of disdain among students at the time. In 1949 there was a strong Communist Party in France, which, with strong support from the workers *(ouvriers)*, succeeded in gaining nearly twenty-five percent of the vote. Its rival, the Socialist Party, was very popular across the industrial north. Paule's family, for instance, were longtime Socialists. Most of my companions in the Common Room at the lycée, being overworked and underpaid students, held Socialist or Communist opinions, and a right-wing sympathizer would definitely be odd-woman-out. This could well have been the explanation for Monique's unpopularity.

Yvonne, on the other hand, was an active member of the Communist Party and anti-clerical. (I found there was still a great deal of talk about the lay school in France at the time and a pronounced anticlericalism among the *maîtresses d'internat* who were preparing, of course, to teach in the public school system.) Since we were all rather short of funds, we relied for news on what we could find in the Common Room. Yvonne ensured that we had a regular, up-to-date supply of Communist publications, like the newspaper *L'Humanité,* commonly called *L'Huma,* the literary magazine *Les Lettres Françaises,* and various film and sporting magazines. *Les Lettres Françaises* was highly regarded for its critical articles, but I soon lost interest in *L'Huma* as a source of news. I found that it unrelentingly repeated the Party line for all events and eulogized Russia and Stalin most uncritically whenever it could.

The cost of living in France continued to rise and wages were definitely out of step with it. There was a big gap between the workers and the middle-class *bourgeois,* and the unions, although divided into competing associations with different political orientations, enjoyed very strong support. It was not surprising that there were so many strikes at the time, since this seemed to be the only recourse the workers had for obtaining redress of the disparities they were experiencing. We had our own experience of a teachers' strike during my time at the lycée. Ena, the assistant from England, and I felt that, being foreigners on work permits and working for a governmental institution, we should not take active part in any

414

political action. After much discussion, we went to our empty classrooms on the day of the strike to make a token appearance and then went about our personal business.

Christel, the German-language assistant from the Saarland, spoke German as her first language and felt very German. Her home region had been taken over by France from Germany at the end of the war. After ten years it would be allowed a plebiscite as to its population's preference for allegiance — to Germany or France. (In fact, it promptly voted itself back to Germany.) Because of this temporary status, Christel had a French passport, which she considered to be something of a joke. "I'm French, you see!" she would cry sarcastically, as she waved her passport in the air. Having grown up under Hitler, she had been from childhood a member of the Hitler Youth and enjoyed all the benefits he provided for young people — libraries, symphony concerts, drama, and international trips to youth congresses. In those impressionable years she had become a true believer. She was only seven years old when Hitler came to power and she was just thirteen when the war began. During the long years of World War 11, she had heard only what the regime ordained she should hear. The collapse of Nazi Germany came, therefore, as a great shock to her and her friends. Suddenly all the things they had valued and the ideals they had held were denigrated, and their teachers told them they had been young fools to swallow it all. "Why didn't they tell us it was a delusion much, much earlier," Christel wondered, "if they had really known it all along?" In 1949 she was in a very mixed-up state psychologically and was trying to work out how she felt and what she believed. Consequently, she was often moody and unpredictable. She was very attached to the Peace Movement, which was strong among youth in Europe at the time, and that is where she was finding her new identity. As a career choice, she was planning to be an interpreter.

As the bearer of a French passport and a fluent speaker of French, Christel had her share of unpleasant experiences in France. When I went into a shop with her one day, the shopkeeper, having detected by my accent and appearance that I was probably of English origin, began to declare how she loved the British but could not stand the Germans. She then turned to Christel and asked her: "Are you English, too?" To which Christel replied, "No, I'm German."

Considerably disconcerted, the woman immediately began to say how well she had got on with the Germans and how much she disliked the Russians. She then continued the conversation by asking Christel if she had married a Frenchman, to which Christel responded that we were "Lectrices" (lecturers). This stumped our interlocutor, who clearly had no idea what this meant. Looking at us rather sadly, she observed: "Oh well, everyone has to earn a living somehow." We wondered what she thought we did for ours.

It was through Christel that I learned a very salutary lesson. She was wondering how to translate into English a particularly unsavory French epithet, with obscene overtones, which was in common use among students. Helpfully, I gave her a very strong Australian equivalent. From then on, it became very embarrassing for me. When any English-speaking person was around, Christel would laughingly bring out this Australian word, explaining to her shocked hearer that "Wilga taught me that!" I realized, as I never had before, that new words in a non-native language do not bring with them all the subconscious connotations they carry for a native speaker. They are acquired as new and interesting words to enter in a vocabulary notebook and try out in the next conversation. Their real emotional whammy can only be experienced in living contexts from the reaction of interlocutors. For this reason, I always deflect the desire of students to learn to swear in another language or use street slang. Not only can they not capture the exact moment and tone of voice in which to utter these expressions, making them gratuitous overkill, but the expressions themselves become rapidly dated. Produced in the wrong tone of voice with a foreign accent or intonation and with imprecise timing, they are most likely to elicit a shocked taking aside and a warning: "We don't use that word," even from those who do.

The English-language assistant from Britain, Ena, was younger than I. I turned thirty while at Douai and my colleagues gave me a copy of Balzac's *Femme de Trente Ans* (The Thirty-Year-old Woman) as a present. I was also a very experienced teacher with a Master's degree, while Ena, with her BA, had had little or no experience in the classroom. Consequently the Principal, with her strong sense of hierarchy, always referred to us as Miss Rivers and Miss Peck. Since I was a "colonial" and Ena felt she represented the Mother Country, I could see that this grated on her. In some strange

416

way, she felt it was inappropriate for the "Colonies" to take precedence over the Head of the Empire. Ena was also very accent conscious. One day, Christel asked me what was wrong with my English, since Ena had been telling my companions that I should not be permitted to teach English with my Australian accent (which was not particularly broad actually). She herself came from the Welsh border country and was always criticising the London accent of a fellow-student at Lille, as he criticized hers for its regional qualities. Even so, as I had found in England, Ena was much more accepting of English regional accents than of those of other English-speaking countries.

Language assistants were expected to conduct conversation classes. Most native-speaking language-teaching assistants in French schools were students, not experienced teachers, yet they were given one of the most difficult tasks in language teaching. With little of no guidance, they were expected to help students express themselves in the language despite their diffidence and fear of sounding foolish, while avoiding the trap of letting a few more confident students do all the talking — a common problem in such groups. In many cases the assistants resorted to doing all the talking themselves, as the easiest way out, and the students were very happy to let them do so. In my case I had had a great deal of experience in encouraging conversation in small groups, and I was determined to use my period in France to perfect this art. At Douai I found that starting with a place as exotic to the French girls as Australia attracted their interest. We then moved on to a number of controversial and provocative topics. I have always included a lot of singing in my language teaching and, when the weather was fine, I would take my groups out under the trees in the *Cour d'Honneur* to chat, and the sound of our singing would waft up into the classrooms.

Nor did I neglect my own French language skills. Very soon after my arrival, I was exchanging with one of the English teachers an hour of critical improvement of my French for assistance with her English. This kind of close personal assistance is always valuable. While I was visiting this teacher, I had opportunities to read children's books to her little son, Christian, and I soon found out how important exact repetition is to young children. I remember reading him a book about Noah. Wearying of being asked questions on the

417

content, he decided to ask me questions. When I referred to the hero as Papa Noé, he solemnly corrected it to Monsieur Noé, as in the book. Since Cri-Cri, as he liked to call himself, was the fifth little boy I had come to know in France, I was beginning to think that little French boys were spoiled by their parents. Cri-cri kicked up a din whenever his father wanted to put his shoes on. He shouted in anger and wriggled and wriggled. Then, when at long last the shoes were on, his father would give him a cake for being a good boy and letting Daddy put his shoes on. This seemed to me an excellent way to encourage tantrums. I mentioned my observation of this spoiling of little boys to Jay's mother, herself a European, to which she replied: "That's what little boys are for, isn't it?" Perhaps that is why Jay had always appeared to me to be mother-smothered.

Learning about French Life

One of the French rituals I soon learned was the regular morning greeting. As each of the nine of us dribbled in for breakfast, we were expected to make the round of the table, shaking hands with everyone, greeting them with "Bonjour, Jacqueline (Paule, Gisèle," etc) and following this up with the culturally essential question: *Avez-vous* or *As-tu bien dormi?* (Did you sleep well?) Later a French friend told me of his stay as a language assistant at Eton in England. Every morning when he came down to breakfast, one of the English masters would be there, completely hidden by the newspaper. My friend would greet him with a cordial "Bonjour," to be rewarded with a vague grunt. Finally, one morning, the Englishman could stand it no longer and returned his greeting with: "Bonjour! Bonjour! Bonjour! Bonjour! Bonjour! Bonjour! Bonjour! That'll do for a week! "So much for intercultural entente!

Much more difficult was the question of *tutoiement* (the use of the familiar form of address *tu*, instead of the more formal *vous* for "you"). The familiar form is used commonly among family members, with children and close friends, and among students, who promptly revert to *vous* when speaking to superiors or in formal working situations. This sounds straightforward, but it is much more subtle and elusive than that. As English-speakers, Ena and I were not accustomed to the use of a familiar form for "you," whereas Christel as a German speaker was. Consequently Christel was soon using *tu* with our French companions, who continued to use *vous* when speaking to Ena and me. Yet we were becoming a close-knit group and the language forms for informal speech were ringing in our ears all day. It was becoming difficult, I found, to maintain a formality of tone I did not feel, but I was not sufficiently acclimated to recognize the subtle signs that the moment for a change had come and with whom. I made one or two tentative efforts to enter into the general ambiance, which were not seized upon by my French companions, who probably thought I was just making common foreigner slips in my speech. One day, I picked up a letter and, without thinking, I turned to Gisèle and said: *"Cette lettre est à toi"* (This letter is yours). Gisèle, very surprised, said laughingly: "Very familiar now, aren't we?" I happened to be leaving the room, so to cover up my lapse I smiled and said cheerfully, "Why not?" My colleagues must have talked it over among themselves, because at lunch Gisèle used *tu* in a most obvious way when addressing me. There were one or two comments, to which Gisèle replied, a little defensively, "She started it!" "But everyone uses *tu* to Christel, so why not me?" I blurted out. One or two of them murmured that they wouldn't have dared to call me *tu*, perhaps in respect for my advancing years. That day Gisèle and Jacqueline, who was the youngest and most informal, used *tu* on and off when speaking to me. Unfortunately, when I came down to breakfast the next morning, the new linguistic relationship I was establishing slipped my mind, and I absent-mindedly used *vous* to Gisèle who was a little miffed, as though I had offered friendship and then suddenly withdrawn it. It was all a little mystifying. I wasn't at all sure if I had done the right thing at the right time. Since they all knew that the English language did not make such distinctions, they probably put my inconsistencies down to my English-speaking habits. As time went on, I did find using *tu* to those I was most friendly with made me feel much more part of the group. Since Communists used *tu* freely with their colleagues, Yvonne didn't find this a problem and very soon I was using *tu* with my close friend Paule.

I was somewhat of an enigma to my colleagues, who discussed openly whether I could be considered a true intellectual in the French sense of the word, since apart from my obvious thirst for knowledge and love of study I also enjoyed gardening, knitting, photography, collecting stamps, and pressing flowers. This did not fit in with their Mandarin concept. However, we got on extremely well. Since there was a shortage of young males in France after the war, they frequently discussed their chances of finding a partner and bringing up a family. This frustration was compounded by the excessively long time it took them to become qualified and then to accede to a permanent appointment and a settled career. They seemed to be spending the best years of their youth in busywork that did not require such highly qualified people. At one stage they jokingly decided to establish an Old Maids Club and respectfully requested that I, as the oldest Old Maid, agree to become Madame la Présidente. Gisèle, who was twenty-eight, as next oldest, was to be the Vice-President. This was a whimsical and momentary expression of their frustration, but it reflected their growing, if repressed, pessimism about their future.

There was general distress and discouragement across the group when Yvonne heard the news that she had received a bad report from her previous school. Was this political? I wondered, since Yvonne was a very outspoken Communist. It seemed that now she would not be made "stagiaire," which was the first step toward a permanent appointment. Naturally, all the others began to worry about their own reports. It was no wonder, with all the uncertainty that surrounded them, that they so often experienced mood swings from extreme hilarity and exuberance, which they expressed through clowning around, to general depression.

The training my colleagues were receiving for teaching seemed to be highly intellectual. In all, in 1949, future lycée teachers had five weeks of teaching experience, the first two weeks being spent in observing classes and the next three in preparing and giving six hours of lessons per week (a total of eighteen hours in all). These lessons were not prepared under guidance nor discussed afterwards with a supervising teacher, although they did provide some classroom practice. Since there were no discussions of the history or philosophy of teaching or possible alternative approaches, this seemed to be a sure way of maintaining traditional methods of teaching from one generation to the next. If the supervising teacher's report on their classroom performance was good, the next stage would be to prepare for the nation-wide competitive examination, for which they could be asked any type of question on anything in their subject area. For

420

literature they might be asked about any period, genre, or specific author or for science about anything in the school or university program. Consequently, having already passed the required number of *certificats* (year-long courses) in their major subject for their first university degree, they would continue their preparation for this *concours* by rushing off to any courses at the local University on any aspect of the subject. Since there was no set program for the *concours* in any particular year, this was a hit-or-miss process, rather than an assessment of their personal command of the material they would be teaching. The central emphasis of their teaching training being intellectual, it was not surprising that the most intellectual among them became teachers, without much regard for their teaching ability; hence the lycée program they taught was also highly intellectual. In the last year at the lycée the philosophy textbook, which was nearly 800 pages long, described and discussed the system of thought of every philosopher from the Greeks to modern times, as well as covering all the methods and rules of logic, and providing a thorough course in ethics. Of course, there had been a weeding-out process all through the school life of these students, so that only the most intellectual were still surviving in the lycée. This contrasted strongly with attempts elsewhere to educate all kinds of students with different aptitudes to the highest extent of their abilities.

Food in the North

Living in residence at the school, I had to adapt to quite different kinds of meals, not just to the traditional French breakfast of coffee and fresh croissants. Institutional food in the north was quite distinctive. For one thing breakfast was more likely to consist of large slices of *pain de campagne* (farmhouse loaves); these do not become hard and stale as fast as the more common crusty *baguettes*, which a French household at that time would usually buy freshly baked twice daily. These slices of bread would be accompanied by *café au lait* in bowls without handles, which one lifted by the rim with two hands, and into which one dipped the dry bread. Bread was, of course, ubiquitous and served with all meals.

Some of the most frequently served foods were new to me. *Choucroûte* or sauerkraut often appeared on the table, along with jugs of the local beer, which was much lower in alcoholic content than

421

Australian or German beers. Christel referred to it, somewhat contemptuously, as a "petite bière," but these Northern girls and *maîtresses d'internat* were very accustomed to drinking it with their meals, rather than the ordinary wine, which was drunk so freely in other parts of France. Since this was a cold region, the alternative was the fermented cider of this apple-growing area. (Later, in the South, I found, one cooled off with *anis*, made from the aniseed plants that grew so prolifically on the hillsides. I soon realized how closely related eating and drinking habits are to geographic factors.) When the winter blasts grew more severe and the rain seemed to fall unceasingly, there would appear on the evening table large jugs of *grog* (rum and lemon juice, diluted with sweetened warm water) to ward off winter infections.

Hot soups were an essential part of nearly every meal. Dishes of *nouilles* (different kinds of noodles or pasta), served with melted cheese or tomato sauce, were served frequently. I was introduced to *yaourt* (yoghourt), which was not common in Australia at the time, but I soon a acquired a taste for it. I was pleased to see that French people ate a lot of vegetables and fruit, although eating vegetables on their own, apart from the main protein dish, was new to me, as were some of the vegetables like *endives* and *artichauts*. I soon learned to pluck the latter leaf by leaf, until one reached the soft, flavorful heart. A salad was always served at the end of a meal, but there were different greens, apart from the one kind of lettuce, to which I had been accustomed at home. Fruit was the usual daily dessert and, having grown up eating a lot of fruit, I appreciated this. Sweet desserts were kept for special occasions, when the famous French *pâtisseries* (pastries) would appear on the table. *Beignets* (fritters) and *crêpes* (pancakes), not necessarily sweet, were main courses, rather than desserts. Naturally no meal was complete without a choice of cheeses from different areas of France. Although I had not been accustomed to much variety in cheeses in the Australia of the 1930s and 1940s, I took to these like a duck to water. I soon came to enjoy them all and share the French love of seeking out rarer ones from different regions. Sweets were mostly bought as gifts for one's hostess and the vendor would wrap them up beautifully in festive paper and ribbons. Coffee was drunk with chicory and this reminded me of the nighttime infusions of my childhood. The Northerners

422

customarily drank their coffee through a square sugar lump placed in the mouth. Soon I had acquired that art myself. I was somewhat surprised to find plum jam, from the fruit of the local orchards, served by itself as a dessert, but this also was a Picardian custom; at other times it would be served with *fromage blanc*, an early stage of cheese. Chocolate was regarded as a food, rather than as a superfluous pleasure. Little children ate it in *pains au chocolat* (chocolate wrapped in a roll of croissant-like texture). When we had examinations in Lille, often of four hours' duration, the cook at the lycée would send us off with what to me were doorstop-like sandwiches and a slab of dark chocolate to keep up our strength during the ordeal. For snacks *pain d'épices* (gingerbread) was popular, especially for children. To calm our nerves before retiring for the night, we would have an infusion of *tilleul* (lime tree leaves) or *camomille*.

There was one thing to which I could not accustom myself. In 1949 most French people did not drink a great deal of tea and they had not assimilated the notion that for a good cup of tea you had to use boiling water. I was horrified when tea was served in open jugs of lukewarm water at the table. Fortunately, I always made sure that I had the means in my room for boiling water and making my own cups of my favorite brew; then I drank it just as I liked it, piping hot with milk. I soon acquired a taste, however, for the strong black coffee French people love.

The Rhythms of the School Year

As in all cultures, there were rituals in this northern French setting to provide an outlet for people's emotions and energies. Soon after school began, we celebrated the *Toussaint* (All Saints Day) with a two-day holiday (November 1st and 2nd). This was the time when French people remembered their family dead. It was a day for church services, masses for the dead, and pilgrimages to cemeteries, where the French brought chrysanthemums to place on the tombs of their loved ones. Next came November 11th (Armistice Day), when the war dead were specially remembered with marches and military pomp.

Of the more light-hearted festivals the first was the *Fête de Sainte-Catherine*, which came fairly early in the school year. It was supposed to be on November 25th, but since the Principal had been ill it was deferred till December 4th — the festival, as it happened, of St Barbe. This caused some merriment because St Catherine was the patron saint of unmarried girls until they were twenty-five, when, if not married, they were considered old maids, whereas St Barbe was the patron saint of watchmakers and married women (the timekeepers of the nation?). In addition, on December 4th, the local miners feted their patron, St Eloi, by running single file through the town. Specially connected with St Catherine's Day was a coif, or head-covering, and unmarried women of twenty-five were said to *"coiffe"* St Catherine for the last time. St Catherine's Day had always been a special day for the young seamstresses of Paris (the *midinettes*), who made themselves very extravagant hats for the occasion. Being under the protection of St Catherine, the twenty-five-year-olds were called *catherinettes* and it was expected that they would be given a gift. For reasons of deference, perhaps, we gave the Principal a present, which seemed a little out of keeping. She was unmarried certainly, but well over the age of twenty-five. At the lycée, our celebration took the form of a concert in the refectory, where the girls performed very amusing, satirical skits on school life. Then we all ate well, as one would expect in France. After the feast the girls rushed in with beautifully made paper hats to *"coiffe"* all the unmarried teachers and supervisors. To end the fete, the girls danced the night away (a rare privilege that they were granted only two or three times a year).

By December 6th it was the *Fête de St-Nicolas,* the patron saint of little children, a tradition that was very much alive in the North. It seemed that St Nicolas came in the night, riding on an ass, and children left carrots for the ass beside their shoes, in which, if they had been good, St Nicolas left them presents. *Le Pere Fouettard* (the Whipping Father) followed St Nicolas and whipped naughty children with a *"martinet"* (or cat o' nine tails). I saw St Nicolas, with his bushy white beard and mustache, in a local store, chatting with the good children. He wore a red robe and high black boots, with a white cloak and hood, and was really very much like Father Christmas. At least in the North, Christmas, it seemed, was mainly a family and religious festival; any presents were only for children, the adults receiving theirs at the New Year.

This observance of a religious festival in a secular school considerably disturbed some of my colleagues, particularly since the Principal also wanted a Christmas party, organized by the *maîtresses d'internat*, in each dormitory on the evening before the girls left for the holiday break. In preparation she had given out a list of suitable songs from different parts of France, most of which, of course, referred to the birth of Christ. There had been a tremendous struggle in France at the end of the nineteenth century to establish the *école laïque* (secular school), and the more left-wing groups were still very sensitive to any encroachment on its laicity. Although ninety-nine per cent of the girls at the lycée were Catholic, at least in name, it was forbidden for them to have any religious pictures or images in their dormitory cubicles and, of course, *crêches* (representations of the Manger Scene) were also banned. There was a great deal of discussion among the boarding-house assistants as to whether they should object and keep to purely secular songs, despite the expressed wishes of the Principal. However, as Christel, the German assistant and a Catholic of sorts, put it: "How can you possibly have a secular Christmas celebration?" She told us how Hitler had tried to change Christmas in Germany into a Festival of Light to be observed on December 21st, the shortest day in the Northern Hemisphere year. It seems it was mainly members of the Nazi Party who celebrated the coming of the Light with solemn hymns, while the rest of the people continued to celebrate Christmas in their homes. As was usual at the lycée Madame Arripe's will was done, despite the mumblings and grumblings of the resident staff.

Invited by the Directrice, I attended the *Veillée du Petit Dortoir* (Watchnight in the Junior Dormitory). For this Jacqueline Goube had set up a Provençal crêche, with colorfully hand-painted *santons*, lent by Madame Arripe herself. These small terracotta figures represented the Holy Family, the shepherds, wise men, and numerous village people, who took their places on the path down the mountainside, bringing presents appropriate to their trade or profession to the Baby Jesus in the cave below. Angels floated overhead in a starry sky. With a red light behind the Holy Family in the cave and a few candles set around, it was very pretty indeed. With the little ones in bed, the senior girls sat around on beds or on the floor. Then, with lights out and candles lit, Paule led them in singing

Christmas carols from the different regions of France. Madame Arripe then read a Christmas story about an ant that set out on pilgrimage to Jerusalem. All this ended with a display of sparklers and cascades of sparks, while the junior girls sucked the sweets Madame had given them. It was a pleasant little function, which quite infuriated the Communist element in the staff room.

My personal Christmas was spent in Paris with my good friends, the Persillets, who shared with me their own typical celebration. When Jacqueline and I went shopping for presents, I saw how beautifully and elaborately the Parisian shop windows were decorated. We watched the "good children" talking to the Père Noël in the Galeries Lafayette, the big department store, with its gilded balconies backed with mirrors that reflected the multi-colored lights. Mr Persillet took me to the Chausson Company's Christmas treat for its six thousand workers and their families at the quite extraordinary Paris Circus. Then Jacqueline and I rushed off to the Comédie Française to see Corneille's *Le Cid* and Molière's *Le Médecin Malgré Lui* (The Involuntary Doctor). This was my second visit to the famous national theatre, where during my November visit I had seen Marie Bell play the role of Racine's Phèdre so movingly.

To celebrate the religious significance of Christmas Jacqueline, her father, and I went to Midnight Mass at her parish church of St Geneviève, named for the patron saint of Paris, who in the fifth century had strengthened the resolve of the inhabitants of Lutèce, as Paris was then called, to resist the attacks of Attila, the Hun. St Genevieve's was absolutely packed with people standing in all the aisles and across the back. Having sung at midnight "Il est né, le divin enfant" (The divine child is born) and "Gloria in excelsis deo," we were in the right mood for gift-giving and the family *réveillon* feast on our return. Here we ate oysters, pâté de foie gras with truffles, ham and cheese sandwiches, delicious preserved strawberries, and special Christmas sweets that Jacqueline had made herself. The next day there was the traditional three-hour Christmas dinner with cousins and friends, where we ate a Christmas goose and a special dessert of the *marrons glacés* (preserved chestnuts) that are such a part of the winter season in France. It was at this Christmas celebration that I became friends also with Jacqueline's cousin, Gaby, who taught French at a big Paris lycée and who was able to give me

426

many insights into French education. New Year's Day brought another large family gathering with cousins and aunts, who welcomed me warmly into my new family. As a friend of Jacqueline's, I was now a friend of them all.

I was pleased to find during this end of the year visit that I could follow everything that was said with the greatest of ease, whereas on my previous visit, two months earlier, I had had to concentrate very hard in group conversations. Our constant chattering at the Lycée was paying off. An additional pleasure of this Christmas visit was the opportunity to see the Cité Universitaire, the international village where students coming to study in Paris could stay in beautifully designed national houses that represented the best in architecture that each country had to offer. Here I was fortunate to be able to meet the Secretary of the French University Women's Federation, Mademoiselle Jeanne Chaton, whom I had heard speak on the radio in Australia in 1946 and who had graciously given me my first clue as to how to get to France to work and study.

I certainly did not waste any of my precious time in Paris, where I visited in depth Notre-Dame Cathedral, with its richly carved facade between its twin towers and its amusing gargoyles glaring down from the roof. The dark interior of the cathedral in the middle of winter was magically illuminated by the gorgeous red, blue, and purple hues of the extraordinary rose windows. The treasures of the art gallery of the Louvre were eye opening for an Australian, and the collections were so immense that I knew I would have to come back many more times to absorb what it offered. Of course, like all tourists, I had to admire on this first visit the Venus de Milo, the Winged Victory of Samothrace, so dramatically displayed at the top of a flight of stairs, and the unforgettable Mona Lisa. While in Paris I paid a visit to the Office des Universités et Ecoles Françaises, which had engineered my assistantship at Douai. My intent was to persuade the Director, Monsieur Renard, that, having come from so far away, I should have the opportunity to stay for at least another year in France. Since it was so early in the year, he was able to offer me a choice of Aix-en-Provence, Toulouse, Bordeaux, or Montpellier for my second year. I chose Montpellier partly because I confused its location with that of Grenoble, which I knew was in the Alps. I soon found out, however, that its situation in Languedoc in the sunny South would ensure me of a much more agreeable climate than that of Douai. Monsieur Renard was not only a most affable and helpful man, but he spoke the best English I had heard in France, without a trace of a French accent. I only wished I could boast of as much with my French.

Chartres, so close to Paris, had to be my next visit. The magnificent cathedral on the plain of the Beauce was as unforgettable as I had anticipated. It had been for centuries the first stage of the pilgrimage to Saint Jacques of Compostello in Spain. Pilgrim groups of students still made an annual pilgrimage on foot to this sanctuary, nearly a hundred kilometers from Paris, and were heartened on their journey when, across the fields of golden wheat, they could see in the far distance its two disparate towers. Inside the Cathedral, I was dazzled by the deep blue of the thirteenth-century glass in its tall windows, and I remembered the blue I had seen in the windows of Canterbury Cathedral, also made by the workmen from Chartres before the secret of the composition of that perfect blue was lost. Around the Choir and High Altar of the cathedral was an indescribably beautiful wooden screen, carved from the sixteenth to eighteenth centuries, showing in high relief about fifty scenes from the lives of Jesus and his mother Mary. On the outside of the cathedral were stone carvings dating from the twelfth and thirteenth centuries, some being among the earliest of the medieval period; these showed unpretentious kings and queens from the genealogy of Jesus and a fascinating calendar in stone of the activities of the rural year, each under its Zodiac sign. The ensemble of the cathedral, built over a period of more than a century, was a demonstration of the slow transition from Romanesque to Gothic.

I could not wait to see the Palace of Versailles, the scene of the extravagantly sumptuous ceremonies and entertainments of the court of Louis XIV. Since it was only a train ride away, it was very accessible. The enormous palace, with its magnificent painted ceilings, and wall panels, and the inimitable Gallery of Mirrors where so many important international gatherings have taken place, the gardens with their great stretches of water (lakes, canals, and pools), their fountains and statuary, groves, and elaborately designed flower beds, although so often seen in pictures, are still breathtaking for the visitor. Naturally we visited the Grand Trianon of rose-colored marble and the Petit Trianon, Marie-Antoinette's own small château with its imitation village where she and her ladies could play at being villagers and milkmaids. Seeing these places with Jacqueline as my guide, I was beginning to know and understand the great artistic heritage of France.

Festival time was not over when I returned to Douai. The *Fête des Rois* (the Festival of the Kings or Epiphany) was upon us. Twelfth Night to the British, it is officially on January 6th. However, at Douai we celebrated it that year on January 8th, which was the nearest Sunday, and the church bells rang across the town throughout the day. For our celebration Madame la Directrice, along with Madame l'Intendante (School Manager), and the senior Surveillantes came to the refectory for a festive afternoon meal with the girls. In accordance with tradition, the central feature was a large, flat, tart-like cake, called a *galette*, with a filling, tasting of almond paste mixed with a syrup. On the galette sat a large crown, with a smaller one nearby. A *fève,* or lucky charm in the form of a small plaster crown, was hidden in each galette on the different tables. At each table the youngest person was asked to turn her back and call out the names of those who were to receive the slices of galette in order. The one who found the *fève* in her slice was declared King and put on the large crown. She then chose her queen and crowned her with the second crown. I was sitting next to Madame Arripe, who was explaining all this to me, when the S*urveillante Générale* found the *fève* and was duly crowned King, at which point she chose me as her Queen, amid cheers of acclamation. Strangely enough, all the afternoon the line of an old French song had been repeating itself in my head: "*S'il fleurit, je serai reine*" (If it flowers, I'll be Queen) and it was so. The room was soon filled with Kings and Queens. After coffee, the girls sang French folksongs, followed by the school song, and for this special occasion they were given permission to dance in the Recreation Room for all of half an hour.

On the Tuesday before Lent came the festival of *Mardi Gras*, which was *Carnaval* to the French. For this we had a week's holiday. (It seemed that if the date of Easter was late in the year, this spring break took place in French schools at Mardi Gras; if Easter was early, the vacation was moved to Pentecost.) I spent this holiday week in the Saarland with Christel, of which more later. There was, however, another carnival-like festival day halfway through Lent, called the *Mi-Carême*. On this occasion, the boarders appeared in fancy dress and presented little items that suited their costumes (songs, dances, recitations, or skits). The usual wedding skit appeared, and I found this very interesting because it was so typically French and unlike what Australian schoolgirls would have prepared. The skit represented the civil ceremony before the Mayor at the Town Hall, which is the legal marriage in France. A church ceremony follows the next day if the couple so desire, but they are already *unis* ("united") at this civil wedding. The Mayor was impressive, dressed in black with the blue, white, and red scarf of the Republic worn bandolier-style across his chest. The bride and groom were given farcical names like *Dentifrice* (toothpaste) and *Savon* (soap), and the whole presentation was hilarious. This was another occasion when the girls were allowed to dance for a short while.

Although we had no holiday for it, there was another notable spring celebration on May 1st, which, as well as being International Labor Day, was also the *Fête du Muguet* (Lily-of-the-Valley Festival), when spring was saluted with the buying and giving of small bouquets of lily-of-the-valley gathered in the woods. There were even lily-of-the-valley cards to send to friends. In this way the school year was punctuated with traditional ceremonies and rituals. When these special occasions could be paired up with the regular Thursday holidays or extended over the weekend, it made for a number of welcome breaks in the school routine.

Rosenmontag: Learning about German Village Life

Thanks to my friendship with the German-language assistant, Christel, I had my first glimpse of a European village that maintained traditional customs and values. She invited me to visit her family in Marchweiler in the Saarland during the Mardi Gras break. Marchweiler was in a frontier area where its natural wealth in coal and iron made it vulnerable to annexation by both France and Germany, without respect to the interests and desires of the people. Hitler had reunited the Saar with Germany by plebiscite in 1934 and France had retaken it after the war, since its coal nicely complemented the iron of Lorraine — another frequently disputed frontier region. France had established the Saar as an autonomous region, linked economically with France under the supervision of a French High Commissioner. From my first day in Saarland, when I fell into conversation with a fellow traveler on the train, it was clear that the people of the Saar felt themselves to be German; they talked German and their customs and style of living were German. For the most part their relatives lived in Germany, yet under the French administration of the time they could not cross the border to visit them, unless they had a medical certificate to say that the relative was dying.

In anticipation of my visit I had tried to brush up my German from my Assimil book, *Deutsch ohne Mühe* (German without Toil) with its dialogues for memorization and practice exercises. I gave myself a crammed two weeks before I left, brushing up on what I had learned on my sea voyage to Europe. Soon I was able to say that I was married or divorced but not single and that I was dead but not alive. None of these expressions, as far as I could see, would be very useful to me in Marchweiler.

Christel's family was a traditional one with father, mother, and adult daughter living downstairs with the great-grandfather of eighty-nine, and a married daughter living upstairs with her husband and baby son. As a family they were deeply religious Catholics and the father said long graces, with Paternosters and Ave Marias, before each meal. As Christel's father explained to me, he had been a Nazi during the Hitler period, because as a civil servant party membership was expected of him. It seems that in the Saar under Hitler people knew only what they were told by the propaganda machine. They believed that Germany had been attacked and that Communism and the Soviet Union's designs on Germany posed a great danger to the Fatherland. They all assured me they had heard very little about Hitler's race theories. Since there were no Jews in the village, they had known nothing about that aspect of Hitler's regime. Christel's brother had died in a Russian prisoner-of-war camp and the son-in-law had been a prisoner of the Americans and the French. Christel's sister had been a military nurse. I have spoken earlier about Christel's psychological state of confusion after her complete disillusionment with the things that had absorbed her heart and mind since childhood. She told me that she felt she could never again be enthusiastic about anything, that something had died within her. At this stage, she was desperately seeking a direction for her life.

I was soon learning German alongside baby Klaus, called *Bubi,* at the level of *Auto-toot-toot* and *Zug - ch, ch, ch, ch.* He soon became very fond of his Tante Vilga. Since no one in the family spoke English apart from Christel, I listened carefully and tried to work out what they were talking about, occasionally inserting little interjections or short phrases that I hoped were reasonably appropriate. I greatly regretted my meager vocabulary, which prevented me from getting more than the drift of the conversations. The great-grandfather particularly was most disappointed that he could not converse with me freely. For several days, I waited anxiously for an opportunity to insert one of my carefully memorized Assimil sentences into the family conversation, but none of them were appropriate. One morning, having come down to breakfast a little ahead of Christel, I seized the opportunity to say to her mother, in my best German accent, *"Ist Ihre Tochter noch oben?"* (Is your daughter still upstairs?) Since this was the only complete sentence I uttered in German during my visit, this broke the family up. So much for the value of learned dialogues in real discourse.

Marchweiler was a village of thirty to forty thousand inhabitants, which would be a large town in comparison with the Kerangs (3,000) and Yarrams (1,500) of Victoria. By contrast, because it was dependent on a still larger center of population and industry, it seemed to lack the autonomous activity of Australian country towns. It was in a region of forest-clad hills that must have been very beautiful in the spring, summer, and autumn. The village was spotlessly clean, the houses fresh with paint, and the gardens well kept. Most of the two or three-storied houses, however, were built directly onto the street. In village style, everyone knew everyone and, when we went walking, Christel was greeted with "Tag" by everyone we met. The little girls all wore long woollen stockings and the boys squarish, visored caps or brightly-colored knitted caps with big pompoms. Since it was still winter, the ground in the mornings was covered with frost. Spring was on the way, however, as evidenced by the little cats' tails (catkins) hanging down from the branches of the hazel bushes. Little tits were everywhere and even some robins and the ubiquitous crows.

In their village way, people seemed to feel authorized to criticize others and keep them in line. Christel, who was wearing the bobby socks so popular at the time, was greeted with many personal remarks from the miners and people waiting with us on the railway platform: "Hey! You've forgotten your stockings!" they cried. Christel explained to me that in small villages everyone behaved and dressed alike. Since it was the custom to wear long stockings in the winter, they found her modern look somewhat shocking.

In the agricultural village of Illingen where Christel was born and where her godfather was the parish priest, all the houses were huddled around the church steeple — again typical of an old village. Each house had a byre for the cattle built under the same roof as the family home, with a large door for the cattle and a small door above it for the hens. In front of each house was a square area marked off for the straw from the cowshed, which could be seen steaming in the morning air when it had just been cleaned out of the byre. There were no fences in the village and people hung their ladders and farm implements on the outside walls of their homes. Christel was very surprised when I asked: "Aren't they afraid someone will steal them?" Apparently such things just did not happen, whereas in areas without strong ties and traditions these things might well have vanished overnight.

Christel and I decided to attend Mass in the old thirteenth-century Abbey Church in the village of Tholy. The church was practically empty when we arrived, so we took seats discreetly at the back. Very soon the church began to fill rapidly, with men on one side and women on the other. When one woman came in and sat on the men's side, the village women, who were correctly seated, soon glared her out of her inappropriate place. Eventually we found ourselves being pushed gently but firmly out of our back row seats by their regular occupants and were obliged to stand at the back. It seemed the seats in the church were auctioned off at Christmas to raise money, so all the seats were paid for. Soon the space behind the pews was packed with those who couldn't afford to buy seats or were visitors like us. It was hardly the most welcoming church I had attended. The service was in Latin, with the hymns and sermon in German. As a further surprise, the congregation rose to remain standing during the whole of the sermon. I hoped they did not have too many long-winded preachers.

On Rosenmontag children roamed the streets in fancy dress, asking for (and getting) little hotcakes, which the housewives had prepared in great quantities. In Saarbrucken cafes and shops were decorated and in the evening there were masked balls. To keep up our energy, we regaled ourselves with piping hot German sausage in long rolls, beautiful cream cakes, and pretzels. Despite the fact that seventy per cent of the city had been damaged during the war, much of it devastated, people were enjoying life in their traditional way. I had to admire their spirit.

12
LIFE IN PICARDY
1950

Living among the close-knit group of resident staff at the lycée at Douai, I came to know them very well. I felt that the French were more like Australians than the English, and this was borne out in part by the fact that the French members of the group seemed to adapt to me more easily than to the assistant from England. They had an openness of approach and a friendliness with everyone that did not come so easily to the English, who seemed to be preoccupied with "keeping up appearances." With this frankness, things that might have been kept hidden in other countries seemed to come to the surface here in the North of France. Perhaps it was because of this difference in approach that my French colleagues kept asserting that English people were hypocritical, maintaining certain ideals vocally, but not living up to them in fact and not acknowledging their faults in front of others. I felt there was a certain through-and-through sincerity about the French and a great sense of loyalty in friendships, which I have continued to marvel at through the years. The French people I came to know in the North were very home-loving, friendly, and hospitable and, at least at that time, the girls I met lived quieter lives than Australian girls of the same age. My young student colleagues, for instance, with their dormitory supervision, were not allowed to leave their dormitory cubicles after the girls had gone to bed at 9 p.m., which was when private life began for the young resident mistresses at St Annes. The girls in my classes seemed very much like the girls I had taught in Australian schools, except that they chattered to me in French instead of English and were a little more excitable. The setting, however, was very different for an Australian. So much around me, in behavior as in places, was rooted in the past. All the European history, legends, and stories I had read since childhood seemed to reflect reality so much more in their native settings and to grip me more vividly. That is why, I suppose, I found all the festivals so fascinating.

In this all-girls school there seemed to be a great fear of close intimate friendships between young women, which might acquire passionate undertones. I had always considered this part of female adolescent development, particularly in unisex environments, as at MacRob and St Annes and now here at the Lycée de Jeunes Filles at Douai. One of the senior girls, a very popular girl and the school pianist, became very friendly with Micheline, the lively young *maîtresse d'internat* — too friendly from the point of view of the other girls. She was seen frequently in Micheline's company and was accused by her fellow students of telling her too much that she might relay to the Principal. Consequently, the other girls sent the student to Coventry (*à la quarantaine*), despite the fact that the day before they had given her a triple "*ban*" (where the girls clap 123, 123, 123, 1 2 3 three times) as a special tribute of appreciation. That Micheline relayed anything to Madame Arripe was most unlikely, not only because of her solidarity with the girls but also because of Madame Arripe's inaccessibility and her intimidating demeanor, but this close friendship had been noticed and commented on by all. On another occasion, before one of the school holidays, a note was picked up in which one of the younger girls had written to a senior, in passionate terms, declaring how very much she would miss her over the break. Consequently, all the girls were forbidden during recreation to walk around the courtyard on the narrow walkway beside the windows, in case one of them might be tempted to use the windowsill to write a note to a fellow student. This seemed to overlook the many other possibilities for writing such notes.

The Lycée was always locked and barred within its solid convent walls. Since the concierge went off duty at nine in the evening, any of us who wanted to go out in the evenings had to take a big, heavy key for the entrance. Since there was only one key for the nine of us, this caused many hassles. The walls were quite unscaleable. Occasionally one of the senior supervisors would lend us a key; otherwise we had to resort to getting a very grumpy concierge out of bed in the middle of the night. The concierge was normally very friendly and liked to chat to me freely in French when I went for my mail. When Christmas came, with its flood of mail with obviously foreign stamps, he suddenly decided I was a foreigner and began to talk to me in pidgin French, which he had never used before: "*Noël, comprend, Noël mange dinde*" (Christmas, understand, Christmas eat turkey"). He soon got over that stage, fortunately, and returned to normal speech. I had already found that the French seemed proud of the fact that they were not strong in geography. I spent my time explaining that Australia was not "on the other side of Germany," for instance. Soon after my arrival I had explained to the concierge where I came from, so I was very surprised one day when he said to me: "Come and look. I have something here from your country" and produced a can of sardines from Portugal. When I protested that I was not from Portugal, he exclaimed: "Portugal or Norway, what's the difference!"

Since we had all become very friendly, Paule came to a brave and broadminded decision that requires a little background explanation. Paule's family home was in Saint-Quentin, an important town since Roman times. Situated on the Somme, it was at the crossroads of commerce from the north to Paris. Its textile industry had been famous from the 12th century on, based at first on wool and later flax for the production of linen and fine tulles. From the time of Napoleon, it had been linked with the extensive canal system of the north, bringing coal to Paris, and heavy industry developed in the late 19th century. A famous center of medieval pilgrimage, its striking, Flamboyant Gothic collegiate basilica, built from the twelfth to the fifteenth centuries, sheltered the sacred relics of St Quentin, the evangelizer of Picardy. Many miraculous cures have been attributed to St Quentin since his brutal martyrdom at the end of the third century. The *Son et Lumière* (Sound and Light) evenings at the cathedral in summer are spectacular and informative. The Saint-Quentin area is noted for its fancy-dress parades and marching bands for the Carnival of Pentecost. In a remarkably beautiful central square is the highly decorated, 15th century Gothic Town Hall, with a carillon of thirty-seven bells. One of the proud possessions of Saint-Quentin is its extensive exhibition of the pastels of native son Quentin de la Tour, who was a famous portraitist at the court of Louis XV in the eighteenth century.

Unfortunately Saint-Quentin was also on the main route over the centuries for invaders coming from the north through the Low Countries, whether it was the English in the Hundred Years' War or the Spaniards and Austrians in the 16th and 17th centuries. Nor was it spared the ravages of the continual civil strife from the 16th century Wars of Religion to the French Revolution at the end of the 18th century, when the basilica became for a time a Temple of Reason. The Germans had invaded this area in three successive wars from 1871 to 1939, the Belgian frontier being a mere sixty kilometers away across flat, unobstructed land. Besieged in 1871, during the Franco-Prussian war, Saint-Quentin suffered much destruction. From 1914 to 1918 it was invaded again and occupied by the Germans. This time the devastation was so extensive that when it was liberated only two hundred houses remained intact, and the empty walls of the basilica rose in mute protest over the rubble. Residential areas, factories, bridges, all were gone. With true Picardian tenacity, the town was rebuilt, largely in the exuberance and fantasy of the Art Deco of the early twentieth century.

During the Second World War, Saint-Quentin was incorporated by Germany into the Occupied Zone, thus being to all intents and purposes annexed. During its liberation in 1944, it again suffered severe devastation, including enormous damage to the great collegiate church. My friend Paule's grandparents and parents had suffered personal property damage and much psychological trauma through three wars against the same enemy. Paule's father had been demobilized from the French Army in 1941 in the South of France, at the time when his home region had become the strictly controlled Occupied Zone. No one in the family had any idea of his whereabouts, since any communication with the so-called Free Zone of the Vichy regime was strictly prohibited. In danger of being shot on sight, he had had to make his way back surreptitiously across the Free Zone into the closely policed zone around Saint-Quentin to rejoin his family. He had quite a saga to recount.

Paule was anxious to make the foreign assistants at the lycée feel welcome in her country and in her own region of Picardy, but she did not want to discriminate among us. She had, however, to think carefully, just five years after the war, before inviting a German like Christel, to her home, where not only her parents but also her grandmother lived. Nevertheless she did invite us all — Ena, Christel, and me — and her family were most gracious to us, doing everything possible to make us feel welcome. During my year at Douai I paid several visits to Saint-Quentin and I have been invited there on innumerable occasions since. In some ways it has become a second home for me in France. Saint-Quentin, with vivid memories of the dreadful Somme campaign of 1917, is surrounded by military cemeteries of various Allied nations. It is also close to the place where the Germans signed the Armistice at the end of the First World War and the spot where, in a railway carriage, Germany signed the surrender document marking the end of the World War 11. I have found it very moving to visit the Australian and Canadian war cemeteries, especially since Saint-Quentin was a name I had seen engraved on the many First World War monuments in Victoria's cities and small towns. I have also traveled widely in the surrounding area, visiting the interesting fortified churches of the Thiérarche, which very few visitors to France seem to know about. There are more than fifty of these, some dating from the twelfth century, but most fortified in the 16th and 17th centuries when this area was the site of so many civil and defensive wars. I have always enjoyed strolling along the tree-lined canals of Saint-Quentin, which form part of a system linking the Low Countries to the north with Paris to the south, via the Seine and Somme rivers. I have enjoyed the annual exhibition of the Roses of Picardy in the extensive public park, the Champs Elysées, which is built over the area of the former city ramparts. I have also had several opportunities to admire what is perhaps the largest butterfly collection in the world, bequeathed to Saint-Quentin in 1912 by a wealthy local collector.

Paule's father worked in a brewery, a not surprising occupation in an area where the light beer of the region was the preferred drink on most occasions. This was the beer the students drank at table in the lycée. Paule's mother was a primary school teacher, very devoted to her students and very kind to me. As one might expect in this industrial area, Paule's family were strong Socialists and trade union supporters. Their house, in French style, was a narrow one, three-storied, with a narrow garden at the back full of the roses one expects to see in Picardy. Paule's aunt and grandmother lived upstairs. The grandmother, born and bred in Saint-

Quentin, spoke the Picardian patois of the area. She had been asked by the family not to speak patois while I was visiting. One evening, when we were at table, to my surprise I heard grandmother say something quite incomprehensible, at which everyone burst out laughing. Grandmother blushed a deep red. She had become so interested in the conversation that she had automatically burst into patois.

Life Outside the Lycée

I was soon seizing opportunities to integrate myself into the life of Douai outside my resident working environment. As was my usual custom, I sought out a church family. I had a choice between the Roman Catholic and the Protestant church (*Eglise Réformée de France*). I chose the latter, which was very much a minority church in the North, representing about one per cent of the population. I soon found myself part of a group of about a hundred people, who were very friendly and welcoming, much more so than at the majority Anglican church in Kenilworth. The Reformed service at the Temple was rather like a Presbyterian service, which reflected the Calvinist origin of both, with some elements similar to Anglican worship. I must admit that it took me some time to feel I was really praying or meditating on spiritual questions in French, since that aspect of my life had been so richly experienced in English. However, I gradually became accustomed to the switch. Soon I was being invited regularly into French homes, especially for the long, leisurely family dinners on Sundays, and treated as a valued friend. In these French homes, I played with more little children and continued to learn informal French from the mouths of babes. The Pastor and his wife had seven children, aged from two to thirteen, so when I visited them I found the *goûter* (afternoon snack time) for the hungry children rather like a Sunday School picnic — there were so many *tartines* of bread and jam to be prepared. I also discovered that French children had a lot of homework to do at an early age. As soon as they had eaten, all but the very youngest were packed off to get on with their *devoirs*. I would occasionally be asked to help set the table — a simple enough task, it would seem. I realized the table setting was quite different in France when I saw the hostess surreptitiously rearranging the cutlery before dinner began. I had also to learn little things like where to rest my knife and fork during intervals of eating, as well, of course, as keeping my hands on the table, as Georges had taught me in Paris. It was like being a small child again. Ena and Christel did not have the same opportunities for social contact outside the lycée that I had, since they attended a big, impersonal Catholic church. Christel had a boyfriend in Germany of strongly left-wing views; he had converted to Protestantism and was studying to be a pastor. As time went on, she began to come with me to some Protestant services and meetings.

With my Protestant friends I took part in Bible studies and youth groups where, apart from lively singing, there were very frank discussions. Young French people, I found, came right out with their personal feelings and experiences, more frankly than young Australians, which made for very profitable discussions from the start. Some of these discussions even got a bit out of hand in the general excitement. Sometimes we went out in groups to visit small communities outside of Douai, where little groups of newly converted Protestants were trying to establish their own places of worship. One group, living in the center of the coal mines, with slag heaps everywhere, had transformed an Army hut into a charming little chapel, right beside the first pit that had opened in the area. At the Temple, I met some very interesting people, like the local bookseller and his wife, who frequently invited me to Sunday dinner, and the Principal of the Teacher Training College for Boys (*Ecole Normale de Garçons*).

The church had a club called *Le Cercle de l'Homme*, which seemed to me to be translatable as "Men's Club," to which I was promptly invited. At first I demurred, saying that I presumed such a club would be for the men of the parish only, as in Australia. "The men wouldn't be interested in coming if the women weren't there," they assured me. This was so different from the attitude toward women in Australia at that time, and even in the sixties when I was at Monash University in Melbourne. At the churches I had attended in my home city there had always been clubs exclusively for men and boys, and the bars had been completely segregated by unspoken understanding. Even at professional gatherings in Melbourne the men would go off together to discuss things, without women to disturb their discussions, and at dances in country towns the men would be on one side of the room and the women on the other. Here, in this

441

"Men's Club" in Douai, I enjoyed a series of interesting lectures and much vigorous discussion of the kind that I have always found stimulating. At the end of April, I spoke to the group on Australia. This was my first public lecture in French and I lectured for an hour and a quarter, fielding many questions afterwards. The lecture was very well received, which was encouraging to me and confirmed my own feeling that I had made much progress during the year in handling the language at a sophisticated level. I found French people at this time, even educated people, knew very little about Australia and there were many differences to explain. My French colleagues, for instance, were very surprised to hear that in 1950 we did not have equal pay for equal work for men and women and they were shocked that, as a high school teacher in Victoria, I had received only sixty per cent of a male teacher's salary. I don't think they would have felt comfortable either with the Australian relations between the sexes at that time, when women were expected to defer to male opinions with a "Yes, dear! Of course, dear! You know best, dear!" attitude.

Outside the Temple every Sunday copies of the Protestant Church's newspaper, *La Réforme,* were sold. This paper gave an impartial, intelligent presentation of the week's news, somewhat along the lines of the *Christian Science Monitor* in the United States. It was highly respected among non-Protestants as well. Through it, I was able to keep up with what was going on in France and in the world and read interesting discussions on economic, social, and artistic trends. It certainly provided a refreshing alternative viewpoint to *L'Humanité.* I found *La Réforme* so interesting and useful that I subscribed to it for some years after I returned to Australia. It provided me with much up-to-date reading on France that I could use for class discussions with my students, while the puzzles and games it published for the holidaying French during July and August proved very useful in stimulating the interest of my advanced classes. I would post these on the class bulletin board and my students would swarm around them between classes.

During my period in France, I always tried to avoid getting into a coterie of English native speakers or of Swedes, Argentinians, and others who wanted to practice their English. I spent as much time as I could with French native speakers. I had worked and saved hard for this opportunity to absorb authentic French and I did not intend to

442

dissipate it through inability to resist social pressures. Among the English-speaking students at Lille, and later at Montpellier, the temptation to party together was great. Instead I spent my time with my French friends and those foreign students who wanted to speak only French. Consequently, after fifty years, I still have close friends I met in my Douai and Montpellier days. The French were excited talkers and so was I. I often thought back to the lengthy discussions Linda and I had had in our young days together and how we had frequently interrupted each other and ended up both talking at once. With this background I did not feel at all on the outer in France. I also appreciated the French *faire le mur* attitude: if they felt hemmed in by demands they did not feel were justified or which they did not want to meet, they would prefer to "jump the wall." This seemed very consistent with the attitude of the swagman in Australia's favorite song, *Waltzing Matilda*, who sprang into the billabong, rather than allow his activity to be curtailed by unwelcome and resented authority.

I was still working at this time on my pronunciation, which had certain persistent inauthentic elements. I had begun learning French with teachers with an Australian accent and little scientific knowledge of sound systems. Had I known then what I know now about contrastive problems of articulation of what may seem to be similar sounds, as well as the production of sounds unique to French. I could have made faster progress in this area. Our learning of phonetics in the thirties, unfortunately, had mainly consisted of learning to transcribe French discourse correctly into the symbols of the International Phonetic Alphabet. The texts we transposed were usually written ones. Without some kind of associated sound practice, this is a purely intellectual exercise. I was finally becoming aware of the fact that there was hardly a sound in French that had an exact equivalent in English. Apart from the problems of vowels (usually emphasized by teachers and textbooks), there were the consonants. The formidable French "r" was not the only stumbling block; even p's, b's, l's, t's, g's, and k's were different. I, like so many others, had learned French sounds piecemeal, instead of learning them as part of a system in which the various parts interact in a language-specific way. I had not realized the degree to which incorrectly pronounced consonants affected the vowels that preceded and followed them and vice versa. This defective early training had left me with quite a problem, because inauthentic sounds that did not interfere with comprehension had become ingrained or fossilized. Furthermore, although I could understand and be understood perfectly well, I had not achieved as yet the stage where I could reveal my personality as fully as I would have liked in communication. I could not as yet insert the little shared allusions, the nuances, and the ironic touches that make conversation more interesting. Nor was I able to joke and tell funny stories as I normally did in English — not because I couldn't construct these in French but because I couldn't yet do so quickly enough to insert them rapidly into the exchange. With joking, timing and correct tone of voice and expressions of the face are crucial. This gradually became possible, but, while I was working toward it, I tended to compensate by acting the fool in small groups as a kind of outlet.

Studies at the University of Lille

The third important segment of my life in France was my period as a student at the University of Lille, which at the time was widely considered to be the best university in France after the Sorbonne; many famous professors had made their way to appointments in Paris by way of Lille. In 1949, Professor Antoine Adam, the famous seventeenth-century literary critic, was at Lille. His stimulating lectures were exceedingly popular, and he particularly enjoyed teaching the overseas students who came to Lille from many countries. I was able to profit from this preference of his. In 1949, the University of Lille, with about six thousand students, was one of the biggest in France. It had not yet become the technological center it is today.

Lille was part of a tri-city, with Tourcoing and Roubaix. It was an area of extensive woollen industries that used Australian and New Zealand wool, and everywhere I would see references to *Laine Pingouin* (Penguin Wool). The three cities met at a crossroads. Lille was the administrative, commercial, and academic city; Tourcoing was the beautiful garden home of the bourgeois factory owners and merchants, with residences in an infinite variety of architectural styles; Roubaix was the working man's city with squalid, badly maintained *corons* (long, uninteresting rows of identical, attached workers' cottages). The badly paid workers of Roubaix had only to walk to the crossroads to see how the other half of society lived in beautiful Tourcoing. It was no wonder that communism was flourishing in this area of the very Catholic north. There was no need to write pamphlets about inequality; it was all written in dirty brick.

Like other towns in the north, the apartment buildings in Lille were built directly on to the street. It took me a few moments to begin to notice among the usual street doors the great arched doorways with bells and bell ropes, which opened on to large courtyards, sometimes with gardens, giving access to the various apartments of the building. I always felt there was something mysterious about these great doors (which one also sees in parts of Paris) and I enjoyed the little glimpses I got of the "other life," whenever I happened to pass just as someone was going in or coming out. The streets of these Northern towns were made of *pavés* (very small, square blocks of stone). I was told that this had something to do with the consistency of the soil in the region, and certainly the constant rain must have exacerbated the problem. In these towns the women could not walk around in high heels and I too had to resort to solid, flat-heeled walking shoes. Outside of the town were workers' plots where working people could grow vegetables, and in the autumn you would see people carrying out to their plots sacks of dead leaves to protect the plants from the rigors of winter. One of the dreamy sights of Lille, as of other towns in the North, was the view in autumn of the many tree-lined canals with their long, low *péniches* (barges), loaded with coal and other goods. These vessels drifted slowly along between banks of richly colored, late autumn foliage, with leaves floating lazily down at every puff of wind. Nearby were the *marécages* (marshes) where market gardeners traveled by boat to the different sections of their vegetable gardens along the waterways in between. I loved to walk along the ancient, double-walled, star-shaped fortifications of Lille, which had been completely rebuilt by Vauban, the famous architect of Louis XIV. Along the remains of the moat trickled the tiniest of streams. Always there was the misty atmosphere typical of Flanders, of which Lille was the capital, which made the spot even more poetic and romantic, and there was an invigorating freshness in the late November air, as I made my way back to my classes.

The city complex was close to the Belgian border and one day. when I was exploring Lille with Paule, we ended up going on to Belgium by tram. It was amusing to be offered Algerian carpets for sale on the tram itself. There were already many Algerians living in France in 1949. Only in France was I ever asked to buy a carpet while drinking a cup of coffee at a sidewalk cafe. From the tram we walked straight into Belgium, with the most casual of checks at the border, along the same road that began in Halluin in France and continued as the main shopping street of Menin in Belgium. The close link between French and Belgian Flanders, indicated by this casual melding and the similar architecture, was not merely that of common suffering through two world wars. The people were cousins. Once over the border, I found myself in another bilingual country like Wales, with all the notices in Flemish and French. People switched with the greatest of ease from one language to the other. Paule was amused because, in the local dialect, the Belgians used both the formal *vous* and the informal *tu* with complete strangers and sometimes mixed the two in the one sentence. As we wandered around, we heard music and came across a street with bright paper decorations across the road. We had come upon a celebration of the Dove and Pigeon Lovers' Club, pigeon racing being the great enthusiasm of this area. I thought immediately of the boy in Sandwich who loved pigeons. He certainly would have felt at home in Menin.

Getting down to Business

For my studies, I had decided to begin with a Diploma in French Studies for foreigners, which at Lille was taught at the Licence (undergraduate) level by regular University lecturers, and to undertake at the same time my first *Certificat* for the *Licence ès Lettres* (Arts degree). With the equivalences I had been granted for my Australian degrees, I needed to complete only three *Certificats*. For this first attempt at studying side-by-side with French students, I had chosen Phonetics, as did a number of other foreign students, who were as anxious as I was to speak in a more authentically French manner.

On the day the University classes began in mid-November, Ena, Christel, and I rushed off from our lycée lunch for the train that would get us to Lille by one o'clock. This would leave us a full hour to roam the streets and look at the shop windows, while the university library and commercial Lille took their customary, two-hour, midday break. At five to two we entered the university, looking for Salle C. The impressive entrance hall to the Faculty of Arts building led to two poky, little, graveled courtyards, across one of which we found our room. Salle C was like any university classroom, except that it looked out directly onto a dull, gray stone wall. Assembled in the room was a motley group of some twenty-five students from eleven countries, most of whom were language teaching assistants like ourselves. A succession of lecturers followed hour by hour. They were a most varied lot. One had the amusing habit of saying *n'est-ce pas* ("isn't it?" or "don't you think?") at the end of every phrase he uttered, sometimes reducing it to an almost inaudible *spa.* The temptation to jot down a check mark each time we heard it was great, and we discovered that he could manage about three hundred and eighty *n'est-ce pas* during a one-hour lecture. This was a diversion from the French grammar he was teaching. The next lecturer paraded from one side of the room to the other in long strides, as he tried to stimulate discussion on "What is a Frenchman?" The lecturer in charge of the Translation class believed in eliciting impromptu oral translations of difficult passages, instead of requiring written translations over which we would have sweated for hours, poring over a dictionary. This was a valid idea educationally and very challenging, but we suspected his motivation was really to cut down on the amount of work he would have to correct. Of course, his method saved us preparation time as well, even if it did little to perfect our translation skills. After a dull disquisition on historical French grammar by a serious and solemn academic, we were woken up and considerably enlivened by Monsieur Adam's literature lecture. A cheery, older man, he proceeded to tell us that since students remembered only digressions in lectures he had developed a method of lecturing mostly by digressions; this was heartening and ensured that his lectures were always packed. Ena, Christel, and I found him so entertaining that we nearly missed our fast train back to Douai. The next train, being an Omnibus stopping at all stations, would have brought us back to a cold, held-over dinner.

I soon made many friends among the students in Lille. The first day of classes I heard what sounded like an Australasian accent and came across a New Zealander, Ralph, who was language assistant at a lycée for boys in Lille. New Zealanders in France at that time found French ignorance of their country rather annoying. The French, it seemed, knew even less about New Zealand than about Australia, thinking of it as a small island off the coast of Australia and as part of the Australian Commonwealth. There was also a Scottish student, Eric, who always looked depressed and oppressed. He was assistant at a coeducational school, which was a rarity in France at the time. When I asked him whether the boys and girls mixed well at the school, he replied laconically and pessimistically: "Too well!" Peter, from Cambridge University, was the University *lecteur* (tutor) and was expected to run an English club, which we sometimes attended to help him out. He found the French students ill-prepared for running things themselves, never having been given any responsibility during their lycée years; consequently, he had to come up with all the ideas himself. Michael was a Londoner, who traveled to Lille for classes from the lycée in Arras. It was with Michael that Ena was always jousting about accent. To complete our English-speaking group, there was a cheerful American from the University of Iowa called Luther Gillett. Gil, as he preferred to be called, was a very affable guy who wore colorful American shirts. At this time when most men still dressed conservatively in gray or black suits with suitably subdued ties, Gil would appear in a green and white shirt or one in gray, pink, and blue with pretty pictures all over it, or he would wear a bright red pullover with skiers flying down the front. He was not a language-teaching assistant but was living in Lille on a Fulbright Fellowship grant. Very chatty and unpretentious, of a gregarious temperament, Gil took to meeting the three of us from Douai at the railway station, in order to enjoy our company before lectures. He was the first American I had ever known well and I found him to be very open and generous. There is one gesture I always associate with Gil. He loved chocolate and, when he met me at the station, he would ask me if I would like some chocolate. Then, instead of breaking off a section to offer me, he would break the chocolate block and give me half. We became very good friends and kept in touch for many years. The French girls were very surprised at our calling these English-speaking fellow students immediately by their first names. They had a much more formal custom, calling each other Monsieur and Mademoiselle for quite a while. Even adding the surname to the title (as in Monsieur Dubois) was an indication that they knew the person quite intimately and Monsieur Jacques or just Pierre was quite a step further. I found this Monsieur/Madame pattern of address of the French to be useful for oiling the wheels of social contact, in that you gave no offense if you had forgotten the name of a new acquaintance.

Another fellow student was a Czech refugee called Olga. In Czechoslovakia she had been a forestry student, as had her fiancé. Not being a Communist she had been labeled a reactionary and, when the universities were "purified," she had had to leave her family and fiancé and flee the country. After four months in Germany and three months in Italy, she had reached Arras in Northern France. There she was teaching a few classes of German at a convent school, where the nuns offered her shelter. She was unable to return home and her fiancé could not leave Czechoslovakia. Her family was not allowed to communicate with her, although she did receive some messages by underground channels. She had no money and even the clothes she wore had been given to her. To survive she was learning French as fast as she could. Another friend with a traumatic personal story was Wanda, a Polish student who lived with her husband in an apartment in Lille. In 1944, when she was eighteen and fighting with the Polish Resistance against the Germans in Warsaw, Wanda had been wounded twice and had a deep bullet-hole in her neck to prove it. The Russians had promised to support the Resistance when they rose against their German occupiers, but instead they had stayed on the other side of the river and allowed Warsaw to be devastated. Taken off to prison camp in Germany, Wanda had nursed Russian soldiers. It was in France that she had met and married Stefan, who had also been a member of the Polish Resistance. Add to this mixture Christel and her traumatic Nazi past and our group became quite a microcosm of postwar Europe. These living, breathing friends represented the kinds of casualties of war that are not counted in official statistics. When examination time came I had reason to be very grateful to Wanda and Stefan. The University had scheduled our examinations at seven thirty in the morning, a time at which it was difficult for many students, including those of us at Douai and Arras, to get to Lille. Fortunately, I was able to stay overnight with Wanda and Stefan, which solved my problem nicely.

Examinations were, however, still a long way off. A two-week Easter break loomed ahead of me. Since I was so close to the Low Countries, then called Benelux, I was agog to see this area, which had been so pivotal in European history over the centuries. Christel and Ena were anxious to come too, as was our New Zealand friend, Ralph. Paule had introduced us to an inexpensive way of traveling with *Tourisme et Travail* (Touring and Work), which had been organized by student unions as a gesture of friendship with students in other countries. In the different places we visited we would be welcomed by students and stay at a very low rate in student dormitories. It was hoped that through these contacts students would form bonds across national boundaries. As it turned out, the twenty students in our so-called "French" tour group came from twelve countries as different from each other as Egypt and Guatemala, Tunisia and Brazil. This was an international bonding experience in itself. The three French students with us were of Russian and Armenian descent. That no one in the group was of purely French origin amused us very much when we were officially welcomed in different places with long speeches about how much our visit would increase mutual understanding between France and the Benelux countries.

Bureaucratie (Officialdom)

Before I left France, I had, of course, to check that all my papers were in order for crossing borders. I had already discovered that my life in France required a lot of waiting in line to get the correct permits for this and that. I needed a *Carte de Séjour* to stay in the country, a *Carte de Travail* to be able to work while there, and a *Carte d'Immatriculation* to permit me to study at the university. Obtaining these government permits always required me to produce several copies of a photograph showing my right ear (the left ear was for French citizens) and the authorities were always interested in my mother's maiden name. At a later date I discovered the importance of proper registration of my permanent address on a *Carte de Domicile* as well.

At one stage, Linda, now in India, sent me a birthday present made of silver. This was such a common metal in Hyderabad in India where she was living that, beaten exceedingly thin, it was actually put on desserts and eaten. The customs officials in Paris held back the

450

packet, suspecting it to be very valuable and to require the payment of a customs duty fee. I was required to present myself in person at the customs in Paris to claim it. Off I went in some bewilderment, knowing that Linda as a missionary could not afford to send me expensive presents. Eventually I located the right office and was immediately asked what was in the packet they held, which I had never seen. I continued to tell different officials that I hadn't a clue what was in the packet, a fact they seemed to find hard to accept. Finally I blurted out that, since it was from my sister who was a missionary in India, where everything was very cheap anyway, it certainly would not be worth more than a quite small sum of money. This seemed to strike a chord in the Customs Officer to whom I was speaking. From then on I was passed from official to official with the introduction that this was a present from my sister, the missionary, so, of course, no duty should be charged. Eventually I was able to leave with the packet, which contained a very nice silver necklace in Indian design. Some officials in France had a heart, it seemed, if you were able to reach it.

My worst bureaucratic experience came when I set out to get visas for my trip to Belgium, Holland, and Luxembourg. Australia had recently issued Australian passports with the Australian coat-of-arms. Inside was printed "British subject" (this was before the establishment of the Commonwealth of Nations). The Australian consular authorities had informed me that I would need visas for all countries in Europe, except Switzerland. This was something of a pill, of course. Unfortunately consuls in less central locations, like Lille, did not seem to be up-to-date on requirements for little-known countries like Australia and New Zealand, and they usually had to look up miles of files to find out what to do about them. In my search for visas I first consulted the Belgian Consul in Lille. Having looked up various files and studied my passport ponderously, he declared: "British subject by birth. No, you don't need a visa as a British subject by birth." "But this is not an English passport," I protested, "It's Australian." More studying of files, then the consul repeated firmly: "No, you don't need a visa as a British subject by birth." Since I couldn't convince him otherwise, I went on to the Dutch consulate some distance away, arriving about ten minutes after the official closing time. Fortunately no one had bothered to close the consulate. I showed my passport and asked my question. Close examination of my passport, then: "No. British subject by birth. You don't need a visa." Same protest on my part: "But, you see, this isn't an English passport. It's an Australian one." "Oh no! you don't need a visa. Anyway if you have any difficulty at the frontier, just tell them that here in Lille I told you that you didn't need a visa." So far so good. I still had to try Luxembourg. I felt a little pocket handkerchief of a state like that could not be out of step.

I found the Consulate for Luxembourg in Tourcoing. I had gone there before my university classes, so it was about half-past one. Disappointingly, there was a notice saying that the consulate was open each morning from 9-12 only. It seemed it was really a Belgian Consulate that handled affairs for Luxembourg and the lady in charge directed me around the corner to the Consul's private residence. Here a stern-looking woman came to the door and told me frostily that the Consul was not available for "*les affaires*" (business). However, despite this disclaimer, I was admitted to a very stuffy nineteenth-century drawing room, overcrowded with paintings and knick-knacks and with a huge portrait of a very old king. Then the poor old Consul came in. He must have been ninety or ninety-five; he had a long beard, a trembling voice, and a slightly wandering eye. I said I had come for information about visas for Luxembourg, to which he replied wearily: "There's no need now for visas for Belgium," without even asking my nationality. I told him gently that I wanted to go to Luxembourg and that I was an Australian. That was almost too much of a shock. "A what?" he asked. Then he questioned me on where I had come from that day and said in a relieved tone: "Oh! It's the consul in Lille who deals with people from Douai."

My next visit was to the British Consul in Lille to clarify my situation. Previously I had seen only the vice-consul, but this time I was admitted into the presence of the Consul himself. He was a tall man of military stature, with white hair and moustache. Rather abruptly he told me that although my fellow-student, Ralph, as a New Zealander, had to get visas, I didn't, because in his passport it stated: "British subject and New Zealand citizen." "That's one of the prices he has to pay for the independence he's so proud of," he informed me. Because in my passport the wording was "British subject," presumably by birth, he maintained I did not need visas. I protested,

"But this is an ordinary Australian passport." To which he replied, "No, it isn't. It's a special one. It's a British passport." So having consulted four consuls, who were unanimous in stating that I did not need visas, there was nothing else for me to do but go ahead and hope for the best, despite what the Australian authorities had told me.

Benelux Exploration

Luxembourg was fascinating in its antiquity, especially for Ralph and myself from the Antipodes. Going beyond its very modern shopping and commercial quarter, with tree-lined boulevards, clean modern buildings, and gardens and squares to give light and air, we came to the 10th century fortress city. Over time, the older city had passed through many hands, with each country (Germany, Netherlands, France, Spain, Austria, or whatever) adding its own ideas for its defense. In its final form the city was high on a hill, surrounded by thick walls running down into a deep gully, across which were a number of attractive bridges. Built into the battlemented walls were miles of tunnels and spiral staircases for the defenders, with grilled openings through which cannon barrels poked out; council and bed chambers for the generals; and casemates (underground chambers or *oubliettes*) where their enemies could languish, forgotten or ignored, for many years or for life. (I think now of a similarly extraordinary experience I had, years later, when I explored the miles of underground tunnels and extensive fortifications of the Maginot Line.)

During the Second World War, the Germans had marched quickly across Luxembourg, although it was a neutral, independent country, and forced the Luxembourgeois to fight in their army. Some escaped to fight with the Allies. Luxembourg had had a beautiful war memorial in honor of its soldiers who died in the 1914-18 war, but when tributes with the French tricolor kept appearing at this site the Germans had it razed to the ground. By 1950, the people of Luxembourg had collected as many of the stones as possible and assembled them as the "Memory of a Memory" (*Souvenir d'un Souvenir*). Their Grand Duchess Charlotte must have been proud of them.

We rounded off our trip to this small country with a visit to the *Petit Suisse Luxembourgeois* (Luxembourg's Little Switzerland), where we traveled through woods of tall, slender birch trees, their whitish trunks covered with green moss, with in between a few pussy willows in pale yellow blossom. Under the trees was a thick carpet of brown leaves from the previous autumn. Higher up the mountains, we came to the green feathery lightness of the firs, with their long, slim brown cones. Down in the valleys were small villages amid their ploughed fields, with occasional, often quite elaborate, wayside shrines. We paused for a while beside a rocky stream, wood-lined, with an attractive rustic bridge over a waterfall. Further on, we passed through narrow clefts in great outcrops of rock, vivid green with moss, and scrambled and climbed up them to see the view from the top. We even talked our way across the German frontier. "Of course, if you're French you can go through," they declared, and thus I set foot, if illegally, on the land of my Lehmann ancestors.

Brussels was our next destination. We first saw it in pouring rain. This was typical of much of the trip, since it was April. My first view of Brussels was from my hotel room, which looked out over chimney pots that could be found anywhere in the world. Brussels, it seemed to me, had tried a little too obviously to build itself on the model of Paris, with its equivalent of the Champs-Elysées and the Arc de Triomphe (here commemorating Belgian independence), but it was not so consistently beautiful and magnificently arranged as Paris, where everything seemed to fit into such a harmonious ensemble. The area around the Grande Place was the most interesting, with the magnificent facades of the Houses of the Trade Guilds or Corporations, Flemish at one end and Renaissance at the other. Facing each other were the Gothic Town Hall with a very tall, lacy spire and the equally beautiful Gothic King's House. I saw this magnificent square in the light of an absurdly huge full moon, very low and disk-like in the night sky, and in the company of a very entertaining Mexican painter, Alfonso, who was thrilled by the beauty around us. Some of the excitement of the trip came from the varied and interesting group of students with whom we traveled, two of whom were painters and two sculptors, and the tremendous amount of information we shared about our countries and cultures. This was an experience I had not had in the more or less homogeneous society in Australia prior to the Second World War. On this trip we sang many songs from the repertoire of our multinational group and that of our host students, in buses and in the various hostels where we stayed. Naturally I led them in singing "Waltzing Matilda," which was always a favorite.

Soon we were on the trail of the Flemish painters at the Brussels Art Gallery — Franz Hals, Brueghel, Rubens, Van Dyck, and the two Teniers, father and son, with their interesting scenes of the life of the Flemish people. It was a real feast. A reception by the chief municipal education officer, the *Echevin,* at the Town Hall enabled us to see its magnificent interior, part Gothic and part eighteenth century. We admired the lovely ceilings of carved wood, the beautiful Brussels tapestries, the many historical paintings of early Brussels and of famous personalities from Belgium's checkered history during her long series of occupations, and the coats of arms of the various towns in the diamond-paned windows. Like all tourists we had to see the famous sixteenth-century statue cum fountain of the little boy, Mannequin Pis, who is clothed about twenty times a year in different costumes. At the time of our visit he had about sixty-five costumes, ranging from military uniforms and national costumes of many countries to the typical garb of lawyers, youth hostelers, university students, American Indians, Japanese samurai, even Maurice Chevalier. Goodness knows how many he has now!

After buying Brussels lace, which is embroidered on net with a needle, and visiting the University of Brussels with student hosts, we plunged further into Flemish territory with a foray to Ghent. All I knew about this city came from the Browning poem: "How they brought the good news from Ghent to Aix," about the famous ride, announcing victory against the Spaniards in the early eighteenth century — a ride so furious that it destroyed two horses on the way:

"I jumped to the stirrup, and Joris, and he;
I galloped, Dirck galloped, we galloped all three....
Behind shut the postern, the lights sank to rest,
And into the midnight we galloped abreast."

Paul Revere was not the only famous rider.

In Brussels, the capital of this ethnically divided country, all public notices and shop signs had been in the two official languages, Flemish and French, whereas here, in the capital of Flanders, everything was in Flemish. I found Flemish very entertaining, because so many words recalled older forms of English. So long as one turned one's mind to Anglo-Saxon roots, they were quite comprehensible. For instance, *Verboten de Grasperken Betreden en Bloemen te Plukken* and *Hunden lopen niet in Park* were very picturesque, and the word used for a luggage porter was very like "Package Dragger," which seemed eminently appropriate. On a construction site I read: *Strong verboten op di Werken ti komen.* On a later trip I followed this progression of related dialects with great interest through Denmark, Sweden, and Norway, having to make subtle adjustments along the way. As I had found in Wales, there was in Flanders a nationalist movement advocating autonomy and the exclusive use of the Flemish tongue. Many years later a dear Belgian colleague organized an international conference of applied linguists in Brussels, at which he gave the opening address entirely in Flemish. In this speech he advocated Flemish as the obvious choice for a lingua franca for the new Europe, since it did not bring with it the old rivalries of French, German, and English, and since Brussels was already the preferred meeting place for a number of European organizations. The same colleague kept doggedly to English when I introduced him to a monolingual French friend, even though he spoke French fluently.

I couldn't help but feel at home in Ghent when I saw the typically Flemish *beffroi* of the old Cloth Market, just like the one in Douai in French Flanders. The old quarter was very attractive with quaint streets of Flemish houses, each with its tall, flat, stepped pinnacle, and the Gothic towers of the churches, set off in charming fashion by picturesque canals or adorning the banks of the two waterways, the Escaut and the Lys. In the Castle of the Counts of Flanders, a great turreted fortress, we were able to visit the *oubliettes* for political prisoners and examine the instruments of torture with which the Counts had imposed their power in days now fortunately long past. There were thumbscrews, racks, guillotines, and wells that provided water for the water torture. Once one of the greatest ports in Europe, noted for its trade with England, Ghent had by the nineteenth century become a dying town, until a local weaver stole a newly developed spinning machine from England, thus enabling the factory owners to revive its commerce through cotton manufacture. Cotton mills flourished to such a degree that by 1950, when we were there, Ghent had become known as the Manchester of the North.

Of particular interest was the Bijloke Archeological Museum. Situated in the infirmary of a thirteenth-century Cistercian abbey, it commemorated the history of almsgiving with a frieze of orphans, in fourteenth-century uniforms sculptured in wood over the fireplace. Here we saw a replica of the kitchen of a Béguinage and the simple bedroom of a Béguine, a member of a medieval religious order of women, originally widows of fallen Crusaders, who did not take vows but lived and worked together in community service in a shared religious life. The real treasures of the museum were in the Trades Guilds section. In the nineteenth century, every guild had deposited in the museum examples of the best specimens of the work of its members; locksmiths, tinsmiths, gunsmiths, weavers, porcelain makers, boatsmen, sawyers, wire workers — the crafts of all were represented. Many of the exhibits were in the form of moving models. In the weaving section were deposited the first sample books of the cotton industry in Ghent. Also on display were the processional standards of all the guilds. As a museum it was unique.

I was to have a second glimpse of Ghent on May 1st, the *Fête du Travail*, or Labor Day, another school holiday, when Christel, Ena, and I came back to see the famous *Floralies* or Flower Show, held every five years. As was customary we wore little sprigs of May Day *muguet* (lily-of-the-valley). Because of the hiatus of the war years this flower show in 1950 was the first to have been held for twelve years and it was especially beautiful, with enormous crowds in attendance. A very large part of the display was given over to Belgium's national flower, the azalea, which appeared in every imaginable color, along with hydrangeas, orchids, camellias, cacti, palms, ferns, and orange and lemon trees (a rare exoticism in these cold parts, although so much a part of our Australian gardens). The flowers were displayed in garden settings, with crazy walks, tropical waterfalls and pools, or little summerhouses. I found Ghent itself even more beautiful on this second visit, when I saw it on a sunny day which brought out the reflection in the river of the succession of the three towers — St Bavon's Cathedral, St Nicholas's, and the Beffroi of the Cloth Market. Before we returned to Douai on this second visit, we took a quick trip to Ostende, where Christel, who had come from a land-locked country, saw the sea for the first time, and what a first time it was! On this glorious evening in late spring, the sea was silky and seductive, fading away to bluish silver at the horizon. The sea is utterly absorbing at moments like these.

From Ghent we continued on to Bruges, the Venice of the North, always the gem of a visit to Belgium, with its "dreaming towers" reflected in the waters of its many canals. The Memling paintings collected in St John's Hospital, where Memling completed much of his work, and the Van Eycks in the town museum more than fed our artistic appetites. It was fascinating to watch the women of Bruges, who still made lace at the doors of their cottages, with their little round tables and innumerable bobbins, crossing the threads at an incredible speed as they made little doilies or lovely edges for handkerchiefs. It was Good Friday, the day of the exposition of a very sacred relic, a flask containing several drops of the blood of Christ shed on the cross, which had been brought from the Holy Land to Bruges by the Crusaders. Since this was the five hundredth anniversary of its arrival in Bruges, even greater numbers of people than usual were lining up to kiss the flask at the Chapel of the Holy Blood in the Petite Place.

Antwerp meant Rubens. We visited his large, Italianate home, with colonnades, statues, sculptured friezes, and paved hall hung with tapestries, which led us into an Italian-style garden. Upstairs was the large, well-lighted room for his students, who contributed so much to his enormous production. We continued on to the fourteenth-century cathedral, the third largest in Europe, with its extremely tall tower. This structure is notable for its seven naves, separated by heavy stone columns. Its art treasures include two triptychs and an altar painting of the Assumption of the Virgin by Rubens, a Murillo painting of St Francis of Assisi, and a unique Leonardo Da Vinci Face of Christ, painted in oils on marble, which was captured by Flemish seamen in a raid into Italy. The mushroom-like pulpit was supported by representations of the five continents; these did not, of course, include Australia, which was still unknown to Europeans at the time when these figures were carved. A boat trip around the forty-nine miles of docks in the Port of Antwerp brought our tour through Belgium to a cold and windy end.

Holland next

In Holland we were again in English-speaking territory — and how well they spoke our language! Our young student hosts spoke English with practically no foreign accent. Even when we were visiting a soap factory, I found I could speak to workmen at random and elicit responses in very creditable English. Their comprehensible English was not all from school learning either. Many who were self-taught spoke equally well. As one Dutchman explained to me: "No one learns Dutch, so the Dutch just have to learn English, French, and German." These three languages were compulsory subjects at the time in all secondary schools. It is this facility with languages that makes the Dutch such successful international managers and gives them, along with the Swedes, such an advantage in the Europe of the second millennium. I gained the impression that the standard of education was very high, with well-trained teachers who had studied for seven years at university level before launching into practice.

Since 1950 was so soon after the loss of Holland's colonial empire, the young Dutch people I met, no matter how well educated, could foresee very little in the way of career opportunities in Holland, where the population at that time was very dense — equivalent to putting the population of the entire world into the United States. The only future many of them could anticipate was through emigration. New Zealand and Australia seemed to be their two preferred destinations at that time, despite their vivid memories of the fact that the Australian wharf laborers had helped the Indonesian revolutionaries by refusing to load Dutch ships in 1945. Sure enough, when I returned to Australia at the end of 1952, there was a great stream of Dutch families arriving to establish themselves in our country.

Our Dutch hosts assured me they could speak German with as much ease as English. They found many pitfalls in using it, however, because of the many misleading cognates to trip them up. In 1950, despite this facility, they preferred not to speak German, because they were still suffering emotionally from their treatment at the hands of the Germans during the war. The deliberate and ruthless destruction of the center of Rotterdam, for instance, as reprisal for Dutch resistance, was shocking to behold. Whole areas of the center city had been swept clear as though there had never been a busy commercial

459

center there in the past. It was horrifying to see acres and acres of cleared ground. Yet Holland was well aware of the advantage to them of rebuilding Germany's industrial base as soon as possible. The great port of Rotterdam, situated on the estuary where the Rhine flows into the Meuse, depended on German commerce. It was for this reason that Holland was a strong supporter of early admission of Germany to the European Union. As some Dutch people told me: "Amsterdam is a town with a port, but Rotterdam is a port with a town," and in Rotterdam harbor we saw many coastal and ocean-going vessels flying the flags of many nations, but particularly the Dutch flag. I feel I still have a small stake in Rotterdam, where there always seemed to be a terrific wind blowing. As I was crossing the harbor on a launch to visit the Sunlight Soap factory, suddenly zoop! my hat was on the deck and then overboard. It was my favorite maroon beret with a green feather.

The visit to the Anglo-Dutch Oil Refineries and the Sunlight Soap factory in Rotterdam gave us further evidence of the egalitarian Dutch society. Not only were these enterprises of the most modern efficiency in processing, but extremely clean, with superb workers' quarters, showers, washrooms, canteens, and recreational facilities.

Holland reminded me of Kerang in an inverted kind of way. One would not have expected similarities between a hot, dry area and a cold, wet one, but there was the same flatness to the horizon, the tall, ever-turning windmills, and the drainage channels intersecting the flat fields, resembling the irrigation channels of Kerang. Any perceived similarity was, of course, superficial. Whereas in Kerang the "canals" had existed to bring water to the thirsty land and the steel windmills to generate electricity to make the area viable, here the canals were to drain water away and the windmills to grind grain. On the flat plains of Holland there were more trees than in the Kerang area, of course, with fat dairy cattle and a few sheep grazing in lush pastures. The larger canals were indispensable for transport and it was always interesting to watch the barges going past with their great loads of raw materials from various parts of Europe. Certainly, there was no similarity in climate. In Holland, at least in April, there were constant tearing winds and sheets and sheets of rain, the land appearing even greener in the gray light. When we went to see the North Sea at Scheveningen, a tempestuous gale was whipping up the sand with such force that, when we ventured down to the shore, we had to back our way slowly and painfully up the beach to the restaurant.

And everywhere there were flowers. The constant color compensated for the dull grayness of the skies. There were flowers in the garden, in window boxes, in extensive public gardens, and in the fields and fields of daffodils, tulips, and hyacinths. People returning from the flowering fields would put garlands of daffodils, with a few red tulips intertwined, on the hoods of their cars and cyclists would wear garlands around their necks or hang them over the handlebars of their bicycles to carry with them the joyousness of the spring season. Even in the big blocks of workers' apartments in The Hague, there were flower boxes at every window. And there was a plethora of bikes, with special bike tracks everywhere, often paraleled by *Wandelpads* or walking tracks. Nuns in their habits, business representatives, school children, all were biking, biking, biking.

Even the royal family biked, it seemed. It was this identification with the life of the ordinary citizens that made the young Queen Juliana so popular. A graduate of the Law School at the University of Leyden, she insisted, whenever she returned to her alma mater, on acting as an ordinary student, not a queen — visiting all her old friends and standing up with the others, as a member of the Student Union, when the President entered. Her mother, Queen Wilhemina, had personally designed a tapestry, with a panoramic view of Leyden, for the small hall where university functions were held. The royal residence of the Dutch monarchs was not a splendid castle but a large, unpretentious manor house, very much in keeping with the spirit of the Dutch people. The Dutch, it seemed to me, liked to watch each other live. Houses were built with large windows straight on to the street and also at the back of the house, so that, as you went along, you could see straight through the house to the garden at the back and watch the family, in full view, at dinner and at play. I later found that the Dutch believed in everything being out in the open — prostitution, drugs, or what have you — considering it more controllable in this way. They seemed to feel no threat from the diverse immigrants and the many strange visitors, who stayed perhaps overly long, on the confident assumption that their Dutchness would not suffer from such surface deviations. In 1950 there was evidence everywhere of their close connections with their former colonies in the Indonesian archipelago. In Javanese coffee shops and restaurants Indonesian woven wall hangings and art objects were much in evidence, and there were many students from that distant region. There had also been considerable inter-racial marriage, as was evidenced by the diversity of appearance of the passersby.

In Delft, we were escorted around by students who had stayed back during their vacation to welcome us. The accommodation in the student hostels was fairly crude but adequate, and I was pleased to find that we had access to a shower, a rarity in Europe at that time. I had not had a shower since I left Australia sixteen months earlier and even baths had not been readily available in some places. In the dining room of the hostel, the French students were surprised that a period of silence was allowed for grace at the beginning of the meal. We were now in Protestant territory. (In 1950 Protestants were in the majority in Holland, although demographics have changed since.) The great hero of the Dutch, we soon found, was William the Silent, Prince of Orange, *Le Taciturne* as the French called him. William, the champion of Protestantism, had worked tirelessly in the sixteenth century to liberate Holland from Spanish domination and was assassinated for his pains. Statues and mementos of him were everywhere.

As our first day in Delft was Easter Sunday, Ena, Ralph and I went for our Easter Communion to the Old Catholic Church, which is separate from the Roman Catholic Church and in full communion with the Anglican Church. We found the chapel in a little room at the end of a long corridor. It was well hidden from the street, because in previous centuries the Old Catholic Church had been persecuted and forbidden to hold services. I thought of how the Pilgrim Fathers, before setting sail for America, had gone to Holland to escape religious persecution from the Anglican church and I began to realize what a mixed-up period the Reformation days had really been. The small church could hold about a hundred people and the interior was very similar in appearance to a high or Anglo-Catholic church in the Anglican tradition. The main difference was the seating of the women in the middle with the men on either side. The Prayer Book service, which was in Dutch, seemed almost like a translation of the one I was accustomed to and the hymns were very familiar, so it was easy for us

462

to follow. The sermon in Dutch provided the only obstacle, and for once I was able to evaluate the ability of the preacher purely on form, without attention to substance. He certainly seemed to be holding the attention of his listeners.

We found Dutch eating habits quite different from the French or English. For breakfast we had a kind of milk roll — there were plenty of them — with cheese, ham, uncured bacon, or jam. We drank milk, lots of it, or coffee made from coffee essence. Lunch was somewhat similar, with a heavier dinner around six p.m., as in Australia, consisting of soup, meat with four or five vegetables, and coffee. One thing the Dutch seemed to enjoy very much was a break for a substantial afternoon snack, with an abundance of cream cakes. At about four o'clock the little cafes would be full of chomping Dutch, picking up strength for the rest of the day.

The canals down most of the streets made Delft a most attractive town. It was not surprising to learn that swimming and rowing were two of the most popular sports among its inhabitants. Along some of the oldest canals the houses, on one side only, would go right down to the water's edge; other canals were tree-lined, with many little bridges. I worried a little about the open canals, unprotected by any kind of barrier, and I wondered aloud how it was that the children did not fall in the water. "Dutch children don't fall in canals!" I was told by my somewhat surprised hosts. I myself felt in constant danger of being run over on the very narrow roads beside the canals, the sidewalks being even narrower.

Of course we had to visit the tomb of William the Silent. It was in a big church in the center of Delft — a Dutch Reformed church converted from a pre-Reformation Roman Catholic church. The tomb was in the apse where the altar had been originally situated. The seats, in semi-circular arrangement, all faced a pulpit placed to the side of the church, halfway down the nave, since preaching the Word was for the Protestants the chief focus of the service. This type of arrangement, in whitewashed interiors, devoid of statues, stained-glass or ornaments, I had seen in the paintings of the famous Delft artists, like Vermeer, Pieter de Hough, and De Witt. In these you would see people standing talking in the open space where the High Altar and chapels would have been before the Reformation. We also saw the tomb of Hugo Grotius, the famous Dutch economist, whose statue graces the Great Square in Delft. Grotius is famous for escaping from prison, in a subterfuge organized by his astute mother, hiding in a box presumed to be filled with books, with his maid sitting on top. We were very taken with the traditional blue and white Delft pottery and searched energetically for antique tiles and dishes, although the modern ones in the traditional style were much more compatible with our financial means.

From Delft, we traveled on to the capital, 'T Gravenhaag (The Count's Hedge) or The Hague. We drove along the banks of many drainage canals, through countryside filled with the silhouettes of windmills and the brilliant gold of daffodil fields. Unfortunately we saw most of The Hague through heavy rain. We were glad to take refuge in the Palace of Peace, where the International Court of Justice meets. This was of great interest throughout because all the nations in the original League of Nations had contributed valuable gifts to its construction, either in the form of furnishings or raw materials, the building itself being built by Dutch workmen. It was a remarkable example of cooperation across the international community. In the large Hall of Justice where the International Court meets, the white stone of the walls was given by France; the woodwork of the dado by the United States; the stained-glass windows, representing the attaining of justice down the ages, by Great Britain; and the chandeliers, the ceiling, and the specially woven carpet by Holland. So it continued throughout the building, with a polar bear and seal fountain from Denmark in the garden; Delft blue-tiled walls; a three-and-a-half ton jasper and porphyry vase from the Czar of Russia; marble in the entrance hall from Italy; woodwork of the doors and inlaid rosewood tables from Brazil; standard lamps from Austria; grill doors constructed in Germany and Belgium; a replica of the Christ of the Andes, as a symbol of international peace, from Argentina; charming, delicate Japanese tapestries; huge, exquisite vases from China; elephants' tusks and gold inkpots from Thailand; a specially woven carpet from Turkey — the list was endless and made an unforgettably beautiful ensemble. The aspirations of the nations that had contributed were summed up in the modern figure of Justice, from the United States, which was not blindfolded as in traditional representations because justice should see clearly. The Hague also offered us a further opportunity to appreciate the painters of the

Flemish and Dutch Schools, particularly Vermeer, Rembrandt, Franz Hals, Hobbema, Rubens, Van Dyck, and Holbein, with little, homely, humorous family scenes by Maes, Steen, and Pieter de Hough. Later, at Haarlem, we were able to study Franz Hals in greater depth. The Van Gogh Museum at Nijmegen and the inimitable Ryksmuseum in Amsterdam, with the huge "Night Watch" by Rembrandt, rounded off our feast of Dutch art.

Leyden, the quintessential university town, brought our visit to its conclusion. Leyden University at the time had about five thousand students in the traditional faculties of law, medicine, arts, science, and theology, the theology classroom being in the disaffected chapel of a former convent that had been commandeered for the university. There was a real student atmosphere about the university, with a series of amusing charcoal caricatures along the walls and up the stairs, representing the various facets and temptations of student life, even to the young lawyer's first pleading, with all his listeners fast asleep. In the anteroom where students wait for their oral exams, the walls and table were smothered with the names and comments of generations of students going back several centuries, including those of Winston Churchill and Jan Smuts of South Africa, who had received honorary degrees from Leyden. Naturally, there was a portrait of *Le Taciturne* himself, William the Silent, who gave the university to Leyden, because it was one of the first towns to come to his side when he was fighting to liberate the country from the Spaniards. The Leyden students welcomed us very warmly and gave us many insights into their university life. In Delft most of our student hosts had been studying engineering and architecture; here at Leyden they were mostly students of medicine and law.

While at Leyden, we spent one wonderful day visiting the tulip and hyacinth fields. I had begun to feel that all the colored postcards I saw of the flowering fields were grossly exaggerated until I saw the real thing. They were magnificent. Fields of tulips, daffodils, and hyacinths, divided into oblong sections of contrasting colors, stretched almost to the horizon on either side of the road. Later we visited a park where the flowers grew, almost as though wild, in among the trees and by the lake. It wasn't till years later, while at a conference of the International Association of Applied Linguistics (AILA) in Amsterdam in 1993, that I saw the culmination of the flower process when I visited the incredible, automated Aalsmeer Flower Auction, the biggest in the world. The sale of the flowers was by a real "Dutch auction." Those bidding had to press a computer key, while the hand of a huge clock moved down from 10 to 1. They had no way of knowing what others were bidding or whether they could do better by waiting; the hand of the clock would stop only when the highest bid had been registered. The bidding moved very fast and required intense concentration. The assembly and distribution process was completely automated, with small wagons of plants and cut flowers moving on their computerized tracks from the entry to the market into the salesroom and out to the dispatch room, to be sent immediately all over the world. The operation was super-efficient and most impressive.

We became conscious, in Leyden, of the Dutch care for all segments of the community, when we visited some of the almshouses set up for the aged by various philanthropies.These quiet cottages, red-roofed with whitewashed walls, with a broad black band at the bottom, were very attractively grouped around peaceful, flowered courtyards. I chose my own place of retirement in one that was open to "chaste virgins and honest widows," for which I presumed I would qualify in my later years. John Robinson, the pastor to the Pilgrim Fathers, died in Leyden where the group had established a church while waiting to leave for the New World. St Peter's Church where Robinson is buried is very plain and Calvinistic in the Dutch Reformed tradition. As part of the leveling movement, even the coats of arms on the slabs of ancient tombs in the floor had been effaced, it being axiomatic that, all men being equal, individuals had no right in death to such class distinctions. To add to the traditional atmosphere, we saw in the street an ancient, elaborately painted, horse-drawn barrel organ, hand operated, bringing a little cheer to the passersby.

I spent my thirty-first birthday in Leyden, exploring an old windmill. We climbed up narrow ladders and passed through innumerable trapdoors, for about nine or ten floors, until we reached a platform immediately under the sails of the windmill and looked out over Leyden. Then we continued up to explore the machinery for grinding grain into flour. The big sails, we found, turned a vertical wheel, which in turn turned a horizontal wheel, which turned two more vertical wheels below it; these turned two more horizontal wheels that, by means of poles, operated four horizontal grindstones even further below. From the grindstones chutes carried the flour down into bags on the lower floor. The windmill was still working after many, many years of operation. Rembrandt, it seems, was born in Leyden in a mill like this. When we emerged from the mill, we were delighted to see a woman in traditional costume — a fishwife in a long black skirt and shawl, with a small, white organdie cap, with round, gold ornaments fastening it at either side. In the new millenium this would be a rare sight indeed.

Before we left Leyden, Ena decided that wooden clogs would be perfect for growing Dutch bulbs during the winter, so we set out to see what we could buy. The vendor was quite befuddled by these curious foreigners, who did not want clogs (*klompins,* as they were picturesquely called) that fit them, but a pair several sizes too large. We hardly liked to disenchant him by pointing out that they made perfect indoor containers for tulips.

We rounded off the trip with a tour of the canals of Amsterdam by motor launch, quite a different experience from our dreamy strolls along the narrow canals of Delft and Leyden, and we were able to compare Amsterdam's immense port with those of Antwerp and Rotterdam. By now, however, it was time to return to France to take up once more our studies and our teaching.

Australia in France

As I grew up in Melbourne, one place name in France resonated in my memory. It was found on all the World War 1 memorials and constantly referred to in speeches on Anzac Day. This place was Villers-Bretonneux in the Somme, an area rich in memories of the exploits of Australian diggers in the muddy trenches. When Geneviève, one of the day school supervisors at Douai, invited me to Amiens on the Somme and arranged for me to visit the school at Villers-Bretonneux on Anzac Day 1950, I was very excited.

Villers-Bretonneux was liberated from the Germans by the Australians on April 25th, 1918, and Victoria had paid for the reconstruction of the school and the hall. The gratitude of the inhabitants and their great attachment to their benefactors was very evident at the time of my visit, although thirty years had passed since the conflict. From the railway station I went along Victoria Street to the school in Melbourne Street, passing the Melbourne Restaurant on the way. Outside the school were two plaques telling of the liberation of the town by Australian soldiers. On an obelisk commemorating the giving of the school by Victoria were listed the names of such famous figures as Billy Hughes, who was Premier of Victoria at the time of the gift. The school building, paid for by contributions from the school children of Victoria, was long and low, rather in the style of Victorian elementary schools, with a long corridor beside the classrooms. The village hall was built of wood sent from Australia and was decorated with small panels of Australian birds, animals, and vegetation carved by pupils of Victorian Technical Schools.

The headmaster welcomed me to the school with the words: "You are at home here, you know," and he really meant it. He seemed delighted to greet an Australian and soon he was showing me the points of interest about the school. In the lobby were two large maps, one of Australia and one showing Australia's position in the Pacific, while over the blackboard in each classroom were friezes, printed by the pupils, with the words: *"N'oublions jamais l'Australie"* (Let us never forget Australia). When I was introduced to the school children as a real, live "Australian," I realized what a mythic creature I must have seemed to them. I was asked if I would like to hear the pupils sing the Australian Anthem. Since Australia did not yet have its own national anthem in 1950 ("God save the King" sufficed), this suggestion intrigued me. The children were gathered together and sang in French "Australia will be There," a favorite marching song of the Australian soldiers in the First World War, and then the *Marseillaise*. It seemed that all the Villers-Bretonneux children learned this "Australian Anthem," which they sang every November 11th over the graves of the Australian war dead in the nearby Australian Military Cemetery. I was sure the sleeping Australians would much prefer to hear this rousing song of their own troops rather than the British National Anthem. It was amazing to me to find how fresh the memory of it all was and I was certainly received like a queen.

After a cup of tea, no less, and a few minutes poring over an album of photographs of Victorian schools and their pupils in 1926, when I myself had been in the second grade, I was driven to the Australian Military Cemetery. Here seven hundred Aussies were buried and the names of eleven thousand more who died in France were listed on a curved memorial wall. In the center of the wall was a high lookout tower, decorated with the Rising Sun badge that the Australian soldiers had worn on their uniforms. Situated on a hill, on ground that belonged to Australia, the cemetery was very well kept by an Australian guardian and the graves were covered with lovely flowers. For me it was a most moving experience.

The next day, Geneviève showed me Amiens, the capital of Picardy. Since it is built along various arms of the Somme, there is much marshy land that is famous for its vegetable gardens. These productive plots are separated by narrow waterways along which the market gardeners pass in flat-bottomed boats. As with the other towns and cities of this area, there was still evidence of extensive bomb damage, tremendous areas near the center of the city having been laid flat. Rebuilding was going on apace, but there was still much to do. Fortunately Amiens Cathedral and the beautiful eighteenth-century weavers' mansions near it had escaped destruction. Amiens Cathedral is one of the most beautiful in France with its flamboyant flying buttresses and its magnificent medieval façade, with two towers, a great rose window, and three doorways thickly decorated with statuary. Below these statues is a series of medallions depicting the activities in the region during the various months of the year. Several of the Amiens statues are particularly famous: the *Beau Dieu* (Beautiful God) on the central doorway of the facade, the *Vierge Dorée* (Golden Madonna) on the central pillar of the South entrance, and the adorable little *Ange Pleureur* (Weeping Angel) on the tomb of a Bishop behind the High Altar.

Exams looming

Back in Lille, we were nearing our examination period. In our literature course, Mr Adam's method of examining was just as untypically French as his lecturing style. At the beginning of the course, he had given us a list of ten very broad questions to prepare on the authors we were studying (Racine, Molière, Stendhal, and Proust were among them), telling us that we would be asked one of these questions at examination time. He would not deal with these questions in class, he said, that was our responsibility. This matter disposed of, he felt free to get on with his amusing digressions. This approach was quite straightforward for me, since I had been expected to do independent research and study in literature since my high school days. To my surprise Gil, with his Iowa degree, hadn't a clue as to how to go about preparing the questions. I had to help him get started. Before long, Mr Adam asked for a student to make an *explication de texte* on a passage from Racine's *Phèdre*. Silence reigned, as the forty odd students sat tight. I had always been the type of student who hated to see a teacher embarrassed by no response, so after a long pause I offered. After all, I had written a Master of Arts thesis on Racine and was very familiar with his plays. "I'll remember this at exam time," said Mr Adam.

I worked very hard on my presentation and arrived fully prepared at the next class. I am also shyer than I appear and I was quite nervous about making this public presentation in front of all these people whose French, I presumed, was better than mine. (I have always found that students who don't speak up appear to be much more knowledgeable, if only because we have no evidence to the contrary.) So I began my explication. Unfortunately Mr Adam, who was an excellent lecturer, still had a great deal to learn about teaching. He could not resist correcting everything I said, either for an unfortunate choice of word or tense, an incorrect gender or agreement, or an inauthentic pronunciation. This continued for about five minutes, during which I felt myself becoming more and more tense. Every time I opened my mouth, it seemed, Mr Adam jumped down my throat. After about five minutes, my control snapped and I burst into stormy tears in front of all my fellow students. The students were very embarrassed for me and Mr Adam was naturally surprised and upset. "But you were doing very well," he told me consolingly. Beneath my weeping, I wondered why, if this were true, he had felt impelled to constantly interrupt my flow of thought. Unfortunately, this was the kind of nervous weeping that only grows worse if anyone tries to console you. With great effort, I struggled to regain my composure and pulled myself together. "I won't say another word," said Mr Adam, which was the best approach he could have taken. I took up my text where I had left off and managed to complete the presentation. From this experience I personally learned an important lesson, that is, not to interrupt students who are trying to express themselves in a foreign language. Correction has its place, as a separate form-focused activity that may sometimes be helpful or necessary, but we must remember the tension a non-native speaker feels when trying to control many aspects of the language at once. The speaker is endeavoring to make the message clear and present it in a way that will be acceptable to the interlocutor. The concentration this requires should not be disrupted. Perhaps non-pedagogical native speakers implicitly understand this psychological process better than we realize, when they listen patiently to foreigners trying to use their language and then tell them they are doing very well. Mr Adam did remember my effort at the examination as he had promised. At the oral, he asked me what I knew about the life of Molière, then cut me off in the middle and said: "That was fine, thank you!"

Other exams were not as straightforward as this one. Being linguistically inclined, I was very interested in the Phonetics course. Apart from the theory, the lecturer, Mr Hinard, gave us extra information in class on research he was conducting himself. He also tried to improve the pronunciation of foreign students in the class by asking them to read passages aloud. He seemed to become very preoccupied with Ralph, my New Zealand friend, and spent an inordinate amount of time trying to improve his pronunciation of the French *r*. Now that I know much more about teaching pronunciation, I could tell him how to approach this much more effectively from a contrastive English-French point of view or, for a mixed-language class, at least how to explain the articulatory movements necessary to produce it. Instead he adopted the old approach of making sounds loudly and clearly, expecting people to imitate them without being able to see what was going on in his mouth. This could only exasperate students having difficulties and make them despair of ever succeeding.

My careful preparation for the Phonetics course paid off, when the results of the written examination were posted. In this class with French students, I had achieved the highest score in the four-hour morning examination and the second highest in the three-hour afternoon session. However, in the French system that was only part of the story. There was still the oral examination to come. The French oral examinations were held in public in an open classroom. Fellow students, friends, students who intended to study the subject the following year, students who had studied it the previous year —

anyone might attend. In front of the professor were set out folded pieces of paper and, in a kind of lottery, each student would pick up one of these mysterious notes and then retreat to a seat to read it and reflect until his or her turn for the interrogation was indicated. I had attended all of the lectures in Phonetics except one, when I had had the flu. Sure enough, on my piece of paper was a question about the professor's own research, which he had explained on that particular day. Unfortunately, my fellow students had not understood what he was doing. He had put some white stuff in his subject's mouth, they told me, and... and...well, they didn't know what he was trying to demonstrate. I had looked up books in the library, but it was hard to find "white stuff in the mouth" in the index. Of course, I know now about this approach to articulatory phonetics, but at the time I did not have any idea of what it was about. Here I was with the one question to answer — the very one I knew nothing about. What was I to do? There was no way I could fudge it. Taking a deep breath, I decided to explain my problem. When my name was called, I went forward and explained that I had not been in class when this research had been discussed. Looking very displeased, Mr Hinard asked me why I had not borrowed another student's notes. "Oh dear! Here goes!" I thought, as he stared at me with growing hostility. "They didn't have notes," I ventured nervously. "Well, couldn't they tell you what I had explained in class?" he asked. "They said something about white stuff in the mouth, but they didn't understand what it was about," I muttered in great embarrassment. Catastrophe! This was hardly what a French professor liked to hear, especially in a public setting. My result was promptly downgraded from what had probably been a *Mention Très Bien* or *Bien* (Very Good or Good) to *Assez Bien* (Quite Good). Thus the saga of my life with regard to examinations was continuing. Perhaps the professor did not like to see a foreign student at the head of his list? I was more successful in the Diplôme d'Etudes Françaises examinations, placing third in the group.

What else do I remember about my Lille exams? Not surprisingly our Translation lecturer tested us through impromptu oral translation of an unprepared passage and then asked questions more or less related to the content. My passage had to do with a *hameau* (hamlet). "What is the difference between a village and a hamlet?" asked the examiner. That was hardly the question to ask an

Australian. I knew about townships, towns, and shires, but villages and hamlets? I had occasionally read about them in English and French novels, but I had presumed that one was a smaller version of the other. This was the answer I gave, explaining that in my country we had townships and small townships, but no villages or hamlets. My examiner was amazed: "Do you mean to say that you don't know what distinguishes a hamlet from a village? Dear! Dear! That will never do!" and my grade was promptly reduced for crass ignorance. For those of my readers still in the same state of ignorance as I was, I have since found out that a village has a church and therefore a parish, while a hamlet has no such spiritual center, being dependent on the village as a kind of appendage within the same parish. There might be several hamlets attached to one village. So my answer about one being smaller than the other, although administratively incorrect, was probably generally true in practice. In this way the examination was at least a learning experience. Who knows? Perhaps this esoteric piece of information may be of vital importance to me someday somewhere.

May Day 1950

Labor Day, the *Fête du Travail*, brought out the marchers again. The Northerners did love their processions and marching bands or *fanfares*. One day in Lille we encountered a procession of the *Bébé Orchestre*, parading with its conductor and children of all ages. In the working class North, May 1st was a great day for Communist demonstrations and red flags were much in evidence. In 1950 the PC (*Parti Communiste*) was quite strong, with about one hundred and fifty elected members in Parliament, out of a total of some five hundred. French governments at the time were rather unstable and changed frequently. One of the problems was that there were so many parties represented among the elected members that one small party could change its mind, vote against the government, and cause it to fall. Various new combinations would then form and a new Government would take over with the same ministers, for the most part, shuffled around in different offices. In this type of situation the Communist members of the house could be quite disruptive, without actually taking power. To many French people, the constant chopping and changing seemed something of a farce and after a while they did not bother to remember who was in and who was out and who was in

473

charge of what this time around. They knew perfectly well that the country would be kept going through the work of the highly trained, permanent department heads, like the *haut fonctionnaire* (high-level bureaucrat) for whom Jacqueline worked. He moved at various stages from civil aviation to oil search, negotiation of oil treaties with Iraq, the setting up of the French Government-owned oil company, collaboration on energy for Europe, and finally the direction of the Government-run natural gas and electricity systems.

As the year wore on, the Principal of the lycée was so pleased with the work of her three language-teaching assistants that she ordained that we should have an exhibition on Wales, Saarland, and Australia at the end of the year. The members of the English and German clubs we had established worked on this project with us. We worked hard for months to obtain artifacts and pictorial posters. Mine had to come by sea mail from Australia, from the tourist bureaux of the various states, and this was a lengthy process. The girls also made their own explanatory display posters on various aspects of life in these areas, as well as preparing songs and dances. At the exhibition itself, we had to be on hand with our students to explain our exhibits. The whole enterprise was such a success that, not only was it written up in two newspapers (with photos in which we were quite indistinguishable in the murk) and described for posterity in the lycée's annual journal, but Madame Arripe, with exceptional enthusiasm and pride, extended its duration to ten days. After the exhibition, my eleven-year-olds presented in English a little play they had prepared, on Snow White and the Seven Dwarfs. They performed it in a classroom for other classes to see. This thrilled my little ones to bits and they were photographed in their costumes for posterity. Of course the lycée had its traditional *Distribution des Prix* to round off the school year. Unlike Australian Speech Days, with long Principal's Reports on changes and progress in school life, buildings completed or planned and such tedious matters, we listened to speeches on general topics (in this case, modern poetry and modern art). Afterwards lists of successes in every subject in every class were read and many prizes awarded. Nothing seemed to be omitted.

La Fête des Gayants: The Festival of the Gayant (Giant) Family

Outside of the lycée, the year in Douai climaxed with the distinctive, traditional summer festival of the Gayants, at which giant figures were paraded in the midst of a procession of decorated floats. Originally for this Douai festival there had been a family of figures paraded each year, but during the Second World War the mother and father figures had been burned. By 1950 they had not yet been rebuilt — there was, of course, so much to rebuild after the war. I was told that it used to take seven men to carry the Father Gayant figure. In 1950, the figures paraded were the Gayant children, a mere fourteen feet high. The men bearers inside the figures made them dance all the way, stopping occasionally for a change of bearers or to rest. To add to the fun, the Fool, wearing a jester's costume of green and red and encased in a contraption that made him look as though he were on horseback, danced around and darted mischievously here and there. It was quite a *kermesse*, as local summer carnivals were called. It was all great fun and a tremendous opportunity for a dedicated photographer like myself. Thus my delightful year at Douai ended and soon I was on my way to as yet unknown, and quite unanticipated, adventures.

I had spent much time and effort during the spring looking for some employment to support myself for the summer. Finally I had obtained a position as interpreter-receptionist in a hotel at Quimper in Brittany, a marvelous center for steeping myself in the Celtic lore of that unique province. On my way I was able to enjoy my first Fourteenth of July in Paris. For the *Fête Nationale* the great monuments were illuminated and the lighted fountains were playing. One of the most interesting sights was the Arc de Triomphe. In the central arch was hung a huge French flag, and behind it were red, white, and blue floodlights, with the rest of the structure floodlit. From the Champs-Elysées, it looked wonderful with a stream of stars before it, formed by the lights of the cars moving up and down this immense thoroughfare. To crown it all, there were extraordinary fireworks over the Seine. All over Paris at the crossroads and in public squares there were public balls that went on for two or three days in a flood of exuberance. There was a public ball in the Place Voltaire, near Jacqueline's apartment in Asnières where I was staying, so I was lulled to sleep by the music of the orchestra. Next day, late in the afternoon, the bus I was on had to stop and wait for the end of a dance that was taking place in the middle of the road. Then I was en route for Quimper for a summer of work. At least that was what I expected.

MA 1948
Wilga and Mother

Up Mt Buffalo in a wheelbarrow
1935

Leaving for Europe 1948

France at last   Exploring Europe

Douai 1950. A rest in the Park

Bread and cheese trips
(the beret with the green feather)

At the Franco-British Hospital
1950

A day off from the Preventorium
Wilga, Ralph, and Que, Tours
1951

Enjoying the southern sunshine
Carcassonne, 1951

Students at EN Montpellier
1951

Spanish dancing
EN Montpellier 1951

Wilga, the Nanny
L'Horme (Ardeche), 1951

Isabelle and Nanou

Wilga in India 1953

The Wilga Tree

482

13
SIX MONTHS ON THE SIDELINES   1950

"What do they dress like that for?" asked Catherine, as she watched the Scots march past in their full-dress kilts and sporrans with bagpipes and drums. I was standing with one of the waitresses at the Hôtel du Parc in Quimper, in Brittany, where I was now installed in my summer job as an interpreter-receptionist. We were watching the procession at the Inter-Celtic Festival. Catherine was dressed in her everyday garb, the traditional Breton costume of full black skirt and black shawl, with, on her head, the Quimper *coif*, a narrow two-inch-high cylinder of white. starched lace, tied under her chin with lace ribbons, with two long white ribbons hanging down the back of her head. Her remark was an amusing illustration of the fact that we do not see ourselves as others see us.

Quimper, in the extreme western part of Brittany, was a very popular tourist resort about ten hours by train from Paris. It was in *la Bretagne Bretonnante*, that part of Brittany in which the inhabitants were very aware of and anxious to maintain their ancient language and culture. In this way it reminded me of the village I had visited at the western extremity of North Wales. The local people in this area spoke Breton among themselves, just as the Welsh had spoken Welsh, and many of the older women still wore traditional Breton costume, with the distinctive *coif* or headdress of their district or village. These coifs were of different shapes and sizes, but all were made of stiffly starched, white, handmade lace. One of the most distinctive coifs, a tall, wide, lace cylinder, was worn by the Bigoudènes, from a village not far from Quimper. One of the kitchen workers at the Hôtel du Parc wore the Bigoudène coif. The Bigoudènes were frequently seen in different parts of France during the summers, selling the lace they had made during the winter.

Quimper was a pretty little town, with a small river, the Odet, running down the main street like a canal; the lacy spires of the cathedral, illuminated at night, completed the vista. The Hôtel du Parc, a subsidiary of the largest hotel in town, the Hôtel de l'Epée, looked out over the river to a tree-covered hillside. Here there were lovely shady walks, culminating in a grand view from the top over fields surrounded with hedges, rather like those of Devonshire. The quiet main street ran along the river and beside the tall, creeper-covered stone walls of the Cathedral gardens.

At the hotel I shared a large room with an eighteen-year-old Alsatian girl, Ginette. Along with some of the other summer workers in Quimper, Ginette was studying at the well-known Ecole d'Hôtellerie of Strasbourg for a career in the hotel trade. This internship at the Hôtel du Parc was part of her training. Ginette spoke English fluently, as well as German and French. She told me that when she began school in Alsace all her studies were in French. Then, when the Germans annexed the area early in the war, all teaching immediately changed to German. After 1944, when Alsace reverted to France, all her schooling was in French again. "When the Chinese occupy Alsace, I'll have to learn Chinese," she told me. "Meanwhile, among ourselves, we just speak Alsatian" (a dialect of German). The very competent manager of the Hôtel du Parc was the wife of the manager of the Hotel de l'Epée, which helped maintain the close relationship with the larger institution. Then there were Rosette, Odette, Josée, Germaine, Catherine (the head waitress), and in the kitchen Corentine, the *plongeuse* who washed up great piles of dishes every day. Corentine was convinced that no one but herself could do even the simplest thing the right way, and she managed to quarrel even with the patient and super-efficient Catherine. The guests were very mixed; there were Belgians, Swiss, English, Americans, Italians, Swedes, and Dutch, as well as the summer-touring French.

I worked in the office, with the hotel bookkeeper and the very experienced Geneviève, who had a phenomenal memory for faces and the keys that went with them; she could recognize "Room 21" before the guest requested her key, an art I never acquired. In the mornings I typed menus, helped with bills and interpreted for any English or

American guests. A large part of the afternoon was free and it was then that I explored Quimper. In the evenings I helped with the billing, seated discreetly at the back of the restaurant, where the waitresses would bring us whatever was left over on the tables, cakes or half-bottles of wine, which we consumed with gusto. These were extra goodies. Provided by contract with food and lodging, we had eaten earlier what was being served in the restaurant, ordering from the menu of the day. Altogether we ate very well. Any table tips were put together in a kitty and this was later divided among us all.

I was actually paid a very minimal wage, the assumption being that I would make a good living from tips for my interpreting. This, however, did not fit the reality of my situation. Most of the English speakers in need of assistance judged me by my speech to be a cut above general service and felt embarrassed to offer me tips. One Welsh lawyer, for whom I interpreted quite frequently, waited one evening until I had finished my work in the restaurant to take me out for coffee, as an expression of gratitude. He obviously had no idea that the tip he hesitated to offer would be my only remuneration. I was grateful to the American student, whose friend fell ill and for whom I interpreted with the doctor, when he shyly slipped me an envelope containing a thousand-franc note. These were "old" francs, of course, since this was before President de Gaulle cut off one zero to reduce the astronomical sums which appeared to be changing hands under the old system.

In a popular tourist resort like Quimper, July was the height of the tourist season, especially with the added excitement of the Inter-Celtic Festival. The hotel was well booked and already filled to capacity early each morning. Consequently, much of my time was spent explaining to dozens and dozens of anxious tourists, who had not thought to book in advance, that there was no room in the inn. They earnestly requested information on where else to go but, as they might have guessed, the situation was the same in all the hotels in town. I was astonished at the number of tourists who wandered about in such a popular tourist area at the high point of the summer season, trusting to luck for accommodation. Many of these wanderers knew no French, so I was kept very busy explaining the situation to them in English.

I was fortunate to be in Quimper in July of that particular year, since it just happened to be Brittany's turn to host the regular Inter-Celtic Festival, with overseas Celts participating. All the important events of the festival took place on the square, just across the narrow Odet from our hotel, so the great processions came practically past our door and I was able to position myself well with my camera for what was a photographer's feast. There were delegations from Scotland, Ireland, Wales, the Isle of Man, and naturally all parts of Brittany. All the participants wore their national or regional costumes, played their national instruments, and came prepared to put on programs of their traditional songs and dances. A play in Breton was performed on a platform in front of the Cathedral and there were Inter-Celtic wrestling contests. The festival atmosphere really began to build after the arrival of the Scottish delegation with their bagpipes, fifes, and drums. In the Overseas Celts' parade, it was the Scots who won everyone's hearts, with their brisk, joyful marching, their uninhibited, wild whoops, and their Highland Flings. Their drummer, with his deftly flying drumsticks, was one of the most joyous-looking men I had ever seen. The national instrument of Brittany is also the bagpipes, the *binious,* which has a sharper, shriller, reedier, thinner sound than the Scottish instrument. The Irish, who also wore kilts, marched to the sound of their bagpipes too, with the green, white, and orange flag of the Republic of Ireland flying proudly before them. I had not realized there were so many different kinds of bagpipes, some played with the bag being pumped under the upper arm. The Welsh women paraded in full skirts, with aprons, shawls, and top hats over lace caps, and the Manx women looked like traditional milkmaids. The overseas groups gave a combined program one afternoon, with the Welsh singing in harmony to the music of two harps and the other groups singing and dancing to bagpipes and fiddles. They all sang in their own Celtic tongues. I was amused to hear someone near me remark: "I suppose they're singing in English," so I hastened to explain to a Breton in this most Breton of areas the strong determination of Celts in other countries to maintain their ethnic identity, their language and their culture.

Sunday was a hectic day for the hotels and restaurants, as it was the day for the great procession of Breton costumes. This display had been arranged by the Celtic Circles of the different villages. Each group wore the authentic costumes of their region and performed their long-cherished dances and songs. It was the culminating parade. On this day the Queen of Cornwall (*les Cornouailles,* as this part of Brittany was called) was to be chosen and crowned. In the procession most groups led off with a girl in bridal apparel, with two bridesmaids and a *cortège* of young men and women in the garb of their village. These were interspersed with bands playing their *binious,* which they had decorated with pennants in the Breton national colors. The women's costumes varied a great deal, but most were of rich, dark-colored velvet, elaborately embroidered with colorful floral patterns in silk thread; they wore satin or silk aprons and elegant white lace *coifs* of varying shapes. The Bigoudènes, with their tall, cylindrical coifs, wore vests embroidered in heavy thread of brilliant orange, with which they wore light silk skirts. It was one of the Bigoudènes who was selected as the Cornish Queen in 1950. Most of the Breton men wore black costumes, with silver buttons, and the distinctive Breton wide-brimmed, round-crowned hats — the *chapeaux ronds* of the folk songs, which some old men still wore in the streets of Quimper. Other men wore tall top hats or even pirate caps. For this procession the Scots appeared in full ceremonial regalia, with short velvet jackets, plaids over their shoulders, and Glengarry caps, and they looked very smart indeed.

After the procession the fun began for the hotel trade. The streets had been absolutely packed with people, who by midday were very hungry. That noontide we fed three times the normal number of customers. The rush was unimaginable. Everyone turned in a hand to help: office staff, the manager, and even the *Grande Directrice* herself. I did all the odd things that came to hand, carrying chairs, clearing dishes, giving out bottles of wine and water, cutting bread, and finally grinding coffee for an hour and a half. It was hectic in the extreme. It was not until half-past four that I was eventually free to rush over to see what was going on in the square. I hurried up the hillside and, between the branches of a tree and someone's shoulder, I got a peek at a vital section of the stage where the national dances were being performed. That night was less rushed in the dining room, but it was half-past eleven before I was free. That night I felt my first severe pains — the beginning of the end of my summer, as it turned out.

Unexpected Change of Plans

I was only ten days into my summer job when I began to feel sharp shooting pains in my chest and side, pains that bent me over and incapacitated me. What could it be? I had to see the doctor immediately and, ironically, I paid him with the thousand-franc note I had received from the young American. The news was startling. I had developed a wet pleurisy; the casing of my right lung was filling up with fluid. According to the doctor, this was because of the stress of overwork for my examinations in the damp climate of the North, where I had not been getting from sunshine the Vitamin D to which my body had been accustomed in Australia. I was to go into hospital immediately, he said. In Quimper, where I knew no one? The doctor gave me twenty-four hours to travel to Paris and get to bed, where I was to stay for at least six weeks, with a month of complete rest after that. All I could think of was to get in touch with Jacqueline and take it from there.

Jacqueline met me at the train in Paris and took me to her father's apartment, but what to do next was by no means simple. She was about to leave for her summer vacation with her cousins on a property out of Douarnenez, near Quimper as it happened. Mr Persillet was most anxious that she not miss out on her well-earned and much-needed vacation. As luck would have it, she was able to get me admitted within a few days to the Hertford British Hospital (also referred to as the Franco-British Hospital) in Levallois-Perret in Paris. It actually turned out to be providential that Jacqueline was leaving immediately for Quimper. At the beginning of the summer I had officially changed my domicile from Douai to Quimper and, in order to get medical benefits in Paris, it was essential that I present myself *in person* at the Social Security office in Quimper to change my domicile a second time. Bureaucracy again! Fortunately dear Jacqueline stepped into the breach and, on her way to Douarnenez, she went to Quimper to talk officialdom into accepting her as my representative to change my registration of address to Paris. Since I had worked only nine months in France, not a full year as required, I would not have been eligible for medical benefits had I not worked for more than three months in England; I thus qualified for assistance, *tout juste,* under a reciprocal arrangement with Great Britain. In my precarious financial situation this was a God-sent boon. My affairs thus fell into place and I could settle down to a long rest in my hospital bed.

When I first fell ill it seemed that I would be well enough to go to the school in Montpellier on October 1st, as arranged, so long as I did a minimum of work there and treated myself as an invalid in need of much rest. This prognostication proved to be quite erroneous. As it turned out, I was to stay in hospital for a full three months, after which I spent another three months as a *grande malade* (seriously ill person) at a *préventorium* in Touraine. France was engaged in a determined fight against tuberculosis. Since people with any form of lung trouble, in this period before antibiotics, might well develop tuberculosis, they were carefully supervised. After initial hospital treatment, they were sent on to a preventorium, from which they would be dispatched to a sanitorium at the first sign of tuberculosis. This medical prevention program was taken very seriously and patients were expected to rest completely until certified as restored to health, after which they were advised to rest for part of each day (*faire la cure*) for at least a further six months.

My New Home in Paris

The Hertford British Hospital had been established in the early 1870s to provide for British and Commonwealth people from any part of France who were in need of medical care, even the poor and the destitute. Under the patronage of the British Crown, it had been largely financed by the estate of the Marquess of Hertford. During one year in the early fifties it saw about five hundred inpatients and about five thousand outpatients pass through its doors — tourists, students, or artists passing through, as well as expatriates and their families, and during the world wars soldiers and airmen. Most patients were English-speaking but others, French spouses or children of British residents, knew little or no English. Built of solid stone in Victorian Gothic style, the hospital had four floors, the upper level decorated with pointed, pinnacled dormer windows and a big clock. The windows and ceilings of the wards were rather like those of an old chapel, in keeping with the neo-Gothic architecture of the exterior. The austere simplicity of the wards reflected the expectation of high standards of efficiency, with the focus on the most modern equipment and devoted nursing care. The hospital was small enough to be friendly, with just three wards and a few private rooms. The medical staff were for the most part visiting French physicians and surgeons, while most of the nursing staff were Anglo-Celtic. My home for the next three months was a bright and airy ward for twelve people, with cheerful floral curtains at the windows.

This was my first experience of a prolonged hospital stay. I soon settled down comfortably to my daily routine of loafing and chatting, reading magazines, working out crossword puzzles, listening to the radio, knitting, writing innumerable letters, and, as the weeks went by, combing Eau-de-Cologne through my hair to dry out the excess oil that accumulated from lack of shampooing. I even had time to knit a pullover for myself, as well as one for the sister in charge of the ward. In the afternoons there were visits from a stream of friends and friends of friends, including Australians from my student past in Melbourne, the latter sent on to me by Gardner Davies at the Embassy. In the rear of the hospital there was a pleasant garden of lawns, trees, and shrubs. By the time I was allowed to take some little walks in the garden, that is, after six weeks of bed rest, summer had gone and it was becoming too chilly to enjoy the outside world. From the window beside my bed I could see the top of a horse chestnut tree, which, with its seasonal changes of coloring, kept me in touch with ongoing life in the big world from which I was now secluded. By the 1st of October, when the leaves were brown, the horse chestnuts falling on the corrugated iron roof of the Maternity Ward below resounded like pistol shots.

The first part of my treatment for pleurisy was the drawing off of fluid from my right lung to inject it into a guinea pig. A wait then ensued to see if there were signs of tuberculosis. The results in my case being negative, the next part of the treatment was rest and more rest for what seemed to be an inordinately long time, to ensure that my lung was completely healed; otherwise, it seemed, I would have a lifetime of tiredness and susceptibility to tuberculosis to look forward to. It seemed a good idea to sacrifice some time now for the sake of future benefits. With so much rest, no hard work or stress and my usual rosy complexion, I looked, of course, a picture of health. New patients, bent and drawn with pain, would ask me how long I had been in the hospital. They would be most astonished when I replied: "Six weeks!" and later "Twelve weeks!" The prescribed regimen was so strict for the first six weeks that I was not allowed to leave my bed at all for any reason.

I soon learned that a hospital is not the place to come for a good night's sleep. It had always been a mystery to me why nurses have to wake patients at five o'clock in the morning to give them a bath or take their temperature. I now know it is usually the last duty of the off-going shift, but it can still be very exasperating. Then, in a big ward, urgent cases may be rushed in on rattling stretcher-trolleys in the middle of the night and be examined and settled down, while all the ward watches and waits. The new patient may be a stroke or accident victim who moans continually or prays incessantly in a loud voice throughout the night. At other times, screens go up around a bed, with a corridor of screens stretching across the ward to the door, and you know that someone near you has died in the night and is being taken away down this sheltered corridor. When the screens come down, you will be confronted with a bare bed, perhaps right next to your own, to remind you of your mortality.

Twelve people died in our ward during my three months' stay at the Franco-British Hospital, but I never became accustomed to the sudden disappearance of someone I had been talking to just that day. The sister in charge of the ward told me I must not take individual cases to heart, that I should remain emotionally detached as the nurses had to. She and her staff, however, were in and out of the ward on eight-hour shifts. They had other people in their daily lives, whereas I was in the ward for twenty-four hours a day. These people had been my constant companions, sometimes for weeks. They had confided in me, telling me their stories in detail and I had watched the progress of their illness or their apparent recovery. It was hard to look at the empty space where, despite their pain and often their anguish, they had greeted me with a bright morning smile and not grieve for them.

Our twelve-bed ward was certainly a stage, in Shakespeare's sense, and across it came a great diversity of players. The nurses, who came from England, Northern Ireland, and the Irish Republic, were a lively, sensitive group. One with the very Irish name of Mary Murphy kept us amused with her Irish jokes. Some of the patients did not know anyone anymore and others were completely paralyzed and unable to talk. Those who spoke only French were glad to have me come and chat with them, giving them what comfort I could. One old

491

French lady with cancer of the stomach, which she knew was terminal, relied on me a great deal until the last few days when she could no longer recognize me or anyone else. She became paranoid and was quite sure the doctors and nurses had come to attack her in some way. *"C'est un guet-apens!"* (They're out to get me), she cried. On her last night of conscious recognition, she insisted on my taking a thousand-franc note (equivalent to about one English pound) to buy myself something to remember her by.

Miss Pavier, who was about forty-five, was an English nanny of the old type, who had spent all her working life in aristocratic families where she had had complete charge of the children from birth. Her first position had been with a noble family in Poland. By this time, however, she was working for the Princess Murat of the Bourbon-Parma line, the branch of the family that owned the huge Batignolles enterprise, famous for constructing great bridges and dams, like the Aswan in Egypt. As a nanny Miss Pavier had always lived in very affluent homes in exclusive areas of Paris, with holidays at fashionable seaside resorts or in the provinces at the family château. She expected to stay with the family as an old retainer for the rest of her life. When I came into the ward, she had been in the hospital for about eleven months with a broken hip and was gradually learning to walk again, having progressed to a walker and then a stick. She was somewhat temperamental and at times a little tactless. Her French was very interesting, since she had acquired it while working with French-speaking people who spoke with the very clipped accent of the *seizième* (the wealthy sixteenth district of Paris, which extends to the Bois de Boulogne). Consequently, unlike most English speakers, she pronounced her *-ez, -er* sounds, as though they were *i*, *allez* and *venez* sounding like *alli* and *veni*, (rather than the usual Anglo-Saxon *allay* and *venay*). We often chatted and joked together. Unfortunately, by the time I left the hospital, she was back in plaster for another two months after a further hip fracture. It seemed she would not be leaving the hospital for at least six more months.

In the bed next to Miss Pavier was an old lady of eighty-seven, Miss Morice, who had been in the hospital for a mere three months. She also suffered from a broken hip. Miss Morice had lived in France since she was eight and had taught languages in a private capacity. She was wonderfully alert for her age. Unfortunately her Frenchness

492

clashed violently with Miss Pavier's assertively English ways. Between their two beds was a window, about which there was a constant daily row between these two strong-minded women. Miss Pavier, with the very English belief in the health value of fresh air, wanted the window open, while Miss Morice, with a typically French horror of *courants d'air* (draughts), wanted it closed. The matter became a standing battle. Miss Morice, being much older, won her point, while Miss Pavier fumed and fretted, expressing her displeasure loudly and frequently. Furthermore, Miss Pavier hummed to herself, which greatly disturbed Miss Morice. The obvious resolution was to shift Miss Morice several beds down the ward where she still maintained that she felt the draughts; so even then poor Miss Pavier's window remained tight shut.

Then there was Mrs Gordon, a pretty, little woman of forty-two, with a devoted husband and two children, who visited her regularly. She had been in the hospital for about fifteen months with a kind of creeping paralysis, which I presume would be diagnosed today as either multiple sclerosis or Lou Gehrig's disease. She was finally unable to do anything for herself; she could neither move nor talk, although she was in possession of all her faculties and could understand everything that was said to her in either English or French. Without the treatments we are accustomed to these days, she was eventually unable even to eat. She was fed liquids with a spoon for a while, but even this became a very slow process as her throat muscles deteriorated. It was a great relief to us all when death finally released her from this terrible cage.

Most of the patients came in for a few days, or even a week or two, for tonsillitis, bronchitis, appendicitis, perforated ulcers, and so on. There were, however, quite distressing cases. One family, for instance, had been driving around Europe on a holiday when, three days from the end of their trip, they had an accident that landed all three of them in the hospital — the father with broken ribs and a perforated lung, the wife with a smashed elbow and the son with eye injuries. There was an almoner from a children's holiday camp (*colonie de vacances*), who had been badly injured in 1940, when the hospital where she was working had been bombed out. She had lost an eye; she had had to have skin grafted all over her body; and her leg had been broken in five places. When I met her she was in the hospital for her thirtieth operation in ten years.

Other patients had had heart attacks or strokes while on holiday and had had to be hospitalized immediately. One stroke victim was brought in, crying out "Jesus! Mary! Joseph! Save me!" in an incessant stream, all night and all day, until, as her condition deteriorated, her voice became fainter and fainter and her prayer more and more hesitant. Then she finally lost consciousness. Another French stroke victim repeated "Ou là là" continually, and an English lady, whose mind was wandering, kept murmuring: "Oh dear! What shall I do? Oh dear! What shall I do?" Her cries became particularly wearing at night, when her "Oh dears" became interspersed with short prayer phrases. The nurses became desperate, since she was keeping everyone awake, but the more they tried to quieten her, the louder she became, calling out: "I can't help it! I can't help it!" During the day the nurses tried to calm her down with injections to put her to sleep; then she couldn't sleep at night until the night nurses repeated the treatment. She obviously couldn't and didn't last too long this way. Mrs Waters had been on holiday in France when she had a mishap. She was a delightful woman but the world's champion snorer. The noise was frightful. She could snore quite cheerfully in broad daylight, but when the lights went out it was terrific and nearly made nervous wrecks of us all. One night when I could stand it no longer, I slipped out of bed to turn her on her side. In the dark, I heard my neighbor murmuring: "Thank you, my dear! Thank you, my dear!" in most heartfelt tones. Fortunately these people were not all in the ward at the same time or it would have been quite a circus.

On the lighter side, I remember one girl who had no first language that she could speak with an authentic native accent. Her mother had spoken Hungarian and her father Polish. Since neither spoke the other's language, they had communicated in heavily accented English and French, which their daughter acquired as her first languages. She then went to school in Vienna, where in her adolescence she learned German, and this she also spoke with a foreign accent. Although she could converse fluently in English, French, and German and was a naturalized British citizen, she was always being asked where she came from. It was in this hospital that I met my first French Canadians (who were, of course, Commonwealth

494

citizens) and became accustomed to their distinctive variety of French. Then there was the young Italian girl, in hospital for a miscarriage, who was anguishing over whether to marry her Egyptian lover, who had from the outset explained that, since his religion permitted him four wives, she would certainly not be the only one. She earnestly sought my advice on this problem that would affect the course of her life. I soon became very friendly too with a charming Welsh air-hostess, as flight attendants were then called. She occupied the bed next to mine. This young woman had a strange malady that took her temperature up to 107 degrees Fahrenheit morning and evening (about 41 degrees Centigrade). When she was diagnosed as having para-typhoid and rushed off to the Contagious Diseases Hospital, I was very glad that, unlike Miss Pavier, I had been able to keep the window between our beds open while she was there.

It was particularly disturbing when things took a turn for the worse for a person in the next bed. The beds were fairly close to each other, so that one might well be listening through a screen to a priest administering the Last Rites of Extreme Unction to one's neighbor. The most dramatic incident occurred when the patient in the next bed to mine, with whom I had been chatting normally during the day, went berserk in the night. She had been restless and having bad dreams since three in the morning. At about five she got out of bed in her nightgown, picked up her handbag and announced that she was going back to her hotel immediately, just as she was. When the nurses tried to quieten her and get her back into bed, she screamed at the top of her lungs. The porters rushed in and the doctor on duty and the Assistant Matron rushed down from their bedrooms, since she was making so much noise. They had to force her onto the bed to give her an injection of bromide. She kept screaming all the time and the very sick patients were moaning — it was quite a drama. Then suddenly she sat up on her bed and berated the nurses, the doctor, the porters, and everyone within sight. Turning to me, she explained in apparent calm lucidity: "I know this family! They've got no money." Then turning back to the doctor she yelled: "William Henry! You've been drinking again!" Fortunately the bromide was having its effect by then. By the time breakfast came at six thirty she was sound asleep. During the day she kept giving me the strangest explanations for her behavior. She must have been having a nervous breakdown. She had been admitted with alleged appendicitis pains, but it was found that she did not have appendicitis at all. Apparently the abdominal pains were delusional too.

Since a number of the patients were monolingual French speakers, I was able to keep up my practice with the language by talking with them. The spouses and children of expatriates, who were British by nationality but not by culture or language, were also very pleased to have me to interpret for them. Many of them had very sad stories to tell. One French-speaking lady in her sixties, the widow of an English jockey she had married in 1912, knew not a word of English and was in a real predicament. As a British subject, she was not eligible for any financial assistance in France. She had been admitted with some form of bronchitis. Since she had no means of support, despite having worked very hard all her life, she was being kept in the hospital until it could be arranged for her to enter an old people's home in England, where she would be entitled to a pension. She had never been out of France in her life, nor had she ever traveled by ship. She was terrified at the prospect, being convinced that she would most certainly drown or die of seasickness. A most helpful little body, she talked to everyone in the ward and she would go from one end of the ward to the other to pick up something someone had dropped or get them a glass of water. I often wonder how she got on later in a place where she would not be able to understand or speak to a soul.

Not everyone's stories were to be believed. A Mrs Chernikov, who had been admitted for a foot infection, wandered all around the ward, smoking and talking incessantly about the grand life she had lived in her youth, all the chauffeurs and servants her family had had, the furs, the jewels, and the exotic trips she had been accustomed to. Later she confided in me that she hadn't a penny nor even a room in Paris. It seemed her husband was in jail in France for illegal sale of dollars and was sought by the British police for evading taxes. Which story of her life was the true one? I wondered. Or were they both efforts to create a life, in these anonymous circumstances, to compensate for the banal, humdrum nature of her existence?

My period in hospital was much alleviated by the great kindness of the French. I knew that the French were very loyal in their friendships and that, once you had been accepted into a French family as a friend, you became part of an extended group. Not only did Jacqueline, despite her busy professional life, come to see me several times a week, but, when she went on vacation, her dear old Aunt Lucie came in every week to do what she could for me. Aunt Lucie was one of those precious individuals who just live to do what they can for others, always with the utmost cheerfulness. Her selflessness was self-effacing, despite the difficulties of her own life. With a husband chronically ill with angina, she had had to go to work at the Post Office to make ends meet, despite the fact that she was well above retirement age and suffered from a considerable disability that caused a distinct limp. She supplemented her meager income with dressmaking. Aunt Lucie always brought me delectable surprises and went home with my washing, after she had assured herself that I had everything I could possibly need. Persillet cousins also came to see me, as did Jacqueline's busy father. My Saint-Quentin friends, Paule Guilbert and her mother, made special detours when they were passing through Paris to visit friends in the South, to bring me companionship as well as small presents and creature comforts. I was very moved when Monsieur Guilbert also came to see me when he was in Paris for a trade union meeting. Genevieve Proy from Amiens, who had taken me to visit Villers-Bretonneux, sent me cards several times a week, first from Amiens and then from various places she visited on her vacation in Savoy and Italy. Former colleagues and students from Douai did not forget me but sent cards and gifts. During this unfortunate period of my life, the kindness of my French friends was overwhelming. I was able to experience an aspect of the French character that tourists, rushing through Paris from the Eiffel Tower to the Louvre, rarely see or imagine.

Gil, my Iowan friend and fellow student at Lille University, was in Paris at the time, finishing off his Fulbright year. He kept me supplied with fruit and American magazines like *The Saturday Evening Post, Time,* and *Life.* When I told him I had not tasted watermelon since I left Australia, he immediately found me some. He searched Paris for peanut butter for me — the ultimate American gift that was rare in France at the time. He brought me a big jar of it, most of which I quietly passed over to Mary Murphy, the Irish nurse, since it was not one of my favorite foods. My half-niece Jeanette came every Sunday and cousin Wiz visited when he came for the 1950

Paris Motor Show. He had won first prize for car design at the English Motor Show that year. My Egyptian friend, Diaa, still in Britain, was most assiduous in his correspondence and liberal with medical advice on how to recover more quickly. Mail poured onto my bed daily and, for this rare period in my life, I had time to reply promptly. I could hardly be lonely with up to seven visitors a day. In a serendipitous coincidence, Miss Nixon sent to visit me a French student, returning from the IVF Annual Conference at Cambridge, who came from the Montpellier area. By this time I had become aware that my convalescence was to be a long drawn-out affair and the seasons were changing. Fortunately, this visitor was able to go to the Ecole Normale d'Institutrices at Montpellier to rescue my winter coat and some warm clothing from my trunks, which were patiently awaiting me in that far-distant city.

Getting out of hospital proved to be more difficult then getting in. After some searching I had found a suitable rest home where I could go for my three-month convalescent period. The French National Insurance, along with a teachers' insurance for which I qualified, was to cover ninety-six percent of my expenses, but before I could leave the hospital an inspector had to come to see me actually lying in a hospital bed. I waited day after day but no inspector appeared. Inquiry revealed that my dossier was in Lille and the Parisian bureaucracy could not cope with this discrepancy. My friends assured me: "If you want something done, get a Communist to do it," so I contacted my Communist friend, Yvonne Serant, from the lycée at Douai. She promptly went to Lille to the National Insurance office and persisted until she found the right room where the official had my dossier on his desk (presumably under a great pile of other files). She insisted on its being brought to the top and within a few days the inspector was there at the foot of my bed. This was in the thirteenth week of my stay. Once my presence had thus been visually verified, I was able to proceed with my arrangements for life after hospital. My lung was now quite clear, but I needed another three months of rest to ensure that I would not relapse.

With the help of the hospital staff, I was soon admitted to a preventorium that specialized in post-pleurisy care — *Le Petit Charentais* near Tours in the lovely Loire Valley. At this establishment I would be with French-speaking people again and

498

speaking only French all day. I looked forward to making considerable progress with the language while taking my enforced rest.

Next, I had to get ready for the transfer to my new home. My guardian angel, Jacqueline, stepped in again. She and her family rallied around me, reducing considerably my trepidation at having to adapt once more to a new set of strange companions. Not only did Jacqueline do my shopping and washing, but she lent me sheets, towels, cutlery, a hot water bottle, and other things I was expected to bring with me to the preventorium. She also lent me the money for my train ticket. It was when I settled down to packing what I would need for St Cyr that I discovered just how tired the pleurisy had made me. For three months I had not tried to exert myself in any way and now the slightest exertion exhausted me. It soon became clear that my doctor was right. I was certainly not yet ready for a normal life of professional activity.

Convalescing in Touraine

The Preventorium of the Petit Charentais was situated at St Cyr-sur-Loire, on the outskirts of Tours, about a hundred and seventy miles from Paris. *Les Charentes*, from which its name derived, was the name of an ancient province of France further to the west, which, interestingly enough, extended to La Rochelle on the west coast, where Christiane lived. I remembered "Charente" so well from the many envelopes I had addressed to her over the years. The preventorium, always called the *prévo* by my companions, was in an old two-storied house, situated in the fields outside of St Cyr. At the time of my admission there were about thirty women there. Most were in their twenties, with a few older women like myself. They came from all kinds of homes and areas of France. They were of very different occupations: factory workers, teachers, students, artists' models, farm women, young mothers separated from their families, even a teenager from the inner city. Illness had brought them together fortuitously. Each was recovering from some form or other of lung infection, mostly pleurisy, which required careful supervision, good food and prolonged rest to avoid the devastating complications of tuberculosis.

When I arrived at the Petit Charentais some of my fellow inmates had been there already for eight or nine months. The average stay was about six months, but there were some very sad cases of women who had already been ill for several years. Some of these patients had had two or three relapses, some caused by foolishness or foolhardiness in impetuously leaving the hospital earlier than they should have, against the advice of their doctors. Those whose medical condition worsened to a tubercular state were immediately packed off to a sanatorium (*sana*), and this was the great dread at the back of everyone's mind. All the women were French, except for one Spaniard (there were many refugees from the Franco regime in France in 1950) and a North Vietnamese from Hanoi, who was a refugee from the long war for independence between the forces of Ho Chi Minh and the French. Since the women were from every level of society and from every corner of the Hexagon, the regional and social accents I heard covered a wide linguistic spectrum. Some used quite a lot of slang — factory and street language rather than the informal speech of students, to which I was now attuned. I soon became accustomed to the regular use of some very coarse expressions that I did not expect to find very useful later..

The routine at the *prévo* was strict, though freer than in hospital. We got up at about 7.45 a.m. (a change from the 5.45 a.m. regimen of the hospital). We took our temperature, then washed and dressed for the day. Breakfast was at 8.30 and consisted of *café au lait* and *tartines* (bread with a scraping of butter). I usually brought along extra butter and a pot of jam to give it some pep. After breakfast we went back to our rooms to make our beds and wait anxiously for the arrival of the mailman, since we could not expect the personal visits to which I had become so accustomed in Paris. From half-past nine to half-past eleven we had to *faire la cure*, that is, go back to bed and rest. We could read or talk a little very quietly but we were not allowed to do anything as energetic as writing or knitting. At 12.30 we had lunch. Fortunately the food was better than in the hospital. As part of our treatment, we were expected to eat a great deal in order to put on weight and one of the patients, who had been there longest, acted as a kind of prefect to see that we ate up everything on the table. From 1.30 to 3.30 p.m. we had to *faire la grande cure*, this time resting in bed without doing anything at all, while maintaining absolute silence. After a little while, in sheer boredom, we would go to sleep. At the sound of the 3.30 bell (bells rang for all of these activities), we would take our temperature again and go down to afternoon tea — a *goûter* of *café au lait* and *tartines*. At this point I usually managed to bring in a little cheese to vary the diet. After the *goûter* we were free for an hour. This was one of the rare times in the day when we could socialize with patients from other rooms. From 5 to 6 p.m., however, we were back in bed, although this time we were allowed to write letters or knit. We had another hour of leisure before the seven o'clock evening meal and again before the bedtime bell at nine. Lights went out at 9.30 p.m., when absolute silence reigned until morning. Of course we had personal things to attend to during the few intervals of freedom, although we were not allowed to do anything as energetic as our laundry, all of which was sent out, and there was a maid to do the cleaning. On Wednesdays, Sundays, and special holidays, we were excused from the afternoon *grande cure* and, after a month in residence, we could go out on those afternoons from two till six. In this way our days were completely mapped out for us for as long as the doctors considered we should stay. In my case, this would be for three months; for some of the women it would be much longer.

The lady in charge of the preventorium was a charming, motherly soul and very kind, but we saw little of her, except when the nurse was on holidays. Our immediate contact, then, was the nurse, whom the women immediately classified as *lunatique* (unpredictable, with sudden changes of mood). If a patient went for pills in the morning, she was told they were only given out in the afternoon; in the afternoon she might well be told crossly that she should have come in the morning. The nurse did the rounds three or four times a day to see we were where we should be, usually in bed, but otherwise we followed the routine and looked after ourselves. Our doctor came twice a week to carefully check on each of us and a specialist visited us every two weeks. When I pestered the doctor about returning to work at the beginning of January, worrying of course about losing my job at Montpellier, he gently teased me, asking why anyone would want to work when they didn't have to. When I persisted, he allowed for the possibility of a January departure on the understanding that I would not work too hard but rest a great deal during the first few months, avoiding all strenuous exercise. This I clung to as the light at the end of the tunnel.

At the *Petit Charentais* I was installed in a room for five people on the second floor. The ceiling of our room in this old house sloped to the wall on one side in attic style. We had two windows. From one we could see the garden, with the trees now coppery with autumn foliage. The second, which looked out over the front courtyard, was always open, no matter what the weather, to ensure that we had plenty of fresh air. My well-informed companions told me that in a sanatorium in the mountains windows would always be open, even when snow was blowing in onto the beds. Here, however, in French fashion, only one window on one side was ever open, so that we would not be subjected to the much dreaded *courants d'air*. From the second window we could see the great entrance gate and spy on arrivals and departures. (In such a limited existence very simple things preoccupied us.) From this vantage point we could see the mailman at the gate. As soon as we heard him ring the bell we would rush in great excitement to the window to make sure it was really he, then wait in breathless anticipation until one of the girls brought up our mail. Joyful exhilaration or mute disappointment ensued, depending on the day's "haul." Mail assumed an enormous importance when each day was exactly the same as the last and the one before it, except for this small variation. Further away, on the other side of the road, we could see a farm. We loved to watch the comings and goings of the people in the little cottage and the children at play, the hens, ducks, and pigeons in the yard, and especially one little corner where the ducks took to the water to swim in a little pond. We could just see the corner of an old roof where the pigeons (or were they doves?) exercised. Still further away, out in the fields, there was a factory, part of which was still under construction. We had little appreciation for the factory, however, when in the early hours of the morning the pomp-pomp of its machines mingled with the cries of the *chouettes* (screech-owls) to irritate our restless sleep.

My room companions were very diverse. The chattiest was a Corsican school teacher, Dominique Peretti, who in a very didactic way soon made it clear to me when I had made a mistake in French pronunciation or usage. Being ever eager to learn, I found this most helpful. It was she who said to me one day: "I wish you wouldn't keep ordering us about!" It was then that I discovered pragmatically something I had never been taught in my French courses: that I should use the conditional to attenuate my proposals. I was saying too often "we should do this or that," using the present tense of *devoir* (*on doit*) instead of the conditional (*on devrait)*, which would have made it more of a suggestion like "Maybe we could do this or that now?" I was learning the nuances of French in actual contexts and it stuck. Thanks to Dominique's irritated reaction, I've never forgotten this usage. Dominique also talked to me about Corsican values and customs. I was most impressed when she assured me that, if anyone harmed her, her brothers would come from Corsica to avenge her, with knives if necessary. It was just like a nineteenth-century novel. Poor Dominique, a woman of forty, was in a complicated situation with her pleurisy. Unfortunately she had not taken it seriously in the beginning stages. As a result she had had several relapses and been ill for more than a year. Furthermore she also had trouble with her liver. The more she ate to strengthen herself against the pleurisy the more her liver played up, yet when she ate less to accommodate her liver her pleurisy deteriorated. It was difficult to see how she would ever be able to get out of this impasse.

Also in the room was a very beautiful woman of Yugoslav descent, Sylvie. About twenty-eight years old, she was an artist's model from Montparnasse in Paris. I had been at the *prévo* only four days when she received a bad report on her latest X-ray, indicating the advisability for her immediate return to hospital for further treatment. Being a very impulsive person, she immediately packed her bags and left on the first train to Paris, preferring to take her chances in a familiar environment. This was the trouble with an illness where one felt quite normal, except for intense weariness, and needed no treatment other than prolonged bed rest, which many thought erroneously they could fit in just as well at home. We missed Sylvie, not only because of her bright personality, but also because she had had a gramophone and played music for us when we had some free time. After her abrupt departure we were tipped out of our room for the weekend so that it could be disinfected.

My third companion, Liliane, was a young mother from Montmartre. She had married at eighteen and had a four-month-old baby at home. Her husband had already spent a year in a sanatorium with tuberculosis when she developed her pleurisy. Consequently she had to go into treatment herself, leaving her baby to be cared for by the grandmother. Liliane very much missed her baby and was most anxious to go home. She was a born and bred Montmartroise. Her husband was a painter, her father a musician and her sister an exotic dancer. She passionately loved her "Butte" — that steep, rocky outcrop on which Montmartre, clustering around the Byzantine structure of the Sacré-Coeur church, is built. Liliane was supposed to stay for six months, but like Sylvie she became very impatient. She talked constantly about how she could rest just as well at home with her husband and baby. Eventually, on receiving the news that her husband had come home from *sana*, she left us after just two months of treatment. We very much missed her cheerful presence.

I often wonder how things turned out for Liliane. It is very probable that she was back in treatment after a few months in an even more serious condition. Unfortunately, those who left without the doctor's permission were not permitted to reenter treatment with National Insurance support should they fall ill again. This made the decision even harder for people of limited means, at a time when emotion was overwhelming their better judgment. There were no counselors or social workers available at the *prévo* with whom patients could discuss their problems and their churning emotions. We, their fellow-patients, with our own anxieties and empathetic understanding of their dilemmas, provided the only sounding board. There was much discussion among us as each crisis arose.

Nguyen Que was my fourth companion and we soon became close friends. Que was from Hanoi and wore Vietnamese-style clothes. She told us Que meant Cinnamon, so the French called her "Cannelle." About twenty-eight, she seemed very young and laughed a lot. Que was a very devout Catholic and, since this was Holy Year, she and I prayed and read Scripture together morning and evening, she using her Missal and I my New Testament and a book of private prayers my sister Linda had given me. We had many very helpful discussions and shared our personal feelings and concerns. Que's family had been very wealthy but had lost everything in the war. They had had to flee when the Communists burned down their factory. Que had a brother who was a student in Paris, of whom she was very solicitous, being determined that he should continue his studies no

504

matter how difficult this might seem. Fortunately in France there were no heavy university fees to pay. She had few means but a great faith and prayed for whatever she needed. It seemed to me that if she prayed for a dressing gown, it would walk in the door. Que spoke English quite well and loved to practice with me when we were alone. At that time she had hopes of becoming an interpreter. When we went walking together on Wednesday afternoons, Que would take the tiny steps of a well-brought-up Vietnamese lady, in contrast to my Australian stride. She was a really good companion and we remained in touch until she entered a convent in England several years later.

Although the young women in the *prévo* were very cheerful and we filled our few leisure hours with much laughter and improvised activity, there was always an underlying anxiety and tension. This might suddenly manifest itself in rapid changes of mood, tears, depression or, when the pressure became too great, unwise decisions. All of them had been suddenly ripped out of a normal existence, with its relationships and commitments, for what could be a long time. The indeterminacy of the length of their absence from their families built in a deep-seated angst. What was happening at home? Were they being told the whole story? Were their children happy and well cared for? Were their husbands faithful to them? How could the family survive without their contribution to the family income? None of them were rich, with housekeepers and servants to make up for their long absence and care for their children. The grandparents were, for the most part, working people too. They seemed to be wasting so much time just resting. It seemed so lazy; yet if they did not obey the doctor's orders they might be out of the loop for much longer. Would they ever be really well or would their condition worsen? There were so many unknowns. *Sana* always loomed threateningly in their subconscious. I naturally shared this underlying anxiety. Would the administration at Montpellier keep my position open for me? After all, they did not know me. They had their own needs and an instructional program to maintain. If they filled my position, what would I do in the middle of the school year? All my savings were being completely eaten up by my share of the expenses, despite the generous contribution of the National Insurance, and I had no family in France to fall back on. Our common predicament

505

brought us very close together despite the great disparities in our backgrounds and temperaments.

Every Monday before lunch we had regular X-rays and were weighed, our weight being carefully tallied. We were expected to put on weight each week. Since we were urged to eat and eat, those who were improving did gain weight. I put on more than a pound the first week and soon was picking up all the weight I had lost in hospital. By the end of my stay, I had put on fifteen pounds. Not everyone, however, was responding to the regimen of rest and plentiful food. Here I saw something I have never seen anywhere else — young women weeping bitterly because they had not put on weight. To lose weight meant that they were slipping back, which was dangerous and would prolong their treatment. There was deep depression among all of us when one of our number, who had been losing weight or whose X-ray showed deterioration, was whisked off to hospital or sanatorium. One day there was real consternation when a young woman came back from a walk spitting up blood. Fortunately it turned out to be related to a heart condition not her lungs and, after a couple of weeks in hospital, she was back in our midst, to our immense relief. We knew deep down that something untoward could happen to any of us at any time. Soon those of us who survived without incident were looking plump and solid. Since I was the tallest, I was soon the heaviest and the pride of the herd.

Our favorite way of filling the odd half-hour of free time was to take a little walk in the fresh air. Since the most attractive part of the garden was within sight of the Director's windows, we were not allowed to walk there. Beyond a small extension of the garden, surrounded by firs and cedars, there was a bare field, across which we strode to the barbed wire boundary. Here we would gaze wistfully over someone's ploughed field. Near the fence were two solitary, windswept pines and a large bush that was heaven-sent for the smokers among us. Smoking, being deleterious to the lungs, was strictly forbidden on pain of expulsion. Still there were some who could not resist and these women would gather behind the bush. On fine days we would take a few turns up and down the field, but when it was cold and windy we would hurry back in, remembering that we were still in delicate health. We lived in constant fear of a relapse.

Even here at St-Cyr I ran up against French bureaucracy, of an equally tenacious but perhaps more bumbling kind than before. Aware, from my Quimper experience, of the necessity for keeping any change of domicile well on record, I made my way to the Prefecture of Police at Tours. Here I answered the many questions the forms required, including this time the date of my mother's birth, about which Mother had always been somewhat vague herself. Of course, they needed more photographs of my right ear. Since I have never had a good look at my right ear, I am not sure what is so distinctive about it. So back I went with the photographs to receive a receipt, which could be exchanged for my card in three months' time. *Enfin*, I thought, that is now completed. But not at all! The next week the Police Officer rode out to the *prévo* on his bicycle to ask me the questions he had forgotten to ask before, and the following week he was back to ask for my last address, which was on a card in his possession anyway. At least his visits were a distraction.

I soon came to know girls from the other rooms and they provided a real lesson in the diversity of humankind. One forceful character, Louise, was a young Alsatian woman, who spoke French with what sounded to the others like a German accent. She loved to sing songs in German and was lively and cheerful. Louise had been a bar girl and had had several children by different fathers. She was very kind and would do anything to help the other women. Another patient, who was married to an Algerian, something unusual in France in 1950, started calling the Alsatian a *Boche* (a Hun), which infuriated Louise, who as a loyal French Alsatian had suffered considerably under the Gestapo during the war. Calling the other woman a *Bicot* (an insulting term for a North African), Louise flew at her and began scratching and punching her and pulling her hair. Quite a melee ensued, until we could separate them and keep them apart. There was also a Spanish girl who had learned all her French in factories. Very fluent in colloquial French, strongly peppered with factory slang and obscenities, like Eliza in Bernard Shaw's *Pygmalion* she would have been quite unpresentable in wider social circles.

One very young woman, a mere teenager from the inner suburbs of Paris, had been sexually abused by her stepfather and had left home. She knew she had nowhere to go when the time came for her to leave the *prévo.* Since she was illiterate, she had to find someone who would write her love letters to her boyfriend and read his replies. When the chief letter writer left, this task was passed on to me. Since her letters consisted mostly of *"Je t'aime, mon cher coco,"* I felt quite capable of writing them for her.

One trauma that involved us all in great discussion was the case of a very quiet Breton woman, Gaby, from a farming background. Her husband was in a sanatorium, but like so many he was too restless to remain until he was cured. One day she received a letter from him telling her he was leaving the *sana* without medical approval and going home to die in Brittany. To prove her love for him, he asked her to leave the *prévo* immediately to come home and die with him. This dilemma preoccupied us all. Should she or shouldn't she? The more sober of us advised her to stay and get better, rather than take such a risk; the more romantic understood her pain and the great statement her sacrifice would be making. The emotional argument won the day and, despite all advice to the contrary, Gaby left us for Brittany.

The dearth of male company was something most of the patients were not accustomed to. Nearby was a sanitorium for men, with whom, quite reasonably, we were not allowed to have any contact. I never worked out how some of the women managed to acquire men friends at the *sana*, despite this prohibition. I guess they were more experienced at this type of thing than I was and it certainly meant more to them than to me.

We went to all kinds of lengths to fill our few spare moments. Since I often played patience to amuse myself, I began telling fortunes by the cards. All it required, I found, was a vivid imagination. I soon became quite convincing at it and my sessions were very popular. I continued this activity just for fun until my companions began bringing strange girls from other rooms to ask me serious questions. "What you told me came true," they would say, "so I have brought Marianne. She wants to know if her husband is faithful to her." At this point I realized I was playing illegitimately with other people's lives and emotions, so my career as a fortune-teller came to an abrupt end. Instead we "talked to the spirits." One patient, who had had some experience with this kind of thing, took the lead. We could find only a rickety fold-up table for our experiment. Solemnly four of us sat around it and held hands above its surface. Closing our eyes, we concentrated on calling up the spirits. "*Esprit, es-tu là? Esprit, es-tu là?*" ("Spirit, are you there?") we called. Unfortunately there was no response. Our leader announced that one of us apparently did not have enough conviction and was holding up the process. Perhaps I was the one? I tried harder. After some time we felt the table begin to move. As we put questions to the "spirit," the table began to bounce in response. We counted the bounces: "A, B, C..." up to N for *Non* (No), O for *Oui* (Yes), and P for *Peut-être* (Perhaps). I looked hard to see what was moving the table, but we were still holding each other's hands above the table and I could see no way in which this rickety old table could be bounced rhythmically by someone's knee. To this day I don't know what moved it, but the table did respond with the right number of bounces to make coherent answers. Again I decided that dabbling with anything other than the here-and-now was not for me.

Small things became dramas in our humdrum existence and such was the incident of the heating. It was now December. Having frozen in our rooms for two days without heat and having asked unsuccessfully of the maid and the nurse why we had no heating (we were not supposed to catch cold), we were told to take the matter up with the Director herself. At eight o'clock, after supper, we all gathered outside this lady's office, asking to see her. An unassuming woman, the Director looked rather startled to see nearly all the women, spear-headed by independent Corsica and democratic Australia, advancing into her office. We had hardly opened our mouths before she agreed to fix the heating herself (it being the handyman's day off). In very short order the house was heated everywhere except in our room, where air had already got into the pipes, so we, poor things, had to wait another day to feel the warmth. By this time, fortunately, I had received some of my warm clothing, sent on from Montpellier.

I had my own worries, of course. All was not well with Montpellier, whose patience had run out. The Primary Teaching Department, which was in charge of the Normal Schools, refused to give me leave of absence since I had never actually been in their service. The news that my appointment had been canceled was very disturbing. Through the ever-attentive Monsieur Renard, however, Paris came to my rescue. Even though it would be the middle of the French school year before I could present myself for teaching, he

509

assured me that once I had a medical certificate to say that I could work again he would find me a post somewhere, He even tried to get my salary paid from October to December, with partial success. My future seemed to be ever balancing on a knife edge.

My Persillet family continued to support me with solicitous attention. A Persillet cousin, passing through on business, dropped off a parcel of goodies for me. In very short order, friends of Jacqueline's uncle, an old couple called Rousseau who by sheer happenstance lived in St Cyr, soon got in touch with me and paid me visits, bringing me books to read, cakes to console me, and strawberry jam for my *tartines.* When I was finally allowed to go out on Wednesday and Sunday afternoons, I would sometimes walk into St Cyr to visit them. Or alternatively, Que and I would walk to Tours to see what we could of that beautiful city, Que with her tiny steps tripping along most engagingly beside me. We especially loved Tours' fourteenth-century cathedral whose glorious windows glowed with deep velvety reds and blues.

As the year waned, Christmas was upon us — the festival of home and family. I began receiving a great number of letters, up to sixteen a day, as well as numerous parcels and hampers. My students from different classes at Douai, feeling my Christmas away from home would be rather thin, sent me cakes, chocolate, coconut biscuits, fruit, nuts, and dates, as well as books and magazines. Fortunately I was expected to put on weight by any means and this was certainly a pleasant way to do it. My English friends did not forget me either. Gil, who had returned to Iowa, sent me packets of American stamps for my collection and I received a plethora of letters and affectionate greetings from friends and family in Australia.

Determined to create something of a home atmosphere in the *prévo* for the festive season, the Director had a big fir branch brought into the dining room and decorated it in traditional style with tinsel. On Christmas Eve we had all kinds of games and homemade entertainment from our varied and talented group of women, some of whom dressed in marvelous paper costumes put together by a little dressmaker in our midst. At this celebration I saw some cabaret-style dances that were much more explicitly risqué than anything I had ever seen before. I was certainly learning about life in this very mixed company. Dressed up as *Le Père Noël* (Father Christmas), I gave out presents the young women had made for each other. We danced and played and sang and gossiped till nearly midnight in a typical French Christmas Eve réveillon, concluding with a sweet supper. This celebration would normally have been at two or three in the morning after Midnight Mass, but staying up as late as midnight was already a big concession for us, accustomed as we were to lights out at 9.30 p.m.

On Christmas morning I was thrilled to be able to go to communion at the Protestant church in Tours, the Temple of the Reformed Church, to which I had become accustomed in Douai. This was the first time I had been able to take communion in five months. Since mail was delivered on Christmas Day, I was pleasantly surprised, on coming home from the service, to find my bed again covered with letters and parcels. It was then time for a typical three-hour French Christmas dinner, with soup, oysters, *boudin* (a kind of sausage), turkey cooked with chestnuts, mashed chestnuts, salad, cheese, and fruit. The culminating item was a *Bûche de Noël* (the traditional cake in the form of a log, with coffee cream frosting and covered with decorative moss and sugar mushrooms). The meal ended, of course, with lots of strong coffee,. By this time the atmosphere was highly charged with emotion, as each patient thought of home and family. One by one girls, who had been having great fun and laughing somewhat hysterically, would burst into stormy tears and rush from the table, while we all tried to carry on as though nothing had occurred. In the evening, we had another feast. That week I put on three pounds, even before consuming all the chocolates and sweets I was receiving in the mail.

This joyous celebration was repeated at the New Year, when we acted a short play, written by the nurse. Appropriately it celebrated the joys and sorrows of the Old Year and the hopes for the New; it was lavishly illustrated with short poems and appropriate songs. I was selected to act the chief role and I was also the producer. Once again our dressmakers and models came out with their best inspirations. The New Year, I remember, looked very fresh and appealing in a simple white nightgown, with several strands of ivy, a simple gold band around her forehead and a lighted candle in her hand. By now I had found I could clown around in French, especially with the Alsatian girl who had a very ready wit. This demonstrated a considerable advance in my confidence in the French language and came as something of a "revelation" to the nurse, who until then had seen only my serious side. By now, we were all very much at home with each other and knew enough about each other's affairs to be able to make mischievous allusions. We had settled down into a very congenial group. The New Year celebration, like that at Christmas, culminated, of course, with another three-hour repast — the typical French way of celebrating every festive occasion.

As January took over, we enjoyed watching the snow falling gently over our garden although, since Touraine was a mild region, it melted much too soon. As I was now a senior patient making good progress, by mid-January I was allowed to take little afternoon excursions to see some of the châteaux for which the area is famous, the nearest being Amboise. This beautiful structure now belonged to the Comte de Paris, the Pretendant to the French throne, who had just recently been allowed to move back to France to live. The château of Amboise, a handsome building in French Renaissance style, sits high on a cliff above the Loire river, surrounded by defensive walls with two great towers. As a residence for the Count and Countess and their eleven children it must have required an enormous amount of central heating. Among its treasures was a very dainty Gothic Chapel of St Hubert, whose fifteenth-century stone decorations were as delicate as lace; and the tomb of no less a personage than Leonardo da Vinci, who had spent his last years at the French court. In the huge round tower at the side of the castle was a spiral roadway so that horses and coaches could be driven right up to the Court of Honor and on to the stables, which were in the higher levels of the castle. Nearby, as a contrast, were the homes of the troglodytes, the cave dwellers who had over the centuries built their homes into the cliffs of the Loire, their chimneys poking up into the fields above.

By chance Ralph, my fellow-student from New Zealand at the University of Lille, had been appointed for his second year in France to a lycée at Blois, not far from Tours. He had already come to Tours once to show Que and me some of the hidden beauties of that city, including the Church where the famous fourth-century Bishop of Tours, St Martin (the one who slashed his cloak to give half to a beggar) was buried. At his tomb, a popular place of pilgrimage, were many plaques given by grateful people, thanking the saint for miracles performed on their behalf. Ralph now invited me to come to Blois to see their famous château. The Director of the *prévo* had allowed me a full day out for this excursion. That was fine except that there was no bus early enough from St Cyr to Tours for me to catch the nine o'clock train to Blois. I was faced with a six-kilometer walk to the station. Fortunately the maid persuaded the farmer, whose activities we often watched from our window, to give me a lift halfway, which cut my early morning walk down to three kilometers.

The château at Blois, which had been the home of the French Court for over a hundred years in the sixteenth and seventeenth centuries, was much larger than Amboise. It had a noteworthy facade with three levels of balcony windows and a striking, highly decorated exterior staircase from the time of Francois 1er, with repeated likenesses of Henry 11's mistress, Diane de Poitiers, on the way up. The steps of the staircase fanned out from a central pillar. Blois was rich in the history of intrigues, conspiracies, hangings, and cynical assassinations. In the study of Catherine de Médicis, the hidden cupboards in the panelling where she kept her poisons adjoined her private chapel. On the way back in the train I had a very good view of the Château of Chaumont, with its great battlemented towers. It was this château that Catherine de Médicis made Diane de Poitiers accept after the death of Henry 11, in exchange for the much bigger, more ostentatious Château of Chenonceaux, which had been the King's original gift to her. All these machinations made me wonder if the "good old days" had been so good after all.

On my return to the *prévo*, I found I was lucky to have escaped for the day. Just after my departure, the doctors had come on their regular visit and categorically forbidden any of the patients to go out because of an epidemic of influenza that was raging all over France.

At last, on January 27th, it was time for me to leave the preventorium, on the strict condition that I should continue to rest a great deal and avoid catching cold. There were plenty of other prohibitions too: no sport, no swimming, no sunbathing, no late nights, and no over-fatigue. With attention to these details, it seemed that in a year's time I would be perfectly well again. I was sorry to say goodbye to all my friends at the Petit Charentais, especially as they were far from being well themselves. Que would especially miss her prayer companion. Having no news of a new position to go to, I once again made my way to Jacqueline's place to await news. Jacqueline, as always, was exceedingly kind. Since all my savings were now depleted, she again lent me money to tide me over. It was a good two weeks before I finally heard that, since the assistantship had remained unfilled, Montpellier would still accept me once the authorities were assured by my medical certificate that I would not promptly fall ill again under their jurisdiction. It was time to gather myself together and take off for the sunny south with its new contacts and new contexts. Encouragingly I had also been assured by the Paris Office that I would most probably be granted a third year in France so that I could complete my Licence degree. Life was decidedly taking a turn for the better.

14
THE SUNNY SOUTH
1951

The ten-and-a-half hour train journey from Paris to Montpellier, 780 kilometers, was a living geography lesson. The train ran swiftly through the peaceful Seine and Yonne valleys to Sens, then to Dijon, crossing Burgundy with its continuous landscape of vineyards on terraced hillsides — the Golden Slope, as it is called, because of the richness of its production of great wines. The Saône valley took us to Lyon, with its numerous factory chimneys and spacious city center. (Train travel, by taking you into the cities, allows you to see so much more than today's prevalent air travel.) Along the wide Rhône River we continued into fabled Provence, with the snow-capped mountains of Savoy to the east. I was beginning to realize just how rich France was in rivers, making it such a fertile land, with great ease of transportation. At Avignon — famous name! — I caught a glimpse of the bridge and, beyond it, the Palace of the Popes, reminiscent of that turbulent time when there were two claimants for ultimate authority in the Roman Catholic church. The change to the south of France, the *Midi,* was already palpable in the warm and perfumed air and visible in the transformation of the vegetation. Everywhere the distinctive dark green of the evergreens was punctuated by the tall, narrow fingers of the yew trees that Impressionist painters like Van Gogh had made so familiar. Olive groves and vines continued for miles. After Tarascon, the town of Daudet's Tartarin, with its solid, box-like fortress on the river's edge, darkness fell, so I could see nothing of Nîmes, a city that had been a great Protestant stronghold, particularly during the seventeenth-century Wars of Religion, and was still forty percent Protestant in 1951. Finally, we reached Montpellier, just ten kilometers from the

515

Mediterranean. While I lived in Montpellier, I found this was a nice biking distance for my leisure moments, and I loved to relax and swim at Palavas-les-Flots.

At my new home, the *Ecole Normale d'Institutrices* (Training College for Women Primary Teachers), I was welcomed with a rousing rendition of *"There is a Tavern in the Town,"* always a childhood favorite of mine. This rollicking song was as popular with the students of English in France as the French drinking song, *Chevaliers de la Table Ronde*, had been with my students of French in Australia. I have always been enthusiastic about singing in language classes, and with my Girl Guide and Church youth group training I have never been shy about leading singing. After all common errors in group singing are indicative, it seems to me, of an easier melodic route to the same destination. It was an enormous pleasure the next morning, my first in the Midi, to look out my window and see a really blue sky again, after the pale imitations of the North. Even though it was still officially winter, the sun was shining most of the day, so I knew that my new surroundings would soon feel like home. As in our Ascot Vale garden, the first harbinger of approaching spring was the beautiful pale pink blossom of the almond trees. When one of the girls brought me some for my room I felt quite nostalgic.

Montpellier was a very attractive town of about 60,000 inhabitants, with tree-lined boulevards, public squares with fountains, and beautiful old eighteenth-century mansions, whose highly decorated courtyards were hidden behind big, forbidding external doors. Out of town were vineyards and the hilly, wilderness-like *garrigue*, with its evergreen live oaks and tall, sweet-smelling wild grasses. Once the rainy winter had passed, the climate in this Southern town was very pleasant on the whole, except for the Mistral — a cold, dry wind that blew continually for days down the Rhône valley, toward low pressure areas over the Mediterranean. The effect of the wind was to make us all feel very restless. Of course, in accordance with French custom, the windows of the public areas, like the refectory of the school, were open only on one side to avoid the famous *courants d'air* so feared by the French..

In 1951 Montpellier had very little industry. Town life centered around the very famous university, at whose Faculty of Medicine, dating from the thirteenth century, Rabelais had been a student. The ancient building of the Faculty of Medicine was still attached to the Cathedral, of which the Dean of Medicine was traditionally a Canon. The town was filled with students of all races and types. In the shopping areas the streets were wide, with fine light-colored buildings. There were several public gardens, one with a beautiful view inland to the mountains. The main Botanical Garden had been established by Henry 1V in the sixteenth century. It has often been said that France is a nation of gardeners and these beautiful lawn and flower-filled spaces had certainly been cherished and nurtured over long periods of time. In the old part of the town were narrow streets and buildings with dark entrances, where decayed old stone staircases led upward to mysterious interiors. On the Esplanade where, during the Wars of Religion, many Protestants had been killed, there was a fine equestrian statue of Louis XIV pointing toward Aigues-Mortes, where the last of the Protestant resistance had been stamped out — a daily reminder to casual strollers of Montpellier's bitter past. That the destruction was not as complete as King Louis had assumed was obvious from the six percent Protestant representation in the town, the two well-attended Reformed Churches, and the various villages in the Cevennes Mountains that were still almost entirely Protestant. These groups demonstrated the same determination and conviction as Marie Durand, who, during the persecution in the seventeenth century, had continued for thirty years to sing psalms in her prison cell in the fortress at Aigues-Mortes, stubbornly refusing to abjure her faith.

On my arrival at the *Ecole Normale* (EN), the Principal deputed one of the senior students, a young woman of about twenty-three, Marie-France, to show me around the establishment. The most intellectually gifted students at the EN, all of whom had been selected for admission by competitive examination, a *concours*, would stay on for two more years after the completion of their Primary Teaching preparation. During this time they would prepare for a further *concours* for the *Ecole Normale Superieure* (ENS) for women at Fontenay-les-Roses. At this institution they would study for the *Agrégation* examination, which was an essential qualification for teaching in the higher classes of a lycée or in a secondary *collège*, where a less classical education was provided. Marie-France was one of these advanced students. During the long period of hard study for the difficult and highly selective *concours* for entry to Fontenay, the students would complete their courses for the Licence ès Lettres at the University of Montpellier. At each stage of their study there was a *concours*, at which only the limited number required to fill vacancies at the time would be "accepted" (*reçu*, as the French termed it). Consequently, many intelligent, hardworking students were left by the wayside, because of low demand for their teaching subject in a particular year rather than any lack of knowledge or ability on their part. Those not *reçus* would be expected to take the examination again the following year, and sometimes for several years, or move into some other occupation. It was a very stressful system and confirmed me in my lifelong opposition to wide-scale impersonal, selective testing, with its hit-or-miss approach, as a career-determining educational criterion.

Marie-France came from the medieval fortress city of Carcassonne, with its perfectly preserved crenelated walls, which I had greatly admired in the postcards sent to me by Marcelle, with whom I had corresponded for a very brief period when I was twelve years old. The Carcassonnais have a very strong southern accent, which I found quite disconcerting on this initial short tour, accustomed as I had become to the accent of Tours, where even the cleaning women spoke with a standard French accent. I was now in Languedoc, proud of its linguistic history when France had been divided into the northern area, where *oui (oïl)* meant "yes," and the South where affirmation was expressed by *oc*. In Brittany, there had been strong popular fervor for the ancient Breton tongue, while here in Languedoc there were groups agitating for proper recognition of the ancient language of *oc*, or Occitan. At first, it took considerable concentration for me to understand what Marie-France was saying. How on earth will I understand my students? I wondered. It was not, of course, that they spoke Occitan, but in the south they pronounced all the letters that were silent in northern French (*on prononce toutes les lettres*," I was told). This resulted in quite a different intonation. Furthermore the nasals were pronounced with a final throat closing, making *enfin*, for instance, sound like "enfang." I became accustomed at the EN to hearing the young resident supervisors call out to the girls: *"Vite, petites!"* and fling themselves down after a period of duty, with an *"Enfang, un peu de repos.* I was told that this strong

Southern accent was something of a problem when the students presented for the oral part of national examinations, like the Agrégation. At that time students were assessed at this examination partly on how standard (meaning north-central) their accent was. The reasoning behind this apparent discrimination was that, since lycée teachers could be sent to teach in schools anywhere in France (nation-wide secular education being the glue that held the nation together), it was essential that they speak with a neutral, standard accent. This policy considerably disadvantaged the southerners, particularly from rural areas.

The 126 students at the EN were aged from sixteen to twenty-two, and all were boarders. While at the school, they covered the last three years of secondary education leading to the Baccalauréat and had two further years of primary teacher training. There were training schools for teaching practice attached to the EN. I was to share my time between the EN for Girls and the EN for Boys. Because Spanish was so popular in the South, there were many fewer classes of English than in the North. I soon found out how much language preferences are affected by geography. German was popular in the northeast of the Hexagon, English in the northwest, Italian in the southeast, and Spanish in the southwest. As Montpellier was so close to the Spanish border, there was in 1951 the added factor of the presence of so many children of Spanish refugees from Franco's regime, with many bilinguals in the classes. As a consequence of this unbalanced distribution of language students I found myself with a very light schedule of six hours a week of English conversation classes, that is, three hours at each school. I had no classes on Thursdays, Fridays, and Sundays, but an unfortunate class hour at 3 p.m. on Saturdays. My classes at the EN for Girls usually had from five to seven students. The three hours at the EN for Boys, however, turned out to be one two-hour session and one one-hour session per week with the same three boys, so I had to work hard to keep it interesting for them. They were country boys. When I would ask them how they had enjoyed a holiday weekend in their homes in the vineyards, their faces would light up as they told me: *"On a bien mangé et bien bu."* ("We ate and drank *very* well!") My Spanish counterpart had a heavy load of teaching with classes as large as sixteen or eighteen, which makes active, distributed conversation difficult to maintain. I was certainly not exhausted by my six-hour per week schedule, but, as I had been warned on leaving the preventorium, I soon found that I tired quickly. I still had to take two hours of rest every afternoon (my *grande cure*) and I was careful to rest whenever I had done anything particularly energetic.

The EN buildings were attractively all white, which was typical of the sunny south. The boarding school situation had built-in advantages for me: I did not have to scout around for lodging or meals and I had a ready-at-hand group of companions who were also looking for leisure-time company. We had similar interests in that we were all engaged in university studies. I was allotted a supervisor's room at the entrance to a dormitory, although I had no responsibility for supervision. The disadvantage to this was that the main switch for "Lights Out" was in my room, as well as the buzzer to wake the students up next day. Each morning, then, I had to jump out of bed when my alarm clock went off at what seemed to me an unearthly hour and, practically in one movement, press the buzzer, switch on the dormitory lights, and plunge back under the covers to continue my morning snooze. However, I did have the pleasure of going to sleep every night to the sound of the nightingales singing in the EN garden. Since there were no baths in the building, we had to go to a public bathhouse for that luxury. There were showers available on Tuesday and Saturday afternoons for which we had to line up with the girls and await our turn. (There had been no baths at the preventorium either.) I did, of course, have in my room a washbasin with hot and cold water and a typically indispensable French *bidet*.

Unfortunately, there was no common room at the EN for the student supervisors and assistants, as we had had at the lycée at Douai, so I greatly missed the casual socialization with whichever of my colleagues happened to be free. Here, there were only two supervisors, Jacqueline Armand and Josette Lavigne, and a very young resident secretary, Camille, on her first job, whom we rarely saw. I was the only resident language assistant. The Spanish language assistant, an expatriate Spaniard called Francesco Olmos, was resident at the EN for Boys. He also taught students from both schools. The junior *intendante* (boardinghouse manager) was usually busy elsewhere, except at mealtimes. To make up for the lack of common-room facilities, I bought myself an electric ring to make my essential cups of tea, and we socialized in each other's rooms, usually after lunch and dinner. My French was now very fluent and I was beginning to acquire something of a reputation as a "wit." I had at last learned the art of timing my telling of stories in French and my slipping in of little joking remarks. I was never lonely. Soon I was receiving invitations from contacts outside the school. I had also started to get the other English language assistants in the area together. They were English, Scottish, New Zealander, and American, some just newly arrived and a little at sea. Before long I had met a group of Protestant students at the University and achieved the heights of giving a Bible Study entirely in French — another first.

I began going quite frequently to the cinema. I found films and plays to be one of the last fortresses to be taken linguistically. It required a tremendous mental concentration on my part to follow all the fast conversation and the abbreviated allusive comments in a film or a play. I had to actually clench my fists and tense all the nerves in my head to "get" everything. These were the glory days of some of the greatest French actors, like Louis Jouvet, Fernandel, Jacques Tati, and Michele Morgan, and film versions of the plays of such leading writers as Jean-Paul Sartre, Anouilh, and Cocteau were appearing. French films, I found, were of a very high standard dramatically and photographically and dealt with a wide variety of life situations and problems. They brought me many insights into the French way of thinking. I had rented a radio and I found I needed the same concentration for the radio plays that were popular at the time and for light comedy programs that contained lots of puns and *double entendre* (double meanings). "Hearing" all the words of songs also required concentration. This was perhaps the most difficult achievement of all; but getting the words of songs, as we have all found, is not particularly easy in one's own language, By now I understood everything and everybody in everyday conversation, and also in university lectures, without having to concentrate. Then there was the usual university campus series of concerts, twelve in all, at very reasonable student prices. We were well served for entertainment in Montpellier.

Jacqueline Armand, one of the two supervisors, was a very vivacious, dark-haired, dark-eyed *méridionale* (southerner). She was married, with a husband teaching in a nearby town, so she was not in residence. She was very friendly and brought me little presents from time to time. Being a Protestant, she was anxious to introduce me to the local Protestant community. Soon her aunt, who was headmistress of a Protestant primary school, invited me to speak on Australia to her students. A Protestant school was something of a rarity in France at that time. Before Louis XIV's Revocation of the Edict of Nantes, in the late seventeenth century, which curtailed the freedom of Protestants to exercise their faith, there had been thirteen Protestant schools in Montpellier. It seemed the Protestants were the founders of secular education in France, before their schools were taken over by the state. This one remaining school had continued through the centuries. Memories of the past were still very much alive in the area. Apart from Louis XIV's triumphal statue, there were Honor Rolls in the Protestant churches in Montpellier, commemorating their martyrs who had been slaughtered on the Esplanade. The headmistress and the young teachers at this Protestant school had very progressive ideas on education and seemed to have a genuine vocation for teaching. I was also invited to dinner by a Protestant teacher at the EN for Boys, Monsieur Alain Parmentier, a senior teacher of English whose wife, Annick, taught English at the Lycée, and they gave me much information on my new location and situation. I came to know this couple, the Parmentiers, very well as time went on.

My other companion, the only resident supervisor that first year, was Josette Lavigne from Dinard in Brittany. Very friendly, she was an interesting conversationalist. Since Josette had been a *grande malade* in sanatorium herself, she also had to watch her health and not overtire herself. Josette and I were soon taking long, therapeutic walks together regularly and we became great friends. We have remained friends ever since and I have frequently visited her in Brittany. A mathematician, not a linguist, Josette always talked to me in French. She knew some English from school, enough to read a little, but her second language was really Spanish, as was Jacqueline's. Hence there was no temptation for me to talk in anything but French, except in my classes. A member of the Communist Party, Josette was engaged to a party organizer in Normandy, Raymond Bléas, whom she had met in sanatorium. As Party members the Communists in the *sana* had apparently been kept in line by the group and rebuked if their behavior might reflect discredit in any way on the Party. Raymond had been Josette's group leader. Josette retained a lifelong political commitment and, in later life, she was an elected official in municipal government in Rennes in her native Brittany, where she was headmistress of a primary school. Her municipal responsibilities were particularly for care of the aged and the young. She was involved in the direction of day-care and senior centers and *colonies de vacances*, that is, youth camps that were often organized by trade unions for working-class families. Later, when I spent a few days with Josette and her husband in Normandy, we went on a round of visits with him in the rural area, where he had grown up. Here every farmer's wife we visited had her own homemade liqueur, made from the local cherries, plums, or whatever they were cultivating — and this we absolutely had to taste. After much such tasting of delightful *alcools*, I'm afraid we were quite tipsy. After his brush with tuberculosis Raymond never fully regained his health and he died young.

Since there was so much teaching of Spanish, my counterpart, Señor Olmos, was kept very busy. With his enthusiastic encouragement, there was much singing of Spanish songs and dancing of authentic Spanish dances, often by girls from Spanish refugee families. Francesco Olmos was tall, handsome, charming, and very fond of female company. He liked to invite young women for walks in the *garrigue* and they soon found out what he was looking for. Word was surreptitiously passed along among the women that they should be careful of *couleuvres* (small snakes) in the *garrigue*. Francis, as the French called him, had been a youth organizer for the Socialists before the Civil War and he was waiting, poised near the frontier, to return at the first possible moment to help build the new Spain. His wait was a long one.

The Principal of the EN for Girls, Mademoiselle Blanc, was very pleasant. A conscientious mother-hen type, with not much dash, she seemed to run the school quite efficiently. Her attitude toward her educational task was much more liberal than that of Madame Arripe at Douai. I soon discovered that the primary education system in France, which ran the Normal Schools, was much less conservative than the secondary system, as exemplified by the lycées, of which Douai had been a particularly rigid example. For one thing the girls at the Montpellier EN were allowed to mix freely with the young men at their counterpart school, which had certainly not been the case with the senior girls at the lycée in Douai.

In 1951 there was in France a subtle socioeconomic difference between the lycées, which provided education for the most part for children of the bourgeoisie, and the EN's, where children of the working class and the peasantry could take their first step up the social scale by becoming primary teachers. Hence the girls and staff at the EN were much more likely to be supportive of left wing, labor-union-related political groups, and they had more liberal views of public education than the students at the lycée, particularly in the conservative north. I have before me a pamphlet, dated May, 1951, distributed by the union of normal school students (*normaliens*), which was associated with the *Confédération Générale du Travail*, the leading left wing trade union. In the pamphlet are listed the demands of the normal school students for a raise in their living allowances, as well as proper recognition for university credit of their two-year post-baccalaureate teacher-training period. It also demands an end to discrimination against Arabo-Berber normal school students in the ENs of Algeria and urges students to join tours to the Soviet Union to see how well the education system there is organized. The EN students and faculty also had the reputation of being much more anti-clerical than those in the lycées, since they came from and were preparing to devote their lives to the secular school (*école laïque*), which they supported fervently. The matter of the separation of church and state institutions was quite an emotional issue in France at the time. Mademoiselle Blanc shared this anticlerical view and, while I was at the EN, there was a one-day strike in the school against proposed amendments to an educational law, dating back to the beginning of the century, which would allow government grants to religious schools. Strong proponents of the secular public schools looked on this proposed legislation as a clerical victory and the first step back to what they regarded as "the bad old days."

Life in France continued to be hard for working people. The cost of living kept rising and outstripping wages. There did not seem to be any basic wage in France at the time, which would provide automatic cost-of-living adjustments, such as I had been accustomed to in Australia. So again there were labor strikes that affected the school. At Douai I had been involved in a teachers' strike, and here at

Montpellier I was caught up in a student strike. There was a strike by the domestic staff, which the students supported by refusing to attend classes. The strike was on the day before the Easter vacation, as it happened, which was handy for me as it gave me time to complete my packing for a holiday on the Riviera. The domestic staff worked from seven in the morning till eleven at night, with a couple of hours off in the afternoon, and only two half-days off a week, never a full day. For this they received board and lodging and a mere pittance in salary. The girls cheerfully undertook to look after themselves during the strike.They thoroughly enjoyed preparing the meals, which were quite palatable, with lots of potatoes, but they also made a real performance of it. They formed up in pairs and came in as singing waitresses, with the dishes held high on one hand, and performed all kinds of antics with the service trolley, as they sang excerpts from the *Cloches de Corneville*, which they had been learning for the school fete.

Attached to the EN was a primary-level practice school, where the Headmistress's close personal friend, Madame Suaire, was in charge of the sixth-grade demonstration class. Here the progressive approach of the *Ecole Nouvelle* (New School) was practiced. I found it very stimulating to discuss educational ideas with Madame Suaire. Although this was a novelty in the early fifties, she had her young students producing their own newspaper and printing it out on a small printing press. The young student journalists naturally wanted to interview me about my exotic homeland in the Antipodes. Patiently I answered their many questions. In the final printed version of my remarks I was amused to read that it was no surprise to them that Australians drank so much tea since Australia was so close to Ceylon. On a classroom map of the world distances are hard for the young to appreciate. I also sat in on some early classes in the demonstration school to see how little French children learned to read. I was interested to find that in early reading, as they sounded out the words, the liaison consonants at the ends of words were attached to the initial syllable of the next word. Thus *les_élèves_ont un encrier* would be read as [le ze lev zõ tõe nã kri je], or *les enfants vont_à l'école* as [le zã fã võ ta le kol]. In my own studies of French I had not been taught the importance of proper syllabification, and I was not consciously aware of the very important difference that the French tendency to begin syllables with consonants made to oral production. This is something I emphasize now with teacher trainees and students.

The University of Montpellier

The buildings of the University of Montpellier were scattered about the town. The Faculty of Arts was only about a quarter of an hour's walk from the EN. The short walk was quite a pleasant change from the continual rush at Douai to get to the station on time for the train to Lille. Study was not the most immediate of my concerns, however, since the year was too far advanced for me to register for further courses for my Licence and I was still supposed to rest a great deal. For general interest I began to audit a course in Geography, which I had taught in Australia. I was attracted by the excursions it required. The Montpellier Geography Department had a collaborative arrangement with the University of Glasgow, whose students were to accompany us in early April on an excursion of several days to see the Causses — the dry, arid plateaus of limestone, riven by deep canyons, so characteristic of Languedoc. Our Montpellier Professor, who wanted everything to go smoothly, primed us up about the visit by continually reminding us of his expectations when *les Anglais* (the English*)* would be with us. Knowing how the Scots felt about their distinctiveness, I stood up in class one day and drew the Professor's attention to the fact that the Glasgow students would not appreciate being referred to as *"les Anglais."* "That's quite unimportant," replied the professor dismissively, "They're all English to us!" Finally, our student visitors arrived, with their woollen Tam o'Shanters and their thick Scottish accents, fifty-three of them in all. We poured into the buses and off we went to see the Causses. At the first stop, as we stood looking out over a steep valley, the Geography professor came over to me excitedly and said, "You know, there isn't an Englishman among them!" I was hardly surprised.

Apart from the excursions, I got very little from the Geography course, and decided not to register in it for credit the following year. In typical French style, the professor lectured only on his speciality, even though this did not have much to do with the published course content. In the lectures we learned the botany of every type of plant that grew in the *sous-bois*, that is, under the bushes and meager trees of the *garrigue*; this interested me very little.

Furthermore I had always worked with contour maps, which now spoke to me clearly as to the nature of the terrain. Somehow I never succeeded in seeing things as clearly with the close hatchings of the hachure maps that the French preferred.

Relaxing in the perfume capital of the world

Easter, which decided the date of the spring vacation, was early in 1951. Since I had come to Montpellier in mid February, this had been a short trimester for me. I still had to rest a great deal, so I selected for the break a guest house on the *Côte d'Azur* (the Riviera). I was to be at Grasse, just inland from the Mediterranean on the hilly slopes between Cannes and Nice. This was a great place for convalescents, because it combined the warm sunshine of the South with the fresh air of the hills, away from what the French considered the more "pernicious" air from the sea. A favorite holiday resort of Queen Victoria's, Grasse was, and still is, the center of the world's perfume industry. Lavender grew wild on the hillsides and there were many flower plantations. The mild climate at Grasse would be good for me and there would be other guests of delicate health in the house. I was to travel via the great port of Marseille and return via Arles in Provence.

In Marseille, I stayed by myself in a hotel for the first time in my life. I was becoming the experienced traveler. My very modest hotel was on the Canebière, the famous main thoroughfare of Marseille, with its shops and theaters, and the loud, joyous voices of the passionate and strongly independent *Marseillais*. Traffic lights were, I found, something of a joke. Pedestrians rarely took much notice of them, so that crossing the road became an amusing game of "dodge the policeman" and, of course, any vehicles that had the temerity to expect the right of way. The cost of living being so high in France and the cost of eating out quite prohibitive for a poor *assistante*, I had brought with me some hard-boiled eggs and cheese. With some crusty French bread, a little succulent ham, some tomatoes, and the readily available fresh, aromatic oranges, I was able to survive on just one hot meal per day. The first thing I wanted to find was some *bouillabaisse*, the famous spicy fish soup of the area, with saffron, tomatoes, and lots of different kinds of Mediterranean fish. Having found a reasonably priced one, I found it was as good as its reputation.

It was a great pleasure to wander round the old port of Marseille, already used thousands of years ago by the Phoenicians and the Romans, with its two strong entrance towers and multitude of little fishing boats, their masts hung with drying fishing nets. On a high cliff, overlooking the port loomed the neo-byzantine church of Notre-Dame de la Garde (Our Lady of Good Watch), the patron saint of mariners. Watching over Marseille and its sea approaches from the top of its tall tower was the enormous, thirty-foot gilded statue of Notre-Dame de la Garde, which could be seen from every part of the port and out at sea. It was to this holy patron that local seamen had turned for centuries for protection in storms and tempests. The interior of the church was richly decorated with gold leaf and mosaic pictures of such biblical scenes as Paul in the tempest at sea, Noah's Ark on the waters of the Great Flood, and Jesus in the storm on the Lake of Galilee. Hanging everywhere were ex-votos: models and paintings of ships, which had been offered by generations of grateful sailors in fulfillment of vows made to their guardian in hours of extreme danger. It was not difficult to find fishermen around the old port who were willing to row interested tourists across to the open harbor to admire the view of the off-shore islands and the Château d'If, where Dumas' fictional hero, the Count of Monte Cristo, had been imprisoned. They could then continue on to the huge international port, with its berths crowded with ships of all nations.

Recognized as the Gate to the Orient and the route of access to Europe from Africa, Marseille's streets were bustling with an incredibly cosmopolitan crowd, many in animated conversation at the open-air cafe tables under the trees. In the old parts of town, the narrow alleyways between the crumbling buildings were hung with multicolored washing and the animation continued in conversations conducted from upstairs windows with people in the street. Any garbage lying around soon dried out in the hot sun and the dry air of the Mistral.

From Marseille I took the train along the Mediterranean coast to Cannes and a bus thirteen hundred feet up the hillside to my convalescent guest house in Grasse. Here I had a pleasant room looking out over a forested hillside. Since the guests ate together in a common dining room, I soon got to know them all. They came from various parts of France, from Brittany, Normandy, the Marne, and even my old stamping ground of Lille. Several were retirees: these included a colonel, a commandant, a much-decorated Pole from the Foreign Legion, and a Hungarian who had lived in France for twenty-four years and was now teaching himself English from gramophone records. This gentleman was quite disconcerted if I pronounced any words differently from the speaker on the recordings. One younger man, a painter, had fought in the French Resistance. He had been parachuted into France on missions several times, until he was captured and sent to the concentration camp at Dachau. As a consequence of his imprisonment his lungs had been badly affected; seven years later he was still trying to regain his health. Since his release from the camp he had traveled a great deal throughout Europe, making a living by selling his paintings. There were lawyers, school teachers, and working men who explained much to me about the attitudes of the striking unions. One young Frenchman, Elie, was a Protestant. Born in Indochina, he had the Croix de Guerre for his exploits against the Japanese and had spent a year in a Japanese concentration camp. Later he had fought with the French in Vietnam. Apart from his proposing marriage to me every quarter of an hour for the first few days, he was a very interesting and amusing companion.

The regimen at Grasse was restful, usually about ten hours of sleep, followed by a leisurely breakfast in bed and a long rest in the afternoon. During the day we took lengthy walks, among the vines, olives, mimosas, and spring-flowering fruit trees. Everywhere there were flowers from which essences would be extracted for perfumes. From our lavender-scented hillside, we had a magnificent view of the Mediterranean, from the bay at Cannes across to Nice. Grasse itself was a curious old town, with steep, narrow streets, many of them stepped. Cannes was a different proposition. It was very beautiful in a more cosmopolitan kind of way, with calm, tree-lined streets. Palms and gardens lined the main shoreside promenade, the Croisette. As you strolled under the palms, you could look out across a narrow sandy beach to the wooded islands in the intensely blue bay, which was partly enclosed by mountains coming down to the sea. That Cannes' clientele was most affluent was evident from the huge luxury hotels, the enormous yachts in the artificial harbor, the magnificent cars, and the expensively dressed people going in and out of the Casino.

Sometimes we would walk up the hillside behind our guesthouse and ramble in the forest, which had once belonged to the Rothschild family. The small dusty-looking, dark-green leaves of the evergreen oaks and the laurestinas contrasted with the feathery, rather sparse foliage of the Aleppo pines and the light green of the wild genistas. Grape hyacinths. wild violets, purple irises, and small pink and white daisies proliferated and, through the trees, we had continual glimpses of the waters of the Mediterranean. One day, as I walked by a tall stone wall enclosing a private garden, I smelled a perfume that I realized reminded me of my childhood. What was it? I asked myself. Like Proust's reaction to the now famous *madeleine*, so reminiscent of his youth, this perfume reactivated for me so many childhood joys and small tragedies. For the moment I just could not recall what it was. I walked around the wall again, sniffing and thinking. The memory sensation was very intense. Then I saw it: a small bunch of highly aromatic white flowers peeping over the wall. They were little pittosporum flowers. The pittosporum, imported from New Zealand, was ubiquitous in Melbourne, and there had been seven of them in our Ascot Vale garden. Nothing else could have taken me back so completely to my childhood playground. I had climbed them, sat and read in them, and played Cowboys and Indians under them with my schoolmates. Their perfume had wafted into the house. Nothing else could so have encapsulated my childhood!

Having time to read in the relaxing atmosphere of Grasse, I was enjoying a novel by Jean Giraudoux, but, to my annoyance, he kept using a word I could not find in the dictionary. The retired colonels and dowagers at the dinner table were most interested in what I might be doing and were pleased that I was reading such a reputable author as Giraudoux. Encouraged by their solicitous attention, I mentioned that the author kept using a word I did not know. "Perhaps we can help you," they eagerly replied. I should have been forewarned by the omission of the word from the dictionary, but I brought it out loudly amid the stunned silence of my companions. "Does Giraudoux use that word?" they murmured disapprovingly.

At Grasse, we were well placed to see some of the gorges, which cut deep into the calcareous mountains inland from the dazzling white limestone cliffs of the coast. With very little vegetation, these rocky gorges gave a striking impression of loneliness and desolation. Along the Gorges du Loup, we could see the river deep down in the valley, as it splashed over rocks and pebbles and was fed at intervals by waterfalls dashing down the slopes. Amid the fresh light green of the spring foliage it was a pretty sight. On the higher slopes we encountered more and more plantations of lavender, which improved in quality, it seemed, the higher it grew. Although the large plantations belonged to a big perfume company in Grasse, many local mountain dwellers were making their own lavender essences and perfumes, which they sold in booths along the road. It was in this area that I came across my first "eagle's nest village" — Gourdon. Built by the Saracens when they invaded the south of France, it was perched high on an impregnable cliff of rock. Before the days of automobile transport, it must have been a weary business to climb right up to the village, but as a defensive outpost it would have been perfect. Since the buildings were made of the rock itself, it was perfectly camouflaged. Its château and the houses nestling close to it disappeared into the general silhouette of the mountain spur, which appeared from the distance as just another wild, mountain peak. The forty inhabitants of Gourdon sold perfumes and essences of the best mountain lavender and distillations of violets, mimosa, and roses. Naturally, in such a calcareous area, caves with extraordinary stalactites and stalagmites abounded. We visited some caves where the fine calcareous structures were infiltrated with iron. Some of these gave off musical sounds and could be played like a xylophone, while others, lit from below, created a credible panorama of hell.

The Causses and Provence

I was hardly back at Montpellier when I received a visit from a Melbourne friend with a car. He was one of the ex-servicemen I had taught in my English Literature class at Taylor's Coaching College and he was doing the Grand Tour of Europe with his cousin. Now that I was in a fabulous area for touring it was a pleasure to have Australian visitors. With a car at our disposal we were able to go out into the Causses and later explore some of Provence. Some of the sites we discovered were breathtaking. Languedoc, like the North unfortunately, is not as well known by overseas visitors as it ought to be.

On this trip we approached the gorge country by the little village of St Guilhem-le-Désert, where in the ninth century a close friend and adviser of Charlemagne had retreated in his old age to seek the solace of a religious life. Here there is a very beautiful eleventh-century Romanesque abbey at the foot of a high cliff, which is crowned by the remains of a Saracen castle. With its relic of the True Cross, a gift from Charlemagne, St Guilhem-le-Désert was one of the stages on the great pilgrimage to Saint James of Compostella in Spain. The picturesque little village clusters around a plane-shaded village square with a well in the center. What a place for my visitors from the very new world of the Antipodes to begin a visit to France! As we continued, the gorges of the Vis River gave us many rough and rugged views of denuded escarpments and desert-dry calcareous cliffs. Then we reached the Cirque of Navacelles, a truly spectacular sight. At this spot the river Vis has carved out a meander, now cut off, which is surrounded by very steep cliffs. On reaching the top of the cliffs you are startled by the dazzling sight of the steep, white walls of the cirque dotted with sparse, speckly vegetation, leading down some four hundred meters to a deep, semicircular chasm. Snuggled into this chasm is an island of limestone, surrounded by a circle of cultivated land in the old meander bed. The cirque was almost hard to look at because of the dazzle, and the effect of height and strangeness made one feel quite dizzy. "Most peculiar!" was our first reaction; "Most interesting!" was our second; and "That was certainly worth seeing!" was our final remark as we drove away. Eerie and fascinating it certainly was!

We continued on to the very Roman city of Nîmes, where we drank refreshing and bubbly Perrier water at a pleasantly shaded table under an awning in front of a cafe. Here the waiters do not hurry you along, so you just sit and be. Watching the world go by along the tree-lined boulevard, we soon lapsed into that feeling of "I've all eternity." We were enveloped in the leisurely atmosphere of the South of France, where the people around you seem to have all the time in the world and intend to enjoy every minute of it. Used to sunshine, blue skies, and a good life, they seem content to savor it, instead of rushing around, wearing themselves out to achieve, achieve, and make more money. No one seemed to be going anywhere in a desperate hurry. It was all most restful and very soon we were relaxing too. I gathered, however, from a fellow passenger in a train at a later date that the southern habit of putting off till tomorrow what you can't be bothered doing today annoys people from the more energetic, northern industrial areas of France. Perhaps it is basically a matter of keeping cool or keeping warm in such different climates.

As Australians, interested in any and all sports, we were fascinated to see how the game of bowls, with steel balls, called *pétanque*, was played by groups of men, wherever there was a spare patch of land in a quiet street in any town or village. This sport is the passion of the South. As early as seven or eight years old, little boys begin to imitate their fathers and uncles. Of course, any group playing soon attracts neighbors and passersby, who become as absorbed as the players themselves and have plenty of opinions to give as to the next move. These peaceful scenes confirmed our already strong impression of the leisurely, relaxed approach to life in this region.

An important Roman center in the first and second centuries of the Christian era, Nîmes has impressive and well-preserved Roman remains, including a perfectly preserved Roman temple in Greek style, with Corinthian columns of the first century BC. In a still active Roman Arena, dating from 15 BC, twenty thousand people can watch the locally popular bullfights, with champion matadors from Spain, picadors, toreadors, and all the ancient ceremonial. The neighboring Camargue is, of course, stock-rearing country with its own cowboys or *gardians*. The Roman Arena in Nîmes is so well built, with staircases leading down into exit galleries and corridors, that the entire crowd can be evacuated within five minutes, without buffeting or crush. The Arena is also used for local political meetings. Not far from the city is the intact Roman aqueduct, the Pont du Gard, over the Gard River, considered by some to be the finest extant example of Roman engineering in the world. It is certainly one of the most beautiful. Two rows of arches are superimposed and crowned by a third set of small arches that carried the aqueduct itself, which supplied pure water to Nîmes for four centuries. The huge blocks of stone with which the aqueduct is built have mellowed to a soft, golden hue that tones in with the sylvan setting of trees on the rocky slopes on either side of the river.

We drove out of Nîmes along roads lined on both sides with vineyards to the horizon. It became more and more evident how important for France its wine industry was. The monoculture of this part of the world, however, constituted a real hardship for its inhabitants during World War II, when the importation of food was difficult. There was little to eat locally except the ubiquitous chestnuts. Since then the region has learned the value of diversification.

With Nîmes as the gate to Provence, it was a hop, skip, and a jump to Avignon, with its fourteenth-century crenelated ramparts, like the cardboard castles of my childhood, its Palace of the Popes, with high impregnable walls, looming over the town, and the remains of the famous bridge about which all little French children and learners of French still sing. And so on to Les Baux, through the weird limestone chain of the Little Alps (*les Alpilles*), their bare white hillsides, dotted with the sparse vegetation of low evergreen oaks, occasionally supporting terraces of olive groves. The ruined fortress of Les Baux is perched high on a rocky hillside, with its wild contours merging imperceptibly with the rocks around it. On two sides the rock face descends into a ravine. The site itself is magnificent, completely dominating the surrounding countryside. This was the impregnable lair of the Counts of Baux who were great marauders, penetrating even to Italy and the Kingdom of Naples. They were so turbulent that at length Louis XIII, in the seventeenth century, had their castle and ramparts demolished, leaving this breathtakingly impressive site. It is rugged and wild to an uncanny degree. After a quick look at the magnificent facade of the lovely Romanesque church of St Trophime at Arles, it was back to Montpellier, our delightful interlude over. For my Australian visitors the trip had been a real feast of Old World grandeur and charm.

May Day in Marseille

At the end of April, I was back in Marseille, which was becoming quite familiar to me. This time I was hoping to see, if briefly, my very old friends from Melbourne, the Alexanders, who were on their way to Scotland to visit Mr Alexander's relatives in Aberdeen. I felt quite at home, staying in the same spotless hotel on the Canebière, where I was already treated like an old friend. I rushed off to the office of the Port Police to get a permit to go on to the quay as the ship came in. It was there that I discovered that the ship would be a day late, so, always the inveterate traveler, I used the extra day to visit the very bourgeois spa town of Aix-en-Provence, whose wide, tree-lined streets and eighteenth-century mansions exuded an atmosphere of smug comfort. Even the university students appeared very obviously to come from families in comfortable circumstances

Since the next day was May 1st, International Labor Day, everyone stopped work in a very proletarian city like Marsellle. There was no transport whatsoever — no buses, no trams, no taxis. In the streets women were selling bunches of lily-of-the-valley, the bringer of good luck. I felt I needed it. The problem was how to get out to the big port where the liners came in, about three or four miles out of town. Immediately after breakfast I set out on foot. As I passed the Old Port, I saw the fishermen painting their boats and mending their nets, and it occurred to me that one of them might like to earn a little extra money. Eventually I found an old sailor willing to take me out to the big port in a motorized rowboat, but he warned me that it was a long way, much further than by road. This old man, a Corsican as it happened, looked just like all the pictures of old sailors in books and on postcards, with his skin sunburned to a deep brown, his white hair, and the white bristles on his chin. He was a cheery, loquacious soul and explained everything to me as we passed by the silent quays, with their boats waiting for the workers to return after the holiday. This delightful boat tour took about an hour. On arrival at the international port area, I found out from the few men on duty that the liner from Australia was not due to arrive for several hours yet. After dreaming, reading, and looking out to sea from the cliff top, I wandered along the coast and picked a little bunch of red poppies, white daisies, and pink kiss-me-quick, which were growing wild on the hillsides, as a gift of welcome for Mrs Alexander. Then the news came that there was sickness on the ship. It would have to be quarantined until inspected by the port doctor, who would vaccinate any passengers not already vaccinated against smallpox. Consequently, the ship would not come into port until late afternoon. This was most disturbing, since my train for Montpellier was due to leave at six-thirty and I had the prospect of a two-hour walk back to Marseille.

The wind was blowing hard and cold, but by this time the men on duty had begun to take an interest in my predicament, and the two young customs officers had invited me into their glassed-in cabin to shelter from the wind. The best way to gain solicitous attention from the French is to appeal to their sympathies with a problem you cannot solve. "Don't worry," said one of the customs officers, "I'll take you back to Marseille on the back of my motor-cycle if you wait till the end of my shift." Naturally, I was very happy to accept. I spent the next few hours talking to the various dockers and boatmen who dropped in for a yarn. In this way I met some real, dyed-in-the-wool Marseillais, who are a breed of their own — the typical Marius of so many stories. Small, dark-eyed, and lively, they were full of fun, always pulling each other's legs and telling tall stories. We all laughed a lot and I had a great opportunity to adapt to their strong Marseille accents. "All Marseille-born men have to go to sea at some stage," they assured me. We talked about many things — conditions of life in France, cost of living, insufficiency of wages — all of which were burning questions in France at the time.

When the doctor arrived in his motor boat, the customs officers persuaded him to take me out to the ship with him to see if I could at least glimpse my friends leaning over the rail. Because of the quarantine, however, I had to promise just to talk and not to pass anything to them. As we drew near the ship, curious passengers stared at me as I cruised around it in the doctor's boat, but I couldn't see any sign of my friends. As we passed in front of the ship, I saw its name on the prow. It was the Ranchi, not the Orontes. I had been asking about "the ship from Australia" and this ship had come from Australia. The Orontes, it seemed, would not dock until the next morning at 7 a.m. Unfortunately the train service to Montpellier would not allow me to see the Orontes arrive and still be back in time for my classes. Regretfully, but gratefully, I whizzed back to Marseille in fine style in a quarter of an hour, riding pillion behind the Customs Officer and arriving in good time for the evening train. Next morning I received a belated cable from the Alexanders, forewarning me that the Orontes would be arriving a day late in Marseille. I was not disappointed, however, since I had had the unique experience of seeing the inside workings of a big port and I had been able to spend time with some born-and-bred Marseillais in their normal work setting.

My third visit to Marseille was eight months later, when I went back to see two old friends from St Annes, Amy Turner and Dora Beadle, who were on their way to England to teach for a while. I found it very convenient to be able to get to Marseille so easily, since the passenger liners from Australia usually stayed in port for a day. I was now quite an old hand at showing my friends around that fascinating city. For Dora's and Amy's visit, I found a nice rowing boat and a willing sailor to take us around the Old Port. Naturally he was full of typical Marseille guff and told us many tall tales. When he brought us back to shore, he declared grandiloquently, "Now, remember! Whenever you come back to Marseille, just stand on the quay and call 'Paul! Paul!' and I'll come running."

Roman Provence

School life in France being punctuated by public holidays, national and religious, some of which were moveable feasts that danced around the set holiday periods, I was free again just after my return for Ascension Day. This was the occasion for a bus excursion for the history students at the school to see the remains of Roman civilization at Vaison-la-Romaine and Orange in Provence. This visit would bring alive for me all those readings in ancient history that had fascinated me in my Latin courses in Australia.

It was a sunny day and the Provençal countryside looked very attractive with the silvery foliage of the olive-tree groves, the acres of vines beginning to sprout with new green leaves, and the rows of cypress trees, planted as wind-breaks to protect the early vegetables from the strong Mistral. As we penetrated further into Provence we could see the pale outline of the hills dominated by the fairy-like, snow-capped peak of Mont Ventoux, the most westerly peak of the Alps. Our first stop, Vaison-la-Romaine, is a fascinating place of great antiquity, having been already a Celtic capital in the fourth century BC, before it became an important Roman center. It contains the most important Roman remains in France. Excavations have exposed houses, baths, and rows of shops, statues, pillars, drains, decorative pools, even household conveniences. Everywhere there are mosaics and frescoes in a wonderful state of preservation. The gardens surrounding the ruins contain only trees and flowers mentioned in the Roman classics. The Roman theater, cut out of the rock of the hillside itself, is perfectly constructed to give every spectator an unobstructed view of the stage. It is still used for open-air performances in the summer season, just as the Roman bridge still spans the river. Evidences of Christianity are also of great antiquity at Vaison-la-Romaine, being traceable back to the third century AD. At the Council of Arles in 314 AD there was already a Bishop of Vaison, so it is not surprising that the oldest parts of the Cathedral date from the sixth and seventh centuries. Nearby Orange completes the picture with its Roman temple, its gymnasium, and its perfectly preserved, three-arched Arch of Triumph, which commemorates the victory of the Roman Second Legion in finally subjugating the obdurate people of Marseille. The Roman theater at Orange is the best preserved in the world. It even retains the high wall behind the stage, with its lofty niche for the statue of the reigning Roman Emperor. This statue had a detachable head, to save having to replace the whole sculpture when a new emperor was installed. I was a little tired at this stage of the visit and sneaked to the other side of the theater for a little rest. Suddenly our erudite archeologist guide turned and, pointing directly at me, declared in a stentorian voice, "And there is Venus!" Sure enough there she was beside me, but such a public christening was not an easy thing to shake off in a student group.

The Basque Country

Another ten days and the Whitsuntide (Pentecost) holiday was upon us. I had decided to use this full week's break to visit the Atlantic coast at Biarritz and see something of the Basque country. "Don't bother about a hotel," said the school manager. "We have a villa at Biarritz. Here's the key. You may as well stay there and save money." This was an offer not to be refused, particularly by a poor language-teaching assistant.

The inhabitants of the different regions of France have noticeably different characteristics, which are generally recognized, almost to the degree of stereotyping. A couple of incidents on the train to Biarritz provided me with interesting insights into these differences. Several young men in my carriage, who were coming home from compulsory military training, began to speak quietly among themselves about a Corsican who had been in their camp and of the reputation of Corsicans as people with hot tempers. After a very few minutes, a tall, dark-eyed, handsome young man burst into the compartment from a nearby compartment, demanding to know: "Why are you bad-mouthing Corsicans? They're Frenchmen the same as you are, aren't they? They fight for France as well as you. Why must you always be attacking them as though they don't belong to France?" with much more along these lines. The young men in my compartment were very much taken aback, since they didn't feel they had been speaking badly about anyone, merely stating the generally accepted opinion that Corsicans were hot-tempered and quick with knives. The young Corsican kept up his tirade for a good five minutes, before leaving somewhat mollified by their explanations. Further along on the trip a Gascon couple joined us, as we passed through what had been ancient Gascony. The man and his wife had big hiking packs and were on their way to represent their region at a camping congress. He talked and joked all the time, but she said nary a word. The husband kept telling tall stories and jokes with a very straight face and a merry eye, every so often taking a swig at his goatskin gourd, which was full of white wine from Perpignan. Every now and then he would blow into it, then hold it up so that a thin stream of wine would came out directly into his mouth. He so perfectly matched the Gascon, as commonly described in French literature, that I had to see it to believe it

We were now passing out of the Mediterranean region of evergreen oaks and Aleppo pines into the Atlantic vegetation of beech trees and deciduous oaks and elms. Since spring was later here, so high in the Pyrenees, the poplars were just putting on the yellow green and the beeches the yellow brown of their spring foliage and the grass was very green. The little stone houses and the church steeples stood out very prettily against the nearer wooded hills, while away to the horizon a series of hills led one's eye to the snow-capped heights of the Pyrenean chain.

At Biarritz, I had a letter of introduction to show to the two old spinsters, who had rooms in my colleague's villa. They regarded me suspiciously at first through a grill in the upper part of the door, but after reading the letter they decided to let me in. I found these two women very interesting. Dressed in the most neglectful way, in the oldest of uninteresting garments, they told me how they had had a dressmaking business, employing some twenty-five seamstresses, where they had made clothes for most of the aristocracy of England, Spain, and other European countries during the grand years when Biarritz had been one of the smartest holiday resorts for the ultra-rich social set. The Duke and Duchess of Windsor and the exiled King of Spain usually spent part of their summers here. With its opulent hotels, boutiques of the leading couturiers and perfume houses of Paris, its inevitable casino, and its golf course for the British, Biarritz reflected the wealthy clientele attracted to its sandy beach and blue ocean waters. The small fishing port was protected by stone walls, separating it from the wilder waters of the Atlantic, which dashed up against the rocky coast in spray, lashing it furiously during storms. With its mild climate the Biarritz area had attracted many sanatoria and *colonies de vacances,* which lined its cliff-top road, the *Corniche*, that ran right to the Spanish border.

Much more interesting to me than Biarritz itself was the inland Basque countryside. Having heard much of the spirit of Basque solidarity and independence, on both sides of the French-Spanish frontier, their pride in the distinctiveness of their ancient language, which is quite unrelated to any other known language, and their enormous attachment to their native soil, I was most anxious to glimpse something of their way of life. Soon I was on my way to St Jean Pied-de-Port a village in a hollow in the low undulating foothills of the Pyrenees. From there I continued on to the Spanish frontier, returning by that other St Jean, the flourishing sardine and tuna fishing port of St Jean-de-Luz, which is one of the most attractive seaside resorts on the Basque coast. In 1951 this area was still quite rural and traditional. Out on the country roads we passed many little carts drawn by pairs of oxen yoked together, with, over their heads, a sheepskin dyed russet or dark brown to match the color of the animals. Oxen were also in use for ploughing the fields. For an Australian used to very large wheat farms, sown and harvested by enormous combines, it was surprising to see men walking behind the plough with the women following, sowing the seed by hand. In the fields were stacks of dried bracken fern, and this bracken, a noxious, imported weed in Australia, was being transported back to the farm outbuildings to spread in the animals' stalls. To add to the local color, every man actually wore a Basque beret! Sharp featured, with high cheekbones and dark hair, they seemed to be of fairly homogenous stock. In the charming little villages we had to contend with goats with tinkling bells and wandering hens. In some, the women were gathered together, laughing and sharing local gossip around the long, stone troughs of communal wash houses, or they were carrying buckets to fill at the street pump, since water had not yet been laid on for many of the individual houses. The scenery, as elsewhere in France, was punctuated by vineyards, with grapevines that grew higher than in the region around Montpellier and were supported on poles. In every little hamlet there was a *fronton*, the tall wall of a court for playing *pelote* or *jai-alai* ("joyous festival") as the Spanish Basques call it. Usually, as we passed by, some people would be practicing the game, projecting the ball against the wall with the distinctive long, hand-shaped basket tied to their wrist. Every region has its own homegrown sports obsession, which it feels is the greatest game in the world — *pétanque*, curling, ice hockey, cricket or Australian Rules football. Here it was clearly *pelote*. Everywhere we saw charming Basque-style houses, whitewashed, with half-timbering, carved wooden balconies, and chalet-type roofs covered with their distinctive rounded tiles. All the timbering and woodwork of doors and window shutters was painted either red or green (thus echoing the red, white, and green of the Basque flag), with just a touch of gray, usually on the woodwork of the window frames, to offset the general color pattern. It made a charming ensemble in village after village, with even the farmhouses in the countryside falling into line. Everywhere everything was tidy and neat.

On the way back to Montpellier through the Pyrenees, I stopped to see what was going on at Lourdes, probably the most famous Roman Catholic place of pilgrimage after Rome. Lourdes is most picturesquely situated in the midst of the mountains, nestling close under an old ruined castle. By now it was pouring rain — April showers that promised May flowers. Lourdes was quite an experience for a person who had been brought up in a strict Protestant tradition, in a country where Roman Catholics and Protestants lived side by side in rather watertight communities. Apart from my Roman Catholic friends at Melbourne University, I had had minimal contact with Roman Catholicism and practically no experience of its religious practices. The intense focus on the Virgin Mary as Intercessor was quite a shock to me and somewhat disconcerting. At the cave where the Virgin Mary, with roses at her feet, had declared herself to St Bernadette, the simple peasant girl, as the Immaculate Conception, people were filling bottles with water from the spring, which was believed to have miraculous healing powers. The huge Basilica, with its torchlight processions of thousands of pilgrims weaving their way up and down the monumental staircases, singing the praises of the Virgin, was most impressive, as were the devotion and hope of the many disabled pilgrims, who drew comfort from the hundreds of discarded crutches and other aids of earlier supplicants whose prayers had been answered. Although this was a non-festive, midweek working day, there were some four thousand pilgrims from many countries, with major pilgrimages from Italy, Germany, Switzerland, France, England, and Wales. The intense commercialization I found very disturbing — streets and streets of souvenir shops, selling Virgins and Bernadettes of all shapes and sizes, even to kitschy bottles in the shape of the Virgin in which one could take away the healing water of the holy spring. There was a beautiful silver Virgin you could wind up to hear her sing the Ave Maria, which seemed to me a little muddled theologically. Surely the Magnificat would have been more appropriate. After much searching, I managed, almost defiantly, to find myself a souvenir without the Virgin or Bernadette. I took away with me a simple eggcup in the form of a Basque in a beret.

I came across an even more medieval aspect of the Roman Catholic church in France when I visited Ena Peck, who was spending the year as a language assistant in Toulouse. It was the day of the annual display of relics at St Sernin's Church, another stage of the medieval pilgrimage to St James of Compostella. St Sernin's was proud of the fact that it had the biggest collection of relics in France. Bits of bones, hair, and body parts of every imaginable saint, known and unknown, down to the most obscure regional patrons, were set out in reliquaries up and down the aisles and in the crypt. Not unexpectedly there were pieces of the True Cross and the Crown of Thorns, although the head of St Thomas Aquinas came as something of a surprise. This great display must have been very impressive to the medieval pilgrim, but to me it seemed a quaint reminder of the enthusiasms, superstitions, and credulity of a past age.

End of Year Fever

Back at the EN there was much nervousness among the girls as the all important, career-determining examinations approached. There was so much to learn and so many details to know that I would find girls sitting on stairs, or in any spare space, learning by heart the summaries at the end of the chapters in their textbooks. They were learning these by repeating them aloud, so that at times the building sounded like a beehive. When I had to supervise examinations, I would see nervous girls copying each other's answers right along a row. It seemed impossible to stop them, probably because they had been doing this for years. After the exams, there was quite a scandal because one over-anxious girl had been found to have broken into the office where the result sheets were lodged in order to alter her grade for one of her examinations. Again I could see the pernicious effects of widespread, impersonal testing, which victimizes individuals more than it validates learning.

The year concluded with a school excursion into Provence. We were again on the track of Romanesque churches and Roman ruins. We first visited the beautiful church of St Gilles du Gard, with its facade of three round-arched doorways, separated by slender columns and decorated with sculptured figures. We continued on to the capital of Camargue, the town of Arles. Here we visited the very famous Romanesque church of St Trophime, of which one can never tire, with its elaborate facade and delightful, covered, twelfth-century cloister around a beautiful garden, where the monks used to walk and meditate while saying their offices. The Roman ruins of the theater, arena, and cemetery, with great stone sarcophagi, were very impressive, but the climax of the afternoon was the opportunity to see two exhibitions of Van Gogh's work in Provence, at Arles and at St Remy. His depiction of boats drawn up on the shore at the Saintes-Maries-de-la-Mer in Camargue, of wheat fields, haystacks and almond trees in bloom, even his old boots, all became so much more vivid in this their province of origin. I had already decided to do a certificate in History of Art in my second year at the University of Montpellier and anticipated with great enthusiasm the obligatory excursions, which would lead me deeper and deeper into the artistic heritage of this region. We were soon in Daudet country and anxious to see the windmill from which that delightful author wrote so many of the short stories every French child and student of French has read in school. This charming little windmill is built on a hill, with a splendid view over the Provence Daudet loved so deeply and wove so delightfully into his tales. From the windmill we could see the plain of the Rhône, the fourteenth century Abbey of Montmajour, the castles of Tarascon and Beaucaire, the Montagnette, and the chain of the Alpilles, to which he so frequently referred.

The best photographs, I find, are the ones you just miss. It was at the foot of this hill that I should have had the perfect picture. A very old shepherd, with his coat over his shoulders, was minding a small flock of sheep, with one black one with its wool cut off in patches on its back. "I'll take it when we come back," I thought, but not surprisingly when I came down the shepherd and his flock had moved on.

On our return to Montpellier we followed a typical Provencal road, bordered with fields of early vegetables, sheltered from the cold Mistral by rows of cypresses or bamboos or by fences of rushes. The roads and fields were bright with brilliant red poppies (the *coquelicots* of French folksong) and white marguerites, in among great clumps of yellow broom. As a contrast to the Basque countryside with its oxen, this was the province of the donkey and innumerable long-eared donkeys were in service drawing carts and pulling ploughs in the fields. Passing by Tarascon and Nîmes, we sang all the way home to Montpellier.

Wilga the nanny

My next concern was how to support myself during the three months of the coming summer. I had after all lost nearly half of my year's salary because of my illness. Moreover, the EN paid salaries in nine monthly segments, not twelve. I had written over forty letters in the attempt to find some kind of vacation work. Some of the responses were extraordinary in their expectations as compared with salary. One person in Bordeaux had wanted me to look after three very young children and the house, help prepare meals, and be on duty from early in the morning till late in the evening, with just one half-day off a week, for board and three pounds a month. (For comparison, this was three and a half times what I had paid to have my shoes mended). My colleagues and friends, well aware of my plight, had been beating the bushes for me too.

Fortunately, my colleague at the EN for Boys, Alain Parmentier, and his wife Annick were looking for someone to take care of their children over the vacation period. They had two children, Isabelle, aged two years nine months, and Marianne (Nanou), aged one year eight months. Madame Parmentier was expecting a third baby and needed to rest after her heavy year of teaching. I had visited them earlier and they were delighted with the way I had interacted with the children, who were little pets, it seemed to me. I protested that, although I enjoyed playing with young children, I hadn't the faintest idea how to care for them. The Parmentiers assured me that it was only a matter of time and I would soon get into the way of it. To persuade me, they doubled their salary offer to board and eight pounds a month, with a full day off a week. Easy-going, friendly people, they intended to treat me more as a friend than an employee; I would dine with them, for instance, and meet other guests of the family. I accepted this pleasant shelter from the hard, cold (and expensive) world with alacrity. My summer with the Parmentiers began with a week at the beach at Carnon, near Montpellier. After that we would be moving on to the country home of Madame Parmentier's father in the Ardèche, south of Lyon in the Rhône Valley — an area of gently rolling hills between Privas and Valence. The Parmentiers were Protestants and Annick's family was an old Huguenot one, which I had found constituted a kind of unspoken but recognized aristocracy in the French Protestant world. The period at the beach gave me time to accustom myself to my new role. After all, It was easy to keep the children entertained digging holes in the sand and building simple sand castles, with occasional side trips to see the ducks and swans in the local park.

Madame Parmentier did not know a great deal about cooking and neither did I, but French summer meals were easy enough to put together and in the Ardèche the cooking would be done by her father's maid, who would accompany him from Paris. I would help with light housework, but Madame Parmentier would not think of asking me to do any heavy cleaning or laundry. French women at that time operated on a kind of caste system. There were women who did heavy housework and women who didn't. I was clearly of the class that could not be expected to exert themselves physically. The washing was sent out and a *femme de ménage* came in to do the cleaning. Cleaning women were paid very little at the time and so were easily affordable. Madame Parmentier was a charming, affable soul, who thought everything I did was just right, so we got on very well indeed.

The Parmentiers' summer home, *L'Horme,* near Vernoux, was in the foothills of the Massif Central, about 150 kilometers by car from Montpellier. The old house, belonging to Madame Parmentier's father, a Parisian businessman, was out in the country, on a plateau surrounded by lightly wooded hills. On the hillsides, there were pastures and farmlands, with conical haystacks drying in the sun. Running down a shady valley nearby was a small creek, with a stone footbridge and a little stone dam holding the water back for the cattle. There were no barriers dividing the fields in this area or along the roadsides. They were not necessary since the farmers knew the boundaries of their own properties. Twice a day they took the cows and goats out to graze, then sat and watched them to see that they did not stray onto someone else's land. At the end of the day they would bring them back to their sheds to eat and ruminate in their bails. Around the house there was a big garden with trees, providing plenty of room for the children to play. Near the kitchen was a large vegetable garden with raspberry bushes, which supplied us with plenty of fresh vegetables and fruit every day. We also gathered *champignons* (mushrooms) in the woods. I soon found out that all sorts of orange and red fungi were called *champignons*; some were edible, some were not. Fortunately the Parmentiers were sufficiently experienced to know the difference. Behind the house was a typical stone farmhouse, or *mas*, occupied by a tenant farmer and his family who worked the land throughout the year.

Annick's father, Monsieur Lauriol, had brought his maid, Olga, to do the cooking and some housework, but not of course the washing. My task was to attend almost exclusively to the children's physical and social needs, lending a gracious hand from time to time to clear the table, help with the drying-up, or dust an occasional room. It was well known in the family that no one could get on with Olga, who was inclined to grumble and quickly found something with which to find fault. It seemed she had nearly made the Danish nanny of the previous year ill with her morose disposition. She was also very talkative. Fortunately for me, we got on famously for some unaccountable reason. She told Madame Parmentier I was not "proud" — my Australian egalitarianism, I suppose. I also continued to get on very well with the children. Madame Parmentier maintained that they had never cried so little as now when I was in charge of them. We would hear perhaps a little outburst of sixty seconds of displeasure from time to time, but that was all.

My day began at about 7.45 a.m., when Nanou would start to grumble and declare her interest in getting up. Isabelle was toilet-trained, but Nanou still had to wear a diaper during the night. Her first question in the morning was always an anxious "*Mouillée?*" (Wet?). If the answer was "*Oui, mouillée,*" there would follow a few moments of disappointed blubbering; if "*Pas mouillée,*" she would be all sunshine and smiles of happy achievement. After getting the children up I would prepare their simple breakfast. Madame Parmentier had explained to me how to make their *bouillie de semoule* (semolina), which I dutifully spooned into their mouths for several days at every meal, until Isabelle began to spit it out in disgust. It was then that I learned I should vary it, with occasional mashed bananas and the like. Things went better after that. Olga kept an eye on us as I fed the children in their high chairs, and she would occasionally call out as she crossed the room: "*Les petites mains sur la table!*" (Little hands on the table!), since, in my foreigner's ignorance, I was not teaching them correct French table manners. While I had my meal with the grownups, the children would romp around asking for crusts. Who, even young children, could resist crunchy French bread? After breakfast, I would bathe them, dress them for the day, and take them out in the garden to play, or we would go to the farm to see the animals. Isabelle loved to see the "*cossons*" (*cochons*, pigs) — she lisped — while Nanou wanted to see the "*coyons*" — she was having trouble with her medial consonants. After lunch, mostly prepared by Olga, they would have their *do-do* (afternoon nap), while I had lunch with the family. The Parmentiers and Mr Lauriol, being very anxious to help me perfect my French, always spoke to me in French, often giving me useful hints and adding to my knowledge of things French.

After lunch I usually had about an hour of peace to work on my German, for which I would have to pass a reading examination for my Licence the following year.

Once the children woke up, it was out again for a "*ta-ta*" in their *poussette* (stroller), stopping perhaps to play by the creek or gather flowers in the meadow. In the environs I found, growing wild, pincushions, forget-me-not, irises, cornflowers, red and yellow poppies, white daisies, buttercups, love-in-the-mist, bluebells, snow-ball bushes, honeysuckle, kiss-me-quick, foxgloves, hollyhocks, and, of course, climbing roses. The meadows were quite a garden. The distinctive trees of this area were poplars, chestnut trees, oaks, and beeches. Since we were still in the South of France, the weather was very pleasant — sunny and warm, but with cool breezes and a certain freshness because we were in the mountains. The children and I would usually end our little outings by wandering along the hillside path, singing little French songs. This was quite a circus, with each of us singing different words to a different tune, although it might be an attempt at the same song. Nanou would bumble along with her little collection of half-heard sounds, while Isabelle would try to make sense of the utterances. She would pick up and remember half the words and make up the rest from her limited experience, coming out at times with strange combinations and inventions. The old folk song, "*En revenant de guerre*" (Coming home from the war), which meant nothing to her, came out in her version as "Three little hens in the field." A popular song at the time was "*J'aime le jambon et la saucisse*" (I love ham and sausage), which made sense to Isabelle. It continued "*J'aime le jambon, c'est bon* "(Ham is really good); "*mais je préfère le lait de ma nourrice*" ("but I prefer the milk of my wet-nurse"), a code expression to the French for alcohol; this Isabelle sang lustily as "*mais je préfère le champagne et les olives*" ("but I prefer champagne and olives"), which fitted in well with the beats to the bar. This, I thought, was quite sophisticated for a two-and-a-half year old and a good augur for her future in the *haute bourgeoisie*. Our singing, I found out later, would waft back to the garden, where the family was relaxing, chatting, and reading. Madame Parmentier always maintained that it was I who had taught the children to sing.

After the children's afternoon milk, their father, mother, or grandfather would take them over for a while. With me they were very sweet, affectionate, and obedient children, but when I took them to their mother for an hour, they would get up to all kinds of devilry. It seemed to me that, conscious of the fact that she saw very little of them during the day, she was over-anxious to demonstrate her love for them; she so much wanted them to love her. This great desire for their love was quite obvious to the children. Consequently they became very demanding, knowing she would refuse them nothing. For an hour they did whatever they liked. Not surprisingly she was very glad to have me come for them at the end of the hour. On seeing me they immediately ceased their little game and reverted to their happy-natured selves, doing exactly what I wanted them to do. Their mother never ceased to be amazed at the transformation.

The children went to bed at about half-past seven, after which I had dinner with the family and was free to read or write letters and prepare myself for a rather broken night attending to their various physical needs. The old house had an attic which, not surprisingly, was full of bats, so I would often be writing letters or updating my diary with bats flying around my head. On one occasion, I counted nine bats flying around my room as I wrote. Fortunately one of the visiting uncles, an astronomer from the Sahara, had told me that bats had a kind of radar that prevented them from hitting me, even though they were blind, and that they would never get tangled up in my hair, as the old story would have it. After that, I took it all very calmly and the bats and I cohabited the room quite happily. I used to reassure the children too that bats swooping down the staircase in the late afternoon were really friendly little creatures and quite harmless. The children took their cue from me, even if a little doubtfully. One day I was carrying Nanou downstairs and holding Isabelle's hand as she made her own way down, like a grown-up person, when a bat swooped past my ear. Involuntarily I flinched, which did not go unnoticed by the observant Isabelle. "You jumped!" she said, this confirming her own view of bats as being not as innocuous as people said. Despite a natural aversion to little things that fly or jump at you, I soon settled down to a modus vivendi with wasps and grayish-brown grasshoppers that seemed to leap up at us everywhere we put our feet. Of course, we had less stressful companions in the garden and the children loved to watch the little red squirrels playing in the trees and the glowworms lighting up at night.

Isabelle was very intelligent, talking very fluently for a two-and-a-half-year- old. She reasoned well and I found I could talk to her about nearly everything. She was a little mischievous, but very sweet. Nanou, at one and a half, understood everything but talked only in broken phrases with her own peculiar pronunciation. I was "Viga" to them both, w's not being part of French phonology and a consonant cluster like "lg" being beyond their infant capacities. Nanou was a merry little soul, always smiling in a charming way, which permitted her to be a little tease and get away with it. Although she was the younger, Nanou was the leader of the two and much more original than Isabelle, who was very affectionate and loved to be with her little sister. Nanou often had an idea that Isabelle would want to copy right away. In some ways they reminded me of Linda and myself when we were small. Nanou was a great collector of pebbles, feathers, pretty leaves or flowers, which she soon tired of and threw away. Isabelle was more at the kindergarten stage, liking to do things with her hands — filling and refilling small buckets with sand with a little spade, or making very serious and important holes with a little rake or stick. Isabelle would dance in front of the mirror for ages, singing long songs, partly remembered, partly invented. She learned rapidly. She would ask the name of something, repeat it three or four times to herself, and then come out with it appropriately several days later. She learned continually by asking *Qui*? ("Who?," which served also for "What?") and *Pourquoi*? ("Why?"). Once when I was carrying Nanou downstairs, I swayed a little, so I explained to Isabelle that I had lost my balance for a moment: "*J'ai perdu mon équilibre*," I explained. "Where did it go?" Isabelle asked, never losing an opportunity to learn. Sometimes, we could not make out exactly what Marianne wanted to say, but as I lived with her I gradually got to understand most of her mutilated pronunciations, usually with consonants missing at the beginnings and ends of words or distorted in the middle. After all she was still very young. She became very attached to me as time went on and liked always to be by my side; in fact she often preferred to be with me rather than with her mother, father, or grandfather.

It was very amusing to hear these little ones, as they learned French, making the same grammatical mistakes with difficult constructions that my students in Australia had made. Since they were listening to native French speakers all day, they quickly picked up structures that are typical of informal French, but are much harder for nonnative speakers to acquire. For instance, even at this early stage, they were using the segmentation of the sentence that is the French way, with its habitual stress on the final syllable, of emphasizing a particular element of meaning. *"Il est parti, papa,"* Isabelle would say, whereas in English, with our variable stress, we would say: *"Daddy's* gone!" *"Parti papa,"* little Nanou would echo wistfully. Soon I was learning practical vocabulary, like diapers (*couches*) and baby's bottles (*biberons*), that I had never learned in my French literary studies, as well as baby French, like *dodo* (nap), *lolo* (milk), *lala* (chocolate), and *dada* (gee-gee). *"Fais dodo, mon petit frère,"* we would sing, *"Fais dodo t' auras lolo, Maman est en haut, qui fait du lolo, Papa est en bas, qui fait du lala,"* and so on.

The children had some problems working out whether I was a child or an adult or something in between. Like all very young children, they were using the familiar form *tu* to me, as they did with all the older people around them, who also called them *tu*. Their parents, on the other hand, used the more formal and respectful *vous* when speaking to me. It was Isabelle who first noticed this discrepancy and tried to use *vous* to me, like Maman and Papa. Of course she was not accustomed to the changes in verb morphology this entailed and struggled on for a little while trying to master this unfamiliar usage, as well as remembering what she was now using with whom when. Nanou tried to imitate her in this, with very muddled results. This effort continued for a short while, until they both found it easier to revert to the *tu* that everyone, including me, was using to them and that they were using to everyone else. At a certain point we were to have a visit from a grownup cousin, Paul, and this posed a little problem for Isabelle, in view of my ambiguous status. Finally she gave me her best advice: "When Cousin Paul comes, you won't kiss him, because he isn't Daddy!" I found this more hilarious than did Madame Parmentier.

The tenant farmer, Monsieur Moulin, and his family in the *mas* were the first French peasants I had met. He was suffering great grief, because his wife had hanged herself in the barn at Easter-time (her mind having been deranged by her change of life crisis). Consequently, every evening, after his heavy day's work, he would sit outside the farmhouse and weep bitterly. His two daughters, Jeannine and Ginette, dressed in mourning black, would work all day beside him in the fields, take the cows to pasture or feed the ducks, goats, hens, pigs (and guinea pigs!), dogs, and horses that so delighted my small charges. If I went to speak to the two mid-teen girls during the day, he would impatiently call them back to work after a very few minutes. Even the cows were in mourning, having had their bells taken off for a year, while those of the neighboring herds tinkled merrily in the nearby fields. I went to dinner with the Moulins in the *mas* several times. The beds were built into the wall like bunks, in the old style, and we supped on heavy country bread and good local cheese, washed down, of course, with a regional *vin ordinaire.* One day I took the children to see the harvesting. The summer's crop was cut with a reaper drawn by two strong farm horses and the men and women followed, gathering the piles of cut wheat to bind into sheaves, which they stood together to dry in stooks. The only thing missing to make it quite biblical was the gleaners following behind to pick up the dropped grain, although there were plenty of odd heads of wheat left behind. The children were very interested to see the big horses but clung very close to me every time they went past. When it was time for the threshing, a big traveling machine came to our farm and farmers from the surrounding area assembled to help. It was quite a social occasion. I put our two little ones in one of the great chests of harvested barley and they had great fun playing and slithering around in it.

The Parmentier family, being Protestant, took an interest in my desire to attend Sunday services and took me up in the mountains to a church in a tiny village built entirely of stone, with charming cobbled or stepped streets and fascinating little arcades and lanes. On one side you looked out over a typical Ardèche scene of hills with park-like pastures, cultivated fields, and occasional woods; on the other side, you looked inland along wild, precipitous valleys of the Massif Central toward the source of the Loire River. On another occasion, Mr Parmentier took me on the pillion of his motorcycle to another village where about a hundred and fifty Protestants, mostly peasants, were meeting in a perfect setting — in a natural amphitheater in the woods facing an orchard. After the church service and a buffet dinner the young people gave a concert of songs and sketches and held a tombola — a Dutch auction, which was here called an American auction. It was very like gatherings in country churches at home in Australia. These little Protestant enclaves in the mountains, of which I had heard in Montpellier, had continued to function for centuries, despite the strenuous efforts of royal and revolutionary regimes to wipe them out.

Since the Parmentiers' country house was so isolated, it was obvious that the children would never realize the significance of "Wilga's day off." After all, wasn't I their playmate? What other life could I have? The family decided that, instead of giving me a day off every week, they would give me a full week off after six weeks. This was ideal for me and I planned, with their help, a week of touring in Savoy and Switzerland for the middle of my summer. I would pass by Grenoble to Annecy, with its very beautiful lake reflecting the snow-capped mountains, which I had admired for years in a pretty postcard Christiane had sent me. I would continue on to St Gervais and Chamonix to see Mont Blanc and the glaciers — the perpetual snows that one only dreamed about in warm temperate Australia. Unfortunately, for starters, the lake at Annecy was very misty, so I was left to imagine its beauty from my framed postcard, and at St Gervais I struck a cloudy, Scotch mist day. I did get a clearer view of Mont Blanc higher up on the Plateau of Assy fortunately, because the next day at Chamonix, which was to be the culminating excitement of my trip, the weather could only be described as rotten. At least I got the chance to walk on my first glacier, the Mer de Glace, its surface dirty with the debris of centuries and its sides slashed with enormous crevasses reflecting a strange greenish light. There was a cave dug into the glacier that was completely furnished with ice furnishings, with water continually running in the ice washbasin and, shining through the glacial walls, a powder blue light that was quite ethereal. With high hopes I took the *téléférique* up over the treetops; this, I hoped, would take me above the clouds. At the top, however, we were in a complete fog and could see nothing at all — none of the fabulous mountain views the tourist pamphlets had led me to expect. Such are the vicissitudes of travel. I could, however, admire the wild, chaotic valley, strewn with great boulders dislodged by many years of rockslides, and the lower slopes of the mountain luxuriant with the bright colors of alpine wildflowers. I left Chamonix in a cloudburst —

a suitable climax — and was then on my way back to L'Horme and my two small charges.

By this time, Madame Parmentier was so enjoying the household harmony that she was beginning to wish that I could stay for ten years to bring up the children for her. However, the return to Montpellier loomed and another nanny arrived — Molly (Maria-Olga) Krieghammer from Vienna. Since there was a week of overlap, I got to know her quite well. She sometimes wore Austrian national dress — a short-sleeved, square-necked white blouse, with a snug corsage of blue with white pin-spots, a dirndl skirt of red with white pin-spots, and over that an apron of red, white, and blue vertical stripes. She was always singing and waltzing. Snippets of the Blue Danube or the music of Strauss floated on the air. The daughter of an Austrian baron, she was preparing for work in the Foreign Service and had come to France *au pair* to improve her French. (Later she was appointed to the Austrian Chancellery in Australia, and, as it happened, I was able to see her again.) Molly was to fill in the month before the longer-term Alsatian nurse arrived. The poor children had to continually adjust and readjust to different minders. It was amusing to me, but not to Molly, to see how Isabelle and Marianne clung to my hands and refused to have anything to do with her at first. "We want Viga," they would insist, drawing away from her very obviously. It reminded me of my first experience with them, when they were missing their Danish nanny. I remember very vividly the first night I put Isabelle to bed. As she stood beside her bed she told me very firmly: "Go away! We don't want you here! We want Mummy." I had been most disconcerted by her insistance, since this had been my first experience with young children. What a difference a few weeks of familiarity had made!

Savoy, the Swiss Alps, and a peep into Italy

Before returning to Montpellier, I took ten days to explore more of the lands further east, meeting up at Besançon with a group of French student travel companions. First we traveled through the Jura Mountains, a region famous for its excellent cheeses. The cow pastures beside the mountain streams tinkled with bells as the cows grazed. The greater the yield of milk the bigger the bells. Some proud cows wore bells as big as school bells — I hope they realized just what an accolade this represented. Switzerland, not having suffered from war, immediately appeared to us as clean, neat, and very prosperous, well dressed and well built. There were flowers everywhere, in window boxes on the sills and balconies of the chalet-type houses, in public gardens and around commemorative fountains. At Lausanne the French were astonished to find that the beautiful cathedral was Protestant, a *temple* in fact! We did not linger beside the beautiful Swiss lakes, but made our way via German-speaking Switzerland to the mountains, with their bare upper peaks and fir-covered lower slopes, with steep cascades coming down like thin white ribbons unwinding. On the heights we glimpsed mysterious ruined castles and isolated villages, as we made our way to the Simplon Gap. Here the road crosses the Alps through a valley, which itself is already some six thousand six hundred feet high. All through my Ascot Vale childhood, I had gone to sleep studying a picture on my bedroom wall of Napoleon crossing the Alps and here I was at that very spot — crossing them, I must admit, in much greater comfort along a much better built road than Napoleon. We looked down into deep ravines, with mountain torrents at their base. Tangled masses of rock, the remains of many landslides and avalanches, mingled with old tree trunks and great patches of unmelted snow.

As we descended into Italy, we could see how much poorer it was than Switzerland, but the riches of the Northern Lakes opened up before us at Lake Maggiore and Lake Como. The misty hills coming down to the lakes gave them a dreamlike appearance that was quite magical. Everywhere were magnificent gardens, around castles and mansions. In one of these there was an imitation of an Australian fern gully. It lacked the eucalypts of our Australian forest, unfortunately, but the tree ferns were authentic. On our tour we visited Milan, with its magnificent cathedral whose delicately pinnacled beauty is hard to describe. I was determined to see Leonardo Da Vinci's Last Supper, which was not on our itinerary, so while the others in the group were settling in at a cafe near the cathedral for afternoon refreshments, I skipped off to find it. I knew it was to be seen at the Church of Santa Maria della Grazia. That was enough for me. Weak as my Italian was, I asked at each street corner for Santa Maria della Grazia and, thanks to the very cooperative Italian man and woman in the street, I soon found it in an area of tremendous bomb damage, amidst which it had been miraculously preserved. Unfortunately, at that time, it was fast fading into the wall on which it was painted, but it was a joy to see the original of this much loved and reproduced picture. Afterwards I had no problem finding my way back to the group by asking at every turn for the *Duomo* (Cathedral). It was certainly a richer experience than drinking yet another cup of coffee.

The return over the St Gotthard Pass was a revelation of the extraordinary skill of the Swiss in building mountain roads, as the way down the mountain switch-backed again and again in a zigzag down the rocky slopes. With a strong wind blowing, it was icy-cold, even though it was late summer. The descent was down a weird, savagely-cut valley, with huge boulders and a raging mountain stream hurtling down into boiling holes, the heavily overcast weather adding just the right somber atmosphere to this eerie scene. Some of the gorges were so narrow that the rocky cliffs nearly met over our heads. As we continued through the mountains, the clouds were so low that we saw nothing at all, just a white blanket of fog, until we finally came down to Interlaken, between its two lakes. Any hope of seeing the snowclad Jungfrau was dim in such weather, except when the clouds broke for a moment or two. We continued on to Berne with its arcaded streets and pointed towers. The many fountains were crowned with medieval figures with banners, all painted in bright colors that echoed the brilliance of the flowers on every windowsill. Even in the central business area there were flowers. Wherever there is a forlorn winter, I have found the passion for a profusion of summer flowers is at its height.

Alsace and the German connection

I left the group next day, to continue with one of those solitary explorations to which I was becoming accustomed, making my way north from Besançon to Alsace. This would have to be another bread, cheese, and tomato trip, since my meager funds were very low. In fact I bought only two meals in ten days and drank only water. My Depression experiences have always helped me in difficult financial moments like these. Fortunately I found some very cheap hotels, in one case sleeping in what was actually a *salle de bain* (bathroom in the literal 1950s sense of the word). I couldn't help but think of little old Auntie Tilly, sleeping in our bathroom during the deepest days of the Depression. I had so hoped to visit Germany, the land of my Lehmann ancestors, while I was in this area. I had even obtained a German visa, but I simply could not afford it now. I decided that after visiting Colmar and the big city of Strasbourg, I would content myself with a quick day trip over the border to Heidelberg — a name that resonated with me, because of Mother's early associations with its Victorian namesake

Not unexpectedly, I loved Alsace — that German-speaking province so stubbornly devoted to France through its various German occupations. Once again I realized how very distinctive the different provinces of France are, in architecture, in foods, and in the general atmosphere of towns and villages. This is one reason why France never ceases to fascinate, even after many visits. Picturesque Colmar, with its colorful roofs decorated with bright-colored tiles (particularly diamonds of light green) and its carved wood balconies, pinnacles, and friezes, is surrounded by vineyards and wine cellars, with villages, like Kaysersburg and Amschwirr, closely clustered nearby. I was back in a countryside of chestnuts, firs, and beeches. Kaysersberg, I found, was the acme of traditional Alsace, with its half-timbered houses clustered round a central fountain and an old church. Here I happened upon a wedding, with the cortege of family and friends just arriving at the church on foot, two by two, led by the bride and her father, the bridesmaids and groom's men, and the bride's mother. At Amschwirr it was a delight to see, on their huge nests on the chimney tops, the famous storks that are the emblem of this region.

In Strasbourg, I saw the Rhine for the first time, that river so deeply embedded in so much of European history. Of course, I climbed the five hundred steps to the top of the Cathedral tower, where I was admiring the extensive view of the city when I met an American, who was a photographer for a well-known American magazine. We struck up an interesting conversation and I found he was driving into Germany next day. He seemed to be looking for company. This seemed to be a great opportunity, so I was considering accepting his invitation to accompany him. He invited me to his hotel for a drink and then to his room to see some of his photographic work for the magazine. The photographs turned out to be pictures of life in the bordellos of France. It was soon apparent that his idea of my accompanying him to Germany was not the same as mine. Astonished at my reaction, he told me I was just like his Aunt Martha, wandering the world like an innocent abroad.

Next day I was on the train to Heidelberg, which was a much safer mode of transport. It was very nasty weather — raining cats and dogs, but I took the chance that it would clear up before I reached Heidelberg. Luck was with me and I was able to walk up the hill through the rain-wet forest to the old ruined castle. Here I looked out over the town, nestling at the foot of the hills on both sides of the River Necker, with its old stone bridge built in the year Australia was founded — 1788. I could see why Victoria's Heidelberg had been named after it: it was very pretty with the hills, the river, and the apple orchards scattered over the surrounding countryside. It seemed a pity that Melbourne's Heidelberg, the apple orchards abandoned long since, was becoming just another outer suburb, indistinguishable from so many others.

The summer over, I made my way back to Montpellier with just 100 francs in my pocket.

15
MONTPELLIER: SECOND YEAR 1951-52

It was pleasant to come back to a familiar spot and not to have to make acquaintance with a completely new set of colleagues. I was most grateful to the French Administration for this third year of resident teaching. It was also a pleasure to be earning some real money again. I had bought practically no clothes for three years; I had four pairs of shoes that needed mending (a luxury I had not been able to afford), and eighteen films piled up that I had not yet had the money to develop. I had darned and redarned my stockings with a stocking mender and the linings of my overcoat and woollen suit were in ribbons; yet I still had a lot of traveling I wanted to do before going back to the Southern Hemisphere. Even with "bread and cheese" trips and sleeping in the bathroom, there were still fares and accommodation to pay for. Planning ahead, I was determined to wear out as many articles of clothing as possible to lighten my luggage for the return home. I was very happy to receive nylon stockings from time to time from my American friend, Gil; these were quite new at the time and available in post-war Europe only at inflated prices. I no longer took buses when I could walk and I cut down on trips to the cinema, useful as these were linguistically. I bought no more fruit or sweets or flowers. Costs in France continued to soar. Fares had gone up twenty-five percent and my board at the EN had risen by nearly fifty percent. Even with this hefty increase, it would have been quite impossible for me to live out in the community on the same amount of money, so to some extent I was in a sheltered position.

Now I was having to think about for my return to Australia via India, where I would visit Linda in Hyderabad in the Deccan (later Andhra Pradesh). Since ship bookings had to be made well in advance, with deposit in hand, I needed to calculate my total expenses and potential savings very carefully. I was hoping to be able to visit my Egyptian friend, Diaa, and his family in Cairo too, since the ship would pass through the Suez Canal. Diaa was very anxious for me to see the pyramids and the temples at Luxor. With the serious situation developing at the time in the dispute over the Suez Canal, Diaa, still in London, was becoming very worried. Should a war break out; he might well be called home for medical service. This would mean curtailment of his studies for his advanced specialist examinations for the Royal College of Gynecologists and Obstetricians and, of course, no visit by me to Cairo. I also wanted to use my last summer vacation in Europe to the fullest to see something of Scandinavia. I had originally kept my return fare to Australia in my bank in London, but my long illness and convalescence without a salary had naturally cut into this nest egg. In this tight situation I was most grateful to receive a little help in loans from Mother and Harold. With all these political and financial uncertainties in mind, I nevertheless put down my deposit for a berth to India on the *Chusan* for September 1952.

When I returned from my summer vacation, the students at the two Normal schools in Montpellier were very happy to see me. Josette, my dear friend and walking companion, had to my great regret moved on. During the Easter break of that year she had married her fiancé in Normandy and at the end of the school year she had moved back north. Jacqueline Armand was still there, as friendly as ever, but very preoccupied with her young family. Although she had a history and geography degree, she had not been able to find a teaching post, so she was still a junior boarding-school supervisor. Her husband, a teacher of Spanish, had been notified that he had been appointed to a post five hundred miles away. He had had to go to Paris to talk the administration into permitting him to stay in Montpellier with his wife and family — a typical vicissitude of such a centralized teaching system.

The other resident colleague, Laure, the new assistant to the housekeeper, was in her early thirties. She was soon involved in emotional upheavals that rocked our little circle. Laure had fallen in love with one of the students, a young woman about twenty called Nicole. They could not resist kissing and caressing each other in public, which became very embarrassing for the other students. These *amitiés particulières* (close personal friendships) were frowned on by the administration, as is commonly the case in girls' boarding schools. Moreover, Nicole, who was very flamboyant, clearly had psychological problems that manifested themselves every now and then in threats of suicide. The Principal was so nervous about the eruption of a public scandal, which would bring her a rebuke from the educational authorities, that she allowed Nicole to do and say anything she liked .to keep things from boiling over. Fortunately, three weeks into the school year, whether coincidentally or by design, Laure left us for Paris to continue her studies as a teacher of Domestic Science.

This break in the relationship precipitated a series of very unpleasant and nerve-wracking incidents instigated by Nicole, which centered around the person replacing Laure as assistant to the housekeeper. This new colleague, Danielle Verdier, was a thirty-year-old woman from Savoy, whom Nicole detested purely because she had taken Laure's place. As it happened, Danielle was as excitable as Nicole. The spoiled daughter of over-indulgent parents she became very emotional when things did not go her way. This made for an explosive situation with Nicole around. Danielle was also having difficulty adjusting to her new position. She did not always see eye to eye with the housekeeper, who liked to pass as much work as possible on to her assistants, so we often had to endure long sessions during which Danielle poured out her woes and resentments. Nicole worked out her antipathy to Danielle by cleverly manipulating the other students to protest against the food served in the refectory, which was Danielle's special responsibility. She then went deliberately over Danielle's head to the housekeeper with these complaints. I found all this very interesting, if disturbing, to watch. In other resident institutions in which I had been involved I had found that, no matter how palatable the food, a certain ennui would set in, just because it was an imposed menu beyond the control of the consumers. Even at Abbotsford School in Kenilworth, during a period of food rationing in England when the school had had special coupons and, if anything, better food than the general community, the girls had still complained about it. Danielle took great pains to work out menus the girls would find interesting. She personally went to the market to pick out the best

561

quality items. At one stage she served a *brandade de morue*, a special Provençal cod dish. The girls loved it and so did I, but when she served it again a little later on, no one would eat it. Naturally this was very frustrating for Danielle, who ironically suffered badly herself from the very prevalent French malady of *mal au foie* (liver trouble) and could eat only boiled potatoes and carrots. Artful Nicole found it easy enough to get the girls worked up about the food, until they realized they were being manipulated. When the housekeeper asked them publicly in the dining hall which girls were discontented, only Nicole raised her hand, at which all the girls burst out laughing and Nicole stalked out in high dudgeon. From then on she became somewhat paranoid, looking for little slights, even from people like myself who did not teach her. She even came to my room to attack me verbally, probably because I was friendly with Danielle. All of this emotional upset created a tense feeling of living on top of an unpredictable volcano.

I was by now well aware of how different French girls were in their approach to others, in contrast to my more British upbringing. In my school experiences in Australia and Britain, if we had to work with someone we did not particularly like, we always acted as though we did like them and tried to maintain a pleasant and unstrained atmosphere. My French colleagues were much more open about their likes and dislikes. At least here in Montpellier, if my colleagues did not like someone they were quite outspoken. It was not just because we were in the South, however, since some of the chief protagonists were from other regions, and I had encountered a similar attitude to Monique in the common room at Douai. My French colleagues regarded the British approach as hypocritical, rather than tactful. Danielle was perhaps an extreme example of this attitude, being excessively blunt and emotional along with it. She was quick to see slights where none were intended. She had taken a violent dislike to several girls who were friendly with Nicole and no one could mention their names without provoking her ire. This antipathy was evident on both sides. By treading delicately, the rest of our small group managed to keep things from becoming too unpleasant.

Italy in the Christmas season.

I was very relieved when the Christmas-New Year break arrived. It would give me a period of relief from all this intense emotion and perhaps cool some hot tempers. I had spent some time planning a solo trip to Italy, hoping by frugal means to keep the costs lower than even for a *Tourisme et Travail* student group tour. Now that my return fare was committed I knew I would really have to watch my pennies. Yet I was still determined to see as much of Europe as possible. This solo tour would have the added advantage that I could go where I liked and see what I personally wanted to see. I retained so much more of what I observed when I was alone than when chattering with others in a group. For the trip I booked all my hotels ahead of time, seeking out inexpensive ones from brochures. A circular train ticket, paid in advance, allowed me two thousand miles of travel, with the added advantage that I could always come back to Montpellier directly at any time, should I run out of funds. This special rate ticket was surprisingly cheap, because train fares in Italy in 1951 cost only half of what one would pay for equivalent travel in France. This helped me enormously.

At this stage I was determinedly on the trail of art and architecture. Apart from the inevitable Rome, Florence, and Venice, Naples was a must because of its proximity to ancient, excavated sites and its notable museums. As I was entering Italy from the north, I stopped off first at Pisa to see the famous white marble Leaning Tower, not just for its lean, but also for the delicacy of its twelfth century sculpted exterior, with its successive levels of slender columns. I found it beautifully in harmony with the neighboring, but much less photographed cathedral of which it was the bell tower, and the extraordinarily lovely round baptistry. I was also enjoying the warm, winter sunshine, which was such a welcome change from the early winter to the north. Then I continued on to Naples, through rather poor countryside with innumerable olive trees and what to an Australian could only seem rather scraggy sheep. After Rome, there were miles and miles of orange groves.

My first encounter with antiquity in its well-preserved form was at Pompeii. To my delight much of the town was practically intact, having been covered by ash from Vesuvius, rather than the lava that overwhelmed nearby Herculaneum. It was very impressive to walk through this long-dead town, its life blotted out in a short period of terror, and to raise one's eyes to Vesuvius, the destroyer, now serene and deceptively unthreatening against the blue sky. I could walk down paved streets lined with houses in varying states of restoration, some nearly complete, and see the Forum, that center of Roman life, the Court of Justice, the public fountain, market, baths, temples, and Caligula's arch of triumph. It was so complete that you almost expected the town to come to life around you — to see families gathered in the peristyle gardens at the center of the houses and visitors coming through the atrium admiring the many wall paintings and floor mosaics. At this site of many contrasts, however, it could not but be distressing to see the figures made by filling in the outlines, left like molds in the cold, rock-like ash by the unfortunate victims. Caught so rapidly and unexpectedly by the tragic event, they lie in most anguished and distorted positions, covering their eyes with their arms in the vain hope of survival.

Looking back from the twenty-first century, it is amusing to remember that in 1951 there were certain pictures and mosaics at Pompeii that had to be kept hidden under curtains from sensitive female eyes, being shown only very surreptitiously to male visitors. This I would hope is a practice that has changed long since.

Living Naples was a fascinating contrast to Pompeii, vital and bouncing with energy. Colorful and lively were the narrow old streets, often stepped, and heavily shaded by the very tall, somber-looking apartment buildings, which were drawn together over our heads by the lines of drying sheets and intimate items of the family wardrobe. On either side, almost hidden by the thick crowds but adding considerable color to the scene, were open stalls, with lavish displays of fruit, particularly the ubiquitous oranges. The interiors of the houses were open to public view, with the wide doors of the windowless street-level apartments flung open, so that whole families seemed to be living right on the street. When I saw one family apparently living under a staircase, I began to realize why so many Neapolitans were eager to migrate to Australia, with its tremendous opportunities.

I saw the strangest things as I sauntered through the streets of Naples — men being shaved on the pavement; a grandmother warming herself at a small fire in an old dish; people talking, laughing, disputing, singing. Everywhere there was noise and bustle and a carefree spirit. Street musicians played exuberantly in small back-street cafes. Down these crowded streets came small carts, drawn by even smaller donkeys, with harnesses jingling. Across the busy thoroughfares noisy merchants drove their horses and carts at a smart pace through the tangled traffic, whips cracking to warn of their approach. Every few yards there was a wall shrine to the Madonna or a local saint, while within the small dwellings were similar shrines, each with votive candles lit as evening came. Fishmongers also lit up their wooden tubs of squirming eels, from which the continually flowing water spilled over into the street. Judging by quantity, a stranger might well assume that the Neapolitans lived on eels and oranges!

In complete contrast to the ever-lively city, but just two hours away by boat, was the Isle of Capri, about which we had all sung lustily in my Girl Guide days. The sky was overcast as our boat left Naples, but as we approached the steep, light-colored cliffs of the island, rising sheer from the transparent green water; the sun had already pierced the clouds. The sunshine brought out the dazzling whiteness of the buildings up the hillsides, with their flat roofs and their attractively arched windows and doors. A small boat took us to the Blue Grotto, passing close under the high cliffs, with their many small cave entrances, until we were transferred by twos into small rowboats that could take us through a tiny hole in the rock. So low was the entrance that we had to duck our heads to get into the large, calm, dark cave. The light coming in through the water caused it to glow with a bright blue light that was indescribably glorious. I had not expected anything so spectacular. All the water and air in the cave seemed aglow with it.

I ate my meager lunch at Tiberias's Villa on a high headland looking out to sea. Sheer cliffs, crowned by a ruined tower, dropped abruptly to the rushing waves, while across the water was Sorrento, misty and fairy-like. The sunshine was delightfully mild — spring in mid-winter. As we returned to Naples, the sky grew rosy with sunset, the usual lights of the town reflected in the water being supplemented by twenty-five illuminated and decorated vessels of the American Navy, which had come into Naples for the Christmas season. I was now "collecting" sunsets, and this lovely sunset over the Bay of Naples was one of my early treasures.

I arrived in Rome just as it was getting dark, on a train that was forty-five minutes late. I was never on a train in Italy that wasn't late, in contrast to the meticulous punctuality of which the French railway service was so proud. Having found my modest hotel, I threw my things into the room and raced out to see St Peter's. What a miscalculation! Rome was not nearly as compact as it looked on the tourist map! After an hour and a half of walking, past beautifully illuminated fountains, down magnificent shopping streets, past the enormous monument to Victor Emmanuel, the architect of Italian unity, with its rearing equestrian statue and Tomb of the Unknown Soldier, I was rewarded by seeing the dark outline of St Peter's loom up before me in the gloom. Exploring it would have to be for another day.

My *Guide Bleu* told me that to see Rome properly required twenty-one days or five to see it quickly, so I knew that I would have to plan carefully to get the very most out of my poor three-and-a-half days. The obvious way was to let Thomas Cook show me Rome and then fill in the gaps in my own way later. I decided to give the morning of my first day to Christian Rome and the afternoon to Ancient Rome, the two coming together in the late afternoon at the Coliseum and the Catacombs.

Of course, I visited the four great Basilicas, with doors that are opened only during Holy Years, and I thought of my little friend Nguyen from the Preventorium at St Cyr-sur-Loire with whom I had repeated the Holy Year prayers. I wondered where she might be on this Christmas Eve. I paid my respects at the tombs of St Peter and St Paul, the latter in a basilica-style church, which provided quite a contrast to the prevailing Gothic. Everywhere I admired the mosaics, which were for all the world like oil paintings, since the Vatican mosaic factory was at the time producing the tiny stones in two hundred and fifty different colors. I found the christianizing of pagan Rome a little disconcerting. Curiously outdated was the way in which successive popes had replaced the statues of Roman heroes, honorably placed on pillars sculpted to tell the stories of their exploits, with those of Christian apostles and saints. Crosses had been added to the tops of the sixteen obelisks brought back from Egypt by

Roman conquerors and now decorating the centers of public squares. Everywhere there were reminders of the extraordinary engineering ability of the Romans, like the huge, unsupported dome of the Pantheon, which dated back to 27 BC. Rivaling it was the great dome of St Peter's in the Vatican, designed by Michelangelo, with its rich gold and mosaics. The enormous square in front of St Peter's was emotionally very moving, with the two colonnaded wings of the church itself, decorated with the statues of so many saints, stretching out to embrace the faithful. I was very impressed by the famous Michelangelo statue of St Peter, the foot of which has acquired quite a sheen over the centuries from being kissed by hosts of pilgrims and curious visitors. It was most amusing to watch the Japanese tourists who sneaked into the enclosure to have their picture taken with St Peter. It was the Pietà that I loved most in St Peter's. I could have stayed and gazed at the beautiful face of Mary for hours.

It was fitting to close the day with the remains of the Forum of ancient Rome and the ruined Coliseum, where a simple cross honors the many Christian martyrs for whom this place was their last sight on earth. I was fascinated by the eleven miles of underground passages of the Catacombs, with their layers of burial niches, interspersed with little cave-like chapels and ancient wall paintings. The homeward route took us along the Appian Way, past the Roman Baths of Caracalla and the Quirinal Palace, now the home of the President of Italy. All of this was a great deal to store in memory for one day, but it gave me a great foundation for my own solitary explorations.

My Christmas Day in Rome was quite unusual. I had not realized that Christmas would be such a closed holiday in Italy. In the morning everything was closed except the churches. Since Christmas for me, as an Anglican, meant taking my Christmas communion, I set out to find the English church. It will be near the British Embassy, I thought. So off I went in that direction. But not so. It seemed it was right across Rome on the other side. Not to be deterred, I changed direction and eventually found it, arriving about ten minutes into the service. This was the first time I had been able to take part in an Anglican service in two years. When children in the costumes of shepherds and wise men came to kneel in front of a pretty creche to pray, along with people from many different countries, I knew it was really Christmas.

By now I was hungry, but since all the restaurants were closed I bought some bread rolls, some chocolate, a couple of attractive cakes, and a cup of coffee. I ate the two cakes and the block of chocolate in lonely state on the Pincio, where from a terrace in the public gardens I had a magnificent view over Rome. Fortunately I love gardens. I kept wandering in the beautiful gardens of the Villa Borghese in glorious sunshine, while all of Rome was eating at the family table. On my Cook's tour I had seen the magnificent interior of the villa, ornately decorated in baroque style, with inlaid marble walls and mosaics, and an art collection of unbelievable richness. The garden was just as fascinating, with its alleys, fountains, little lakes, and replicas of ancient temples. I was so happy that I kept on walking and nibbling at the dry bread rolls. At length I had eaten my way through both of them and was no longer hungry, so I decided not to bother looking for a place to eat. That was my Christmas Dinner for 1951.

In my wanderings through Rome I came across a number of lesser known public fountains, which are among the attractions of Rome, and I poked into little churches, finally finding myself in the church of St Peter in Chains that contains the famous Michelangelo Moses. This discovery made my wanderings worthwhile. I spent some time studying this life-sized statue which I found to be even more impressive than the better-known statue of St Peter in St Peter's Basilica.

Continuing my ramble, it was a pleasure to stumble on the Protestant cemetery where both Shelley and Keats were buried. This burial place is a strong reminder of the centuries-long magnetic appeal of Rome to intellectuals, artists, and all lovers of the beautiful. I now found time to linger among the very extensive ruins of the Forum, with its many temples, its rows of pillars marking the site of long-vanished public buildings and its arches of triumph to long-dead heroes. I stayed a long time contemplating the lovely sunset over these spectacular and evocative ruins. Going up some steep steps I discovered the church of St Mary in Aracoeli, where the Holy Bambino is brought out in procession and especially venerated on Christmas Day. Clothed in elaborately decorated gold clothes, with a crown on its head, the holy statue was back in its place over the altar when I arrived. The whole church was illuminated with chandeliers for the great festival. From this dazzling light I went out into the dark to walk back to my hotel, on my now habitual tour of illuminated fountains in delightful little local piazzas. What a Christmas Day it had been!

I still had two days to wander, so on Boxing Day I was able to visit another of the great churches, St John Lateran, the Cathedral and Mother Church of Rome, where the skulls of St Peter and St Paul are buried under the High Altar. For variety I visited the gardens of the Villa d'Este, so familiar from the many famous paintings they have inspired. I continued on to the somewhat bewildering town of Tivoli, on one of the seven hills of Rome; this I saw from underneath an umbrella (the same folding umbrella, my sturdy traveling companion, that had so frequently protected me on my rush from Douai to Lille). Here the waterfalls in a leafy valley, with old temples perched on the hillside, and a mysterious grotto where the water rushes down into a bottomless hole, reminded me of all the romantic stage settings I had seen in operas and musical comedies. I was sure it would be a lovely place to linger when it wasn't raining.

Of course the last day had to be dedicated to the Vatican Museum and Library and the Sistine Chapel, all of which had been tightly closed for the two days of Christmas. The Library by itself would take several days to explore, with its enormous collection of ancient manuscripts, including the fourth-century Codex Vaticanus, one of the oldest copies of the Scriptures, and the many beautifully illuminated manuscripts from the Middle Ages. I was especially thrilled to see all the old sixteenth, seventeenth, and eighteenth-century maps, so illustrative of the history I had studied in school. It was exciting, for instance, to see the actual map where the Pope had drawn a line to divide the world into Portuguese and Spanish spheres of influence in the seventeenth century. I found it very amusing to trace, through a sequence of maps, the gradual expansion of the known world from the European point of view. Australia was, of course, completely absent from the earlier ones. Gradually its shape developed from the haziest of lines to some kind of recognizable outline after the voyages of Dampier and the early Dutch and Portuguese adventurers. The Sistine Chapel with its many frescoes by Michelangelo and Botticelli, was mind-boggling, even though in 1951, before the subsequent cleaning, the colors were rather disappointingly somber. The details were, however, magnificent, particularly in the great Last Judgment over the altar. Since the whole ceiling was covered with prophets, sibyls, and scenes from Bible history, I got quite a crick in the neck and nearly went cross-eyed trying to take it all in. On the next visit I knew I would have to bring a mirror, which would make it so much easier to enjoy. Still I think there is something in suffering to see the real thing, rather than relying on a reflected image. All around the walls were huge rectangular frescoes, each of which deserved a leisured period of time to enjoy, while the Raphael room upstairs was equally a feast for the eyes. Here famous paintings like the School of Athens and the Parnassus, depicting the leading poets of antiquity and the Renaissance, along with frescoes of Bible subjects, like St Peter being released from prison, linked the greatness of antiquity with the greatness of Christendom in true Renaissance spirit. The sculpture halls, with their priceless statues and vases from Greek antiquity. and the rich artifacts from the Egypt of the Pharaohs would warrant a visit on their own. The treasures of the Vatican Museum are truly inexhaustible and I knew I would have to come back for many more visits even to begin to appreciate them. But Florence called and I had to move on.

I rushed to the train for Florence, for which I did not have a reservation. I asked anxiously from compartment to compartment whether there was a seat available. No, no, no! were the responses. The train was absolutely packed. Finally I found a compartment full of young Italian men in uniform, where there was one spare seat. This they offered me with some hilarity and I gratefully sank into it. I soon found out the reason for their mirth, when a handsome young man appeared in the doorway. As a practical joke, they had given away his seat while he was in the corridor. The only place for him to sit was on my knees, or me on his, which he thought was a great idea. My companions were a group of Civil Guardsmen from Città Vecchia, who were returning to their barracks in high spirits after their Christmas break, and we had an uproarious time. Of course, Franco, whose seat I had taken, ended up proposing to me as we watched the romantically colorful sunset through the train window. Since we didn't have a common language, one of the group translated for him in rather fractured French, keeping us all in fits of laughter. Franco then played me soulful songs on his mouth organ and gave me a photograph to remember him by. He later followed up this encounter by writing to me in Australia. It was all very lighthearted and reminded me of the young Italian at Lake Como, who overtook me as I was coming down a hillside singing to myself and was soon declaring that I had sung my way into his heart. It's nice to be proposed to from time to time, but not as an everyday diet. The four hours passed quickly in such lively company.

On another train trip in Italy I also received a proposal, this time from a young businessman who didn't speak English. He invited me to the dining car for coffee, where he managed to convey to me that if he could find a nice young Australian (presumably me) who would marry him he would love to go to Australia, where he foresaw all kinds of opportunities. On that same journey, I met two older men who were twins. They were woodcutters, going home for the Christmas season. When I asked them what they did in their spare time in the woodcutters' camp, they surprised me by replying: "We read Dante and the Bible!" Train journeys can be most illuminating. This encounter reminds me of a friend's father, a Finn-Swede, who was a woodcutter in Canada. He was so strong that he got into the Guinness Book of Records as the man who could hold the most bricks on a hod with one hand in the world, yet he wrote poetry in his leisure time and was honored in Finland with a prestigious poetry prize.

Florence, the city of the Medicis and the quintessence of Renaissance art and architecture, cannot but charm. I spent a full three days exploring what it had to offer. The Cathedral was something of a disappointment after the glorious ones I had seen. It was cold, dark, and plain. At that time mass was said inside a glass enclosure around the choir and altar, with priests and monks on the inside and the people watching through the glass. To a Protestant mind this seemed the essence of "holy mysteries." I'm sure this must have changed since Vatican II. My appreciation rose when I visited the lovely Campanile, designed by Giotto, and the eleventh-century Baptistery, horizontally striped in white, green, and red, its interior opulently decorated with gold Florentine mosaics. I wandered the streets absorbing the many Renaissance buildings until I came to the Palazzo Vecchio, the Palace of the Medicis, with its crenelated wall and tall thin tower. Before it was a plethora of copies of famous Florentine statues, the originals of which were in the museums. I paused a while

571

before the round stone in the square where the dissenter, Savonarola, was burned as a heretic. There is so often this unfortunate combination of rigidity, cruelty, and extravagant beauty in the artistic centers one visits; here, for instance, close by Savonarola's death site is the Palace, brimming with indescribable riches of Renaissance art. At the Uffizi, this dazzled Australian was quite overwhelmed to see original paintings by practically every great Renaissance painter she had ever heard of — from Giotto, Fra Angelico, and Botticelli to Da Vinci, Titian, Raphael, and Michelangelo — as well as a very rich collection of ancient Greek sculpture. It was a complete education in one visit. This education was complemented by a visit to the Holy Cross Church, where I was surrounded by the tombs of so many of the greatest Italian men of arts and letters, each memorial a sculptural gem.

Wandering around Florence, I saw what was left of the picturesque old quarters that had been so drastically destroyed by the Germans. Fortunately they had spared the old covered bridge over the Arno, with its double row of small jewelers' shops. At every step there were private palaces of Renaissance architecture to admire, all simple, almost plain, but elegant and timeless. Florence is not, of course, just a collection of antique treasures, but a flourishing city, with wide tree-lined boulevards, lined with opulent modern residences.

The museum of the Pitti Palace, the residence of the Medicis for three hundred years, was specially decorated to hold their private art collection. Many of the pictures still remain in the setting originally planned for them. Since the Medicis collected not only Italian paintings but many from neighboring countries as well, every imaginable painter of the period seems to be represented. Around the palace are lovely gardens with long cypress-lined avenues, fountains, and terraces, all decorated with statues in abundance. Of course Michelangelo was everywhere, which was a great delight. In the Medici funeral chapels, where eight archdukes are buried, there were as many as nine Michelangelo statues. In a room by itself at the Academy Museum was Michelangelo's powerful and extremely impressive statue of David, with its very penetrating gaze, and there were also a number of unfinished works, with forms half-emerging from the marble block, which made me realize just how amazing is the sculptor's art. First the block of marble, then the artist's eye and brain with his conception of his work, then his attack upon the stone and the emergence of the brilliant figure he has conceived! These half-finished sculptures, with the figures seeming to be fighting their way out, while remaining for ever imprisoned, seemed as contemporary as any modern work.

There seemed no end to the riches of Florence. At St Mark's Convent the museum was devoted entirely to Fra Angelico's work — a collection that extends into the convent, with Fra Angelico frescoes in all the passages and in the refectory and a scene from the Bible in each monk's cell. Here I was able to see Savonarola's cell with the hand-copied books he had used.

Next day, I visited Sienna, the city of St Catherine, with its twelfth to thirteenth century Cathedral horizontally striped in black and white, the floor decorated with black and white mosaics. Beside it stands the shell of the fourteenth century cathedral that was to be bigger, brighter, and better than any other, but was never finished. Such are the rewards of hubris!

In the train going back to Florence I had a beautiful view over the Tuscan countryside that has inspired so many poets and artists, with its gently rolling hills along the horizon rising up to the snow-clad Appennines. Then there were miles of olive groves, with interspersed cypresses in groups, or in solitary meditation, all pointing their tall silhouettes to the sky. They were so reminiscent of the French yew trees, that it began to look very Provençal. From the station I hurried to the Michelangelo Square on a hillside overlooking the River Arno to see the sun set behind the city, one of the unforgettable sights of my life. The deep red glow highlighted the pointed cypresses and the lovely towers and domes of Florence, with a delicate slip of crescent moon and a necklace of lights reflected in the Arno. It was a veritable jewel for my collection.

Like Switzerland, Venice is one of the places people dream most about visiting. The train, after passing through the fogged-in valley of the Po, brought us into the Queen of the Adriatic in beautiful sunshine.

Swooping around in boats is the Venetian style and even taxis take to the water. On arrival I went directly down to the Grand Canal to take a ferryboat, a Vaporetti, to St Mark's Square. It was a great initiation to travel down the Grand Canal, which flows in a great S between magnificent marble palaces. Black gondolas were ferrying people across or carrying merchandise past us, as the ferryboat zigzagged from side to side to pick people up at different stops. Half an hour later I was in St Mark's Square, the social and touristic center of the city. Here were the white marble palace of the Doges, the presidents of the ancient republic of Venice, and St Mark's Cathedral, whose Byzantine architecture attests to the claim of Venice to be the European door to Asia and the East. On its pillar looking down at us was the Lion of St Mark, the emblem of Venice's patron saint, and behind it the ugly brick Campanile that dwarfs the Cathedral. Where the square lengthened out before St Mark's it was lined with arcades of small, exclusive shops. The square was full of pigeons. There are, of course, pigeons in the Cathedral Square in Milan and in Trafalgar Square in London, but these were the boldest, cheekiest pigeons you could ever imagine. They swarmed under your feet and made no movement to avoid being trodden on. If you bought a cornet of corn to feed them, they didn't wait to be asked, but a dozen attacked you at once, fought to empty the cornet, sat on your head and shoulders and flew in your face. It was most disconcerting. My hotel was just behind St Mark's and I had a beautiful room. Although it was now about three in the afternoon and I had had no lunch, I didn't feel hungry. With these bread and cheese trips, I found I gradually lost my appetite and, toward the end of my tour, I no longer felt hungry at all. This was most convenient.

The Venetians boasted that there was not a wheel in Venice. You either traveled by boat or on foot. It made for a very peaceful city — no horns blowing, no bells ringing, just excitable Venetian voices, with their musical lilt, and everything moving at the leisurely pace of two strolling legs. This suited me very well. As space is limited on the thousand islands of Venice, the "streets" are extremely narrow — the big shopping streets hardly wider than a lane and the residential streets more like alleyways. Consequently all the streets looked alike to me and whenever I turned off the beaten track I ended up at, or nearly in, a canal. With no barriers for protection, I had to keep my eyes open. I found I had to twist and turn to find bridges to cross the canals. Even when one is taking care and following a map Venice can be baffling and confusing. I set off from my hotel to visit the Friars'

Church, where Titian and Canova were buried and where there was a famous Titian Assumption over the high altar. On the way back I thought I was being very astute in finding my way, but I still managed to go round in circles, and half an hour later I was back where I had started. That morning I thought I would be spending the rest of my life in the maze of Venice. I soon found out the Venetians were right; it really was much quicker and easier to go by water. As a consolation, however, I did get some splendid photographs of little side canals and less conventional glimpses of the Bridge of Sighs.

Spanning the Grand Canal is the wide Rialto Bridge of Shylock fame, covered with small shops and a street market. The atmosphere here was most animated and exciting. From it I watched the sun set over the Grand Canal, with the silhouette of a gondola crossing the water — a very poetic and romantic scene. The shops of Venice were full of magnificent Venetian glass of brilliant coloring, but, of course, far beyond my means. I decided that next time I came to Venice I would come as a millionaire and buy all the lovely things I would love to possess.

St Mark's seemed exceedingly small after St Peter's, but its distinction, of course, is its magnificent gold mosaics in Byzantine style. This was another building I had studied in detail in Miss Spring's History of Art class at EHS, so it was exciting to be able to linger over all the beautiful detail. It was a fine climax to my dream trip back into history. Now I had to think of my return to Montpellier by as direct a route as possible. When I arrived safely back at school, I had two small coins jingling in my empty pockets.

Spring term at Montpellier

As we moved into the second trimester in early 1952, Lucienne Pouzeaud, who was to be another of my lifelong friends, came to join us. About twenty-two at the time, she was a student of English. Of a sunny personality, with a relaxed sense of humor, she was much at ease with everyone. Lucienne was from a small village of eighty inhabitants in Auvergne, in the Massif Central, where her parents had a cafe — that essential social institution of French life where local people gather to spend their leisure time in congenial company. All the village girls she knew from her school days thought only of marriage and the household arts, so she was glad to be in a

575

more exciting intellectual environment. Later she became a teacher of English in a lycée, married a fellow student from Montpellier, and ended up living in different parts of the world in the French Foreign Service. At Montpellier she was completing her studies of English and supporting herself as a resident supervisor. When she joined us a little sanity seemed to return to our communal life. She brought a breath of fresh air into the tense, hothouse atmosphere. By this time, Danielle was conducting a hot and heavy affair with the Spanish assistant at the boys' school. Lucienne and I enjoyed spending time together and very soon we were planning a trip to England and Scotland for part of the summer vacation. Since neither of us had much money, it would have to be a hitchhiking experience

It was from Lucienne that I discovered that young French people did not have the same sense of responsibility in institutional situations as I had been brought up to expect. I remember how Lucienne, when on duty one day, flounced into my room and settled down with the angry remark, "I'm not staying out there with all those rude, disrespectful girls! If they don't know how to behave, they can jump in the lake," and she did not return to her post. I had found something of the same attitude among the resident staff at Douai. At least it reduced the amount of emotional wear-and-tear that this kind of supervision, without final responsibility, often entailed. I remember too how Lucienne and Jacqueline Armand worked hard one day on my pronunciation of the French "r," till I nearly cried with frustration. Like most native speakers neither of them had the faintest idea how to explain what I should do, and I am afraid their determined efforts had very little effect.

It was obvious that our troubles at the EN were not over. For about a year, mysterious anonymous letters had been arriving at the school, as well as at the central educational administration offices, informing on unfortunate aspects of life and personal relations. Not surprisingly this had created a distrustful atmosphere among us, as we all wondered who, with an intimate knowledge of the details of daily life at the school, could be writing these poison pen letters. Finally, to our astonishment, it turned out to be Jacqueline Armand's father. As he had never been in the school, he must have got his information from exaggerated stories Jacqueline had carried home. We then discovered that she had frequently carried stories about us to the

Headmistress, always ones that put us in a bad light. We remembered then that, despite her apparent affability, she had frequently told each of us unpleasant things about the others and warned us to be careful about trusting each other. When the facts came to light, she was promptly asked to find a position elsewhere. At last things settled down to a normal routine, after what had been an exhausting three months.

Jacqueline's replacement was a really delightful colleague, Renée Panaphieu from nearby Sète. She looked quite unlike a Southerner, having very flaxen hair, which she had inherited from ancestors who had come south from French Flanders. She was trying to finish her studies in Spanish. Renée soon invited me to visit Sète, which was at that time the biggest Mediterranean port in France after Marseille. Of special interest to me was the lonely cemetery on a headland by the sea, where the French poet, Paul Valéry, is buried. At Melbourne University I had studied in detail Valéry's poem, *Le Cimetière Marin*, under the guidance of Professor Chisholm, who was a recognized Valéry scholar. Now here I was visiting it. At the Panaphieu home, in traditional French style, we remained at the family table from 1.30 to 4.30 p.m. and then again from 8 to 11.30 p.m., with lots of stimulating conversation and good wine to accompany the excellent Southern cuisine.

It was through Renée that I heard about some of the sexual harassment that women students in French universities had had to endure. With her very blond hair Renée was very attractive to Southern men, although she was a reticent person and never sought to attract attention. She was having a difficult time finishing her degree in Spanish. Her professor had made her a proposition, which she had refused, so he had failed her at her oral examination. At the beginning of the following year's Spanish course, the professor had singled her out in the amphitheater, taunting her by posing the question on which he had failed her at the oral. In front of a theater full of students he observed, with a meaningful look, "Miss Panaphieu, you should know the answer to that question, shouldn't you?" Poor Renée wept. She was sure he would never pass her at the oral examination and she would not be able to complete her degree. The French oral examination was such a personal, subjective test that it was quite possible for the examiner to pass or fail anyone on a whim, no matter how well the student might have performed on the written exam. I had found that out at Lille and I was to have a similar experience here at Montpellier at the end of the year. Of course, this unpredictability could work both ways — to the advantage as well as to the disadvantage of the student.

Easter in Spain, 1952

Since I was so deep in the South, the obvious next step was to visit Spain. In the Australia of my youth, there had been few immigrants of Hispanic origin and Spanish was not taught in the schools, nor to my knowledge in the universities. Australia and South America produced similar products — wheat, beef, wool, gold, and other metals, so there were no strong commercial ties that made learning Spanish an imperative; certainly Spain was not an important trading partner. Hence I knew very little about Spain and the Spanish people. Now that I was in Languedoc, however, Spain was an accessible, much discussed neighbor, and a great many of the Montpellier students were of Spanish heritage. Easter break found me traveling with a group of thirty men and women, French students for the most part, with one New Zealander, several Americans, a Scotsman, and some South Americans. An older Frenchman, a dentist called Monsieur Le Riche, was accompanied by his "niece," a very attractive young woman, who shared the same room with him. It soon became apparent that the relationship was ill described.

We crossed the border between the French and Spanish Basque areas and made our way to the famous seaside resort of San Sebastian, with its attractive half-moon bay, sheltered by rocky cliffs. After a brief overnight visit, we continued on to Madrid across very dry, mountainous country, with great rocky boulders seemingly strewn at random. The houses and fences of stone melded into the landscape of sparse Aleppo pines, with the occasional small olive grove. Along the horizon lay long, low mountain ranges.

That South Americans knew very little about my country soon became apparent, as I chatted in the train corridor with an Argentinian. I had explained to her that I was an Australian. By now I was quite accustomed to Europeans misinterpreting this as Austrian. I was quite surprised this time, however, when my companion, who seemed confident that she knew what she was talking about, commented: "You must find this weather very warm. It's very cold in your country, isn't it?" Since Argentina latitudinally is not so very different from Australia, I wondered what she meant. Seeing the surprise on my face, she added: "Australia's a big island with a small island nearby, isn't it?" "Yes," I replied hesitantly, since this could be interpreted as a reference to the mainland continent of Australia (the big island) and the state of Tasmania (a small island nearby), or even to Australia with New Zealand "nearby," since people from other continents did not have much idea of size and distances in Oceania, as the French called it. "I was sure it was very cold there," she persisted. "Not really," I replied, "We never see snow, except on the tops of the highest mountains for a short period in winter." "Isn't it a big island with a small island nearby?" she asked again, reflectively, "and you say it isn't very cold?" She thought this over for a while, then light dawned. "Oh!" she exclaimed, "I was thinking of Greenland and Iceland!" I was quick to assure her that Australia was near the South Pole, not the North Pole, and not very close at that. This conversation reminded me of the concierge at Douai, to whom it had seemed a very minor misstep to confuse Australia with Norway.

Finally we reached Madrid. Tired and hungry after our long train journey, we made our way to our hotel, only to find that our rooms were not "ready." It was only later in the day that we discovered this was a euphemism for "not available." After much loud disputation and cross-talk in Spanish, it appeared that there were only seven rooms left for the thirty-six of us. Our rooms had been given away to placate another tour group, which had arrived just ahead of us and with whom we soon found ourselves competing, like a football crowd, for food in the cafeteria. Eventually, as a compromise, we were installed in an annex, where the water was icy cold.

In Madrid we were brought face to face with the realities of Franco's Spain. It was not so long after the Civil War and the subsequent involvement of Franco with the Fascist Axis. Spain in 1952 was much poorer and much more isolated than the prosperous, modern country we know today. Wherever we went, we were surrounded by masses of people, adults as well as children, staring at us and our bus. There were children everywhere — bright-eyed, ragged little mites, easily breaking into laughter. Shoeshine boys appeared and industriously began their work as soon as we took our seats on the sidewalk terrace of a café. Adults were watchful and quickly intervened if they felt the little boys were trying to exploit the valued tourists. Children begged persistently. Wherever we turned we would hear little murmurs of "Una peseta. Una peseta, por favor." It was money they wanted; nothing else would do. When I gave one little boy a candy, he wasn't at all sure whether to be pleased or not. Several times I saw him take it out of his pocket to make sure it wasn't a disguised peseta.

To our surprise our tour of Madrid began at 5.45 p.m. "Spanish time," we found, bore little relationship to the daily rhythms to which we were accustomed. Madrid, however, was worth the visit, with its wide streets, beautiful buildings with even a few skyscrapers, its many fountains, and its bustling city life. All signs of the five-month Civil War had been erased in the pleasantly rebuilt residential areas for the affluent, through which we passed on our way to Franco's great achievement — the new buildings for the University of Madrid, with their blue-tiled walls and lavish, red-upholstered public lecture theater.

Our mental images of traditional Spain were confirmed by the many lovely, black lace mantillas in the shop windows, the extraordinarily complicated combs to hold them in place, and the elaborate hand-painted fans to go with them. The great Plaza de Toros provided a spectacular setting for the immense stone bullring in neo-Moorish style, with its ogive arches, its decorative colored tiles, and its many beautiful mosaics. We were told that angry bullfight crowds had been known to set fire to wooden arenas. The small children, playing in the empty ring at being matadors, with an old red cloak to swing around, softened the stark realities of the well-equipped hospital and the red-decorated chapel of Our Lady of Solitude, where the matadors prayed before entering into the contest. Their calling was dangerous. A famous matador had recently died in the ring because the spectators kept pressing him to add to the thrill by performing more and more daring feats. During a night out on the town, in a Madrid nightclub, we had our first opportunity to see colorful, lively, flamenco dancing, with the swirl and ripple of long skirts, the clicking of castanets and the shouts of *olé* when the dancers swept their colorful skirts shoulder high. We knew this was merely prelude since we would see much more dancing in authentic settings in Andalusia.

We could not pass up a side trip from Madrid to Avila, across the wild, rocky Castilian plateau, with its stunted live oaks and its tantalizing views of the snow-clad Sierras. We were now in the hometown of the great Saint Teresa, who brought about the reform of the Carmelite order in the 16th century. This most impressive site with its undulating battlemented walls, fortified with eighty round towers, was our first exciting introduction to the picturesque and historic riches of the Spanish heritage. The pinkish-yellowish stone hardly looked like a twelfth century construction; it was so fresh-looking in the clear air. I was becoming accustomed to relics of saints, scattered all over Europe, and here, in a chapel over St Teresa's birthplace, I was able to see the finger of St Teresa and the sole of one of her sandals, treasured in elaborate gold caskets.

We found the Spanish people to be very cheerful and helpful, although many were living in very poor conditions at that time. Street vendors were selling single cigarettes and other small articles in an attempt to earn a few coins. Fortunately fruit was readily available and oranges in particular abounded. When I offered a little boy who was begging for pesetas an orange, he turned away in positive disgust.

We soon became accustomed to eating at what seemed to us very odd hours. The Spanish came to life in the evenings. Breakfast would be between ten and eleven in the morning, lunch from three to four p.m. and dinner at ten or eleven at night. Spanish people enjoyed wandering around in the cool night hours. A long afternoon siesta, when shops and businesses were closed, guaranteed that they would be wide awake until quite late. I saw people walking about with babies in their arms at midnight, and at 3.30 a.m. there were still plenty of people, even elderly folk, strolling around the square. Coming from Australia, where at that time shops closed at 5 p.m., it was interesting to see some still open at one in the morning. We soon adapted to the Spanish routine. We were finding everything so interesting that we were rarely tired, despite our few hours of sleep. One thing I greatly missed. On the Benelux trip we had stayed in student hostels and been welcomed by French- and English-speaking students, with whom we had had many long discussions. This close contact with local people was not possible under a totalitarian regime, so we were left to draw our own conclusions from street observations, without local input to refine our interpretations and assumptions. We did make some person-to-person contacts in the trains and sang along with happy Spanish workmen, but since we couldn't speak much Spanish and they knew no English our exchanges stayed at this impersonal level.

Our next destination, Ubeda, took us over the Sierra Morena. I was fascinated by the extensive groves of Australian eucalyptus trees here and there, apparently very happily adjusted to their adopted country. The blue mountains on the horizon were set off by the soft spring coloring of the vegetation and the extraordinarily changing colors of the soil — at times red, then white, even mauve in the distance. As far as the eye could see there were olive groves upon olive groves. In other areas agriculture was still being carried on as it had been for centuries. An elderly shepherd would be watching a few sheep. Fields were being ploughed and sown by hand; the father walking ahead, steadily holding the wooden, horse-drawn plough, while the whole family followed him sowing the seed. Along the road we would pass mules or asses laden with great baskets on either side, while a man sat nonchalantly in the middle. We passed groves of almond trees and ate delicious loquats — large, juicy drop-shaped ones, with clear yellow skin. They reminded me of the fruit outside our kitchen door in Ascot Vale. Banana palms peeped out at us from patios, from which drifted the sweet perfume of orange and lemon trees. One evening we saw a magnificent spectacle against the sunset sky — the silhouette of a single file of laden donkeys, ridden by men in short smocks and Basque berets, crossing the fields with the women following on foot

We assuaged our hunger along the way in a small village, where we were served great hunks of freshly baked bread accompanied by the local cheese. Lunch — a fine one— was served to us eventually at 5.30 p.m. in Ubeda, while a crowd of locals unabashedly stared at these strange foreigners in their midst.

In the small town of Jaén we caught up with the Holy Week celebrations we had been so eagerly anticipating. The procession was under way. To the accompaniment of the town band, the Pietà (the statue of the grieving Mary, with the body of her dead Son in her arms) was being carried on a huge, massive silver litter, or *paso,* through streets crowded with eager spectators, while penitents in black, pointed hoods followed in expiatory humility. It was classic and very moving. As we continued south we saw many more of these processional floats, carrying statues dressed in cloth of gold, black velvet, or silver lamé; they were as ornate as the churches, with their baroque decorations gleaming with gold. There was no doubt as to the genuinely precious nature of the gold decorations and the expensive jewels that adorned the richly appareled statues. Riches of this type were everywhere. Throughout the towns we visited, the churches were decorated to the nth degree in an exaggerated Baroque style. Every inch of ceilings, walls, altars, chapels, and statues was painted in bright colors or covered with heavy gold leaf. Nothing was left to the imagination.

We continued on our way and reached Granada at 1.40 a.m., with dinner served at 2.15 a.m. We were still very much on Spanish time.

Soon we were immersed in the Moorish heritage of the south at Granada, beneath the great Sierra Nevada, whose melting snows provided the plentiful water for the gardens and fountains the Moorish conquerors so delighted in. Words cannot describe the delicate beauty of the Alhambra — its intricate carvings and traceries, its complicated geometric patterns and stylized quotations in decorative Arabic script, its tiled friezes of beautiful flowers, and its shadowy alcoves that attract the breezes but keep out the sun. These, along with the extensive orange-blossom perfumed gardens, with their cypresses and flowing fountains, made this eighth century palace of the Sultans, an incredible introduction to a completely new world of beauty and charm. Over the Moorish arches of the open windows was a delicate, lacy fretwork that let in the light. The elaborate stucco carvings that filled any concave spaces were as fully dimensional as stalactites. In the Queen's boudoir, where blind musicians would charm the Sultana with music from a gallery above, sweet perfumes would rise from beneath stones in the floor. Certainly all the senses were aroused and satisfied.

Greenery, tinkling fountains and pavilions, with exquisite views through ogive aches and Moorish windows. continued to delight us in the famous Generalife Gardens, which had been landscaped to provide the maximum of pleasure and relaxation for another summer palace. The civilized way in which the Moors cultivated the beauty of their surroundings was unsurpassed.

In Granada it was Holy Thursday, when the devout were expected to pray in seven churches in commemoration of the seven last words from the cross. Consequently, all the churches were crowded. Women in black velvet dresses were strolling with their husbands and friends. They were wearing in their hair very high, wide combs over which were draped long, black, lacy mantillas held in place, in most cases, with a diamente clip. With their black eyes and hair, they looked most elegant.

Some of us lost track of the rest of the group in Granada and went searching for them in the quarter above the town, where the gypsies lived in small, whitewashed houses, some cut cave-like into the rocks. It was forbidden to dance during Holy Week, but we were soon accosted by little boys offering to arrange for the gypsies to dance for us notwithstanding. We followed them into a small cottage, then into a living room full of family photographs. The door was bolted and opened surreptitiously from time to time to let in women who had gone to put on long, colorful dance dresses with white-edged flounces. All this seemed rather clandestine. Soon the gypsies were dancing in a most spontaneous and enthusiastic way, with an old lady singing and one of the little boys playing the guitar. It seemed very much a family affair. Even small children danced to the enthusiastic singing, clapping, and olés of aunts, uncles, and cousins. The small space was well adapted for the shuffling, tapping steps, with many brusque movements of the body and arms, the proud strutting, and the circling of the men with snapping fingers. The dancers were not young or beautiful; but this was of no importance, as with swirling skirts and graceful movements they brought their age-old culture to life for us. It was becoming evident that Spain was not a country with a different culture, but an amalgam of a number of ancient and exciting heritages. In the streets the occasional man in the exotic costume of a mountain village and the working donkeys with their heavy burdens all spoke of the maintenance of traditional ways of life.

On Good Friday evening we were to see the three processions of Granada, which promised to be more imposing than in the small town of Jaén. The Virgins would be much more richly appareled and bejeweled, it seemed, and the people had spent weeks preparing the lavishly decorated litters. Unfortunately it rained on their parade and we were only able to see one procession, where the Pietà was preceded by black-hooded penitents and followed by the massive silver litters of the Virgin of Sorrows and various saints. A large number of penitents and ladies in black velvet dresses and mantillas, some barefooted, walked behind. As the rain became heavier, the other processions had to be canceled to the great disappointment of those who had lavished such care on their preparation.

One of the most beautiful views over Granada was from the hillside in the evening, when the beauty of the Alhambra itself was set off by the soft moonlight reflecting back from whitewashed walls.

Next day being Easter Saturday, we were taken in the morning to see the "official" gypsy dancing for tourists, in a richer part of the hillside village. Here we sat around the walls of a whitewashed courtyard. The gypsy dancers, some the same as on the previous day, were not only more elaborately dressed but also very heavily made up, which didn't really suit the older women whose beauty had faded. This time there were about thirty dancers and two men with guitars, with other women sitting around clapping and singing. The dancers used many more castanets and the performance was much more like a concert program than the more relaxed extempore dancing of the previous afternoon. A young plump, self-satisfied-looking girl chewed gum all the time she was dancing her solo, and the other dancers played very much to the gallery, particularly to the tourist cameras. As well as an entrance fee, we paid a round of drinks for the men, while the little boy of the previous day went around and took up a collection for himself. We were very glad we had stumbled on the more spontaneous, clandestine dancing in the gypsy home on Good Friday.

After noon on Easter Saturday we left for the long drive to Cordoba, taking an extensive detour to Malaga on the way, because some members of the group wanted to see the Mediterranean. While it was light the drive was interesting. We threaded our way between fields of sugar cane that was being harvested and loaded on donkeys, with the occasional little boy sitting on top sucking a sugar cane. However, night fell as we left Malaga and the road to Cordoba was impossibly bad. We bumped our way along in pitch-black darkness, which slowed us up considerably. It was half-past four in the morning

585

when we finally reached our destination. Inexperienced as yet in the ways of Spanish life, we were amazed to find, at the Assumption College hostel where we were to stay, waiters, formally dressed in white, still waiting to serve us our evening meal. Finally we began to eat at 5 a.m. From the beginning of the trip we had become accustomed to the lavish use of olive oil in cooking and the ever-present eggs on the menu. For our late dinner at Cordoba, we were served what looked like interesting desserts of white blancmange. On turning them over, we discovered eggs again, poached this time and sitting in their usual bath of olive oil. Everywhere we went, we encountered the ubiquitous egg for lunch or dinner, sometimes in mounds of peas or scrambled with tomatoes. Not surprisingly, as the tour continued, nearly everyone's stomach was deranged in one way or another by the unaccustomed amounts of oil. Vegetables we rarely encountered, although meals usually ended with an orange or a banana.

For my 33rd birthday on April 13th (Easter Sunday) I was in Cordoba, continuing on the trail of the Moors. In the tenth century Cordoba had been their magnificent capital. In the morning I visited the Cathedral, which had been a Moorish mosque until the twelfth century. Originally begun in the eighth century, it had nineteen naves and numerous entrances from a courtyard filled with orange trees. Here women were filling their water jars at the well. Built in the style of the mosques of Damascus, it was an interesting example of Moorish religious architecture. Since Greek Orthodox craftsmen had been recruited to help with its construction, its mehrab, or sanctuary indicating the direction of Mecca, blazed with Byzantine mosaics set in marble. The interior, a mass of red and white striped columns and arches, was so vast it was difficult to take it in. Unfortunately in the midst of this grandeur a Catholic church had been constructed, with the usual closed-in sanctuary and many small chapels with statues of the saints. To celebrate the festive day some of the worshippers were wearing their local regional costumes. We saw one woman dressed in traditional Toledo costume, which she set off with large, gold earrings.

Cordoba itself was very charming with bright, whitewashed houses with grilled windows and central patios. These small courtyards, with their pretty wrought-iron gates onto the street, were decorated with palms and bright-colored cinerarias and cooled by small fountains. As the favorite gathering place for the family in the coolness of the summer evenings they were furnished with comfortable chairs, family photographs, and decorations on the walls — everything that would make for family comfort. The little squares filled with orange trees were aromatic in the evenings. In the afternoon we were taken to visit the grave of the famous toreador, Manolete, who had died fighting in 1947. He had been gored by the bull he was killing. People still came regularly to weep at his tomb and at his house, where his blood-stained garments were enshrined, along with the ears and tails he had been awarded for his success in his many contests.

The natural next stop was the bullring to see what a bullfight was all about. Despite the colorful pageantry and the artistry of the toreadors and matadors, to those of us of Anglo extraction it was an upsetting performance. I personally was pleased when one bull attacked a matador and tore his golden pants. The crowd cheered fervently when the bull was finally killed with an axe and dragged from the ring. With the many against the one it was hardly an equal contest. Unable to enjoy what to us was a cruel performance, some of us left early, to the amusement of the fanatical crowd.

We traveled on to Seville, on the Guadalquivir River, traditionally the site of the Columns of Hercules. Again we passed through areas where farming was being carried on in primitive fashion, with hand ploughing and sowing, and now and then we would see men riding paniered asses or a whole family setting out on horseback, with father in a bright-colored shirt and broad-brimmed hat in front. Wells with vertical wheels of buckets were being turned by asses and women in peasant scarves guarded the animals in the fields. The peasants' thatched, whitewashed cottages were tiny, only two rooms with a low entrance. Little black and brown pigs wandered around and bulls watched suspiciously from the fields. Peppercorn and eucalyptus trees flourished in the arid soil. There were wild tufts of low-growing fan-shaped palms. Along the sides of the roads and in the fields bloomed pink, yellow, and bright blue flowers, with red poppies scattered through the crops. It was a most colorful region.

We found Seville to be a very beautiful city, with a character all its own. Its boulevards were shaded by lofty trees; attractive squares, both large and public and small and intimate, centered around ornamental crosses; and its public buildings were decorated with bright ceramic tiles. The former Jewish section, the Santa Cruz area, was particularly lovely, with narrow streets of whitewashed houses, brilliant in the sunshine, their facades decorated and their balconies and patios full of flowers. Cool fountains tinkled behind the intricate grills of their gates. At night the streets were illuminated by the soft light from ironwork lanterns. It was quite the Spain of dreams and light opera, of Don Juan, Carmen, and Figaro. As we drove past the old tobacco factory, in which the University of Seville was located, I had no idea that I would return after thirty years to lecture within its walls.

We visited the Seville Cathedral. Built to astonish the world, the cathedral is the biggest in Spain and the third largest in the world, being surpassed only by St Peter's in Rome and St Paul's in London. The nave is fifty meters high, with a Gothic groined ceiling supported by many pillars of clustered columns. The main altar gleams with the gold from Montezuma's treasures. The cathedral tower, the Giralda, formerly the minaret of the old Moorish mosque the cathedral has replaced, was in its time the highest building in the world and it still dominates the city. It is another reminder of the bitter rivalry of the two great religions that fought for supremacy in Spain. Moorish influence of 800 years ago was again much in evidence when we visited the palace of the Alcazar, with its intricate decorations and attractive gardens.

At the cathedral I saw the tomb of Christopher Columbus, where his coffin, sent back to Spain from Cuba at the beginning of the twentieth century, is supported by four bearers representing the four Kingdoms of Spain. Some say this cannot be his coffin, since he died poor in Spain and was buried in a monastery. Others consider it to be the coffin of his nephew, Bartolomé, who founded Santo Domingo in 1496. At a later date I saw "Columbus's tomb" again in the Dominican Republic, where his remains were purportedly found in 1877 during restoration work on the Santo Domingo cathedral, but then I have seen the tomb of the Virgin Mary in various disparate places as well.

In Seville I found to my surprise that there were two rival Virgins, whose partisans were fanatical about their relative merits. We went to a little church to see the Triana Virgin, Our Lady of Hope, in the gypsy quarter. The other Virgin, the Virgin of the Macarena, in a more affluent area, has a richer treasure, it seems. When the Confrérerie of one Virgin buys her a bigger and better jewel, the supporters of the other sets up an appeal to try to acquire an even bigger jewel for theirs. The Triana Virgin was on a tremendous massive silver stand, which it takes fifty men to carry in procession. The Virgin of Hope is also Our Lady of Sorrows, so behind her tears was the beginning of a smile. She was wearing an enormous jeweled crown of fine gold and the hilt of the dagger in her heart was studded with diamonds, rubies, and precious stones, whose gleams and flashes attested to their authenticity. The Virgin was richly dressed, with an enormous cloak spread out behind her in a train that was embroidered with gold thread and studded with jewels. From the canopy above hung a heavy fringe of gold and silver thread, The riches of this Virgin were breathtaking. In the same church was another Virgin, similar in appearance but less rich, and still a third on the high altar. A simple Christ carrying his cross was tucked away in a corner. Outside the church I was solicited for alms by the poorest, scrawniest old women in rags that I had seen anywhere in Spain. To me it was a heart-rending contrast.

We had been warned never to buy cigarettes in Spain in the street, but only from licensed government stores, yet there were many surreptitious street vendors selling cigarettes, at apparently advantageous prices, under the benevolent eye of the local police. Since some of our group were inveterate smokers, they were very tempted by the packets of cigarettes offered to us wherever we went. One day in Seville one of our group succumbed and bought a carton of twenty packets of unauthorized cigarettes. He began to open the carton to check its contents, as we had seen our guide do. At this point the vendor seized the carton saying the police were coming. Immediately we seized it too. The vendor then pretended to drop the cigarettes and, as we bent to pick them up, he tried to make off with them. One of the women in our group circumvented him, seizing the carton again, at which point he made off and disappeared in the crowd. Quickly we opened the carton and discovered to our amazement that all the packets inside were perfect in appearance and each was filled with carefully rolled cigarettes, but every one of them was filled with sawdust. These beautifully packaged frauds must have been put together in a factory. But what could we do? Since we had been warned not to buy in the street, to whom could we complain?

On our return journey north we stayed overnight in Toledo. This ancient city is strikingly situated on a promontory of dry hills, surrounded on three sides by a deep gorge, with the fourth side protected by inner and outer walls — an excellent defensive situation for old-style warfare. The hotel where we stayed in Toledo was presumably inexpensive, but very much in need of renovation. We rushed around like silly kids comparing our rooms. Some had no windows or only a large window onto the inside passage. The only running water in my room came from a pitcher, and the washbasin into which it was to be poured had a rusty can underneath it to catch the water. The basin was supplied with a cork to plug the hole, but when mine broke I had to poke my finger up from underneath to force it out and let the water through, thus washing my hands again in the dirty water. It certainly seemed very primitive in comparison with even the cheapest French and Italian hotels at the time.

Toledo, the capital of a short-lived Moorish empire in the eleventh century, still retained a distinctly Moorish medieval atmosphere. At night particularly we felt we were indeed back in the Middle Ages. The small cobbled streets, often just steep, narrow passageways, sometimes covered over, were ill lit by sparse, dim, wrought iron lanterns or illuminated wall shrines dedicated to the Virgin. In some dark corners there were crosses lit by lanterns. These illuminated crosses were intended originally to discourage dueling, for which the protagonists sought out the darkest places. Occasionally the streets opened out into pretty little squares. On the outside of the church of St Juan de los Reyes were many chains cast off by Spanish prisoners liberated from servitude to the Moors after the Spanish victories at Cordoba and Granada. The ancient fourteenth-century synagogue in Moorish style, with beautiful decorated arches and pine cone capitals on its many columns, which had long since been converted into a Catholic church, was a reminder of the flourishing Jewish community that was expelled from Spain in 1492.

The thirteenth-century Toledo Cathedral, built in French Gothic style, is one of the most famous in Spain. It has a lovely interior with five naves. In its treasury are displayed the objects made for Queen Isabella's private chapel from the first gold brought back from America. In the same treasury were statues in silver of each continent, with belts of precious stones. Spain's ecclesiastical treasuries gleamed and glowed with extraordinary riches.

Since Toledo was so famous for its fine steel, it was interesting to see young boys making Toledo jewelry by hand, working with gold and silver wire to produce beautiful brooches, bracelets, poniards, cufflinks, pocket knives, and ashtrays. Outside in the street Andalusian men with donkeys were selling local ceramics from their paniers. Another treasure of Toledo was the house where the late sixteenth-century painter, El Greco, lived for forty years. Here we were very moved by the magnificent portraits of Christ and the twelve apostles, each of whom was painted as a quite distinctive personality. We continued on the trail of El Greco in Madrid, where at the Prado we saw a further collection of his paintings, along with masterpieces of Velásquez and Murillo, and the famous clad and unclad Mayas of Goya.

From Madrid our last foray was to the Escorial Palace by train. As we went up into the Sierra the landscape became wilder and more and more rocky and desert-like. Here Philip II, in the sixteenth century, had built a renaissance combination of palace, church, and monastery that was as austere and remote as its builder. It was rigidly rectangular, with square towers and severe unadorned outer and inner surfaces. Splendor was lavished on the monastery chapel rather than on the King's private quarters, which were intentionally austere. The chapel was so placed that when Phillip was ill at the end of his life he could watch the masses and offices from his bed. In the crypt were the burial places of the Kings and Queens of Spain, beginning with Charles V, the Holy Roman Emperor. This monastery-palace seemed to encapsulate the rigid Catholicism of the Counter Reformation of Philip's day.

On the way back to Montpellier I had the great pleasure of visiting the wonderfully preserved medieval fortress city of Carcassonne, home of my very first French correspondent, with its extensive fortified walls with little pointed towers. The city was made even more secure by two sets of ramparts separated by large passages, which could be kept under close scrutiny. At the church of St Nazaire in Carcassonne we returned to the French Romanesque style, which we found restful in its simple beauty after the over-decorated Spanish Baroque of which we had been seen so much during our travels. It was a fitting finale to a most enlightening and culturally rich tour. How much richer, however, would it have been, had we been able to meet and communicate with the Spanish people themselves in their fascinating and ancient land.

Continuing my studies at the Université de Montpellier

Amid the turmoil of the first term, I had, of course, registered for the two Certificates I still needed to complete my *Licence ès Lettres* degree. For serious study I had decided on two certificates: Art History and Practical English. I then settled down to a concentrated six hours a day of regular study, sandwiched in between my now nine hours per week of conversation classes at the EN and lectures at the university campus.

I had registered for the Practical English course (*Etudes Pratiques d'Anglais)*, not because I needed to learn English or was looking for an easy ride, but because it consisted largely of translation from English into French of a very high standard. I knew I would find this very challenging in competition with native speakers of French. *Thème* (translation from native language to target language) is always more difficult for the language learner than *Version*, (translation from target language into native language), and what was *Version* in this course for the French students was *Thème* for me. At this level the passages we were expected to translate were extremely difficult. I remember once having to translate a section of Charles Lamb's "Dissertation on Roast Pig." I spent a full twenty-four hours working on my translation. Since the French use the same word for both *pig* and *pork*, I wrestled for a long time with the sentence: "He was neither pig nor pork, a kind of hobbledehoy," the latter word coming from the old British expression, "He was a hobbledehoy, neither man nor boy." Some things, I soon found, are untranslatable. Associated with the practical translation exercises were two other segments of the course. One was the study of British culture and institutions. As an Australian coming from a different culture, I dutifully read up all the required material on the House of Commons, the House of Lords, and the history of the British Labour movement, both unions and political party.

For this course I also had to demonstrate knowledge of a language other than English. Since everyone in the class knew French, this did not count, so I had to resurrect my German, with which I had dabbled on previous occasions. This language requirement was a translation one, and for this I had to read Fouqué's early eighteenth-century romantic work, *Undine*, and be ready to translate any part of it from German into French at the examination. With that, I was expected to have a detailed knowledge of German verbs with all their exceptions. These I pasted on my mirror, so that I could review them whenever I washed my face or combed my hair.

Meanwhile I found a private student who wanted some help with English in exchange for helping me with German. She was a Ukrainian Botany professor who had left Kiev and found her way as a refugee to France, where she was working as a laboratory assistant. On the way she had spent some time in a prisoner of war camp in Germany and was fluent in German, with, as it seemed to me, a Ukrainian accent. I would converse with her for an hour a week in German. Although I could understand most of what she said, I soon realized how much I lacked vocabulary for expressing myself. To meet her needs, I would spend an hour translating extempore into French the latest botanical research published in English, in a rapid oral translation, so that she could keep up with her field. This was an interesting experience, which made me realize how much understanding material in another language is dependent on one's existent knowledge. At times, I did not understand the botanical experiments described in the material I was translating, but my student would say: "That's all right. I know what they're talking about." In a windfall, I also acquired a paying student for English, which helped me save for my travels.

The professor in charge of the Practical English course had seized the opportunity to get some practice herself in English conversation with an educated native speaker and thus increase her knowledge of the English-speaking world. From time to time she invited me to her home to drink sherry and chat. We got on very well. One day toward the end of the year, as we sipped sherry in a relaxed atmosphere, she asked me about the kinds of relations England had with Australia as a member of the Commonwealth. I explained that the British monarch was recognized as monarch of Australia, by virtue of his or her role as head of the Commonwealth, not because he or she was monarch of Great Britain. In addition there were defense agreements, cultural exchanges, mutually beneficial trade arrangements, legal recourse (at that time, anyway) to the Law Lords in England as the court of final appeal, and sports competitions in cricket, rugby, and athletics. She found this very interesting. At my final oral examination in English, my own language, the discussion was to be drawn from the material about British culture and institutions, so the professor asked me about the relations between Britain and Australia, as a member of the Commonwealth. I thought this was rather amusing, since I had been the one to enlighten her on this subject just a few days previously. However, because I explained five aspects of the relationship, not the six I had listed over sherry, she marked me down on English conversation, despite my having done very well in the written translation exam. This brought my final grade down from a *Mention Bien,* to a *Mention Assez Bien* (a *Mention Très Bien* being rare). My translation from German into French had been weaker than that of the French students, who had learned German for six years in their lycée studies and who were translating into their mother tongue. This had made me vulnerable from the point of view of my final grade. The English professor was very disappointed afterwards that I had not been given the higher *Mention Bien*, which she felt I deserved. "But I thought you would be strong in German," she said, "and my grade for English conversation wouldn't matter!" Here again the weakness of the French oral examination system was evident — haphazard decisions made with little justification that would affect students for many years afterwards. For me it was not crucial in this instance, but for many others this tipping of the scales, through some little slip at the very subjective and personal oral examination, could be career-threatening. I thought back to my Douai experience in the Phonetics course and wondered by how many thousands this experience had been multiplied over the years.

As for Art History, first of all I was passionately interested in it. (This would no doubt have astonished Miss Spring at EHS. since she had never considered me her best student.) Furthermore I was attracted to the course by the fact that it included excursions to see the artistic treasures of this picturesque and historic region, which had passed through such periods of greatness. There were three segments to the course: Post-Classical Greek Art (all wet draperies and funeral stelae); Romanesque Architecture, my favorite, with which Languedoc and Provence were richly endowed; and Nineteenth and Twentieth Century French Painting. We would be studying David, Ingres, Gericault, Rouault, the Douanier Rousseau, Van Gogh, Pizzarro, Monet, Manet, Matisse, Picasso, Gauguin, and Braque. What a feast for an art lover! I could hardly wait! We romped about the countryside visiting fortified churches, the great sites at Aigues-Mortes and Arles (St Trophime, of course), as well as exhibitions of Impressionist paintings.

Since the post-classical Greek segment was the province of a professor who was away digging up new treasures in the Cycladean Islands, the course content was being taught by an assistant lecturer. This non-tenured gentleman, who limped painfully, had a large chip on his shoulder because, no matter how hard you worked in French academe and no matter how well qualified and scholarly you were in your specialty, it was difficult to get appointment to the rank you deserved. Here he was doing the work for an absentee professor who was enjoying himself in the sunshine of the Greek islands. The lecturer labored away on postclassical sculptural masterpieces with their wet draperies, while we studied reproductions in reference books — or at least some of us did. I was among the latter because I was enjoying this further extension of my knowledge of ancient art. The French students and a certain number of the foreign students, particularly the young Americans, were leaving all that kind of thing till the end of the year, when they would cram in what they could at the last minute.

Surprise! Surprise! Six weeks before the end of the year, the professor in charge of the course returned from his archaeological digs with newfound artifacts that he was most anxious to display and discuss with his students. We received a six-week crash course in the ancient civilization of the Cycladean Islands. Dilemma for the students! What would they be asked about in the final exam — wet draperies or Cycladean artifacts? The students for the most part decided to put their bets on the Cyclades, the professor's passion. After all, the French students assured us, it was the absentee professor's course, no matter what the lecturer had talked about.

We had had the option of writing a four-hour exam on one segment of the Art History course and taking oral exams for the other two. I selected Modern French Painting for my four-hour written exam and had written away, boosted with blocks of dark chocolate and some sandwiches from the EN. When the results were posted, I received an eighteen out of twenty, quite unusual in the French system and therefore meriting a *Mention Très Bien*. In fact Monsieur Antoine LeBon, our handsome, blond professor, had personally asked me to keep in touch with him as one of his most promising students. I certainly was teased unmercifully about that! This result for the written exam was on my record when I presented myself for the oral exams in the other two segments.

The morning arrived for the oral exam on the Greek segment. To the consternation of many of the students, the professor from the Cyclades had gone down with the flu just at exam time. Who then appeared to conduct the oral exam but the disgruntled assistant lecturer! There was much dismay among the students who had crammed exclusively on the Cycladean material, completely ignoring anything taught by the assistant lecturer. Now they had to admit at the oral that they knew very little about this gentleman's painstakingly organized course. Some had not even attended his lectures regularly, which he had undoubtedly noticed. Naturally he did not take this admitted ignorance at all kindly. When I arrived and actually knew what a funeral stela was, the lecturer smiled for the first time in the year and began to ask me if I had been to Greece and, if not, whether I intended to go. We had a very pleasant, even animated chat, while he told me what he most loved about Greece. Then, well aware as he was of the results from my written exam, he decided to give me a *Mention Très Bien* for the classical segment as well.

Next came the oral on Romanesque architecture. I had very much enjoyed all the excursions, my various visits to St Guilhem-le-Désert, St Gilles, the fortress at Aigues-Mortes, and of course the ever-glorious St Trophime at Arles. I had studied hard, immersing myself in these magnificent medieval structures. As I was on my way to the oral examination, I suddenly thought: "Oh dear! I didn't look over the fortified churches!" I was confident about the rest, however. In the classroom filled with students, I went forward to the Professor's desk and chose, in this traditional oral exam lottery, an envelope, containing the question I was to answer. Finding an empty seat for the few minutes I had to prepare my response, I opened the envelope to see what had been my luck in the draw. Holy smoke! It was a question about the fortified churches, along with a photograph on which I was to comment. I drew a deep breath and tried to work out my strategy. I remembered standing on a windy hillside while the professor commented on a fortified church. What had he said? The wind had carried half the words away. These fortified churches are Romanesque, I decided, so all I have to do is find as many Romanesque features as I can in the photograph and comment on those. This is what I did. However, the professor, having the results of my exams in the other two segments before him, was convinced that I really knew much more about it than I had indicated and was just nervous. He prompted me with questions: "And what about X? and Y? and Z?" "Yes, of course, there's always X, and Y, and Z," I echoed. No doubt about it, the professor concluded, she deserves her *Mention Très Bien.* I had covered all aspects of the question, hadn't I? From this experience I learned that, in the person-to-person interaction of an oral examination, there could be a halo effect as well as unfair penalization.

Gypsy pilgrimage at the Saintes-Maries-de-la-Mer

"The Camargue!" everybody said. "You must see the Camargue! Especially on May 25th, the gypsies' annual pilgrimage! It's one of the most colorful festivals in the region." "But watch out for your purse!" my friends added "Half the pickpockets in Europe will be there!" The Camargue was an area of marshes and wild grasses on the delta of the Rhône, between Montpellier and Marseille, where *gardians* (French cowboys) tended herds of wild horses and small local bulls. The latter were used for a distinctive and very popular type of bullfight where all the local lads could jump into the ring and try to fight the bull.

Gypsies and pilgrimages! What a strange mixture! I thought. I couldn't wait to see what this festival had to offer in contrasts and medieval ceremony.

The Saintes-Maries-de-la-Mer, known the world over from Van Gogh's painting of its brightly colored boats, was a sleepy old Mediterranean port, which even in the late eighth century had already been the Mecca of the gypsies and wanderers of Europe. According to very ancient tradition, soon after the death of Jesus, Marie-Jacobus, sister of the Virgin Mary, Marie-Salomé, mother of the apostles James and John, Lazarus, whom Jesus raised from the dead, and his sisters, Martha and Mary Magdalene, were all set adrift in a boat by the Jews who had opposed their Lord. The black servant of the two Maries, Sara, was apparently so heartbroken at being left behind that Marie-Salomé compassionately threw her cloak out to her and, with this as a raft, she joined the others. The boat drifted and drifted through calm Mediterranean waters, until at last it was blown up on the beach in Camargue, near the Saintes-Maries-de-la-Mer. The little band then separated to evangelize various areas of Provence. Mary Magdalene took up a hermit's life at the Sainte-Baume. Marie-Jacobus, Marie-Salomé, and Sara, it was believed, remained at the port until their death. In time Sara became the patron saint of the gypsies.

Each year, on the 24th and 25th of May, it was the custom for gypsy people to gather from far and near to honor their patron saint and to renew old friendships. For a brief period families were reunited and affairs straightened out, amid much dancing and singing.

When I arrived all spare land at the Saintes-Maries-de-la-Mer was covered with parked caravans. In what seemed like general disorder, horses, dogs, and children roamed, amid old cooking stoves, folding tables, washing hanging over whatever was available, and bedding left out to air. Gypsy women, with their long, colorful dresses, unfortunately none too clean, their black hair stiff with oil, and with large gold earrings swaying, would offer to tell your fortune. Others moved among the crowd of visitors with three or four pathetic-looking children clinging to their skirts, spinning long tales of misfortune, while the children felt surreptitiously for a carelessly pocketed purse.

Children! Children everywhere! They were lovable and appealing, despite their neglected appearance. It seemed they began to beg as soon as they could walk. They besieged the visitor with a persistent, low whine: "Une petite charité, madame. We have no father. A few coins, madame, just a little something!" Father was no doubt not far away, begging just as persistently for something to fill the mouths of his large and hungry family.

Everywhere there were stalls — in the market place, along the side streets, around the curious old fortified church itself. Sausages dangled in strings; there were dolls on sticks and great teddy bears for sale. Postcards were offered at exorbitant prices. Scarves of bright design, sweets from doubtful-looking bins, balloons, doughnuts, and ice cream kept coy company with medallions of the Saintes-Maries, statuettes, and rosaries.

Meanwhile, great crowds of the devout and the merely curious like myself pressed into the unusual little twelfth-century church, with ramparts like those of a medieval castle, which had originally provided protection against the invading Saracens. Its greatest treasure was the relics of its three saints. With a tremendous fervor, the assembled Gypsies and pilgrims loudly sang the praises of their patron saints, the hymns and prayers being amplified into the square outside the church. Before the altar were the statues of the two Maries in their boat. Down in the crypt was the special chapel for the gypsies' own beloved saint. Beside a reliquary containing her bones was the statue of black Sara, draped in a satin cloak to which gypsies through the years had pinned photos of the children they had committed to her protection. On a rack nearby were the thanksgiving offerings of the wandering folk — ties, handkerchiefs, scarves, perhaps a spray of artificial flowers. As there were no windows in the crypt the air was thick with the smoke of burning tapers, while the floor was wet with the miraculous water from St Sara's well, which the gypsies were carrying away to cure all their ills during the ensuing year.

At eleven o'clock the procession began. A choir of women from nearby Arles, in traditional costumes of tight-sleeved blouses and long flowing skirts, with lace-edged shawls draped over their shoulders and small velvet and lace caps perched high on their curls, led the procession from the church. With enthusiastic cries of "Vive les Saintes-Maries! Vive Sainte Sara!" a horde of joyously jostling gypsies escorted the statues of the Saintes-Maries in their boat down to the sea, while the densely-packed crowds of spectators were kept back from the route by the mounted *gardians* of the Camargue. These local cowboys were distinctive in their broad-brimmed hats and bright-colored ties. Down into the sea they went, the gypsies accompanying the statues right into the water. Behind them, in the sea, the *gardians* formed with their horses a half circle facing the shore. Then, from a boat the Bishop, holding aloft a silver hand tied with red ribbons, blessed the statues and the crowd of pilgrims.

The day was then given up to fun and sport. Gypsy women danced to the music of Spanish guitars — flamenco-type dancing in the midst of a circle of clapping friends, with many rhythmic movements of shoulder and hip and slow, almost spasmodic, passes with their hands. The tension increased as the male partner, with snaps of the fingers, led the dancer on.

In the crowded local arena there was a mild form of bullfight, the favorite summer distraction in this part of France, with the tough little bulls of the Camargue. Athletic men in white tried to seize a cockade and tassels placed between the bull's horns, and great was the amusement of the crowd when half a dozen men leapt back over the fence to escape the bull's quick dash. It was great sport, especially as, unlike Spanish bullfights, the bulls were not killed.

"Please may we have a copy of that photo?" an old man asked me. He was seated at a table with a large group of gypsies, young and old. "We are thirty members of one family gathered here together for the first time." "Certainly!" I replied. "What address will I send it to?" "Address? Oh yes, address! Ah.....!" The old gypsy looked enquiringly at his family. A low, perplexed discussion followed. "We'll be at Lodève for Christmas," said the grandfather, "but before that it's hard to say." "Grandfather! Grandfather! When can we see the photo?" clamored his many grandchildren. "I'll show it to you next year at the Saintes-Maries," he replied. Then turning to me, he asked, "Could you send us thirty copies, poste restante to Lodève?" Even if you don't lose your purse, I found, a visit to the Saintes-Maries can prove expensive.

My year rollicked to a close at Montpellier and I could now proceed with my summer plans.

16
WILGA:
THE HITCHHIKING
SPECIALIST   1952

I was determined to visit Scandinavia during my last summer in Europe but, of course, it would have to be inexpensively. I had decided to hitchhike (*faire du stop* or *voyager au pouce*, by thumb, as the French called it). I would travel with an Australian friend, Doris, a mathematics teacher who had taught with me at Taylor's Coaching College in Melbourne and a French student from Montpellier, Marie-Claude, who was studying for her *agrégation* in history and geography. At the time hitchhiking was very popular with students and reasonably safe, as long as you did not travel alone. If people did not like hitchhikers they just did not stop. The English students in the Lake District had taught me some of the fine points of the art, so I set off with confidence.

Doris and Claude could not have been more different. Doris was quiet, almost phlegmatic, and did not express many opinions. In fact she spoke very little and then, being rather unimaginative, made only the most obvious comments. She did not speak any French. Claude, on the other hand, was very Southern French — a true *méridionale*. She had a lively mind and was quick of speech, always ready with an observation, a quip or a point of view to discuss. Of small build, with her hair cut very short, she looked like a young boy in her pants and shirt. With her strong background of advanced studies in history and geography, she was very perspicacious about what she was encountering, but she spoke no English. I was right in

601

the middle. If these two were to communicate at all during our four-week trip, it would have to be through me.

With our rucksacks on our backs, Claude and I met up with Doris in Paris. Taking a train to the outskirts of the city, we set out for the road in high spirits. We soon found, however, that it takes patience to be a hitchhiker. Rides come along very randomly; you may wait five minutes or half a day. It seemed on that first day that we would never get moving. Finally a doctor and his wife picked us up in a small car and took us through the vineyards of Champagne to St Dizier, where they were visiting friends. They told us that if we were still waiting when they continued on their way east, they would pick us up again. After trying for a couple of hours to get another ride (there was very little traffic), we were just making our way in discouragement to the railway station when our friends of the morning reappeared and packed us into their small vehicle for the long ride to Nancy in Lorraine. There we had the pleasure of sauntering round Stanislas Square in the late evening, when the waters of the fountain were lit up with various colors, and the trees were illuminated from behind with a light green light that set off the white of the buildings.

After a good sleep in an inexpensive hotel, we took the bus to the end of the line, which set us on the road to Strasbourg. Hitchhiking is not all in long stretches but every little helps. Our first ride was for four kilometers on the back of a truck, followed by another four kilometers on the back of another truck. We were then left in a village street, where we were picked up fairly soon by a rather crazy racing-car driver, who delighted in asking us whether he frightened us with his fast, erratic driving. He set us down on the road beyond Lunéville. Another slack period of waiting followed, until I had the idea of attaching a Union Jack to my rucksack — a trick I had learned from the English girls. Almost immediately a rich industrialist in a big car picked us up, although we got the impression from his demeanor during the drive that he didn't quite approve of our activity. Doris and I chatted with him in English (drivers often liked to practice their English or their French with us) but Claude felt very uneasy. She had qualms about hiding behind the British flag and kept quiet, not wanting to be recognized as French. We were very pleased to be taken as far as Strasbourg, which put us near the German border. Finding ourselves an inexpensive hotel, we immediately went out to see what we could of that very interesting city.

Since crossing frontiers with strange hitchhikers can be a little risky for even kind and helpful drivers, we decided to cross the border between France and Germany on the train. In preparation we bought tickets to Offenburg for the next morning. The frontier between France and Germany seemed to be very well guarded, with at least twelve officials trying to keep busy, checking up and down the train. Once in Germany, we were tempted by a visit to the Black Forest, since it was not very far away. We looked for a road going south. We got a lift to Freiburg almost immediately on the back of a truck, with two Germans and a Norwegian. Soon we were bowling along past fields of tobacco, maize, and poppyseed.

The Norwegian, on this, our first ride in Germany, gave us a lot of helpful hints for successful hitchhiking ("trampen," as he called it) and information on youth hostels. Following his advice, on arrival at the Youth Hostel in Freiburg we bought a booklet with all the information we needed for the *Deutschen Jugendherbergen* (DJH); this became our travel bible while we were in Germany. From Freiberg, we were able to travel into the mountains of the Black Forest with a young man in a beautiful Opel car, rolling along smoothly and comfortably as far as the beautiful Titisee lake. Here the name of the region acquired new meaning for us as we admired the black fir trees, extending right down the hillside to the water's edge.

The Youth Hostel in this beautiful spot had attracted many young vacationers, most of whom arrived on bicycles. For most hostels, we found, guests were supposed to arrive on foot or by bike, so we hitchhikers usually walked the last section to the youth hostel, which in this case was about two and a half miles out of town. At Freiburg the many young travelers were accommodated in rooms with four double-decker beds, and this made for ready conversation, in our case in a mixture of German, French, and English. Since we all picnicked in the refectory with food we had bought, this led to further mixing, with much discussion and hilarity. In this way we learned much about Germany and the neighboring countries. As we continued our travels, we also picked up useful information from fellow hostelers about where to go and which hostels to aim for.

Next day we returned to Offenburg in several stages. We were picked up first by a quiet, thin-faced doctor, who packed us into his small car to take us to the village of Bad Durrheim. This small, isolated place was most picturesque. We ate our lunch of bread, cheese, and fruit in the village square while we watched the activities of the storks on their large nests on the chimney tops. Another quiet man took us on to Villingen. (With our haphazard mode of travel, we soon became accustomed to finding ourselves in places we had never heard of before and were very unlikely to visit again.) Our third driver was an insurance agent who spoke English. He took us on his rounds, which included the pleasure of a detour to the mountainous, wooded area of Wolfach, with dark forests of fir trees rising from deep glacial valleys and little villages with bright flowers in the window boxes of their chalet-roofed houses. The village men were wearing very short shorts held up with Tyrolean braces, embroidered or with embossed designs in leather. Great timber trucks went by with long fir logs. The hotel where we spent the night was just as traditional, with wash basins and pitchers in rooms decorated with family pictures.

To our delight, we were finding that hitchhiking was much easier in Germany than in France. We had the impression that Germans approved of young women like ourselves getting out on the road for fresh air and exercise. As we went on, we found that even old ladies helped us by giving us hints as to the best places to wait to be sure of getting a good lift. On one occasion a local woman came up to tell us that we would be much more likely to get a ride if we crossed the bridge ahead of us and walked a little further on, where there was a bigger road with more traffic.

While hitchhiking we always tried to give something in return for rides, usually by chatting entertainingly with the driver. Our drivers were usually men, mostly on their own, since there were three of us to accommodate. They were going about their daily business, which often entailed long drives, and they were a little bored with their own company. It was unusual at that time for cars to have radios. Usually we could converse with the driver in one of our three languages, English, French, or German. If he spoke only German, I took the front seat and kept the conversation going. Even though the drivers were friendly and welcoming, Claude who had grown up in Occupied France soon began to feel very nervous. Being surrounded by the sounds of German brought back memories. Consequently she preferred to keep quiet and preserve her anonymity. If the driver was taciturn and preferred to concentrate on his driving rather than listen to our chatter, we respected his preference. Some drivers liked us to sing French or English songs to wile the time away.

As we traveled along the back roads through pretty little villages and gentle rolling countryside, Doris would occasionally make a comment in English, and Claude would ask me what she had said. Usually the conversation ran like this:

Doris (in English): "This is so pretty. It's just like a postcard!"

Claude (in French): "What did Doris say, Wilga?"

Wilga: (in French) "She said it was very pretty. It was just like a postcard."

Claude (in French): "*Mon dieu*! Don't bother telling me anything she says. It's never worth repeating!"

Doris (in English): "What did Claude say, Wilga?"

Such are the hazards of tripartite communication.

Back in Offenburg from our Black Forest jaunt, we made our way out to the road to Heidelberg. We were picked up almost immediately by a German businessman who took us all the way to our destination. Since it was mid-July we were passing between fields where men were harvesting and packing straw onto carts. Some of the straw even came in through the car windows, as we drove between the loaded carts. Arriving early at the hostel (always a good idea in summer), we booked in and were free to explore this beautiful university town. Heidelberg was a magical name for me, because Mother had frequently talked about walking ten miles to Heidelberg, Victoria, as a child to buy a button or a reel of cotton.

All was not smooth sailing in youth hostels, we found. After all the overnighters were a chaotic agglomeration of all kinds and conditions of people. At the Frankfurt hostel where we stopped next, I had my watch stolen. I had taken it off and put it on the side of the washbasin while I rinsed my hands. Returning to my room I discovered I had left it behind and went back to the bathroom immediately to look for it. No sign of the watch! The only person around was from my room. I immediately confronted her and demanded my watch. She strenuously denied my accusations, so what more could I do? At least I could enjoy Frankfurt, which was a delightful city with swimming pools on the River Maine and lovely lawns and gardens along the verge. The silhouette of the Cathedral stood out, lonely and lovely, over the parts of the city razed during the wartime bombing.

The next day was a Sunday — the day for family outings in the car. Since it was quite hopeless for hitching rides, we regretfully made our way to the railway station. Here we caught the train to Mainz, where we boarded the afternoon boat for the trip down the most scenic part of the Rhine to Coblenz. In the cool breeze from the river, we drifted past picturesque Rhenish villages with medieval church towers and half-timbered houses with typically stepped facades. In some of the villages local summer festivals were being celebrated — Lindenfest or Rottweinfest, they all provided the opportunity to drink, sing, and dance. The festival spirit was not confined to the villagers. The Germans on board laughed and sang and drank their Rhenish wine, until all inhibitions were subdued and they could clown around with unrestrained exuberance.

Although it was Sunday, the incessant traffic of a busy commercial artery continued, as barges full of coal and sand surged past us, often in convoys of four or five long barges towed by a brave little tugboat. After Bingen we passed more and more ruined castles on headlands, islands, and hilltops, where their outlines stood out clearly against the blue sky. On terraced slopes were carefully tended vineyards, all neatly planted in perfectly straight lines. Finally into view came the rocky cliff of the Lorelei, where the legendary siren singer drew boatmen off their course onto the rocks. We could see why the Rhine was for the Germans so much part of their national identity, with its broad width of moving water, the incessant commerce, the joyful holiday-makers, and the extraordinary natural beauty, set off by the artistic creations of their forebears.

The youth hostel in Coblenz was in an old fort, with wonderful views over the city and the surrounding area. We had a sentinel's eye view of the confluence of the Moselle and the Rhine, with busy traffic on the two rivers. Since the previous day had been a Sunday, we had run into money problems. With the banks closed, we had not been able to change money. There were no credit cards and ATM's in those days, and we had not yet heard of travelers' checks. We had followed the advice of an American soldier and changed some French francs for German marks with a taxi driver — a procedure that was rarely advantageous for the purchaser. Our first necessity on Monday morning in Coblenz, then, was to find a bank. Here we experienced the kindness of the ordinary German to strangers. A passerby went out of his way to take us on a twenty-minute walk to the bank, which would have been very hard for us to find in this shockingly destroyed town, with ruins and rubble everywhere. With some money in hand I was at last able to replace my stolen watch. Coblenz was in the French zone of occupation, and, since it was the fourteenth of July, French soldiers and members of the French Africa Corps were marching, with tanks parading, flags flying, and bands playing.

The husband of a relative of mine was an Attaché at the Australian Embassy in Bonn. This seemed an excellent reason for going in that direction. Making ourselves look as presentable as we could, we hitched a ride in a delivery truck to the respectable area where they lived on the outskirts of Bonn. Unfortunately my relatives were both ill in bed, but their little blonde four-year-old daughter entertained us most engagingly. Although we acted as though we had arrived on a bus, I'm sure that, knowing the penchant of young Australians for inexpensive traveling, they easily guessed how we had come. Very kindly they arranged for their chauffeur to drive us on to Cologne.

The hostel in Cologne was already full by the time we found it, so we ended up sleeping in a Catholic refuge for women that had been set up in some air-raid shelters in the midst of the general destruction of the city. The hostel was certainly not palatial — it had no windows and the beds were Spartan — but it was quite adequate for weary wanderers. We most gratefully accepted their hospitality for two nights while we explored their famous city, with its proliferation of beautiful churches full of artistic treasures. We particularly admired the Cathedral with its two openwork, decorated spires and its many pinnacles that made it look like a reliquary. Although it had suffered from intensive bombing, there was still much to appreciate. On the pillars of the interior were polychrome figures of saints and angels; the gilded reredos was richly carved in high relief; and on the altar there was a gold casket with relics of the Three Kings. Detailed scenes of the Passion were represented by a wealth of figures sculpted in wood. On the richly clothed statue of the Virgin and Child above the altar hung many ex-votos in the form of beautiful jewels.

We had some difficulty getting far from Cologne. We had taken a tram to the outskirts, but we seemed doomed to two-kilometer rides in the countryside. One driver, trying to be helpful, even dropped us off at the village railway station. When we did finally make it to Wuppertal that day, we sat down wearily on a patch of grass to eat our lunch. Up came a local woman to ask us to move. It seemed that our chosen patch of grass was about to be mowed. It certainly wasn't our day when we couldn't even find a public place where we could sit down in peace.

Since drivers made decisions in a split second, first impressions were important. Sometimes, because there were three of us, each with a heavy pack, one of us would stay back from the road with the rucksacks while we hitched for a ride, so as not to discourage potential drivers with the sight of too big a group. We hailed only vehicles that had enough room for three passengers and never vehicles that had on board more than one man, or two at the most when we were in a tight situation. Our next offer came from some men (too many men) with whom we felt uneasy; they stayed and waited for us for some time, trying to change our minds, but we were very wary. Claude was the quickest to pick up "bad vibes." Perhaps it was because she spoke neither German nor English and so was much more attentive to body language.

After another short hitch we were picked up by a man in a heavy truck, which was drawing three trailers. My companions sat on bricks in the first trailer, while I conducted a lively conversation in German with the driver. I told him that my grandfather had been a German immigrant to Australia (actually it was my great-grandfather, but I didn't know the German word for that relationship) and that I was trying to get to my *heimat* (place of family origin), which was Hamburg. This appealed to his German soul. I found throughout Germany that drivers were very anxious to help me reach my *heimat*. Later I found out that most of the early German immigrants to Australia had come from Hamburg, which was the great port of departure, and that my own family was actually from Leipzig. Be that as it may, this unintentional fiction proved useful as we continued on our way.

Next a friendly man with a young son took us through the Ruhr, via Dortmund, to Unna. This was certainly a change of scene, as we drove over one of the richest coalfields in Europe and watched the heavy smoke rising from the innumerable factory chimneys on the horizon. For the next fifty kilometers beyond Unna we sat on tires in the back tray of a truck, the surface of which was covered with greasy oil stains. We were now passing through great wheat fields, which were being harvested by machines in fields that seemed to have been machine sown. This was quite a contrast to what we had seen earlier in Southern Germany, where men had been laboring mightily to bring in the harvest by more primitive methods. As we moved into orchard country, our cheerful young driver bought us freshly picked cherries to relieve the tedium of our journey.

We were now coming into the British Zone of Occupation and we began to see many vehicles with British Tommies on board. We were aiming for the hostel at Paderborn. Our itinerary was very much determined by the situation of suitable hostels at reasonable distances from where we happened to be at any particular moment, and we changed our intended destinations according to our success in moving forward with a rapid succession of rides. On this occasion our driver dropped us off at Erwitte, a very small place in the North Rhineland. The local bus went only to a town twenty kilometers from Paderborn, so we made for the railway station where we waited half an hour for a local train that took us somewhere near the youth hostel we had in mind. We then walked the rest of the way. We were certainly getting plenty of exercise on our journey, which, with our frugal picnic diet, was reflected in our much more sylph-like figures. I lost more than fifteen pounds over the four weeks we were on the road. On arrival at the Paderborn hostel we were very glad of the palliasses it offered and ready for a good night's sleep. The only drawback in these hostels was the penchant for the healthy and enthusiastic German girls to get up at 4.45 in the morning to get out on the road. They were a Spartan race. On the other hand we very much appreciated it when a tall, blond girl brought us bread and buns in bed — lovely iced ones they were too. We felt quite spoiled.

We waited a long time for a ride out of Paderborn. Hitchhiking requires patience and, in a sense, the relinquishing of control of one's time and volition to chance and random encounters

609

that will shape the immediate future. When we ended up in places quite unfamiliar to us, we would consult our Youth Hostel guide for the nearest hostel, especially when it was late in the day. At other times we would just change our ideas on where we would go next. Consequently, we found ourselves in some places of unexpected interest that only the people in the vicinity knew about. Our wait at Paderborn was worthwhile. We were eventually picked up by a very charming, cultured lawyer, who was most informative. He poured out a flood of rapid German, of which I understood only about forty percent, telling us the history of the area. We went through beautiful woods where in 9 AD the German hero, Hermann, had defeated the Roman forces of the Emperor Augustus and stopped them from advancing further into Germany. Everywhere in Germany there were trees. We were now passing through woods of leafy beech trees, which must have been most colorful in autumn. Our driver told us that woods were the most cherished adornment of Germany. Unfortunately some had been cut down by the occupying British. He went out of his way to show us a local beauty spot of historic and cultural interest near Erterstein. We passed through a narrow gap in huge outcrops of rocks to find ourselves looking out over a lovely lake surrounded by woods. In one of the rocky outcrops had been constructed a representation of the tomb of Christ; in another was a replica of the cave in Jerusalem where St Helena had discovered Christ's Cross; while on the outside rock surface was a carving of the Descent from the Cross. These relics of Christian piety dated back to the last decade of the eleventh century. It was all most impressive. Our interesting and informative driver left us in the central square of Horn. How many wandering travelers had had the opportunity to visit Erterstein and Horn? we wondered.

Getting out of Horn, however, was another story. We had made our way to the edge of the town, only to find ourselves on a very quiet road beside a field of oats. Nobody seemed to be going anywhere. After four hours we managed to get several short rides — on the back of a truck, then squeezed into a small, low trailer behind a car, and finally, for fifteen kilometers, in a grocer's delivery van. We were now near Hameln, the Hamelin of Pied Piper fame. Despite the attractions of the picturesque renaissance houses of its old town and its busy, modern port, we decided not to tarry long but to take advantage of the increased traffic to continue on to Hannover. Our luck changed when a pleasant chemistry student packed us into his small Volkswagen. It seemed he had fought against the Australians at Tobruk and spent two years in America as a prisoner of war. Consequently he spoke very good English. For a while I could take a rest from my strenuous efforts to follow rapid conversational German. Our new driver took us by back country roads through delightful old villages of Lower Saxony, which seemed untouched by the twentieth century, to within eleven kilometers of Hannover. That was the end of our luck for the day, however. There was nothing for us to do but walk the remaining distance to Hannover with our heavy packs on our backs.

By the time we reached the hostel at 9.30 p.m. we were extremely tired and very hungry. All day we had been prevented from taking the train, or even eating, by the fact that we had lots of money, but again no German money — our continuing problem. At the hostel they allowed us in on the promise of payment the next day. Not surprisingly, there was in the dormitory another Australian girl who was from Coburg, only a few miles from my home in Ascot Vale. We met Australians and New Zealanders wherever we went. Having come from the other side of the world, they were as determined as I was to see as much as they could, despite their very modest finances.

Next morning it was pouring rain — a great hazard for hitchhikers. Since I was the one who spoke German, naturally it was I who had to sally forth in the rain to go to the bank. Like other North Germany cities, Hannover had been very badly hit by the bombing and much reconstruction was in progress. For our next destination we had decided on Kiel. We wanted to see the canal, which was quite famous as an engineering feat at the time. By afternoon the rain had stopped and we were soon on a tram out to the road for Hamburg. Here we waited quite a while without much success, until the driver of a heavy lorry packed us like sardines into the front seat and took us out to the motor road. By this time there were many other young people trying to get rides as well. We were fortunate to be picked up by a young driver, in an Opel again, who drove us to Celle, through fields of wheat, barley, oats, potatoes, and cabbages, all essential elements in the German cuisine. Celle was a lovely old North German town, rather like Chester in England with its many half-timbered houses.

As we were leaving Celle, the same young man who had brought us picked us up again. Having now finished his business in Celle, he took us to within fifty kilometers of Hamburg. Soon we were passing through more forests, this time of oaks and ashes, with some elms. We were out of the mountains and in flat country again. After our driver left us on the road, we were picked up almost immediately by a man going right through Hamburg to Kiel, so we decided to take advantage of this stroke of luck and bypass Hamburg. I retold the story of my grandfather and my *heimat* to our sympathetic driver and received the same warm response. I was certainly getting a lot of mileage out of this heart-warming search for my roots.

We finally saw Hamburg briefly as we drove through it. It was a big, imposing city and I wished I had more time to explore it. Although, as elsewhere, there was much destruction in the center (more than half of the buildings having been destroyed during the war), there was still much to admire. We were particularly struck by the many magnificent bridges over the canals and the river, some being suspension and double suspension bridges, which are always eye-catching. One bridge with the Hanseatic Towers of Hamburg's coat-of-arms at the entrance was most impressive. I could see as we passed through that it was a city of gardens and lakes.

Beyond Hamburg we bowled along a fine, tree-lined motor road for the eighty-eight kilometers to Kiel. The countryside was now much more intimate, with smallish green fields divided by hedges and everywhere healthy-looking cows. The villages, built of cheerful red brick, began to look much more Danish. Some of the houses had deep-sloping thatched roofs and we began to see occasional windmills on the horizon, usually with small electric windmills attached. Everywhere the children were flaxen-haired, their hair the color of the ripe wheat. Toward the coast were low hills or dunes. The hostel beside the Kiel railway station was in a long, low, prefabricated building, not nearly as comfortable as the palatial accommodation at Hannover. Tired as we were, however, from our long day, we slept very soundly.

Next morning we set out to see the Kiel Canal, which was much wider than the Suez Canal. Its magnificent system of cranes and buckets for transporting the coal to the ships was very advanced for its time. Interesting as it all was, we could not linger. We had to race on to catch the boat for Korsør in Denmark.

What a dull, wet day it was for a sea trip! After six hours we arrived in Denmark and hurried out on to the road to hitch a ride to Copenhagen. After a long wait we had advanced only four kilometers toward Copenhagen, so we returned to Korsør, where we spent the night in their very attractive youth hostel. Here no one seemed to speak English, but we managed to communicate sufficiently for our needs. We spent the evening in a lovely old lounge, such as one would expect to find in an old-style hunting box in the forest. The young Danes who were staying in the hostel were sitting around saying nothing. They seemed to be very quiet people, quite different from the more gregarious Germans. Even in waiting rooms at railway stations in Denmark we noticed this same quiet reticence. As quiet as the Danes may appear, it seems they are very determined and decisive. During the war when Hitler ordered that all the Jews in Copenhagen be rounded up for transportation to concentration camps, the King put on the yellow star the Jews were forced to wear and declared: "I am a Jew!" The population followed his example, so that it was hard for the Germans to tell who should be rounded up and who should not.

Next morning we were able to move on quickly with a ride direct to Copenhagen. Denmark seemed to be as calm and peaceful as its citizens. We drove past well-ordered fields, with brown cows grazing in luscious clover. The farmhouses were clean and well built, with groups of larger buildings that formed co-operatives. Soon we were in Copenhagen, with its green copper roofs, in search of Hans Christian Anderson and the Little Mermaid. We were happy to meet both of them in their eternal stone images. At that time I had no idea how well I would later come to know Copenhagen, when I would visit Inge Rivers, the widow of my car-designer cousin from London. Wiz married a second time and lived out his last years very happily in Denmark.

After a brief visit we left Copenhagen by tram and bus for the outer road, where we were very fortunate to be picked up immediately by a Dane who could speak German. He asked us whether we had had the opportunity as yet to eat real Danish food. Out of kindness of heart he insisted on driving us off the main road to his favorite restaurant to have a typical Danish breakfast with lots of fish. He took us halfway to Helsingør (Elsinore), the site of Hamlet's castle. We drove along a pleasant seaside road with beautiful houses, surrounded by the gardens of Denmark's more wealthy citizens. In front of every house there were flag poles with flags flying, red with a white cross, often in long, thin pennants. We were taken the rest of the way by a charming teacher from the International Folk High School of Helsingør, who had very interesting things to tell us about that distinctively Scandinavian approach to adult education about which I had read in my studies at Melbourne University. She told us she had some Aussies in her international summer course that year. More compatriots abroad! We were truly everywhere.

It was fun to visit Hamlet's castle, the Kronborg — a splendid Dutch Renaissance structure with the light green copper roof so popular in this region. We wandered around the ramparts and thought of Hamlet's father's ghost. From the ramparts we could see Sweden. Below us on the point, there was a sentry box with a Danish flag flying and a solitary soldier walking up and down whistling. What a change of atmosphere from the tense situation in Germany! Back in the town, we wandered through old streets with little, low, yellow houses with brown, low-sloping roofs, like those in parts of Copenhagen. We then caught a ferry to Sweden. The Danish-Swedish frontier was very relaxed, with no formalities beyond the stamping of passports. In about twenty minutes we were in Sweden.

Hälsingborg, on the opposite shore, was the summer residence of the King of Sweden. Flags were flying for Prince Phillip's visit to his Aunt Louise. We had little time to explore it, however, since we still had a long way to go. We were picked up very soon by a man who persuaded us to drop our original project of going directly to Stockholm. He suggested we go instead to Göteborg on the west coast, then across country from there to Stockholm on the east coast, so that we could see the beauties of the interior. He then drove us around the coast some distance to set us on our way. Throughout our trip we found people very interested to help us in our explorations, and in this casual way our trip developed.

Our driver left us at Bastad. There a grandfatherly man, an English-speaking ex-teacher turned book publisher, picked us up. He took us the full two hundred kilometers to Göteborg. Since he had been driving a long time on his own, he was most grateful for our company. He told us that he often drove from Copenhagen to Madrid and back for his work. At his request we sang all the songs we could think of to keep him from going to sleep. At Halmstad he took us to a cafe to have a Swedish afternoon tea — coffee, enormous open-faced sandwiches with eggs and herring, and strawberry cream cakes. People's kindnesses were unlimited.

We were now traveling along interesting seacoast with twisted trees that looked like Australian ti-tree. In the Swedish towns through which we passed were blocks of modern flats and public buildings of very contemporary design. The towns were open and airy with wide streets. The houses were surrounded by gardens. Everywhere there were avenues of trees, fountains, and public gardens to provide fresh air and recreation for the people. Even the smaller houses were nicely painted and well kept. The people we saw were well dressed. There were no obvious signs of poverty, and, since Sweden had remained neutral during the war, there was, of course, no bomb damage. As Claude remarked: "There doesn't seem to be any proletariat here!" The further we went, the more I felt that Sweden was more like Australia than any other country I had visited so far. It too was a very big country with wide-open spaces and a small population, with large aggregates of people being found only in a few big cities. Even the silver birches seen from the distance resembled gum trees. There were the same isolated small towns, far horizons, and modern mechanized farming. The houses were well built and individually styled. The modern blocks of flats were very clean and indicative of a high standard of living. At Varberg, our kind driver took us to see the fortifications erected against Danish invaders hundreds of years earlier, some dating from the 13th century. As we traveled through Scandinavia, we heard much of the to-ing and fro-ing over the centuries of the Danes, the Swedes and the Norwegians — invading here, retreating there, occupying strips of each other's territory for shorter or longer periods. Fortunately they were now in a cooperative period. At Göteborg even the hostel was more comfortable than we had expected. Instead of the double-decker wooden structures with palliasses to which we had become accustomed there were beds with wire mattresses. This being the summer season the hostel was established in a school building, so we slept off our fatigue surrounded by blackboards.

Funny, unplanned things keep happening when you are hitchhiking. It was cold and windy when we set out for the Stockholm road. First of all we had problems finding it. Because we had been given vague indications, when we finally reached it we found we were heading in the wrong direction and ended up back in Göteborg. We were pretty late getting to the right road, but we were fortunate to be picked up quickly by a young man who didn't speak anything but Swedish. He kindly took us the seventy kilometers to Boras. From Boras a truck driver took us out to a very deserted spot near a quarry, where we waited a very long time for some traffic to pass by. Finally a father with his small son on board took us four kilometers further on. It certainly didn't look as though we were going to make much progress that day.

After another very long wait, we were picked up by two men who spoke only Swedish. They kept laughing and talking and asking us something we didn't understand. We began to feel very nervous. We had mostly traveled with men who were driving alone or with their wives or children. These two men insisted on taking us off the road into the forest, saying "Kaffe! Kaffe!" We kept saying: "No! No! Wandererhem, Wandererhem," as youth hostels were called in Sweden, giving the name and address of the nearest hostel in our guidebook. Our drivers only laughed at our obvious discomfort, which made us even more nervous. Suddenly they turned off the road into the forest. Stopping at what appeared to be a log cabin, they invited us to get out and come inside. Reluctantly we followed them. As we came through the building we found ourselves in a terrace café, looking out over a beautiful lake, and there they bought us the promised coffee. Our hosts were highly amused at our obvious distrust and our surprise at the outcome. However, now that all was well, we amused ourselves with a linguistic exchange. Amid much hilarity and frequent cups of coffee, they taught us to count to ten in Swedish and we taught them to count to ten in French. In our nervous moments we had named a nearby youth hostel at Ulricehamn as our destination, so they now drove us there. They waited politely while we rang the bell to make sure someone was there to welcome us (they were really very kind). However, we had decided it was far too early to give up for the day if we were going to keep up a good pace. As they drove off we sneaked around the back of the hostel and hurried back on to the road to the astonishment of the youth hostel director, who had just opened the front door to greet us.

A young architect then took us sixty kilometers to Jönköping. We felt we were seeing the real heart of Sweden that day, as we drove through forests of firs and birches, with many delightful glimpses of large and small lakes. At Jönköping the next day we lunched beside a very large lake, actually the beginning of one of the largest lakes in Sweden. It was like looking out to sea from the shore of a bay. We were struck again, as everywhere, by the modernity of Sweden, even to the sculptures that proliferated in every town. Even in smaller places like Jönköping, there were vigorous, active figures in stone.

We were moving along smartly now, and we left Jönköping early in an attempt to reach Stockholm before evening. Very soon a French architect in a big Ford Vedette picked us up and drove us all the way to the capital — a full day trip from 9.30 a.m. to 4.30 p.m. Naturally we found it very comfortable and relaxing not to have to wait beside the road and hitch rides every hour or so. Since our French driver had done his share of hitchhiking as a student, he understood what we were doing. After the big, long Jönköping lake, we drove by many more lakes, large and small. No wonder so many of the Swedes who went to the United States settled in Minnesota, the "Land of a Thousand Lakes." Wood from the forests was floating on the lakes, the logs lashed together for transportation. Soon we were passing over miles and miles of plains, with hay drying on long racks that stretched across the fields like fences. We wondered how the hay could possibly dry, even with this distinctive system, since it rained so frequently even in summer. While having lunch at Norrköping, we came across the four Australians we had last seen in Hannover!

Stockholm on first sight was very modern with blocks of flats shaping the skyline, rather than the medieval spires of Germany. The famous Stockholm youth hostel we had heard so much about on the road was on a three-masted ship anchored in the center of the city. Unfortunately it was already full when we arrived, so we were sent to the Badminton Hall. On arrival we were amazed to find ourselves looking down over tiers and tiers of seats into a badminton court filled with rows of beds — a hundred in all — with young people milling around. It was quite a sight.

In the Badminton Hall we heard from our fellow hostelers about a Scandinavian-type restaurant, where for several crowns we could eat as much as we liked. At that time I had never heard of a smorgasbord, and this sounded too good to be true. We soon found the restaurant, which was already packed with tour groups. Since it was a self-service buffet, there was great confusion as people crowded around the dishes of food. We realized how hungry we were after several weeks of picnicking when we saw the mountains of food. Determinedly, and somewhat surreptitiously, we kept on helping ourselves to more and more food and we ate very well. We ate right across the gamut of dishes, helping ourselves liberally to the fresh buttered bread and washing it all down with cups of hot coffee.

In Stockholm I wandered into a shop with Claude to buy her a new sweater. Claude had had her one and only sweater stolen in a Swedish youth hostel. Being from the sunny south of France, she found Sweden in the summer like winter at home, and she was already coughing and sneezing. It was when I found myself surrounded by well-dressed Swedish shoppers that I realized just how shabby and unkempt we looked after three weeks on the road. Suddenly I felt like an alien vagrant.

Built on islands near the sea, Stockholm had a beauty all its own. There were bridges and waterways everywhere, giving lovely vistas. The King's Palace, an immense, quite severe 17th century building in French Louis XV style, also looked out over the water. Nearby was Parliament House, set back among trees, with across the water the National Gallery, looking rather like a Venetian palace. There was a separate building for the upper House of Parliament, the House of the Nobility. The old streets of Stockholm were very picturesque, their houses covered with a mellowed yellow whitewash. Having decided to visit a museum on an island, we went down to buy a ticket for the boat ride. Not knowing the language, however, we bought by mistake a round trip ticket and ended up where we had started. No matter. The skyline of Stockholm from the water was very satisfying, and we enjoyed passing through cool, green passages between tree-covered islands where lucky residents had built their lovely homes.

We now moved on with Norway in our sights. We had a very good day, covering three hundred kilometers before evening. The major part of the day was spent with a light-hearted Swedish watchmaker who had hitchhiked himself when he was a student and who already had two French boys on board when he picked us up. Indefatigable, he later picked up an English boy. Somehow he packed us all in. When we went through towns where we had to go more slowly and stop at intersections, he would joke about how high the fines were for picking up hitchhikers and he took great pride in his ability to avoid the police. After he dropped us all off, Doris, Claude and I were proceeding with a grandfatherly Swede, when the French boys whizzed past us in a faster car. It was always fun to meet up again with people we had encountered along the way, so many of whom were following a similar itinerary to ours. We were already coming across the little red-painted farmhouses that continued into Norway. Of course, there were more lakes, sparkling through the dark fir trees, with wood floating on them in large quantities. After a ride in a big car with a great hunk of wood across the interior, and another in a gravel truck, we reached Christinehamm. We were now well on our way to Oslo, distances being immense in this area. The next day our luck continued and two Norwegians drove us over two hundred kilometers to within four kilometers of the border.

After the Norwegian frontier, the scenery began to change as we went higher up the mountains. We were taken nearly to Oslo in the back of a truck, with three women from the driver's family in the back with us. On the way we stopped to have tea — Norwegian sandwiches and wafers, like waffles, with butter and cheese. At Oslo our hostel was situated high on the mountain slope looking out over the harbor. The harbor of Oslo, being a drowned estuary, was magnificent, with wooded slopes and innumerable inlets, surrounded by the mountains. We found the city itself less interesting, however, than Stockholm. It was a pleasant, clean, modern city, with an ultra-modern Town Hall, constructed just before the war, but in an architectural style I did not find particularly pleasing. It was a very square building in red brick, with two big squarish towers. Its surroundings were more attractive, with fountains and open galleries along which highly colored, sculptured wooden wall panels showed aspects of Norwegian life. The Royal Palace was box-like too and much smaller than the older palaces of Stockholm and Copenhagen. Doubtless, it was much more adapted to modern needs.

The public gardens, decorated with innumerable sculptures by Vigeland, were the main attraction. These statues represented all stages of human life. Two rows of statues led up to a central column showing man mounting up toward the light. On the central column were dozens of figures forcing their way up and, around it, were thirty-six sculptured groups arranged in threes and spread out like the spokes of a wheel. Higher up, above a monumental staircase, was a Wheel of Life with several more figures on it. On the whole the statuary was very interesting and forceful in a massive way and the ensemble was very moving and thought-provoking. Very thrilling to me were the maritime museums across the harbor. I shall never forget the sight of the three-thousand-year-old Viking ships that had been brought up from the bottom of the Oslo fiord. It fired the imagination to see the high carved prows of these great vessels with place for thirty-six oarsmen. I could picture them forging across the seas, inspiring terror in the inhabitants as they approached the shores of England and Normandy. It was also a thrill to see the Kon Tiki, the famous balsa raft on which in 1947 Thor Heyerdahl had floated across the Pacific, from Peru to Polynesia, to prove his theory that it was possible that some Pacific Islanders had come originally from South America.

Doris had to leave us in Oslo to join friends in Paris, so Claude and I set out to explore Norway on our own. We had decided it was foolish to come all the way to Norway and not see the fiords. Since not much time remained before I would have to join my friend Lucienne in Paris for our trip to Great Britain, we abandoned hitchhiking for a while. Instead we took the train to Bergen. We had heard much from fellow hostelers about this beautiful train trip from Oslo to Bergen that crossed over the backbone of the country. Unfortunately, leaving the Oslo hostel in haste, I left my camera on the bed, just as we were beginning the most beautiful part of our trip.

The Oslo-Bergen railway was a marvel of engineering. It took us right over the mountains to the west coast. Every minute of the trip was fascinating. There were beautiful views down steep valleys through thick forests. Gradually we rose higher and higher until we were above the tree line. The vegetation became more and more stunted, until it disappeared into tundra, and then there were just rocks covered with mosses and lichens, with glaciers coming down the slopes and patches of residual, unmelted snow, even though it was mid-summer. In the distance were lakes, with snow-capped hills behind them, and the deep clefts of mountain valleys, where waterfalls dashed down the precipitous slopes. It was most spectacular. As we came down toward the coast we traveled along the shores of a great fiord at the foot of steep, tree-covered cliffs. It was an unforgettable journey. At Bergen, we stayed in a most attractive and comfortable youth hostel, high on a cliff above the town, with an unbelievably spectacular panoramic view over Bergen, its tremendous estuary surrounded by hills. The next day we went out by bus to visit a little fiord, where we spent a happy afternoon relaxing on the heather-covered slopes, looking out over the water.

We had to keep moving, however, so we spent that night on the boat from Oslo to Stavenger, sleeping on the long seats of the saloon. We then caught the bus from Stavenger to Christiansand, passing through interesting hilly coastal country. Here it was more open, with rocky outcrops and scattered trees. More wild and rugged than the fiord country, it was rather like the French Cevennes. Another night on a boat from Christiansand brought us back to Denmark. This time we slept on rubber mattresses on the deck. Once we were back in Denmark we recommenced our hitchhiking. Despite fair success the first day, we found hitching difficult in Denmark. The trucks never picked up passengers, and the cars were small and full of people and luggage. We soon gave up our efforts and decided to catch the train to the frontier of Germany where hitchhiking would be easier.

That night we reached Hamburg very late and arrived at the Youth Hostel at about 9.45 p.m. to find it full, as were all the hotels. The manager had no suggestions as to where we could go. I had reached my *heimat* and there was no room in the inn! We walked down the street, a little nonplussed as to what to do. Soon I saw two grandmotherly-looking women coming toward us. Aha! I thought. Elderly ladies would not like to see two young women out on the street late at night with nowhere to go. Approaching the two ladies I explained our situation and asked if they had any suggestions for us. "Go to the Hamburg Railway Station," they hastened to tell me, "to the Catholic-Evangelical Mission." It seemed this was a kind of Travelers' Aid for women. Solicitously they gave us detailed directions as to the right tram to take to get there. Off we went to the central railway station, only to find ourselves at the end of a long line of similarly shelterless wanderers. Gradually we made our way up the line to the bossy, prefect-like woman, who was allotting accommodation. (Or was she merely harried and hassled by the enormity of her task and the multiplicity of tongues in the seemingly unending line before her?). *"Bank? Bank?"* she shouted at me, in an impatient tone."*Nein! Nein!*" I replied, somewhat confused. The only *"Bank"* I knew about in German was the *"Deutsche Bank"* and I wasn't in need of money. She gestured us out of the way and moved on to the next in line. Marie-Claude and I were left wondering why we were being rejected. We were feeling very discouraged when we were rescued by some Austrian girls who spoke English. They explained to us that there were no beds left; all they could offer us was a bench (*Bank*). The sharp-toned woman had been asking me whether we would be happy to sleep on a bench. Of course we would at that hour of night! So back to the end of the line we went and worked our way forward again. When asked this time: *"Bank? Bank?"* I quickly replied, *"Ja! Ja! Danke schön! Danke schön!"* and we were in. So we spent our night in the city from which my ancestors had set out for Australia on mattresses laid over benches in a room full of young wanderers. The noise of the engines of the international expresses roared through the open windows, as they hooted, hissed, and whistled their way in and out of this enormous station. Even here, of the six women in distress in our section three were Australians! Should I have been surprised? At the Copenhagen Hostel, there had been fourteen Aussies that we knew of. Claude was very astonished when she realized how many of us there were wandering around Europe.

Next day being a Sunday — a bad day for hitching — we took the train from Hamburg to Bremen, a very interesting and picturesque old town, and later continued on to Leer on the German frontier. Our ambition to see Scandinavia achieved, our main interest now was to get back to France by the most direct route, and this took us quickly through the two small countries of Holland and Belgium. With just two people it was easier to get rides and we kept up a good pace.

Holland, even at this fast clip, was as fascinating as ever, with its innumerable canals, windmills, and sleek cows in lush pastures. The only unpleasant incident was in Belgium. It was the first time we had encountered overt disapproval of our mode of travel. We were given a ride by a very stern-faced man, who made it clear that he disapproved of hitchhikers and lectured us on the subject as we traveled along. We wondered why he had picked us up at all. We had always felt that those who did not approve of hitchhiking passed us by, and we had been picked up by so many friendly people who enjoyed our conversation, our information about our countries, and our singing. Oh well! we thought, it takes all sorts to make a world. At Mons we finished our journey by taking the train, Claude for Paris and Wilga for Saint-Quentin for a short visit with Paule Guilbert, my friend from the lycée in Douai.

In Paris I was to meet Lucienne, my good friend from Montpellier, who was doing her degree in English and wanted to accompany me on a hitchhiking trip to England and Scotland. She was looking forward to practicing her English and becoming more acquainted with the British Isles. Personally I looked forward to meeting my "Alexander relatives" in Scotland. Mary, Marj, and Jean Alexander had been my friends since junior high school and I had always looked on Mrs Alexander as my second mother. Their father, who had immigrated to Australia from the Aberdeen area, had retained a strong Scottish accent all his life. He had died unexpectedly while on a trip with his wife to the old country. It was his sisters, Mary and Marj's aunts, that I was anxious to visit in Stonehaven and Aberdeen and I planned to visit Mr Alexander's grave at Stirling.

Back to the United Kingdom

With our rucksacks packed, Lucienne and I took the train to London, where we spent the night with my English friends, the Uptons. Next day Mr Upton kindly took us with him on a business trip to Cambridge. It is always a pleasure to return to the banks of the River Cam and contemplate the beautiful architecture of the colleges from this vantage point. This was a helpful start, but we were determined to keep moving on to Scotland. We found hitchhiking in England to be quite easy, especially as Lucienne was a pretty, blonde twenty-three year old, with a bright smile. There were, of course, no language barriers as there had been at times in Europe. After two days of successful hitchhiking toward the north we drove into York on a truck. The driver had enjoyed our company so much that he offered to take us on further next day. He suggested a convenient and inexpensive hotel where he himself stayed. This seemed like a stroke of luck. We quickly settled in and then cheerfully set out to see what we could of the great city of York: the Castle, the old quarter of the Shambles, and the famous Minster — another architectural gem I had studied in detail in my History of Art classes in high school. Unfortunately the Minster was partially hidden by scaffolding in a timely effort at restoration. With care I was able to avoid this necessary but unsightly obstacle in my pictures. Back at the hotel we retired peacefully for a good night's sleep. About midnight, to our surprise and mild consternation, we heard soft knocking on the door of our room, which we naturally ignored. We were not surprised, however, next morning to find that our "kind" truck driver had left early without leaving a message.

We were taken as far as the Scottish border at Berwick-upon-Tweed, by a very serious man with a very precise way of speaking. Lucienne, being there to study English as it is spoken, was very amused at the formal way he addressed us. We both sat in the back of the car and when he wanted a break from driving he would ask us: "Would you please get out here, ladies, and have some tea. May I offer you some sugar? How many cakes would you like?" and so on, all in a polite, but distant manner, without much warmth. It was certainly a change from our errant truck driver.

Progress was quite rapid in Scotland and in no time we were in Edinburgh, where friends of my Rivers cousins in London had invited us to stay with them. We were treated royally by our new friends, with all the kind hospitality that from my childhood I had known to be a Scottish trait. Next day they took us on a tour of the city of Edinburgh, noted as one of the most beautiful cities in the world. We went first to the Castle where we were fortunate to see the famous summer Military Tattoo. Within the battlements of this splendid castle, high on a crag it was exhilarating to watch the magnificent parade of Scottish regiments in full regalia, marching to the stirring music of the bagpipes. Of course, we walked the Royal

Mile through old Edinburgh to the palace of Holyroodhouse, where Mary Queen of Scots lived through so many of the tragedies of her eventful life. The palace was later enlivened, for a short period, by the glittering court of Bonnie Prince Charlie, the "king" of the highland clans loyal to the Stuarts. When Bonnie Prince Charlie fled to France he was indirectly referred to as "the king over the water" and toasts to the king were held over a glass of water so there would be no mistake as to who was being honored. Without realizing it, it was the Bonnie Prince we had been singing about, when around the piano at the Alexanders' home, we had so frequently sung "My Bonnie lies over the ocean, My Bonnie lies over the sea" and the hauntingly nostalgic "Will ye no' come back again?" We also visited the house of John Knox, Queen Mary's nemesis, and remembered how he had fulminated against her immoral behavior. Edinburgh through history has certainly been a city of great contrasts and violent moments.

There was much to see in Edinburgh. Over it loomed the mount of Arthur's Seat, which reminded me of the mountain of the same name near Melbourne. We visited St Giles Cathedral, so distinctive across town with its steeple in the form of an open crown. Here we admired the beautiful wood paneling of the Thistle Chapel, dedicated to one of the oldest orders of chivalry in Europe, the Order of the Thistle — that tough, prickly symbol of Scottish identity. I examined with pleasure the Monument to my early love, Sir Walter Scott, tracing among the statues up its two-hundred-foot column the heroes from so many of his books that I had read so avidly in my early teens. With our new friends we walked along the shores of the wide Firth of Forth, admiring the great spans of the Forth Bridge, which I recognized from the picture in my high school geography book. In fact, thanks to my Britain-centered education in the Victoria of the nineteen-thirties, I knew the British Isles in many ways better than my own country.

From Edinburgh we hitched rides without difficulty through Perth (another name imported to Australia) to the little known town of Stonehaven. One of the governors of Victoria in my youth had been Lord Stonehaven, so this name also rang a bell. Here we found our way to the home of the Alexander aunts. Mr Alexander's two single sisters, both nurses, welcomed us most warmly. They couldn't do enough for us and spoiled us in every conceivable way. Next morning we were sitting up in bed in the pink and blue bed jackets they had lent us, eating a copious breakfast from the silver service and drinking our morning tea from delicate china cups. This was a far cry from hostel life.

The Alexander sisters, never having ventured far themselves, were very interested in our mode of travel. They were very anxious to see for themselves how we operated. Next day we were to go on from Stonehaven to Aberdeen to see their married sister, Aunt Mary. The two sisters decided to come with us to the motor road to see us off. They insisted that they must talk personally to whoever picked us up to ensure that we were dropped off at the right exit for Aunt Mary's place. Off we went to the motor road with our two new friends in tow. Since we did not want to alarm passing drivers with the sight of four people, too big a group to pick up, the two sisters hid behind a hedge, while we signaled to passing vehicles. The truck driver who stopped was somewhat nonplussed, as we climbed up into the cabin, to see two middle-aged ladies dash forward from behind a bush to give him detailed instructions as to where he was to take us and the precise spot where he must drop us off. Thus we traveled safely to the "grey granite city" of Aberdeen, where we were now in the tender care of Aunt Mary. She, like her sisters, was kindness itself and made us more than comfortable. All the Alexanders treated us like beloved members of the family. With Aunt Mary we soon became familiar with the sights of Aberdeen.

Outside of Aberdeen we had a stroke of luck in being picked up by a young English Air Force officer, named Colin. During his tour of duty Colin's girl friend had deserted him and, now that he was "demobbed," he was trying to get over his emotional distress by touring Scotland on his own. He was so cheered up by our company that he invited us to continue with him on a tour of the famous Scottish Lochs, which was exactly the destination we had had in mind. Needless to say, we accepted with alacrity. For the next three days we had no worries about transport and were picked up each morning at our hostel by our personal chauffeur. With Colin we wandered around the shores of Loch Ness (we saw no monster) and slithered our way over rocks at Loch Lockey at Invermoriston, continuing on to Loch Lomond. As we crossed the mountains through the pass of Glencoe, the site of the famous massacre in 1692 of the highland McDonalds (who were loyal to the Stuarts) by the Campbells, the barren wastes shone with a strange yellow light under the lowering clouds of an approaching storm. At Balloch we danced with the local lads and lassies at their Saturday night fling.

However, nothing so good goes on forever. Soon we had to say goodbye to Colin and find other means of transport. That was when we met the Laird (as he told us he was). The Laird took us to Helensburgh through Glen Fruin. He was beginning to become a little too friendly for our liking. When we came to a small wood he suggested we stop and look for mushrooms in among the trees. We soon discovered, however, he was looking for more than mushrooms, but we were more agile than he was. Laughing off his lack of success, he cheerfully drove us past Gare Loch on to Dumbarton.

Outside of Dumbarton we were picked up by Sandy MacDonald, a redheaded fish merchant. We rode in the back of his van, where he usually carried his fish, as the strong odor soon indicated. Sandy was most hospitable and decided that, as we had come so far, we must see the famous Highland Games and Gathering of the Clans, being held just at that time at Dunoon under the patronage of the Duke of Argyle. After seeing that we had a nice tea, he drove us off to the Games. The fact that he had no advance tickets for us was no problem at all, he assured us, since he was so well known in the area. He would soon talk the people at the gate into giving us the best seats in the grounds. True to his word he escorted us to front row seats, where we sat among the well-dressed spectators, trying to look dignified in our shabby hitchhiking attire. When Sandy heard that an Australian Olympic runner was competing in the Games, he immediately sent her a message to come and meet a distinguished Australian guest. She responded promptly, expecting no doubt to see a consular representative or a prominent athlete. She must have been somewhat surprised when she came to the stand and found two scruffy hitchhikers sitting in places of honor. The Games were very stimulating with the leading Highland bands marching in ceremonial kilts and sporrans, with a very upright and skilled Drum Major in a busby twirling and tossing his staff at the front of the line. We saw much expert Scottish dancing and hurling of shot putt and hammer, as well as the usual contests on the track. The atmosphere was very lively, even ebullient.

Sandy then insisted that we come back to his house for the night. "What will your wife think about two strange women suddenly descending on her out of the blue?" we asked. "She's English," said Sandy, "but she's married to a Scot, so she's just had to get used to our Scottish hospitality." Home we went with him and slept comfortably for the night on the living room floor. We were not difficult guests. As it happened we got on very well with Mrs MacDonald, who invited her neighbor in to meet us. As a result of this contact, the neighbor's brother offered to drive us the next day to Stirling, where I wanted to visit Mr Alexander's grave.

Within sight of Stirling Castle, I gathered the purple heather from the hillside and with it I covered the grave of my best friends' father, while I reflected on his self-effacing kindness to us over the years.

It was time to return to England, so we hitched rides over the border at Gretna Green and made our way to Liverpool, where we turned south to Chester and Shrewsbury. We were now in the Border Counties, skirting Wales. We celebrated Lucienne's birthday in the lovely town of Ludlow, with its beautiful cathedral and castle and picturesque old streets. It was all so very English. Lucienne felt very much at home in the countryside around Ludlow, which seemed to her very like that of her home province of the Creuse in France. Next we got a ride to Hereford, where the Early English architecture of the Cathedral, with its square, pinnacled tower and round arches, its Lady Chapel, and colorful windows, was reminiscent of my favorite Romanesque style in the South of France. Soon we were traveling down the valley of the Wye, on our way to Tintern Abbey, a name that resonated with me from the famous poem of Wordsworth's that I knew so well. Although the Abbey was a ruin, it was emotionally very moving.

To round off the trip, we traveled to London on the tray of a truck. It was a long ride with no rest stops, and this we found rather stressful as a last hitch. We were, of course, too shy to mention our needs. Once in London we were able to relax at the home of Mrs Upton, where we had begun our odyssey. With her usual kindness she soon had us back in top form.

628

17
THE CIRCLE COMPLETED
1952

Return to the Southern Hemisphere

My vagabond summer over, I had now to turn my thoughts to the future. The date for my departure on the P&O liner *Chusan* loomed very near. Before leaving Montpellier, I had begun looking for a position in Melbourne after my return to Australia. Although I was now much more qualified as a teacher of French, with my Licence ès Lettrès degree and my three years of living and working in France, I knew that the Victorian Education Department, with its strictly enforced promotion policy, would merely reenter me on the list, well below the level to which my experience and qualifications entitled me. I had by now experienced the freedom of the private schools, so my thoughts turned in that direction. I decided to apply for what I considered to be the best school educationally in Melbourne, the Melbourne Church of England Girls' Grammar School (MCEGGS). My interest in educational ideas was still strong, and MCEGGS stood high on my list for its application of progressive educational ideas. My old mentor Freddy, as well as Professor Browne, had always spoken very highly of the school and of its Principal, Dorothy J. Ross. During my Diploma of Education days we had visited the school to see how a progressive school was organized and operated. Since then, my sister Linda had spent a short period as an assistant in the boarding house section of Morris Hall, the middle school, as part of her missionary training. I had applied to teach in the senior section, Merton Hall. To my delight, Miss Ross had replied immediately offering me a position for 1953. My immediate future settled, I was now free until the beginning of February of the next year, and I intended to spend a couple of months with Linda in Hyderabad in India on my way home. Because of the worsening political situation with the unpopularity of King Farouk, my earlier plans for stopping off in Egypt to visit my friend Diaa were now out of the question. Diaa was too nervous about what might happen, so I booked to go directly to Bombay.

First visit to India

As the *Chusan* made its way through the Mediterranean, I had to catch up on my vaccinations. In those days of smallpox, typhus, and typhoid injections this meant several days of misery. Fortunately, on this voyage, I had a roomy cabin at the highest level, and I looked forward to a good rest on board ship after rushing around all summer. At table, I soon made friends with Mattie Fernandes, a Goanese primary school teacher on her way back to Bombay from a visit to London. We walked and talked and found we had much in common. Since, on the day of my arrival in Bombay, my train to Hyderabad was not scheduled to leave until the evening, Mattie invited me to her home to meet her family. Like many Goanese, Mattie was a Roman Catholic. Goa was still a colony of Portugal at that time; India's "police action," incorporating it into the Republic of India, was yet to come. Although Mattie's family lived and worked in Bombay, they were very supportive of the separate status of their tiny homeland.

Mattie lived in the Little Flower of Jesus Building in the Girgaum section of Bombay, a very crowded area with lots of families and little black-eyed children. The Fernandes's apartment seemed wide open, having large window areas on both sides; one side looked into the busy street, while the other, which gave on to a noisy, crowded lane, directed one's gaze straight into other people's equally wide open living quarters. In the neighboring homes there was plenty of interest in Mattie's return, in the comings and goings of her friends, and in her strange, fair-skinned, fair-haired visitor. The Fernandes's apartment was soon filled with people. Everyone who knew Mattie came to greet her and garland her with ropes of sweet-smelling flowers. Mattie's brother worked in the Indian film industry, already becoming one of the biggest in the world. Indian films, as he told me, always had to have a girl singing in the moonlight and any romance was definitely touch-me-not.

I traveled to Hyderabad by train in a second-class compartment. Third class, I was told, would be very crowded indeed, with large Indian families with crying babies jammed in among the enormous quantities of luggage with which Indians customarily traveled. The usual very large suitcases and wicker baskets that Indians seemed to need would be augmented by bedding rolls and tiffin baskets for hot curry and rice along the way. In the second class compartment there were double-decker wooden berths for sleeping, on which the Indians squatted during the day. At night any breezes that might have cooled the stuffy compartment were excluded by the necessity to lock windows and doors while we slept, lest prying hands snatch away our possessions when the train stopped at stations along the way.

My sister Linda had arrived in India in 1949 just before the end of the British Raj and the inauguration of the new republic on January 26th, 1950. She was settling in just at the right time to enter into the excitement of the establishment of a new nation. Some of the older missionaries, who had been in India for many years, were still wedded to the upper class English habit of dressing for dinner in the evenings and generally keeping up the standards of the British Raj. They also kept a certain distance between themselves and the "natives." This seems quaint from the perspective of the twenty-first century. Linda, on the other hand, with her egalitarian upbringing, soon had a very nice group of Indian friends, to whom I was now introduced. Linda had found Indians to be friendly, welcoming, generous people when friendship and trust were offered. Mattie's family in Bombay had already shown me this warm acceptance and hospitality.

Hyderabad, where Linda was working, had been an independent state ruled by a prince, the Nizam, before the Indian "police action" in 1948 incorporated it into the Indian Republic. After incorporation of the princely states, their rulers had been permitted to retain their privileges and their lands for a ten-year period to ease the transition and to allow for orderly social change. When I arrived in Hyderabad, the former Nizam, considered at the time the richest man in the world, was still very much in evidence. His state, the largest of the princely states, was about the size of Kansas. Since the Nizam was a Muslim, he had ruled Hyderabad state for the most part with Muslim, Urdu-speaking officials, whereas the majority of the population was Hindu and Telegu-speaking. This situation was rapidly changing as more and more Telugu-speaking officials took over. The partition of the subcontinent into India and Pakistan, with the tremendous turmoil that ensued, had occurred only three years before my arrival. Millions of refugees had poured on to the roads, going in both directions — Muslims trying desperately to get to Pakistan and Hindus to India. There was, while I was there, a certain nervousness among the Muslim population remaining in Hyderabad, since they represented the former ruling class. Many of them could see no future for themselves or their families in India and had plans to move to Pakistan as soon as feasible. Since Government regulations prohibited them from taking their wealth out of the country, they were converting much of it into jewels, some of which could be worn by their wives and the rest smuggled out in various devious ways. Unfortunately customs officials also confiscated jewels, if they discovered them. To many the future looked very murky indeed.

Hyderabad was a beautiful and architecturally striking city, which moved to the rhythm of traditional ways. Most of the modern commerce and administration took place in the twin city of Secunderabad. The city had been built in 1589 by the Muslim conquerors from the north, who were attracted to the area by its diamond mines. These rulers of the Golconda Kingdom built the nearby sixteenth-century fortress of Golconda, so rich in history. The central landmark of the old city of Hyderabad was the beautiful Char Minar, a four-minareted gateway in delicate Moorish architecture, with ogive arches and finely sculptured balconies at intervals up the four towers. Not far away was the main mosque, where the Nizam went regularly for prayers. In the same area was a grand bazaar with much fine jewelry, brassware, beautiful saris, and the bangles Indian women wore in quantity. This was a good place to practice one's bargaining skills. Silver was particularly plentiful and, apart from the intricately designed necklaces and bracelets and the silver inlay in bidriware (made of a gun-metal like alloy), silver was beaten extremely fine and served as an edible embellishment for desserts.

A beautiful sight against the intense blue of the sky were the spreading trees, often with flaming red blossom, which set off the public buildings in the main streets of Hyderabad. The city was quite an intellectual center, with the highly respected Osmania University and its excellent hospitals, practicing both Western and Indian homeopathic medicine. It was well equipped with good transport and a reliable water supply from several reservoirs on the outskirts. This abundance of water was a definite boon, since there was no rain from October to June. The one thing Linda, with her Melbourne upbringing, missed during the long drought before the monsoon arrived was the sound of rain pattering on the roof.

The numerous small lakes and tanks were delightful places for picnics in the cool of the evening. I went on one such picnic with some of the girls from Linda's school. The girls had brought tiffin baskets of curry and rice and various Indian delicacies for us to try. They carefully laid out a cloth on the grass and sat on the ground around it. Unfortunately, in my clumsy foreigner way, I tiptoed over the cloth to find a seat on the far side — to Linda's horror. It seems I had unintentionally walked on the table.

The streets of Hyderabad were always crowded with people in all kinds of colorful costumes reflecting their ethnicity or religion. Bicycle rickshaw wallahs and individual cyclists, calling out to make a way and ringing their bells continually, nipped in and out of the traffic. Flat-bottomed bullock carts with plodding buffaloes took their time in the middle of the road. Pony carts and the few chauffeur-driven motor cars of the wealthy, blared their horns incessantly, as they tried to weave their way through the masses of people. The traffic seemed completely chaotic, with no one apparently respecting any recognizable rules of the road. Beggars wandered in and out of the confusion calling for alms. Wandering cows, unmolested, poked their noses into the vegetable stalls in search of forage. I once saw all the traffic halted at both sides of a bridge while seven cows slowly and ponderously made their way across. Dogs and goats mingled with people and cows. Street sellers pushed their barrows and pushcarts determinedly through any opening they could find. Double-decker buses, so full that people were hanging out the doors and windows and riding on top, pushed their way doggedly through the throng. The streets were lined with small shops and hole-in-the wall shoplets opening directly onto the street, their colorful wares displayed for all to see. These commercial enterprises were securely closed and barred at night, with well-padlocked wooden shutters.

Small, overcrowded houses packed every small alley, Little temples and innumerable shrines to favorite gods were tucked in among the houses or up the narrow lanes between them. There was constant noise, especially at festival times, when loud, sometimes raucous, hypnotic music blared out from dawn till dusk. Festivals, both Hindu and Muslim, were numerous. There was a great variety of dress, according to religious or ethnic persuasion. The Hindu women wore very colorful saris, often decorated with gold or silver thread, and the Muslim girls brightened up their white pajamas with colorful scarves. Some of the women of a gypsy caste wore clothes decorated with designs made of small bits of shiny mica and much heavy jewelry. A great deal of life was lived on the street, very much in public, and this was clearly much more exciting than being inside the very small, dried-mud houses, with pats of dung drying on the outside walls for fuel. As religious custom demanded, early in the morning very elaborate designs were drawn in chalk on the well-swept pavement in front of the Hindu houses, even those of the poorest.

Muslim women in Hyderabad were in purdah, which meant that they stayed inside their houses and went out only when accompanied by male members of their immediate family. They never came out to greet their husband's male associates, for instance. Their husbands would entertain business contacts on the outside veranda. When these Muslim women came out in public, they were completely veiled. As one walked along the street, one would sometimes see merchants dash out of their shops to draw long curtains right to the curbside to make an enclosed passageway from a wealthy Muslim woman's chauffeured limousine to the door of the shop.

With Linda I visited some Muslim women in their secluded quarters. They were very happy to see us and served us tea and a number of hors d'oeuvres. One dish I was offered I thought I recognized. I had enjoyed eating green beans in batter on a visit to Linda's doctor friend Prema's house and this dish seemed very similar. I took one readily and began to eat it. To my surprise it was extremely hot and burned my tongue. The hostess, who was watching me, asked whether I liked it. Of course, being polite, I assured her I did. "Have another one," she said. What could I do but accept with thanks. The second one seemed even hotter than the first. By this time all the ladies were watching me with interest. "Look!' they said, "She really likes them. Have another one." By this time my mouth was fiery hot. Fortunately at that point I remembered that my sister had told me that in India it was quite polite to accept something and leave it uneaten on your plate. When I did this, the ladies, to my great relief, lost interest. It seemed I had been eating hot chilies in batter, not innocuous green beans.

The Nizam was reputed to have had more than seventy wives, apart from concubines. As a Muslim he had the right to four at one time, but the number of divorces was not limited. The wives who no longer interested him lived in purdah in a Zenana, where the women who had children had separate rooms, but those with no children were crowded into one area. These forgotten wives never saw the Nizam, unless for a daughter's wedding or when a child was in hospital. The Nizam was noted for his love of money and, when he had garden parties, the guests were expected to bring him gifts of gold coins that he personally collected. Thanks to an acquaintance with connections, we were able to see the great treasures of the Nizam, many of which were gifts from all over the world. These treasures were stored in several interconnected houses, which were specially opened for our visit. As we were escorted through, we were amazed to see extraordinarily beautiful and rare objets d'art piled pell-mell in extravagant disorder. The Nizam, being a devout Muslim, went to the mosque to pray every evening. His official vehicle would often be followed by several curtained limousines for those of his wives who were accompanying him. Because of his notorious "wandering eye," citizens, and even foreigners, with attractive daughters would see that they were not in view on the street as the Nizam passed by, lest, having been attracted by their innocent beauty, he should order that they be sent to the palace.

Linda was teaching at St George's Church of England Girls' Grammar School, which was run by the Church Missionary Society to which she belonged. The teachers at the school were for the most part Indian. The Principal and a few of the teachers were Australian or English missionaries, all fully trained teachers like my sister. Linda taught English, History, and Scripture, as she had done in schools in Melbourne. St George, for whom the school was named, was a popular saint with the Mar Thoma and Jacobite Christian Churches. These ancient Christian churches on the Malabar Coast, in the southwest of India (now the state of Kerala), claimed St Thomas as their founding evangelist. The Malayali people from that area were a well-educated group, widely distributed in responsible positions all over India. Among them George was a common family name, as were Jacob, Samuel, Joseph, John, and Paul. Some of the teachers and students at St George's belonged to this ancient Christian community.

Linda lived on a small lane off King Khoti (King's Palace) Road, so we would ask the bicycle rickshaw men for King Khoti Road and then direct them to her small lane. On one occasion a rickshaw man, whose English was not very strong, took me to the Zenana gate at the Palace. I suppose he thought I wanted to visit one of the begums (or wives of the Nizam). Linda's house was spacious and airy. In accordance with Indian custom, she had a cook, who also did the household shopping, an ayah who dusted and made beds, and a dhobi, or washerman, who came to pick up the dirty linen. Her garden consisted of innumerable pots, kept well watered every day by a mali, a special servant who also acted as a gatekeeper. Insects were a major problem and they were not easily deterred. We slept under mosquito nets, of course. On one occasion when her living room was infested with short-lived flying insects that dropped their wings before they died, Linda thought she could circumvent them by attracting them outside with a lamp. Once they were all safely outside on the veranda, she quickly shut the door and went on with her work. To her astonishment she saw a little army of insects advancing under the closed door, attracted by the light inside.

Each servant had his or her specific work to do and they did not intrude upon each other's domain. At one stage, Linda was displeased with the work of the village woman who made the beds and dusted; she was often away because of problems with her children and, in Linda's view, did not have very much to do. Linda asked the cook, who, with only Linda to cook for, also seemed to have much leisure, whether he would like to do the bed making and dusting, as well as the cooking, and earn more money. To her surprise he refused, saying: "But then I wouldn't get my rest." Upon reflection, Linda realized that, since he came from the same village as the ayah, he could not take over her work and deprive her of this small support for her family. There was also the problem of each person keeping to his or her specific kinds of tasks and the unstated hierarchy of these tasks.

While in India, Linda studied Hindi and Urdu, which were cognate languages with very different writing systems, and

Hindustani, which was a mixture of the two and widely used as a lingua franca in the area. In this way she was able to communicate with the servants and with some of the zenana women she visited. Most of the Christians with whom she worked spoke English, as did most of the educated Hyderabadis, a great number of whom had studied in English-medium schools like St George's. English was in common use among people of very diverse language origins, and it was an official second language in India, as it still is, because of the many unresolved language rivalries.

The girls at St George's School were mostly from an affluent level of society. In 1952 most of them were Muslim, with a substantial group of Hindus, along with children of the Christian community. The Muslims, being mostly descendants of the Aryan conquerors from the north, were fairer and taller than the mostly Tamil and Telegu people of southern Dravidian extraction. Even among the Hindu girls there were varying degrees of skin color. Girls of darker skin, it seemed, worried about their marriage prospects, because they considered their dark color unattractive.

At St George's the girls all wore white pajamas, with a long top and a length of georgette scarf wound around their waist, crossing the chest to hang down over one shoulder. They all wore their hair in a single plait down their backs. The effect, when watching from the back of a school assembly, was very uniform — a sea of white with all these black plaits. The girls liked to wear a string of fragrant frangipani flowers across the back of their hair and they sometimes brought me a small frangipani garland to wear across the back of mine. Since all the small children had personal ayahs to look after their needs and give them food, the ayahs stayed all day in the schoolyard. When I arrived at the school, I would see them gathered with their tiffin baskets in a gossipy group under a big, shady tree. It was no wonder that ayahs were so useful when marriages were being arranged; they soon learned from each other the peculiar habits and temperaments of the children from the different families in the area.

During Ramzan, the Muslim period of fasting, the Muslim girls were not able to eat or drink anything during the day, which would often be very hot. The more orthodox among them could not even swallow their saliva, but would have to rush out of the classroom at intervals to spit it out. The Muslim girls at St George's were often married young, as were many of the Hindu girls. At the wedding ceremony, the bride would be heavily garlanded and expected to keep her eyes down in great modesty for long periods, which encouraged some of her young schoolmates to try to make her giggle. Weddings were always spectacular affairs lasting several days and it was always interesting to observe the different customs of the different communities.

There was a parallel St George's Church of England Boys' School, which had over the years educated many of the leaders in government and business in Hyderabad. Many of the boys had sisters at the Girls' School. When I arrived for my six-week visit, it so happened that the Boys' School was short-handed. This was providential, since I was now very much in need of some ready cash. The Geography teacher, who was preparing several classes of boys for the international examinations offered by Cambridge University in England, had had to take a period of leave. As an experienced geography teacher, I was pressed into service to prepare the boys for this important exam. Being accustomed to preparing students for statewide exams in Australia, I immediately consulted the Cambridge syllabus to see the requirements for the examination. To my horror, I found that the absent teacher had been teaching his students the wrong areas of the world for that year, yet the exam was only six weeks away. Methodically I set about teaching them the prescribed syllabus in just six weeks. I was somewhat amused to find myself, as an Australian, teaching Indian boys the geography of India for an English examination. The Principal had decided that I should teach only the A class, streamed for the boys most likely to pass the examinations, but the B class, who were also intending to sit for the exam, were most unhappy with this arrangement. In desperation they waylaid me in the corridor on my way to class, blocking my path and insisting that I teach them as well. "We have to sit for the exam too," they pleaded. The best I could do was to invite them to join the class I was teaching. They accepted this offer with alacrity and crowded into the two-student desks with the students of my allotted class, to the consternation and resentment of the "brighter" boys. My students were for the most part Muslim. One, with a sister in one of Linda's classes, went home to tell his family: "I never expected to learn anything from a woman, but I was surprised."

Of course, I did not teach only Geography classes. Each morning I had to present myself at the Principal's office to find out my assignments for the day, in order to cover for absent teachers. One morning, to my surprise, I was assigned an Urdu class. After some quick thinking, I made a compact with the boys in the class that if they would teach me to count to ten in Urdu, I would teach them to count to ten in French. In this way the class period passed very pleasantly. Another time I was plunged suddenly into a class called Morality. I asked the headmaster what I was supposed to teach. "Tell them stories about great leaders who acted morally," he said. As I went down the corridor to the classroom, I reflected on my few memories from childhood about moral leaders. On arrival in class I settled in to discuss with the boys the story of George Washington and the cherry tree (apocryphal or not). Then I moved on to the defeated Robert the Bruce of Scotland, who, when hiding from his English foes in a cave, had watched a spider trying to climb up a fine thread to the roof of the cave. The spider fell and fell over and over again. Robert the Bruce, watching its undaunted persistence in climbing back up so many times, took heart. He decided to "try, try, try again" (as we were told as children), sure that he would succeed at last. After I had talked about the fleeing King Alfred, who burned his hostess's cakes while he was reflecting too deeply on his own predicament and planning how to defeat his foes, I could think of no more material about moral leaders. In a moment of inspiration I asked the boys to tell me about Mahatma Gandhi and Mr Nehru. This kept us occupied until the bell rang.

I very much enjoyed meeting Linda's Indian friends. One of her best friends was Dr Prema Naidu, a Christian married to a Hindu, with a daughter at St George's who later went on to study at Oxford. Prema was a highly respected gynecologist at the local hospital. I remember Prema's old mother, Mrs Marsilamoni, telling me on one occasion: "I am a very old woman. I'm 62 years old." Life expectancy was certainly very different from that of the Western world. It was on Prema's invitation that Linda and I were able to join her extended family on a three-day trip to the famous Ajanta and Ellora caves at Aurangabad. We traveled by train with our tiffin baskets and bedding rolls in Indian style. I remember spending much of the long journey teaching Dr Prema French from a very old-style textbook she had brought with her. I often wonder how much she retained from that effort.

Both the Ajanta and the Ellora caves are unforgettable (which seems a very weak word for such extraordinary art). The Ajanta caves, with their shrines and monasteries, illustrate through their architecture, frescoes, and sculptures all stages of Buddhist art from the first to the seventh centuries. Walls and ceilings are covered with intricate frescoes depicting the previous lives of the Buddha and, in so doing, they show the lives of people and animals in gardens, courts, cities, and jungles. Some of the figures in these frescoes have become the best-known images in Indian art. We could appreciate these frescoes only briefly, as they were illuminated for us by flashlight. This emergence of these extraordinary images, in a sudden flood of artificial light, only added to the mystery of their creation in the dark interior of these deep caves.

Ellora consisted of well over a mile of cave temples, some Buddhist, some Hindu, and some Jain. We could only gaze in awe at the superhuman engineering feats of their builders in cutting huge blocks of stone out of the solid cliff face to create great halls, supported by elaborately carved columns with intricately sculptured capitals. The freestanding temple of Kailasa, backed by the solid cliff face, is by itself a marvel of art, with its detailed friezes of elephants, lions, and griffins, often in mortal combat. We had much to reflect on during our long return to Hyderabad.

This complete change of environment having refreshed me, I continued on my way to Melbourne, to enter on the next stage of my career at the Melbourne Church of England Girls' Grammar School. On the way I spent a week in Western Australia with Auntie Del, still bedridden from her stroke and still imposing her will on the hospital staff from her bed. On December 24th, 1952, I reached Melbourne on the Stratheden. It was a somewhat chaotic return, since Harold had been redecorating the interior of the house during his six months of long-service leave and had not yet finished. Fortunately I was now well accustomed to settling into any corner where I could find living space.

At this stage of my life I was determined to return to Australia permanently, despite the attractive opportunities that had presented themselves while I was abroad. I had a strong sense of vocation to help build up Australian education. I felt I was now well qualified to make an important contribution in this area. I was not to know at that time that things would turn out very differently.

APPENDIX

I REMEMBER:

Growing Up in Australia

Summer Holidays

I remember summer days of fierce heat (sometimes well over 100 F or 40 degrees C), when the searing north winds of January, blowing from the desert, brought with them an acrid smell of smoke and fire. The sky would have an eerie orange glow to the east of Melbourne, in the direction of the Dandenong Ranges, where bushfires were raging through the eucalyptus forests — the gum trees, as we call them, because of the resin they exude. Flames would be igniting fallen leaves and licking up the dry strands of peeling bark. At the speed of an express train they would leap from treetop to treetop, while people, in terrified haste, abandoned their homes hidden away among the trees — beloved homes that would soon be reduced to ashes, along with the mementos and acquisitions of a lifetime. These were days of dread and deep anxiety for friends on holiday in the hills and children of friends in summer camps scattered through the bush. At other times, the sky would darken with a lurid orange glow as the dust from the cleared and eroded settlers' blocks to the northwest of our state of Victoria blew over the city. Gritty particles would settle on everything and in our mouths, until storm winds brought relief in drenching, yellow-brown showers.

But summer was not all disaster. It also meant sunny days on the wide, sandy beaches around the bay, followed, if we were not careful, by nights of brutal sunburn from the direct semitropical rays. This was before the slogan Slip, Slop, Slap became current — Slip on a shirt; Slop on the sunscreen, Slap on a hat! We loved to swim. We also loved hikes in the bush and picnics, where one cooked sausages and lamb chops over an open fire of aromatic gum tree wood and warded off the tiny bush flies with leafy eucalyptus fans. Cricket and tennis filled the leisure hours, and there were open air concerts in the gardens around the kiosk-like band stands.

Back to school

Autumn meant return to school, as February-March hove in sight. Autumn is barely perceptible in a country where trees do not lose their leaves. The brilliant colors of the "decorative" imported Northern Hemisphere trees — oaks, elms, maples, and poplars — flamed out in private gardens and along the streets, contrasting with the grey-blue sameness of the native foliage. The lavender-blue blooms of the feathery South American jacaranda trees lined the streets and enlivened the suburbs of their adopted land. After the fierce heat of midsummer and the humidity of its declining weeks, the mild sunshine and refreshing showers of autumn were most welcome. The flowers of summer, which had suffered in wilting patience, took on a new lease of life as the water of the frequent early-morning rains reached their thirsty roots. Birds did not prepare to leave in great numbers: the winter would not be overly long or chill. Fruit was harvested from the trees and bottled or stacked away in sawdust for the winter months. The brown grass of summer was gradually growing green again

Playing hard and keeping warm

Autumn moved quietly into the cool, clear days of winter, interspersed with bleak winds and what seemed unending rains. With an occasional frost but no snow, winter was the time for daffodils, irises, camellias, and outdoor sports. Tennis was an all-year sport, but with the coming of the winter months Australian Rules football, soccer, and rugby took over from cricket on the many open public sports fields around the city and suburbs. Horse races competed for the attention of ardent sports fans — spectators and betting enthusiasts alike. For girls like us, the great enthusiasm was field hockey or basketball. We were fanatical devotees.

Gradually as July approached, life became more rugged. People wrapped up well in warm coats and scarves of good merino wool, never forgetting to take with them the ever-ready brolly. The winter evenings were enlivened by world-class musical and theatrical entertainment. After all, in the southern winter in July and August, Australia had to compete for outstanding performers only with a few major centers, like Buenos Aires, Rio de Janeiro, and Cape Town.

Hikes in the bush

It was bracing to take long walks in the bush. The heavy, golden blooms of the wattles, Australia's perfumed national flower, glowed radiantly among the thin-leafed gum trees. Beneath the trees bloomed red, pink, and white heath, Victoria's own flower, whose delightful spikes of tiny bells rise from tough, prickly, uninteresting-looking plants. Lizards would dart among the fallen leaves. Occasionally we would find little sprigs of native boronia, with its tiny brown cups and magnificent perfume. Fortunately, our native flora are protected by law from greedy passersby, whose depredations could easily lead to their extinction. As enthusiastic Girl Guides, we followed trails, built campfires, and sang all the songs we knew. We loved to "Cooee!" across the valleys and listen to the echoes from the surrounding hills.

Celebrating life

I remember halcyon days of spring, the beautiful blue skies of September decked out with the whitest puffs of clouds. Azaleas and rhododendrons now colored the gardens of our "Garden State." Contrasting with the light green of the spring leaves of the "decorative" trees were the reddish tints of the new shoots on the indigenous eucalypts. Although they are not deciduous, gum trees do replace their foliage, dropping their old leaves and renewing their paper-thin bark as the year progresses.

Fern glades and birdsong

On brisk spring days, we would wander into magical fern gullies in the Dandenongs, where the new green tendrils of tree ferns were uncurling on five- or six-foot high trunks to join the unfurled circles of older fronds. These extraordinarily beautiful ferns dip low into rivulets that ripple over wet rocks amid the dense undergrowth, beneath the sixty-foot high canopy of gum tree branches. Some lean close to the bridal veils of hidden waterfalls. Maidenhair ferns thrive in the damp of the spray. Birds of divers colors flash through the trees: we see the pink and grey of galahs, the crimson and blue or the yellow, red, and green of rosella parrots, and the black and white of Australian magpies, the sweetest songsters of the bush. Those who watch carefully catch delightful glimpses of little blue-capped wrens and black and white willie wagtails, whose name derives from their fanlike tails in constant motion. In the distance one can hear the mimicking calls of the lyrebird: whistles, the crack of whips, the sawing of wood, or perfect imitations of the songs of other birds. In the early morning or toward sunset, one may have the good fortune to hear a group of three or five kookaburras, or laughing jackasses, begin to celebrate their togetherness. They begin with low chortles that gradually increase in amplitude, until they reach an intensity that sends peals of laughter echoing through the bush. During the day the constant *ping* of bellbirds in the treetops relieves the eternal calm.

Shy, elusive animals

Why no animals in these glades? you may ask. Kangaroos leap across open stretches of grassland; opossums are night creatures; wombats and echidnas (spiny anteaters) hide in burrows in the ground, emerging when they find it suitably quiet and danger-free; platypuses are quietly busy in streams or in the riverbanks where they nest underground; koalas love the highest branches of selected gum trees in more isolated areas, where they sleep for much of the day — they really don't like company! Australia's animals are shy, independent, and elusive; they mind their own business and hope that you will mind yours. The Australian bush is an area of quiet activity, of unobtrusive creatures alert to slight noises or disturbances. To see a lyrebird, for instance, you may have to remain quiet, unmoving, for several hours. The bush yields its treasures not to the passerby, but to the patient, unhurried observer.

Land of the Southern Cross

How do native Australians know for sure they are home? They look up above the treetops or the houses, or the incoming waves of the ocean, and they see the broad swathe of the Milky Way with its myriad points of light winking through the haze. They recognize Scorpio with its question-mark tail, Orion's Belt with its jeweled sword, but, best and brightest of all, the Southern Cross with which their flag is decorated. The Cross is constantly in view, with its five stars, its lopsided crossbar, the tiny fifth star blinking out shyly beneath it, and the brilliant pointers (Alpha and Beta Centauri), which forever indicate its presence as it revolves in different orientations around the South Pole. Australia Felix, the Lucky Country, Oz, or the Land of the Southern Cross we Aussies call our homeland

My Country

I remember a poem I learned in primary school: *My Country* by Dorothea McKellar. This has stayed with me ever since.

> I love a sunburnt country,
> A land of sweeping plains,
> Of rugged mountain ranges,
> Of drought and flooding rains.
> I love her far horizons.
> I love her jewel sea,
> Her beauty and her terror —
> The wide brown land for me!

ENDNOTES

PREFACE

1 Ruth Park, *A Fence around the Cuckoo*. Ringwood, Vic.: Viking/Penguin Australia, 1992, p. 254.

2 Carol Shields, *The Stone Diaries*. New York: Penguin, 1995, p. 340.

3 Janet Frame, *An Angel at my Table* (1984). Quote from Quality Paperback Book Club edition, 1994, p. 69.

4 Susan Miller, *The Distinguished Guest.* New York: Harper-Collins, 1996.

CHAP. 1. TANGLED ORIGINS

5 R. Hughes, *The Fatal Shore: The Epic of Australia's Founding*. New York: R Alfred Knopf, 1987, pp. 354-5.

6 Baroness Emmuska Orczy, *The Scarlet Pimpernel.* New York: Putnam, 1905.

7 H. H. Peck, *Memoirs of a Stockman*. Melbourne: Stock and Land. 1948, p. 97.

8 Geoffrey Stephens, *The Hutchins School. Macquarie Street Years 1845-1965*. Hobart: The Hutchins School, 1979, p. 3.

9 Ibid

10 K. Fitzpatrick, *Sir John Franklin in Tasmania 1837-1843.* Melbourne University Press, 1949, p. 18.

11 Stephens (1979), p. 7.

12 Hughes (1987), p. 327.

13 Preceding details from Phyllis M. Power, *From These Descended*. Kilmore, Vic.:Homestead Books, 1977. Limited Edition. Pp. 111-2.

14 Hannah Charlotte Gray was the only daughter of Charles Lyons of Hobart Town, another Tasmanian connection.

15 Reproduced in Powell (1977), between pp. 104-5.

16 Peck (1948), pp. 98-9.

17 Grant Aldous, *The Stopover that Stayed: A History of Essendon*. Clayton, Vic: Wilke and Co. (1979).

18 Peck (1948), p. 12.

19 Peck (1948), p. 99

20 For details about the Separatists who emigrated to South Australia in the late 1830's, see David Schubert, *Kavel's People: From Prussia to South Australia* . Adelaide, S.A.: 1985.

21 He taught at Macedon, Kangaroo Flat, and Port Fairy in the Western District, among others. The quotations and information on the teaching careers of the Burstons in this and the following paragraphs that are not attributed to the *Australasian Schoolmaster* (August, 1900) are from reports from the official archives of the Victorian State Education Department in Melbourne.

22 Michael Clyne, "Multilingual Melbourne Nineteenth Century Style,*" Journal of Australian Studies* 1 7 (1985):75.

23 *Australasian Schoolmaster* (1900): 35.

24 John J. Burston, *The State School Arithmetic: Arranged to suit the Requirements of The Program of Instruction* . Issued by the Education Department. Rev. ed., enlarged, Melbourne, Sydney, Adelaide: George Robertson and Co Ltd, 1884, "for pupils and pupil teachers preparing for their own examinations." He had already published for the Education Department a successful *State School Grammar*.

25 In the account of the Burstons as a notable teaching family in the *Australasian Schoomaster* (August, 1900) there is no mention of a fourth son. The information on Harry from the Victorian Education Department records ends on a disapproving note: "Left the district in company with the late assistant at Nillumbik and is reported to be living with her as man and wife." In a note dated three months later, we read: "Reported to be living in Tasmania....Mr Burston has left a wife and large family of children at Diamond Creek."

26 Quotations from a reference for C. J. Tanner written by Thos. Campbell Fraser, M.A., of the Landsberg House School, Mt Blackwood, Pentland Hills, Nov. 6th, 1872.

27 *Vigneron and Orchardist*, 10 August, 1892, cited in D. H. Edwards, *The Diamond Valley Story*. Greensborough: Shire of Diamond Valley, 1979, p. 79.

28 Edwards (1979), p. 79.

29 Edwards (1979), p. 85

30 Edwards (1979), p. 26.

31 *The Gospel according to St Mark*, chap. 12, v. 40.

CHAP. 2. EXPLORING THE WORLD: THE ASCOT VALE DAYS

32 John Bunyan, *The Pilgrim's Progress: From this World to that which is to come delivered under the similitude of a dream.* Guilford and London: Lutterworth Press, 1961, p. 53. Original final edition 1688.

33 C. McCullough, *The Thorn Birds.* New York: Harper and Row, 1977, p. 81.

34 Howard Gardner, *Frames of Mind: The Theory of Multiple Intelligences.* New York: Basic Books, 1983; *Multiple Intelligences: The Theory in Practice.* New York: Basic Books, 1993; and *Creating Minds: An Anatomy of Creativity seen through the Lives of Freud, Einstein, Picasso, Stravinsky, Eliot, Graham, and Gandhi.* New York: Basic Books, 1993.

35 *Book of Australian Facts.* Sydney: Readers Digest, 1992, pp. 346-7.

36 Colin Simpson, *The New Australia.* 2d ed. New York: Dutton, 1972, p. 135. Unfortunately, rabbits being very resilient developed resistance to myxomatosis, and by 1995 they were estimated to be still consuming three per cent of the value of Australia's agricultural production. At that stage an even stronger rabbit calcovirus (RCV) was introduced in the hope that eradicating 80 per cent of the existing rabbits would bring in an extra 600 million dollars annually for Australia's agriculture sector in increased production. Report of International Wool Secretariat-funded study in *Word from Down Under* 3, 22 (Nov. 26,1995), p. 4.

CHAP. 3 . BANK ST STATE SCHOOL

37 Janet McCalman, *A Hundred Years at Bank Street: Ascot Vale State School 1885-1985.* Ascot Vale, Vic.: Ascot Vale Primary School — School Council, 1985, p. 54

38 Martha Finley, *Elsie's Children.* New York: Buccaneer Books, 1987, reprint.

39 The Anne series was written by L. M. Montgomery, the first volume, *Anne of Green Gables,* being published in Boston by L. C. Page in 1908.

40 When I met this classmate seventy years later and remarked how she had always come first in the class, she smiled and replied, "But you went much further."

41 McCalman (1985), p. 41.

42 May Wynne, *Three and One Over.* London: Cassell, 1924.

43 Alan Marshall, *I Can Jump Puddles.* Cleveland: World Publishing Co., 1957.

44 Caroline Hofman, *The Wise Gray Cat.* Chicago: Volland, 1918.

45 The first of Eleanor Porter's popular books was *Pollyanna* (1913).

CHAP. 4. LEARNING TO LOVE LEARNING: EHS

46 Frances Hodgson Burnett, *The Secret Garden.* Philadelphia: Lippincott, 1938; Gene Stratton Porter, *A Girl of the Limberlost.* Reprinted Library of Indiana Classics American Ltd, 1984.

47 Noumea, the capital of New Caledonia, with about forty thousand inhabitants, became, after the Second World War, when air transport was readily available, a place of pilgrimage for Australian and New Zealand teachers and students of French. It was the nearest place where they could hear authentic French and practice using it in real-life contexts.

48 M.-L. Chapuzet and W. M. Daniels, *Mes Premiers Pas en Français.* London: George Harrap, n. d, my first class textbook for French, was written entirely in French, even for the teaching hints included for the instructor.

49 G. Gladstone Solomon, *La Vie de Madame Souris*, Book 1 of *Le Français pour les Jeunes.* London: J. M. Dent, 1926. Translation of quotation from pp. 28-9: "Mrs Mouse's son is a good fisherman./ He fishes with his tail./ Here he is fishing with his tail./ He has a worm./ Fish love worms./ They eat worms./ Look! he's caught a little fish."

50 M. Lahy-Hollebecque, *Agnès et le Vaste Monde*. Paris: Armand Colin, 1929.

CHAP. 5. SURVIVING THE DEPRESSION

51 Park (1992), p. 245.

52 McCalman (1985), p. 47.

53 Four two-hour tapes of interviews by Judith Walzer (1981) for *Oral History of the Tenured Women in the Faculty of Arts and*

Sciences at Harvard University were deposited in the Henry A. Murray Research Center Archive of Radcliffe College, Cambridge, MA.

CHAP.6. ACADEMIC NOVITIATE
54 The Herbert Lehman Education Fund, a Special Project of the NAACP Legal, Defense & Education Fund.

55 Phyllis's eventful life-story may be read in Phyllis Gration, *Seeing without Sight. A Personal History of the Dog-Guide movement in Australia*. Melbourne: P. M. Gration, 1998.

56 *Education for Complete Living: The Challenge of Today.* The Proceedings of the New Education Fellowship Conference held in Australia Aug.1st to Sept. 20, 1937. Ed. K. S. Cunningham, assisted by W. C. Radford. Melbourne: Melbourne University Press, in association with Oxford University Press, 1938. P. viii.

57 H. E. Palmer, *The Principles of Language-Study*. London: Harrap, 1921. Reprinted London: Oxford University Press, 1964

58 F. Gouin, *The Art of Teaching and Studying Languages*. Trans. H. Swan and V. Betis London: George Philip and Son; New York: Charles Scribner's Sons, 1892.

59 In the English tradition, the most prestigious boys' private schools in Australia are usually referred to as "public schools," a very confusing term for non-Australians.

CHAP. 7. RURAL VICTORIA
60 Seneca, *Ad Lucilium* V, vii.

CHAP. 8. EDUCATIONAL CONTRASTS: ST ANNES AND TAYLOR'S COACHING COLLEGE
61 St Annes Church of England Girls' Grammar School has since been incorporated into the Gippsland Grammar School, a coeducational institution.

62 A. Andrew, *Life at St Annes, Gippsland Grammar School and STAGGS.* Sale: Gippsland Grammar Foundation, 1996, p. 9.

63 Andrew (1996), p. 11.

64 All quotations in this paragraph are from a four-page pamphlet, entitled *The Big Five*, For Students of George Taylor &

Staff, University Coaches, 306 Little Collins St., Melbourne; 13-5 O'Connell St., Sydney. n.d. (probably mid-1940s).

CHAP. 9. VENTURING OUT OF THE NEST

65 "Pommies" is a common, uncomplimentary term in Australia for English immigrants. It is usually considered a derivative of pomegranate, used for the word immigrant, in the rhyming slang of the early Australian miners.

CHAP. 10. THE NORTHERN HEMISPHERE: UPTOP

66 C. E. M. Joad, ed., *The English Counties.* London: Odhams Press, 1948, p. 269.

APPENDIX. I REMEMBER: GROWING UP IN AUSTRALIA

67 Originally published in *Standpoints* 5,5 1992-93. Paris: Centre National de Documentation Pédagogique/Mission Laïque Française: 4-7

GLOSSARY

(With acknowledgment to THE MACQUARIE DICTIONARY. McMahon's Point, NSW, Australia: The Macquarie Library, 1981.)

Aeroplane, airplane

Aluminium, aluminum

Anzac Day, Australia's commemoration on April 25th of the landing of Australians on Gallipoli in 1915; Australia's Veterans' Day

Ayah, Indian nursemaid or household servant

Balaclava, knitted woollen hood that covers all of the head except the face

Barrack, to root for, cheer on (a team)

Basin, bowl

Baths, public swimming pools, often municipal

Belly-whackers, flat dives

Bet, wager

Billabong, small lake formed by the cutting off of a meander

Billy, cylindrical container for liquids with a close-fitting lid and a wire handle

Biscuits, cookies

Blinkered, unable to see except straight ahead

Bob, shilling (one-twentieth of a pound)

Bobbies, English policemen, nicknamed for Sir Robert Peel, the founder of the force

Bookie, bookmaker who accepts wagers, or bets, on the horse races and other sports

Bowler, pitcher

Brolly, umbrella

Brown paper bags, brown bags

Buggy, four-wheeled horse-drawn vehicle

(The) Bush, the natural forest

Bushfire, fire in the Bush or in scrubland, a wild fire

Bushranger, bandit or outlaw who hides in the Bush

Chiyack (chiyacking), tease in an amusing, friendly way

Chook, hen, chicken
Coaching, tutoring
Coles, Australian Five and Dime store, whose slogan was "Nothing over Two and Six" (two shillings and sixpence)
Coo-ee, aboriginal call, adopted by European settlers
Clump, walk heavily and clumsily
Dandenongs, mountains close to Melbourne, within which is the national park area of Sherbrooke Forest
Dead marines, empty bottles
Diggers, Australian veterans of the First World War
Droving, herding large numbers of sheep or cattle long distances to market
Dunny, outside toilet, usually away from the house
Finicking, fussing about with
Flat, apartment
Florin, silver coin worth two shillings
Flutter on the geegees, little bet on the horses
Footpath, sidewalk
Form Mistress, Home Room teacher
Fossicker, individual searching unsystematically for gold
Girl Guides, Girl Scouts
Grazier, breeder of sheep and cattle, who owns a substantial area of grazing land
Greengrocer, fruit and vegetable seller
Guinea, twenty-one shillings
Gully, small valley cut by running water
Gum tree, eucalyptus tree
Hessian, burlap
Hidey, children's game of hide-and-seek
Icechest, icebox
Icing, iced, frosting, frosted
Jinker, light, two-wheeled, horse-drawn conveyance
Jumper, sweater
Kelly country, area in northeastern Victoria where the bushrangers, the Kellys, lived and where their last standoff against the police took place
Kelpie, Australian sheep dog
Kept in, detained after school as a punishment

654

Kerosene, a petroleum product used in lamps

Koori, Australian aborigine

Last Post, Taps, in barracks the last bugle call before retiring

Left down (in school), not promoted

Lollies, candies; boiled lollies, hard candy

Lolly shop, candy store

Long service leave, in Australia, a benefit for all workers, giving them three months' paid leave after working for ten years, and six months after twenty years

Lorry, large truck

Macks. Macintoshes (British usage), raincoats

Marks, grades

Matilda, see Swagman

Mopoke, owl-like night bird

Outback, country areas far from towns

Paddock, fenced-in field

Palliasse, mattress filled with straw

Pannikin, small metal cup, often collapsible

Pasty, small pie made from a circular piece of pastry folded in over a filling of meat or vegetables

Pavlova, dessert composed of a meringue pie-shell filled with a mixed fruit salad, usually with passion fruit, and topped with thick whipped cream

Petrol, gas for vehicles

Picture theatre, cinema

Plaits, braids

Play old Harry, to play up, to misbehave

Plonk, put down heavily

Post box, mail box

Pouf, cushioned seat with no back, usually for the fireside

Pound, twenty shillings

Pram, perambulator, baby carriage

Primary school, elementary school

Public school, prestigious private school (often church-affiliated)

Pudding basin, mixing bowl

Puffed, out of breath

Pushbike, bicycle

Rabbiting, hunting rabbits

Ring, call on the telephone

Rubbish tin, garbage can

Rug, thick blanket to throw over a bed or wrap around one's knees

Sandshoes, tennis shoes

Saveloys, thick, highly seasoned, smoked pork sausages

School fellows, class mates

Scoff down, eat rapidly with great relish

Scotty, bad-tempered

Sheep station, privately owned rural estate with a large area of grazing land for sheep

Shelter-shed, shed in a schoolyard, where children can eat lunch or shelter from the rain

Shilling, silver coin worth twelve pennies

Sixpence, silver coin worth half a shilling

Skerrick, a very small quantity

Skittling, sending flying or knocking over

SP Bookie, starting price bookmaker. See Starting-price betting

Spouting, down pipe

Squatter, wealthy landowner, usually on a sheep station

Starting-price betting, illegal off-course wagers based on the odds for racehorses (or racing dogs) as the race began; these were announced from the course by the radio commentator

State school, public school (supported by state taxes)

Stooks, groups of sheaves of grain leaning against each other

Subway, pedestrian walkway under a railway line

Superannuation, pension fund for retirement

Supper, late evening snack

Swagman, itinerant worker humping (carrying) his bluey, or bedroll, which is also referred to as Matilda

Sweets, candies

Swot, cram, study hard

Tank, a reservoir for drinking water

Tea, dinner in the evening, usually about six o'clock

Teetotaller, non-drinker of alcohol

Thrippenny, silver coin worth three pennies (one quarter of a shilling), a threepence

Tiffin baskets, set of closed containers, in which Indians keep food hot, for outside consumption or for traveling

Tiggy, children's chasing game called tiggy-touchwood

Tins, cans

Tommies, British soldiers, short for Tommy Atkins

Two-up, a popular gambling game among Australian men with time to spare; two coins are placed in a piece of slotted wood and tossed in the air, while participants bet on whether they will fall showing heads or tails

Vegemite, dark, yeast-based spread

Violet Crumble, a chocolate-covered bar with honeycomb center

Wattle, acacias with golden balls of bloom with a distinctive perfume. .Similar to mimosa. Australia's national flower, from which the national colors, green and yellow, are derived

Weatherboard, clapboard

Woop Woops, the outback, the boondocks

ABOUT THE AUTHOR

Wilga M. Rivers, Professor Emerita of Romance Languages and Literatures at Harvard University, Cambridge, Massachusetts, has a PhD (Illinois at Urbana-Champaign); Licence ès Lettres (Montpellier); Dip. Etudes Françaises (Lille); MA and Dip Ed (Melbourne); D Lang (Hon.) (Middlebury); and MA (Hon) (Harvard). She received the Palmes Académiques from the French Government for services to French language and culture.

For seventeen years Professor Rivers was Coordinator of Language Instruction in the Romance Languages at Harvard, where she was in charge of the coordination and development of language instruction in French, Spanish, Italian, Portuguese, and Romanian for day and evening courses. She has taught courses and seminars in French Syntax and Phonetics, Theory and Practice of Language Teaching, and Linguistic and Psychological Bases of Language Learning. She has directed Ph.D and MA theses and taught in summer seminars in a number of universities. She continues to teach classes in language teaching methodology and direct MA theses in the Harvard Division of Continuing Education. Professor Rivers also taught at the University of Illinois UC, Columbia, Northern Illinois, and Monash University in Australia. She has conducted applied linguistics and psycholinguistics seminars in France, England, India, Brazil, Singapore, Egypt, Japan, India, China, and Thailand. She has lectured in forty-five US states, all of the Canadian provinces, and in forty-four countries. Professor Rivers has been active in language teachers' organizations and in linguistics and applied linguistics groups, from which she has received a number of awards for Distinguished Service. She has been a consultant for a number of Foundations, as well as the Department of State. She has served on various Editorial Boards. She is presently on the Advisory Boards of the National Foreign Language Center (Washington, DC) and the National Language Acquisition Research Center (San Diego State University).

Professor Rivers has written thirteen books and ninety articles. Her work has been translated into eleven languages. Website: www.agoralang.com/wilga_rivers.html

Printed in the United States
R516100002B/R5161PG19301X00003BA/4851